CW00555741

Sociolinguistics in Ireland

Sociolinguistics in Ireland

Edited by

Raymond Hickey
University of Duisberg and Essen, Germany

Erin Carrie

palgrave
macmillan

First published 2016 by
PALGRAVE MACMILLAN

The authors have asserted their rights to be identified as the authors of this work in accordance with the Copyright, Designs and Patents Act 1988.

Palgrave Macmillan in the UK is an imprint of Macmillan Publishers Limited, registered in England, company number 785998, of Houndmills, Basingstoke, Hampshire, RG21 6XS.

Palgrave Macmillan in the US is a division of Nature America, Inc., One New York Plaza, Suite 4500, New York, NY 10004-1562.

Palgrave Macmillan is the global academic imprint of the above companies and has companies and representatives throughout the world.

Hardback ISBN: 978–1–137–45346–4
E-PUB ISBN: 978–1–137–45348–8
E-PDF ISBN: 978–1–137–45347–1
DOI: 10.1057/9781137453471

Distribution in the UK, Europe and the rest of the world is by Palgrave Macmillan®, a division of Macmillan Publishers Limited, registered in England, company number 785998, of Houndmills, Basingstoke, Hampshire RG21 6XS.

A catalog record for this book is available from the Library of Congress.

A catalogue record for the book is available from the British Library.

Contents

List of Figures		vii
List of Tables		viii
Preface and Acknowledgements		x
Notes on the Contributors		xii
The International Phonetic Alphabet		xvii
Maps		xviii

Part I Language and Society in Contemporary Ireland

1 English in Ireland: Development and Varieties   3
Raymond Hickey

2 The Irish Language in Present-day Ireland   41
Brian Ó Catháin

3 The Irish Language and the Media   60
Iarfhlaith Watson

4 Irish-English Code-switching: a Sociolinguistic Perspective   81
Siobhán Ní Laoire

5 The Sociolinguistics of Language Use in Ireland   107
Anne Barron and Irina Pandarova

Part II Language and Society in Irish History

6 Language Relations in Early Ireland   133
Patricia Ronan

7 From Early Modern Ireland to the Great Famine   154
Liam Mac Mathúna

8 Language Shift and Language Revival in Ireland   176
Regina Uí Chollatáin

v

9 Language, Politics and Identity in Ireland: a Historical
   Overview   198
   Tony Crowley

10 Emigrant Letters: Exploring the 'Grammar of the
   Conquered'   218
   Kevin McCafferty

11 Society, Language and Irish Emigration   244
   Raymond Hickey

Part III Sociolinguistic Interfaces

12 Second-language Acquisition of Irish and the Role of
   Reading   269
   Tina Hickey and Nancy Stenson

13 The Language of Irish Writing in English   299
   Carolina P. Amador-Moreno

14 Irish Society as Portrayed in Irish Films   320
   Shane Walshe

15 Translation and Society in Ireland, 1900–Present   344
   Kathleen Shields

16 Sociolinguistic Information and Irish English Corpora   365
   Elaine Vaughan and Brian Clancy

Timelines   389

Glossary   395

General Bibliography   416

Index   421

List of Figures

1.1 Short Front Vowel Lowering in recent Dublin English   29
1.2 The word *dress* for three speakers with increasingly
     lowered vowels from left to right (recognisable in the
     higher value for F1 towards the right)   29
1.3 Rotation in vowel space   30
6.1 Lexical fields of pre-thirteenth-century loanwords in
     Irish   142
10.1 BE-deletion in IrE: effect of following grammatical
      environment, 1731–1840 (n = 253)   228
10.2 BE-deletion in IrE: effect of subject type, 1731–1840
      (n = 253)   230
10.3 First person *shall/will* in IrE letters, 1761–1890 (n = 1463)   233
11.1 Major waves of emigration from Ireland to various
      destinations in the anglophone world   246
13.1 Quotative uses of *go*, *be there* and *be like*   307
13.2 Results of quotative forms in CIDN compared   308
13.3 Past and present tense uses compared   310
13.4 Distribution of quotatives across grammatical person   311
13.5 Reporting of male and female voices within third person
      subjects   312
16.1 Sample of concordance lines for *shur* in LCIE (sorted one
      item to the left)   377

List of Tables

1.1 Shared features in vernacular varieties of (southern) Irish
English   16
1.2 Suggestions for sources of key features of (southern)
Irish English (Hickey 2004a, 2007b)   18
1.3 Summary of the Dublin Vowel Shift from the 1990s   25
1.4 Changes in non-local Dublin English by speaker age   26
1.5 Levels of indexicality after Silverstein (2003)   32
5.1 Composition of the ICE-Ireland S1A sub-corpus
comprised of speakers of NI/ROI background with TQ
raw and relative frequencies per 10,000 words   115
5.2 The interactional functions of tag questions and their
proportions in ICE-GB and ICE-Ireland private
conversations (Barron et al. 2015)   116
5.3 The interactional functions of tag questions and their
proportions in private conversations of NI and
ROI speakers   117
5.4 The functions of TQs in women's and men's speech in
ICE-Ireland according to regional background   122
10.1 BE-deletion in IrE: effect of following grammatical
environment, 1731–1840 (n = 253)   228
10.2 BE-deletion in IrE: effect of subject type, 1731–1840
(n = 253)   230
10.3 First person shall/will in IrE letters, 1761–1890 (n = 1463)   233
10.4 GoldVarb analysis of shall/will in late
eighteenth-century IrE (1761–90)   234
10.5 GoldVarb analysis of shall/will in IrE (1831–40)   235
10.6 GoldVarb analysis of shall/will in IrE (1881–90)   235
11.1 Timeline for emigration from Ireland during the
colonial period   245
11.2 Parallels between Glasgow English and Northern Irish
English   258
13.1 Word list of 2-word clusters in CIDN   306
14.1 Grammatical features in Northern and Southern Irish
films   338
14.2 Chronological list of Northern and Southern Irish films   340

16.1 Linguistic and societal variables investigated in sociolinguistics   369
16.2 Existing Irish English corpora   371
16.3 *Sure/shur(e)* in LCIE, SPICE-Ireland and the BNC normalised per million words   375
16.4 Top ten keywords in LCIE using BNC Spoken as reference corpus   376
16.5 Sample of metadata preserved in the LCIE database   379

Preface and Acknowledgements

The present volume gathers together a range of contributions by established scholars with the theme of language and society in Ireland, both in its history and the present day, as their central focus. There are many reasons why a book on sociolinguistics in Ireland is topical but the common thread throughout this volume is how the relationship of a society to the languages spoken by its members evolved, how it has been and is redefined afresh in successive generations. In today's Ireland this is true, as it was in the past, but perhaps now even more so, given the large number of people at present living in the country but born outside Ireland. This adds a further dimension to the interface of language and society which previously was solely determined by the relative positions of Irish and English to each other, the latter in many different varieties.

Contemporary Irish society has reacted to the languages it contains: linguistic issues are present in the media, and academic interest in these has burgeoned over the past few decades. In public the question of how modern Irish people view and engage with their heritage language, Irish, is a recurring topic. The attempts to adapt the Irish language to suit the world of the twenty-first century and the programmes to improve knowledge and use of the language in today's Ireland are matters which are keenly debated. These issues have a further political dimension, seeing as how the language question for both the Republic of Ireland and Northern Ireland has been addressed in the peace accord of the late 1990s, which continues to be implemented in both parts of the island of Ireland.

For readers new to the area of language and society in Ireland a comprehensive glossary of common terms in the field has been added and a set of general references has been provided, which might help those interested in Irish history, literature and culture to orient themselves in these areas.

For these reasons and many more, which will hopefully become apparent in the various chapters of the volume, this project was undertaken during the past few years. It would not have been completed without the dedication of all the contributors and, as an editor and author, I express my gratitude to all my colleagues whose work fills the pages of this book. My thanks also go to Libby Forrest and Rebecca Brennan at Palgrave Macmillan for their continual support for this project, and to the rest of the staff, especially the copy-editor Frances Tye, whose engaging work saw this volume swiftly and carefully to completion.

Notes on the Contributors

Carolina P. Amador-Moreno is Senior Lecturer in English Linguistics, University of Extremadura, Spain. Her research interests centre on the English spoken in Ireland and include sociolinguistics, stylistics, discourse analysis, corpus linguistics and pragmatics. Publications include *An Introduction to Irish English* (2010), the co-edited volumes *Writing Orality* (2009) and *Fictionalising Orality*, and a special issue of the journal *Sociolinguistic Studies* (2011). Other publications include articles in the journals *Intercultural Pragmatics, English Language and Linguistics, Irish University Review* and the *International Journal of English Studies*. Current research projects include CONVAR (*Contact, Variation and Change*) in collaboration with Kevin McCafferty, at the University of Bergen.

Anne Barron is Professor of English Linguistics, Leuphana University, Lüneburg, Germany. Her main research interests lie in the areas of Irish English, variational pragmatics, interlanguage pragmatics and discourse analysis. Her publications include the monographs *Acquisition in Interlanguage Pragmatics* (2003) and *Public Information Messages* (2012) as well as the co-edited volumes *The Pragmatics of Irish English* (2005), *Variational Pragmatics* (2008) and *Pragmatics of Discourse* (2014). She is also series co-editor of 'Studies in Pragmatics' (Brill) and member of a number of editorial boards, including the *Journal of Pragmatics*, *Intercultural Pragmatics* and *Study Abroad Research in Second Language Acquisition and International Education*.

Brian Clancy lectures in academic writing and research methods at Mary Immaculate College, University of Limerick, Ireland. His research work focuses on the blend of a corpus linguistic methodology with the discourse analytic approaches of pragmatics and sociolinguistics. He is interested in the use of corpora in the study of language varieties, and the construction and analysis of small corpora. His published work addresses these areas and also explores corpus-based discourse analysis in intimate settings, such as between family and close friends, as well as varieties of Irish English. He is author of *Investigating Intimate Discourse: Exploring the Spoken Interaction of Families, Couples and Close Friends* (forthcoming) and co-author, with Anne O'Keeffe and Svenja Adolphs, of *Introducing Pragmatics in Use* (2011).

Tony Crowley is Professor of English, University of Leeds, and a former visiting professor at the Institute of Irish Studies in Liverpool. He has published widely in the area of language and cultural theory, including *Wars of Words: the Politics of Language in Ireland 1537–2004* (2005) and *Scouse: a Social and Cultural History* (2012). He also curates the Murals of Northern Ireland Collection at the Claremont Colleges Digital Library.

Raymond Hickey is Professor of English Linguistics, University of Duisburg and Essen, Germany. His main research interests are varieties of English (especially Irish English and Dublin English) and general questions of language contact, variation and change. Recent publications include *Motives for Language Change* (2003), *A Sound Atlas of Irish English* (2004), *Legacies of Colonial English* (2004), *Dublin English. Evolution and Change* (2005), *Irish English: History and Present-day Forms* (2007), *The Handbook of Language Contact* (2010), *Eighteenth-Century English* (2010), *Varieties of English in Writing* (2010), *The Sound Structure of Modern Irish* (2014) and *A Dictionary of Varieties of English* (2014).

Tina Hickey is a lecturer in the School of Psychology, University College Dublin. Her main research interests include first- and second-language acquisition, bilingualism and immersion education, family language transmission and minority language maintenance. Her publications include some of the earliest articles in international journals on the acquisition of Irish as L1, books on the development of L1-Irish-speaking children and L2 learners in immersion preschools (*naíonraí*), and articles on L2 reading in Irish. Her current work includes collaboration with Prof. Nancy Stenson within a Marie Curie International Fellowship on Irish orthography and the teaching of Irish reading.

Liam Mac Mathúna is Emeritus Professor of Irish, University College Dublin, where he was Head of the School of Irish, Celtic Studies, Irish Folklore and Linguistics, 2006–13. He also taught at Uppsala University and St Patrick's College, Drumcondra, Dublin, where he was Registrar, 1995–2006. His extensive publications on Irish language, literature and culture include *Béarla sa Ghaeilge* [English in Irish] (2007) a study of Irish/English code-mixing in literature composed in Irish 1600–1900, and a new edition of An tAthair Peadar Ua Laoghaire's novel, *Séadna* (2011). He is editor of *Éigse: a Journal of Irish Studies*, published by the National University of Ireland and is currently engaged in a study of the Ó Neachtain circle of Irish language scholars in Dublin, 1700–50, and the diaries of Douglas Hyde, 1874–1912, as part of a wider project researching the impact of modernity on Irish-speaking communities.

Kevin McCafferty is Professor of English Linguistics, University of Bergen, Norway. His research interests are in the field of language variation and change, with a focus on Irish English. His main publication to date is *Ethnicity and Language Change: English in (London)Derry, Northern Ireland* (2001). He is co-editor of *Pragmatic Markers in Irish English* (2015, with Carolina P. Amador-Moreno and Elaine Vaughan). Articles have appeared in *Language Variation and Change, English World-Wide, Diachronica, Language and Literature, English Language and Linguistics, English Today, English World-Wide* and *American Speech*. His current research activity is focused on compiling the *Corpus of Irish English Correspondence* and using it to research the history of Irish English.

Siobhán Ní Laoire is Lecturer in Irish and Chair of MA in Applied Irish, Dublin Institute of Technology, where she is also currently Head of the Department of Languages. She previously held positions in the Dublin Institute for Advanced Studies (1991–2005), St Patrick's College, Dublin City University and University College Dublin. Most of her research work in recent years has focused on register and stylistic variation in contemporary Irish.

Brian Ó Catháin is a senior lecturer in the Department of Modern Irish, National University of Ireland Maynooth. He completed his PhD on the language and oral narrative of Inis Oírr, Co. Galway at University College Dublin and has published widely on aspects of the linguistics and sociolinguistics of Modern Irish. He is the editor, with Ruairí Ó hUiginn, of *Béalra: Aistí ar Theangeolaíocht na Gaeilge* [Speech: Essays on the linguistics of Irish] (2001) and of *Sochtheangealaíocht na Gaeilge* [The Sociolinguistics of Irish] (2009).

Irina Pandarova is a research and teaching assistant in English Linguistics, Leuphana University, Lüneburg. Her main research interests are in the areas of variational pragmatics, the semantics/pragmatics interface (with a special focus on pragmatic markers), discourse analysis and Irish English. She is currently writing a PhD thesis on the semantics and pragmatics of the pragmatic marker *sure* across British, American and Irish English and is involved in a research project on tag questions across varieties of English.

Patricia Ronan is Lecturer and Research Fellow in English Linguistics, Department of English, University of Lausanne. She has previously worked at the Universities of Uppsala, Bonn, the Basque Country and Maynooth. Her research interests comprise both English Linguistics and Celtic – especially the medieval Irish language. Recent publications include the monograph 'Make Peace' *and* 'Take Victory'. *Support Verb Constructions in Old English in Comparison with Old Irish* (2012), as well as the edited volume *L'Irlande et ses contacts/Ireland and its contacts* (2014).

Kathleen Shields is Lecturer in French, National University of Ireland Maynooth. Her main research interests are bilingual lexicography, translation studies and language policy. Recent publications include, as editor, *Translating Emotion: Studies in Transformation and Renewal Between Languages,* as well as many articles on translation and literature, for example in *CLCWeb, Romance Studies* and *French Cultural Studies*. She is currently working on a book project about the English language in France, *L'anglais en France, attitudes, réalités et représentations*.

Nancy Stenson is Professor Emerita of Linguistics, University of Minnesota, USA, and Adjunct Professor, School of Psychology, UCD, where she recently completed a Fulbright Fellowship and a Marie Curie Incoming International Fellowship. Her research interests include structural aspects of language contact in Irish and the acquisition of Irish as a second language. Recent publications include *Basic Irish* and *Intermediate Irish* (2008), *An Haicléara Mánas* (2003), and articles with Tina Hickey on Irish L2 literacy in *Language, Culture and Curriculum* and the *Journal of Celtic Language Learning*. Current projects include completion (with Tina Hickey) of a manual of Irish orthography for teachers and learners.

Regina Uí Chollatáin is a Senior Lecturer and Director of the de Bhaldraithe Centre for Irish Language Scholarship, University College Dublin. Her main areas of research are Irish language revival and media. Her books include *An Claidheamh Soluis agus Fáinne an Lae 1899–1932* (2004), *Iriseoirí Pinn na Gaeilge* [Print-media journalists of Irish] (2008), co-edited publications include *P. H. Pearse: Life and After-life* (2009, with Roisín Higgins), *An Greann sa Ghaeilge* [Humour in Irish] (2013, with Malachy O'Neill), *Cnuasach Comhar 1982–2012* (2014, with Aisling Ní Dhonnchadha), and *Films gaèlics a Catalunya/Scannáin Ghaelacha sa Chatalóin* [Gaelic films in Catalonia] (2014, with Jerry White).

Elaine Vaughan is Lecturer in Applied Linguistics and Course Director for the MA TESOL, University of Limerick, Ireland. She has two main areas of teaching and research: language pedagogy for ELT/foreign language teaching, and using corpus-based methodologies to investigate varieties of English. She has published on teacher talk in workplace meetings (her PhD thesis) and language teachers as a community of practice, the pragmatics of Irish English and examining Irish English, discourse-pragmatic markers in spoken language, the use of humour and laughter in meetings and corpus linguistics more generally.

Shane Walshe is Lecturer in English, University of Zurich, Switzerland, and previously taught at the University of Bamberg, Germany. His main research interests are Irish English, literary dialect, perceptual dialectology and linguistic stereotyping. *Irish English as Represented in Film* (2009) examines the way in which Irish English is portrayed in 50 films set in Southern Ireland. Ongoing research projects include examinations of the portrayal of Irish speech in American comics and other forms of popular culture.

Iarfhlaith Watson is Lecturer in Sociology, University College Dublin, and a former President of the Sociological Association of Ireland. He publishes in both Irish and English. His research is mainly in the area of the Irish language, including his book *Broadcasting in Irish* (2003), and many articles and book chapters on linguistic elitism, Irish language media, and the educational advantages of speaking Irish. He has been a member of the Board of the International Visual Sociology Association and Irish Representative on the International Social Survey Programme, and has published on topics such as anti-immigrant attitudes and banal nationalism.

The International Phonetic Alphabet

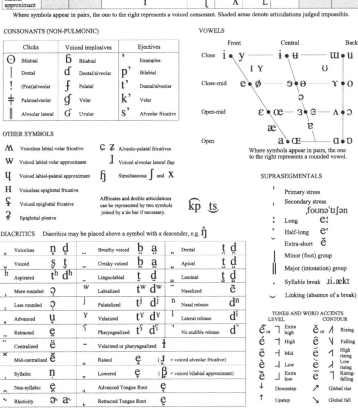

THE INTERNATIONAL PHONETIC ALPHABET (revised to 2005)

https://www.internationalphoneticassociation.org/content/full-ipa-chart

Maps

Map 1   Political division and cities in Ireland

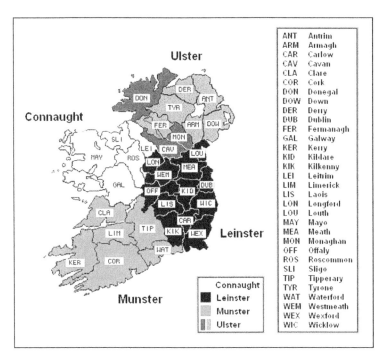

ANT   Antrim
ARM   Armagh
CAR   Carlow
CAV   Cavan
CLA   Clare
COR   Cork
DON   Donegal
DOW   Down
DER   Derry
DUB   Dublin
FER   Fermanagh
GAL   Galway
KER   Kerry
KID   Kildare
KIK   Kilkenny
LEI   Leitrim
LIM   Limerick
LIS   Laois
LON   Longford
LOU   Louth
MAY   Mayo
MEA   Meath
MON   Monaghan
OFF   Offaly
ROS   Roscommon
SLI   Sligo
TIP   Tipperary
TYR   Tyrone
WAT   Waterford
WEM   Westmeath
WEX   Wexford
WIC   Wicklow

Map 2   Provinces and counties of Ireland

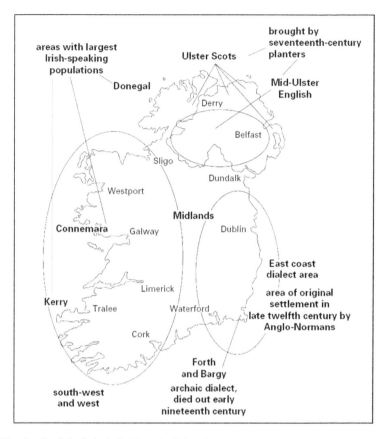

Map 3 English dialect divisions in Ireland

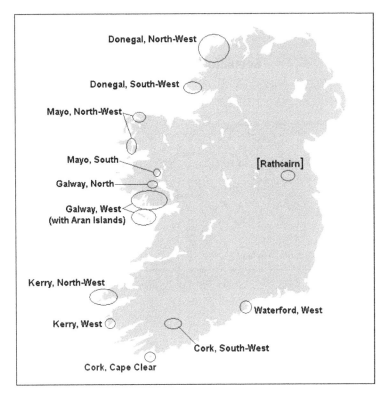

Donegal, North-West

Donegal, South-West

Mayo, North-West

Mayo, South

Galway, North

Galway, West
(with Aran Islands)

[Rathcairn]

Kerry, North-West

Kerry, West

Waterford, West

Cork, South-West

Cork, Cape Clear

Map 4   Irish-speaking regions of Ireland

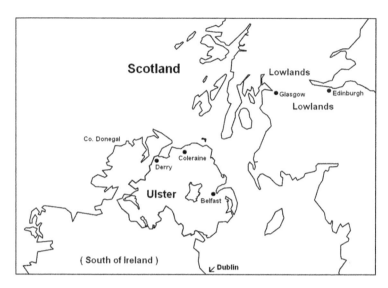

Map 5   Ulster and Scotland

Part I

Language and Society in Contemporary Ireland

1

English in Ireland: Development and Varieties

Raymond Hickey

1.1 Introduction

The relationship of language to society in Ireland is multifaceted and multilayered. This has been the case in history and is so to this day. The two languages whose relationship dominated the linguistic landscape of Ireland in previous centuries, Irish and English, are both still present. But many more languages have been introduced to the country by immigration in recent years, especially after the accession of several East European countries to the European Union in 2004. This allowed the free movement of citizens of the new member states in the enlarged union, a fact which contributed to the surge of foreign labour into Ireland in the so-called Celtic Tiger years (late 1990s to 2008). The country which contributed most to the swelling population of non-Irish-born people in Ireland was Poland. Before the financial crisis of 2008, male Poles were largely employed in the then-booming construction industry and female Poles worked in service industries. Recent census figures show that now there are approximately 123,000 present in the Republic of Ireland (Census 2011). This means that many Poles are still living in the country and a new, Irish-born, Polish-heritage generation (Diskin and Regan 2015) is growing up in Ireland which, if not linguistically, will at least culturally leave its mark on Ireland in the coming years.

(1)   *Languages in present-day Ireland (2015)*

    (i) Irish
   (ii) English, including Ulster Scots in Northern Ireland
  (iii) Several mainland European languages, above all Polish
  (iv) Non-European languages spoken by small ethnic groups

The order of the list in (1) reflects the constitutional position of the languages, or their lack of it. Irish is the first language of the nation as specified in the constitution of 1937. English is a second language, in the words of the constitution 'accepted as a second official language' (*Bunreacht na hÉireann*, 'Constitution of Ireland', Article 8). But in practical terms, Ireland is a completely English-speaking country. Those who can speak Irish are also bilingual, with the exception of very few older speakers in the rural *Gaeltacht*, a collective term for Irish-speaking regions.

The Irish successfully transferred their linguistic identity from the Irish language of their forebears to forms of English which they now speak and which are sufficiently distinct from other varieties of the language to function as the bearers of an Irish linguistic identity.

The entry for (1, ii) above also has a reference to Ulster Scots (Montgomery and Gregg 1997). This is a variety of English traditionally spoken in Northern Ireland by people of Scottish descent, especially in the rural regions of the so-called Ulster Scots crescent (Hickey 2011a: 298). But in the urban context of Belfast (Milroy 1978) this variety has been the object of an Ulster Scots revival movement (Hickey 2011a: 311–17) which seeks to increase its 'otherness' by maximising the differences between it and more mainstream varieties of English. Whether this undertaking will be successful remains to be seen (see the discussion in Hickey 2011a).

The languages listed under (iii) and (iv) are not constitutionally recognised in the Republic of Ireland. All of them have arrived in the country far too recently for that to have happened. But their numbers have resulted in an interesting situation. Going on the assumption that not more than half of the 53,000 individuals, who in the 2006 census stated that they used Irish on a daily basis outside education (Hickey 2011b: 12), are native speakers of the language, the 120,000-plus Poles in Ireland constitute a group four to five times greater than that of first-language speakers of Irish.

1.2   Language studies and scholarship in Ireland

Authors working on Irish English can be grouped according to the material which they devote their attention to. Firstly, they can deal with phenomena already present in Irish English and which are the result of change which has long since taken place, mainly during the language shift of the past few centuries. Secondly, authors can treat ongoing change in Irish English. The latter group is considerably smaller than the former and in essence consists of scholars working on English in the large urban centres of the island, Dublin, Derry and Belfast. Investigation into English in Belfast has ebbed away since the seminal work of James and Lesley Milroy in the late 1970s and 1980s. However, the language of the remaining two cities, Dublin and Derry, has been the subject of investigations in recent years by Hickey (2005a) and McCafferty (2001) respectively. The works which their investigations have engendered are sociolinguistic studies of linguistic variation in an urban setting and are basically different from the work of other scholars in the field such as Corrigan, Filppula or Kallen, to mention only three of the prominent authors working currently on Irish English. The latter authors have been looking at either rural forms of Irish English or at the grammar of more general varieties found throughout the island of Ireland, in either the north or the south and in some cases in both.

The history of Irish English studies reaches back into the late eighteenth century. What can be regarded as the first studies of Irish English are glossaries for the archaic dialect of Forth and Bargy (Hickey 2007a: Chapter 2). The gathering of lexical material into glossaries is part of an antiquarian interest in language which flourished at this time, not only in Ireland. This interest continued throughout the nineteenth and twentieth centuries and led in particular to collections of local words and sayings for the north of Ireland (see the relevant entries in Hickey 2002a: 186–94). This concern with local vocabulary in Ulster has persisted up to the present (Fenton 2014 [1995]).

Almost at the same time as the first glossaries were being compiled, at least one author, Thomas Sheridan, was concerned with the elocution of English. Part of Sheridan's concern was with pointing out the nonstandard pronunciation of Irish English (Sheridan 1781). Like the glossarists, Sheridan was located within a certain tradition, that of eighteenth-century prescriptivism (Hickey (ed.) 2010), which in England had its major representative in the grammarian Robert Lowth (Tieken-Boon van Ostade 2010).

In the course of the nineteenth century, the concern with antiquarianism and elocution receded, and there was a lull in the activity of scholars involving themselves with English in Ireland. At this time, the study of the Irish language was a concern of scholars and it reached clear expression in works such as O'Donovan's (1845) *A Grammar of the Irish Language* and the monumental *Grammatica Celtica* by Zeuss (1871). However, in the second half of the nineteenth century, a small number of authors began to concern themselves with specific features of Irish English, very often in the context of English in the north of Ireland, where the background of English speakers was particularly complex given the mixture of Scots and English input to the region. In addition, there are one or two cases of writers who examined features of a certain locality; the most well-known of these is probably David Patterson, who produced a book on provincialisms in the speech of Belfast (Patterson 1860).

But it was not until the beginning of the twentieth century that works dedicated specifically to Irish English as a distinctive variety of English began to appear. The main monograph of this period is that published by Patrick W. Joyce (1910), *English As We Speak It in Ireland*, which despite its shortcomings, still represents the beginning of modern scholarship on this variety. Articles also began to appear in learned journals, such as the studies by Hayden and Hartog (1909) and van Hamel (1912). From the 1920s there exists a study by James Jeremiah Hogan (1927), which is basically an examination of the historical documents available for Irish English. Hogan is also known for his textbook, entitled *An Outline of English Philology Chiefly for Irish Students* (Hogan 1934), which contains many remarks on specific traits of Irish English. After this work, there was a break until the late 1950s, when Patrick Leo Henry published his doctoral dissertation *An Anglo-Irish Dialect of North Roscommon* (1957), which initiated scholarly research into Irish English in the second half of the twentieth century. The 1960s saw publications by authors who were to become authorities in this field: George Brendan Adams for English in Ulster and Alan Bliss for English in the south of Ireland. Both of these authors had long publication careers and were active in the 1970s and, in the case of Bliss, up to the mid-1980s. By this time, a younger generation of scholars had become active, John Harris, Jeffrey Kallen, Markku Filppula and the present author, all of whom inherited ideas from Henry, Adams and Bliss and have continued to develop these, adding their own interpretations in the process. In addition to these authors, one should mention those working on the lexicon of Irish English, above all Terence Dolan. Parallel to this work, two British linguists, James and Lesley Milroy, with their colleagues in Belfast, were engaged in seminal linguistic investigations of social networks in the city which were to lead to a paradigmatic change in the field of sociolinguistics (Milroy 1987).

1.2.1   Issues in Irish English studies

Most investigations into Irish English have so far had an historical component, perhaps the only exception being sociolinguistic examinations of phonology in urban settings, mainly Belfast, Derry and Dublin. The historical considerations of scholars have been concentrated on syntax and morphology, and concerned with the relative weight to be accorded to contact explanations on the one hand and to those which appeal to the retention of inherited features in input varieties of English to Ireland on the other. Because the interface between Irish and English has been a permanent feature in the history of Irish English, the weighting of contact in its genesis is the single most controversial issue in this field. Up until the early 1980s, contact explanations were favoured, above all in the work of Patrick L. Henry and Alan J. Bliss. In this they were following on earlier work by older authors such as P. W. Joyce and J. J. Hogan (see above). However, with the publication of a seminal article by John Harris (1984), the pendulum began to swing in the opposite direction, and researchers started to attribute much more weight to the retention of inherited traits. Studies such as Kallen (1989, 1990) and Markku Filppula (1991, 1993) offered syntactic analyses of Irish English which addressed both possible sources. By the early 1990s, the pendulum had swung back to a more central position, and in research by scholars such as Karen Corrigan (1993) and Hickey (1995, 2007a), the role of contact, this time considered in an objective and linguistically grounded manner, was largely re-established.

1.2.2 New directions in research

In the field of Irish English studies many new avenues of research have appeared, often on the basis of new data. For instance, the University of Limerick has a research team working on the pragmatics of Irish English using their *Limerick Corpus of Irish English* (Vaughan and Clancy 2015, this volume). Another case of corpus-based research is that by John Kirk and Jeffrey Kallen based on the *International Corpus of English – Ireland*, in which the authors have concerned themselves with the questions of standardness and 'Celticity' (see Kirk and Kallen 2011, for example).

Areas which interface with language have been receiving increasing attention. The interaction of language planning and politics (McDermott 2011) is just such a case, as well as language and ethnicity (Kirk 1997), especially in the context of the Travellers in Ireland (Clancy 2015). Mention should also be made of work done in the area of translation studies (Shields, this volume). This is of relevance to research into Irish English as it is directly concerned with the features and structures of this form of English which can be employed to achieve equivalents to local flavouring and ambience in the work of source authors.

1.2.3   Terminology

There are different designations for the many varieties of English spoken on the island of Ireland. In the north of the country, terms are used which reflect historical origin, e.g., *Ulster Scots* (see the discussion in Kirk 1998 and Hickey 2011a) for the English stemming from the initial Lowland Scots settlers. *Mid-Ulster English* refers to geographically central varieties which are largely of northern English provenance. *Contact English* is found occasionally to refer globally to varieties spoken in areas where Irish is also spoken. In general treatments of English in the south of Ireland, three main terms can be found.

1. *Anglo-Irish* is an established term in literature to refer to works written in English by authors born in, or closely associated with Ireland. It is also found in politics to refer to relations between England and Ireland. Within the context of other varieties – Canadian English, for instance – the term has been used to refer to English in Ireland (Kirwin 1993).
2. *Hiberno-English* is a learned term which is derived from Latin *Hibernia* 'Ireland'. The term enjoyed a certain currency in the 1970s and 1980s, but in the 1990s, many authors ceased to employ it, as it may require explanation to a non-Irish audience or readership. However, some authors, such as Dolan and Filppula, continue to employ the term.
3. *Irish English* is the simplest term. It has the advantage that it is parallel to the designations for other varieties, e.g., American, Australian, Welsh English, and can be further differentiated where necessary.

A non-linguistic term with a considerable history is *brogue* meaning a clearly recognisable Irish accent, frequently of rural origin. The term comes either from the Irish word for *shoe* or possibly from an expression meaning something like 'a lump in one's tongue'. It is often used in a loose sense to mean the Irish pronunciation of English (Walsh 1926) and the term is also found outside Ireland, e.g., in Ocracoke Brogue on the islands off the coast of North Carolina.

1.3   History

The history of Irish English can be divided into two periods. The first period began in the late twelfth century with the arrival of the first English-speaking settlers and finished around 1600, when the second period opened. The main event which justifies this periodisation is the renewed and vigorous planting of English in Ireland at the beginning of the seventeenth century. During the first period the Old English – as this group is called in the Irish context – came increasingly under the influence of the Irish. The Anglo-Normans, the military leaders during the initial settlement, had been completely absorbed by the Irish by the end of the fifteenth century. The progressive Gaelicisation led the English to attempt planting the Irish countryside in order to reinforce the English presence there. This was by and large a failure, and it was only with James I that successful planting of (Lowland Scottish and English) settlers in the north tipped the linguistic balance in favour of English in that part of the country. The south was subject to further plantations along with the banishment of the native Irish to the west during the Cromwellian period, so that by the end of the seventeenth century, Irish was in a weak position from which it was never to recover. During the seventeenth century, new forms of English were brought to Ireland: Scots in the north and West/North Midland varieties in the south (where there had been a predominantly West/South-West input in the first period). The renewed Anglicisation in the seventeenth century led to the 'discontinuity hypothesis', namely the view, above all of Bliss (see Bliss 1972), that the forms of English from the first period were completely supplanted by the varieties introduced at the beginning of the modern period. However, on the east coast, in Dublin and other locations down to Waterford in the south-east, there is a definite continuation of South-West English features which stem from the imported varieties of the first period.

1.3.1 The medieval period

The documentary record of medieval Irish English is confined for all intents and purposes to the collection of 16 poems of Irish provenance in the British Museum manuscript, Harley 913, known collectively as the *Kildare Poems* (Lucas (ed.) 1995) after one of the poems in which the author identifies himself as from the county of Kildare, to the south-west of Dublin. The collection probably dates from the early fourteenth century. The language of these poems reflects a general West Midland to Southern usage of late Middle English. It is a moot point whether the *Kildare Poems* were written by native speakers of Irish using English as an official, 'high' language in a diglossic situation and whether indeed the set was written by one or more individuals.

Apart from the *Kildare Poems*, medieval Irish English is attested in a very small number of verse fragments and in some fragmentary city records from Dublin and Waterford, comments on which can be found in Henry (1958) and Hickey (2002b).

1.3.2   The early modern period

At the end of the sixteenth century, attestations of Irish English begin to appear which are deliberate representations of the variety of the time. These are frequently in the guise of literary parody of the Irish by English authors. The anonymous play *Captain Thomas Stukeley* (1596/1605) is the first in a long line of plays in which the Irish are parodied (Sullivan 1980). Later a figure of fun, the stage Irishman, was to be found in dramas of this type, establishing a tradition of literary parody that lasted well into the twentieth century. The value of these written representations of Irish English for reconstructing the language of the time has been much questioned – e.g., by reviewers of Bliss (1979) (see Hickey 2002a: 126–7) – and it is true that little if any detail can be extracted from these sources. In addition, most of the satirical pieces were written by Englishmen so that one is dealing with an external perception of Irish English at the time. Nonetheless, this material can be useful in determining what features were salient at the beginning of the early modern period and hence picked up by non-Irish writers.

Satirical writings are not the only source of Irish English, however. There are some writers, especially in the nineteenth century, who attempted to indicate colloquial speech of their time. The first of these is Maria Edgeworth, whose novel *Castle Rackrent* (1800) is generally regarded as the first regional novel in English and was much admired by Sir Walter Scott. Other writers one could mention in this context are Carleton and the Banim brothers. William Carleton (1794–1869) is the author of *Traits and Stories of the Irish Peasantry* (5 volumes, Dublin, 1830–3) and uses Irish English in the speech of the peasants. John (1798–1842) and Michael (1796–1874) Banim are the authors of *Tales of the O'Hara Family* (6 volumes, 1825–6), where again Irish English is used for narrative effect. The novel by Edgeworth and extracts from the works of Carleton and the Banim brothers are contained in *A Corpus of Irish English* (Hickey 2003a).

1.3.3   The modern period

With the close of the eighteenth century, drama by Irish writers went into a marked decline, and did not regenerate itself until some of the major figures of the Irish Literary Revival, such as Lady Augusta Gregory (1852–1932) and William Butler Yeats (1865–1939), turned towards this genre at the end of the nineteenth century. This culminated in the linguistic and thematic innovations of John Millington Synge (1871–1909), followed somewhat later by Sean O'Casey (1884–1964) who dealt with themes from lower-class Dublin couched in vernacular language. The break in the tradition of playwriting, which had begun in the Restoration period, meant that there was no continuation in the late nineteenth century of earlier literary concerns. The themes of seventeenth- and eighteenth-century playwrights from Ireland were not specifically Irish. Those Irish characters who appear in their plays, by and large, do so in a setting which is English. The concern with Ireland and matters Irish by major writers begins with Jonathan Swift (1667–1745). The dramas produced after the beginning of the Irish Literary Revival in the 1880s were Irish in their themes. The question of theme should not, however, be seen as the only defining feature of English literature by Irish authors. The predilection for satire, a strongly ironical sense of humour and a prevailing occupation with linguistic form are qualities which are shared by such diverse writers as Swift and Sterne in the eighteenth century and Shaw and Joyce in the twentieth century.

One can safely say that after Richard Brinsley Sheridan (1751–1816), drama by Irish writers went into a period of decline. Writers such as Charles Maturin (1782–1824), James Sheridan Knowles (1784–1862) and Samuel Lover (1797–1868) are minor in stature. It is not until the mid-nineteenth century that playwriting produced a prominent writer in Ireland. This is the somewhat isolated figure of Dion Boucicault (1820–1890), the author of many plays which were popular in both England and the United States in his day.

Turning to prose one finds a number of works in which a specifically Irish idiom is used. At the end of the nineteenth century Edith Somerville (1858–1949) together with Violet Martin (Ross) (1862–1915) published their *Experiences of an Irish R. M.* (1899) in which dialect is used for regional flavouring. The chapter entitled 'Children of captivity' deals with Irish English. The authors discuss such matters as Irish bulls, which they regard as an integral part of the Irish sense of humour, and criticise the English custom of parodying the Irish in their literature. A certain amount of dialect is found in the early work of James Joyce (1882–1941), for instance with the maid in the story *The Dead* from the collection *Dubliners*. In later works, in *Ulysses* and above all *Finnegans Wake*, the use of non-standard English is highly artistic and contrived. Contemporary literary writing makes use of Irish English features in much the same manner as did the major authors of the early twentieth century. Novelists like Roddy Doyle (1959–) use a racy vernacular idiom for scenic effect. The more recent novels of the journalist

Paul Howard (1971–) show the snobbish southern Dublin moneyed class via a satirical portrayal of their variety of English.

1.4 The language shift

Literary representations do not reveal anything about the then relationship of Irish to English, the spread of English or the regional input from England. There were no censuses before 1851 which gave data on speakers of Irish and English (after that date one can draw a reasonably accurate picture of the decline of Irish). Adams (1965) represents a useful attempt to nonetheless produce a linguistic cartography of Ireland at the beginning of the early modern period. The upshot of this situation is that there is no reliable data on the language shift which began in earnest in the early seventeenth century and which had been all but completed by the late nineteenth century. This has meant that statements about the shift have been about what one assumes must have happened rather than on facts revealed from historical documents.

Nonetheless, the external history of this shift shows what the overall conditions were and allows some general statements in this respect. In rural areas there was little or no education for the native Irish, the romanticised hedge-schools notwithstanding (Dowling 1968 [1935]). The Irish appear to have learned English from other Irish who already knew some, perhaps through contact with those urban Irish who were English speakers, especially on the east coast, and through contact with the English planters and their employees. The latter two groups play no recognisable role in the development of Irish English as a separate linguistic group, i.e., there is no planter Irish English, probably because this group was numerically insignificant, despite its importance as a trigger in the language shift process. What one can assume for the seventeenth and eighteenth centuries in rural Ireland is a functional bilingualism in which the Irish learned some English as adults from their dealings with English speakers. By the early nineteenth century, the importance of English for advancement in social life was being pointed out repeatedly, by no less a figure than Daniel O'Connell (Ó Catháin, this volume), the most important political leader before Parnell.

The fact that the majority of the Irish acquired English as adults in an unguided manner had consequences for the nature of Irish English. Bliss (1972) pointed out that this fact is responsible for both the common malapropisms and the unconventional word stress found in Irish English. However, the stress pattern in verbs with final long vowels, e.g., *distribute* [dɪstrɪ'bjuːt], *educate* [ɛdju'keːt], can also be due to English input, particularly as late word stress is only a feature of southern Irish (not of that of the west and north, see Hickey 2011b: 308–14). Consequently, influence due to contact with Irish could only be posited for the south of Ireland and might have affected the pronunciation of English words.

Another point concerning the language shift in Ireland is that it was relatively long, spanning at least three centuries from 1600 to 1900 for most of the country. The scenario for language shift was one where lexical transfer into English was unlikely, or at least unlikely to have become established in any nascent supraregional variety of English in Ireland. After all, English was the prestige language, and the use of Irish words would not have been desirable, given the high awareness of the lexicon as an open class. This refers to Irish lexical elements in English in Ireland, both historically and at the present. In some written works, and historically in varieties close to Irish, there were more Irish words and idioms (Odlin 1991).

In phonology and syntax the matter is different. Speakers who learn a language as adults retain the pronunciation of their native language and have difficulty with segments unknown to them. A simple case of this would be the substitution of English dental fricatives by stops (dental or sometimes alveolar, depending on region). A more subtle case would be the lenition of stops in Irish English, e.g. *cat* [kæt̪], which, while systemically different from lenition in Irish, could be the result of a phonological directive applied by the Irish learning English to lenite elements in positions of maximal sonority.

In syntax, there are many features which either have a single source in Irish or at least converged with English regional input to produce stable structures in later Irish English. Adult speakers learning a second language, especially in an unguided situation, search for equivalents to the grammatical categories they know from their native language. The less they know and use the second language, the more obvious this search is. A case in point would involve the habitual in Irish. This is a prominent aspectual category in the language and available for all verbs by using a special form of the verb *be* and a non-finite form of the lexical verb in question (e.g. *Bíonn sí ag léamh [gach maidin]* 'is she at reading [every morning]'). There is no one-to-one formal correspondence to this in English, so what appears to have happened is that the Irish availed of the afunctional *do* of declarative sentences, which was still present in English at the time of renewed plantation in the early seventeenth century (especially if one considers that the input was largely from the West Midlands of England), to produce an equivalent to the habitual in Irish (Hickey 1995, 1997). This use of an English structure in a language contact situation to reach an equivalent to an existing grammatical category in Irish depends crucially on a distinction between the existence of a category and its exponence. The difference in exponence (the actual form used) between the habitual in Irish and Irish English has often led scholars to either dismiss Irish as a source for this in Irish English or to produce unlikely equations to link up the category in both languages formally. But if one separates the presence of a category in a grammar from its exponence, then one can recognise more clearly the search for equivalence which the Irish must have undertaken in acquiring English and one can understand the process of availing of means in English, present but afunctional (i.e., declarative *do*), to realise an existing category in their native language.

1.4.1 Supraregionalisation

It is obvious from English loanwords in Irish that early Irish English had not progressed through the major long vowel shift in England (Baugh and Cable 2002: 105–8), e.g., Irish *bácús* 'bakehouse' shows unshifted /aː/ (not /eː/) and /uː/ (not /au/). The play *Captain Thomas Stukeley* (1595) referred to above, consistently uses <oo> for words with /au/ from /uː/ in modern English, e.g., *toon* for *town*. Furthermore, comments from Thomas Sheridan in the late eighteenth century (Sheridan 1781) show that Middle English /aː/, as in *patron*, still had not shifted, nor had Middle English /ɛː/ as in *meat*. But present-day Irish English shows little or no trace of these unshifted vowels. The reason is not that the English shift took place in Irish English some time in the nineteenth century but that the unshifted forms were replaced by mainstream English pronunciations due to a process called *supraregionalisation* (Hickey 2013). The essence of this process is the replacement of salient vernacular features of a variety by more standard ones (Hickey 2012b), frequently from an extranational norm, as with southern British English vis-à-vis Irish English. The motivation for this move is to render a variety less locally bound and more acceptable to a non-vernacular community, hence the term supraregionalisation. I assume that this process has applied not just to Irish English but to other varieties during their histories, and that it is this which has in large part led to regional or national standards throughout the anglophone world (see the contributions in Hickey (ed.) 2012). The process is especially obvious in Irish English because there are records of features before supraregionalisation set in. In Ireland, and probably in other anglophone countries, supraregionalisation is linked to education and the formation of a middle class, and so it is a process which can be largely located in the nineteenth and early twentieth centuries. For Irish English this has meant that certain features disappeared in the course of the nineteenth century. For instance, the lowering of /e/ before /r/ (historically attested in England in words like *dark, barn* and of course in county names like *Hertfordshire*) was very widespread in Ireland and is recorded at the beginning of the nineteenth century in pronunciations like *serve* /saːrv/. This lowering has been lost in Irish English, except for a few older rural varieties in the north where it can be found occasionally, e.g. *Me nerves* [naːrvz] *are botherin' me.*

1.4.2 Vernacularisation

Strongly local features are not always lost entirely through supraregionalisation. Another possible development is the relegation to vernacular varieties. Take the instance of Middle English /ɛː/ as in *beat* /bɛːt/. This pronunciation is now confined to vernacular, often rural varieties where supraregionalisation has not taken place. Furthermore, non-local speakers can style-shift downwards to achieve a vernacular effect. It is part of the competence of all speakers of Irish English that they know what features can be donned to impart a popular touch to their speech. Another example of this would be the use of *youse* or *yez* for the second person plural (also found in other anglophone regions such as Tyneside, Beal 1993). This is shunned by non-local speakers but can be employed when deliberately switching to a vernacular mode.

The process of vernacularisation has in some instances led to a lexical split. Consider the reflex of velarised [ɫ] before [d] in Irish English: this led to the diphthong [au] as in the words *old* [aul] and *bold* [baul] with the common feature of post-sonorant stop deletion. These forms are available alongside /oːld/ and /boːld/ to non-local speakers, but the meanings are somewhat different as the original forms with [au] have gained additional meaning components: [aul] 'old + affectionate attachment', e.g., *His* [aul] *car has finally given up the ghost*, [baul] 'daring + sneaking admiration', e.g., *The* [baul] *Charlie is back on top again.*

1.5 Island-wide features in Ireland

Varieties of English across the whole of the island of Ireland show several common features which they often share with Irish as well. This fact might suggest that one is dealing with areal traits which have diffused with time over the entire island (Hickey 2012a). For the south of Ireland (and in many instances for the north also), one can list the following features shared by all vernacular varieties. It is true that some of them are

Table 1.1   Shared features in vernacular varieties of (southern) Irish English

---

Phonology

1. Lenition of alveolar stops in positions of high sonority, e.g., *city* [sɪt̞i]
2. Use of clear [l] in all positions in a word (now recessive), e.g., *field* [fiːld]
3. Retention of syllable-final /r/, e.g., *board* [boːrd]
4. Distinction of short vowels before /r/ (now recessive), e.g., *tern* [tɛrn] versus *turn* [tʌrn]
5. Retention of the distinction between /ʍ/ and /w/ (now recessive), e.g., *which* [ʍɪtʃ] and *witch* [wɪtʃ]

Morphology

1. Distinction between second singular and plural personal pronouns, e.g., *you* [ju] versus *youse* [juz] / *ye* [ji] / *yeez* [jiz]
2. Epistemic negative *must*, e.g., *He mustn't be Scottish.*
3. *Them* as demonstrative, e.g., *Them shoes in the hall.*

Syntax

1. Perfective aspect with two subtypes:
   a) Immediate perfective, e.g., *She's after spilling the milk.*
   b) Resultative perfective, e.g., *She's the housework done* (OV word order)
2. Habitual aspect, expressed by *do + be* or *bees* or inflectional *-s* in the first person singular

   a) *She does be reading books.*
   b) *They bees up late at night.*
   c) *I gets awful anxious about the kids when they're away.*

3. Reduced number of verb forms, e.g., *seen* and *done* as preterite, *went* as past participle
4. Negative concord, e.g., *He's not interested in no girls.*
5. Clefting for topicalisation purposes, e.g., *It's to Glasgow he's going.*
6. Greater range of the present tense, e.g., *I know him for more than six years now.*
7. Lack of *do* in questions, e.g., *Have you had your breakfast yet?*
8. *Be* as auxiliary, e.g., *They're finished the work now.*
9. *Till* in the sense of 'in order that', e.g., *Come here till I tell you.*
10. Singular time reference for *never*, e.g., *She never rang yesterday evening.*
11. *For to* infinitives of purpose, e.g., *He went to Dublin for to buy a car.*
12. Subordinating *and* (frequently concessive), e.g., *We went for a walk and it raining.*

---

found outside Ireland, in England and at overseas anglophone locations, but the combinations of features would appear to be unique to Ireland (see Table 1.1).

The above features can be arranged according to the sources which can be postulated for them. In the sense of the comments made in

Section 1.2.1 above, both transfer from Irish and English input are found as suggestions, with convergence also considered as a likely scenario for some of these features (see Table 1.2).

Apart from the putative source of specifically Irish English features, there have been various suggestions concerning the linguistic models to use in interpreting such features. For instance, in the area of aspect, there have been attempts to use grammaticalisation models (Kallen 1990) and prototype theory (Hickey 2000) to arrive at alternative descriptions. Greene (1979) and Ó Sé (1992, 2004) are influential articles describing the verbal system of Irish and its possible effect on Irish English.

1.6   The lexicon

The linguistic level which has been given greatest attention by popular writers is certainly the lexicon (Dolan 2012 [1998]; Share 2003 [1997]; Ó Muirithe 1996; Hickey 2005b). The tradition of gathering word-lists goes back at least two centuries, if one considers the glossaries gathered by Vallancey for the archaic dialect of Forth and Bargy in the south-east corner of Ireland (Vallancey 1788).

A number of specifically Irish English items represent archaic or regional usage which has survived in Ireland. For instance, the adjectives *mad* and *bold* retain the earlier meanings of 'keen on' and 'misbehaved' respectively. In some cases the words are a mixture of archaism and regionalism, e.g., *cog* 'cheat', *chisler* 'child', *mitch* 'play truant'. One can also notice semantic extensions which have taken place in Ireland, e.g. *yoke* with the general meaning of a thing or device. An additional feature here is the merger or reversal of words which are complementary in meaning: *ditch* is used for *dyke*; *bring* and *take*, *rent* and *let*, *borrow* and *lend* are often interchanged while *learn* can be used in the sense of *teach* in vernacular varieties, e.g. *That'll learn yah!* 'That will teach you a lesson'.

Although Irish today is spoken natively by less than 1 per cent of the population (Hickey 2011b: 9–25), and although the knowledge of Irish among the majority is, in general, very poor, there is a habit of flavouring one's speech by adding a few words from Irish, which is sometimes referred to as using the *cúpla focal* (lit. 'couple of words'). These words are always alternatives to English terms readily available, e.g., *ciúnas* 'silence', *piseog* 'superstition' (anglicised as *pishogue*), *sláinte* 'health', *plámás* 'flattery', *grá* 'love'. Such incursions into the lexicon of Irish are brief and superficial. Borrowings can go both ways, e.g., the common

18

Table 1.2 Suggestions for sources of key features of (southern) Irish English (Hickey 2004a, 2007b)

Phonological features	Possible source
Dental/alveolar stops for fricatives	Transfer of nearest Irish equivalent, coronal stops
Intervocalic and pre-pausal lenition of /t/	Lenition as a phonological directive from Irish
Alveolar /l/ in all positions (now recessive in syllable-final position)	Use of non-velar, non-palatal [l] from Irish
Retention of [ʍ] for <wh>	Convergence of input with the realisation of Irish /f/ [ɸ]
Retention of syllable-final /r/	Convergence of English input and Irish
Distinction of short vowels before /r/	Convergence of English input and Irish
Morphological features	*Possible source*
Distinct pronominal forms 2 p.sg. + pl.	Convergence of English input and Irish
Epistemic negative *must*	Generalisation made by Irish based on positive use
Them as demonstrative	English input only
Syntactic features	*Possible source*
Habitual aspect	Convergence with South-West English input on east coast, possibly with influence from Scots in Ulster. Otherwise transfer of category from Irish
Immediate perfective aspect with *after*	Transfer from Irish
Resultative perfective with OV word order	Possible convergence, primarily from Irish
Subordinating *and*	Transfer from Irish
Variant use of suffixal *-s* in present	South-West input in first period on east coast
Clefting for topicalisation	Transfer from Irish, with some possible convergence
Greater range of the present tense	Transfer from Irish, with some possible convergence
Negative concord	Convergence of English input and Irish
For to infinitives indicating purpose	Convergence of English input and Irish
Reduced number of verb forms	English input only
Be as auxiliary	English input only
Single time reference for *never*	Transfer from Irish, English input

term *craic* for social enjoyment is a loan from Irish, itself originally a borrowing from English.

The difficulty with the lexicon of Irish English lies not in finding words which come from Irish or which are regional/archaic English in origin but in determining whether these are current in present-day Irish English and, if so, for what sections of the population. There is a great difference in the lexical items available to and used by, say, older rural inhabitants and young urbanites.

Lexicographically, the north of Ireland is well served by Fenton (2014 [1995]), Macafee (ed.) (1995) and Todd (1990), and the south in the past decade or so has experienced a number of publications in this sphere (with varying degrees of linguistic analysis) (Ó Muirithe 1996; Share 2003 [1997]; Dolan 2012 [1998]). Clark (1977 [1917]) is an older work by an author about whom very little is known; Traynor (1953) and Moylan (1996) are regional lexical studies. For a brief overview of the Irish English lexicon, see Hickey (2005a); Kallen (1996) provides a linguistically interesting examination of the structure of the present-day lexicon while the chapter on Irish English lexis in Kallen (2013) is the best there is to date. There also exist studies of the vocabulary of individual literary authors, especially James Joyce (e.g. Dent 1994; O'Hehir 1967); Wall (1995) is a general lexicon of literary works.

1.7 The sociolinguistics of present-day Irish English

In present-day Ireland, the major instances of language change lie in the area of pronunciation. The grammar of Irish English (see Section 1.5 above) contains established non-standard features and these are neither increasing nor decreasing, although some general features of present-day varieties of English are to be found in Ireland, e.g. quotative *like* as in *And he was like, 'let's go to my place'*, the lack of restrictions on augmentative *so*, as in *That's so not happening these days* or the use *you guys* as a gender-independent second person plural pronoun as in *Are you guys going to the party tonight?* The lexicon of Irish English (see Section 1.6 above) is also fairly stable, perhaps with a decline in the items derived directly from Irish and with an adoption of many salient words from North America, often instances of hyperbolic usage, e.g. *awesome, gross*, etc.

All changes in pronunciation in (southern) Irish English, which have become general across the entire country, derive from Dublin usage and have done so in the past. By 'usage' is meant here the speech of non-local Dubliners, those who speak with a recognisably Irish

English accent but without the defining features of local Dublin English. This variety is what can be termed 'supraregional Irish English' (see Section 1.4.1 above). It is subject to continual change, often determined by generation and gender, and many changes in non-local Dublin English usage of the past 25 years or so have now become part of supraregional Irish English and can be found in the speech of younger individuals around the country who do not have an accent typical of their locality. Examples of such features would be a dark *l* in syllable codas, e.g. *deal* [diːəɫ], the homophony of the formerly distinct /ɔː/ and /oː/ vowels, e.g. *horse* [hɔːrs] and *hoarse* [hoːrs], now both [hoːrs] for younger speakers of supraregional Irish English, or the absence of a voiceless labio-velar approximant [ʍ] leading to homophony in word pairs like *which* and *witch, whale* and *wail, whet* and *wet,* etc.

Given the unidirectional influence of Dublin English on varieties throughout the remainder of the Republic of Ireland, the new features found today in non-local Irish English are taken to have derived from recent sociolinguistically motivated changes in Dublin English. It is the latter which are discussed in the following sections.

1.7.1   Background

The English language has been spoken in Dublin since the late twelfth century, when the first English and Anglo-Norman settlers came up from the south-east where they had landed in 1169. The next few centuries form the first period, which lasted until around 1600 and which in its closing phase was characterised by considerable Gaelicisation outside the capital and within (see Section 1.3 above). Despite this resurgence of native culture and language, English never died out in the capital and there are some features of colloquial Dublin English which can be traced to the first period (Hickey 2002b).

1.7.2   Documentation

The historical records of Dublin English are slight and before 1600 they consist mainly of municipal records which here and there betray the kind of English which must have been spoken in the city (Henry 1958: 64–7). For an historical background to present-day speech one must look to the elocutionist Thomas Sheridan and his *A Rhetorical Grammar of the English Language* which contains an appendix in which he commented on the English used by middle-class Dubliners, the 'gentlemen of Ireland' in his words, which he regarded as worthy of censure on his part. Sheridan's remarks are a valuable source of information on what

Dublin English was like two centuries ago. Among the features he listed are the following (the phonetic values have been ascertained with reasonable certainty by interpreting his own system of transcription, which is decipherable and fairly consistent, see Hickey 2009):

(i) Middle English /ɛː/ was not raised to /iː/. The pronunciation [ɛː] can still be heard in Dublin in words like *tea, sea, eat*. Of these, the first is still found as a caricature of a bygone Irish pronunciation of English. Hogan (1927: 65) noted in his day that the non-raised vowel was rapidly receding. Today it is somewhat artificial; the pronunciation is also found in Northern Ireland, where equally it is a retention of an earlier value.

(ii) A pronunciation of English /ai/, from Middle English /iː/, as [əi]. It is not completely certain that this sound was intended by Sheridan but it would tally with what is known from present-day Dublin English, cf. pronunciations like *wild* [wəɪl(d)].

When discussing consonants Sheridan remarks on 'the thickening (of) the sounds of d and t in certain situations'. Here he is probably referring to the realisation of dental fricatives as alveolar plosives as found in colloquial forms of Dublin English today. There is no hint in Sheridan of anything like a distinction between dental and alveolar plosive realisations, which is an essential marker of local versus non-local speech today.

(2) Local Dublin Non-local Dublin
 thank, tank [t̪æŋk] *thank* [t̪æŋk]
 tank [tæŋk]

Already in Sheridan's day linguistic behaviour was apparently prevalent which aimed at dissociating middle-class speech from more local forms, as evidenced in the many instances of hypercorrection which he quotes: 'instead of *great* they [middle-class Dubliners – Sheridan's group of speakers, RH] say *greet*, for *occasion, occeesion; days, dees,* &c.' (1781: 142) [ee = /iː/, RH].

1.7.3 Contemporary Dublin

The city of Dublin lies at the mouth of the river Liffey in the centre of the east coast, and spreads along the shores of the horseshoe shape of Dublin bay. The suburbs, which have increased dramatically since the middle of the twentieth century, reach down to Bray and beyond into

Co. Wicklow in the south, to the west in the direction of Maynooth and to the north at least to Swords, the airport and beyond. The Dublin conurbation now encompasses about a third of the population of the Republic of Ireland.

Like any other modern city Dublin shows areas of high and low social prestige. Within Dublin there is a clear divide between the north and the south side of the city. The latter is regarded as more residentially desirable (as are some parts of the north side near the sea, e.g. Clontarf, Sutton, Howth). Within the south there is a cline in prestige with the area from Ballsbridge and Donnybrook out to Foxrock enjoying highest status. This is the area of certain key complexes like the Royal Dublin Society (an important exhibition and event centre in the capital) and the national television studios (RTÉ) and of the national university (University College Dublin) in Belfield. This entire area is known by its postal code, Dublin 4. Indeed this number has given the name to a sub-accent within Dublin English which was known as the 'Dublin 4 Accent', later referred to simply as 'D4 English', 'Dartspeak' or the 'Dart accent'. The less prestigious parts of the city are known by their district names such as Tallaght to the west and Ballymun in the north near the airport, a suburb with older high-rise flats and which is associated with adverse social conditions.

1.7.4   Varieties of Dublin English

Any discussion of English in Dublin necessitates a division into different types. The first comprises the inherited popular form of English in the capital. The term 'local' is intended to capture this and to emphasise that its speakers are those who show strongest identification with traditional Dublin life of which the popular accent is very much a part. The reverse of this is 'non-local', which refers to sections of the metropolitan population who do not wish a narrow, restrictive identification with popular Dublin culture. This group then subdivides into a larger, more general section, labelled 'mainstream', and a currently smaller group consisting of younger, usually lower-middle-class individuals who are, and have been, at the forefront of all changes in accent which can be observed in the capital; this group also consists mostly of females. For want of a better term, this group is labelled 'fashionable'.

(3)   1) *local* Dublin English
    2) *non-local* Dublin English   —   a) *mainstream* Dublin English
                                                      b) *fashionable* Dublin English

1.7.5   Features of local Dublin English

1.7.5.1   Vowels

Breaking.   Long high vowels are realised as two syllables with a hiatus when these vowels occur in closed syllables. The hiatus element is [j] with front vowels and [w] with back vowels.

(4)   a   *clean*   [klijən]   but: *be*   [biː]
     b   *fool*   [fuwəl]   *who*   [huː]

The disyllabification of long high vowels extends to diphthongs which have a high ending point, as can be seen in the following realisations.

(5)   a   *time*   [təjəm]   but: *fly*   [fləɪ]
     b   *pound*   [pɛwən]   *how*   [hɛʊ]

If one recognises a cline within local Dublin English then this disyllabification is definitely at the lower end. For instance, the front onset of the vowel in the MOUTH lexical set is quite common in colloquial, but not necessarily local varieties of Dublin English. However, one does not have a hiatus [w] or the deletion of the post-sonorant nasal (with or without a glottal stop as trace). The following are further salient characteristics of Dublin English.

(6)   a   Fronting of /au/
       down   [dɛʊn] – [deʊn]
     b   Distinction of historically short vowels before /r/
       circle   [sɛːkl̩]
       nurse   [nʊːs]
     c   Early modern English short /ʊ/
       Dublin   [dʊblən]

1.7.5.2   Consonants

Low rhoticity.   Local Dublin English is generally non-rhotic or shows only low rhoticity, i.e. non-prevocalic /r/ is weakly present, if at all.

(7)   a   *card*   [kæː(ʲ)d]
     b   *car*   [kæː(ʲ)]

Cluster simplification.   Consonantal syllable codas, particularly those consisting of stops after fricatives or sonorants, show a strong tendency to be simplified. Intermediate registers may have a glottal stop as a trace of the stop in question.

(8) a *pound* peʊn(ʔ)
     b *last*   [læːs(ʔ)]

Fortition of dental fricatives. The realisation of the first sound in words like *thin, think*, etc. as an alveolar plosive [t] is probably not a recent phenomenon. Hogan (1927: 71–2) notes that it is found in seventeenth-century plays (assuming that *t, d* represent [t, d]) and furthermore in the Dublin City Records (from the first period, i.e. before the seventeenth century, see above) where the third person singular ending -*th* appears as -t. According to Hogan alveolar realisations are common in rural varieties in the south and south-west of Ireland. Here they are probably a contact phenomenon deriving ultimately from the realisation of non-palatal /t, d/ in Irish. Hogan incidentally also remarks on the dental stops which are found in present-day Irish English (*loc. cit.*). The acoustic sensitivity of the Irish to the shift from dental to alveolar derives not least from the merger which results in local Dublin English and in many rural vernaculars in the south.

(9) mainstream speech   local speech
     thinker [t̪ɪŋkɚ]   *thinker, tinker* [tɪŋlɐ]
     tinker   [tɪŋkɚ]

     breathe [briːd̪]   *breathe, breed*   [briːd]
     breed   [briːd]

T-lenition. A salient feature of southern Irish English is the realisation of /t/ in positions of high sonority (intervocalically and post-vocalically before a pause) as an apico-alveolar fricative, sharing all features with /t/, bar closure. This cannot be indicated in English orthography of course, but vacillation between *t* and *th* for /t/ is found already in the *Kildare Poems* (probably early fourteenth century, Hickey 1993: 220–1) and would suggest that it was a feature of English in Ireland in the first period.

In local Dublin English the lenition of /t/ in a weak position is extended beyond the initial stage of apico-alveolar fricative to /r/ then to /h/ with final deletion as in the following instance.

(10) /t/   [t]   →   [ɹ]   →   [h]   →   ø
      water   [wɑːt̞ɚ]   [wɑːɹɚ]   [wɑːhɚ]   [wɑːɚ]

1.7.6 When change set in

During the 1990s major changes took place in non-vernacular Dublin English, essentially making this more different from traditional colloquial speech in the city. The increase in wealth and international position during the Celtic Tiger years (mid-1990s to 2008) meant that many young people aspired to an urban sophistication which was divorced from strongly local Dublin life. For this reason the developments in fashionable Dublin English diverged from those in local Dublin English, indeed they can be interpreted as a reaction to it. Furthermore, in-migrants to the city, who arrived there chiefly to avail of the job opportunities resulting from the economic boom, formed a group of upwardly mobile speakers, no longer attached to local communities, and their section of the city's population has been a key locus for change.

Linguistic behaviour which leads to divergence from local speech can be termed *dissociation* as it is motivated by the desire of speakers to hive themselves off from vernacular forms of a variety spoken in their immediate surroundings (Hickey 1998, 1999, 2013). It is furthermore a clear instance of speaker-innovation leading to language change, much in the sense of James and Lesley Milroy (J. Milroy 1992: 169–72; J. and L. Milroy 1997). The dissociation was realised phonetically by a reversal of the unrounding and lowering of vowels typical of local Dublin English. This reversal was systematic, with a raising and rounding of low back vowels being the most salient elements of the change (Hickey 1999). These vowel changes are displayed in Table 1.3.

The retraction of the PRICE vowel (Hickey 2005a: 51–3), as in *time* [taɪm], did not establish itself in later supraregional speech and there are only some individuals, mostly in south Dublin, who show a retracted

Table 1.3 Summary of the Dublin Vowel Shift from the 1990s

a) retraction of diphthongs with a low or back starting point				
time	[taɪm]	→	[tɑɪm]	
toy	[tɒɪ]	→	[tɔɪ], [toɪ]	
b) raising of low back vowels				
cot	[kɒt̪]	→	[kɔt̪]	
caught	[kɒːt̪]	→	[kɔːt̪], [koːt̪]	
			ɔɪ	oː
			↑	↑
Raising			ɔɪ ɔ	ɔː
			↑ ↑ ↑	
			ɒɪ ɒ ɒː	
Retraction aɪ		→	ɒɪ	

Table 1.4   Changes in non-local Dublin English by speaker age

Speakers	over 35	under 35	comment
Consonants			
WHICH	[ʍɪtʃ]	[wɪtʃ]	lack of [ʍ] # [w] distinction
MEAL	[miːl]	[miːɫ]	use of syllable-final [ɫ]
SORE	[soːɹ]	[soːɻ]	use of syllable-final retroflex [ɻ]
Vowels			
NORTH	[nɒːɹt̪]	[noːɹt̪]	considerable raising of vowel
MOUTH	[maʊt̪]	[mɛʊt̪]	fronting of diphthong onset
GOAT	[goʊt̪]	[gəʊt̪]	centralisation of diphthong onset (mostly confined to females)
GOOSE	[guːs]	[gʉːs, gyːs]	greatest degree of fronting found with young females
HORSE	[hɔːɹs]	[hoːɻs]	merger of HORSE-HOARSE sets

starting point for this diphthong. The fronting of the onset for the MOUTH vowel is a different matter: this is a local feature which is also found in non-local forms of Dublin English and which is firmly entrenched in new supraregional Irish English.

The new pronunciation quickly spread throughout the Republic of Ireland and is now (2015) the supraregional form of Irish English used by most males and all females under about 35 (see Table 1.4).

Despite these changes a southern Irish English accent can still be easily recognised. Dental stops are used for interdental fricatives, especially in syllable onsets, e.g. *think* [t̪ɪŋk]. The STRUT vowel is quite far back, a slightly centralised version of cardinal vowel [ʌ], i.e. [Ä], and may be somewhat rounded for some speakers, i.e. [ɔ̈]. Intervocalic and word-final/ pre-pausal /t/ is realised as [t̠], e.g. *cut* [kÄt̠]. The [t̠] is an apico-alveolar voiceless fricative and not laminal so that *hit* [hɪt̠] and *hiss* [hɪs] are not homophones.

There are several negative diagnostics of Irish English: TH-fronting does not occur anywhere and the use of a glottal stop for /-t-/ is primarily found in local Dublin English (word-finally, i.e. in the context /-t#/, glottalisation may occur in quick speech but not in reading style, for example). The vowels in TRAP and BATH show the same quality and only differ in length: [træp] and [bæːt̠]. A retracted [ɑː] in the BATH set is regarded as posh English and is generally not found in supraregional Irish English except in lexicalised instances like *father* [fɑːðɚ].

1.7.7 Irish, British and American English

The rise of a new pronunciation in the 1990s might be seen as due to an increasing influence of either British or American English, or a combination of both, on emerging forms of Dublin English among fashionable speakers in the metropolis. However, this is definitely not the case in any systematic way. Indeed for developments in the 1990s it seems difficult to posit any significant external influence on Irish English, north or south. There may well be parallels with either American or British English (see the following two sections), however these would appear to be coincidental and for each parallel which may be found, there are internal reasons within existing varieties of Irish English which can account adequately for their occurrence.

1.7.7.1 Parallels with American English

1. *Use of retroflex /r/* Among major varieties of English, supraregional American English is known for its retroflex [ɻ]. Locations in Britain which also show this realisation are the south-west of England (traditionally) and large parts of Scotland.
2. *Use of intervocalic alveolar tap* Among the allophones of /t/ in intervocalic position in recent Dublin English is a tap as in many forms of American English. This was produced by many young female speakers in the test sentence *They've a new water supply* when the present author was collecting data for *A Sound Atlas of Irish English* (Hickey 2004b). In conservative mainstream Irish English the realisation here would be as a fricative: [wɒːt̞ɚ]. In local Dublin English a glottal stop would be found: [wɑːʔɐ], but a tap is also possible as in *letter* [lɛɾɐ].
3. *Horse/hoarse-merger* For all supraregional speakers in Ireland born after the 1980s the vowels in these two words are pronounced the same. This homophony is true of many forms of English, not just American English, and it also holds for non-rhotic varieties, such as all those in the southern hemisphere.

Despite the above parallels, for the changes of the 1990s and early 2000s one cannot maintain that young Irish speakers adopted an American pronunciation of English. There are many obvious differences, such as the raising of the TRAP vowel before nasals or the realisations of alveolar/dental consonants, which are different in Irish English when compared to American English.

1.7.7.2 Parallels with British English

When considering British English within the context of Irish English, it should be noted that supraregional southern British English is not something which is regarded as worthy of emulation by the Irish, and certainly not in the form of Received Pronunciation. Quite the opposite is the case: for Irish people to imitate a standard southern British English accent would be to make themselves ridiculous in front of their Irish compatriots.

1. *Velarisation of syllable-final /l/* The velarised [ɫ] in non-local Dublin English has a parallel in southern British English though it is not anything like as old. The vocalisation of [ɫ] which is so often found in colloquial forms of English in the south-east of Britain has no counterpart in Irish English.
2. *Back vowel raising* The raised articulation of long low back vowels is an established feature of southern British English and is part of a long-term shift in long vowel values which commenced in late Middle English. However, the raising of back vowels in Irish English is not a historical continuation of an older process but a reaction to existing open vowel values in local Dublin English.
3. */au/-fronting* A front onset for the diphthong in the MOUTH lexical set is not so much a parallel with Received Pronunciation as with vernacular forms of English, especially in London and the Home Counties. In Ireland this is a feature of Dublin English which fashionable speakers did not dissociate themselves from and hence it has become a part of recent supraregional Irish English.

1.7.8 Short Front Vowel Lowering

In the above discussion of changes in non-local Dublin English, external influence was not favoured as an explanation. With the present set of changes the opposite seems to be the case. The lowering of short front vowels, which is so apparent in the recent speech of young non-local females, does not appear to be an internal development within Dublin English but an imported feature from North America (USA, possibly along with Canada). From a number of investigations in the past two decades it is known that the vowels of the KIT, DRESS and TRAP vowels are lowered in both Canada (see Clarke et al. 1995; Boberg 2005, 2012), and in California (see Kennedy and Grama 2012) and increasingly in other parts of the United States and the anglophone world in general, e.g. in South Africa and in Australia. This lowering of vowels would appear to have been adopted in Dublin by young, non-local females, as part of

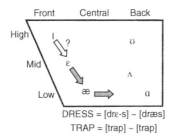

DRESS = [drɛ-s] ~ [dræs]
TRAP = [trap] ~ [trap]

Figure 1.1   Short Front Vowel Lowering in recent Dublin English

what is unconsciously perceived as a cool and trendy way of speaking (see Figure 1.1).

The lowering is not identical to that found in North America. In particular the KIT vowel is not lowered appreciably (only in the environment of /r-/, e.g. *rid* [red]) and the DRESS vowel, when it occurs before nasals as in *friend*, *bend*, *ten*, etc., does not show any noticeable lowering, probably due to the tendency for nasals to raise vowels. The greatest lowering is found for the DRESS vowel in pre-sibilant position,[1] e.g. *address*, *best*, *fresh*, *yes*, etc. with a realisation near [æ]. Those speakers who have this lowering also have a lowering and retraction of the TRAP vowel to a centralised [a] so that the vowels in the two lexical sets are kept distinct (see Figure 1.2).

Vowel movements are frequently interpreted (when internally motivated) as triggered by shifts in phonological space which lead to a realignment of vowel distinctions. For instance, the short front vowel

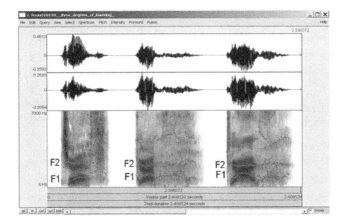

Figure 1.2   The word *dress* for three speakers with increasingly lowered vowels from left to right (recognisable in the higher value for F1 towards the right)

lowering found in Canada is regarded as connected to the reduction of phonological distinctions in the low back region due to the *Don* ∼ *dawn* merger in Canadian English (Boberg 2012: 174–5). The lowering in Dublin English would seem to only concern the DRESS and TRAP vowels; the LOT and STRUT vowels are, as yet, unaffected by this lowering. In addition, Dublin English, and Irish English in general, does not show any signs of a collapse of the distinction between the LOT and THOUGHT vowels (the *Don* ∼ *dawn* merger).

When searching for reasons for Short Front Vowel Lowering, one can advance both internal and external arguments as follows.

1. *Internal argument* Short Front Vowel Lowering is favoured in the environment of liquids, i.e. post-/r/ and pre-/l/. /r/ would depress the third formant of an adjacent vowel and hence favour lowering, cf. *breakfast* [brækfəst]. In non-local Dublin English syllable-final /l/ is velarised/pharyngealised and so would have a lowering effect on the preceding vowel, e.g. *hotel* [həʊtɛ̈l]. In addition, one could posit that the vowel shifts of the 1990s, i.e. upwards and forwards in the rear of vowel space, reduced the number of vocalic distinctions in this area, producing a drag effect on short front vowels similar to that posited for Canadian English due to under-utilisation of vowel space. See Figure 1.3:

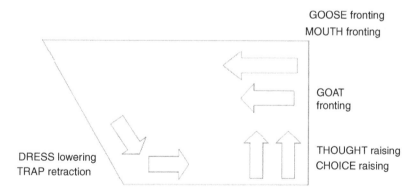

GOOSE fronting
MOUTH fronting

GOAT
fronting

DRESS lowering
TRAP retraction

THOUGHT raising
CHOICE raising

Figure 1.3 Rotation in vowel space

2. *External argument* Exposure in the media to young female speakers with Short Front Vowel Lowering might be responsible. In Ireland, young female broadcasters, weather forecasters and continuity

announcers on Irish national radio and television in general show Short Front Vowel Lowering. And it is also true that on local radio channels throughout the country young female broadcasters are now showing Short Front Vowel Lowering.

But this suggestion would still leave the unanswered question: how did people in the media pick up Short Front Vowel Lowering to begin with? Did some young females speakers go to Canada/USA (California) and pick up the rudiments of Short Front Vowel Lowering there and then plant the seed of this shift back in Dublin with the shift then spreading throughout the city?

It is probably too early to say whether Short Front Vowel Lowering will become an established feature of non-local Dublin English and hence of supraregional Irish English. The lowering is not found now (2015) with all young females and it is practically unknown among males. For variation of this kind to become an established instance of language change it would have to apply across the board and occur in the speech of both sexes. Whether this will happen in Dublin remains to be seen.

1.8   The enregisterment of Irish English

The phenomenon of enregisterment has become the object of linguists' attention in the past decade or so, triggered by seminal publications such as Agha (2003) and Silverstein (2003). The term stems from Agha and refers to a process whereby linguistic features of a variety become associated with its speakers and where a general awareness of these features arises. This awareness can be manifest in journalistic texts, in advertisements, on commercial products, often largely for the tourist industry, such as mugs, T-shirts or postcards. Enregistered features or references can appear on billboards in public places, often as puns; e.g. a public advertisement for cider displayed recently in Dublin had the text 'North Cider or South Cider', a pun on Northsider/Southsider, a reference to the class and linguistic division of Dublin into a northern part and a southern part divided by the River Liffey running through the centre of the city.

Enregisterment has been studied for a number of locations in the anglophone world, e.g. Pittsburgh (Johnstone et al. 2006) and the north of England (Beal and Cooper 2015). It is a process by which lay speakers become aware of what features are typical of their native variety and comment on these. Silverstein distinguishes three levels of indexicality which can be linked to the development of enregisterment (see Table 1.5):

Table 1.5   Levels of indexicality after Silverstein (2003)

Level 1	Linguists notice features
Level 2	Speakers notice features
Level 3	Features are overtly commented on in public (full enregisterment)

Of interest for the current section are only cases of level 3 indexicality. In the history of Irish English certain features have been the focus of overt comment, e.g. in political cartoons or in literary representations of Irish speech. A case in point is the variable (ai) in Irish English. Vernacular Dublin English shows a pronunciation with a central, schwa-like vowel as onset, e.g. *tie* [təɪ]. There is historical documentation of this realisation which shows that it was typical of Dublin English in late eighteenth-century Ireland. For instance, Fanny Burney (1752–1840), in her reminiscences of famous individuals she knew, imitates the Irish accent of the playwright Richard Brinsley Sheridan (1751–1816) by referring to his pronunciation of *kind* as [kəind], indicated orthographically as *koind*. This pronunciation seems to have become part of the stereotype of an Irish accent and authors such as Kipling used the <oi> spelling to indicate this, cf. his story *Soldiers Three* (1890) where he uses this spelling as in 'Those are the Black Oirish'. But there is an inherent difficulty with the use of <oi> for the realisation of (ai): at least in present-day varieties of Irish English it is not certain whether <oi> represents a centralised or a retracted onset, i.e. [əɪ] or [ɑɪ]. The novelist Paul Howard in the Ross O'Carroll-Kelly novels make frequent use of the spelling *roysh* for *right* and from the orthography it is not clear whether he intends [rəɪt] or [rɑɪt̪]. This situation can be contrasted with the enregisterment of features of Pittsburgh English such as the diphthong flattening found in words like *downtown* [daːntaːn]. This is unambiguously represented by <ah>, i.e. *downtown* is written *dahntahn* in representations of Pittburghese, e.g. on T-shirts, mugs, postcards and the like.

   Another enregistered feature of Irish English is the unraised realisation of <ea> in words like *tea, leave, meat*, etc. The original vowel in such words is /ɛː/ from Middle English. In vernacular varieties of Irish English this has remained a mid-vowel but in supraregional varieties it is /iː/ as in more standard forms of English. As opposed to the centralised onset of the /ai/ diphthong, unraised /ɛː/ can be indicated by <ay> as in *tay* or *crayture*. This realisation has been extended to instances of Middle English /eː/ and has a considerable pedigree in Irish English, e.g. *Jaysus* or *daycent*, found in the Dublin plays of Sean O'Casey in the early twentieth century.

Enregisterment of other local features is dependent on the options of English orthography. For instance, the high unrounded vowel in words like *but, cut, done, come*, is not normally given any particular representation in vernacular narrative in plays or novels set in Dublin, although this realisation is iconic of local Dublin English, and occurs in the name of the city. It is furthermore one which is unique in the anglophone world, with the exception of the North of England.

An orthographic option which is available in principle would be <d> to indicate the stop realisation of English interdental fricatives in words like *dis, dem, dose* 'this, them, those'. But Dublin writers, and Irish writers in general, have not used <d> for English /ð/, perhaps because it involves far too much alternation of the orthography given the high occurrence of <th> spellings in English.

In the realm of grammar there are a number of clearly enregistered features. An obvious instance is *youse* or *yez* as a special second person plural pronoun (but not the archaic form *ye* which serves the same grammatical purpose in supraregional Irish English). Both of these are specifically Irish (Hickey 2003b) with the former having spread to many colonies due to significant Irish input in the nineteenth century, e.g. Australia and New Zealand.

Enregisterment implies a general awareness of features specific to a certain variety or set of varieties. Some features which are commented on prescriptively in an Irish context are not, however, confined to Irish English but are common across vernacular forms of English in a broader context. An instance is provided by demonstrative *them*, as in *Them shoes are nice*, which is ubiquitous in non-standard English.

The vocabulary of Irish English offers a number of clear cases of enregisterment. These can involve a specifically Irish realisation of an English word, as in *eejit* for *idiot*, or an English word borrowed into Irish and re-borrowed back into English in an idiomatic sense, as in *craic* for social enjoyment (see Section 1.6 above). Further examples, from the semantic-pragmatic interface would be *gas* in the sense 'fun, ridicule' or *grand* as an expression of approval or reassurance (Hickey, in press).

It should be remarked that enregistered features may in some instances have a vacuous reference, somewhat like a stereotype which does not apply to a variety although it may have done in the past. A case in point is the orthographic representation of the vowel in words like *start*, *hard*, *art*. In journalistic and popular references to posh south Dublin accents, and in the novels of Paul Howard mentioned above, this vowel is rendered orthographically by <*o*>, cf. *orts* for *arts*. While this pronunciation may have existed for a short time in the late 1980s and early 1990s, it is not actually used today: for the vast majority of Dubliners the START vowel is mid to front, i.e. in the region of [a: ~ æ:].

Enregisterment would seem to involve referring to and the use of local features by non-vernacular speakers; that is, it is often about outsiders looking in on the variety in question. But some features are simply too confined to a purely vernacular mode to be used by others, e.g. the non-rhotic character of local Dublin English which could, incidentally, be easily shown in spelling, e.g. *cah*, *fah*, *hahd*, *bohd*. Furthermore, for complex linguistic and historical reasons, the Irish tend to belittle their own marked accent of English (they see it as vulgar, not to be taken seriously). This fact militates against the positive enregisterment and commodification of Irish English.

Finally, one could ask whether enregisterment might lead (i) to the perpetuation of features in a variety, as in the case of unraised /ɛ:/ seen in *Jaysus*, *tay*, etc., or (ii) to the introduction of features into a variety in the case of supposed features. If the latter is true, then enregisterment could become a trigger for language change, i.e. spuriously enregistered features, like *ort* for *art*, could lead to a genuine instance of language change if speakers begin to use the *ort* pronunciation outside the context of enregisterment.

1.9 Conclusion

The development of the English language in Ireland, both historically and at the present, has provided food for linguistic discussion and continues to do so, due to the long-term interaction of Irish and English and to different types of regional input. General linguistic insights into language contact and language shift have recently been brought to bear on research into English in Ireland. There has also been an increasing awareness of the different varieties represented historically in Ireland and surviving to this day, e.g. Ulster Scots (Hickey 2011a).

It is a measure of the maturity of the field that all subareas have been covered by significant publications of late; cf. the attention given to the pragmatics of Irish English in recent publications (Barron and Schneider (eds) 2005; Amador-Moreno et al. (eds) 2015) and to the arguments for various standpoints, especially the relative weight accorded to contact versus retention (Filppula 1999, 2003) in the historical development of Irish English. The databases for analyses have also been expanded through the compilation of a number of text corpora documenting Irish English in several respects (Kirk and Kallen 2008; Hickey 2003a). Avenues which remain to be fully explored do exist, most noticeably contemporary urban Irish English and non-native varieties used by immigrants (Diskin and Regan 2015), the most likely loci of linguistic change in years to come.

Note

1. Audio examples of Short Front Vowel Lowering can be found on the research website *Variation and Change in Dublin English* accessible at the following URL: http://www.uni-due.de/VCDE.

References

Adams, George Brendan (1965). 'Materials for a language map of seventeenth century Ireland', *Ulster Dialect Archive Bulletin* 4: 15–30.

Agha, Asif (2003). 'The social life of a cultural value', *Language and Communication* 23: 231–73.

Amador-Moreno, Carolina P., Kevin McCafferty and Elaine Vaughan (eds) (2015). *Pragmatic Markers in Irish English*. Amsterdam: John Benjamins.

Barron, Anne and Klaus Schneider (eds) (2005). *The Pragmatics of Irish English*. Berlin: de Gruyter Mouton.

Baugh, Albert C. and Thomas Cable (2002). *A History of the English Language*. Fifth edition. London: Routledge.

Beal, Joan C. (1993). 'The grammar of Tyneside and Northumbrian English', in: Milroy and Milroy (eds), pp. 187–213.

Beal, Joan C. and Paul Cooper (2015). 'The enregisterment of Northern English', in: Raymond Hickey (ed.) *Researching Northern English*. Amsterdam: John Benjamins.

Bliss, Alan J. (1972). 'Languages in contact: Some problems of Hiberno-English', *Proceedings of the Royal Irish Academy* 72, Section C: 63–82.

Bliss, Alan J. (1979). *Spoken English in Ireland 1600–1740. Twenty-Seven Representative Texts Assembled and Analysed*. Dublin: Cadenus Press.

Boberg, Charles (2005). 'The Canadian shift in Montreal', *Language Variation and Change* 17.2: 133–54.

Boberg, Charles (2012). 'Standard Canadian English', in: Raymond Hickey (ed.) *Standards of English. Codified Varieties around the World*. Cambridge: Cambridge University Press, pp. 159–78.

Clancy, Brian (2015). '"Hurry up baby son all the boys is finished their breakfast": Examining the use of vocatives as markers in Irish Traveller and settled family discourse', in: Amador-Moreno, McCafferty and Vaughan (eds), pp. 229–47.

Clark, James M. (1977) [1917]. *The Vocabulary of Anglo-Irish* (original edition, St. Gallen, Handelshochschule). Reprinted Philadelphia: R. West.

Clarke, Sandra, Ford Elms and Amani Youssef (1995). 'The third dialect of English: Some Canadian evidence', *Language Variation and Change* 7: 209–28.

Corrigan, Karen P. (1993). 'Hiberno-English syntax: Nature versus nurture in a creole context', *Newcastle and Durham Working Papers in Linguistics* 1: 95–131.

Daly, Mary (1990). 'Literacy and language change in the late nineteenth and early twentieth centuries', in: Mary Daly and David Dickson (eds) *The Origins of Popular Literacy in Ireland: Language Change and Educational Development 1700–1920*. Dublin: Anna Livia, pp. 153–66.

Dent, Robert W. (1994). *Colloquial Language in* Ulysses: *a Reference Tool*. Newark: University of Delaware Press.

Diskin, Chloé and Vera Regan (2015). 'Migratory experience and second language acquisition among Polish and Chinese migrants in Dublin, Ireland', in: Fanny Forsberg Lundell and Inge Bartning (eds) *Cultural Migrants and Optimal Language Acquisition*. Clevedon: Multilingual Matters.

Dolan, Terence (2012) [1998]. *A Dictionary of Hiberno-English. The Irish Use of English*. Third edition. Dublin: Gill and Macmillan.

Dowling, Patrick J. (1968) [1935]. *The Hedge Schools of Ireland* (original edition, London: Longmans). Revised edition Cork: Mercier Press.

Fenton, James (2014) [1995]. *The Hamely Tongue. A Personal Record of Ulster-Scots in County Antrim*. Fourth edition. Newtownards: Ulster-Scots Academic Press.

Filppula, Markku (1991). 'Urban and rural varieties of Hiberno-English', in: Jenny Cheshire (ed.) *English Around the World: Sociolinguistic Perspectives*. Cambridge: Cambridge University Press, pp. 51–60.

Filppula, Markku (1993). 'Changing paradigms in the study of Hiberno-English', *Irish University Review* 23.2: 202–23.

Filppula, Markku (1999). *The Grammar of Irish English. Language in Hibernian Style*. London: Routledge.

Filppula, Markku (2003). 'The quest for the most "parsimonious" explanations: endogeny vs. contact revisited', in Hickey (ed.), pp. 161–73.

Greene, David (1979). 'Perfects and Perfectives in Modern Irish', *Ériu* 30: 122–41.

Hamel, August van (1912). 'On Anglo-Irish syntax', *Englische Studien* 45: 272–92.

Harris, John (1984). 'Syntactic variation and dialect divergence', *Journal of Linguistics* 20: 303–27.

Hayden, Mary and Marcus Hartog (1909). 'The Irish dialect of English', *Fortnightly Review*, Old Series / New Series 91–85: 933–47.

Henry, Patrick L. (1957). *An Anglo-Irish Dialect of North Roscommon*. Zürich: Aschmann and Scheller.

Henry, Patrick L. (1958). 'A linguistic survey of Ireland. Preliminary report', *Norsk Tidsskrift for Sprogvidenskap [Lochlann, A Review of Celtic Studies]* Supplement 5: 49–208.

Hickey, Raymond (1993). 'The beginnings of Irish English', *Folia Linguistica Historica* 14: 213–38.

Hickey, Raymond (1995). 'An assessment of language contact in the development of Irish English', in: Jacek Fisiak (ed.) *Language Change under Contact Conditions*. Berlin: Mouton de Gruyter, pp. 109–30.

Hickey, Raymond (1997). 'Arguments for creolisation in Irish English', in: Raymond Hickey and Stanisław Puppel (eds) *Language History and Linguistic Modelling. A Festschrift for Jacek Fisiak on his Sixtieth Birthday*. Berlin: Mouton de Gruyter, pp. 969–1038.

Hickey, Raymond (1998). 'The Dublin Vowel Shift and the historical perspective', in: Jacek Fisiak and Marcin Krygier (eds) *English Historical Linguistics*. Berlin: Mouton de Gruyter, pp. 79–106.

Hickey, Raymond (1999). 'Dublin English: Current changes and their motivation', in: Paul Foulkes and Gerry Docherty (eds) *Urban Voices*. London: Edward Arnold, pp. 265–81.

Hickey, Raymond (2000). 'Models for describing aspect in Irish English', in: Hildegard Tristram (ed.) *The Celtic Englishes II*. Heidelberg: Carl Winter, pp. 97–116.

Hickey, Raymond (2002a). *A Source Book for Irish English*. Amsterdam: John Benjamins.

Hickey, Raymond (2002b). 'Dublin and Middle English', in: Peter J. and Angela M. Lucas (eds) *Middle English. From Tongue to Text. Selected Papers from the Third International Conference on Middle English: Language and Text Held at Dublin, Ireland, 1–4 July 1999*. Frankfurt: Lang, pp. 187–200.

Hickey, Raymond (2003a). *Corpus Presenter. Software for Language Analysis*. Amsterdam: John Benjamins.

Hickey, Raymond (2003b). 'Rectifying a standard deficiency. Pronominal distinctions in varieties of English', in: Irma Taavitsainen and Andreas H. Jucker (eds) *Diachronic Perspectives on Address Term Systems*. Amsterdam: Benjamins, pp. 345–74.

Hickey, Raymond (2004a). 'The phonology of Irish English', in: Bernd Kortmann et al. (ed.) *Handbook of Varieties of English. Volume 1: Phonology*. Berlin: Mouton de Gruyter, pp. 68–97.

Hickey, Raymond (2004b). *A Sound Atlas of Irish English*. Berlin: Mouton de Gruyter.

Hickey, Raymond (2005a). *Dublin English. Evolution and Change*. Amsterdam: John Benjamins.

Hickey, Raymond (2005b). 'English in Ireland', in: D. Alan Cruse, Franz Hundsnurscher, Michael Job and Peter R. Lutzeier (eds) *Lexikologie-Lexicology*. Berlin: Mouton de Gruyter, pp. 1256–60.

Hickey, Raymond (2007a). *Irish English. History and Present-day Forms*. Cambridge: Cambridge University Press.

Hickey, Raymond (2007b). 'Southern Irish English', in: David Britain (ed.) *Language in the British Isles*. Second edition. Cambridge: Cambridge University Press, pp. 135–51.

Hickey, Raymond (2009). 'Telling people how to speak. Rhetorical grammars and pronouncing dictionaries', in: Ingrid Tieken-Boon van Ostade and Wim van der Wurff (eds) *Current Issues in Late Modern English*. Frankfurt: Peter Lang, pp. 89–116.

Hickey, Raymond (2011a). 'Ulster Scots in present-day Ireland', in: Hickey (ed.) 2011a, pp. 291–323.

Hickey, Raymond (2011b). *The Dialects of Irish, Study of a Changing Landscape*. Berlin: de Gruyter Mouton.

Hickey, Raymond (2012a). 'English in Ireland', in: Raymond Hickey (ed.) *Areal Features of the Anglophone World*. Berlin: de Gruyter Mouton, pp. 79–107.

Hickey, Raymond (2012b). 'Standard Irish English', in: Hickey (ed.), pp. 96–116.

Hickey, Raymond (2013). 'Supraregionalisation and dissociation', in: J. K. Chambers and Natalie Schilling (eds) *Handbook of Language Variation and Change*. Second edition. Malden, MA: Wiley-Blackwell, pp. 537–54.

Hickey, Raymond (2015). 'The pragmatics of Irish English', in: Amador-Moreno, McCafferty and Vaughan (eds), pp. 17–36.

Hickey, Raymond (In press). 'The pragmatics of *grand* in Irish English', *Journal of Historical Pragmatics*.

Hickey, Raymond (ed.) (2003). *Motives for Language Change*. Cambridge: Cambridge University Press.

Hickey, Raymond (ed.) (2010). *Eighteenth-Century English. Evolution and Change*. Cambridge: Cambridge University Press.

Hickey, Raymond (ed.) (2011a). *Researching the Languages of Ireland*. Uppsala: Uppsala University.

Hickey, Raymond (ed.) (2011b). *Irish English in Today's World*. Special issue of *English Today* 106 (June 2011). Cambridge: Cambridge University Press.

Hickey, Raymond (ed.) (2012). *Standards of English. Codified Varieties Around the World*. Cambridge: Cambridge University Press.

Hogan, James Jeremiah (1927). *The English Language in Ireland*. Dublin: Educational Company of Ireland.

Hogan, James Jeremiah (1934). *An Outline of English Philology Chiefly for Irish Students*. Dublin: Educational Company of Ireland.

Johnstone, Barbara, Jennifer Andrus and Andrew R. Danielson (2006). 'Mobility, indexicality and the enregisterment of "Pittsburghese"', *Journal of English Linguistics* 34: 77–101.

Joyce, Patrick W. (1910). *English As We Speak It in Ireland*. London: Longmans, Green and Co.

Kallen, Jeffrey L. (1989). 'Tense and aspect categories in Irish English', *English World-Wide* 10: 1–39.

Kallen, Jeffrey L. (1990). 'The Hiberno-English perfect: Grammaticalisation revisited', *Irish University Review* 20.1: 120–36.

Kallen, Jeffrey L. (1996). 'Entering lexical fields of Irish English', in: Juhani Klemola, Merja Kytö and Matti Rissanen (eds) *Speech Past and Present: Studies in English Dialectology in Memory of Ossi Ihalainen*. Frankfurt: Peter Lang, pp. 101–9.

Kallen, Jeffrey L. (2013). *Irish English, Vol. 2. The Republic of Ireland*. Berlin: de Gruyter Mouton.

Kennedy, Robert and James Grama (2012). 'Chain shifting and centralization in California vowels: an acoustic analysis', *American Speech* 87.1: 39–56.

Kirk, John M. (1997). 'Irish English and contemporary literary writing', in: Jeffrey Kallen (ed.) *Focus on Ireland*. Amsterdam, John Benjamins, pp. 189–205.

Kirk, John M. (1998). 'Ulster Scots. Realities and myths', *Ulster Folklife* 44: 69–93.

Kirk, John M. and Jeffrey L. Kallen (2008). *ICE-Ireland: a User's Guide*. Belfast: Cló Ollscoil na Banríona.

Kirk, John M. and Jeffrey L. Kallen (2011). 'The cultural context of ICE-Ireland', in: Hickey (ed.) 2011a, pp. 269–90.

Kirwin, William J. (1993). 'The planting of Anglo-Irish in Newfoundland', in: Sandra Clarke (ed.) *Focus on Canada*. Amsterdam: John Benjamins, pp. 65–84.

Lucas, Angela (ed.) (1995). *Anglo-Irish Poems of the Middle Ages*. Dublin: Columba Press.

Macafee, Caroline I. (ed.) (1995). *A Concise Ulster Dictionary*. Oxford: Oxford University Press.

McCafferty, Kevin (2001). *Ethnicity and Language Change: English in (London)Derry, Northern Ireland.* Amsterdam: John Benjamins.

McDermott, Philip (2011). '"Irish isn't spoken here?", Language policy and planning in Ireland', in: Hickey (ed.) 2011b, pp. 25–31.

Milroy, James (1978). 'Belfast: Change and variation in an urban vernacular', in: Peter Trudgill (ed.) *Sociolinguistic Patterns in British English.* London: Edward Arnold, pp. 19–36.

Milroy, James (1992). *Linguistic Variation and Change.* Oxford: Blackwell.

Milroy, James and Lesley Milroy (1997). 'Exploring the social constraints on language change', in: Stig Eliasson and Ernst Håkon Jahr (eds) *Language and its Ecology: Essays in Memory of Einar Haugen.* Berlin: Mouton de Gruyter, pp. 75–101.

Milroy, James and Lesley Milroy (eds) (1993). *Real English. The Grammar of the English Dialects in the British Isles.* London: Longman.

Milroy, Lesley (1987). *Language and Social Networks.* Second edition. Oxford: Blackwell.

Montgomery, Michael and Robert Gregg (1997). 'The Scots language in Ulster', in: Charles Jones (ed.) *The Edinburgh History of the Scots Language.* Edinburgh: Edinburgh University Press, pp. 569–622.

Moylan, Séamus (1996). *The Language of Kilkenny.* Dublin: Geography Publications.

Odlin, Terence (1991). 'Irish English idioms and language transfer', *English World-Wide* 12.2: 175–93.

O'Donovan, John (1845). *A Grammar of the Irish Language.* Dublin: Hodges and Smith.

O'Hehir, Brendan (1967). *A Gaelic Lexicon for 'Finnegans Wake' and Glossary for Joyce's Other Works.* Berkeley and Los Angeles: University of California Press.

Ó Muirithe, Diarmaid (1996). *Dictionary of Anglo-Irish: Words and Phrases from Irish.* Dublin: Four Courts Press.

Ó Sé, Diarmuid (1992). 'The perfect in Modern Irish', *Ériu* 43: 39–47.

Ó Sé, Diarmuid (2004). 'The "after" perfect and related constructions in Gaelic dialects', *Ériu* 54: 179–248.

Patterson, David (1860). *The Provincialisms of Belfast and the Surrounding Districts Pointed Out and Corrected.* Belfast: Alexander Mayne.

Robinson, Philip (1994) [1984]. *The Plantation of Ulster. British Settlement in an Irish Landscape, 1600–1670.* Belfast: Ulster Historical Foundation.

Share, Bernard (2003) [1997]. *Slanguage: a Dictionary of Slang and Colloquial English in Ireland.* Second edition. Dublin, Gill and Macmillan.

Sheridan, Thomas (1781). *A Rhetorical Grammar of the English Language Calculated Solely for the Purpose of Teaching Propriety of Pronunciation and Justness of Delivery, in that Tongue.* Dublin: Price.

Silverstein, Michael (2003). 'Indexical order and the dialectics of sociolinguistic life', *Language and Communication* 23: 193–239.

Sullivan, James (1980). 'The validity of literary dialect: evidence from the theatrical portrayal of Hiberno-English', *Language and Society* 9: 195–219.

Tieken-Boon van Ostade, Ingrid (2010). 'Lowth as an icon of prescriptivism', in: Raymond Hickey (ed.) *Eighteenth-Century English. Ideology and Change.* Cambridge: Cambridge University Press, pp. 73–88.

Todd, Loreto (1990). *Words Apart: a Dictionary of Northern Irish English.* Gerrards Cross: Colin Smythe.

Traynor, Michael (1953). *The English Dialect of Donegal: a Glossary.* Dublin: Royal Irish Academy.

Vallancey, Charles (1788). 'Memoir of the language, manners, and customs of an Anglo-Saxon colony settled in the baronies of Forth and Bargie in the County of Wexford, Ireland, in 1167, 1168, 1169', *Transactions of the Royal Academy* 2: 19–41.

Wall, Richard (1995). *A Glossary for the Irish Literary Revival.* Gerrards Cross: Colin Smythe.

Walsh, James J. (1926). 'Shakespeare's pronunciation of the Irish brogue', in: James J. Walsh (ed.) *The World's Debt to the Irish.* Boston: The Stratford Company, pp. 297–327.

Zeuss, Johann Kaspar (1871). *Grammatica Celtica.* Revised edition by Hans Ebel. Berlin: Weidmannsche Verlagbuchhandlung.

2
The Irish Language in Present-day Ireland

Brian Ó Catháin

2.1 Introduction[1]

If one were to observe the general state of Irish in Ireland today, one could readily conclude that the language is in a healthy state and that there is no immediate danger to it, particularly given the following circumstances:[2]

1. Irish has primary official language-status in Bunreacht na hÉireann ('The Constitution of Ireland') and it also has official language-status in the legislation of the European Union.
2. The Official Languages Act, 2003 (Acht na dTeangacha Oifigiúla, 2003), the Language Commissioner (Coimisinéir Teanga) and the Office of the Commissioner of Official Languages (Oifig Choimisinéir na dTeangacha Oifigiúla) are in operation in the Republic of Ireland in order to ensure that speakers of Irish may (i) employ Irish in their dealings with state and semi-state/public organisations; (ii) have recourse to an independent arbitrator where service through Irish is lacking, in whole or in part. It may also be noted that an Irish Language Act for Northern Ireland has been promised by the British Government since the 2006 St Andrews' Agreement.
3. A publicly funded language body, Foras na Gaeilge, which seeks to promote Irish in a variety of spheres, is active throughout the whole of Ireland.
4. A government department (An Roinn Ealaíon, Oidhreachta agus Gaeltachta/The Department of Arts, Heritage and the Gaeltacht) and a dedicated junior minister therein are entrusted with the duty, care and implementation of the state's main policies regarding Irish,

its latest policy being set out in the ambitious – over-ambitious, according to some observers – 20-year strategy document entitled *Straitéis Fiche Bliain don Ghaeilge 2010–2030*.

5. Irish continues to be learned by all primary and post-primary pupils, the average pupil spending some 14 years in total learning Irish.

6. There continues to be growth in demand for Irish-medium education, particularly in the case of primary level Irish-medium schools, known as Gaelscoileanna.

7. The dedicated national Irish language radio station, Raidió na Gaeltachta, established in 1972, continues to offer a comprehensive service to speakers of Irish in the official Irish-speaking areas, throughout the country, and worldwide (via the internet); the Irish-language television channel, TG4, founded in 1996, in addition to other broadcast, print and digital media, cater, to varying degrees, for the national and international Irish language community.

8. Irish language sites and material occupy a significant place in the internet serving the global Irish language community.

9. Irish continues, with support from the state, to be cultivated at academic, literary, cultural and popular levels, and a significant body of literature continues to be published.

10. The majority of Irish people have a favourable attitude towards Irish and wish to see it continue to exist, to prosper and to be fostered by the state.

11. Census returns report continued overall growth in the number of speakers of Irish in the entire country: according to the latest figures from 2011, 40.6 per cent of the population of the Republic of Ireland (3 years +) self-reported ability to speak Irish, and 10.7 per cent of the equivalent population of Northern Ireland self-reported a similar ability.

12. Significant general interest in Irish exists among the international community – both those living within and outside Ireland.

13. There exists a considerable body of people in Ireland who are not native speakers but who have learned the language as a second language – generally through the educational system – and who use it regularly, in some cases, also choosing to speak it in the home and thereby transmit it to the next generation.

With regard to the state of Irish in the Gaeltacht – a collective term employed to designate those officially recognised regions of Ireland, predominantly on the west coast, where Irish continues its historical existence (or where it is assumed to continue the same) as the everyday community language of the majority – it is clear that a different situation exists: here there exists a significant decline in the use of Irish in the home and as a community language, and, more crucially, there exists a significant decline in intergenerational transmission of the language. Furthermore, it is clear that this decline has accelerated over the past 30 years or so. To quote Fennell (1981: 36) '...in the course of the 1970s, in the principal Irish-speaking territories, the majority have begun to rear their children in English.... Since this kind of situation has been the usual prelude to the disappearance of an Irish-speaking district, it is fair to say that the final dissolution of the Gaeltacht is now in sight.' Hindley (1990: 248) has the following to say on this matter: 'There is no room for honest doubt that the Irish language is now dying.' From a later comprehensive report dealing with the use and state of Irish in the Gaeltacht – Ó Giollagáin et al. (2007) – it is clear that the position of Irish as a community language in the Gaeltacht is so fragile that these authors anticipated the demise of Irish in the Gaeltacht within a period of 15–20 years. An updated version of this report, covering the period 2006–11, was concluded in 2014, and its findings – see Ó Giollagáin and Charlton (2015) – point clearly to further weakening of the use and position of Irish in the Gaeltacht. All these authors highlight an issue which is a key factor in the general demise of the language: a clear reduction in the numbers of children who are acquiring and speaking Irish in the home. To put it in another way, there has been a noticeable increase in the number of parents in the Gaeltacht who have chosen, and are choosing, to rear their children with English as their first language rather than Irish. This development, in tandem with a general convention found both in the Gaeltacht and in general society in Ireland, to acquiesce to the use of English as the default community language, particularly in situations where one or more non-speakers of Irish are present, is resulting, in the Gaeltacht, in subtractive bilingualism with English consequently gaining the upper hand – see further Ó Riagáin (1997).

The focus of the present contribution is on language shift, from Irish to English, not merely in the present-day context but also in the context of the history of Irish, the present language shift being a phenomenon which is rooted in historical change in Ireland. Some changes which have been taking place in spoken Irish today will also be examined and, in conclusion, the question will be addressed as to what is in store for the Irish language as a spoken language.

2.1.1 Language shift and language death

Language shift occurs when the members of an L1 speech community begin to use an alternative language, L2, in domains in which they hitherto employed their own L1. This process is often triggered by social and political changes and the change from L1 to L2, it has been noted, is frequently completed within a period of three generations: the change begins in the first generation of speakers who are monolingual, speaking L1 alone, or for whom L1 is their main language. The change continues in the second generation; at this point, speakers are bilingual in L1 and L2, with varying competence in both languages (L1 as the primary and L2 as the secondary language or L2 as the primary and L1 as the secondary language). In the third generation, speakers are monolingual, speaking L2 alone, or they have L2 as their primary language and possess, at most, a passive understanding of L1. When change of this type occurs, L2 frequently has a pronounced influence on L1: one can observe major changes taking place in L1 – for instance, one may have considerable borrowing from L2 into L1, or code-mixing/code-switching of L2 and L1 occurs. At the stage where the community of L1 speakers cease to use L1 entirely, one can speak of 'language death'. The term 'language death' is also used in the case where a particular speech population is destroyed – either 'naturally' or sometimes by means of violence – and when the language is no longer present anywhere else in the world (see Crystal 2000 for a general account of language shift and death). The term 'language maintenance' is employed to refer to a situation where one language is still in use but where a different language is regarded as more 'important' than the other, for example, when the latter language is perceived as having a higher status or more speakers – the endangerment of Scottish Gaelic and Irish, on the one hand, and Breton, on the other, are dealt with by Watson (1989) and Kuter (1989) respectively, while Harrison (2007) deals with the same topic on a more general level. If one considers all the Celtic languages, including Irish, which are still spoken today, one can conclude that significant language shift is characteristic of all of them: there are few monolingual speakers left and the bilingual speakers that exist are under considerable pressure to eschew their first language, a minority language, and to adopt the majority language, be it English or French.

Various stages of language shift may result when a given speech community interacts with another community employing a different language, but the final result of complete language shift is, of course, language death. Language death carries major implications which may not always be fully understood or recognised by the last speakers of the endangered language: not only does the death of a language simply spell the end of a means of communication for the community in question, but it also signifies an end to its associated culture – be this oral or written – and indeed to the ideology of the community whose language is thus endangered. It is obvious that it is not just a given speech community which suffers when a language dies but the global collective group of all speech communities who lose one further member, and with that, a part of their identity. When one considers that some linguists believe that between 50 per cent and 90 per cent of the 6900 languages of the world are about to die in the next century (Romaine 2008: 12, see also McCloskey 2001: 15–17), it is obvious that language shift/death are phenomena which are happening at an unprecedented rate on a global scale (Nettle and Romaine 2000; Harrison 2007).

2.2 The languages of Ireland

A general summary of the use of the two main spoken languages in Ireland from the period of Old Irish (600–900 CE) to the Modern Irish period (from approximately 1650 CE to the present), would recognise four (or, if one views Irish as already extinct, possibly five) major periods, which can be ordered chronologically as follows:

P1: Irish is the majority language in use and is spoken by all.

P2: Irish and English are used as spoken languages, but the use of Irish is much more widespread than that of English, i.e. the status of Irish is superior to that of English.

P3: Irish and English are used as spoken languages, but in certain high-status domains the use of English is much more widespread, i.e. the status of English is superior to that of Irish.

P4: Irish and English are used as spoken languages, but Irish is a minority language only employed by small geographically unlinked speech-communities and by small networks of speakers within the majority population which generally employs English, the status of which is dominant.

(P5: English is the sole majority language used and spoken by all.)

If one accepts this five-period reading, it is apparent that the following short summary can be made (1) two monolingual periods exist: P1 and P5; (2) three periods of bilingualism exist – P2, P3 and P4 – in which varying degrees of strength for Irish and English are found; (3) the situation regarding spoken Irish has been weakening from P1 to P5, i.e. the use and dominance of English has been increasing from P2 to P5.

2.2.1   Irish from the sixteenth to the twentieth century

On looking at the use of Irish in the Ireland of the sixteenth century, one can observe that it was spoken across the country in all societal domains. English was spoken at the same time by groups of speakers, particularly in towns, but these groups did not enjoy any elevated status. From the beginning of the seventeenth century, however, major political, social and economic changes took place. As a result of these changes, the old established social and political order collapsed. Political power was taken from the native Irish, and plantations were established whereby outsider speakers of English were installed in territories which had previously belonged to the Irish. The native Gaelic lords either succumbed to the new English order or left the country, and the native Irish language professional poets, who until now had played a significant role in Irish society, were subsequently left without support or patronage. Naturally, these political, cultural and social disturbances affected the Irish language too, and, as a consequence, the status of the language in society came to be reduced greatly. At the same time, the importance of English as a spoken language increased, especially in urban centres. While it is clear that use of Irish was still very robust in rural areas, the population employing Irish generally belonged to the lower ranks of society who were not in a political, economic or cultural position to challenge English, the use of which by the superior ranks of society was ever-increasing. Wall summarises the situation succinctly:

> By 1800 Irish had ceased to be the language habitually spoken in the homes of all those who had already achieved success in the world, or who aspired to improve or even maintain their position politically, socially or economically. The pressures of six hundred years of foreign occupation, and more particularly the complicated political, religious and economic pressures of the seventeenth and eighteenth centuries, had killed Irish at the top of the social scale and had already weakened its position amongst the entire population of the country. (Wall 1969: 82)

With regard to the subsequent major language shift which took place in Ireland during the course of the nineteenth century, one can list five general reasons:

1. The particular negative economic situation of speakers of Irish: Irish was now generally in use by an economically impoverished low-status rural population, living a hand-to-mouth existence.

2. Demographic change: although the population of Ireland at the beginning of the nineteenth century was at its greatest ever, it was devastated by the Great Famine (1845–8) when, at a conservative estimate, a million people died and another million emigrated, most of those thus affected being native speakers of Irish. A further critical blow dealt to the Irish-speaking population by the Famine was the increased underlying perception on the part of speakers of Irish of the importance of English and their need to demonstrate competence in it, especially given the likely necessity of emigration to the United States of America and Canada, a process which was already under full swing in the nineteenth century, and which would continue well into the twentieth century, where, while the target country changed substantially to Britain, the requirement for English remained the same.

3. Lack of institutional support: the educational system and the Catholic Church (representative of the faith of the vast majority of people in Ireland), as well as the political and legal systems offered no support for Irish. If one regards, for example, the system of public primary education in Ireland (the 'National Schools'), initiated in 1831, one can see that no place was accorded to Irish, or to the native culture of Ireland, in the curriculum of these schools; see Ó Buachalla (1981). St Patrick's College, Maynooth, the national centre for the training of Catholic priests, founded in 1795, was, in effect, an English language institution. Despite the establishment of a chair of Irish at St Patrick's College, and despite the personal support for Irish given by some of its staff and trustee-bishops, it cannot be claimed that the ecclesiastical authorities there sought, in a continuous and systematic fashion, to enable English-speaking clerical students, who in the future would serve primarily as priests in all parts of Ireland, including Irish-speaking districts, to be in a position to execute their duties fully through the medium of Irish.

4. Lack of status: if one views, by way of example, the language disposition of two individuals who can be regarded amongst the leading native figures of the period, then one can readily see that they too were persuaded of the 'superiority' of English:

   (a) Daniel O'Connell (1775–1847), the foremost Irish politician of this period, was a native speaker of Irish, but he rarely, if ever, employed the language at public meetings although Irish was, at the time, the common language of the broad masses of the population (Ó Dochartaigh 1992: 22). With regard to his attitude

to the same population abandoning spoken Irish, it is said that
he claimed the following:

> I am sufficiently utilitarian not to regret its gradual abandon-
> ment. A diversity of tongues is no benefit; it was first imposed
> on mankind as a curse at the building of Babel. It would be a
> vast advantage to mankind if all the inhabitants of the earth
> spoke the same language. Therefore, although the Irish lan-
> guage is connected with many recollections that twine around
> the hearts of Irishmen, yet the superior utility of the English
> tongue, as the medium of all modern communication, is so
> great that I can witness without a sigh the gradual disuse of
> the Irish. (MacDonagh 1929: 342)

(b) John McHale (1791–1881), Catholic Archbishop of the Diocese of
Tuam, while personally very attached to Irish and supportive of
it in his diocese, is said, nonetheless, to have recommended the
following pragmatic stratagem to his flock: 'Keep the Irish which
is your own, and learn the English.'

5. Lack of literacy in Irish and lack of a print culture in Irish: the tradition of writing in Irish was a manuscript-based one, and this tradition
lasted until the middle of the nineteenth century, resulting in the
dominance of English in the area of the printed word. There was
no general access to books and newspapers/journals in Irish, and
no significant 'elite' cultivating Irish as a literary medium, a factor which diminished the status of the language. The majority of
ordinary speakers of Irish were unable to read and write their own
language, and although this, of course, does not mean that these
speakers neglected the heritage of their native language – a strong
oral tradition in Irish flourished well into the twentieth century, for
example – nonetheless the lack of literacy in Irish amongst ordinary
speakers of the language put them at an ever-increasing disadvantage, especially when faced with an English language system of public
education which accorded no recognition to Irish and Irish learning
until such a period, when it was probably too late to attempt to halt
the dominance of English.

2.2.2   Language change

Three main types of change can be distinguished: (1) changes to the
internal system of a language – such changes can happen under the

influence of another language. If one regards the verbal category in Irish, for instance, one can observe that a process of reduction in this category has been taking place for centuries, whereby synthetic forms of the verb have been replaced by analytic forms – in Modern Irish one may now hear a verbal form such *ní rinne muid* for traditional *ní dhearnamar* ('we did not make'), the former demonstrating not only the change of synthetic form to analytic form, but also the regularisation of the traditional irregular form; (2) changes which can be directly traced to the influence of another language on the individual language in question. Examples of this kind of influence are the many borrowings from other languages which can be observed throughout the history of Irish: *sagart* (< Latin *sacerdos*), 'priest', *bróg* (< Old Norse *brók*) 'shoe' and *prionsa* (< Anglo-Norman *prince*) 'prince'; (3) changes which cannot be attributed with certainty to an internal or an external source. An example in case is the strong decline in the use of the genitive case in present-day spoken Irish: the traditional inherited inflection of the genitive is often neglected by native speakers, e.g. *hata an fhear* may be heard instead of the traditionally inflected *hata an fhir* 'the man's hat'. On the one hand, one could maintain that native speakers of Irish, who are virtually all fully bilingual speakers of English, produce uninflected genitives under the influence of English, which does not require genitival inflection. On the other hand, there is also clear internal evidence from Irish for the gradual reduction over time in 'redundant' inflections for various cases, including the genitive – the inflections having existed in Irish from the earliest stages.

If one examines spoken Irish in the present-day Irish-speaking regions, particular the Irish spoken by younger native speakers of the language, and one compares it to the Irish spoken by their parents, or indeed by their grandparents, it is clear that the variety spoken by younger speakers shows significant changes. Illustrative examples of some of these changes are discussed below in (1) – (4) – for detailed discussions of these and related phenomena, see further Stenson (1993), Ó Catháin (2001) and Péterváry et al. (2014).

1. Changes relating to (a) phonetics, (b) morphology, and (c) syntax. (a): the retroflex [ɻ] of Irish English replaces, particularly in syllable-final or word-final position, the flapped [r] of Irish in such examples as *fear* 'man' or *go leor* 'enough' (Hickey 2011: 376–81); in general second-language speakers use the velar stops /k, g/ for the corresponding fricatives /x, ɣ/, *ach* 'but' [ak] for [ax], *gach* 'every' [gak] for [gax]; *a ghualainn* 'his shoulder' [ə guːlən] for [ə ɣuəlʲənʲ]; (b) proper

names are not inflected, as in traditional speech, for the vocative case: one hears the form of address *Seán* 'John' instead of the traditional *A Sheáin* 'John.VOC'; (c) direct relative clauses are employed where one would traditionally have found indirect relative clauses, e.g. *an fear atá mé ag caint leis* instead of the traditional *an fear a bhfuil mé ag caint leis* 'the man I am talking to'.

2. Non-grammatical use of initial mutations which are, of course, characteristic of Irish and of all the Celtic languages, e.g. *Gaeilge maith* (omission of lenition of adjective *maith*) instead of the grammatical *Gaeilge mhaith* 'good Irish', and *leis an tAire* (use/generalisation of prefix-*t* which is traditionally required in the case of singular masculine nouns with an initial vowel after the definite article *an* in the nominative/accusative case) instead of the grammatical *leis an Aire* 'with the Minister'.

3. Code-mixing with English or code-switching involving English, e.g. *Shíl mé go mbeadh leathuair an chloig oibre agam; as it turned out, ní raibh tada le déanamh agam* 'I thought that I would have half an hour's work; *as it turned out*, I did not have anything to do', where in traditional Irish a phrase such as *mar a tharla* would be employed instead of the English 'as it turned out'.

4. Excessive use of loans, idioms and direct translations from English: (a) *Enjoyáil muid é* instead of a traditional phrase such as *bhain muid sásamh/sult as*, this latter phrase furthermore demonstrating the typical preference in Irish for the structure 'verb + noun + preposition' to indicate appraisal/feeling, where English prefers a single simple verb 'enjoy'; (b) *Fuair sé fuacht* instead of a traditional phrase such as *tholg sé slaghdán/tháinig slaghdán air* 'he contracted a cold (disease)'. A further example occurs when the inchoative use of English 'get' is translated directly into Irish with *faigh* 'get', e.g. *fuair sé níos fuaire* for *d'éirigh sé níos fuaire*, or the more idiomatic, *chuaigh sé i bhfuaire* 'it got colder'.

The changes illustrated in (3) and (4) above are an indicator of a particular weakness in the Irish of younger L1 native speakers: their acquisition of, and societal exposure to, Irish has not been sufficient to enable them to discuss at ease in Irish more complicated topics of a technical or abstract nature. Another related weakness is the absence of higher registers in the Irish of these speakers, a weakness which is, in turn, related to the reduced role of Irish within their speech community but which leads to the fortification of English in which they, thus, demonstrate higher linguistic competence than in Irish, see further Petérváry et al. (2014). On the other hand, it must also be acknowledged that some scholars – e.g. de Bhaldraithe (1993) – have provided some evidence that the picture regarding Irish in the official Irish-speaking regions is not exclusively one in which Irish is being impoverished and weakened by English. The general assessment is, however, that the Irish of young, and younger, speakers in general is undergoing major change which is primarily due to the influence of English.

If one now considers the Irish of speakers of Irish outside the official Irish-speaking areas, i.e. the Irish of those who have L2 competence in Irish, one can see that there is strong evidence for phenomena such as those outlined in (1), (2) and (4) above, see further Maguire (1991), Ó Catháin (2001), Nic Pháidín (2003) and Walsh (2007). Given the fact that these speakers' L1 is English, it stands to reason that their Irish will demonstrate a greater influence of English than that of their L1 Gaeltacht counterparts. The following selection of examples illustrates the changes which can be observed in a typical L2 speaker of Irish.

(1) Changes relating to (a) phonetics, (b) morphology and (c) syntax: (a) the English alveolar stop [t] is employed instead of the Irish velarised dental stop [t̪ˠ] which occurs in words such as *tá* 'is'/'are'; (b) a form such as *tiocann* is used instead of *t(e)agann* 'comes', whereby the first syllable of *tiocann* is a new construct based on the verbal form *tiocfaidh*, the future form of the irregular verb *tar* 'come'; (c) a form such as *ar cúl iad* is heard instead of *ar a gcúl* 'behind them' – *ar cúl iad* reflects English syntax in its word order and the use of the third person plural pronoun *iad* in final position, whereas traditional Irish syntax requires in the case of all compound prepositions such as *ar cúl*, the third person plural possessive adjective *a* (and attendant eclipsis/nasalisation as initial mutation – in the present case the change of <c> /k-/ to <gc> /g-/) which is inserted between the two constituents of the compound preposition in question.

(2) Non-grammatical use of initial mutations: *leis an fear* (with <f-> /fʲ-/) is heard instead of *leis an bhfear/fhear* (with <bhf-> /vʲ-/ or <fh-> Ø) 'with the man', and of prefix <t-> /t̪ˠ/ as in *tá an am caite* instead of *tá an t-am caite* '(the) time is up'.

(4) Excessive use of loans, idioms and direct translations from English: *Sin é a <u>wantann</u> muid chun a faigh* instead of *Sin a dteastaíonn uainn (a bheith againn)* 'That is what we want (to have)' and *níor dhein mise aon rud go dtí an bord* 'I didn't do anything to the table' instead of *níor leag mise lámh ar an mbord*.

There are only small numbers of L2 speakers of Irish of whom one can say that they demonstrate a high degree of competence in Irish uninfluenced by English. However, such speakers – and, indeed, L2 speakers of Irish in general – avoid the code-mixing and code-switching so common with speakers from the present-day Irish-speaking regions. When comparing the variety of Irish currently spoken by young native speakers from the official Irish-speaking areas to that of the L2 speakers of Irish outside these areas, one can observe that the two varieties are moving towards each other, and, in some cases, that the same 'new' features can now be found in both varieties. The following examples illustrate this type of development:

(1) non-grammatical use of the preposition *ag* + verbal noun instead of the preposition *a* (followed by lenition) + verbal noun in such sentences as: *an rud a bhí mé ag déanamh* (with <d-> /dʲ-/) 'the thing I was doing' which can be heard instead of the grammatical *an rud a bhí mé a dhéanamh* (with <dh-> /j-/).

(2) non-grammatical use of the preposition *roimh* + verb instead of the conjunction *sula(r)* + verb: *roimh a tháinig muid* instead of *sular tháinig muid* 'before we came'.

Ó Murchú summarises the situation succinctly when he comments:

> In the last generation or so, the pattern of bilingualism found among the urban elite has been extending to the Gaeltacht. Gaeltacht leadership now forms a social continuum with the Irish-speaking networks in the rest of the country. English as well as Irish is increasingly felt appropriate to all settings in the Gaeltacht also and, in matters of accent and usage the two groups are converging rapidly . . . . The older elaborate Irish speech forms are thus being replaced among younger speakers, either by an impoverished variety in a pattern of diagonal bilingualism, or by a modern koine, the features of which in lexicon and to some extent in grammar are now increasingly being defined by elite urban groups. (Ó Murchú 1988: 248–9)

2.2.3 Irish: a speech community or a network of speakers?

On examining the details concerning speakers of Irish in the censuses which have been carried out since the founding of the Irish state in 1922, three general conclusions can be drawn:

1. The number of Irish speakers within the official Irish-speaking areas has decreased.

2. The numbers of speakers of Irish outside of the official Irish-speaking areas has increased.
3. The majority of daily speakers of Irish are L2 learners still attending school and learning Irish there.

With regard to the speakers mentioned under (3) above, a major reduction in their numbers occurs when they complete their post-primary education, normally aged 17 or 18. This is one of the major difficulties facing Irish today: since the foundation of the independent Irish state in 1922, the main responsibility for the maintenance and revival of the language has been placed, by the state, on the teaching of Irish in the education system, where the vast majority of pupils engage in learning the language. Insufficient attention has been given to the promotion of the natural use of spoken Irish in society at large, e.g. in entertainment or sport, in order to foster and increase the use of the language as a natural means of communication in society. This thinking continues to this day: even in the case of Irish-medium schooling, which constitutes a significant and growing development area for the language, Irish is still primarily and intrinsically linked to the educational sphere. It does not appear to be the case that such all-Irish schools are succeeding in producing appreciable numbers of Irish speakers who are willing to employ the language in general outside of its educational context. In this context, a trend of great concern has been highlighted by Punch (2008: 53), who in discussing data from the 2006 census and referring to the numbers of pupils in schools in the official Irish-speaking areas who did not use the language daily outside of school, notes: 'A possible worrying feature is that over two thirds of the 14,000 daily speakers of school-going age in the Gaeltacht do not speak the language on a daily basis outside of school.'

One of the main difficulties with the maintenance and promotion of Irish is that in the past there was no detailed language policy set out for the Irish-speaking areas (or for any other part of the country), nor was any significant effort made on a national scale to address practical language planning issues. For a significant period of time, it was believed, somewhat naively, that if Irish occupied a central place in the educational system and was taught to pupils during their entire education, the result would be competent speakers of Irish who would be empowered and willing to speak the language both in the home and in society in general, thus ensuring its subsequent transmission to, and acquisition by, the next generation. In this way, it was believed, the historical language shift to English could be halted and ultimately reversed. With a lately gained understanding of the difficulties associated with promoting an (undefined) goal of general bilingualism and of the importance of co-ordinated detailed national language planning, attempts are now being made to develop positive policies which will support the community of Irish speakers, both within and without the Irish-speaking areas, and of applying the procedures of language reversal as outlined by Fishman (1991; 2001). It is clear, however that the task is a mammoth one, and that if the numbers of speakers of Irish are to increase to the highly ambitious targets set out in current state strategy (e.g. increasing the number of daily speakers of Irish outside the educational system from 83,000 (2006 figure) to a projected 2 million by 2030), then innovative methods will have to be found to assist current Irish language networks, particularly those found outside the official Irish-speaking areas, to form significant, vibrant and lasting Irish language communities.

An example of past neglect by statutory bodies (e.g. by Údarás na Gaeltachta ['Irish Language Areas Authority'][3] with regard to language planning in the official Irish language areas is the over-riding emphasis which was placed on schemes which promoted industrialisation in those areas, schemes which were, of course, clearly needed to provide local employment opportunities, to stem population loss and promote the local economy. These schemes, however, paid little or no attention to: (1) possible sociolinguistic implications; (2) the drawing-up and implementation of language policies which would foster the acquisition, use and generational transmission of Irish within the local speech community. Positive changes have occurred in very recent times, and the abovementioned body, Údarás na Gaeltachta, is now, for instance, the co-ordinating body for communities in the official Irish-speaking areas, who are required to draw up detailed local language plans regarding the cultivation and promotion of Irish. A further example of such positive change is An Clár Tacaíochta Teaghlaigh ['The Home Assistance Programme'], established and financed by the government department An Roinn Ealaíon, Oidhreachta agus Gaeltachta/The Department of Arts, Heritage and the Gaeltacht, a programme which seeks to strengthen the use of Irish in the home and community in the official Irish-speaking areas. Despite such positive language-planning changes in the Gaeltacht, they may not suffice to reverse the language shift which, it would appear, is gradually reaching its inexorable conclusion. Some scholars, see Ó Curnáin (2009), are even of the opinion that in order to minimise the linguistic minoritisation of Irish and in order to achieve solid L1 Irish language acquisition from the earliest age, a radical solution is required: the establishment of Irish language refuges where

Irish would be the sole medium of communication in home and community, where the emphasis would be on total immersion in all aspects of Irish heritage, and where exposure to English would be delayed to enable complete L1 acquisition of, and competence in, Irish.

A more practical solution might, perhaps, be a concerted, state-led, attempt to develop, implement and support the concept of stable bilingualism, or diglossia (Ó Murchú 1970: 18–19) as official policy, so that both the language shift from Irish to English and the inordinate pressure on Irish resulting from the current transitional bilingualism might be halted. The advantage of stable bilingualism is that there is little competition between the two languages in question: different domains are associated with use of the two languages, and it is the society using these languages which establishes which language is the more suitable for which domain. Another advantage of stable bilingualism is that it offers the potential to reduce the pressure the majority language exerts on the minority, or lesser-used, language, a factor which would help Irish in its ever-competing struggle with English.

2.3 The death of Irish?

What lies in store for Irish? In order to answer this question, it is necessary to differentiate between the situation of Irish in the official Irish-speaking areas and Irish outside these areas.

2.3.1 Irish in the Gaeltacht

If one considers the situation in the Gaeltacht, it has become increasingly obvious that Irish has receded very considerably there as a community language. The era of the traditional native speaker, armed with a sound competence in his or her own local variety of Irish, is coming to an end, even in those districts in the official Irish-speaking areas which may be regarded as strong areas of the language: Ó Curnáin (2007: 59) speaking of the area of Iorras Aithneach, Co. Galway, where Irish plays a relatively strong role in the community, notes: '... there will be no fully traditional speakers left alive after c. 2050'. With regard to the majority of speakers of Irish born after 1970, and especially those who were born after 1980, it is clear that they have not acquired the language fully: they are bilinguals and, although competent in both Irish and English, their competence in English is usually greater. This is because (1) they employ English more often than Irish and (2) there are 'gaps' in their Irish, for instance, they lack certain registers in Irish and they are often unable to discuss complex or abstract matters in the language or, at least, they are more fluent in discussing the same in English.

What of the generation which will follow this current bilingual generation who are thus generally more proficient in English? Three key questions arise in the case of this future generation:

(1) Will Irish be spoken to them in the home?
(2) If Irish is spoken to them in the home, will they be in a position in their own lives to hear and acquire a sufficient amount of Irish to designate them as speakers of Irish?
(3) Will they be willing to speak the language?

By all appearances, it would seem that this next generation will only have a rudimentary knowledge of the language and that their competence in it will primarily be one of a passive nature, i.e. they will understand but not actively speak Irish. To put it briefly, this will be the final generation with any appreciable competence in Irish, and when they pass away this will signify the end of Gaeltacht Irish.

2.3.2   Irish outside the Gaeltacht

If one now considers the situation of Irish outside the Gaeltacht, one can predict the continuation of networks of speakers which currently exist and which speak their own varieties of Irish, most of which demonstrate the influence of English to varying degrees. For the majority of these speakers, English is, and will continue to be, their native and primary spoken language. It is most likely that these varieties of neo-Irish will survive, i.e. that Irish per se will survive but that there will be major differences between this Irish and the traditional Irish which used to be spoken in the Gaeltacht. While there are those, particularly in academic circles, who would discount these varieties of non-native or neo-Irish, claiming that one cannot regard them as 'Irish' due to the major linguistic differences that exist between them and the traditional or historical varieties of Irish, it must, however, be recognised that, in all probability, it is these varieties of Irish which will prevail in spoken form. A similar situation would appear to exist for other Celtic languages; see Hornsby (2005) on the position of Breton in present-day Brittany.

2.4   Conclusion

The mixture of Irish and English which one can hear with both second-language speakers and younger native speakers in the Gaeltacht is a type of linguistic phenomenon which is widely attested across the world and which has occurred repeatedly in history. It is known from the history of English itself that language contact led to mixture and change, with the Celts in the Old English period (Hickey 2012), with the Scandinavians (Lutz 2012) and with speakers of Norman French in the Middle English period (Machan 2012) to mention a number of more well-known cases of contact. Despite the changes engendered by such contact, there is no doubt that the resulting language was, and is still, perceived afterwards to constitute the same language as before. But the structural alterations which took place meant that the simple classification of English as a purely West Germanic language could not be upheld.

It is thus valid to ask whether the various varieties of neo-Irish found in Ireland today should be accepted as representing a legitimate continuity of the language. When comparing the situation of Irish now with that of English in history there is one essential difference: the latter language continued to be employed by the same community of speakers through the generations, but the Irish language community of the official Irish-speaking areas is in the process of mutating into one of English speakers, so that in the near future it may well be the case that only speakers of Irish as a second language will exist, or that only second-language learners of Irish will choose to transmit their varieties of Irish to the next generation, in effect leading to the first situation arising. How far these future varieties will be removed from the traditional Irish of the Gaeltacht, and how robust and stable these L2 forms of Irish turn out to be, are questions that remain to be answered in the course of the present century.

Notes

1. This chapter is based on the Irish-language contribution, Ó Catháin (2012). My thanks go to the editor of the present volume, Raymond Hickey, for his assistance and many suggestions in the preparation of the present version.
2. For further details, see the essays in Nic Pháidín and Ó Cearnaigh (2008).
3. There is no official translation for Údarás na Gaeltachta and the English-language version of the organisation's website, accessible at http://www.udaras.ie/en, only uses the Irish name.

References

Crystal, David (2000). *Language Death*. Cambridge: Cambridge University Press.
de Bhaldraithe, Tomás (1993). 'Nóitíní ar staid inmheánach na teanga' [Short Notes on the Internal State of the Language], *Teangeolas* 32: 25–8.

Fennell, Desmond (1981). 'Can a shrinking linguistic minority be saved? Lessons from the Irish experience', in: Einar Haugen, J. McClure and Derick Thomson (eds) *Minority Languages Today*. Edinburgh: Edinburgh University Press, pp. 32–9.

Fishman, Joshua (1991). 'Irish: what more can be done?', in: Joshua Fishman, *Reversing Language Shift: Theoretical and Empirical Foundations of Assistance to Threatened Languages*. Clevedon: Multilingual Matters, pp. 122–48.

Fishman, Joshua (ed.) (2001). *Can Threatened Languages be Saved? Reversing Language Shift Revisited: a Twentieth Century Perspective*. Clevedon: Multilingual Matters.

Harrison, K. David (2007). *When Languages Die: the Extinction of the World's Languages and the Erosion of Human Knowledge*. New York and London: Oxford University Press.

Hickey, Raymond (2011). *The Dialects of Irish: Study of a Changing Landscape*. Berlin: de Gruyter Mouton.

Hickey, Raymond (2012). 'Early English and the Celtic hypothesis', in: Nevalainen and Traugott (eds), pp. 497–507.

Hindley, Reg (1990). *The Death of the Irish Language*. London: Routledge.

Hornsby, Michael (2005). '*Néo-breton* and questions of authenticity', *Estudios de Sociolingüística* 6.2: 191–218.

Kuter, Lois (1989). 'Breton vs. French: language and the opposition of political, economic, social and cultural values', in: Nancy C. Dorian (ed.) *Investigating Obsolescence: Studies in Language Contraction and Death*. Cambridge: Cambridge University Press, pp. 75–89.

Lutz, Angelika (2012). 'Language contact in the Scandinavian period', in: Nevalainen and Traugott (eds), pp. 508–17.

McCloskey, James (2001). *Guthanna in Éag: an Mairfidh an Ghaeilge beo?* [Vanishing Voices: Will Irish Survive and Live?] Baile Átha Cliath: Cois Life.

MacDonagh, Michael (1929). *Daniel O'Connell and the Story of Catholic Emancipation*. Dublin: Talbot Press.

Machan, Tim William (2012). 'Language contact and linguistic attitudes in the Later Middle Ages', in: Nevalainen and Traugott (eds), pp. 518–27.

Maguire, Gabrielle (1991). *Our own Language: an Irish Initiative*. Clevedon: Multilingual Matters.

Nevalainen, Terttu and Elizabeth Closs Traugott (eds) (2012). *The Oxford Handbook of the History of English*. Oxford: Oxford University Press.

Nettle, Daniel and Suzanne Romaine (2000). *Vanishing Voices. The Extinction of the World's Languages*. Oxford: Oxford University Press.

Nic Pháidín, Caoilfhionn (2003). '"Cén fáth nach?" – ó chanúint go criól' [Why not – from dialect to creole] in: Róisín Ní Mhianáin (ed.) *Idir Lúibíní: Aistí ar an Léitheoireacht agus ar an Litearthacht* [Between Brackets: Essays on Reading and Literacy]. Baile Átha Cliath: Cois Life, pp. 115–30.

Nic Pháidín, Caoilfhionn and Seán Ó Cearnaigh (eds) (2008). *A New View of the Irish Language*. Baile Átha Cliath: Cois Life.

Ó Buachalla, Séamas (1981). 'The language in the classroom', *The Crane Bag* 5.2: 18–31.

Ó Catháin, Brian (2001). 'Dearcadh an teangeolaí ar chomharthaí sóirt Ghaeilge an lae inniu' [A Linguist's View on the Characteristics of Irish Today], *Léachtaí Cholm Cille* 31: 128–49.

Ó Catháin, Brian (2012). 'Malartú agus bás teanga', in: Tadhg Ó hIfearnáin and Máire Ní Neachtain (eds) *An tSochtheangeolaíocht: Feidhm agus Tuairisc* [Sociolinguistics: Function and Report]. Baile Átha Cliath: Cois Life, pp. 67–82.

Ó Curnáin, Brian (2007). *The Irish of Iorras Aithneach, County Galway*. Dublin: Dublin Institute for Advanced Studies.

Ó Curnáin, Brian (2009). 'Mionteangú na Gaeilge' [The linguistic minoritisation of Irish], in: Brian Ó Catháin (ed.) *Sochtheangeolaíocht na Gaeilge* [The Sociolinguistics of Irish]. *Léachtaí Cholm Cille 39*. Maigh Nuad: An Sagart, pp. 90–153.

Ó Dochartaigh, Cathair (1992). 'The Irish language', in Donald MacAulay (ed.) *The Celtic Languages*. Cambridge: Cambridge University Press, pp. 11–99.

Ó Giollagáin, Conchúr and Martin Charlton (2015) *Nua-shonrú ar an Staidéar Cuimsitheach Teangeolaíoch ar Úsáid na Gaeilge sa Ghaeltacht: 2006-2011*. [An Up-date of the Comprehensive Linguistic Study on the Use of Irish in the Gaeltacht.] Údarás na Gaeltachta.

Ó Giollagáin, Conchúr, Seosamh Mac Donnacha, Fiona Ní Chualáin, Aoife Ní Shéaghdha and Mary O'Brien (2007). *Staidéar Cuimsitheach Teangeolaíoch ar Úsáid na Gaeilge sa Ghaeltacht: Tuarascáil Chríochnaitheach* [A Comprehensive Linguistic Study on the Use of Irish in the Gaeltacht: Final Report]. Baile Átha Cliath: Oifig an tSoláthair.

Ó Murchú, Máirtín (1970). *Urlabhra agus Pobal* [Speech and Community]. Baile Átha Cliath: Oifig an tSoláthair.

Ó Murchú, Máirtín (1988). 'Diglossia and interlanguage contact in Ireland', *Language, Culture and Curriculum* 1.3: 243–9.

Ó Riagáin, Pádraig (1997). *Language Policy and Social Reproduction: Ireland, 1893–1993*. Oxford: Oxford University Press.

Péterváry, Tamás, Conchúr Ó Giollagáin, Brian Ó Curnáin and Jerome Sheahan (2014). *Iniúchadh ar an gCumas Dátheangach: an Sealbhú Teanga i Measc Ghlúin Óg na Gaeltachta/Analysis of Bilingual Competence: Language Acquisition Among Young People in the Gaeltacht*. Baile Átha Cliath: An Chomhairle um Oideachas Gaeltachta agus Gaelscolaíochta.

Punch, Aidan (2008). 'Census data on the Irish language', in: Nic Pháidín and Ó Cearnaigh (eds), pp. 43–54.

Romaine, Suzanne (2008). 'Irish in the global context', in: Nic Pháidín and Ó Cearnaigh (eds), pp. 1–25.

Stenson, Nancy (1993). 'English influence on Irish: the last 100 years', *The Journal of Celtic Linguistics* 2: 107–28.

Wall, Maureen (1969). 'The decline of the Irish language', in: Brian Ó Cuív (ed.) *A View of the Irish Language*. Dublin: Stationery Office, pp. 81–90.

Walsh, Clare (2007). *Cruinneas na Gaeilge Scríofa sna hIarbhunscoileanna Lán-Ghaeilge i mBaile Átha Cliath* [Accuracy in Written Irish in Post-Primary Irish-medium Schools in Dublin]. Baile Átha Cliath: An Chomhairle um Oideachas Gaeltachta agus Gaelscolaíochta.

Watson, Seosamh (1989). 'Scottish and Irish Gaelic: the giant's bedfellows', in: Nancy C. Dorian C. (ed.) (1989) *Investigating Obsolescence: Studies in Language Contraction and Death*. Cambridge: Cambridge University Press, pp. 41–59.

3
The Irish Language and the Media

Iarfhlaith Watson

3.1 Introduction

Newcomers to Ireland flicking through the channels on their television or radio could be excused for believing that Irish would be commonly heard on the street, but they are likely to walk the highways and byways of Ireland for a long time in search of the spoken language. Unbeknownst to them, however, among all the conversations going on around them, there is usually an Irish speaker within a stone's throw. Perhaps one in six people in the Republic of Ireland can converse in Irish. This is more than half a million people of varying levels of fluency – a reasonable audience for Irish language media. The audience, of course, need not be limited to the linguistic group, but can incorporate the whole nation. Examining the connection between the Irish language and nation gives insights into why one in six people can converse in Irish, why there are Irish language media and why it is of more than niche interest.

Irish language media is the focus of this chapter – primarily media of the spoken word, such as radio and television – understood within the concepts of nation and ideology. This chapter is structured chronologically according to what appear to be different ideological periods over the past century, focusing in more depth on the more recent periods.

3.2 Conceptual context

There are two aspects to the conceptual context for this chapter. The first is the nation. In this chapter 'nation' is not a synonym for state (see Connor 1978), but rather nation is understood culturally. Putting it simply, Gellner (1983: 47) referred to the nation as 'a culture in need of a political roof'. From another perspective, a nation is a group of people who share something in common, who consider themselves a nation and have or want their own state attached to territory or land. This definition provides four elements: culture; national consciousness (without which there can be no more than the seed of a nation planted by intellectuals); state (existing, regional, or longed-for – the political roof for the culture à la Gellner); and land (usually a specific territory, parts of which are invested with national import (such as historic sites), but sometimes it is a desire for some place to make a homeland). The national consciousness usually arises as a result of a political argument or political project. This is where language enters the scene as evidence that there is an existing unique nation, qua culture, in need of a political roof – Gellner (1983: 45) called it 'the nationalist principle of *cuius regio, eius lingua'*.

The second aspect of the conceptual context is ideology. In this chapter ideology is not a synonym for ideas, but rather has a wider element and critical dimension. Ideology is viewed here as 'ways of acting, thinking and feeling' (to borrow Durkheim's phrase – Durkheim 1938 [1895]: 2) which (adding a critical dimension from Thompson 1994: 135) intersect with positions of power. What this means is that national ways of acting, thinking and feeling form structures which are advantageous to some members of the nation (even if there is limited, or no, awareness of that advantage).

Drawing on this concept of ideology, the main part of this chapter will involve a focus on Irish language media in four time periods based on ideological (rather than linguistic) phases, concluding with a suggestion that we are now entering a cosmopolitan phase. First there will be a discussion of the situation in the period up to the 1920s; the following section will deal with the 1920s to 1950s; then the period from the 1950s to the 1980s; and, finally, the period from the 1980s to the present. The rationale for structuring the chapter in this way is to provide a context and a more analytical insight into the situation of the Irish language and of Irish language media today.

National languages (particularly languages in the media) have played an important role in allowing people to imagine the wider community of speakers to which they belong. Anderson (1991) called this the imagined community. In the context of the first national movements of the American and French Revolutions in the late eighteenth century and the wars of independence in Latin America in the nineteenth century there is a strong element of civic republicanism. In this context language was approached rather pragmatically – a *lingua franca* was required for all citizens to communicate. Taking the French Revolution as an example, initially the focus on civic culture allowed for a diversity of languages. Bell points out that the National Assembly voted in 1790 to translate its laws into various regional tongues (Bell 2003: 173) and in 1792 the Minister of Justice set up an office to translate laws and decrees into German, Italian, Catalan, Basque and Breton (Bell 2003: 72). This situation did not last long, and by 1794 there was a clear agenda to eradicate linguistic diversity; see Bell's (2003: 171–7) discussion of the 'Politicization of the language'. Although this was a civic form of nationalism, the consequences paralleled ethnic nationalism. Bemoaning the results, Bell wrote: 'I would argue that the cultural uniformity advocated by most Republicans, from Gregoire onwards, has caused a real degree of French cultural impoverishment' (Bell 2003: 21).

Anderson argued that these first national movements were new in the sense that they were concerned with making a new people, rather than with the genealogy of the nation or the historical people. We find that in 1792, at the National Convention in Paris, Jean-Paul Rabaut de Saint-Etienne argued that 'we must make the French a new people' (Bell 2003: 21). This is often referred to as the civic dimension of nations and nationalism. Although this dimension continued as a theme in later national movements – for example Massimo d'Azeglio argued in 1861 that 'We have made Italy. Now we have to make Italians' – the second generation of nationalist movements in Europe in 1815–50, according to Anderson (1991: 194–5), approached the nation as an 'awakening from sleep'. This was the ethnic dimension, the argument being that the nation is not new; rather it existed before and now needs to be awakened. This also explained instances in which intellectuals could not speak the national language – because awakening the nation also involved awakening the national language.

Languages in print, according to Anderson (1991: 44–5), laid the bases for national consciousness for a number of reasons. First, they provided a single 'field of communication', which allowed an individual to imagine being part of a nation. Initially, this involved novels and newspapers, but later it included radio and, even later, television. Second, the fixing of language in text slowed the rapid linguistic changes of an oral community. Over centuries the language maintained sufficient fixity to be understood and this lent the language and, by association, the nation an air of antiquity. The putative antiquity supported the argument that there was a nation in the past which could be awakened from sleep. Third, Anderson (1991: 45) argued that the print-language was the language of power. This explained the importance of 'breaking firmly into print – and radio' (and television) for a language of 'subordinate status'.

3.3 The nationalist ideology: pre-1920s

The construction of the Irish nation went through three phases from the late eighteenth century to the late nineteenth century, beginning with a mythical antiquarianism, followed by a more rigorous academic antiquarianism (see Hutchinson 2001), in which the Irish nation would be English-speaking and British in civic and political life, with an Irish flavour to provide distinctiveness. Finally, beginning in the mid-to-late nineteenth century there was a nationalist phase. In the late nineteenth century and during the twentieth century Irish nationalism was a project of awakening the Irish nation – awakening its culture in terms of sports, dancing, language, etc. Sometimes cultural elements were more than asleep and required an amount of invention. As a result of this nationalist project, written output in Irish increased from the late nineteenth century (see Delap 2007: 23–35), but there were no media of the spoken word until the 1920s. The only event which could be called a broadcast was a Morse Code message sent from the GPO (General Post Office in Dublin) during the Easter Rising of 1916 to any and all who could receive it (Gorham 1967: 2).

The main ideological thrust of social change in Ireland during the late nineteenth century and early twentieth century was nationalist; it was a political project in cultural clothing, and its focus was on political independence, justified by an Irish nation in contrast with an imagined 'other' of Englishness and Britishness. The Irish language played an important role in this project. By the late nineteenth century the number of Irish speakers had been declining for several centuries. The language survived mainly in the remotest districts of the western seaboard. Congested as many of these areas were, they were hit hard by famine and emigration. Although this patchwork region of Irish speakers was idealised in nationalistic poetry, plays and paintings, this did little to preserve the language in these areas. Instead, it was promoted as a second language in the rest of the island. There were Irish language promoters who cycled the countryside to offer classes; there was the gradual introduction of Irish into the education system (initially as an extra-curricular subject) and even the Irish language requirement for entry into any of the colleges of the National University of Ireland (National Universities of Ireland Act 1908) – a requirement still in force today. All of this was about constructing an Irish nation to go with an independent state. The project was not complete at independence, but set the scene for the manner in which the new state would deal with the nation, including the Irish language and Irish language media.

3.4   The protectionist ideology: 1920s–50s

The ideology of this period was nationally oriented and relatively authoritarian. Its main focus was a cultural and top-down one, in which the state (and other social forces) attempted to forge a nation by imposing its ideology on the people. Following the turmoil of the war of independence and the civil war in Ireland, an important objective for the new state was to unite the people. According to Gellner (1983) nationalism plays an important role in the homogenisation of society. He argued that industrial society requires homogenisation and that this is provided by nationalism. A key criticism of Gellner's argument is that there are examples of nationalism in the absence of an industrial society. Without Northern Ireland (or Britain) the 26 counties of the new state were clearly an agricultural society (with more than half the working population employed in the agricultural sector). Nationalism, however, can function as a tool of homogenisation for the state even in an agricultural society.

A key tool available to the state – building on the pre-independence nationalist project – was the education system. A new tool that became available to the state from the 1920s was radio. In both cases the focus of the ideology of the time was on the masses – to use the education system and radio as linguistic tools of a nationalist policy. The emphasis was on the uniqueness of the Irish nation, and on emphasising and further establishing its unique cultural characteristics (such as the Irish language). Both the attitude of uniqueness and the emphasis on culture were manifest to some extent even in the economic and political policies which were pursued from the 1930s to the 1950s.

The instability of the early 1920s in Ireland meant that radio arrived rather later than in other European countries. Nonetheless, as radio was considered an important tool in establishing the Irish nation, a White Paper on broadcasting was prepared within months of the end of the civil war. The Postmaster General argued that a radio station was vital to the effort of setting the nation on its feet and that if Irish people could hear only British broadcasts it would have a negative effect on the restoration of the Irish language. He went on to argue that, although the people wanted to be entertained, cultural progress was more important than entertainment (Watson 2003: 14).

Although the protectionist trend of this ideological era was evident in efforts to establish the Irish nation, this ideology did not reach its peak until the 1930s and 1940s. During the 1920s there were some threads of a more liberal and minority approach which came later, but these were normally threads of arguments that tended to be on the losing side in the outcomes. During the debate on the 1926 Wireless Telegraphy Bill, the Postmaster General explained to the Dáil (30 November 1926) that there would be a channel for the Gaeltacht. There was also some discussion of financial matters, such as Conor Hogan's statement in the Dáil (7 December 1926) that

> The Minister for Posts and Telegraphs stated that he was going to erect a wireless station for the Gaeltacht. I confess that I have the feeling that if the Government could give bread to the people there it would be better than giving them a wireless station. We have no information; no figures have been put before us as to what the charge will be on the taxpayer. I do not think it is right that, at present, any money, even one penny, should be expended in respect of this service, which places an additional burden on the taxpayer.

Furthermore, the possibility of a private commercial radio station was considered. Nonetheless, the government decided that the new station should be run from the Department of Posts and Telegraphs, which kept this nation-building tool within the control of the state. The first radio station in Ireland was 2RN from 1926 (Pine 2002; Watson 2003: 16–19).

During this era radio listeners were an indistinguishable mass on whom the state could impose the type of programming it deemed best for the nation. Technical limitations – the lack of power of the transmitters – meant that radio was restricted to the regions around Dublin (and for a time Cork, with 6CK) until Radio Éireann (RÉ) began in the mid-1930s. Linguistic limitations – the lack of fluent Irish speakers – meant that the state could not fully implement the linguistic element of its national project on radio. By the 1940s, however, the amount of Irish on RÉ reached a peak of 10 per cent of total broadcasting time (Watson 1996: 52).

The disparity between native Irish speakers (from the Gaeltacht)[1] and the secondary bilinguals (Gaeilgeoirí)[2] was reinforced by policy during this era – a distinction which is not widely appreciated and which has continued to increase to the present day. The state policy of actively promoting Irish – even imposing it – is clear in the education system and radio. This was a policy to increase the number of Gaeilgeoirí, one that has been relatively successful in creating Irish speakers through the education system. On the other hand, a policy of preservation (and restoration) could have facilitated the survival of Irish in the Gaeltacht. The policy, however, seemed to be closer to preservation through neglect and seclusion.

Although the amount of Irish on radio that was aimed at the nation as a whole increased during the 1930s and 1940s, the Gaeltacht was considered only occasionally. In the early 1930s the possibility of providing county committees with access to radio raised the possibility that the Galway committee could be the first step toward a separate Irish language radio channel – but this channel would not materialise for another four decades. On another occasion, because of the lack of radio ownership in the Gaeltacht, the possibility of providing free radios was considered. The conclusion, however, was that radio might undermine linguistic policy by spreading the English language; after all, the most popular programmes on radio were in English and the people in the Gaeltacht would tune in to listen to them. These are just two examples of how the preservation of Irish in the Gaeltacht was pursued through isolation or even neglect or inactivity. On the other hand, the promotion of Irish as a second language is clear in Éamon de Valera's[3] suggestion that instead of reading the news alternately in the three main dialects of Irish, the news should be read in a version of the language which would best be understood by English speakers. This suggestion was not acted on (Watson 2003).

During this era the ideological approach was primarily cultural and supportive of the national project. This meant protecting the nation from outside influences and reinforcing its distinctiveness, its cultural elements – 'symbol, myth, memory, value and tradition' (Smith 2009: 25). This is the defence of a symbolic boundary; the cultural elements are of more symbolic than practical importance. This helps to explain the contradictions of the language policy and of people's attitude to Irish – it is not necessary to create an Irish-speaking nation; all that is required is that Irish be understood to exist, that somebody speaks it. This is sufficient for the symbolic purposes of the nation. The evidence of the existing language was (and is) in school, on the radio and in the Gaeltacht. The danger inherent in this is that the symbol is expected to represent a reality (or at least the possibility of a reality).

By the 1950s the failures of the national project became more apparent. This was clear not only in its cultural aspects, but also in its political and economic aspects – the island was still partitioned and the economic situation was dire. In that context there was a shift from a more protectionist to a more liberal ideology, which influenced the situation culturally, politically and economically. In practice this meant a more market-oriented approach. In the context of radio this was evident in a change in approach from deciding what listeners needed, to ascertaining what listeners wanted. In the early and mid-1950s a number of listener surveys were conducted. The results indicated that the number of listeners attracted by Irish language programmes (except news) was extremely low (0 per cent was within the margin of error). These figures were never made publicly available (see Watson 2003: 33–5 for details).

3.5 The liberal ideology: 1950s–80s

The ideology of this period was group- and market-oriented. The main focus was economic, and was more reactive to group interests than that of the previous ideology. With the lack of progress on cultural objectives such as 'restoring' the Irish language, political issues such as the northern question, and economic issues such as employment and emigration, it became apparent by the 1950s that the national project had stalled, if not failed, and there was a shift toward a more liberal, market-oriented ideology. This ideology was reinforced by economic and social liberalisation from the 1950s onwards, influenced in part by the Programmes for Economic Expansion from the late 1950s and the 1960s, the arrival of television in 1962, and by Ireland joining the European Economic Community in 1973. In this context the state's focus on cultural aspects of the national project waned, and, in the balance between the symbol and practice of the Irish language, there was a swing away from practice to symbol in terms of the vision for the whole nation. This meant that although Irish was an important symbol for the nation, it was not necessary to make everyone speak it. In fact, it was not even necessary to make anyone speak Irish or listen to it, except schoolchildren; and, even then, the Irish language schools shifted increasingly from state to voluntary initiative through this and the following eras. The use of radio and television to promote the linguistic policy of the state, although explicit in legislation, was no longer central in practice. This resulted in a reduction in the amount of programming in Irish and a shift in emphasis from broadcasting at everyone to broadcasting for a potential audience.

As well as the ideological shift in Ireland beginning in the 1950s, there was also a technological shift as the state considered the introduction of television. The view of the cultural power of radio was applied to television by the President of Ireland, Éamon de Valera, in his speech on the occasion of the first RTÉ television broadcast on 31 December 1961, in which he said:

> I must admit that sometimes when I think of television and radio and their immense power, I feel somewhat afraid. Like atomic energy it can be used for incalculable good but it can also do irreparable harm. Never before was there in the hands of men an instrument so powerful to influence the thoughts and actions of the multitude.

The ownership and control of television (and radio) in the form of a semi-autonomous authority (established in the RTÉ Authority Act, 1960), part publicly funded (by licence fees levied on households with a television) and part commercially funded (by selling advertising time), reflected a new ideology according to which the state no longer used the media directly as a tool of linguistic policy. Nonetheless, the 1960 Act did place certain obligations on RTÉ as regards the Irish language, such as Article 17: 'In performing its functions, the Authority shall bear constantly in mind the national aims of restoring the Irish language and preserving and developing the national culture and shall endeavour to promote the attainment of these aims'. These obligations, however, were in conflict with the new liberal market-oriented ideology in which viewership ratings were valued. The result was that barely 2.5 per cent of television airtime was broadcast in Irish.

Although an Irish language television channel was not established until 1996, there had been frequent suggestions that one should be set up, dating back to the 1950s. In the late 1950s the Irish language organisation Gael Linn offered to run television in Ireland on a commercial basis (see www.gael-linn.ie and Seanad Debates 20 January 1960). In 1963 Conradh na Gaeilge passed a motion and sent a letter to the Government requesting the establishment of a television channel in Irish on the edge of the Gaeltacht (Watson 2003: 77). Doolan et al. (1969), who had been working in RTÉ, suggested the setting-up of a Gaeltacht television channel. Much of the focus of such suggestions was the lack of a television service for Irish speakers, particularly the Gaeltacht community. This was mainly in opposition to the continuation of the earlier nationalist and protectionist ideologies. In the 1960s the policy in RTÉ was to include as much Irish as possible across a range of programmes. This policy was called the 'diffusion policy' (disparagingly dubbed the 'confusion policy' by a number of RTÉ staff). The objective was to expose as large an audience as possible to a few phrases in Irish.

In the context of this dearth of programming in Irish there were reactions from Irish language and Gaeltacht organisations. In terms of the Irish language organisations, the continuing problem was the lack of progress in achieving the 'national aims of restoring the Irish language' (mentioned in the 1960 Act, above) and a shift in emphasis away from that project. The most relevant demand here was for an increase in the amount of airtime devoted to Irish. The Gaeltacht organisations, however, managed to tap into the liberal ideology, by framing their demands as a minority rights issue in the form of Gluaiseacht Ceart Sibhialta na Gaeltachta (the Gaeltacht Civil Rights Movement). This paralleled the civil rights movements in Northern Ireland and in the United States. The main argument was that the Gaeltacht had been neglected. One of the key successes of this movement was the establishment of a Gaeltacht radio channel (within RTÉ) called Raidió na Gaeltachta (RnaG), which began broadcasting in April 1972, but it also focused the state's attention on the Gaeltacht, which led to an industrialisation policy, amongst other things, for the Gaeltacht during the 1970s. The industrialisation policy was successful insofar as the population of the Gaeltacht did not decline during the 1970s, but its success was tarnished by the declining number (and percentage) of Irish speakers within the Gaeltacht.

RnaG has worked well as a community radio station which has reinforced a sense of shared community across the scattered region of the Gaeltacht. It has also been of linguistic interest as the daily exposure to the various dialects has improved their mutual intelligibility. Furthermore, à la Anderson, it has given a minority linguistic community access to an important medium of communication. Since 2005, in order to attract youthful listeners, RnaG has permitted the broadcasting of songs with lyrics in English.

Within the liberal ideology the shift away from obligation and national practice was also manifest in the removal of a number of obligatory linguistic elements of policy, such as the requirement to pass Irish in the Leaving Certificate and the Irish language requirement for recruits to the Civil Service (removed in 1973 and 1974, respectively) (see Watson and Nic Ghiolla Phádraig 2011: 447). Despite this ideological shift, threads of the national project continued in policy and in public perception, so that although the tension remained between the importance of the Irish language as symbol and practice, the market-oriented perspective meant that there was a swing from efforts to bring about practice at the national level to encouragement or tolerance of practice at the group level. This was also evident in the state's withdrawal of wholehearted support for, and active promotion of, Irish language education, which would result in a declining number of Irish language schools in the early part of this era, but which was followed by an exponential growth of such schools from civil society initiatives from about 1970 (see Watson 2007: 367 for a graph of the number of new Irish language schools up to 2005).

With the more market- and group-focused approach of this ideological period there was more interest in public opinion, ratings and the like. This was pursued in relation to the media through regular listener surveys, but also continuously through the television rating systems, which provided RTÉ with valuable insight into the size and demographic profile of audiences for their programmes. There were also surveys to gain further insight into issues such as support for the Irish language generally and Irish language media specifically. For example, in March 1977 RTÉ appointed an Advisory Committee on Irish Language Broadcasting. This committee claimed that a large majority of the population agreed with the use of Irish on television and radio. Although their report was not published, their proposals were summarised a decade later in the *Report to the Ministers for the Gaeltacht and Communications* (Working Group on Irish Language Television Broadcasting 1987: vii–viii). Another example is a survey commissioned by the Broadcasting Commission of Ireland (BCI) which claimed that 79 per cent of the population agreed with the statement that 'Irish language radio programmings should be promoted fully by the Government' (BCI 2004: 8).

The continuing support for the Irish language stems from its symbolic importance for the nation, but this was not manifest in audience figures for Irish language programmes. Although programmes in Irish could be justified on the basis of the importance of the Irish language as a national symbol, as had been the case in the previous period, the market-oriented element of the liberal ideology was in tension with it. Nonetheless, the liberal ideology contained an element of minority rights which helped to justify providing a service for Irish speakers. Programmes for learners of Irish continued to be broadcast, but there was also an emphasis on providing Irish speakers with a range of programmes in Irish and even a separate radio station for the Gaeltacht (RnaG).

In 1978 RTÉ established a second television channel. The initial public demand had been to transmit the BBC across the country because those near the border or the east coast could already receive British channels using a large aerial. The decision taken was to have an RTÉ2 rather than the BBC. Irish language organisations expressed the fear that programmes in Irish would be broadcast on RTÉ2 and that this channel would have lower ratings. In terms of the earlier national ideology this would further hinder the promotion of Irish as a national language, and from the perspective of the liberal ideology it could strengthen the market-oriented dimension of that ideology against the group-rights dimension.

In the 1980s the state and RTÉ came under further pressure to improve its Irish language service, particularly on television.

3.6 The neoliberal ideology: post-1980s

The ideological shift in this period has been from liberal to neoliberal, with a further move from the cultural aspects of the national ideology deeper into the economic dimension. This ideology was yet more market-oriented, with a focus on individual rights rather than on group rights. With respect to the Irish language there has been a shift toward the linguistic rights of the individual. Nonetheless, threads of the national and liberal ideologies continue, which means that the Irish language still appears to have a privileged position and group rights have not been abandoned. It was in this context that a national Irish language television channel and a Dublin-based radio station were established.

The availability of the Gaeltacht radio channel cast in stark contrast the dearth of programming in Irish on television, which barely amounted to 2 per cent of the broadcasting time in any average week from the 1960s to the 1980s, and consisted, for example, of a brief daily news bulletin (a more detailed version of which could have been watched earlier in English), a brief weekly children's programme, and a weekly half-hour current affairs programme (see Watson 2003: 80 for this example from one week in 1985, and page 97 for an improved selection in 1995 – still accounting for only 2 per cent of total broadcast time on RTÉ1 and 2). Throughout the 1970s Irish language and Gaeltacht organisations, as well as individuals, demanded an increase in the amount of Irish on RTÉ television. During the 1980s programmes in Irish were gradually transferred from RTÉ1 to RTÉ2 without any substantial increase in the percentage of programming in Irish. This led to a gradual shift in the focus of demands, from more Irish language programmes on RTÉ television, to demands for a separate Irish language television channel.

From 1980 onwards a group calling themselves Coiste ar son Teilifís Gaeltachta (a committee for Gaeltacht television) and later Meitheal

Oibre Theilifís na Gaeltachta (Teilifís na Gaeltachta cooperative) tried to replicate the campaign which had led to the establishment of RnaG. Arguing that the lack of Irish language media was hampering the inter-generational transmission of the language in the Gaeltacht, one of the members, Donncha Ó hÉallaithe (1997) argued:

> chonaic muid an dream a bhí faoi mhíbhuntáiste ná seo iad pobal na Gaeltachta a raibh an cultúr áitiúil cineál préamhaithe go huile agus go hiomlán i nGaeilge go leanúnach leis na céadta bliain agus go raibh sé ag teacht chuig an bpointe nach raibh ag éirí leis an bpobal sin an teanga a chur go dti an chéad glún eile mar *just* bhí paistí ag diúltú. Bhí *reaction* uafásach ó pháistí sna hochtóidí in aghaidh na Gaeilge, *just* bhíodar ag diúltú — chomh luath agus a d'fhoghlaimidís Béarla dhiúltóidís Gaeilge a labhairt.

> [we saw that the group which was disadvantaged was the Gaeltacht community whose local culture was kind of rooted totally and com-pletely in the Irish language continuously for hundreds of years and that it was reaching the point when that community was not succeeding in passing on the language to the next generation because children just were refusing. There was a terrible reaction from children in the eighties against the Irish language, they were just refusing – as soon as they would learn English they'd refuse to speak Irish.]

Following a failed television broadcast attempt in 1980, the group man-aged to broadcast live and prerecorded material within a Gaeltacht area of County Galway in November 1987 and again in December 1988. In the years soon after this the Gaeltacht group became part of a wider national campaign for a television channel, FNT (Feachtas Náisiúnta Teilifíse). Although within this campaign the issue of whether the planned channel should be a Gaeltacht or national television chan-nel was rather obscure, even its title suggested that the focus was not on a community television channel. The campaign continued for a number of years, enjoying a fortuitous coincidence of timing with the appointment of Michael D. Higgins (current President of Ireland), who, as the Minister with responsibility for both the Gaeltacht and broadcasting (1992–7), made the final decision to go ahead with the channel. Higgins' electoral constituency was West Galway (including the Gaeltacht region of Connemara). He had been preceded at the end of the previous government by Máire Geoghegan-Quinn (1992), from the same constituency, who had laid the groundwork in the Department of Communications.

The new Irish language channel began broadcasting in 1996 under the name Teilifís na Gaeilge (TnaG), but was relaunched as TG4 three years later. Initially, although with some autonomy, the channel came within the remit of the RTÉ Authority; following the Broadcasting Act of 2001, however, TG4 was enabled to go its own way. Born in the era of the neoliberal ideology, TG4 is a child of the period, as is evident in some of the points made by Pádhraic Ó Ciardha. As adviser to both Ministers (mentioned above) and subsequently as Information Officer and current Deputy Chief Executive Officer of TG4, Ó Ciardha has played an important role in the direction which the channel has taken. Before the channel began broadcasting Ó Ciardha (1996) made a number of points which appeared to place the channel within the earlier ideologies, but were really threads more clearly woven into the current neoliberal ideology. Echoing the national ideology, he argued that TnaG was a national channel for the Irish public as a whole and not a minority or community channel focusing only on serving Irish speakers; it just happened that the channel would broadcast in Irish (with subtitles). His point that the new channel would have to attract a large audience, or a smaller audience with a large expendable income, resonated with the market-oriented approach of the liberal ideology. However, these threads fit well within the neoliberal ideology, in which limited resources and an obligation to commission programmes meant that, more than RTÉ, the new channel, and especially its independent producers, would be subject to market forces. Furthermore, Ó Ciardha (1996) claimed that the channel would not be an instrument of the Government's language policy – however, in recent years the channel has pledged to support the Government in reviving the language ('Tacú leis an Rialtas chun an Ghaeilge a athbheochan trí oibriú go dlúth leis ar chur i bhfeidhm na Straitéise 20 Bliain don Ghaeilge (2010–2030)' [support the government in order to revive Irish through working closely with the government and implementing the 20-Year Strategy for Irish (2010–2030)] TG4 2012: 6).

TG4 has managed the tensions between the different ideological demands placed upon it. In its recent annual report there is a pledge to serve the culture of the whole island, of the Gaeltacht community and Irish-speaking families and even to provide an Irish language service around the world ('A chinntiú go bhfreagraíonn ár gcuid cláracha do chultúr phobal oileán na hÉireann...do riachtanais na bpobal Gaeltachta agus na dteaghlach arb í an Ghaeilge a dteanga laethúil.... [agus] ar fud an domhain' [affirming that our programmes address the culture of the people of the island of Ireland...the needs of the people of the Irish-speaking regions and of the households in which Irish is the daily language.... [and] throughout the world] (TG4 2012: 6)). At the same time, TG4 is expected to compete for ratings. This was an issue that caused some discussion even before the channel came on air. There were fears, which echoed the protectionist ideology, that the Irish language would be ghettoised on a separate channel. There were also critics reflecting a more neoliberal ideology claiming that viewership figures for Irish language programmes were too low to justify the expenditure (see Fitzgibbon 1993: 2). This was similar to the arguments in relation to Irish language radio broadcasts in the 1950s. Nonetheless, within a few years TG4 had become the channel in Ireland with the eighth largest viewership, with more than half a million people watching it on a daily basis (TG4 2012: 11–12). Although catering for minority interests, such as Gaeltacht culture, can restrict the potential audience, TG4 has been able to attract a wider audience which includes people with limited or no Irish, by broadcasting programmes in English and by providing subtitles in English for programmes in Irish.

There have been significant changes with regard to Irish language media over the past 20 years. The most significant was TG4, discussed above. There was also another development in the form of a small independent Irish language radio station in Dublin, called Raidió na Life (RnaL), which began broadcasting in 1993. This station was established by Comharchumann Raidió Átha Cliath Teoranta [Dublin Radio Cooperative Limited] (CRÁCT) and most of its staff work on a voluntary basis. The core audience for this station is the Irish-speaking community in the Dublin region. Despite the use of the word 'community', the vast majority of Irish-speakers in Dublin do not form an Irish-speaking community. In recent years there have been more Gaeltacht and Belfast voices on RnaL. The station also broadcasts programmes in other languages such as Spanish and Polish.

As well as that, there is a small amount of broadcasting in Irish on independent radio stations throughout the island, which receive a licence from the Broadcasting Authority of Ireland (formerly the BCI) south of the border and Ofcom in Northern Ireland, where programmes in Irish (television and radio) have been broadcast on the BBC as well as on some independent stations, such as Iúr FM [Newry FM] – a community radio station based in Newry, which broadcasts a considerable amount in Irish (between 10 and 20 per cent of the time); Féile FM [Festival FM], based in Belfast, which broadcasts for several weeks each year; and Raidió Fáilte [Welcome Radio], also based in Belfast and which broadcasts completely in Irish.

Turning the radio dial on an average evening in Dublin a listener now has available a range of programmes in Irish on RTÉ Radio 1, RnaG, RnaL, as well as on many other independent English language radio stations, many of whom present popular music charts programmes in Irish. In fact, often when searching in the evening for programmes in Irish on the dedicated Irish language radio stations RnaL and RnaG, the listener finds that the sounds emanating from both stations are thumping club tracks without lyrics. Since the arrival of TG4 and RnaL, and RnaG's efforts to attract a younger listenership in the evening, the Irish language seems to have acquired a certain cachet.

As schools, rather than families, continue to produce the majority of the half a million Irish speakers in the Republic of Ireland, the Irish-speaking community is quite small, with a mere 30 per cent of Irish speakers having the opportunity to speak Irish on a daily basis. The question on the census about frequency of use allows us to calculate that only 15 per cent of Irish speakers speak Irish on a daily basis (outside the education system) and an equal percentage speaks Irish on a weekly basis (see Watson and Nic Ghiolla Phádraig 2011: 439; Hickey 2011: 11–14; and Watson and Nic Ghiolla Phádraig 2009). For the majority of Irish speakers the programmes in Irish on radio and television are their only regular exposure to the language and their only opportunity to imagine an Irish-speaking community. Increasing individualisation under the neoliberal ideology reflects the reality for the majority of Irish speakers today, for whom speaking Irish is an individual choice, exercised when the circumstances are favourable. For the vast majority of Irish speakers, the Irish language is not the everyday language of communication; it is often an effort of will when opportunities arise, opportunities that are fragmented across the media, across civil society and across networks of friends and family. The existence of these atomised Irish speakers and their fragmented opportunities to speak Irish are in no small part thanks to ideological support for the language evident in state efforts and public support for the Irish language. So long as state support through the education system is the primary foundation on which the intergenerational transmission of the Irish language depends, the language will remain in the precarious position of relying on its continued ideological importance.

3.7 A cosmopolitan ideology?

In each ideological phase there is evidence of many different ways of acting, thinking and feeling, but they cohere into particular structures in each phase and are more likely to result in particular kinds of outcomes in one ideological phase than another.

This results in benefits for particular individuals and groups who have (and acquire) particular characteristics and can take advantage of those structures (see Watson and Nic Ghiolla Phádraig (2011) for a discussion of the middle-class advantage associated with the Irish language).

The ideological contexts since independence have changed from a focus on the whole nation, through a more liberal focus on minority rights, to a more neoliberal individualistic focus. The image of the audience for Irish language media has also changed to reflect these different ideological contexts, from one in which the ideal was of an Irish-speaking nation and mass audience, through a segmented or niche audience of an Irish-speaking minority, to an Irish language service for a fragmented audience which contains some Irish speakers. In these ideological adaptations there is a shift of focus away from the efforts to create an Irish-speaking nation in the decades following independence (the protectionist phase); these efforts had benefitted those outside the Gaeltacht who could speak (or acquire) the language, while the Gaeltacht continued to decline economically and linguistically, and Irish language radio programming was directed at the Irish-speaking community in the Gaeltacht and at the nation as a whole. In the liberal phase, the Gaeltacht was given some focus as efforts were made to counter its disadvantage, but Irish speakers outside the Gaeltacht continued to grow in number; this was the era in which Raidió na Gaeltachta was born. In the neoliberal phase there is a coincidence between the ideology of the atomised individual and the reality for the majority of Irish speakers scattered across Ireland, as only about 10 per cent of them are concentrated in the Irish-speaking communities of the Gaeltacht. Even though there is a large number of Irish speakers in Dublin, they do not live in a linguistic community and the majority of Irish speakers only occasionally coalesce into Irish-speaking groups; this is the era of Teilifís na Gaeilge.

Perhaps at this juncture we are undergoing a process of cosmopolitanisation, a globalisation from within (Beck and Sznaider 2006), moving further down the road of individualisation, away from the minority rights perspective of multiculturalism. Beck argued that '[d]er multikulturellen Prämisse zufolge gibt es kein Individuum, sondern der Mensch ist ein reines Epiphänomen seiner Kultur' (Beck 2005: 99) [according to multicultural premises there is no individual, just the person as a mere epiphenomenon of culture]. In other words, the individual is 'das Produkt der Sprache, der Traditionen, der Überzeugungen, der Bräuche und Landschaft, innerhalb derer er (oder sie) auf die Welt kam und aufwuchs' (Beck 2005: 99) [the product of the language, the traditions, the convictions, the customs and landscape in which he (or she) came into the world and grew up]. Within a cosmopolitan ideology (if such an era is now beginning) the focus on the local or national would be in a global context of individuals who are different but equal.

To defend the equal value of all individuals would also mean to defend the linguistic diversity of humanity. This could not be done solely at the global level, but would be focused on at the local and state level. In this context individual states would play a role in defending languages that exist within its borders, most particularly its autochthonous languages, but also recent arrivals. Work done to protect, preserve and revive languages would be in the interests of humanity rather than narrow self-serving national interests. This means that the Irish language would be protected by the Irish state and by Irish citizens not because it is a language that belongs to a particular group of people, but because it belongs to humanity. The Irish state would preserve it where it is spoken and encourage it to be spoken regardless of the other cultural characteristics of individuals who speak the language. The Irish state would also encourage or at least not block the use of other languages within its borders and, similarly, the Irish language could be spoken by people in many other countries around the world. To facilitate this it would be necessary to choose a *lingua franca* to facilitate communication within the borders of each state and preferably a global *lingua franca*. The existence of a *lingua franca* would facilitate the preservation of languages because it would work against the nationalistic linguistic homogenisation of nation-states and would facilitate communication within multilingual states.

In conclusion, the dominant mode of support for the Irish language is symbolic. The world today is divided into nation states, and an ideological belief is widespread that the nation of each nation state has its own unique national characteristics (although most 'nation' states contain several nations). Language is often a key national characteristic. It is not necessary for that language to be the most widely-used language, but to exist to a sufficient extent that it can remain of symbolic value in representing a unique characteristic of the nation. The Irish state is unlikely to provide much more than symbolic support for the Irish language. That the Irish language exists is sufficient. The *cúpla focal* [few words] can be used as a badge of Irishness. Although nation-states continue to exist in this ever-globalising world, the legitimacy of nation-states is being undermined by that process of globalisation. One of the perspectives which has been emerging in recent decades is the idea of multicultural states rather than nation-states. The predominant approach within multiculturalism appears to be mainly a tolerance of differences at the symbolic level only. Such a multicultural perspective in Ireland could provide the same level of minimal symbolic support as is being given nowadays. Both the multicultural state and the nation-state fail to treat all individual human beings with equal respect. As epiphenomena of diverse cultures, individuals are tolerated merely at the symbolic level. True respect for the individual would allow for actual real diversity. In Ireland to be Irish does not mean to speak Irish, but to have the command of a *cúpla focal* [few words]. Perhaps the same could be said about another major element of Irish identity – Catholicism. To be Irish means not to practise Catholicism in full, but to participate mainly in symbolic form. At least Gaelic sports appear to be fully practised. Although Cumann Lúthcleas Gael [the Gaelic Athletic Association, GAA] carries out its business in English, they have a Gaelic Language and Culture Committee in each county and continue to regard it as part of their aims to support the Irish language and culture (particularly Irish dancing, music and singing) (see www.gaa.ie/about-the-gaa/cultur-agus-gaeilge).

Perhaps the mainly symbolic support of the nationalist, protectionist, liberal and neoliberal approaches will be undermined by the continuing process of globalisation. In that case a cosmopolitan approach might allow support for the Irish language to continue into what Beck et al. (2003) called the second (or reflexive) age of modernity. A cosmopolitan approach would treat all individual human beings with equal respect and would allow and facilitate them to speak any language. It would allow and facilitate, in particular, the speaking of the Irish language; a cultural element that came into existence in Ireland, but forms part of global cultural diversity.

Notes

1. Irish-speaking communities, mainly in the west.
2. Literally, Irish speakers, but usually refers to Irish speakers from outside the Gaeltacht.
3. Head of Government for most of the 1930s–50s and Head of State from the late 1950s to the early 1970s.

References

Anderson, Benedict (1991). *Imagined Communities: Reflections on the Origins and Spread of Nationalism.* London: Verso.

Beck, Ulrich (2005). 'Dir kosmopolitische Gesellschaft und ihre Feinde', in: Anton Amann and Gerhard Majce (eds) *Soziologie in interdisziplinaeren Netzwerken.* Vienna: Boehlau Verlag, pp. 77–106.

Beck, Ulrich, Wolfgang Bonss and Christoph C. Lau (2003). 'The theory of reflexive modernization: problematic, hypotheses and research programme', *Theory, Culture & Society* 20.2: 1–33.

Beck, Ulrich and Natan Sznaider (2006). 'Unpacking cosmopolitanism for the social sciences: a research agenda', *The British Journal of Sociology* 57.1: 1–23.

Bell, David A. (2003). *The Cult of the Nation in France: Inventing Nationalism, 1680–1800.* Cambridge, MA: Harvard University Press.

BCI [Broadcasting Commission of Ireland] (2004). *Turning on and Tuning in to Irish Language Radio in the 21st Century.* A research report prepared by MORI Ireland on behalf of the Broadcasting Commission of Ireland and Foras na Gaeilge. Dublin: BCI.

Connor, Walker (1978). 'A nation is a nation, is a state, is an ethnic group, is a …', *Ethnic and Racial Studies* 1.4: 379–88.

Delap, Breandán (2007). *Ar an Taifead: Fís, Fuaim, Focal.* Dublin: Cois Life.

Doolan, Lelia, Jack Dowling and Bob Quinn (1969). *Sit Down and be Counted: the Cultural Evolution of a Television Station.* Dublin: Wellington Publishers.

Durkheim, Emile (1938 [1895]). *The Rules of Sociological Method.* London: Collier Macmillan.

Fitzgibbon, Frank (1993). 'Paying for Teilifis: Michael D. Higgins's brainchild will cost State 21m to run', *The Sunday Tribune*, 5 December 1993.

Gellner, Ernest (1983). *Nations and Nationalism.* Oxford: Blackwell.

Gorham, Maurice (1967). *Forty Years of Broadcasting.* Dublin: RTÉ.

Hickey, Raymond (2011). *The Dialects of Irish, Study of a Changing Landscape.* Berlin: de Gruyter Mouton.

Hutchinson, John (2001). 'Archaeology and the Irish rediscovery of the Celtic past', *Nations and Nationalism* 7.4: 505–19.

Ó Ciardha, Pádhraic (1996). Personal interview with the author on 19 February 1996.

Ó hÉallaithe, Donncha (1997). Personal interview with the author on 11 April 1997.

Pine, Richard (2002). *2RN and the Origins of Irish Radio.* Dublin: Four Courts Press.

Smith, Anthony D. (2009). *Ethno-Symbolism and Nationalism: Cultural Approach.* London: Routledge.

TG4 (2012). *Annual Report.* http://www.tg4.ie/en/corporate/background.html.

Thompson, John B. (1994). 'Ideology and modern culture', in: *The Polity Reader in Social Theory.* Cambridge: Polity Press, pp. 133–41.

Watson, Iarfhlaith (1996). 'The Irish language and television', *British Journal of Sociology* 47.2: 255–74.

Watson, Iarfhlaith (2003). *Broadcasting in Irish: Minority Language, Radio, Television and Identity.* Dublin: Four Courts Press.

Watson, Iarfhlaith (2007). 'Identity, Language and Nationality', in: Sara O'Sullivan (ed.) *Contemporary Ireland: a Sociological Map.* Dublin: UCD Press, pp. 351–69.

Watson, Iarfhlaith and Máire Nic Ghiolla Phádraig (2009). 'Is There an Educational Advantage to Speaking Irish? An Investigation of The Relationship Between Education and Ability to Speak Irish', *International Journal of the Sociology of Language* 199: 143–56.

Watson, Iarfhlaith and Máire Nic Ghiolla Phádraig (2011). 'Linguistic elitism: the advantage of speaking Irish rather than the Irish-speaker advantage', *The Economic and Social Review* 42.4: 437–54.

Working Group on Irish Language Television Broadcasting (1987). *Report to the Ministers for the Gaeltacht and Communications*. Dublin: Government Stationery Office.

4

Irish-English Code-switching: a Sociolinguistic Perspective

Siobhán Ní Laoire

4.1 Introduction

Irish is a minority language in a contact situation with a major world language, and language contact phenomena have been a feature of Irish for hundreds of years. Code-switching (CS) is the most visible and marked of language contact features and it forms part of the active linguistic repertoire of most speakers of Irish. It has been under-represented in Irish language corpora and in linguistic and dialectological description and analysis of Irish. Irish-English CS follows international trends in being perceived as aberrant and thereby generally stigmatised by the speech community.[1]

The data in this chapter come from two distinct data sets. Firstly, individual examples of CS collected and observed in speech communities which comprise adult L1 speakers of Irish in Gaeltacht areas (in this instance, primarily Connemara). Data were noted in mainly informal and spontaneous L1 Irish social settings, and on regional Irish language radio, over several years and including very recent examples. These data are indicative of the process and product of CS in contemporary Irish. In the second part of the chapter, an exploration of data from transcriptions of one season of a radio soap opera indicates that variation in use of CS marks role negotiation, identity construction and fluctuating and relative levels of in-group membership.

Speakers of Irish comprise multiple and diverse speech communities and communities of practice. Language competence and associated linguistic and sociolinguistic behaviours are an important factor in how Irish-English CS is practised and perceived. As we shall see, invariant *avoidance* of CS, for instance, is strongly marked as learner or linguistic novice behaviour in informal domains. The most salient linguistic fact about the speech communities and social networks under consideration here is that Irish is the unmarked, default language choice in intimate/neighbourhood domains and, in some instances, in a wider range of contexts. The networks are L1 only or L1 dominant and have a complete range of L1 stylistic repertoire potentially available. Since adult L1 speakers of Irish are also bilingual, that repertoire potentially includes access to English.

The following description of a car journey (a conflation of real life events), undertaken by bilingual friends, serves to quickly introduce key linguistic and sociolinguistic elements of Irish-English CS.[2] Describing the linguistic junctions of this journey also highlights the essential sociolinguistic and contextual sensitivity of CS. The women in their 30s are L1 speakers of Irish from a Gaeltacht community and their usual language of interaction with each other is Irish. Their car journey takes them from Galway to Dublin, where they are both working. The chat between these old friends is intimate and lively as they catch up on each other's news. Their conversational style in Irish is informal and includes regular use of English phrases and lexical items such as:

(1) Beidh an *jackpot* anocht a'ainn.
    'We'll get the jackpot tonight.'
(2) Tá seo lochtach, tá sé briste freisin, tá sé *really* go dona.
    'This is faulty, it's broken too, it's really bad.'
(3) Ag caint fúmsa, *I suppose*?
    'Talking about me, I suppose?'

When they stop at a petrol station they switch from Irish to English as they pay for their purchases and chat politely with the cashier and with each other. As they return to the car, they revert to their previous language choice and continue their conversation, in the intimacy and privacy of the car, in Irish.

Switches on this journey pinpoint triggers, junctions and motivations for variation of language code. The switch from Irish to English which occurs when the friends interact with the cashier is a classic situational or domain-based CS. In this case, it also overlaps with addressee-based CS. The underlying sociolinguistic reality is that the unmarked language choice for interactions in the public sphere between strangers in Ireland is English, outside of Gaeltacht areas at least. In this case, and without additional contextual information, the switch to English is based on a prediction or assumption that the cashier is not an L1 Irish speaker and includes the related trigger of public rather than intimate or private domain. For the bilingual friends not to have switched in anticipation of an interaction in English with the cashier would be viewed as aberrant and marked behaviour. This situational CS is akin to a diglossic, functionally marked language choice and is typical of minority/majority linguistic interactions.

As the friends return to the car they move from an anonymous public sphere to an intimate and private space. They also move from polite interaction, aimed at the communicative goal of getting petrol and paying for it, to a resumption of a dynamic, jointly negotiated and nuanced interaction between equals. Their situational switch to Irish is triggered by the change of domain on a macro level but returning to Irish also has a metaphorical force as it reinforces the friends' intimacy and marks the junction with the previous polite but public interaction. Additionally, by converging towards an informal style of Irish, characterised by use of English, the participants in this speech event mark equality and closeness on a micro level. This latter element of use of CS as a stylistic marker on the formality–informality continuum can be described as metaphorical CS as it forms an active part of the interaction and sees the friends drawing on their repertoire as bilinguals to contextualise their relationship and negotiate roles.

4.2 Researching and defining Irish-English code-switching

The essential structural properties of CS – an alternating or mixing of two languages – are neatly encapsulated in the statement from a member of a bilingual Latino-English speech community used in the title of Poplack's (1980) influential study: 'Sometimes I'll start a sentence in Spanish [*sic*] *y termino en español*'. The term *code-switching* is used in this chapter to describe alternation of languages within a speech event or conversation. It incorporates the term 'code-mixing', sometimes reserved for insertions or alternations within a clause or phrase, and the term 'borrowing', sometimes used to describe insertions of single lexical items.

Most CS research concentrates on linguistic/psycholinguistic/ grammatical aspects or on situational/social/sociolinguistic aspects. The research literature nonetheless contains a consistent thread of recognition and acceptance of the multifactorial nature of CS and CS research. Matras (2009) summarises thus:

> The study of codeswitching elevated a phenomenon that had been traditionally viewed by normative grammarians as 'language corruption' to an investigation field in its own right...Researchers have

since been focusing on situational and contextual motivations for switching as well as on the structural characteristics of codeswitching, aiming to identify general patterns. Switching is considered functional in the sense that speakers are motivated by various factors to switch at particular points in the discourse. At the same time it is clear that language mixing is multilayered and that it can serve various different purposes even in the same conversation. (Matras 2009: 101)

Stenson (1990, 1991, 1993, 1997) has undertaken several descriptions of grammatical structure and linguistic constraints in Irish-English CS, and data presented in this chapter are generally consistent with the patterns she describes:

> ...switching tends to be intrasentential and can involve anything from a single English word to a whole phrase within a sentence, which is nonetheless perceived as an Irish sentence. The vast majority of switches involve single lexical items, especially nouns. These may occur either alone...or as part of a larger noun phrase...Less frequently, larger segments of a noun phrase are in English. (Stenson 1990: 170)

Establishing distinctions between borrowing and code-mixing for individual lexical items is Irish is not straightforward due, in part, to the long history of language contact (Sjoestedt-Jonval 1928, Stenson 1993, Mac Mathúna 2008) and consequent variation in levels of assimilation, integration and speaker perception of individual loan words. The CS-borrowing continuum, therefore, while essentially diachronic, is also a dynamic rather than linear connection (Matras 2009: 110). Older borrowings, and English discourse markers such as *well, you know, so,* can be interpreted as relatively assimilated and unmarked in speaker judgements but nevertheless are recognised by speakers as English insertions. Stenson (1993) notes a wide range of semantic categories susceptible to borrowing from English with well-established loanwords, often filling a lexical gap or replacing older forms, co-existing with English words borrowed without phonological assimilation. As Gardner-Chloros (2009: 101) notes:

> One of the challenges posed by CS is to explain the variation within it, or, viewed another way, to describe how broadly it should be defined. It has been defined here as inclusively as possible, because, in the present state of knowledge it has not been demonstrated that the

differences between CS and other contact phenomena are categorical differences as opposed to differences of degree.

For these reasons, our use of the term code-switching as a blanket term to refer to the process of language contact which manifests in the use of English vocabulary at various levels of phonological, morphological and syntactic assimilation and integration is justified. As we will see, the relative sociolinguistic markedness and sensitivity of individual tokens of Irish-English CS in a speech event are themselves context-sensitive and variable, and judgements on relative sensitivities form part of analysis and interpretation of data. Too restrictive a definition would thus risk failing to capture nuances of variation. Given the sociolinguistic theme of the present volume, our emphasis here is on CS behaviour and on its social-attitudinal reflexes and we will therefore forefront CS as process in this discussion and consider structural, grammatical aspects, when relevant, in that context.

4.3 Sociolinguistic overview of the Irish-English CS database

It is possible to identify a range of communicative, social and stylistic functions, motivations and meanings in CS behaviour which point to the context-sensitive nature of the CS database. The following broad overlapping categories facilitate an integrated discussion of data from diverse sources and contexts:

i) CS as informality marker
ii) CS triggered by perceived properties of domain, register or semantic range
iii) CS as a stylistic/narrative device in informal spontaneous speech
iv) CS as a tool in identity construction and negotiation of relationships.

A selection of examples and contexts are presented under these headings below, while noting that no list of this type will be exhaustive.

4.3.1 CS as informality marker

CS functions as a marker on the formality–informality spectrum in bilingual and multilingual contexts internationally, and Irish-English CS follows this pattern. A base level of use of CS is a neutral, unmarked stylistic option at the informal end of the spectrum in Irish, particularly in spontaneous spoken language. In general, CS is conspicuous by its absence in formal and written domains. Thus, for many adult L1 speakers the most significant element of the toolbox for style-shifting towards an appropriate register for an interview on local Irish language radio or speaking at a public meeting will be a significant reduction in CS tokens in their linguistic performance. Examples 4–20 below are indicative of the general database of contemporary Irish-English CS in informal domains:

(4)   Níl *electricity* anseo. Shíl sé go raibh *electricity* anseo agus níl. Níl sé *plug*áilte isteach.
       'There's no electricity here. He thought there was electricity here and there isn't. It's not plugged in.'

(5)   Bhí sé beagáinín *contrary* ar dtús. Tá sé ag fáil *in good humour* anois.
       'He was a bit contrary [difficult] at first. His humour is improving now.'

(6)   *Consultant* é, déarfainn. *Major find* ar bith a bhíonn in aon áit ar fud na tíre, caithfidh seisean a bheith ann.
       'He's a consultant, I'd say. Any major find anywhere in the country, he has to be there.'

(7)   Tá sé an-*happy* ach tá sé ag iarraidh, tá sé ag iarraidh an *slab* a *ghlue*áil taobh thíos.
       'He's very happy but he wants, he wants to glue the slab underneath.'

(8)   Tá sin *absolutely perfect*.
       'That's absolutely perfect.'

(9)   ... na *pallets* 'thabhairt suas go dtí an *level*.
       '... to bring the pallets up to the level.'

(10)   Bhí sagart anseo ag iarraidh *one way traffic* a dhéanamh ansin, lá sochraide.
       'A priest here wanted to make [a] one way traffic [system] there on funeral days.'

(11)   Tá sé sách *nippy*.
       'It's quite nippy.'

(12)   Bhí mé fhéin *going mad*.
       'I was going mad.'

(13)   *Leave them out*, is glaofaidh mé air tráthnóna.
       'Leave them out, and I'll ring him this evening.'

(14)   ... go raibh siad ag *mix*eáil le sluaisid, le lámha. '*Fuck*', a deir sé, 'cá bhfuil na *compressors* bailithe?'

'...that they were mixing with shovels, by hand. "Fuck", he said, "where are the compressors gone?"'

(15) ...bhíodh an dá shúil gearrtha, *all the time.*
'...her two eyes used be cut, all the time.'

(16) Bheadh sé sin *too risky.*
'That would be too risky.'

(17) Ach is dóigh go gcaithfeá, *you know, question and answer.*
'But you probably would have to, you know, question and answer.'

(18) An mbeidh *game* cártaí a'd?
'Would you like a game of cards?'

(19) Ar aon nós, *a* bua *is a* bua. [Sports commentator on a radio sports show].
'Anyway, a win is a win.'

(20) Ó, tá sí *flat out*, an creatúr.
'Oh, she's flat out, the poor thing.'

It is important to note that these examples were observed and collected in a variety of contexts in L1 speech communities over a number of years, rather than at a single speech event. In an individual speech event the quality of CS tokens (longer strings vs single words; older borrowings vs lexical loans for which there is already an Irish equivalent; degrees of syntactic displacement, if any, etc.), as well as their frequency, impinge on social meaning and markedness. Accordingly, these elements influence the way individual CS tokens are performed, perceived and interpreted by participants. We will also see that the smaller unit of sociolinguistic analysis – a community of practice – which includes the necessary elements of mutual engagement, jointly negotiated enterprise and shared repertoire (e.g. Eckert 2000: 34–41) is relevant in differentiating and distinguishing between Irish language speech communities and their sociolinguistic, particularly CS, practice.

4.3.2 Semantic, lexical and domain triggers for CS

The semantic weight and/or range of a word or phrase can be felt to be unequal or not precisely equivalent as between Irish and English due to cultural associations. Thus Irish speakers who have lived or are living in the US insert the terms *social security, highschool, subway, congressman* rather than search for an equivalent in Irish. As with CS behaviours universally, these bilingual speakers are capable of accessing and using an equivalent Irish term but its efficacy and force are not felt to be adequate in a different cultural context. Such CS patterns for culturally marked concepts are a widespread feature of CS (Myers-Scotton 2006: 212–15) where a speaker uses CS to fill a perceived or real lexical gap. Other triggers for switching are outlined in the following contextualised examples:

4.3.2.1   Neologisms and technical terms

The use of neologisms in Irish is sociolinguistically constrained as to usage, and speaker judgements consistently report a danger of seeming affected or superior when newly coined terms are employed in informal domains. The combined force of terminology, domain and referential range may have motivated the CS in the following example where the term 'hard drive' *diosca crua* was known to be part of the repertoire of both the speaker and the addressee:

(21)   Theip an *hard drive* orm inniu.
'The hard drive crashed today.'

Outside the formal workplace, the unmarked choice for technical, scientific or specialist terms is predominantly the CS item but the inter-actional force of use/non-use of CS is always context-bound. In some social networks, particularly within the education sector where L1 and L2 speakers often interact, fine-grained subtle judgements are needed as to use and non-use of CS for terminology to avoid communicating condescension or risking exaggeratedly stereotyped behaviour.

A radio interview with a tax specialist contained the following examples of CS:

(22)   ...go háirithe má tá tú ag fáil *single payment*. [Specialist interviewee]
'...especially if you are getting the "single payment."'
(23)   ...na *pensions* uilig. [Specialist interviewee]
'...all the pensions.'
(24)   Bhfuil tú sásta go bhfuil leigheas faighte ar an *mhedical card*? [Interviewer]
'Are you satisfied [do you believe] that the medical card [problem] has been resolved?'

However, in other parts of the same interview the specialist and inter-viewer both used the equivalent Irish terms. The motivations and effect of CS behaviour here is to make accommodational moves, and bridge the gap, between speaker and listener. Specialist terminology, whether in English or in more recently coined Irish terms, are equally alien to the non-specialist listener and the metaphorical space between the two sides is lessened when the specialist occasionally acknowledges the 'otherness' of the topic and creatively dilutes its impact. The context of this interview, an 'Ask the expert' type slot, is central to this interpretation. It is worth noting that specialist terminology is not an inevitable trigger for CS. An indicative community of practice is exemplified by young, tech-savvy, L1 professional broadcasters on a currently running afternoon radio programme (*Rónán Beo@3*), also on RTÉ Raidió na Gaeltachta but aimed primarily at a younger listening audience. Both interviewer and guest can regularly be heard discussing media and technology and using technical terminology in an unselfconscious, unmarked way.

4.3.2.2 *Reducing markedness*

A related, and frequent, speaker strategy for reducing the sociolinguistic markedness of newly coined terms is seen in the following example, taken from the same radio interview as examples 22–4. The speaker 'glosses' or provides an English translation alongside the neologism, thus acknowledging the use, and clarifying the meaning, of the lexical item in a non-threatening way without lowering the appropriate register:

(25)   ... tiocfaidh seo chugat go huathoibríobh nó *automatically*.
     ' . . . this will come to you automatically, or automatically.'

Mar a déarfá, 'as you/one might say', or formulations such as *mar a deir an Ghaeilge Nua* 'as it is said in the "New Irish"' or *mar a deir na Gaeilgeoirí* 'as the "*Gaeilgeoirí*" [L2 speakers] say', are also frequently used to neutralise or acknowledge the stylistic implications of use of a neologism (and non-use of CS).

Avoiding slippage of register may also be a motivation for use of the formula *mar a déarfá*, to shadow or follow a lexical CS:

(26)   Cén *idea* atá agat leis, mar a déarfá?
     'What's your idea for it, as you might say [as it were]?'

Metalinguistic commentary and self-awareness regarding sociolinguistic aspects of style is a common feature of CS in Irish, as in other, language-contact contexts.

4.3.2.3 *Domain associations*

Domain associations can trigger CS, so that skilled bilinguals will count and perform mathematical processes in whichever language they originally learned maths. As above, such speakers know this lexicon in Irish but the semantic associations and referential range triggers a switch to the language of primary school. For similar reasons, older Gaeltacht speakers almost universally code-switch for dates:

> (27)   Chuaigh mise go Meiriceá *in Nineteen Forty Nine*. [Radio documentary, personal reminisence.]
> 'I went to America in Nineteen Forty Nine.'

There is an inevitable level of subjectivity in interpreting or attempting to account for micro-level switches in informal settings. In the following extract from a group of women at a coffee break in a work setting, the use of English *Christmas cards* seems to trigger another switch, despite a turn in between, and the speaker augments the effect by adding a semi-assimilated CS verbal noun borrowing '*mak*áil':

> (28)   Speaker A: Bhfuil mórán *Christmas cards* tagtha?
>   'Have many Christmas cards arrived?'
>   Speaker B: [Short answer in Irish]
>   Speaker C: Meas tú an bhfuil sé ródheireanach ag gabháil ag *mak*áil *Christmas cakes*?
>   'I wonder is it too late to start making Christmas cakes?'

An overlapping interpretation here could posit Speaker C as making an accommodational move towards Speaker A by converging towards her CS style.

In a similar interaction and context, the repetition of the English word 'toothpaste' may have triggered the one-word response in English from Speaker C:

> (29)   Speaker A: Rud eile atá go maith: *toothpaste*. [As a treatment for mouth ulcers]
>   'Another thing that's good: toothpaste.'
>   Speaker B: Tá, *toothpaste*.
>   'Yes, toothpaste.'
>   Speaker C: *Good*.
>   Speaker A: Nó braoinín fuisce.
>   'Or a little drop of whiskey.'

As in all the above examples, it is notable that a single lexical item of CS does not signal a macro switch to English as Speaker A continues here in Irish.

4.3.3 Irish-English CS as a stylistic/narrative device

CS is frequently used as both a stylistic and functional tool in defusing tension, changing atmosphere or introducing humour:

(30) Tá mise ag cur orm mo *birthday suit!*
'I'm putting on my birthday suit!'
(31) Tá an *yoke* crochta as an mbealach. [Referring to the recording device during an extended participant observation session of several hours]
'The "yoke" is hung up out of the way.'

A similar overlapping of stylistic and interactional functions occurs when a speaker uses CS to switch the direction of the topic being discussed, to interrupt the turn-taking sequence, to mark their own turn or to introduce an entirely new topic. CS for repetitions, paraphrasing and additions can be used to add emphasis in interaction and also as a stylistic doubling or echoing device in a narrative setting:

(32) Ná déan sin! *Don't even think about it!* [Parent to child]
'Don't do that. Don't even think about it.'
(33) *Young and old*, bhí seandaoine is daoine óga ann. [Radio documentary, reminiscence].
'Young and old, old people and young people were there.'
(34) Ó tá sin go hálainn, tá sé *beautiful.*
'Oh, that's beautiful, it is beautiful.'

CS is available as a stylistic device with which to mark a climax or emphasise a point in the narrative or social exchange:

(35) Tabhair dhom an *full whack.*
'Give me the full whack.'
(See Smith-Christmas 2014: 287–8 for similar functions in a Scottish Gaelic narrative sequence.)

Quotative CS, where a verbatim quote is inserted into the discourse string, is a functional option in a bilingual setting and adds to the narrative pace:

(36) *'Ease up'*, a deir sé, *'ease up.'* [Repeating an instruction to a driver]
'"Ease up", he says, "ease up."'

(37) *'Enter'*, a deir sé ....*'Exit'*, anois. 'Tab', i dtosach. [Group
of women gathered round a computer screen in a training
session]
'"Enter", it says .... "Exit", now. "Tab", first."'

4.3.3.1 *Metaphorical and communicative effects*

In a Gaeltacht classroom the teacher's switching between Irish and
English to expand on, and repeat, what has already been said may be
stylistic, may add emphasis or may be seen to be a response to the range
of linguistic competence levels in a typical Gaeltacht school. It may also
carry additional sociolinguistic force as a teacher chooses to converge
or diverge from what may be unstable or shifting perceptions of the
relative status of home, school and schoolyard domains and language
choice. As Baker states in summing up a range of CS contexts similar to
that given here:

> Familiarity, projected status, the ethos of the context and the per-
> ceived linguistic skills of the listeners affect the nature and process
> of codeswitching... This suggests that codeswitching is not just lin-
> guistic; it indicates important social and power relationships. (Baker
> 2011: 110)

In the increasingly complex linguistic landscape of majority L1 inner-
zone Gaeltacht areas, the relative prestige values of Irish and English
vary enormously according to social network and domain. In classroom
or similar stratified semi-formal contexts, therefore, CS between Irish
and English can have privileging, authoritative or 'democratising' force,
even in a majority L1 context, and can be felt as either diverging or
converging moves – in addition to, or apart from, narrative and stylistic
considerations.

4.3.4 CS in identity construction and role negotiation

On a macro level, the triggers and sociolinguistic context for language
switching from Irish to English and from English to Irish are patterned
and constrained in ways typical of minority-majority language interactions. Our introductory example showed a switch from minority to
majority language on a situational or addressee basis. The converse of
this – majority to minority, English to Irish, situational or addressee-
based CS – is, by definition, excluded or rare since adult L1 Irish speakers
are bilinguals.

English-Irish CS becomes, therefore, confined to symbolic and
metaphorical contexts, often concerned with identity construction. L2

speakers and learners living, or on holiday, abroad may mark group membership, difference and distance from other nationalities by using Irish as a 'secret' language, learned in the shared context of school, which also symbolically differentiates them from other nationalities. Partial bilinguals will sometimes CS to Irish for greetings and other short strings as a symbolic or metaphorical gesture, depending on the fluctuating symbolic currency of the linguistic context. Irish language social networks and communities of practice comprising mainly L2 or majority L2 members are also likely to use metaphorical CS according to mutually agreed norms and shared social and symbolic capital. As previously noted, however, Irish-English CS behaviour in micro-level, informal mode is generally avoided by L2 speakers.

Finally, the option of macro-level CS between Irish and English is available to balanced bilinguals in interaction with each other in L1 speaker networks. They may choose to define and redefine context, topic, role and social distance with reference to mutually understood shared heritage or new contexts, in the manner described in Blom and Gumperz's (1972) canonical study on code-switching and social meaning in linguistic structures. Compare Lamb (2008: 47) on Gaelic-English language choice '...perhaps the crucial determining factor is not so much the formality or informality of the subject matter, but rather *who* the participants are and *where* they are'. In speech events involving balanced bilinguals this macro-level CS option is additional to the option of style-shifting within Irish, with gradations of use of micro-level CS as part of that repertoire, and analogous to 'variant switching', as discussed in Maehlum's (1996) review of Blom and Gumperz (1972).

4.4   Irish-English CS as a sociolinguistic variable in identity construction and role negotiation: a micro-interactional study

Two broad, universal observations, which have both qualitative and quantitative aspects, can be made about the interpretation and practice of CS:

 i) it is patterned, not random
 ii) relative frequency of CS tokens are indicative of positions on the formality-informality spectrum.

However, sociolinguistic functions, motivations and constraints for Irish-English CS, in common with other linguistic pairings and groupings, are intrinsically context-sensitive. Therefore the question: 'Who code-switches, why, when and how?', requires micro-scale, discourse-based work to understand how CS is used and perceived within speech communities and communities of practice.

In the context of an investigation of the range of variables available for register marking and style-shifting in contemporary Irish, the parameters of CS as a sociolinguistic variable were explored (Ní Laoire 1998, 2009). The study examined language styles in dramatic characterisation and plot development in a long-running radio drama, *Baile an Droichid*. The radio drama – written, produced and set in the Connemara Gaeltacht – was broadcast weekly on RTÉ Raidió na Gaeltachta from 1988–97 and, due to popular demand, further episodes have been broadcast intermittently since then.[3] The corpus consists of eight episodes of *Baile an Droichid* (*BD*), broadcast sequentially over one season. The *BD* data are situated at the informal/spontaneous/intimate end of the stylistic spectrum. The data comprise a generous range of speech event types – groups, one-to-one; asymmetrical, mutually reciprocal; combative, appeasing – in all of which we can observe the negotiation of relationships and the use of language therein. Data were explored through the techniques of discourse analysis and within the parameters of stylistic variation. Variables and their relative sensitivity were identified and quantified. Clearly, as pre-scripted drama, these data are a representation of, rather than actual, spontaneous speech but the corpus is also self-contained, continuous, internally accountable and finite and is sourced in a speech community which parallels that which is represented in the drama. This circularity of input and output indicates a strong link between the linguistic variety portrayed and that identifiable in real life, non-dramatic contexts, including that of its listening audience.[4]

A base level of CS is the norm in the *BD* corpus and the exploitation of that part of the bilingual repertoire by most members of the fictional speech community is comparable with the type of CS behaviour and its linguistic reflexes described in the first part of this chapter. The manipulation, exploitation and variable use of CS, and the related non-use, and optional use, of neologisms and technical terminology, is remarkably consistent across characters and situations and is used in highly marked and patterned ways.

4.4.1   Methodology

In order to quantify use of CS within the corpus and then examine individual characters' CS behaviour, all tokens of CS were tagged and counted. For counting purposes, a CS token was defined as a single English word or string of English words occurring in the data. Thus, individual lexical items at varying levels of grammatical and phonological assimilation and integration, such as *kite, ladder,* sean*wellingtons, sheet*eannaí, *block*áil and *squeeze*áilte; phrases such as *for God's sake, looking forward, bugger all, blast you* and *don't blame me*; and whole English sentences each counted as one token. The transcribed line (*c.* 12 words), as opposed to the sentence or discourse string, was used as a practical and internally consistent unit of measurement of data.

Each character's tokens were counted and the ratio of CS tokens per line for each character was plotted. The total count for CS tokens in the corpus is 481 in a total of 2162 lines of data. This is a ratio of CS tokens per line of 0.089:1. The scores for two characters, Peartalán and *An Sagart*, 'the Priest', were significantly lower in statistical terms than all other adult characters (both had a score of 0.02:1 while all other characters ranged from 0.12:1 to 0.49:1). The most striking linguistic behaviour which marks two characters out of eight as different in the context of the *BD* speech community, therefore, is their avoidance of CS. To interpret and understand this linguistic behaviour the data was correlated to context-bound information gleaned from actions and interactions within the drama.

4.4.2 Use and non-use of CS as a socially diagnostic variable

The plot and range of characters of *BD* are believable and familiar within the terms of the genre. General themes are developed through a presentation of the sometimes mundane details of everyday life in various households in a small rural community and subsequently through the intermingling of characters in the non-domestic milieu. It has a relatively high humorous and slapstick element. The dialogue is credible and spontaneous. The issues of relative social status and face feature prominently as an underlying theme in *BD* and the importance of the social marking of in-group and out-group membership of various kinds can be seen as an inevitable consequence of this emphasis on intracommunity status.

Tracking levels of use of CS across characters in *BD* shows that dependent, socially based variables such as levels of integration and relative status within the community can be correlated with levels of variation in use of the linguistic variable of CS. Interestingly, however, the social meaning of the low incidence[5] of CS by *An Sagart* and Peartalán respectively must be interpreted in different ways. This interpretation centres on the complex of other stylistic variables with which a low level of use of CS clusters.

The parameters of stylistic variation in *BD* can be said to be defined in two ways: a formality/informality axis and an outsider/insider axis. It is possible to isolate four notional stylistic poles – Formal, Informal, Learner L2 and Unmarked L1 – in relation to which various characters move, in correlation to dependent variables such as role and topic. *Formal Style*, as represented primarily by *An Sagart*,[6] is characterised by

i) avoidance of CS
ii) careful marking of declensional inflections
iii) tendency towards choice of dialect-internal forms which come closest to that of written standard/literary/Munster style; also,
iv) it does not show a high level of use of neologisms, though avoidance of unassimilated borrowing may lead to higher levels of usage of older assimilated loanwords and a use of calques and translations of idioms associated with formal and specialised registers of English.

An Sagart affects a social distance as appropriate to the traditional interpretation of a priest's status within the community, a distance which is mirrored by the community in their attitude and behaviour towards him. The character of *An Sagart* does not include CS as an active part of his repertoire but his linguistic repertoire does include several high-prestige variables. This linguistic behaviour marks a distance from the group but nevertheless defines itself in relation to it since he is an L1 speaker of a West Galway dialect. The currency of stylistic variation in Formal Style, with which an avoidance of CS clusters, is therefore considerably more subtle and context-sensitive than that which we shall see in Learner L2 Style.

Informal Style, as represented by all characters save Peartalán, is characterised by

i) graded use of the CS variable, depending on the position of the speech act on the formality–informality continuum and insider/outsider axis
ii) choice of local over non-local morphology, phonology and lexis
iii) avoidance of neologisms
iv) free use of calques and idiom translations, particularly those associated with informal registers of English
v) variable use of declensional marking.

CS clusters in situations in *BD* where a high degree of informality and intimacy are being portrayed and the domain can be characterised as domestic/neighbourhood – the quintessential locus of Informal Style. On a structural level, most CS in the *BD* corpus takes place at the level of the simple lexical item. Within this categorisation, nouns predominate, with a total of 326 single nouns compared with 20 verbs. Stenson (1993: 118) describes the occurrence of 'blatant examples of English syntactic patterns without historical Irish analogues' as infrequent but enough to be noticeable in the data she observed. *BD* data, in contrast, contain no examples of word order displacement of the degree she describes (post-verbal pronoun in progressive constructions: '... go mbíonn tú ag *disappoint*áil mise i gcónaí...'; English prenominal position adopted for borrowed adjective: '... gur *viable* rud a bhí ann...'). This is accounted for, at least in part, by the fact that the language contact data in the *BD* corpus comes from a finite database rather than from an open-ended observation process focused specifically on identifying language contact features.[7]

Longer strings and less assimilated lexical CS occur predominantly in the output of one character, Helen. This character is presented as assertive, ambitious, authoritative and self-assured. In her linguistic output she stays within the parameters of Informal Style but shows a definite tendency to extend the stylistic margins of the CS variable beyond those observed by other local characters. Additional to her tendency towards longer CS strings, many of Helen's CS tokens are interrogatives and imperatives – discourse structures associated with a control function, as illustrated in the following examples:

(38) a. Who is Buck Jones?

      b. *Oh, stop nagging, Michael.*

      c. *What's wrong,* Michael? Á, cén fáth 'chuir tú 'caoineadh é?
          'What's wrong, Michael? Ah, why did you start him crying?'

      d. *Well, don't blame me.* Cén fáth nár labhair tú fhéin leis má tá tú chomh *smart*áilte sin.
          'Well don't blame me. Why didn't you talk to him yourself if you are that smart?'

      e. *Well, that's your problem. Please, Michael,* cuartaigh mo *runner.* Tá deifir orm.
          'Well, that's your problem. Please, Michael, search for my runner. I'm in a hurry.'

      f. *What* beithígh?
          'What cattle?'

At the level of the individual loanword we also find that Helen shows a tendency to expand the conventions of interlingual junctions in an individualistic way.[8] Helen's lower levels of morphological and phonological assimilation of CS items are accompanied by a lower level of declensional marking and it is also notable that several of her borrowings carry extra-cultural connotations, being imported in both the literal and metaphorical sense. In almost all cases this extension in degree and type of CS is associated with her character's 'authoritative/irritable' mode. By exploiting the style-shifting repertoire associated with CS, Helen signals a mode in which she demands and expects attention. She successfully marks a distinction between herself and her interlocutors by a subtle expansion of the common linguistic currency available in Informal Style.

Learner L2 Style, as represented exclusively by Peartalán, is characterised by

  i)   avoidance of CS
 ii)   use of non-local forms
iii)   use of neologisms and technical terminology
 iv)   occasional, though infrequent, learner-marked errors

Peartalán is an outsider in the literal sense, coming from another region. He has radically different cultural benchmarks to those of his wife and neighbours and is presented as an eccentric, lightweight, ineffectual, naive and occasionally stupid townie in contrast to the more worldly wise and substantial members of the rural community into which he has married. He is also the only L2 character of the eight-character cast though it is important to note that, besides monostylism and levelling of regional markers, the aspects which mark him as an outsider are mainly phonological. He has relatively high mastery of syntactic and grammatical elements of Irish and is a full participant in linguistic interaction in terms of meaning. His linguistic deficit, therefore, is in his grasp of metaphorical and social, not literal, meaning.

Peartalán functions within a separate set of norms, those of L2 learner speakers. He avoids CS due to his lack of linguistic (and social) perspicacity and total lack of awareness of the stylistic subtleties being manipulated by, for instance, *An Sagart*. As a learner he has not mastered the stylistic repertoire of any part of the formal–informal continuum. His invariant avoidance of the CS variable clusters with a range of other linguistic behaviours, but this set of variables is entirely different to those exploited by the priest. These include unstable regional dialect marking, occasional grammatical errors, and, most visibly, a high level of use of neologisms – all of these mark his L2 status, which mirrors and reinforces his social status as outsider.

Unmarked L1 Style is, in empirical terms, indistinguishable from Informal Style (with extensions at the margins for some of the variables incorporated in Formal Style). In sociolinguistic terms, however, a style which is conceptually situated in opposition to Learner L2 Style is necessary to the interactional and sociolinguistic dynamics of *BD*. Such an opposition answers to the important social outsider/insider distinction so crucial to the character of Peartalán in *BD*. Both Informal and Formal styles encompass the phonology, morphology, lexicon and syntax of the L1 West Galway dialect and act as a cumulative check and point of opposition to Learner L2 Style for dramatic interaction and for the listening audience.

Further analysis of individual speech events reveals grading of use of CS which involves accommodation and adjustment.[9] Marked and statistically significant accommodational moves are made by all local characters in relation to *An Sagart*. These are manifest in a reduction in CS tokens as characters style-shift from Informal Style towards Formal Style in his presence.[10] This feature is the most unambiguous, consistent and patterned example of style-shifting and accommodation in the *BD* data. Predictably, and in line with characterisation and plot, the accommodational style-shifting is unidirectional rather than reciprocal and no significant pattern of adjustment by *An Sagart* is evident.

By contrast, these 'inside' characters do not adjust or converge towards Peartalán. Neighbours and intimates alike are heard to choose CS tokens when addressing Peartalán and in his company while Peartalán continues his invariant choice of Irish terms over CS. In one indicative instance, Peartalán uses the stylistically inappropriate *rothar aclaíochta*, 'exercise bike' and *féirín* 'present' while Phil, his wife and the quintessential insider in this speech community, persists in using the loanwords *exercise bike* and *present* in the same conversation. This parallel track, non-converging behaviour at the micro level of the individual lexical item highlights the asymmetry of insider and outsider through a juxtaposition of dramatic and linguistic elements. In conjunction with the plot and the condescension with which Peartalán is treated in this scene, this is just another contrast which leaves the listening audience in no doubt as to which complex of linguistic and extra-linguistic behaviours is to be interpreted as deviant and socially incompetent.[11]

4.5 Discussion

Focusing on individuals and their behaviour in micro-interactional studies brings the variationist analysis of CS full circle. The role of ethnographic methods in understanding sociolinguistic variation is discussed by Lawson:

> In a sense, the focus on the individual is a natural part of the focus on social meaning and the construction of social identity, since it is at the level of individual language use that identities are constructed and meaning negotiated. Moreover, by ignoring individuals, sociolinguistic description is reduced to a large group means and disembodied accounts of how language is actually used on the ground. (Lawson 2014: 203)

The characters of Peartalán, *An Sagart* and Helen and their associated linguistic behaviour are related in subtly different ways to their social group. We identified Unmarked L1/Informal Style as the style against which other styles were defined, and defined themselves, in the *BD* corpus. Chambers (1995: 91) notes that, sociolinguistically, insiders embody the social characteristics of their group prototypically and actualise the linguistic trends in the data prolifically. The *BD* 'insiders' and their linguistic performance fall into this category and the listeners benchmark 'normal/inside' against Unmarked L1, their own linguistic currency as a predominantly L1 audience in the non-fictional world. 'Outsider' linguistic behaviour (including avoidance of CS) is thus mediated through this benchmark. Eckert's (2000: 204) discussion of 'extreme users' who are flamboyant 'navigators of broad networks' and Chambers' (1995: 95) description of 'aspirers' – those with social ambitions that stretch beyond their immediate social domain – resonate with the innovative and boundary-challenging linguistic, and non-linguistic, behaviour of Helen. Network studies which uncover patterning of this type contribute to an understanding of the social, social-attitudinal and linguistic context of CS in contemporary Irish. The contribution of sociolinguistics, as Chambers (1995: 91) notes, is 'the empirical evidence that being an outsider has linguistic consequences as well'.

4.5.1 Popular perceptions of CS

Social attitudinal aspects of linguistic behaviour portray CS in *BD* as a low-prestige variable associated with informal, non-stratified social contexts. Commentary from inside and outside Irish language speech communities is also consistent in its abhorrence of language contact phenomena generally, and of CS in particular. A view of CS as a widespread feature of bilingual speech communities which can represent a skilled level of linguistic behaviour and which is neither random nor unconstrained has not entered the terms of the popular debate. That debate focuses almost exclusively on the negative and detrimental effects of language contact on the linguistic integrity of Irish. An explicit term, *Béarlachas* 'Englishism', exists to describe the phenomenon of language contact within the didactic tradition. Since this tradition does not recognise CS or other language contact features as legitimate parts of the linguistic repertoire, the pedagogic and normative focus is shifted towards an avoidance of syntactic structures which are indigenous to English idiom but not to Irish. The term *Béarlachas*, therefore, always and without exception carries a negative connotation.

The dialectological tradition of investigation and description of spoken Irish has paid scant attention to CS and other language contact phenomena. The strength of the normative, prescriptive tradition in relation to language contact phenomena within the established dialectological tradition has also played a role in negative self-evaluation of CS behaviour within the speech community. Specifically, the characteristic behaviour of the 'good speaker'[12] excludes innovation and disruption of a diachronically based ideal of linguistic purity (Cram 1986, Ní Laoire 1993). Public discourse about the portrayal of CS when it occurs in the popular media (particularly drama) decries a style of speech which includes CS while tacitly acknowledging the use of such styles in real life. This is consistent with popularly expressed views in other language contact situations and falls under a general rubric of what Milroy and Milroy (1991: 29–54) have called 'the complaint tradition' (Ní Laoire 2000).[13]

4.5.2 CS and the changing linguistic landscape

Increasing levels of linguistic heterogeneity in Irish language speech communities raise additional issues for investigation and description. Many formerly exclusively L1 speech communities now encompass L2 speakers of varying levels of proficiency as well as extra-dialectal L1 speakers. Documenting the possible impacts of interdialectal style-shifting, foreigner talk[14] and structural and lexical influences from L2 and other areal dialects on L1 would add substantially to our understanding of language contact. The linguistic competence balance in an individual speech event may affect CS behaviour, a context-sensitive part of the stylistic repertoire, in various ways. *BD* data remind us that control of social and linguistic constraints on CS are at the upper end of the sociolinguistic competence spectrum. Eckert and Rickford (2001), in discussing theoretical frameworks for analysing stylistic variation, signal the importance of

> ... whether and how we can be sure that speakers do have productive access to the full range of variants under discussion. This is of course necessary for interpreting use and non-use as stylistically significant. (Eckert and Rickford 2001: 14)

In speech events which include both L1 and L2 speakers of Irish, even where L2 is at a relatively high competence level, some reduction and levelling of repertoire options, including CS, is likely. Given L2's tendency towards monostylism and limited capacity for stylistic adjustment or manipulation, the balance between L1 and L2 speakers will influence the sociolinguistic sensitivity of CS.

This chapter did not consider CS data from children at stages of the bilingual acquisition process or from adult learners below L1 competence level, and this marks an important methodological distinction and differentiation within the potential sample universe. Recent strands of research on bilingualism and Irish-English contact reference CS as both a symptom and cause of unstable bilingualism (e.g. Péterváry et al. 2014: 20–4). Distinguishing 'normal' CS from CS in language erosion remains, as with all CS research, a multidimensional task with sociolinguistic, psycholinguistic and structural elements (Bolonyai 2009). Even allowing for the current diversity of approaches to distinguishing discrete grammatical systems in CS, it is notable that all examples of CS considered here show Irish providing the grammatical/structural frame for English insertions and alternations.[15]

Clearly, a majority-minority bilingual context which lacks functional differentiation impacts most on the minority language, and international evidence shows that CS, amongst young people in particular, is a feature of situations of language shift, decay and death. The complexities of the constituent elements of contemporary social networks in Gaeltacht areas impact most immediately, however, on macro-level variation around language choice, since sociolinguistic etiquette currently predicts use of English as *lingua franca* in interaction between L1 and L2 speakers. It seems important, therefore, not to conflate the negative and stigmatised associations of CS in the public debate with wider questions concerning language death and decay since the bilingual and plurilingual language-contact context which begets CS is not of necessity implicated in language shift, contraction or death.

4.6 Conclusion

CS is a common form of bilingual communication in speech communities all over the world. It is also the case that a high frequency or, in some contexts any, use of CS is socially inappropriate in formal situations in Irish. These poles are bridged by Gardner-Chloros's (2009: 112) reminder that CS is the plurilingual embodiment of techniques that have equivalents in the monolingual sphere. Accordingly, theoretical approaches to register and style variation become highly relevant. Quantifying what constitutes a neutral unmarked minimum level of CS in individual performance in informal domains remains an embedded query in this analysis, requiring triangulation and comparison within and outside the informal spontaneous spoken language database. Variables such as gender, age and idiolectal variation as well as the overarching question of mutually accepted norms within communities of practice must also form part of the analytic framework.

In choosing data that exhibit 'non-standard' and stigmatised features we highlight corpus-internal and context-specific consistency while focusing on linguistic performance. This confirms CS as a context-sensitive stylistic marker and linguistic resource in informal domains in Irish. Access to the multiplex dimensions of variation in Irish-English CS is facilitated by a model of the speech community that invokes sociolinguistic concepts such as face, solidarity as well as covert and overt prestige, and takes account of accommodation and adaption within individual social networks and communities of practice.

Notes

1. See, for instance, Bullock and Toribio (2009: 1) 'While CS is viewed as an index of bilingual proficiency among linguists, it is commonly perceived by the general public as indicative of language degeneration.'
2. This chapter includes material previously published in Irish, in Ní Laoire 2009 and Ní Laoire 2012.
3. As ever, my thanks are due to Joe Steve Ó Neachtain, scriptwriter, actor and creator of *Baile an Droichid*.
4. All actors are L1 speakers, besides Peartalán (see below) who plays to type, and they frequently improvise and interact creatively with the handwritten scripts in a workshop-type environment, contributing further to the spontaneous and naturalistic linguistic context.
5. *An Sagart* has 3 tokens in 187 lines and Peartalán has 4 in 193 lines. The respective tokens appear in rare scenes where *An Sagart* is presented as empathetic and Peartalán is portrayed as being simpatico and in tune with other characters. By contrast, Helen, the 'extreme' user of CS, shows a count of 97 tokens in 197 lines.

6. Despite appearing frequently in the drama, this character is referred to at all times simply as *An Sagart*, 'the Priest', and addressed only as *a Athair*, 'Father' – a very effective, plot-driven, distancing strategy.

7. It should be remembered that frequency patterns forefronted by a quantitative analysis can seem extreme when presented in isolation rather than in context. In the case of *BD*, subtlety and skill are used by the scriptwriter so that linguistic style remains an intrinsic part of the drama rather than calling attention to itself through exaggerated linguistic behaviour (see Ní Laoire 2012: 203–7).

8. Thus, Michael, Helen's long-suffering husband, regularly forms plurals using the native ending '–annaí' e.g. '*bale*annaí', while his wife, on another occasion in the corpus, imports both lexicon and plural morphology for the same loanword, *bales*.

9. Length limitations do not allow extensive transcription from the *BD* corpus here. Ní Laoire (2009) contains illustrative examples.

10. CS tokens per character according to scene and participants were counted in order to track behaviour of characters in differing combinations, with and without the presence of *An Sagart*.

11. As confirmation of this interpretation, Peartalán's wife offers a metalinguistic commentary on his use of neologisms in another scene and admonishes him to get on with the work and '... never mind your big words', '... *ná bac le do chuid focla móra*'.

12. Compare Chambers and Trudgill's (1980: 33) NORM, <u>n</u>on-mobile <u>o</u>lder <u>r</u>ural <u>m</u>ale.

13. Popular commentary on language styles in *Baile an Droichid* tended to centre on a putative high level of language-contact features but a quantitative analysis did not corroborate that. Conversely, many characters in *Ros na Rún* (a long-running television soap opera on TG4) show lack of nuance and verisimilitude around use of CS which points to the mixture of L1 and L2 scriptwriters and actors involved.

14. A style which shares features with 'caretaker speech', the language spoken to young children. Features include slow speech rate; simple vocabulary; repetitions and elaborations and paucity of slang and idioms.

15. Example (19) is ambiguous as to 'base' structure. In a far-reaching analysis of grammatical approaches to CS, Gardner-Chloros and Edwards (2004) argue that attempts to characterise CS speech using the assumptions of formal syntactic analysis may be misguided. As they suggest, one of the greatest difficulties with existing models is in accounting for the role of CS in language change, and the matrix language (ML) 'turnover hypothesis', where the ML in a community may change over time, fails to account for the gradualness and irregularities of this process.

References

Baker, Colin (2011). *Foundations of Bilingual Education and Bilingualism*. Fifth edition. Bristol: Multilingual Matters.

Blom, Jan-Petter-P. and John J. Gumperz (1972). 'Social meaning in linguistic structures: Code-switching in Northern Norway', in: John J. Gumperz and

Dell Hymes (eds), *Directions in Sociolinguistics*. New York: Holt Rinehart and Winston, pp. 407–43.

Bolonyai, Agnes (2009). 'Code-switching, imperfect acquisition, and attrition', in: Bullock and Toribio (eds), pp. 253–69.

Bullock, Barbara E. and Almeida Jacqueline Toribio (2009). 'Themes in the study of code-switching', in: Bullock and Toribio (eds), pp. 1–17.

Bullock, Barbara E. and Almeida Jacqueline Toribio (eds) (2009). *The Cambridge Handbook of Linguistic Code-switching*. Cambridge: Cambridge University Press.

Chambers, J. K. (1995). *Sociolinguistic Theory: Linguistic Variation and its Social Significance*. Oxford: Blackwell.

Chambers, J. K. and Peter Trudgill (1980). *Dialectology*. Cambridge: Cambridge University Press.

Cram, David (1986). 'Patterns of English-Gaelic and Gaelic-English code-switching', *Scottish Language* 5: 126–30.

Eckert, Penelope (2000). *Linguistic Variation as Social Practice: the Linguistic Construction of Identity in Belten High*. Oxford: Blackwell.

Eckert, Penelope and John Rickford (2001). *Style and Sociolinguistic Variation*. Cambridge: Cambridge University Press.

Gardner-Chloros, Penelope (2009). 'Sociolinguistic factors in code-switching', in: Bullock and Toribio (eds), pp. 97–113.

Gardner-Chloros, Penelope and Malcolm Edwards (2004). 'Assumptions behind grammatical approaches to code-switching: When the blueprint is a red herring', *Transactions of the Philological Society* 102: 103–29.

Lamb, William (2008). *Scottish Gaelic Speech and Writing: Register Variation in an Endangered Language*. Belfast: Cló Ollscoil na Banríona.

Lawson, Robert (2014). 'What can ethnography tell us about sociolinguistic variation over time? Some insights from Glasgow', in: Lawson (ed.), pp. 197–219.

Lawson, Robert (ed.) (2014). *Sociolinguistics in Scotland*. Basingstoke: Palgrave Macmillan.

Mac Mathúna, Liam (2008). *Béarla sa Ghaeilge: Cabhair Choigríche: An Códmheascadh Gaeilge/Béarla i Litríocht na Gaeilge 1600–1900*. [English in Irish. Help from a foreign land: Irish/English Code-mixing in Irish-language Literature 1600–1900.] Dublin: An Clóchomhar.

Matras, Yaron (2009). *Language Contact*. Cambridge: Cambridge University Press.

Milroy, James and Lesley Milroy (1991). *Authority in Language: Investigating Language Prescription and Standardisation*. Second edition. London: Routledge.

Mæhlum, Brit (1996). 'Codeswitching in Hemnesberget: Myth or reality?', *Journal of Pragmatics* 25: 749–61.

Myers-Scotton, Carol (2006). *Multiple Voices: an Introduction to Bilingualism*. Oxford: Blackwell.

Ní Laoire, Siobhán (1993). 'Traditions of spoken language study in Ireland', *Irish Review* 14: 65–73.

Ní Laoire, Siobhán (1998). 'Aspects of Stylistic Variation in Modern Irish.' Unpublished PhD dissertation, University College Dublin.

Ní Laoire, Siobhán (2000). 'Traidisiún an ghearáin: An díospóireacht faoi Ghaeilge na Gaeltachta inniu' [The complaint tradition: the debate on Gaeltacht Irish today], in: Liam Mac Mathúna, Ciarán Mac Murchaidh and Máirín Nic Eoin (eds) *Teanga, Pobal agus Réigiún: Aistí ar Chultúr na Gaeltachta*

Inniu. [Language, Community and Region. Essays on the Culture of the Gaeltacht Today.] Dublin: Coiscéim, pp. 34–47.

Ní Laoire, Siobhán (2009). 'Ionramháil stíle mar chleachtas sóisialta: códmhalartú agus iasachtaíocht i gcorpas comhaimseartha Gaeilge' [Stylistic variation as social practice: codeswitching and borrowing in a contemporary Irish language corpus], *Léachtaí Cholm Cille* 39: 188–219.

Ní Laoire, Siobhán (2012). 'Teangacha i dteagmháil: Cómhalartú, piseanú agus criólú' [Languages in contact: Codeswitching, pidginisation and creolisation], in: Tadhg Ó hIfearnáin and Máire Ní Neachtain (eds) *An tSochtheangeolaíocht: Feidhm agus Tuairisc*. [Sociolinguistics: Aim and scope.] Dublin: Cois Life, pp. 49–66.

Péterváry, Tamás, Brian Ó Curnáin, Conchúr Ó Giollagáin and Jerome Sheahan (eds) (2014). *Iniúchadh ar an gCumas Dátheangach: An Sealbhú Teanga i measc Ghlúin Óg na Gaeltachta/Analysis of Bilingual Competence: Language Acquisition among Young People in the Gaeltacht*. Dublin: An Chomhairle um Oideachas Gaeltachta agus Gaelscolaíochta.

Poplack, Shana (1980). 'Sometimes I'll start a sentence in Spanish *y termino en español*: toward a typology of code-switching', *Linguistics* 18: 581–618.

Sjoestedt-Jonval, Marie-Louise (1928). 'L'influence de la langue anglaise sur un parler local irlandaise', in: *Étrennes de Linguistique Offerts par quelques Amis à Émile Beneveniste*. Paris: Paul Guethner, pp. 81–122.

Smith-Christmas, Cassie (2014). 'Code-switching in "Flannan Isles": a micro-interactional approach to a bilingual narrative', in: Lawson (ed.), pp. 277–95.

Stenson, Nancy (1990). 'Phrase structure congruence, government, and Irish-English code-switching', *Syntax and Semantics* 23: 167–97.

Stenson, Nancy (1991). 'Code-switching vs. borrowing in Modern Irish', in: P. Sture Ureland and George Broderick (eds) *Language Contact in the British Isles: Proceedings of the Eight International Symposium on Language Contact in Europe, 1988*. Tübingen, Max Niemeyer, pp. 559–79.

Stenson, Nancy (1993). 'English influence on Irish: the last 100 years', *Journal of Celtic Linguistics* 2: 107–28.

Stenson, Nancy (1997). 'Language contact and the development of Irish directional phrase idioms', in: Ahlqvist, Anders and Vera Čapkova (1997) *Dán do Oide: Essays in Memory of Conn R. Ó Cléirigh*. Dublin: Institiúid Teangeolaíochta Éireann, pp. 559–77.

5

The Sociolinguistics of Language Use in Ireland

Anne Barron and Irina Pandarova

5.1 Introduction

While the study of Irish English (IrE) on the phonological, grammatical and lexical levels is long established (cf. Hickey 2011: 13–14), the study of variation in language use in IrE is a recent endeavour (cf. Vaughan and Clancy 2011: 47). IrE is not exceptional as a variety in this regard, dialectological research in general having long concentrated on synchronic variation at the level of pronunciation, vocabulary and grammar. In pragmatic research too, variation in language use according to macrosocial factors, such as region, age, socio-economic class, ethnicity – and gender to a lesser extent – have been largely neglected. However, in recent years variational pragmatics has emerged as a research field, making intra-lingual pragmatic variation according to these five macrosocial factors the focus of systematic analysis (cf. Schneider and Barron 2008; Barron and Schneider 2009; Holmes 2010: 449; Schneider 2010; Placencia 2011; Barron 2014, forthcoming). This research field propagates intra-lingual pragmatic research adopting the methodological principles of empiricity, comparability and contrastivity (cf. Schneider 2010; Barron 2014). In other words, research should be contrastive between varieties and use comparable data since it is only such data that can highlight the similarities and differences between varieties on any level.

In line with these developments in variational pragmatics, the study of pragmatic variation in IrE has recently enjoyed increased interest. This has been aided by concentrated efforts to further research in the area (Barron and Schneider 2005, cf. also chapters in Migge and Ní Chiosáin 2013), by a recognition of the level of pragmatics in textbooks on IrE (Amador-Moreno 2010) and also by the emergence of corpora, such as the Limerick Corpus of Irish English (LCIE) (Barker and O'Keeffe 1999), *A Corpus of Irish English* (Hickey 2003), the Irish component of the International Corpus of English (ICE-Ireland) (Kallen and Kirk 2008), SPICE-Ireland (Systems of Pragmatic Annotation in the Spoken Component of ICE-Ireland) (Kallen and Kirk 2012) and the *Corpus of Irish English Correspondence* (McCafferty and Amador-Moreno in preparation). To date, variational pragmatic research on IrE has focused predominantly on language use relative to other inner circle varieties, and primarily relative to British English (BrE), and to a lesser degree American English (AmE) (cf. also Elwood 2010 on IrE vs. New Zealand English). Studies of language use within IrE itself according to macro-social factors, such as gender, socio-economic class, age and ethnic identity are less frequent.

The present chapter first gives an overview of research on language use in IrE, focusing first on region and then on the remaining macro-social factors. Following this, a corpus study of tag questions (TQs) in IrE across region (Northern Ireland (NI)/Republic of Ireland (ROI)/Great Britain (GB)), gender, and across region and gender is presented. The empirical study adds to language use research on regional and gender variation in IrE and, more broadly, to the growing body of research integrating a number of macro-social factors. The paper closes with an outlook to the future.

5.2 Language use in Irish English

The following overview of language use in IrE focuses first on patterns of language use particularly common in and also specific to IrE relative to BrE and AmE. Variation between Southern and Northern IrE – i.e. between language use across the political divide on the island of Ireland – is then addressed (Section 5.2.1), as is research on language use in relation to the remaining macro-social factors other than region (Section 5.2.2).

Given space constraints, the overview is not exhaustive but purposely restricted to variational pragmatic research adopting the methodological principles of empiricity, comparability and contrastivity (cf. also O'Keeffe 2011; Vaughan and Clancy 2011 and Schneider 2012 for further overviews of language use in IrE). Indeed, Vaughan and Clancy (2011: 50) comment on the value of the variational pragmatic framework for structuring a research agenda for the study of language use in IrE. Variational pragmatics distinguishes five levels of analysis. These are the formal, the actional, the interactional, the topic and the organisational levels (cf. Schneider and Barron 2008; Barron and Schneider 2009; Schneider 2010; Barron 2014, forthcoming). This framework informs the following overview and structures Section 5.2.1.

5.2.1   Language use in Irish English: Focus on region

Analyses on the formal level focus on the communicative function of individual forms. They frequently employ corpus data. A recent analysis of the discourse marker *now* by Clancy and Vaughan (2012) is a case in point. Their analysis of the LCIE shows *now* to have additional pragmatic functions in IrE. In addition to its use as a discourse marker, functioning to mark a new phase of discourse in formal contexts as in BrE, *now* is frequently used in IrE in clause-final position in informal contexts. In this position, it functions to downtone assertions and to mark events as completed. Furthermore, when clustering with expressions of time, it functions as an approximator marking the vagueness of time reference. Clause-final *like* is a further discourse marker which has been the subject of several studies. Kallen (2006) highlights the uniqueness of this discourse marker to IrE using a contrastive analysis of the comparable corpora ICE-Ireland and the British ICE component (ICE-GB) (cf. also Lucek 2011). Other analyses on the formal level include Pandarova's (in preparation) analysis of the semantics and pragmatics of the pragmatic marker *sure* across IrE, BrE and AmE and its historical development, Kallen's (2005a) contrast of *you know, I'd say, I say* and *I mean* in ICE-GB and ICE-Ireland (ROI and NI), O'Keeffe and Adolphs' (2008) corpus analysis of response tokens in IrE and BrE, a study of TQs by Barron et al. (2015) using ICE-Ireland and ICE-GB (cf. 5.3 below) and Hickey's study of the development and specifically Irish pragmatics of *grand* (Hickey in press).

Overall, formal analyses of IrE reveal that variety-preferential uses are common, with particular forms being preferred/dispreferred in one variety over another. In addition, we have a variety-specific use of forms involving the emergence of related senses not present in other varieties (cf. Foolen 2011: 221–5, cf. also Pandarova in preparation). Also, despite a lack of variational pragmatic research on the issue, there is some evidence for the existence of variety-specific forms, such as the *sure*-tag in IrE (*sure* + pronoun + operator) (cf. Hickey 2007: 276–7; Barron 2015). Such new senses and forms carry social meaning and may be employed as local identity markers (cf. Schneider 2012: 481). Finally, as Foolen (2011) also notes, it is possible that a particular function is realised using different forms across varieties. We return to this in the discussion of TQ use in Section 5.3.3.

Research on IrE on the actional level has focused predominantly on speech act data elicited by means of production questionnaires (cf. Barron, forthcoming). Analyses centre on pragmalinguistic questions relating to speech act strategies and their linguistic realisations.

Sociopragmatic questions, such as when and where which speech act and strategy is used, are also addressed. The range of speech acts analysed in IrE includes compliment responses (Schneider 1999), expressions of gratitude (Elwood 2010, 2011), offers (Barron 2005b, 2011), requests (Barron 2008a, b) and responses to thanks (Schneider 2005). Variety-preferential uses of language are common on this level, with particular strategies or linguistic realisations preferred in one speech community to a greater extent than in another (cf. Barron 2005a). However, variety-exclusivity is also found in some of the forms and functions identified. An example of such a variety-exclusive form is seen in Barron's (2011) analysis of the offer strategy 'question future act of speaker' in ICE-Ireland and ICE-GB. In both BrE and IrE, this strategy is realised by the conventionalised pattern AUX *I* + actional verb? but the modal verb employed differs. While *shall* is exclusively used in BrE (as in *Shall I pour out your water?*), *will* is used in its place in IrE. Similarly, Schneider (2005) in a study of thanks minimisers in English English (EngE), IrE and AmE finds the NO PROBLEM tokens *you're grand* and *no bother* to be exclusive to IrE in his data.

Scholarship pointing to a variety-preferential use of particular strategies and linguistic realisations in IrE is frequently concerned with issues of directness and indirectness and also with the question of whether the use of strategies and linguistic forms are more or less diverse – and consequently therefore more or less conventionalised. Turning firstly to the degree of variation, Schneider (1999) in an analysis of compliment response strategies in IrE and AmE using production questionnaire data finds IrE strategies to be more diverse. He reports a similar finding in a 2005 study of thanks minimisers in IrE, EngE and AmE also using production questionnaires (cf. also Barron 2005b for similar findings on offer strategies in IrE relative to EngE). In addition, on the level of form, Elwood (2011) finds routine realisations of 'thanks' to be more varied in the Irish soap opera *Fair City* relative to the British programme *EastEnders* (however, cf. Burmeister 2013 below on death announcements for conflicting findings). Further research is required on this level.

As far as levels of directness are concerned, somewhat contradictorily both directness and indirectness have been found to characterise IrE on the actional level (Amador-Moreno 2010: 115; cf. also Kallen 2005a on directness on the formal level). Barron (2008a, b), for example, in an analysis of requests using production questionnaires finds IrE speakers to be more indirect as compared to in EngE speakers. Specifically, IrE speakers employed more external modifiers in the standard situation analysed in which role relations were clear, and more internal mitigation and a lower level of upgrading than EngE speakers in non-standard situations. On the other hand, however, Barron (2005b) found IrE speakers to choose a range of more direct offer head act strategies than EngE speakers in particular situations (cf. also Clancy 2005 on directness in IrE family discourse). Such contradictory findings point to the dangers of associating language use in IrE with negative politeness strategies alone (cf. also Barron 2012 and Kallen 2005b: 131). They furthermore underline the need to take a differentiated view of language use. In particular, speech act, situational constellations and also genre (cf. Barron 2012) need to be taken into account.

Research on the remaining levels of analysis, i.e. on the interactional level (level of sequential patterns), the topic level (level of discourse content) and the organisational level (level of turn-taking), represents a research desideratum in IrE. On the interactional level, Schneider (2008) has examined the opening turns of small talk in England, Ireland and the USA. While EngE speakers were found to start small talk at a party with a greeting, IrE speakers did so with an assessment of the party, and AmE speakers preferred to introduce themselves. In addition to such sequential differences, differences were also found in the frequency and realisation of speech acts. On the organisational level, O'Keeffe and Adolphs (2008), in a study of IrE and BrE using two comparable subcorpora of the LCIE and the Cambridge and Nottingham Corpus of Discourse in English (CANCODE) corpora, find response tokens to be used considerably more frequently by BrE speakers. No differences were recorded on a functional level, convergence and engagement tokens being the most frequent types in both sub-corpora.

Finally, as is evident from the overview above and as also noted by Vaughan and Clancy (2011: 51), 'spoken Irish English has dominated the pragmatic research agenda thus far'. Indeed, Burmeister (2013) on death notices in Scotland, Wales and the ROI is a noteworthy exception on this level (cf. also Barron 2012). Despite many similarities across the three varieties, notable differences were also recorded. Expressions of gratitude to institutional carers were frequent in IrE notices relative to the other varieties. Information on the funeral was more detailed in the IrE texts, as was the description of the circumstances of death. The inclusion of religion-inspired sayings or proverbs was also limited to IrE. On the level of form, IrE death notices were more routine – in contrast to the finding for spoken speech act realisations detailed above.

Thus far, the focus has been on contrasts between IrE and other varieties. Studies on variation in language use within the geographical island of Ireland are extremely rare despite the fact that they offer much potential for research. Kallen and Kirk (2008: 30), for instance, hypothesise that the political border between the ROI and NI may be reflected in linguistic differences and indeed Vaughan and Clancy (2011: 15) suggest that North/South research on a pragmatic level may aid in easing social dissonance by increasing awareness that misconceptions and conflict can result from differing language-use conventions (cf. also Wolfram and Schilling-Estes 2006: 101). Kallen (2005b) is one of those rare studies that includes a ROI/NI contrast. He investigates the use of *I mean* and *you know* and *I say* and *I'd say* in ICE-GB and ICE-Ireland and finds *you know* to occur more often in the NI sub-component, a fact which shows more similarities with the ROI than with the GB data. By contrast, however, the use of *I say* in NI shows a pattern more similar to the GB data.

Finally, a further research desideratum is the study of pragmatic variation across constituencies of a particular region or indeed across the urban/rural divide. Schweinberger (2013) represents one of the limited studies on this level, looking at variation across county (Down, Fermanagh, (London)Derry, Tyrone) in the use of traditional clause-final *like* and the innovative clause-medial *like* within Northern Irish English.

5.2.2 Language use in Irish English: Focus on age, gender, social status, ethnic identity

We now turn to research on IrE taking the macro-social factors ethnicity, age and gender into account. To the best of our knowledge, no variational pragmatic study on IrE has yet focused on socio-economic class, and research on the remaining macro-social factors is also limited. Ethnicity is a case in point. To date only Clancy (2011a, b) has taken up the topic with regard to the traveller community in an Irish context. His research focuses on hedging and on the use of kinship terms in naturally occurring data from one traveller family and one settled family from the Limerick city area with the same gender profile. He finds the settled family to use more hedging and the traveller family in contrast to make more use of kin titles rather than first names. He suggests these findings to reflect a higher value placed on individuality in the settled family and on collectivity and family in the traveller community, while at the same time recognising that the data underlying the analysis are not comparable on all levels leading to a possible influence of age, socio-economic status and level of education as well as ethnicity. Further research is required.

The influence of age and, to a lesser extent, gender on language use in IrE has been the focus of research by Murphy (2010). Using a corpus of everyday conversations, she analyses a range of hedging devices, taboo language, amplifiers, boosters and vague category markers in a female language corpus consisting of three sub-corpora of 20–29-year-olds, 40–49-year-olds and 70–80-year-olds. A male corpus is used for comparative purposes. Among the findings, women in their twenties and forties are shown to use more hedges than 70–80-year-olds. Also, while the women in their twenties preferred the forms *like* and *actually*, those in their forties preferred *you know* and *I think*. Findings are explained as a product of different conversation types which speakers at different ages engage in, younger women engaging in more face-threatening discussions relative to older speakers. Males were also found to use hedges less with increasing age, a feature also explained with reference to length of acquaintance. Murphy (2012) is a further corpus analysis of language use in IrE focusing on age and gender and the use of response tokens. Findings are complex and point to the importance of taking speaker role, background context and speaker relationship into account in analyses of gender. Farr and Murphy (2009) also look at age and gender as they relate to the use of religious references to express emotions. They find men, particularly older men in the 70–80 age group, to use religious references most frequently. Preference for specific forms also varies by age and gender (cf. also Murphy 2009 on the pragmatics of FUCK in IrE by age and gender). Finally, Schweinberger (2012) in an analysis of ICE-Ireland finds gender differences in the use of clause-final *like* among older speakers, with men employing this form more than females. The peak age for use of clause-final *like* was 26–33 years, cf. also Schweinberger et al. (2009) on age and gender and *like* in the Northern Irish Transcribed Corpus of Speech (NITCS).

The above overview has revealed that research on the pragmatics of IrE is alive and well. We have seen that the focus of research to date has been on spoken language and in particular on the formal and actional levels of analysis. In addition, it has been shown that despite some studies on age, gender and language use within IrE, the vast majority of studies focus on language use on a regional level, and within this factor particularly on variation in language use on a national level, with IrE compared to BrE and AmE. Studies of regional pragmatic variation on a more subordinate level, as for instance, across province, or across the rural/urban divide represent a research desideratum, as does also research on pragmatic variation across the geographical island of Ireland, particularly across the North/South political divide. The following empirical analysis on the formal level addresses this latter research gap by investigating TQ use in the ROI and NI while also comparing findings to ICE-GB (cf. 5.3.1). In addition, gender (operationalised as sex) and TQ use is analysed (5.3.2) and we also look at how region interacts with gender in TQ use (5.3.2). As such, the study also addresses the need for studies focusing on the interplay of macro-social variables.

5.3 A corpus study: Tag questions across region and gender

Tag questions (TQs), such as *Mary is a doctor* [anchor], *isn't she?* [tag], are formed by a combination of two clauses, an anchor and a tag uttered by the same speaker. The anchor can be a declarative, imperative, exclamative or interrogative clause (cf. Axelsson 2011: 30). The tag hosted by that anchor, on the other hand, is invariably a clause with interrogative syntax consisting of a finite operator and a pronominal subject. In canonical TQs, such as (1),[1] these typically agree with the subject and finite operator in the anchor. In invariant TQs, such as (2), in contrast, the interrogative tag is not dependent on the syntactic properties of the anchor (cf. Andersen 2001: 104).

(1) B: Pauline your tea's not too hot <u>is it</u>
     A: That's lovely <#> No it's fine it's lovely
         (S1A-008)
(2) Ha you've to go earlier and spend quality time with mother <u>is it</u>
     (S1A-042$D)

TQs can be described both formally and functionally, and a number of studies taking a contrastive approach have investigated both formal and pragmatic variation in TQ use as conditioned by region (cf. Algeo 1990, Tottie and Hoffmann 2006, Allerton 2009 on BrE and AmE; Cheng and Warren 2001, Wong 2007 on Hong Kong English; Borlongan 2008 on Philippine English). Age and gender have also been investigated within particular varieties of English (cf. Tottie and Hoffmann 2006 on age), with gender research suggesting that TQs serve different communicative and interactional purposes in women's and men's speech (Cameron et al. 1989; Coates 1989; Holmes 1995). This form-functional line of variational research has recently also been applied to TQs in IrE as, for example, in Barron (2015), an analysis of a service encounter corpus from the south-west of Ireland, and Barron et al. (2015), a corpus study of IrE and BrE private conversations.

Table 5.1   Composition of the ICE-Ireland S1A sub-corpus comprised of speakers of NI/ROI background with TQ raw and relative frequencies per 10,000 words

	Face-to-face and telephone conversations in ICE-Ireland					
	NI speakers			ROI speakers		
	Male	Female	Total	Male	Female	Total
Overall number of speakers	48	121	169	33	137	170
Number of speakers uttering a TQ	18	46	64	19	67	86
Word count	22,478	60,115	82,593	15,824	79,394	95,218
Speech unit count	3386	8496	11,882	2,313	11,654	13,967
TQ count	23	60	83	38	120	158
Relative frequency of TQs per 10,000 words	10.23	9.98	10.05	24.01	15.11	16.59

Data for the present study were obtained from ICE-Ireland, a corpus which allows detailed insights into the occurrence of TQs in a variety of discourse contexts, as well as access to speakers' demographic information. Since TQs are predominantly a feature of spontaneous dialogic discourse (cf. e.g. Kimps et al. 2014: 66), the analysis is limited to the ICE-Ireland text types face-to-face and telephone conversations. Using an extraction methodology described in Barron et al. (2015) and controlling for the two relevant social variables, regional background and sex of the speaker, a total of 241 TQs were identified in the speech of NI and ROI males and females taken together.[2] Relative frequencies were calculated on the basis of the total number of words produced by these speakers (cf. Table 5.1). Statistical significance tests[3] were calculated based on the concept of speech unit. Speech units in ICE-Ireland are utterances corresponding roughly to sentences but also including clauses or phrases incomplete due to 'interruption, hesitation, false start, etc.' (Kallen and Kirk 2008: 17–18). Each speech unit is marked by the symbol '<#>' and may in principle contain only one TQ. Thus, it is possible to quantify and compare TQ and non-TQ speech units in the data.[4] The results of the study are presented in the following. Invariant TQs in the data are relatively infrequent, amounting to 2.4 per cent of all NI TQs and 7 per cent of all ROI TQs.

The initial quantitative analysis shows that overall use of TQs differs significantly across NI and ROI (cf. Table 5.1). Fewer NI speakers use TQs relative to ROI speakers (64/169 or 37.87 per cent vs 86/170 or 50.59 per cent). The difference between ROI and NI is statistically significant if we compare the number of speech units containing a TQ to those that do not ($\chi^2 = 13.0143$, df $= 1$, p $= 0.000309$***). In terms of relative frequencies, NI speakers use only 10.05 TQs per 10,000 words, or approximately 40 per cent less frequently than ROI speakers, whose relative frequency is 16.59. Interestingly, Barron et al. (2015) find TQ use in corresponding data from ICE-GB to be as high as 25.42 TQ per 10,000 words. These findings suggest that despite the political separation between NI and ROI, and NI's political affiliation to GB, the frequency of TQs in the NI ICE sub-component is more similar to that in the ROI sub-component than it is to TQ use in ICE-GB.

Beyond frequency comparisons, however, it is also interesting to look at *how* different groups use TQs. This we do in the following, with Sections 5.3.1 and 5.3.2 focused on region and gender respectively.

5.3.1   Tag question function across region

The present discussion of function is based on the functional coding scheme employed in Barron et al. (2015) in the context of their description of TQs in ICE-Ireland and ICE-GB. The scheme draws on insights from previous work by Algeo (1990), Axelsson (2011), Holmes (1995), Kimps et al. (2014) and Tottie and Hoffman (2006) and is at the same time adapted to describe the corpus data. Following Kimps et al. (2014), who focus on the interactional functions of TQs, two overarching categories are distinguished: information-oriented TQs, including questions, statements and statement-question blends, and desired action-oriented TQs, such as requests, offers and suggestions.[5] Their proportional use in private conversations in ICE-GB and ICE-Ireland as reported in Barron et al. (2015) is given in Table 5.2.

Table 5.2   The interactional functions of tag questions and their proportions in ICE-GB and ICE-Ireland private conversations (Barron et al. 2015)

	ICE-GB N = 244		ICE-Ireland N = 248		Statistical significance
Exchanging information					
Questions	52	21.31%	85	34.27%	$P_{bonferroni} < 0.01$**
Statements	97	39.75%	73	29.44%	$P_{bonferroni} < 0.05$*
S-Q blends	92	37.70%	87	35.08%	n.s.
Negotiating desired action	3	1.23%	3	1.21%	n.s.

5.3.1.1 Information-oriented TQs

Information-oriented TQs are involved in the exchange of information between speaker and addressee and are further differentiated according to two main, interdependent criteria: the relative knowledge status of the interlocutors (based on contextual clues) and whether or not a response is projected (Kimps et al. 2014: 69–71). Based on these criteria, three major types of information-oriented TQs are differentiated in the present context: questions, statements and statement-question (S-Q) blends.

Question TQs convey the speaker's uncertainty about the truth of the information contained in the anchor, and frame it as a B-event, i.e. as something known to the addressee (Labov and Fanshel 1977). Question TQs are information-seeking and naturally seek a response, a next turn in which the addressee is expected to restore the knowledge imbalance. Relevant examples are (1) and (3).

(3) Johnnie doesn't drink <u>does he</u> <#> Or does he
     (S1A-043$B)

As Table 5.2 shows, Barron et al. (2015) found question TQs to represent over one-third of all TQs in private conversations in ICE-Ireland and to be significantly more frequent than in parallel data from ICE-GB. Question TQs were also the most frequent group in Barron's (2015) analysis of TQs in service encounters recorded in the south-west of ROI.[6] Interestingly, however, they were used at a significantly higher level in the service encounter sample (48.5 per cent) relative to ICE-Ireland ($\chi^2 = 4.635$; df. $= 1$; p $= 0.031*$), a finding which raises the question as to whether question TQs are more typical of ROI speakers than of NI speakers. The results displayed in Table 5.3 for NI and ROI speakers reveal that question TQs are employed to an almost equally high

Table 5.3 The interactional functions of tag questions and their proportions in private conversations of NI and ROI speakers

	NI speakers N = 81		ROI speakers N = 157		Statistical significance
Exchanging information					
Questions	29	35.80%	54	34.39%	n.s.
Statements	34	41.98%	37	23.57%	$P_{bonferroni} < 0.01**$
S-Q blends	18	22.22%	63	40.13%	$P_{bonferroni} < 0.05*$
Negotiating desired action	–	–	3	1.91%	n.s.

extent by NI and ROI speakers relative to ICE-GB and rather suggest that the higher proportions in the service encounter sample may be genre-specific.

In contrast to questions, statement TQs do not seek but give information. Broadly speaking, their purpose is to communicate directly or indirectly facts, personal beliefs, assessments and positive or negative attitudes towards a certain topic or towards the addressee (Barron et al. 2015). In this sense they are rhetorical (cf. Axelsson's 2011 rhetorical TQs). This makes them A-events or, alternatively, if the information is shared between speaker and hearer (e.g. via world knowledge), AB-events. The addressee is not expected to supply an answer, although, as Kimps et al. (2014: 77) note, unsolicited responses, such as backchannels, acknowledgements or disagreements, may occur. Barron et al. (2015) distinguish four distinct subtypes of statement TQs: TQs stating a fact/opinion, as in (4–5), TQs acknowledging the addressee's preceding assertion (6), challenging TQs which undermine the addressee's positive face and demonstrate power (7), and, lastly, TQs used in conversational joking (8).

(4) D: What was it called <#> Operation uhm
     F: Oh uhm <,> hold on <unclear> 1 syll </unclear>
     D: May <u>was it</u> <#> Something May
     (S1A-002)

(5) Mm <,> well I don't lose mine at all <#> But then again now I only bring them into college <,> so <,> <u>you can't really go too wrong</u> <,> <u>can you</u>
     (S1A-059$B)

(6) C: She always gets out of everything
     A: Yeah she does doesn't she <#> She's always complaining <#> Yeah
         well no she wouldn't do it she said to save her life
     (S1A-075)

(7) C: Oil on my jeans you mean
     A: <u>Your jeans</u> <u>were they</u>
     (S1A-080)

(8) A: Right <#> How long were they here for
     B: Oh they stayed for weeks
     A: Right
     B: Finally they got tired and wanted to go back to their city life you know

A: Yeah <#> <u>Suppose it would be quiet</u> <,> <u>would it</u> <&>
laughter </&> <#> So did you ever keep in touch with
them or
(S1A-029)

Barron et al. (2015) found that IrE speakers in general use a significantly
lower amount of statement TQs than BrE speakers (cf. Table 5.2). However, as seen in Table 5.3, there is highly significant variation within
ICE-Ireland itself, with NI speakers using over 18 per cent more statements than ROI speakers (χ^2 = 8.6501, df = 1, $p_{bonferroni}$ < 0.01**). Indeed,
NI speakers' use of these TQs is more similar to that of BrE than to
ROI speakers.

The final information-oriented category, statement-question blends
(S-Q blends), displays characteristics of both questions and statements
(Kimps et al. 2014: 77–9). They are employed when the speaker
is more or less certain of the truth of the proposition but nevertheless requires a confirmatory response from the addressee. S-Q
blends involve an AB-event, where knowledge is shared by both
speaker and addressee, or an A-event, where the speaker 'projects
that s/he expects the co-participant(s) to catch up with this information and reduce the knowledge imbalance' (Kimps et al. 2014:
77). Barron et al. (2015) distinguish three subtypes of S-Q blends:
TQs seeking to (re-)establish knowledge, evaluations and opinions as
common ground, e.g. the two items in (9), conversation- or topic-initiating TQs (10), and TQs expressing a surprised reaction towards
what another speaker has just said and inviting a confirmatory
response (11).

(9) B: Yeah this this guy was like twenty-two or three <u>was he</u>
    C: Mm
    B: And uh would put a pizza in the microwave <,> and eat it
       off this paper plate <,> and use the plastic knife and fork
       and then like just throw it in the bin
    D: Oh God
    B: No washing up <#> No mess <#> Nothing
    D: Great idea
    B: <u>They were so they were very tidy</u> <u>weren't they</u>
    C: That's true
    (S1A-056)
(10) B: Then he's two sisters <#> One of them lives in the South
        and the other one lives in England

> A: Terry's sisters
> B: And his brother lives in the South <#> So he was the only one up here <unclear> 4 sylls </unclear>
> B: Nice bread that wasn't it
> A: That was lovely Caroline
> (S1A-009)

(11) C: He's probably still in England
> B: Oh I think he's at home
> C: He's at home is he
> B: Yeah I think he's at home
> (S1A-087)

The proportions of S-Q blends in IrE and BrE are rather similar (Table 5.2). However, there are differences within ICE-Ireland, with ROI speakers producing significantly more S-Q blends than NI speakers (40.13 per cent vs. 22.22 per cent respectively; $\chi^2 = 7.6302$, df = 1, $p_{bonferroni} < 0.05^*$) (cf. Table 5.3).

5.3.1.2 Desired action

The second major functional category is that of desired action TQs. In contrast to the categories discussed so far, these TQs are employed not in the exchange of information but in the exchange of goods and services (cf. Axelsson 2011; Kimps et al. 2014). Included are commissives and directives, such as requests, commands, offers, advice and suggestions, all of which project a verbal or a non-verbal response in compliance with the action under negotiation (Kimps et al. 2014: 81).

In the present data, desired action TQs are very rare, as also in previous findings (cf. Barron et al. 2015 for an overview). Only three items were identified – two requests, e.g. (12), and a command, all uttered by a ROI speaker (1.91 per cent).

(14) Ivana will you turn off the soup will you
(S1A-081$D)

5.3.2 Tag question functions in women's and men's speech across region

Among the first researchers to focus on male/female uses of TQs, Lakoff (1975) claimed that TQs signal insecurity and are more frequent in women's speech. Empirical studies since have revealed the issue to be more complex. Dubois and Crouch (1975), for example, found TQs to be used by the less powerful independently of sex in an academic conference setting, while Cameron et al. (1989: 88) suggest that in conversational contexts involving unequal power relationships (e.g., interviewer – interviewee, teacher – pupil), TQs 'function as an interactional resource of the powerful rather than the powerless' (cf. also Holmes 1995). However, not only power but also sex and regional background play a role in TQ use. Holmes (1995) found women in her New Zealand data to use more TQs than men, while Cameron et al. (1989) observed the reverse tendency in their BrE data. That region is an important factor in TQ frequency is also borne out by the present data. It is to these data that we now turn.

Overall, men in ICE-Ireland were found to use more TQs than women. However, the results displayed in Table 5.1 point to important regional differences. ROI men use most TQs, with 24.01 TQs per 10,000 words. ROI women are second, although the relative TQ frequency in this group is much lower (15.11 per 10,000 words). The difference in the number of speech units containing a TQ relative to speech units which do not is significant across ROI males and females (χ^2 = 6.4884, df = 1, p = 0.010858*). This is not the case on the other side of the border, however, where NI men and women use TQs at an almost equal rate (10.23 vs. 9.98 TQs per 10,000). These diverging findings confirm Holmes' (1995: 84–5) conclusion that the frequency of TQs used by men and women is variable and dependent on a variety of contextual factors, including region.

Leaving frequency aside, Holmes (1995) has pointed out that TQs may also serve different functions in women's and men's speech which are indicative of their different interactional styles. Women, for instance, have been found to employ more 'facilitative' TQs functioning to 'invite the addressee to contribute to the discourse' and to indicate 'concern for the needs of others', while men use more 'epistemic modal' TQs expressing 'genuine speaker uncertainty' and 'requesting reassurance or confirmation' (Holmes 1995: 81–3; for similar results, cf. Cameron et al. 1989; Coates 1989).

The present data do not confirm Holmes' assessment from a statistical perspective. However, some tendencies may be noted. Table 5.4 shows that on either side of the border, men use proportionately more questions (corresponding to Holmes' epistemic modal category) than women, whereas women use more S-Q blends (roughly equivalent to Holmes' facilitative category). Also, an in-depth analysis of sub-function reveals that the two sexes use statement TQs for different interactional purposes. Independently of region, men use more challenging TQs (50 per cent in NI and 36.36 per cent in the ROI) than women (15.38 per

Table 5.4   The functions of TQs in women's and men's speech in ICE-Ireland according to regional background

	NI speakers			ROI speakers		
	Men	Women		Men	Women	
	(N=22) (%)	(N=59) (%)	Statistical significance	(N=38) (%)	(N=119) (%)	Statistical significance
Questions	50.00	30.51	n.s.	39.47	32.77	n.s.
Statements	36.36	44.07	n.s.	28.95	21.85	n.s.
S-Q blends	13.64	25.42	n.s.	31.58	42.86	n.s.
Desired action	–	–	–	–	2.52	n.s.

cent in both NI and the ROI) (χ^2 = 5.6915, df = 1, p = 0.017047*). On the other hand, although not statistically significant, we see that women use more TQs to state a fact or express an opinion (53.85 per cent in NI and 46.15 per cent in the ROI) than men (37.5 per cent in NI and 27.27 per cent in the ROI). Finally, men do not use any TQs functioning as acknowledging responses at all in either the NI or ROI corpora. In contrast, acknowledging responses make up approximately one-fifth of all women's TQs in NI (19.23 per cent) and one-third in the ROI (30.77 per cent). Such uses are consistent with Holmes' claim that women employ a more supportive style in conversation.

5.3.3   Discussion

The present analysis of TQ use adds to the research on regional pragmatic variation in its focus on variation across the North/South political divide on the island of Ireland, i.e. across Northern and southern IrE, as well as on pragmatic variation between language as it is used in ICE-GB and ICE-Ireland. It also furthers the limited research to date on gender and language use in IrE as well as on the complex interaction of macrosocial factors, specifically in this case on the interplay of gender and region. In the following, we highlight a number of issues raised by the above analysis.

The first question concerns the relationship between TQ use in the ROI data, the NI data and the ICE-GB data. Barron et al. (2015) have shown that ICE-Ireland (ROI and NI) speakers use significantly fewer TQs than ICE-GB speakers. The present analysis sheds further light on this issue, revealing that ROI speakers use significantly more TQs than NI speakers. This also applies to the interaction of gender and region. In other words, irrespective of sex, ROI speakers used more TQs than

NI speakers. On the other hand, however, both varieties employ TQs to a lower extent than in ICE-GB. This lower use in the ROI – and particularly in NI – may be suggested to relate to a preferential use of linguistic forms other than TQs (cf. also Barron et al. 2015). Indeed, Tottie (2009: 361–2), discussing the lower use of TQs in AmE relative to BrE proposes, for instance, that epistemic particles, such as *probably, likely, presumably*, may on occasion be used instead of the canonical tag functions. Alternatively/in addition, it is possible that the lower TQ use recorded in IrE is due to an extensive use of TQs other than the clausal TQs containing interrogative tags focused on in the present study. Examples include concordant non-interrogative TQs with a declarative tag, such as those involving the typically Irish '*sure* + pronoun + aux + (*not/n't*)' tag (e.g. *It can't be right, sure it can't*, cf. Hickey 2007: 276–7; Pandarova in preparation) and the '*so* + pronoun + aux + (*not/n't*)' tag (e.g. *She's pretty, so she is*, cf. Asián and McCullough 1998: 49) as well as single-word tags, such as clause-final *like* (cf. Lucek 2011), phonological tags (e.g. *eh*), or fixed phrases containing lexical material, such as *you know?* Indeed, the functional interplay of the whole range of TQs is an interesting research area particularly when viewed across cultures, as a single function may be realised preferentially using a canonical tag in one society and using an invariant tag in another (cf. also Allerton 2009: 320; Barron 2015; Tottie 2009: 361–2). Such questions remain ripe for further variational pragmatic research.

In terms of function, both the NI and the ROI speakers used questions to a similar extent and both groups used more question TQs than did speakers in ICE-GB. Interestingly, and as also mentioned in Barron et al. (2015), Tottie and Hoffmann (2009: 154) in a historical study of TQs, note that 'In the 16CD data, confirmatory uses are the most frequent type, with over 60 per cent of all cases, compared with 30–37 per cent in PDE [Present-day English]. This suggests that confirmation seeking [equivalent to the present question category] may indeed have been the original use of tag questions'. Given differences in the underlying text types, such findings remain speculative. However, they do point to an interesting path for further research to investigate whether the higher level of question TQs in the ROI and NI relative to levels in ICE-GB is due to retention in the former varieties or possibly also to convergence in the contact situation with the functions of TQs in the Irish language.

NI speakers were also found to employ more statements than ROI speakers. In this respect, they approached the ICE-GB data to a greater extent. ROI speakers, on the other hand, employed more statement-question blends and indeed showed more similarities in this respect to the ICE-GB data than to the NI data. Interestingly, the gender analysis threw some light on this divergence. While males and females across the two datasets do not differ significantly in their use of statements and statement-question blends, there is significant variation specifically in terms of women's preferences. NI women use more statements than statement-question blends, while ROI women exhibit the reverse tendency ($\chi 2$ = 9.5414, df = 1, p < 0.01, cf. also Table 5.4). Hence, the observed regional differences can be attributed to significant variation in NI and ROI women's TQ function preference. This example of the interplay of region and gender demonstrates the importance of considering gender distributions in future analyses of regional corpora.

5.4 Conclusion

The present review of language use in IrE, as also the corpus analysis of TQs, was situated within the variational pragmatic framework and thus focused on describing language use in IrE using contrastive comparable empirical data. Such contrasts give some insight into whether particular features of IrE or of a sub-variety of IrE (defined by gender/age/socio-economic class/ethnicity) are similar to those of other varieties or sub-varieties, are preferred/dispreferred in the (sub-)variety at hand (variety-preferential/variety-dispreferential) or indeed potentially particular to IrE or to a sub-variety of same (variety-specific). The overview leaves no doubt but that IrE has its own pragmatic profile, characterised by variety-specific forms and variety-preferential uses. In addition, language use is found to be dictated by the contradictory poles of directness and indirectness, and thus also by both positive and negative politeness, depending on situational constellations, speech act and genre.

Relative to the situation in the early 1990s, research on language use within IrE is alive and vibrant. This is not to say, however, that there is no scope for future study. On the contrary, research desiderata have been highlighted above on all levels of the variational pragmatic approach and concerning all macro-social variables. Also, as the tag question study shows, the study of the interaction of these factors can be particularly insightful.

Finally, on a more applied level, the overview points to the need to increase the awareness of IrE speakers themselves as to the pragmatic profile of their language use relative to other varieties of English. As O'Keeffe (2011: 63) states, 'Pragmatics is a mine-field in a transcultural context and the better we understand the nuances of Englishes (or any other language used transculturally), the less we are prone to pragmatic failure...'. One might also add here '...and the less we are prone to the resultant social dissonance' (cf. Wolfram and Schilling-Estes 2006: 101). The potential of research in language use to resolve misunderstandings was highlighted above in the case of NI. Taken further, it would seem beneficial to recognise and increase awareness of intralingual pragmatic variation not only on the level of nation but also on the level of age, gender, ethnicity, socio-economic class and all levels of region. We look forward to future developments.

Acknowledgements

The authors wish to acknowledge the support of the Fund for Scientific Research (*Kleinforschungsprojekt*) awarded by the Leuphana University Lüneburg which enabled the research reported in this paper to be undertaken. Special thanks also to Martin Schweinberger, who offered advice on statistical measures, and to Kerstin Single for assistance on formal matters.

5A Appendix

Transcription conventions

<,>	Short pause
<„>	Long pause
<#>	Utterance initiation mark
<{> ... </{>	Initiation and completion of a stretch of text in which overlapping speech occurs
<[> ... </[>	Initiation and completion of an utterance which overlaps with another utterance. Subsequent overlapping utterances are numbered, as in <[1> ... </[1>, <[2> ... </[2>, etc.
<unclear> ... </unclear>	Unclear speech
<&> laughter </&>	Indicates laughter

Notes

1. All examples cited come from the ICE-Ireland corpus (Kallen and Kirk 2008).
2. Twenty-four TQs uttered by speakers of mixed geographical background between NI and ROI or between Ireland and a non-Irish jurisdiction have been omitted from the present analysis (cf. Kallen and Kirk 2008: 31). Also, one ROI speaker whose sex is unknown is omitted. This speaker did not produce any TQs.

3. The statistical measures are Pearson's chi-squared test and Fisher's exact test with a Bonferroni correction for multiple comparisons.
4. Many thanks to Martin Schweinberger for extracting the word and speech unit counts per unique speaker computationally and making these available online (cf. Schweinberger 2014).
5. As noted by Tottie and Hoffmann (2009: 141), 'it is important to keep in mind that the pragmatic functions of tag questions form a continuum and that functions overlap and shade into one another'. This is especially true when TQs are studied in corpus data lacking prosodic and paralinguistic markup, as is the case in ICE-GB and ICE-Ireland. Based exclusively on contextual clues found in the corpus transcriptions, the present functional analysis should therefore be seen as reflecting tendencies in the data.
6. Note that Barron (in press) uses the term 'confirmation-eliciting' in place of question TQs.

References

Algeo, John (1990). 'It's a myth, innit? Politeness and the English tag question', in: Christopher Ricks and Leonard Michaels (eds) *The State of Language*. Berkeley/Los Angeles/Oxford: University of California Press, pp. 443–50.

Allerton, David J. (2009). 'Tag questions', in: Rohdenburg and Schlüter (eds), pp. 306–23.

Amador-Moreno, Carolina P. (2010). *An Introduction to Irish English.* London/Oakville: Equinox.

Andersen, Gisle (2001). *Pragmatic Markers and Sociolinguistic Variation: a Relevance-Theoretic Approach to the Language of Adolescents.* Amsterdam/Philadelphia: Benjamins.

Andersen, Gisle and Karin Aijmer (eds) (2011). *Pragmatics of Society.* Berlin: Mouton.

Asián, Anna and James McCullough (1998). 'Hiberno-English and the teaching of modern and contemporary Irish literature in an EFL context', *Links & Letters* 5: 37–60.

Axelsson, Karin (2011). *Tag Questions in Fiction Dialogue.* University of Gothenburg PhD thesis.

Barker, Gosia and Anne M. O'Keeffe (1999). 'A corpus of Irish English – past, present, future', *Teanga* (Yearbook of the Irish Association for Applied Linguistics) 18: 1–11.

Barron, Anne (2005a). 'Variational pragmatics in the foreign language classroom', *System* 33.3: 519–36.

Barron, Anne (2005b). 'Offering in Ireland and England', in: Barron and Schneider (eds), pp. 141–77.

Barron, Anne (2008a). 'The structure of requests in Irish English and English English', in: Schneider and Barron (eds), pp. 35–67.

Barron, Anne (2008b). 'Contrasting requests in Inner Circle Englishes: a study in variational pragmatics', in: Martin Pütz and JoAnne Neff van Aertselaer (eds) *Developing Contrastive Pragmatics: Interlanguage and Cross-Cultural Perspectives.* Berlin/New York: Mouton de Gruyter, pp. 355–402.

Barron, Anne (2011). 'Variation revisited: a corpus analysis of offers in Irish English and British English', in: Joachim Frenk and Lena Steveker (eds)

Anglistentag 2010 Saarbrücken: Proceedings. Trier: Wissenschaftlicher Verlag Trier, pp. 407–19.

Barron, Anne (2012). *Public Information Messages: a Contrastive Genre Analysis of State-Citizen Communication.* Amsterdem/Philadelphia: Benjamins.

Barron, Anne (2014). 'Variational pragmatics', in: Carol A. Chapelle (ed.) *The Encyclopedia of Applied Linguistics* (EAL): electronic version. Oxford: Wiley-Blackwell.

Barron, Anne (2015). "'And your wedding is the twenty-second <,> of June is it?" Tag questions in Irish English', in: Carolina P. Amador-Moreno, Kevin McCafferty and Elaine Vaughan (eds) *Pragmatic Markers in Irish English.* Amsterdam: John Benjamins, pp. 203–28.

Barron, Anne, forthcoming. 'Variational pragmatics', in: Anne Barron, Gerard Steen and Yueguo Gu (eds) *Routledge Handbook of Pragmatics.* London/New York: Routledge.

Barron, Anne and Klaus P. Schneider (eds) (2005). *The Pragmatics of Irish English.* Berlin/New York: de Gruyter Mouton.

Barron, Anne and Klaus P. Schneider (2005). 'Irish English: a focus on language in action', in: Barron and Schneider (eds), pp. 3–15.

Barron, Anne and Klaus P. Schneider (2009). 'Variational pragmatics: Studying the impact of social factors on language use in interaction', *Intercultural Pragmatics* 6.4: 425–42.

Barron, Anne, Irina Pandarova and Karoline Muderack (2015). 'Tag questions across Irish English and British English: a corpus analysis of form and function', *Multilingua* 34.4: 495–525.

Bieswanger, Markus and Amei Koll-Stobbe (eds) (2013). *New Approaches to the Study of Variability.* Frankfurt/M.: Peter Lang.

Borlongan, Ariane M. (2008). 'Tag questions in Philippine English', *Philippine Journal of Linguistics* 39.1: 1–34. http://ejournals.ph/index.php?journal=hsjakgdfeuwbrenmmzvrio&page=article&op=view&path%5B%5D=71&path%5B%5D=75 (accessed 6 December 2014).

Burmeister, Melanie (2013). 'Variability in death notices from Scotland, Wales and the Republic of Ireland: a comparative perspective', in: Bieswanger and Koll-Stobbe (eds), pp. 65–88.

Cambridge University Press. Cambridge International Corpus. CANCODE – Cambridge and Nottingham Corpus of Discourse in English. http://www.cambridge.org/de/elt/catalogue/subject/custom/item3646595/Cambridge-International-Corpus-Cambridge-and-Nottingham-Corpus-of-Discourse-in-English-%28CANCODE%29/?site_locale=de_DE (accessed 6 December 2014).

Cameron, Deborah, Fiona McAlinden and Kathy O'Leary (1989). 'Lakoff in context: the social and linguistic functions of tag questions', in: Jennifer Coates and Deborah Cameron (eds) *Women in their Speech Communities: New Perspectives on Language and Sex.* London: Longman, pp. 74–93.

Cheng, Winnie and Martin Warren (2001). "'She knows more about Hong Kong than you do isn't it": Tags in Hong Kong conversational English', *Journal of Pragmatics* 33: 1419–39.

Clancy, Brian (2005). "'You're fat. You'll eat them all": Politeness strategies in family discourse', in: Barron and Schneider (eds), pp. 177–99.

Clancy, Brian (2011a). 'Complementary perspectives on hedging behaviour in family discourse: the analytical synergy of variational pragmatics and corpus linguistics', in: Fiona Farr and Anne O'Keeffe (eds) *Applying Corpus*

Linguistics. Special Issue of *International Journal of Corpus Linguistics* 16.3: 371–90.

Clancy, Brian (2011b). 'Do you want to do it yourself like? Hedging in Irish traveller and settled family discourse', in: Bethan L. Davies, Michael Haugh and Andrew J. Merrison (eds) *Situated Politeness*. London: Continuum, 129–46.

Clancy, Brian and Elaine Vaughan (2012). "'It's lunacy now": a corpus-based pragmatic analysis of the use of "now" in contemporary Irish English', in: Migge and Ní Chiosáin (eds), pp. 225–46.

Coates, Jennifer (1989). 'Women's speech, women's strength?', *York Papers in Linguistics* 13: 65–76.

Dubois, Betty Lou and Isabel Crouch (1975). 'The question of tag questions in women's speech: They don't really use more of them, do they?', *Language in Society* 4: 289–94.

Elwood, Kate (2010). 'An analysis of expressions of gratitude in Irish English and New Zealand English', *Waseda University Departmental Bulletin Paper* 36, 3, available online at https://dspace.wul.waseda.ac.jp/dspace/bitstream/2065/39054/1/BunkaRonshu_36_Elwood.pdf.

Elwood, Kate (2011). 'Soap opera thankfulness – A comparison of expressions of gratitude in "Fair City" and "EastEnders", *Waseda University Departmental Bulletin Paper* 38, 3, available online at https://dspace.wul.waseda.ac.jp/dspace/bitstream/2065/39061/1/BunkaRonshu_38_Elwood.pdf.

Farr, Fiona and Bróna Murphy (2009). 'Religious references in contemporary Irish English: "For the love of God almighty. I'm a holy terror for turf"', *Intercultural Pragmatics* 6.4: 535–59.

Foolen, Ad (2011). 'Pragmatic markers in a sociopragmatic perspective', in: Andersen and Aijmer (eds), pp. 217–42.

Hickey, Raymond (2003). *Corpus Presenter. Software for Language Analysis. With a Manual and* A Corpus of Irish English *as Sample Data*. Amsterdam: John Benjamins.

Hickey, Raymond (2007). *Irish English: History and Present-day Forms*. Cambridge: Cambridge University Press.

Hickey, Raymond (2011). 'Present and future horizons for Irish English', *English Today* 27.2: 3–16.

Hickey, Raymond, in press. 'The pragmatics of *grand* in Irish English', *Journal of Historical Pragmatics*.

Holmes, Janet (1995). *Women, Men and Politeness*. White Plains, NY: Longman.

Holmes, Janet (2010). 'Sociolinguistics', in: Louise Cummings (ed.) *The Pragmatics Encyclopedia*. London: Routledge, pp. 446–9.

International Corpus of English. http://ice-corpora.net/ice/ (accessed 13 November 2014).

Kallen, Jeffrey L. (2005a). 'Silence and mitigation in Irish English discourse', in: Barron and Schneider (eds), pp. 47–71.

Kallen, Jeffrey L. (2005b). 'Politeness in Ireland: "In Ireland, it's done without being said"', in: Leo Hickey and Miranda Stewart (eds) *Politeness in Europe*. Clevedon: Multilingual Matters, pp. 130–44.

Kallen, Jeffrey L. (2006). '*Arrah, like, you know*: the dynamics of discourse marking in ICE-Ireland', unpublished paper presented at the Sociolinguistic Symposium 16, University of Limerick 6–8 July 2006.

Kallen, Jeffrey L. and John M. Kirk (2008). *ICE-Ireland: a User's Guide.* Belfast: Cló Ollscoil na Banríona.

Kallen, Jeffrey L. and John M. Kirk (2012). *SPICE-Ireland: a User's Guide.* Belfast: Cló Ollscoil na Banríona.

Kimps, Ditte, Kristin Davidse and Bert Cornillie (2014). 'A speech function analysis of tag questions in British English spontaneous dialogue', *Journal of Pragmatics* 66: 64–85.

Labov, William and David Fanshel (1977). *Therapeutic Discourse: Psychotherapy as Conversation.* New York: Academic Press.

Lakoff, Robin (1975). *Language and Woman's Place.* New York: Harper and Row.

Lucek, Stephen (2011). '"I came up and I seen this haze of smoke, like": How Irish are invariant tags?', *Trinity College Dublin Journal of Postgraduate Research* 10: 95–108.

McCafferty, Kevin and Carolina P. Amador-Moreno, in preparation. *CORIECOR. The Corpus of Irish English Correspondence.* Bergen and Cáceres: University of Bergen and University of Extremadura.

Migge, Bettina and Máire Ní Chiosáin (eds) (2012). *New Perspectives on Irish English.* Amsterdam: John Benjamins.

Murphy, Bróna (2009). 'She's a *fucking* ticket: the pragmatics of FUCK in Irish English – an age and gender perspective', *Corpora* 4.1: 85–106.

Murphy, Bróna (2010). *Corpus and Sociolinguistics: Investigating Age and Gender in Female Talk.* Amsterdam/Philadelphia: Benjamins.

Murphy, Bróna (2012). 'Exploring response tokens in Irish English – a multi-disciplinary approach: Integrating variational pragmatics, sociolinguistics and corpus linguistics', *International Journal of Corpus Linguistics* 17.3: 325–48.

O'Keeffe, Anne (2011). 'Teaching and Irish English', *English Today*, 27.2: 57–63.

O'Keeffe, Anne and Svenja Adolphs (2008). 'Response tokens in British and Irish discourse: Corpus, context and variational pragmatics', in: Schneider and Barron (eds), pp. 69–98.

Pandarova, Irina. In preparation. 'The semantics and pragmatics of *sure* across varieties of English.' PhD thesis to be submitted to the Leuphana University Lüneburg.

Placencia, María E. (2011). 'Regional pragmatic variation', in: Andersen and Aijmer (eds), pp. 79–113.

Rohdenburg, Günther and Julia Schlüter (eds) (2009). *One Language, Two Grammars? Differences Between British and American English.* Cambridge: Cambridge University Press.

Schneider, Klaus P. (1999). 'Compliment responses across cultures', in: Maria Wysocka (ed.) *On Language Theory and Language Practice: In Honour of Janusz Arabski on the Occasion of his 60th Birthday.* Katowice: Wydan. Uniwersytetu Wroclawskiego, pp. 162–72.

Schneider, Klaus P. (2005). 'No problem, you're welcome, anytime: Responding to thanks in Ireland, England, and the USA', in: Schneider and Barron (eds), pp. 101–39.

Schneider, Klaus P. (2008). 'Small talk in England, Ireland, and the USA', in: Schneider and Barron (eds), pp. 99–139.

Schneider, Klaus P. (2010). 'Variational pragmatics', in: Mirjam Fried, Jan-Ola Östman and Jef Verschueren (eds) *Variation and Change: Pragmatic Perspectives.* Amsterdam/Philadelphia: Benjamins, pp. 239–67.

Schneider, Klaus P. (2012). 'Pragmatics', in: Raymond Hickey (ed.) *Areal Features of the Anglophone World*. Berlin: de Gruyter Mouton, pp. 463–86.

Schneider, Klaus P. and Anne Barron (2008). 'Where pragmatics and dialectology meet: Introducing variational pragmatics', in: Schneider and Barron (eds), pp. 1–32.

Schneider, Klaus P. and Anne Barron (eds) (2008). *Variational Pragmatics: a Focus on Regional Varieties in Pluricentric Languages*. Amsterdam/Philadelphia: Benjamins.

Schweinberger, Martin (2012). 'The discourse marker LIKE in Irish English', in: Migge and Ní Chiosáin (eds), pp. 179–202.

Schweinberger, Martin (2013). 'A sociolinguistic analysis of the discourse marker LIKE in Northern Irish English: a look behind the scenes of quantitative reasoning', in: Bieswanger and Koll-Stobbe (eds), pp. 13–39.

Schweinberger, Martin (2014). *Combining Word and Speech Unit Counts with the Biodata of Speakers Represented in the Spoken Part of ICE Ireland with R*. Lüneburg: Leuphana University Lüneburg. http://www.martinschweinberger. de/blog/codes-tutorials/ (accessed 13 May 2014).

Schweinberger, Martin, Peter Siemund and Georg Maier (2009). 'Towards a more fine-grained analysis of the areal distributions of non-standard features of English', in: Esa Pentitilä und Heli Paulasto (eds), *Language Contacts Meet English Dialects: Studies in Honour of Markku Filppula*. Newcastle-upon-Tyne: Cambridge Scholars Publishing, pp. 19–45.

Tottie, Gunnel (2009). 'How different are American and British English grammar? And how are they different?', in: Rohdenburg and Schlüter (eds), pp. 341–63.

Tottie, Gunnel and Sebastian Hoffmann (2006). 'Tag questions in British and American English', *Journal of English Linguistics* 34.4: 283–311.

Tottie, Gunnel and Sebastian Hoffmann (2009). 'Tag questions in English: the first century', *Journal of English Linguistics* 37.2: 103–61.

Vaughan, Elaine and Brian Clancy (2011). 'Pragmatics and Irish English', *English Today* 27.2: 47–52.

Wolfram, Walt and Natalie Schilling-Estes (2006). *American English: Dialects and Variation*, 2nd edition. Malden, MA: Blackwell.

Wong, May L.-Y. (2007). 'Tag questions in Hong Kong English: a corpus-based study', *Asian Englishes* 10.1: 44–61.

Part II

Language and Society in Irish History

6
Language Relations in Early Ireland

Patricia Ronan

6.1 Introduction

Since the Middle Ages, the linguistic landscapes of Ireland have clearly undergone massive changes, of which the most obvious one is the rise of English and the concomitant decline of Irish. Generally, in situations where different population groups, who are speakers of different linguistic varieties, come into contact, it is the language of the socio-economically more powerful group that will influence the language of the less powerful population group (e.g. Crystal 2002, Thomason 2001: 66, 77, Hickey 2010: 8). As far as the linguistic situation in Ireland is concerned, Crowley (2000: 1) observes that the relations between the two main languages of Ireland, English and Irish, are as complicated as the political relations between these two communities. In order to trace the linguistic influences of relative socio-economic differences, the lexicon of a language constitutes a good source. The language of the less powerful linguistic variety will typically incorporate a large number of loanwords from the more powerful variety, as the vocabulary is 'an open class with a high degree of awareness by speakers' (Hickey 2010: 8). In the following we will consider statements about population groups as well as semantic fields of loanwords taken from the languages in contact.

At first sight, the spread of the English language to Ireland appears to correspond to the situation in a number of countries which use English as a first or second language. During the first decade of the twenty-first century, work has been carried out on formalising typical patterns of the outcome of colonial contacts involving the English language (Schneider 2003, 2007). It can be argued that the overall outcome of the social and linguistic developments in Ireland corresponds to the model developed by Schneider, but to what extent especially the early stages of English presence in Ireland confirm Schneider's model shall be questioned here. The aim of this paper is thus to trace the relative sociocultural status of English and Irish speakers in Ireland during the medieval period and to correlate changes in these differences with the respective linguistic influences of the languages on each other. For this the emphasis will be put on lexical influences. It will furthermore be shown that the scenario that unfolds during the medieval period does not correspond to the typical developments chartered by Schneider's (2003) Dynamic Model and it will be explained why this is the case. These goals are approached as follows: after this brief introduction, we will outline relevant theories on the sociology of linguistic and cultural contacts in Section 6.2. We will present the socio-historical background to the contacts of the population groups in Ireland and then consider the linguistic outcomes; here Section 6.3.1 refers to the period pre-1200, Section 6.3.2 refers to the period post-1200, and a brief glimpse of further developments is given in Section 6.3.3. In Section 6.4 the discussion draws these findings together before a conclusion is offered in Section 6.5.

6.2   The sociology of linguistic and cultural contacts

The linguistic development in Ireland has been influenced by various sociolinguistic factors. The development of the relative positions of English and Irish is largely due to the sociopolitical circumstances of the population groups who used the languages. In this section we will provide an overview of typical mechanisms of language contact (Thomason and Kaufman 1988, Thomason 2001) and we will introduce a model that has been devised for the international spread of English (Schneider 2003, 2007).

6.2.1   Typical mechanisms of language contact according to Thomason and Kaufman

According to Thomason and Kaufman (1988: 72–6) and Thomason (2001: 70–1), the basic mechanisms of language change in contact situations are as follows. In the *casual contact* situation, we find few bilingual speakers. The effect on the languages involved will be that there is no influence on phonology, morphology and syntax. Only specific content words are borrowed. As linguistic contact increases, in the phase of *slight contact*, a minority of relatively fluent bilinguals will emerge. As a result, some new phonemes can enter a language through the use of loanwords. If both contact languages have the same syntactic structures there can also be increased use of existing syntactic structures in the contact situation. In the lexicon, basic as well as non-basic content words can be borrowed, as well as some function words. As bilingualism keeps increasing and linguistic contacts become more frequent, which is Thomason and Kaufman's stage of *more intense contacts*, we find extended influence on phonology, morphology and syntax, as well as borrowing of basic function words and of content words, including pronouns, nouns and adjectives. Finally, at the stage of most intense contact, we find extensive bilingualism of the population, with the possible heavy linguistic influence in all linguistic areas, lexicon, phonology, syntax and morphology.

The usefulness of Thomason and Kaufman's model for typologies of lexical borrowing in the history of the English language has been assessed by Fischer (2003: 108–10). Fischer cautions that it is problematic to try and determine intensity of language contact on the basis of lexical borrowing alone because often the circumstances of the contact situation remain unknown. This pitfall is to be avoided in the present contribution, which seeks to provide a correlation of the circumstances of the contact situation and its linguistic outcome.

6.2.2   The Dynamic Model of the spread of English

Schneider's Dynamic Model of the spread of New Englishes (Schneider 2003, 2007) models the development of the English language in postcolonial situations in the Inner and Outer Circles of English (Schneider 2014: 10), i.e. in countries where English is used as a first or second language, and it would thus also be applicable to the linguistic situation in Ireland. The model is based on the understanding that the socio-historical developments of the population groups, as well as their demographics, determine the outcomes of linguistic development in language-contact situations. Schneider (2003: 234) argues that structural and sociolinguistic similarities of international varieties of English are due to 'fundamentally similar contact processes', and are influenced by similarities in the communication, accommodation and identity-formation processes. These structural similarities, according to Schneider, arise in typical, characteristic phases of development. Schneider bases his model on the understanding that any society will construct social identity through its use of language. Correspondingly, the choices taken in the use of linguistic variables will reflect how the speakers construct their identities and identify themselves as members or non-members of different social groups. These processes, Schneider (2003: 240) argues, are subject to constant re-evaluation in view of changing relationships between the population groups. The overall linguistic development can be understood as follows (Schneider 2003: 255).

1st stage: Foundation. The use of the English language is introduced by the arrival of its speakers in an area, the two population groups remain largely apart and only a little interaction and communication takes place.

2nd stage: Exonormative stabilisation. The (English) settler language stabilises on the basis of its source varieties. English turns into the language of administration, is considered the elite language and learnt as a second language by some members of the local population.

3rd stage: Nativisation. The colonised country loosens its ties with England, as a distinct national identity evolves. More local speakers' use of the settlers' language, features of local languages are introduced into settler and indigenous communities' language, a linguistic complaint tradition arises.

4th stage: Endonormative stabilisation. Growing national identity eventually leads to the adoption of an internal, homogeneous linguistic norm.

Final stage: Differentiation. The variety of the local English language can develop further differences, such as regional differentiation.

This model has been applied to the rise of various varieties of English which evolved from settler communities, e.g. Australia, New Zealand, and to a partial extent, Fiji, Hong Kong, Malaysia, Philippines (Schneider 2003: 256–71, Schneider 2007). Whether it is also applicable to the early settlement situation in Ireland will be outlined in Section 6.4 below.

6.3 The socio-historical development of English and Irish contacts

6.3.1 The period pre-1200

Arguably the contacts between Irish-speaking Gaels and Anglo-Saxons happened when the first Saxon raids on Ireland took place in the fifth century AD (cf. Ronan 2013: 76). These events are recorded in the annals in Ireland for the years 434 and 471. Naturally, very little linguistic exchange will have taken place on those occasions. The Annals of Ulster (AU 434.1) remark somewhat cryptically that the first raid by the Saxons had taken place from Ireland or in Ireland (*'di Ere* no *ind h-Eirinn'*) in

434 AD, and a second one in 471 (AU 471.1 Prae*da secunda Saxonum de Hibernia*). Other raids continue to be recorded in the Annals, especially for 685, for which the Annals of Ulster (Mac Airt and Mac Niocaill (eds) 1983) state that

(1) The Saxons lay waste Mag Breg, and many churches, in the Month of June (U685.2)
(2) The battle of Dún Nechtain was fought on Saturday, May twentieth, and Egfrid son of Owsy, king of the Saxons, who had completed the fifteenth year of his reign was slain therein with a great body of his soldiers; . . . . (U686.1)

Ulster is the home province of the Dal Riada, who went on to colonise Scotland. It is therefore not surprising that the Ulster records show a clear interest in the interaction of Saxons, Picts, Britons and Gaels, and particularly in the fate of their rulers especially in the North of Britain, as well as in the Gaelic monasteries there. Predictably, recurrent information can be found on the spread of Christianity in Britain. Thus the Annals of Tigernach (Stokes (ed.) 1895–6) record that *The Saxons came to the Faith* (T597.3). The wording with the use of the verb *come* implies that the annalist seems to have felt that the Saxon community joined the Irish in their Christian faith and that a joint community of Irish and Saxons was thus created. In other words, they became 'one of us'. But also other information is recorded with interest.

(3) A battle between the Saxons and the Picts, in which fell Bernith's son, called Brectrid (U698.2)
(4) Cinaed son of Ailpín, king of the Picts, *and* Ethelwulf, king of the Saxons, died (U858.2)
(5) A murrain of cattle in the land of the Saxons (U699.1)
(6) Bede, a learned man of the Saxons, rested (U735.7)
(7) The successor of Colum Cille, an excellent scholar, suffered a violent death among the Saxons on the fourth of the Ides of March (U854.3)

These notes stem from a time for which there typically is only a handful of notes for each year, which clearly underlines that such events were indeed considered important.

During the ninth and the tenth century, various battles between Saxons and Norsemen in Britain are also recorded in the Irish annals (e.g. AU 918.4, 936.1, 952.2).

(8)   The dark foreigners [i.e. the Danes, PR] won a battle over the northern Saxons at York, in which fell Aelle, king of the northern Saxons (U867.7)

(9)   The foreigners of Loch dá Chaech, i.e. Ragnall, king of the dark foreigners, and the two jarls, Oitir and Gragabai, forsook Ireland and proceeded afterwards against the men of Scotland.... (U918.4)

The majority of these entries are very short and amount to one or two lines. Significantly longer is the following account, which shows remarkable compassion for the sufferings endured by all population groups.

(10)   A great, lamentable and horrible battle was cruelly fought between the Saxons and the Norsemen, in which several thousands of Norsemen, who are uncounted fell, but their king, Amlaíb, escaped with a few followers. A large number of Saxons fell on the other side, but Athelstan, king of the Saxons, enjoyed a great victory. (U937.6)

It is interesting that the scene is presented in terms of the general horrors of fighting and battle and that no attempt is made to single out one of the sides negatively as the responsible aggressors. This is in spite of the fact that the chroniclers might have had reason to view the Norsemen as murderous, negatively connoted invaders. Just one year before this entry, the plundering of the monastery of Clonmacnoise by the Norsemen living in Dublin is recorded (U936.2) and two years before the entry here, the monks had chronicled the killing of many Munstermen by the Norsemen (U935.6). Under these circumstances one might have tried to forge a group identity of the local, Irish population versus the invading foreigners. However, other entries of the period show that other Irishmen were just as likely to harm and kill their compatriots. For the year 937 we also find, for example *Gairbíth son of Mael Eitig, king of Fir Rois, was killed by his kinsmen* (U937.3) or simply *Bruatur son of Duibgilla, king of Uí Cheannselaig, was killed* (U937.2). It seems likely that the Norsemen were not stigmatised as exclusively bad because their conduct seems to have been not too much out of line with that of the local populations. This is confirmed by Ó Corráin (1989: 30, 35), who describes that Irish kings, like Viking forces, used to raid and plunder their fellow countrymen's territories and churches. Even more positively depicted than the Norsemen were some Saxon personalities. The Annals of Ulster state that

(11) Athelstan, king of the Saxons, pillar of the dignity of the western world, died an untroubled death. (U939.6)

Clearly at this time, relations between the Irish and their Saxon neighbours must have been at least to a large extent trouble-free for such a eulogy to be applied to a Saxon king. Overall, there seems to have been a good basis for friendly contacts and interaction between the different population groups and linguistic contacts may well have ensued.

In spite of the interest shown, Gaelic and Saxon interaction appears to have been sporadic at this stage. We do know, however, that there was considerable interaction between the Gaels and the Britons. Gaelic colonies were established in Wales from the fourth century and Ó Corráin (1989: 6) notes that the south-west of Wales was bilingual in Welsh and Irish in the fifth century. Ó Corráin cites *Sanas Cormaic*, 'The Glossary of Cormac', a ninth-century work, saying that '[t]he power of the Irish over the Britons was great, and they had divided Britain between them into estates; ... and the Irish lived as much east of the sea as they did in Ireland' (Ó Corráin 1989: 6). There is further proof of this statement in the form of standing stones with Old Irish Ogam script from the fifth to seventh centuries in Wales, Cornwall, Devon, and on the Isle of Man. Further well-documented contacts existed between the Vikings of Dublin and the Vikings in Britain.

From the ninth century there existed contacts mainly between the Viking settlements Dublin, Waterford and Limerick (Downham 2004: 55). Throughout this and the following century, these trade relations expanded and in the tenth century we find extensive trading contacts between Ireland and Chester and particularly between Dublin and York (Downham 2004: 56, 57). The English exported mainly jewellery, pottery, woollens, food items, and continental wares to Ireland, while the Irish did trade in hides, grain, timber, slaves, fish, and antler combs. During this period we thus have situations of mutually beneficial trade relations. As a result, there existed not only trade and religious, but also intellectual networks between Britain and Ireland by the eleventh century, especially so within the Viking settlements of Chester and York. During the twelfth century the Irish contacts expand even further south to Bristol, as well as to London, Gloucester, Exeter and Cambridge (Downham 2004: 54–6). As a result, we find English merchants in Dublin as well as Irish traders in London. According to the evidence of the *Vita Ædwardi*, these contacts resulted in some English nobles and merchants learning Irish (Downham 2004: 57). These trade relations were matched by political contacts. In late tenth and the early eleventh centuries we find political alliances between Irish Gaels as well as Irish and English Danes and the Norman king Richard of Normandy (Downham 2004: 60). Even when the good political relations faltered on the top level during Edward the Confessor's reign 1042–66, it seems that many noble families from the two isles retained strong links: especially the former royal family of Godwine and the Leinster king Diarmaid. After the loss of kingship to the Normans, Harald Godwinson and his family went on exile with Diarmaid of Leinster (Downham 2004: 67–8). Official relations between Ireland and Britain were not furthered by the fact that, even when relations between William the Conqueror and the new Dublin king improved somewhat, the Irish continued the support of William's Welsh enemies. In the religious context, too, official relations did not improve with the new ruling elite in England. In 1074, Rome gave the English church supremacy over Ireland. Up to the twelfth century, Anglo-Irish official relations thus deteriorated (Downham 2004: 69–71).

In the annals this change of Irish-English relations is reflected by repeated references to the exploits of English forces. In the next step, the annals record Henry's taking power in a detached, polite way:

(12)   There came into Ireland Henry (son of the Empress), most puissant king of England and also Duke of Normandy and Aquitaine and Count of Anjou and Lord of many other lands, with 240 ships. (So that that was the first advent of the Saxons into Ireland.) And he came to land at Port-lairgi and received the pledges of Munster. He came after that to Ath-cliath and received the pledges of Leinster and of the Men of Meath and of the Ui-Briuin and Airgialla and Ulidia. (U1171.10)

(13)   The king of the Saxons (namely, Henry, son of the Empress) went from Ireland on Easter Sunday [*April 16*], after celebration of Mass. (U1172.1)

In the following entries there are some references to Saxon killings of Irish chieftains, particularly to the beheading and later public displaying of the Breifne and Conmaicne king Tigernan Ua Ruairc (Annals of Ulster, U1172.2). But otherwise, little resentment of the arrival of English power on the scene becomes visible in the Ulster Annals of the twelfth century. This is excepting references to the death of Strongbow, whose death is gleefully reported in the Annals of Ulster.

(14)   The Saxon Earl [*Strongbow*] died in Ath-cliath of an ulcer he got on his foot, through the miracles of Brigit and Colum-cille and the saints besides, whose churches he destroyed. (U1176.8)

On the evidence of the Annals of Ulster, we can thus assume that up to the twelfth century, Irish-English relationships within Ireland were on an equal social footing. Given the frequent interested comments on church affairs across the waters, the affinity of the Irish annalists may of course be due to the shared faith of the peoples, largely exported by Irish missionaries. Animosities seem to be directed towards personalities rather than towards ethnicities. It remains an open question, however, to what extent ethnicity would at all have been a relevant concept at this time.

Summing up the events until the late twelfth century, we may say after initial skirmishes between Anglo-Saxons and Irish Gaels, mutually beneficial trade relations and social contacts seem to have been established between the two population groups. On the one hand there were links particularly via the Norsemen who lived both in Britain and Ireland and whose significant contacts with both their British and Gaelic neighbours would have helped to diffuse cultural and linguistic features. The same holds true for the Gaelic settlers in various parts of Britain. On the other hand, extensive trade contacts also developed between Irish Gaels and the English. These contacts of trade partners took place on an economically and socially equal footing and, according to Thomason and Kaufman's (1988) scale would have allowed for casual or slight linguistic contacts between Irish Gaels and Anglo-Saxons. In the terms of Schneider's dynamic model, we can say that these contacts are clearly pre-Foundation phase, as the English settlement started with the arrival of the first English settlers in 1171. In the following we will relate these findings to a study of the available lexical evidence.

6.3.1.1   Linguistic outcomes of the contacts

For the collection of data representing this period, a keyword search was carried out of the electronic version of the *Dictionary of the Irish Language* (*eDIL*, Toner (ed.) 2013). The search was supported by a manual investigation of the print version of this dictionary (Quin (ed.) 1976). The loans stem from Irish roughly prior to the arrival of Anglo-Norman administrators in the late twelfth century. These searches yielded 38 examples of lexical items which are marked, without differentiating between the two, as Anglo-Saxon or Old English loans in the *Dictionary*. The examples contain loanwords that denote new concepts, as well as newly

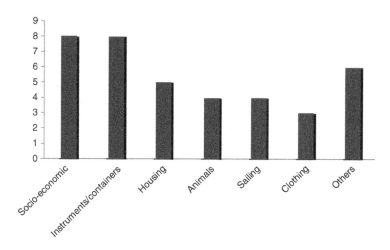

Figure 6.1   Lexical fields of pre-thirteenth-century loanwords in Irish

introduced words for already existing entities. For our purposes here it is more interesting to trace the lexical fields to which these items belong than to investigate the semantic type of loan involved. The loans can be subdivided into lexical fields that indicate in which contexts linguistic borrowing took place. Figure 6.1 shows these lexical fields.

Overall the number of loans is quite small. We find that the most extensive borrowings denote terminology for instruments and household vessels, and socio-economic vocabulary (eight examples each). For instruments and vessels we find *bara*[1] 'barrow', *bleide* 'drinking cup', *cann* 'can', *ciste* 'chest', *copp* 'crest, tuft', *croccán* 'vessel', *poll* 'hole', *rather* 'sieve?'. Loans from the socio-economic sphere include *gabal* 'tax', *lag*[2] 'law', *pinginn* 'penny', *goistibe* 'godparent', *reccaire* 'reciter', *rót* 'road', *scilling* 'shilling', or *spled* 'play'. Both these categories of loanwords are compatible to contacts of the Irish population groups with early English traders and settlers. Furthermore, there are about just as many loans from the domains of housing, animals, clothing and sailing. Loanwords denoting animals are *boc* 'billy-goat', *eobarr*[3] 'boar', *rón* 'seal' and *sebac* 'hawk'. In the case of loanwords from the lexical fields of housing and clothing, it is mostly difficult to determine whether the loanwords were in fact derived from contacts with Old Norse or Old English speakers. *Staire* 'stairs' is thought to be a loan from English, but *halla* 'hall', *stól* 'stool', *rúm* 'room' and *scellbolg* 'wall, shield' may in fact be borrowed from either language. While *briar* 'pin' is thought to be from

Old English, *cnap* 'knob, button' and *lóthar* 'fleece' may derive from contact with either language. Both loans from the domains of housing and clothing would seem to require more than casual contacts among the population groups. The following loans do not fit into any semantic group: *cromm* 'bent', *fae* 'woe', *gib-gab* 'gibberish', *grutt* 'malt', as well as *blinn* 'stittle' and *nes*[4] 'island'. Loanwords from the domain of sailing are typically thought to derive from contact with Old Norse rather than Old English, such as *bát* 'boat', *long* 'boat', *múr* 'mire, sandbank', but *séol* 'shoal' seems to be an English loan. Loans from this semantic field would not seem to necessitate more than trade contacts.

Overall, this collection of Anglo-Saxon loanwords, found in pre-thirteenth-century Irish, seems indeed to mirror trade contacts plus some more extensive contacts due to limited population movement to the extent of Thomason and Kaufman's *slight contacts*. This situation is entirely consistent with the socio-historical situation discussed above.

6.3.2 The Irish and the English during the late medieval period

6.3.2.1 *The historical context*

In the eleventh and twelfth century, Dublin was a thriving, and like the other Viking settlements, independent town with a population of Norse and Irish descent. It was surrounded by territory held by the provincial kings of Leinster, and altercations were frequent. In the mid-twelfth century, a Leinster king, Dermot MacMurrough, was dethroned and in consequence, in 1166, approached Henry II of England for support (Simms 1989: 56–7). Henry, who had been granted the right to rule Ireland by the English Pope Adrian IV earlier during his reign, authorised his subjects to support MacMurrough. The Earl of Pembroke, known as 'Strongbow', was offered MacMurrough's daughter in marriage and the succession to Leinster, and Wexford was promised to further combatants. Their conquest succeeded, and further raids into neighbouring provinces took place. In 1171, Henry II himself arrived to take tributes and fealty not only from Strongbow, but also from kings and chieftains of Limerick, Cork, Leinster, Bréifne, Airgialla and the Ulaid – in other words, from most parts of Ireland except for Connacht, and the Northern and Southern Uí Néill (Simms 1989) and the Irish church soon followed suit. Dublin was granted to the men of Bristol, and the whole province as far as the Shannon was administered by Hugh de Lacy. Predictably, this changed situation draws critical comments by some Irish annalists, but most comments remain neutral in tone. Thus the *Annals of the Four Masters* (O'Donovan (ed.) 1846–50) comment as follows under the headings for 1172 and 1185:

(15) Tiernan O'Rourke, Lord of Breifny and Conmaicne, a man of great power for a long time, was treacherously slain at Tlachtgha by Hugo de Lacy and Donnell, the son of Annadh O'Rourke ... (M1172.4)

(16) The son of the King of England, that is, John, the son of Henry II, came to Ireland with a fleet of sixty ships, to assume the government of the kingdom. He took possession of Dublin and Leinster, and erected castles at Tipraid Fachtna and Ardfinan, out of which he plundered Munster; ... (M1185.6)

While de Lacy's slaying of O'Rourke is labelled as 'treacherous', and plunderings are mentioned, the comments at this time remain moderate and non-partisan overall, and no more critical than they are of other Irishmen. With the Treaty of Windsor 1175, English influence spread, but was not unchallenged. The new lords fortified their feudal holdings and imported tenants, and considerable feuding took place, also amongst the colonisers (Simms 1989: 59–60, 63). Simms (1989: 66) points out that the surnames in the lists of free tenants indicates that knights, free tenants, burgesses and artisans came from England, Wales and Flanders and lived side by side with unfree Irish tenants, while the original Irish nobility was displaced to uncolonised territory. According to the Statutes of Kilkenny from the year 1366, this was a time when

the English of the said land used the English language, mode of riding and apparel, and were governed and ruled, both they and their subjects called Betaghes, according to the English law. (Crowley 2000: 14)

The language of the new nobility was Norman French while English was that of the peasants. Under King John, much of the administration was put into the hands of officials and an increasing number of small freeholdings were created during the thirteenth century. The remaining Gaelic kingdoms had been coming under English control and were administered by Anglo-Norman barons. In order to retain their lands, the Gaelic lords struck an increasing number of personal relationships with the Anglo-Norman nobility, such as marriages (Simms 1989: 79–80). Correspondingly, no clear dividing line between the ethnic Irish on the one hand and the ethnic English on the other hand can be recognised. These blurred lines are reflected by entries in the Annals of the Four Masters under the headings 1178, 1205 and 1221, which state that

    (17)   A victory was gained by Art O'Melaghlin, the people of Offaly, and the English, over the people of Delvin Eathra and Melaghlin Beg, and a part of the men of Teffia; (M1178.10)

    (18)   Meyler [...] took possession of Limerick by force; on account of which a great war broke out between the English of Meath and the English of Meyler... (M1205.11)

    (19)   The son of Hugo de Lacy came to Ireland [i.e. from England, PR], without the consent of the King of England, and joined Hugh O'Neill. Both set out to oppose the English of Ireland, and first went to Coleraine, where they demolished the castle.... (M.1221.3)

From the middle of the thirteenth century onwards, the spread of English settlers was halted when the English suffered defeats both in Donegal in the north and Callan, now Co. Kilkenny, in the south, and a revival of Gaelic culture and learning took place. This cultural upsurge drew in the English settlers as well, to the extent that the head of the English colony, the third Earl of Desmond, was himself famed for the quality of his Irish language poetry (Lydon 1994: 152–4). At this time, too, Anglo-Norman influence had been weakening after the loss of Normandy, and the importance of English rose correspondingly. In addition, the relations between the nobility in Ireland and the English crown were strained by the financial demands of both Edward I and Edward II to finance their other campaigns. In opposition to a native Irish nobility, who had submitted to the English crown, and a partly gaelicised Anglo-Irish nobility, a large absentee class of landowners owned the titles to the land held by local grant-holders or tenants, but lived outside Ireland. This tendency increased after a period of bad harvests and diseases in the mid-fourteenth century, which made the estates unprofitable and unattractive. The decreasing revenues from Ireland were blamed by the English crown on incompetent administration and excessive gaelicisation of the Anglo-Irish nobility (Simms 1989: 79–80).

As a result various expeditions took place from England to try and reconquer the territory, and for the improvement of the situation, the Anglo-Irish nobility were encouraged to keep apart from native Irish culture by laws such as the Statutes of Kilkenny, enacted in 1366. These statutes, written in Norman French, enforce the use of English rather than Irish customs by the Anglo-Irish colonisers in all aspects of Gaelic culture, such as the use of Irish law, language and dress (Simms 1989: 83–8). The preamble to the Statutes states that Englishmen should use English names and the English language and that failure to do so would result in the loss of property (Bliss 1979: 13). Further legislation from different locations throughout the country shows, however, that this effort met with only partial success. Thus, the Statutes of Kilkenny were confirmed by a new act in 1495, which made the same demands. In 1465 it was enacted in the eastern counties of Dublin, Meath, Kildare and Uriel (mainly comprising modern-day Co. Armagh) that Englishmen should take English surnames referring to a town, a colour, a craft or an office. Both Bliss (1979: 13) and Kallen (1994: 152) further point to the Waterford Ordinance (1492–3), which stipulates that

> No manner of man, freeman or foreign, of the city of suburb dwellers, shall plead nor defend in the Irish tongue against any man in the court, but that all they that any matters have in court to be ministered shall have a man that can speak English to declare his matter, except if one party be of the country; then every such dweller shall be at liberty to speak Irish. (Crowley 2000: 17)

These pieces of legislation, the Statutes of Kilkenny and the Waterford Ordinance, illustrate the socially and regionally constrained status of the English language in fourteenth- and fifteenth-century Ireland. This picture of increasing gaelicisation of the English in Ireland, painted by legislation, is confirmed by the sociopolitical developments of the time: the Gaelic lords were not only able to stem the instances of insurgence by representatives of the English crown, but also managed to reclaim large parts of the English-administered lands even in the stronghold of the Pale (Cosgrove 1994: 159). Ireland became ungovernable for the English crown to the extent that long-standing, gaelicised Anglo-Irish families were entrusted with the government of the country while dynastic battles raged in England (Cosgrove 1994: 166–7).

6.3.2.2 *Linguistic outcomes of the contacts*

As the Anglo-Norman lords became increasingly gaelicised, their bilingualism created a good foundation for the diffusion of Anglo-Norman loanwords into Irish (Hickey 2011: 9). Thus a notable number of loanwords from a wide variety of different semantic fields can be found. A manual and semi-automatic search for loanwords in *The Dictionary of the Irish Language* (Quin 1976, Toner 2013) finds 126 loanwords from Anglo-Norman. These centre largely on fighting (18 items), e.g.

caistél 'castle', *copail* 'copel, sword pommel', *scrasaid* 'destroys', *seirsé-nach* 'mercenary', or *túr* 'tower', on government (15 items), such as *buirgé*s 'borough, town', *contae* 'county', *cúirt* court, or *prisún* 'prison', and economy (12 items), such as *airnéis* 'chattel', *cuntas* 'account', *oighir* 'heir', or *táille* 'reckoning'. But also everyday items like food (13 items, e.g. *bitáille* 'victuals', *cabún* 'capon, turkey'), household terms (13 items, e.g. *amáille* 'enamel', *cubairche* 'lidded', *seómra* chamber), instruments (9 items, e.g. *butúr* 'knife', *casúr* 'hammer', *pinnsúr* 'pincers') and animals (9 items, such as *cursún* 'horse', *pertris* 'partridge') are found. Furthermore, there are religious terms (e.g. *aibít* 'habit', *cardináil* 'cardinal'), words for ornaments (*máille* 'ring', *próiste* 'broach', social interaction (*compán* 'companion') and landscape terms (*díc* 'dike', *foraís* 'forest') and other terms, like *pultad,* 'sifting, bolting' or *slapar* 'bandage'.

Overall, the loanwords from Anglo-Norman into Irish indicate words for fighting, government, but also for housing, containers and implements – lexical fields in which Anglo-Saxon loans are also found. Additionally, words for 'fine' food terms are found, as well as for non-domestic animals, where the Anglo-Norman terms largely specify additional, non-basic vocabulary. Close social contacts are also mirrored in the terms for companionship and activities. Furthermore, religious borrowings confirm that the Anglo-Normans were also instrumental in the reorganisation of the church.

This comparison of loanwords from the two languages reflects the larger cultural differences between Gaels and Anglo-Normans than between Gaels and Germanic speakers. But, given that they denote less basic items than the Germanic loans, they also provide linguistic evidence of an even stronger integration of erstwhile Anglo-Norman speakers into Gaelic culture, situated between *slight* and *more intense* contacts in the terminology of Thomason and Kaufman (1988). This integration is also evidenced in early literature. Thus, a collection of poems compiled around 1330 in an Anglo-Norman context in Ireland, the so-called *Kildare Poems* (Lucas (ed.) 1995), contains Latin and French poems, as well as English ones. There are also some cultural loans from the Irish language, such as *russin* 'light afternoon meal':

(20)   In Cokaigne is met and drink, /With-vte care, how and swink.
       The met is trie, the drink is clere, /To none, *russin* and sopper.
       'In Cokaygne there is food and drink without sorrow, anxiety
       and toil. The food is excellent, the drink is pure, for mid-day
       meal, light collation and supper.' (l. 17–20, Lucas (ed.) 1995, cf.
       Ronan 2013: 77–8)

The language of the poems is Middle English and shows strong signs of cultural transfer. The linguistic background of the author, or authors, is unknown. One poem is attributed to one Michael of Kildare, and his epithet suggests an origin close to Dublin. The poems show a number of dialect features, some of which have been argued to be due to Irish influence and indicative of a distinctive emerging Irish English variety (Hickey 1993, Hickey 2007). Some literary motifs and uses of loanwords point to an English- and French-speaking author strongly familiar with Irish tradition.

6.3.2.3 Schneider's Dynamic Model and medieval Ireland

If we view these socio-historical and sociolinguistic factors in the context of Schneider's Dynamic Model of the spread of English, the following picture emerges. According to Schneider's model, at the time of stabilisation of the settler community (Phase 2: Exonormative Stabilisation), we typically find that administrative affairs are carried out in the settlers' language, which is indeed the case in Ireland during the thirteenth, fourteenth and fifteenth centuries. We also expect growing bilingualism of the indigenous population, and increasing intermarriage, and the latter is also to be found here. Consequently, as shown above, we can see that the settlers' language acquires some loanwords from the local language. However, at this stage it is not so much the settler population which provides the new cultural norm; instead, the settlers show strong orientation towards indigenous cultural and linguistic norms. Rather than the indigenous population treating English as an asset, the settlers are sufficiently disenfranchised from England to forgo sociopolitical and thus linguistic allegiances with their country of origin in favour of sociocultural integration into Gaelic culture. This situation leads to a stabilisation of large parts of the culture not according to English, but Gaelic norms. In terms of Schneider's model, this represents a reverse direction of accommodation that is not envisaged in the model.

6.3.3 Further developments in the post-medieval period

Gaelic norms, culture and language remained strong with the, albeit intermittent, rule of the Anglo-Irish families up to the early sixteenth century. However, with the accession to power of Henry VIII, the English crown took a stronger interest again. Henry initially failed to restore obedience to the English crown, but when challenged by a revolt in 1534, he took steps to restore his power (Cosgrave 1994: 172). Henry VIII was finally proclaimed king of Ireland by the Irish parliament in 1541, and the proclamation was read out in Irish. Kallen (1994: 153–4) sees the use of the Irish language as a symbolic act rather than due to lack of English on the Irish nobles' part. Irish certainly continued to be used in official state matters, e.g. by the lord of Sligo, O'Connor, when presenting himself to Queen Elizabeth I in 1568 (Kallen 1994: 154), and the chronicler Stanyhurst denounces the contraction of the English-speaking Pale area around Dublin in 1577, stating that the English population have 'so acquainted themselves with the Irishe, as they have made a mingle mangle, or gallamaulfrey of both languages' (Kallen 1994: 154, cf. Ronan 2013: 80). This statement paints Stanyhurst's position as a speaker of an exonormative variety of English, who adheres to a common standard and, in keeping with a complaint tradition, still orientated towards the colonial standard, denounces the very strong nativisation of speakers of English, who identify with the Irish culture and admit several local lexical items and some grammatical features into their language. Here, again, we encounter a situation in which it is not the non-English speakers who bring linguistic contact features into the English language, but the population groups of the settlers themselves who show strong evidence of the influence of the Irish language on their English. Thus Nativisation, Phase 3 of Schneider's Dynamic Model, is influenced by the vernacular features of the gaelicised former settler populations, and, in contrast to Schneider's model, perhaps more so than by the not yet extensively anglicised Irish-speaking population.

This situation changed, however, with the second colonial expansion, which arrived in Ireland with the Plantations of Ulster, mainly driven by settlers from northern England and Scotland, in the early seventeenth century, and the campaigns into the south of Ireland by midland and southern British (Canny 1989). Following these incursions, post-1650, the largest percentage of English speakers are to be found in towns, and the administration is in the hands of English speakers (Kallen 1994: 157–8). As argued in Ronan (2013), it is at this stage that a second settlement of Ireland by English speakers takes place and a new stabilisation process gets under way (the Second Period of Irish English, Hickey 2007). In contrast to other English-speaking countries worldwide this new stabilisation is based on the two differing dialect models in the north and the south of Ireland. Over time, the Catholic middle classes increasingly shift to English in search of socio-economic improvement (Wall 1969: 82–5), resulting in Schneider's Phase 3, Nativisation of English, and concomitantly Endonormative Stabilisation, Phase 4, characterised by self-dependence, as the use of English increased in daily life in the eighteenth and nineteenth centuries.

6.4   Discussion

Our survey of historical data shows that pre-thirteenth-century English-Irish contacts led to borrowing on the basis of social equality, i.e. before colonialisation took place and when contacts were on the level of neighbourly trade contacts. The evidence of loanwords from English into Irish bears this out completely: the types and the lexical fields of the loans are consistent with casual and slight contacts through trade and neighbourly relations, and the relative scarcity of loanwords is in keeping with a restricted contact situation.

The contact situation changed after the first English colonialisation in the late twelfth century. In colonial terms, the settlement of Anglo-Norman nobles, with their retinue, particularly of English-speakers, proved only partly successful. While Ireland initially seems to have been able to produce generous revenues for the English crown, the settlers in Ireland increasingly nativised. Thus, while some Irish-speakers doubtlessly learnt at least some English and Norman French, the settlers adopted Gaelic customs and the Irish language on a large scale. This was supported considerably by intermarriage and by political and economic allegiances between the two population groups. The historical data further reveals considerable friction between different strands of English settlers in Ireland, as well as some political instability in England during the first centuries of English settlement. These factors would not have encouraged the settler population to retain a distinct identity as Anglo-Normans, or English, nor indeed the Gaelic population to aim for acculturation to the Anglo-Normans. Rather, the sociocultural context encouraged the settlers to adopt elements of Gaelic culture, along with the Irish language. In this respect the early contact situation in Ireland differs considerably from the more recent contact situations that are reviewed by Schneider (2003, 2007) and on which his Dynamic Model of the spread of English is founded.

It is only with the second colonialisation phase, starting in the seventeenth century, that the original nativised settlers are disempowered. It is the new settlers who introduce new linguistic, separate standards for the north and the south of the country, and form a new socio-economically superior settler community. Consequently it is after the eighteenth century that large indigenous population strands undergo language shift. As argued in Ronan (2013), a further difference between the linguistic situation in Ireland and other postcolonial varieties of English results from the different settlement histories in the north and the south of the country: in Ireland dialect differentiation of the English language started at the very beginning of the second colonialisation due to the different geographic origins of the settlers. Dialect differentiation thus starts at a considerably earlier stage in the evolution of Irish English than in other international varieties. Correspondingly, while further research may show that, early dialect differentiation apart, Schneider's model can account quite well for the development of Irish English after 1600, the socio-historical situation in pre-seventeenth-century Ireland was not conducive to large-scale linguistic change.

6.5 Conclusion

This study has set out to trace the circumstances and the linguistic effects of medieval Gaelic and English contacts. We have seen that the earliest contacts took place on the basis of neighbourly relations. At this time, the relative socio-economic status of both population groups was on an equal footing maintained by common trade interests. The linguistic effects of these early contacts correspond to what is described as typical of such, largely casual, contacts: we find loanwords from English into Irish denoting new concepts that arose from linguistic contacts between the population groups.

It is with the beginning of settlement by Anglo-Normans and English groups in the later twelfth century that more intensive contacts took place. However, in contrast to other international contact situations in which settlers from England were involved, the initial phases of settlement did not lead to gradual language change of the indigenous population groups to English. Instead, the relative sociocultural relations between the two population groups did not favour continued identification of large proportions of the settler community with their country of origin. Consequently the settlers adopted strong Gaelic identities, which even repeated legislation could not counteract. The linguistic result of this was considerable linguistic transfer from the settler language to the indigenous language, caused by large-scale language shift from Norman French and from English to Irish. Hence during the Middle Ages in Ireland the model of language shift proposed by Schneider (2003) is not applicable as the model requires continued identification with the settler community during the initial phases of settlement.

Notes

1. *Bara* may conceivably either be an Anglo-Saxon or an Old Norse loan (*eDIL*, s.v. *bara*)

2. *Lag* may conceivably have been loaned either from Old Norse or Old English.
3. *Eobarr* may be loaned from Old English or from Old Norse.
4. Both *blinn* and *stittle* might either have been borrowed from Old English or Old Norse.

References

Bliss, Alan (1979). *Spoken English in Ireland 1600–1740*. Dublin: Cadenus Press.
Canny, Nicholas (1989). 'Early Modern Ireland', in: Roy F. Foster (ed.) *The Oxford Illustrated History of Ireland*. Oxford: Oxford University Press, pp. 104–60.
Cosgrove, Art (1994). 'The Gaelic Resurgence and the Geraldine supremacy', in: Theodore W. Moody and Francis X. Martin (eds) *The Course of Irish History*. Dublin: Mercier Press, pp. 158–73.
Crowley, Tom (2000). *The Politics of Language in Ireland 1366–1922. A Source Book.* London: Routledge.
Crystal, David (2002). *Language Death.* Second edition. Cambridge: Cambridge University Press.
Downham, Clare (2004). 'England and the Irish Sea zone in the eleventh century', *Anglo-Norman Studies* 26: 55–72.
Fischer, Andreas (2003). 'Lexical borrowing and the history of English: a typology of typologies', in: Dieter Kastovsky and Arthur Mettinger (eds) *Language Contact in the History of English*. Frankfurt: Peter Lang, pp. 97–116.
Hickey, Raymond (1993). 'The beginnings of Irish English', *Folia Linguistica Historica* 14: 213–38.
Hickey, Raymond (2007). *Irish English. History and Present-day Forms.* Cambridge: Cambridge University Press.
Hickey, Raymond (2010). 'Language Contact: Reconsideration and Reassessment', in: Raymond Hickey (ed.) *Handbook of Language Contact.* Maldon: Wiley-Blackwell, pp. 1–28.
Hickey, Raymond (2011). 'The Languages of Ireland', in: Raymond Hickey (ed.) *Researching the Languages of Ireland.* Uppsala: Uppsala University Press, pp. 1–45.
Kallen, Jeffrey (1994). 'English in Ireland', in: Robert Burchfield (ed.) *The Cambridge History of the English Language* Vol. V. Cambridge: Cambridge University Press, pp. 148–96.
Lucas, Angela M. (ed.) (1995). *Anglo-Irish Poems of the Middle Ages.* Dublin: Columba Press.
Lydon, James F. (1994). 'The medieval English colony', in: Theodore W. Moody and Francis X. Martin (eds) *The Course of Irish History.* Dublin: Mercier Press, pp. 144–57.
Mac Airt, Seán and Gearóid Mac Niocaill (eds and transl.) (1983). *The Annals of Ulster.* Dublin: Dublin Institute for Advanced Studies.
Ó Corráin, Donnchadh (1989). 'Prehistoric and Early Christian Ireland', in: Roy F. Forster (ed.) *The Oxford Illustrated History of Ireland.* Oxford: Oxford University Press, pp. 1–52.
O'Donovan, John (ed. and transl.) (1846–1850). *Annala Rioghachta Eireann: Annals of the kingdom of Ireland by the Four Masters.* Reprint 1990. Dublin: Hodges and Smith.

Quin, E. Gordon (ed.) (1976). *Dictionary of the Irish Language*. Dublin: Royal Irish Academy.

Ronan, Patricia (2013). 'L'évolution de la langue anglaise en Irlande', *Ireland and its Contacts/L'Irlande et ses contacts. Cahiers de l'ILSL* 38: 73–91.

Schneider, Edgar W. (2003). 'The dynamics of New Englishes', *Language* 79.2: 233–81.

Schneider, Edgar W. (2007). *Postcolonial Englishes*. Cambridge: Cambridge University Press.

Schneider, Edgar W. (2014). 'New reflections on the evolutionary dynamics of world Englishes', *World Englishes* 33.1: 9–32.

Simms, Katharine (1989). 'The Norman invasion and the Gaelic recovery', in: Roy F. Forster (ed.) *The Oxford Illustrated History of Ireland*. Oxford: Oxford University Press, pp. 53–103.

Stokes, Whitley (ed. and transl.) (1895–6). *The Annals of Tigernach*. Reprint 1993. Felinfach: Llanerch Publishers.

Thomason, Sarah Grey (2001). *Language Contact. An Introduction*. Edinburgh: Edinburgh University Press.

Thomason, Sarah Grey and Terrence Kaufman (1988). *Language Contact, Creolization and Genetic Linguistics*. Berkeley: University of California Press.

Toner, Gregory (ed.) (2013). *Electronic Dictionary of the Irish Language (eDIL)*. Available at http://edil.qub.ac.uk/about.php. Last accessed 15 September 2014.

Wall, Maureen (1969). 'The decline of the Irish language', in: Brian Ó Cuív (ed.) *A View of the Irish Language*. Dublin: Stationery Office, pp. 81–90.

7

From Early Modern Ireland to the Great Famine

Liam Mac Mathúna

7.1 Introduction

In the centuries that followed the Anglo-Norman invasion of 1169 the vast majority of the population of Ireland continued to speak Irish, mostly in the countryside, while English predominated in the towns and cities, as well as in the area around Dublin, known as the Pale. However, pressure on Irish as a vernacular mounted when the Tudor dynasty equated English-speaking with loyalty to the crown and Irish with disloyalty. This policy was given formal expression in 'An Act for the English Order, Habit, and Language', passed by the Dublin Parliament in 1537. In its introduction, the act drew a distinction between the King's loyal, English-speaking population in the Pale and those dwelling in the rest of the country, of whom it was stated that there was 'nothing which doth more contain and keep many of his subjects of this his said land, in a certain savage and wild kind and manner of living, than the diversity that is betwixt them in tongue, language, order, and habit' (Crowley 2000: 21). It was therefore to be enacted 'That every person or persons, the King's true subjects, inhabiting this land of Ireland, of what estate, condition, or degree he or they be, or shall be, to the uttermost of their power, cunning, and knowledge, shall use and speak commonly the English tongue and language' (Crowley 2000: 22). Although the ideological, institutional and administrative underpinning of this colonial policy was strongly developed during the sixteenth century, it was not until the following century that it began to bear tangible fruit in the wake of the Ulster (1609) and Cromwellian (1652) plantations and the further confiscation of land from the native Catholics following the enactment of the Penal Laws, from 1695 onwards. The dominant role of the English language in the realms of politics, public administration and commerce set the scene for the vernacular language shift from Irish to English from about 1730 onwards, initially in the east of the country, and for the expanding use of Irish/English code-mixing by the increasingly bilingual native population.

The phenomenon of language shift has often been associated with the nineteenth century and primarily attributed to three major societal events: (1) the establishment of the Royal College of St Patrick's at Maynooth, Co. Kildare, as an English-speaking seminary for the preparation of the country's Catholic clergy in 1795, (2) the founding of the National Schools in 1831 as a monolingual primary education system for all children, regardless of their mother tongue, and (3) the ravages of the Great Famine of 1845–50, which had a disproportionate impact on the poorer, rural, Irish-speaking population, killing 1 million people and prompting another million to emigrate. However, these developments really only accelerated the second stage of the language shift, in Connacht and Munster in particular, but they did occur at a time when awareness of the language change was increasing and people were seeking to link cause and effect. In recent decades there has been increasing scholarly interest in the evidence for vibrant urban Irish-speaking communities, 1700–1850, formed initially by migrants from the countryside, so that the language shift is now better interpreted within the general west European transition from traditional communities to modernity, which in the particular circumstances of the Irish situation was accompanied by language change (Burke 2009, Briggs and Burke 2007, Buttimer 1993, Mac Mathúna 1991, Mac Mathúna and Uí Chollatáin forthcoming, Ó Buachalla 1968, Ó Madagáin 1974).

Nonetheless, the story of Irish in the three centuries following the proclaiming of Henry VIII as King of Ireland by the 'Crown of Ireland Act' of 1542, down to the traumatic societal implosion caused by the Great Famine is one of apparently inexorable language shift from Irish to English. While this was probably an inevitable consequence of the implacable antagonism of the dominant English polity to native Irish culture, critical analysis would suggest that it was facilitated by intellectual and conceptual failings within Gaelic Ireland. A crucial and ultimately fatal weakness of the native response to the pressure from the English language in the new public sphere of anglicised common law, administration and commerce was the failure to envision Irish/English bilingualism as an attainable compromise solution which might have served to keep English at bay and to maintain Irish, (at least in the private sphere, as happened in Wales, for example) until the final quarter of the nineteenth century. What was lacking was an ideology developed within the Irish-speaking community which would have conceptualised a certain accommodation with English, marking out and retaining a range of domains and registers for Irish, rather than ceding all to English, and allowing the Irish nation to morph into 'a new England by the name of Ireland' (*Saxa nua dan hainm Éire*) or a 'young England' (*Saxa óg*), as foreseen by perceptive early-seventeenth-century poets (Mac Mathúna 2007: 23).

7.2   Gaelic Ireland and attitudes to English

Gaelic Ireland seems to have lacked the intellectual verve that might have given rise to such a bilingual resolution of the language crux. It is not that the country didn't have first-rate thinkers and doers – Flaithrí Ó Maolchonaire OFM (*c.*1560–1629), consummate Churchman and politician, immediately comes to mind – but the upper echelons of native Irish society were content to embrace the dominant ideology of the day, post-Council of Trent Counter-Reformation Catholicism (Hazard 2010). However, some such as the Waterford-born Peter Lombard, who was appointed archbishop of Armagh in December 1601, made diligent efforts to justify the continuing war being waged against Elizabeth by Ó Néill and his allies, characterising it as 'a struggle for the vindication of the Catholic religion, the glory of God, the liberty of their country and their own security' (quoted in Hazard 2010: 38).

Indeed, it has to be acknowledged that language competition and conflict between speakers of Irish and English had long been a feature of social reality in Ireland, and was quite independent of top-down royal enactments and regulations. Ongoing tensions at home between the English-speaking Catholics of Dublin and other towns in Leinster and Munster, who tended to favour the Jesuits, and the more or less exclusively Irish-speaking provinces of Connacht and Ulster where the Franciscans were in the ascendant, could boil over in the pressurised competition for resources and patronage within the *émigré* communities on the Continent. Thus, for example, Flaithrí Ó Maolchonaire and Aodh Rua Ó Domhnaill alleged in 1602 that Thomas White of Clonmel, Jesuit rector of the Irish College at Salamanca, excluded entrants from Connacht and Ulster families, encouraged obedience to the English monarchy and showed a disregard for the use of the Irish language among the student body (Hazard 2010: 39, 67). While Tadhg Ó Cianáin in his account of the Earls' journey, 1607–8 (written up in Rome, 1609–10) uses the term *Éireannach* 'Irishman' exclusively, thereby avoiding sectional designations such as *Gaedheal* 'native (Irish-speaking)

Irishman' (Walsh 1916, Ó Muraíle 2007), Ó Maolchonaire, writing in Spain in 1605, consistently highlighted the differences between the native Irish and the Old English, whom he characterised as *los irlandeses inglesados* 'the Anglicised Irish', a term which re-emerged in Gaelic petitions from 1611 onwards (Hazard 2010: 52, 73). On the other hand, the phrase *Old English* was first used by the Englishman Edmund Spenser in *A View of the State of Ireland* (1596), while Richard Stanihurst, a Dubliner himself, had called this group *Anglo-Hiberni* in Latin in *De Rebus in Hibernia Gestis* (1584), and Fynes Moryson, an Englishman like Spenser, used the term *the English-Irish* (Crowley 2005: 11).

As behoved one who held the post of Attorney General in Ireland, John Davies, writing in *A Discovery of the True Causes Why Ireland Was Never Entirely Subdued* (1612), put his faith in the implementation of the law, which could follow on from the conquering of the country, and he clearly had no qualms about calling a spade a spade: 'So a barbarous country must first be broken by a war before it will be capable of good government;... For that I call a perfect conquest of a country which doth reduce all people thereof to the condition of subjects; and those I call subjects which are governed by the ordinary laws and magistrates of the sovereign' (Davies 1612, quoted in Crowley 2000: 58). He was decidedly optimistic about the way matters were developing following the defeat of Aodh Ó Néill:

> Civil assemblies at assizes and sessions have reclaimed the Irish from their wildness, caused them to cut off their glibs and long hair, to convert their mantles into cloaks, to conform themselves to the manner of England in all their behaviour and outward forms. And because they find a great inconvenience in moving their suits by an interpreter, they do for the most part send their children to schools, especially to learn the English language; so as we may conceive an hope that the next generation will in tongue and heart and every way else become English, so as there will be no difference or distinction but the Irish sea betwixt us. And thus we see a good conversion and the Irish game turned again.

> For heretofore the neglect of the law made the English degenerate and become Irish; and now, on the other side, the execution of the law doth make the Irish grow civil and become English. (Davies 1612, quoted in Crowley 2000: 60)

Displaying the pragmatic perspective of an economist, William Petty advocated the use of English on practical grounds in his *Political*

Anatomy of Ireland, written in 1672 and published in 1691, advising the Irish 'to decline their Language' because it

> continues a sensible distinction, being not now necessary, which makes those who do not understand it suspect, that what is spoken in it, is to their prejudice. It is in their Interest to deal with the *English*, for Leases, for Time, and upon clear Conditions, which being perform'd they are absolute Freemen, rather than to stand always liable to the humour and caprice of their Landlords, and to have everything taken away from them which he pleases to fancy. (Petty 1691, quoted in Crowley, 2000: 89, Crowley 2005: 73)

7.3　Learned reaction and macaronic verse in eighteenth-century Ireland

The overthrow of the native Irish landowning aristocracy was inevitably followed by the demise of the learned classes who had depended on their patronage. Although medical men seem to have fared better than the lawyers, chroniclers and poets, institutions such as the bardic schools had become a thing of the past by the mid-seventeenth century. Many of those who would have become a *fili* (later *file*) 'poet' or *seanchaidh* (later *seanchaí*) 'chronicler, historian' in an earlier generation, joined the Church, the Franciscan Order in particular, and under its patronage printed a significant series of Counter-Reformation Irish-language texts in the Low Countries in the first half of the seventeenth century, from 1611 onwards. In Ireland itself, the Church of Ireland published Irish versions of a Catechism (1571), the New Testament (1602), the Book of Common Prayer (1608) and the Old Testament (1685) in what was a rather leisurely publishing schedule (Williams 1986). Alongside these printing innovations, one saw great manuscript works such as *Annála Ríoghachta Éireann*, 'The Annals of the Four Masters', overseen by the Louvain-based Michél Ó Cléirigh, and Séathrún Céitinn's *Foras Feasa ar Éirinn*, 'The History of Ireland', both compiled and written in the 1630s, and which circulated in manuscript until they were published in the nineteenth and twentieth centuries, respectively. These were ambitious projects, majestic in scope, and in the case of Céitinn in particular achieved fame on the basis of the attractiveness of their prose style, as well as the compelling ideology of their content. Poets such as Piaras Feiritéar, Dáibhí Ó Bruadair, Aogán Ó Rathaille and Eoghan Rua Ó Súilleabháin, to name just some of the more renowned, continued to invigorate the Irish language itself, although, with the exception of groups such as the Ó Neachtain circle in Dublin, one does not get much of a sense of genre innovation (Mac Mathúna 2012b).

Ironically, one way the literati had of maintaining their social status was by maximising their linguistic prowess and adding English to their existing repertoire of Irish and Latin. This they displayed, inter alia, by dexterous code-mixing, that is to say, the employment of English in an ancillary role to Irish in predominantly Irish language texts. Prompted originally by the increasing permeation of English in Ireland from the Elizabethan era onwards, Irish/English literary code-mixing remained largely a matter of individual creative choice up to about 1750. However, the phenomenon of societal code-mixing became more widespread during the eighteenth century, as native Irish society grew increasingly bilingual (Mac Mathúna 2007). This resulted in particular in compositions in the *barántas* or warrant genre and macaronic love songs, alongside religious compositions and burlesque prose tales (Mac Mathúna 2012a). Virtually all of these compositions were aimed at bilingual domestic audiences who would have had a varying degree of command of the two languages.

The linguistic virtuosity of some of the macaronic warrants is quite impressive, as can be seen from the following, intricate, example from Co. Cork:

(1) *Whereas this day* do réir réim chirt an chalandair,
   I received information le héifeacht go dearfa,
   The warrant I gave, much le faobhar chum an fhairceallaigh,
   He's got a supersedeas le *means* chum é sheachaint air.

   To all bums and bailiffs ó Bhéarra don Mhainistir,
   Constables, gaolers, is gach éinne dhen aicme sin,
   Let none take his orders barántas ná atharach,
   Atá a theideal ar lár óm' láimhse gan dearmad.

This may be translated as follows:

(2) *Whereas this day* according to the course of justice of the calendar,
   I received information with import positively,
   The warrant I gave, much with energy after the lump (of a man)
   He's got a supersedeas with means to avoid it against him.

   To all bums and bailiffs from Beare to Mainistir,
   Constables, gaolers, and everyone of that class,

Let none take his orders warrant or alternative,
His title is wanting from my hand without mistake.

(Mac Mathúna 2012a: 122)

In another composition, this time a love song, the poet tells us that when he saw a girl 'I knew by her gazing she'd play the Hide and Go Seek', and proceeds:

(3)   Do dhruideas féin léi agus d'iarras póigín nó trí,
      The answer she made, 'Young blade you are making too free',
      Is é a dúirt mé féin léi gur bheannaigh sí domhsa róbhinn,
      'And I'd like for to teach you to play the Hide and Go Seek'.

      Do fhreagair an spéirbhean agus dúirt sí gur aerach mo shlí:
      'I'll tarry a while until more of the world I'll see,
      Táimse ró-óg, cúig déag an fómhar seo 'imigh dínn,
      Though I'd like a good dale to play the Hide and Go Seek'.

The following would represent a translation of the above:

(4)   I moved close to her and asked for a little kiss or three,
      The answer she made, 'Young blade you are making too free',
      I said to her that she addressed me most sweetly,
      'And I'd like for to teach you to play the Hide and Go Seek'.

      The beauty answered and said that I had a merry way,
      'I'll tarry a while until more of the world I'll see,
      I am too young, fifteen this autumn past,
      Though I'd like a good dale to play the Hide and Go Seek'.

(Mac Mathúna 2012a: 127)

One poem where the code-mixing medium facilitates opposing messages is *As I was walking one evening fair* by Donnchadh Rua Mac Conmara, set in Newfoundland, in which the poet exploits the fact that only part of his audience would have understood both languages. This allowed the poet to indulge himself and his bilingual Irish-born audience at the expense of the monolingual English speakers of Newfoundland. This song also reminds us that Irish always had an international reach. The English half-verses express politically loyal and socially agreeable sentiments, whereas the Irish are disaffected and abusive. Thus, Mac Conmara alternately praises and reviles the power of King George:

(5) *Come, drink, a health, boys, to Royal George,*
        Our chief commander – nár ordaigh Críost,
        Is aitchimis ar Mhuire Mháthair,
        É féin is a ghardaí a leagadh síos.

        Come, drink, a health, boys, to Royal George,
            Our chief commander – which Christ never ordained,
        Let us beseech Mary Mother of God,
            To strike down his guards and himself.

(Mac Mathúna 2012a: 131–2)

The gap between the two messages is even greater in regard to the comments on some of Newfoundland's womenfolk:

(6) *Here you may find a virtuous lady,*
        A smiling fair one to please the eye—
        An paca straipeanna is measa tréithe,
        Is go mbeiread féin ar bheith as a radharc.

        Here you may find a virtuous lady,
        A smiling fair one to please the eye—
        A pack of whores with the worst of traits.
        And I would be better off to be out of their sight.

(Mac Mathúna 2012a: 131–2)

However, it is not until the early eighteenth century in the scholarly circle formed around Seán and Tadhg Ó Neachtain, in the urban environment of Dublin, that one finds evidence of the innovative thinking that might have given rise to a programme of structured bilingualism: the Ó Neachtains and their circle displayed the requisite intellectual openness, vibrancy and capacity for innovation. Their rich and varied scholarly output shows clearly that they were at home with urban living and modernity (Mac Mathúna 2012b, Mac Mathúna 2013).

In fact, the process of language change was referred to specifically by Tadhg Ó Neachtain in an astute passage in his geography text, *Eólas ar an Domhan* 'Knowledge of the World' (early 1720s), in which he shows his awareness of contemporary sociocultural developments. He was quite conscious that a language shift from Irish to English was taking place among the better-off native Irish at the time, stating explicitly that the nobility were turning their backs on Irish, but were steadfast in their attachment to the Catholic religion. When broaching the subject, he adverts to the traditional attachment of the Gaelic nobles to the Irish language, stressing the regard in which it had been held by all classes since olden times:

> Alas now there is no one of the nobility of the Gaelic people who is not denying their tongue, selling off their names and the pride of Gael Glas and the people of that Míle who journeyed to us from Spain under a great shade of bravery, poetry, and learning. And when they established themselves, Irish was respected, here and yonder, and in every place as a language of the soil, fluent, abundant, lively, precise, swift, tasty, sweet, and that for thousands of years up to now […]
>
> And from all this it may be appreciated that it was held in great esteem by the king as well as the labourer; and now it is as the tallest tree, when it is cut under its base, it is much more dreadful and heavier to fell than the little shrubbery which is close to the ground. The same fate certainly befell the nobility of the Gaels as regards their language. (Ní Chléirigh (ed.) 1944: 12–13; translation by the author)

Thus, there was a language shift under way from Irish to English among the native Irish in the Dublin of Tadhg Ó Neachtain's day. However, we have other, even more arresting evidence, this time from Tadhg's father Seán, which is by no means so sanguine about the pre-eminence of English. Seán actually upbraids the Virgin Mary and bemoans the fact that she had disregarded his prayers. According to Tadhg, Seán composed the following lines on his deathbed (1729):

> (7) I prayed to Mary Mother of God
> very devoutly, like everyone,
> because I didn't speak English
> she didn't pay attention to my prayer.
>
> The people who don't accept her
> they are the strongest in the land;
> the group who gave her reverence
> it is a pity that they are in bondage to foreigners.
>
> (From TCD H 4 20, p. 124, quoted in Risk
> 1975: 59, translation by the author)

Given his lifelong commitment to Irish language scholarship, these verses suggest a despondency verging on despair. They recall an earlier poem, from 1715, which may also have been composed by Seán. In this, the poet expresses estrangement from St Patrick who, he points out, is after all a Briton (*Breathnach*): therefore it comes as no great surprise to find that Patrick is of little use to the Irish in their struggle with their English neighbours. The poet argues that the Irish should have been steadfast in their allegiance to their own native saints, including Colum Cille, Brighid and Éanna, and not accorded Patrick a pre-eminent position:

(8) Nature is stronger than nurture
I will not hide it from you, o Patrick,
that it is your relationship with the English
which has given our enemy his strength.

(Ní Shéaghdha 1983: 67, translation
by the author)

A related question is that of the amount of contact, interaction and cultural exchange which is likely to have taken place between Irish and English speakers in Dublin in the early decades of the eighteenth century. Cathal Ó Háinle (1986) has examined the case for influence from the Ó Neachtain circle on Jonathan Swift, which would have put the Dean in a position to provide a translation of the song *Pléaráca na Ruarcach*, 'O'Rourkes' Revels', attributed to Aodh Mac Gabhráin from Co. Cavan. Swift's translation is just one of what must have been many instances of the social and cultural divide in Dublin and throughout the country being bridged by music and song. In a similar vein, Alan Harrison has traced Tadhg Ó Neachtain's friendship with Anthony Raymond, a Church of Ireland minister, graduate and fellow of Trinity College Dublin, who provided a significant link which afforded the Ó Neachtain circle indirect access to Trinity's library. It was through Raymond that they gained access to the *Book of Ballymote*, an important manuscript (written *c.*1390) which he borrowed from Trinity in 1719 and which Tadhg held on to after Raymond's death, it remaining in the former's possession until 1743. In fact it never made its way back to Trinity College and is now in the keeping of the Royal Irish Academy (Harrison 1988: 78–9, Harrison 1999: 95–9).

7.4 Bilingualism in eighteenth- and nineteenth-century Irish society

Although there is no direct statistical information available as regards the numbers of Irish-speakers in the country in the eighteenth century, Garret FitzGerald has succeeded in projecting nineteenth-century figures back as far as the cohort of people born in the decade 1771–81. A question about ability to speak Irish was included by way of a footnote in the census questionnaires of 1851, 1861 and 1871. This question was only embodied in the main section of the census form in 1881. On the basis of sophisticated reworking of the various statistics, FitzGerald has calculated that 10 per cent or fewer of the children born in the period 1771–81 were raised with Irish in the seven Leinster counties of Carlow, Dublin, Kildare, Laois, Offaly, Wexford and Wicklow, and the three Ulster counties of Antrim, Down and Derry. The overall figures calculated by FitzGerald for the cohort of Irish speakers born in the period 1801–11 in each of the four provinces were Leinster 11 per cent, Munster 77 per cent, Connacht 80 per cent and Ulster 15 per cent, giving a grand total percentage of 41 per cent for the entire country. Although the language change was therefore destined to be a predominantly nineteenth-century phenomenon in much of Munster and Connacht (and in Co. Donegal), this analysis provides overwhelming evidence for earlier language transition in over half the country.

A particular feature of the Irish situation in the nineteenth century is worthy of mention, namely the telescoped rapidity with which the language shift could take place as the change gathered momentum. Máirtín Ó Murchú has compared evidence from two areas within Co. Limerick: he found that the abandonment of Irish in the barony of Kilmallock was particularly rapid, taking just five decades to decline from 100 per cent among those born in 1811–21 to 3 per cent in 1861–71, whereas a similar but slightly earlier decline in the barony of Pubblebrien occurred over six decades, i.e. from 100 per cent in 1791–1801 to 3 per cent in 1851–61 (Ó Murchú 1988: 81). Of course, both examples underline the fact that Irish/English bilingualism was very much in a transient state, a mere train-station pause on the journey from one language to the other, so to speak.

Travellers can give us lively accounts of how Irish/English linguistic interaction was actually happening in the community, thereby complementing the raw statistical figures. For instance, we learn from Arthur Young in *A Tour in Ireland* (1778) of an initiative whereby Lord Shannon paid bounties amounting to £50 per annum to labourers: 'He gives it them by way of encouragement; but only to such as can speak English, and do something more than fill a cart' (Crowley 2000: 124). Karl Gottlob Küttner, a German parson's son from Saxony, visited the country in the summers of 1783 and 1784 in order to tutor the children of the Earl of Tyrone, George de la Poer Beresford in Curraghmore Estate near Portlaw, Co. Waterford. As his account of the language situation is that of a Continental observer, it is particularly valuable. It describes a linguistically opaque, ambivalent world where all seem to know English, but most actually use Irish:

> Today I wish to write about [...] the language spoken by the Irish. You know that this nation has its own, but you will find it disconcerting that among people of high rank almost no-one is to be found who understands it. Most of them have not the slightest knowledge of it and know no other language besides English. In fact all school instruction and all religious services are conducted through English, which almost everyone understands – at least the exceptions are seldom. At the same time the vast majority of the nation speaks Irish. The common masses speak no other language among themselves. There are no books in the language except for some prayer books and the Bible, and I am not even sure whether this exists in its entirety in Irish. Often when I found a group of country people together I listened with great concentration and yet was not in the least able to understand. It is very guttural, even more so than the Zurich dialect, and quite unpleasant to the ear. (Bourke 2013: 30–1; translation of Küttner 1785)

Whether the religious services alluded to include those of the Catholic Church as well as the Church of Ireland is impossible to tell from this account. Given the size of the country, and variations in circumstances and occasions over time, it is scarcely surprising that different visitors should recount different experiences, reflecting the practical complexity of the situation on the ground. Interestingly, John Bernard Trotter, born in Downpatrick, Co. Down, found that 'the Irish language is spoken almost generally in the county of Wexford', a supposedly very 'English' part of Leinster, as late as 1812 (Woods 2009: 32). Similarly, another traveller, Atkinson, was surprised in 1815 to find prosperous Kilkenny farmers speaking only Irish, and he remarked in particular on the 'extensive pig breeders and dairymen of the Walsh mountains who cannot speak a single sentence of plain English' (Whelan 1999: 135). The fact that in the west English was still the lesser-known language, the one that stood out, is clear from the custom observed by Thomas Reid, a native of Eglish, Co. Tyrone, at the market in Tuam, Co. Galway in 1822, 'for women who can speak English to wear coloured ribands on their caps or bonnets' so that 'a stranger unacquainted with the vernacular tongue' might know to whom he should address himself (Woods 2009: 32, 101).

It is clear from the various accounts that language change was not an inevitable, linear progression, but that there were peaks and troughs along the way. In the early nineteenth century one finds indications of Irish, at least temporarily, bucking the trend of retreat. For example, Thomas Cromwell reporting on his travels through Ireland stated in 1820 with regard to the overall position of Irish: 'This language is spoken by 3,000,000 of the people; and like the Welch and the Highlanders, is loved and venerated by all those "to whose infant minds it first conveyed the tender and endearing accents of maternal affection" to a romantic extreme.' He proceeds to complain of the 'actually increasing prevalence of the language and that religion, both of which it is to be presumed, this protestant mode of teaching was intended to exterminate' (de Bhaldraithe 1970: xviii–xix). On the other hand, when summarising the linguistic situation reported by travellers to Ireland Woods (2009) has the following to say:

> Some researchers unfamiliar with travellers' narratives may suppose that visitors' ignorance of the Irish language was a bar to worthwhile conversations. There is little evidence of this in narratives. Only on rare occasions do travellers mention the Irish language as a difficulty in communicating with local people, though often enough they do mention the Welsh language as a difficulty when en route through Wales. Such was the experience in 1835 of Jonathan Binns, who heard no Irish spoken until he had spent several weeks in Ireland, but on disembarking from Kingstown at the port of Holyhead had difficulty getting directions, those he inquired of speaking only Welsh. Similarly, the German Georg Kohl, travelling through Co. Kerry in 1842, recorded, 'all the people I met with spoke English, though Kerry is considered to be one of the counties where the Irish language has been best preserved'. (Woods 2009: 35)

Another perceptive observer, this time one from within the Irish-language community and culture itself, was the celebrated diarist Amhlaoibh Ó Súilleabháin, who was born in Co. Kerry but spent most of his life in the town of Callan in Co. Kilkenny, where he kept a school and a shop at various times. His diary, written in Irish, spans the years 1827–35. Ó Súilleabháin was keenly aware of the public neglect of the Irish language, and writing on 14 May 1827 he bemoaned the educational neglect of Irish and the general demise of the language: 'Will it be long until this Irish language in which I am writing will disappear? Fine big schools are being built daily to teach this new language, the English of England. But alas! Nobody is taking any interest in the fine subtle Irish language, apart from mean Swaddlers who try to lure the Irish to join their new cursed religion' (de Bhaldraithe 1979: 24, de Bhaldraithe

1970: 9). On observing the establishment of an English language library at the beginning of the following year (5 January 1828) he could not help regretting the lack of similar provision for Irish:

> Some of the townspeople are organising a circulating library for a limited number of members. It has been established for the last year. Every member of the society pays five shillings a year. Alas! Who will establish an Irish language library? No such person is available. The English language of the Saxons is every day getting the upper hand of our own native language. Add to that a thousand million other blemishes and deficiencies under which we are suffering since the day the English once got hold of our native land – poor persecuted Ireland. (de Bhaldraithe 1979: 41, de Bhaldraithe 1970: 25)

Earlier, on 16 July 1827, he had been cheered by news of the publication of several sets of Annals, which 'have been translated from Irish into Latin by Charles O'Connor, D.D., and have been printed by order of the Marquis of Buckingham. I am delighted with this, as are the very few Irishmen who read their own sweet subtle mother tongue' (de Bhaldraithe 1979: 27, de Bhaldraithe 1970: 12). It is also from Ó Súilleabháin that we learn of a rare instance of Irish being used in the public political arena, as he tells us that he delivered a speech in Irish at a monster meeting on 8 July 1832: 'I was at a meeting in Baile Héil, near Cloch an Tóchair and Carraig Seac. There was at least a hundred thousand men present. There were twenty thousand horsemen at it. Men came from Wexford and Tipperary to oppose the tithes and church rates and demanding the return of the Parliament to Dublin. I spoke there in Irish' (de Bhaldraithe 1979: 121, de Bhaldraithe 1970: 101).

With regard to the views of national political leaders, Henry Grattan articulated a measured, more or less neutral, standpoint at the turn of the nineteenth century: 'I should be very sorry that the Irish language should be forgotten, but glad that the English language should be generally understood' (Crowley 2005: 101). His friend and compatriot, Henry Flood, left a bequest for Trinity College Dublin in 1791, directing:

> they do institute and maintain, as a perpetual establishment, a professorship of and for the native Irish or Erse Language, and that they do appoint, if he shall be then living Colonel Charles Vallencey to be the first possessor thereof, with a salary of not less than three hundred pounds sterling a year, seeing that by his eminent and successful

labours in the study and recovery of that language he well deserves to be so first appointed. [...] and I will that the rents and profits of my said lands, houses, hereditaments and estates shall be further applied by the said University to the purchase of all printed books and manuscripts of the dialects and languages that are akin to the said native Irish or Erse Language. (Kelly 2001: 51–2)

However, this bequest was never implemented (Kelly 2001). The clarion call of the Young Ireland leader Thomas Davis to his fellow-countrymen urging them to uphold the native Irish language was to inspire later generations:

> A people without a language of its own is only half a nation. A nation should guard its language more than its territories – 'tis a surer barrier and more important frontier, than fortress or river.... To lose your native tongue, and learn that of an alien, is the worst badge of conquest – it is the chain on the soul. To have lost entirely the national language is death; the fetter has worn through. (Crowley 2000: 161, from 'Our National Language', *The Nation*, 1843)

In particular, Davis argued cogently in favour of working to maintain the language in the districts where Irish was spoken:

> About half of the people west of a line drawn from Derry to Waterford speak [Irish] habitually, and in some of the mountain tracts east of that line it is still common. Simply requiring the teachers of the National Schools in these Irish-speaking districts to know Irish, and supplying them with Irish translations of the schoolbooks, would guard the language where it now exists, and prevent it from being swept away by the English tongue, as the red Americans have been by the English race from New York to New Orleans. (Crowley 2000: 163, from 'Our National Language', *The Nation*, 1843)

On the other hand, he baulked at the prospect of revival in the eastern part of the country, taking a rather defensive stance, albeit one which probably correctly gauged the temper of middle-class sentiment at the time:

> The usual objection to attempting the revival of Irish is, that it could not succeed.

If an attempt were made to introduce Irish, either through the national schools or the courts of law, into the eastern side of the island, it would certainly fail, and the reaction might extinguish it altogether. But no one contemplates this save as a dream of what may happen a hundred years hence. It is quite another thing to say, as we do, that the Irish language should be cherished, taught and esteemed, and that it can be preserved and gradually extended. (Crowley 2000: 163, from 'Our National Language', *The Nation*, 1843)

In fairness to Davis, he could envisage an expanded role for the language, within the world of print, in the context of the establishment of Repeal reading rooms – even if, ironically, his own, essentially monolingual, newspaper *The Nation* was patently not leading the way to this brave new world. He wrote:

To the districts where the Irish language is spoken, they should send a purely Irish Grammar, and an Anglo-Irish Grammar and Dictionary for each room, to be followed by other works containing general information as well as peculiarly Irish knowledge, in Irish. Indeed, we doubt if the Association can carry out the plan which they began by sending out Dr. MacHale's Translations without establishing a newspaper, partly in English and partly in Irish, like the mixed papers of Switzerland, New Orleans and Hungary. (Crowley 2000: 163–4, from 'Repeal Reading Rooms', *The Nation*, 1844)

Daniel O'Connell, the foremost politician of his day, was, like Amhlaoibh Ó Súilleabháin, a native speaker of Irish from Co. Kerry. However, unlike Ó Súilleabháin, and the Anglo-Irish patriots Flood and Davis, O'Connell was indifferent if not actually negatively disposed to the language. As noted by Crowley, O'Connell's clearest statement of his views with regard to Irish was given in response to a query in 1833:

Someone asked him whether the use of the Irish language was diminishing among our peasantry. 'Yes', he answered, 'and I am sufficiently utilitarian not to regret its gradual abandonment. A diversity of tongues is no benefit; it was first imposed on mankind as a curse, at the building of Babel. It would be of vast advantage to mankind if all the inhabitants spoke the same language. Therefore, although the Irish language is connected with many recollections that twine around the hearts of Irishmen, yet the superior utility of the English tongue, as the medium of modern communication, is so great, that

I can witness without a sigh the gradual disuse of the Irish' (Daunt, quoted in Crowley 2000: 153, Crowley 2005: 102)

7.5 Increase of interest in the Irish language

From the middle of the eighteenth century there is evidence of a growing cultural interest in Irish in polite circles, and several societies were founded with a view to promoting the study of Irish and Irish language sources. The regulations of one due to be established in Dublin in 1752 are extant, but nothing further is known about it. The preamble to its rules are as follows:

> Whereas the Irish, the mother Tongue of this Nation, has been long neglected and discouraged by the introduction of strange Languages not so full or Expressive and that the Natives, not only find themselves alone amongst all the Nations of the Earth, ignorant, for the most part, of the Language of their forefathers, but suffer frequently in their Trade, Business, and accomplishments; besides the shamefull Charge, against them by other Countries, of the most grose Levity, in being so easily lead to abollish and render obselete the sacred Repository of their Annals and Archives from the earliest times faithfully recorded, now no where to be met with, but in foreign Libraries, whilst they are busied in cultivating and improving the Histories and Chronicles of Moors, and other Barbarians at home, to the great Detriment, and immortal Dishonour of their Posterity –

> NOW, the following Subscribers, feeling the Deep wound their Country suffer'd and in full of hopes, that one Day or other, so grievous a Loss might be repaired, think proper to enter into an Irish Club. To which they also invite all others, that shall think proper to joyn them. (Leabharlann Náisiúnta na hÉireann 1981: Document 1)

Other societies with a scholarly interest in the language were subsequently founded. They included The Society of Antiquities (1782) which became the Royal Irish Academy (1785), The Gaelic Society of Dublin (1808), The Iberno-Celtic Society (1818), Irish Archaeological Society (1840) and The Ossianic Society (1853). Established with the aim of editing and publishing Irish language manuscript sources, they left a legacy of mixed success. Complementing and intersecting with these scholarly endeavours, the parallel publication of *Bolg an tSolair* under the aegis of the *Northern Star* in Belfast in 1795 and Philip Barron's *Ancient Ireland* in

Waterford in 1835 were important precursors of the later flowering of Gaelic columns in English-medium newspapers in Ireland and abroad, as well as the Irish language newspapers and periodicals of the revival period (Uí Chollatáin 2010, Uí Chollatáin 2011a, Uí Chollatáin 2011b).

7.5.1 The situation of Irish in the mid-nineteenth century

Coming to the end of our period, the overall linguistic situation as recorded in the 1851 census for Ireland was as follows: The total number of Irish speakers was 1,524,286 (or 23 per cent of the population), of whom 319,602 were Irish-speaking monoglots. The percentages for the provinces were Connacht 51 per cent, Munster 44 per cent, Ulster 6.8 per cent and Leinster 3.5 per cent. With regard to Donegal, it is worth pointing to a number of specific features. While the percentage of Irish-speakers for the county as a whole was 29 per cent, they were grouped in three western and one northern barony, and just under half of the total of Irish-speakers were monoglots (Ó Cuív 1971: 23, 25). However, with regard to all of these figures, one has to bear in mind the caveat that there was significant under-reporting of Irish language usage in the 1851 and other nineteenth-century censuses (FitzGerald 1984: 118).

Although the language shift from Irish to English has not yet run its course and is continuing its onward progression into the twenty-first century in the Gaeltacht areas, it is important to realise that it was countered, to a greater or lesser extent, by the revival movement and contrary pressure for a shift from English to Irish, the subject of the next chapter in this book. Despite the private enunciation of perceptive sociolinguistic awareness by a cultural figure such as Amhlaoibh Ó Súilleabháin and the public articulation of a putative positive programme to maintain Irish by a political leader such as Thomas Davis, actual plans of action had to await the founding of language organisations such as the Society for the Preservation of the Irish Language (1876), the Gaelic Union (1880) and above all the extraordinarily effective mobilisation of public opinion by the Gaelic League (1893). But by the end of the nineteenth century the challenge had become immense, as is clear from Douglas Hyde's celebrated lecture entitled 'On the Necessity for De-Anglicising the Irish Nation', delivered in 1892. A number of illuminating anecdotes cited by Hyde show the practical working out of the language shift from Irish to English and how it was proceeding at headlong speed in the western portion of the country in the last decades of the nineteenth century. In their own way they are more enlightening than any array of statistics could ever be. The guilelessness of the second account is truly remarkable, indicative as it is of the vagueness of the individual's appreciation of the mechanics of the language shift in which he was such an active participant:

> [...] I mention the case of a young man I met on the road coming from the fair of Tuam, some ten miles away. I saluted him in Irish, and he answered me in English. 'Don't you speak Irish', said I. 'Well, I declare to God, sir', he said, 'my father and mother hasn't a word of English, but still, I don't speak Irish.' This was absolutely true for him. There are thousands upon thousands of houses all over Ireland to-day where the old people invariably use Irish in addressing the children, and the children as invariably answer in English, the children understanding Irish but not speaking it, the parents understanding their children's English but unable to use it themselves. In a great many cases, I should almost say most, the children are not conscious of the existence of two languages. I remember asking a gossoon a couple of miles west of Ballaghaderreen in the Co. Mayo, some questions in Irish and he answered them in English. At last I said to him, '*Nach labhrann tú Gaedheilg?*' (i.e., 'Don't you speak Irish?') and his answer was, 'And isn't it Irish I'm spaking?' 'No *a-chuisle*', said I, 'it's not Irish you're speaking, but English.' 'Well then', said he, 'that's how I spoke it ever'! He was quite unconscious that I was addressing him in one language and he answering in another. (Hyde 1986: 160–1)

7.6 Conclusion

One can see, therefore, in the three centuries from the Early Modern period to the Great Famine, covered by this chapter, that it was really only in the first half of the nineteenth century that ideas centring on the maintenance and promotion of Irish began to be well formed, while programmes of action, public dissemination of ideas and strategies for the mobilisation of public opinion all lay in the future. In the absence of practical measures in support of Irish and active contrarian engagement with the status quo, the institutional infrastructure and state apparatus continued to do their task relentlessly and efficiently, to the benefit of English and to the detriment of the Irish.

References

Bourke, Eoin (2013). *'Poor Green Erin': German Travel Writers' Narratives on Ireland from Before the 1798 Rising to After the Great Famine.* Frankfurt am Main: Peter Lang.

Briggs, Asa and Peter Burke (2007). *A Social History of the Media: From Gutenberg to the Internet*. Third edition. Cambridge, MA and Malden, MA: Polity.

Burke, Peter (2009). *Popular Culture in Early Modern Europe*. Third Edition. Farnham, Surrey and Burlington, VT: Ashgate.

Buttimer, Cornelius G. (1993). 'Gaelic literature and contemporary life in Cork, 1700–1840', in: Patrick O'Flanagan and Cornelius G. Buttimer (eds) *Cork History and Society: Interdisciplinary Essays on the History of an Irish County*. Dublin: Geography Publications, pp. 585–654.

Crowley, Tony (2000). *The Politics of Language in Ireland 1366–1922: a Source Book*. London and New York: Routledge.

Crowley, Tony (2005). *Wars of Words: the Politics of Language in Ireland 1537–2004*. Oxford: Oxford University Press.

de Bhaldraithe, Tomás (1970). *Cín Lae Amhlaoibh*. [The Diary of Amhlaoibh.] Baile Átha Cliath: An Clóchomhar Teoranta.

de Bhaldraithe, Tomás (1979). *The Diary of an Irish Countryman 1827–1835. A Translation of Cín Lae Amhlaoibh by Tomás de Bhaldraithe*. Cork and Dublin: Mercier Press.

FitzGerald, Garret (1984). *Estimates for Baronies of Minimum Level of Irish-Speaking amongst Successive Decennial Cohorts: 1771–1781 to 1861–1871*. Dublin: Royal Irish Academy.

Harrison, Alan (1988). *Ag Cruinniú Meala: Anthony Raymond (1675–1726), Ministéir Protastúnach, agus Léann na Gaeilge i mBaile Átha Cliath*. [Gathering Honey: Anthony Raymond (1675–1726), Protestant Minister and Irish Studies in Dublin.] Baile Átha Cliath: An Clóchomhar Teoranta.

Harrison, Alan (1999). *The Dean's Friend: Anthony Raymond 1675–1726, Jonathan Swift and the Irish Language*. Dublin: Edmund Burke Publisher.

Hazard, Benjamin (2010). *Faith and Patronage: the Political Career of Flaithrí Ó Maolchonaire c. 1560–1629*. Dublin and Portland, OR: Irish Academic Press.

Hyde, Douglas (1986) [Breandán Ó Conaire (ed.)]. *Language, Lore and Lyrics: Essays and Lectures*. Dublin: Irish Academic Press.

Kelly, James (2001). 'The last will and testament of Henry Flood: text and context', *Studia Hibernica* 31 (2000–1): 37–52.

Leabharlann Náisiúnta na hÉireann [The National Library of Ireland] (1981). *Athbheochan na Gaeilge*. [The Revival of Irish.] Baile Átha Cliath: Leabharlann Náisiúnta na hÉireann.

Mac Mathúna, Liam (1991). *Dúchas agus Dóchas: Scéal na Gaeilge i mBaile Átha Cliath*. [Heritage and Trust: the Story of Irish in Dublin.] Baile Átha Cliath: Glór na nGael.

Mac Mathúna, Liam (2007). *Béarla sa Ghaeilge: Cabhair Choigríche: An Códmheascadh Gaeilge/Béarla i Litríocht na Gaeilge 1600–1900*. [English in Irish. Help from a Foreign Country: Code-mixing of Irish and English in Irish Literature 1600–1900.] Baile Átha Cliath: An Clóchomhar Teoranta.

Mac Mathúna, Liam (2012a). 'Verisimilitude or subversion? Probing the interaction of English and Irish in selected warrants and macaronic verse in the eighteenth century', in: James Kelly and Ciarán Mac Murchaidh (eds) *English and Irish: Essays on the Irish Linguistic and Cultural Frontier, 1600–1900*. Dublin: Four Courts Press, pp. 116–40.

Mac Mathúna, Liam (2012b). 'Getting to grips with innovation and genre diversification in the work of the Ó Neachtain circle in early eighteenth-century Dublin', *Eighteenth-Century Ireland/Iris an Dá Chultúr* 27: 53–83.

Mac Mathúna, Liam (2013). 'The Ó Neachtain circle and the evolving intellectual world of Gaelic Dublin, c. 1730', in: Ailbhe Ó Corráin and Gordon Ó Riain (eds) *Celebrating Sixty Years of Celtic Studies at Uppsala University: Proceedings of the Eleventh Symposium of Societas Celtologica Nordica*. Uppsala: Uppsala University, pp. 113–47.

Mac Mathúna, Liam and Regina Uí Chollatáin, forthcoming. *Saothrú na Gaeilge Scríofa i Suímh Uirbeacha na hÉireann, 1700–1850. Imeachtaí an tSeimineáir a Tionóladh in Institiúid don Léann Daonna UCD, 23–24 Bealtaine 2013.* [The Cultivation of Written Irish in Urban Centres of Ireland, 1700–1850. Proceedings of the Seminar held in the Humanities Institute, University College Dublin, 23–24 May 2013.] Baile Átha Cliath: Ollscoil na hÉireann.

Ní Chléirigh, Meadhbh (ed.) (1944). *Eólas ar an Domhan i bhFuirm Chomhráidh idir Sheán Ó Neachtain agus a Mhac Tadhg.* [Knowledge of the World in the Form of a Conversation between Seán Ó Neachtain and his Son Tadhg.] Baile Átha Cliath: Oifig an tSoláthair.

Ní Shéaghdha, Nessa (1983). 'Diomoladh Phádraig Naofa' [The Disparaging of Saint Patrick], *Celtica* 15: 67–8.

Ó Buachalla, Breandán (1968). *I mBéal Feirste Cois Cuain.* [In Belfast by the Sea.] Baile Átha Cliath: An Clóchomhar Teoranta.

Ó Cuív, Brian (1971). *Irish Dialects and Irish-Speaking Districts: Three Lectures.* Dublin: Dublin Institute for Advanced Studies.

Ó Háinle, C. G. (1986). 'Neighbors in eighteenth century Dublin: Jonathan Swift and Seán Ó Neachtain', *Éire-Ireland: a Journal of Irish Studies* (Winter 1986): 106–21.

Ó Madagáin, Breandán (1974). *An Ghaeilge i Luimneach 1700–1900.* [Irish in Limerick 1700–1900.] Baile Átha Cliath: An Clóchomhar Teoranta.

Ó Muraíle, Nollaig (2007). *Turas na dTaoiseach nUltach as Éirinn: From Ráth Maoláin to Rome.* [The Journey of the Ulster Leaders from Ireland: From Rath Moylan to Rome.] Rome: Pontifical Irish College.

Ó Murchú, Máirtín (1988). 'Historical overview of the position of Irish', in: Liam Mac Mathúna, Nora French, Elizabeth Murphy and David Singleton (eds). *The Less Widely Taught Languages of Europe.* Dublin: IRAAL, pp. 77–88.

Risk, May H. (1975). 'Seán Ó Neachtuin: an eighteenth-century Irish writer', *Studia Hibernica* 15: 47–60.

Uí Chollatáin, Regina (2010). 'Crossing boundaries and early gleanings of cultural displacement in Irish periodical culture', *Irish Communications Review* 12: 50–64.

Uí Chollatáin, Regina (2011a). 'Newspapers, journals and the Irish revival', in: Kevin Rafter (ed.) *More a Disease than a Profession: Irish Journalism before Independence.* Manchester: Manchester University Press, pp. 160–73.

Uí Chollatáin, Regina (2011b). 'Irish language revival and cultural chaos. Sources and scholars in Irish language journalism', in Erin Boon, A. Joseph McMullen and Natasha Sumner (eds) *Proceedings of the Harvard Celtic Colloquium: Volume XXX, 2010.* Cambridge, MA: Department of Celtic Languages and Literatures, Faculty of Arts and Sciences, Harvard University, pp. 273–92.

Walsh, Paul (1916). *The Flight of the Earls by Tadhg Ó Cianáin.* Maynooth: Record Society, St. Patrick's College and Dublin: M. H. Gill & Son, Ltd.

Whelan, Kevin (1999). 'An underground gentry?', in: J. S. Donnelly Jr and Kerby A. Miller (eds) *Irish Popular Culture 1650–1850.* Dublin and Portland, OR: Irish Academic Press, pp. 118–72.

Williams, Nicholas J. A. (1986). *I bPrionta i Leabhar: Na Protastúin agus Prós na Gaeilge 1567–1724.* [In Print in a Book: the Protestants and Irish Prose 1567–1724.] Baile Átha Cliath: An Clóchomhar Teoranta.

Woods, C. J. (2009). *Travellers' Accounts as Source-Material for Irish Historians.* Dublin: Four Courts Press.

8

Language Shift and Language Revival in Ireland

Regina Uí Chollatáin

Revivalists faced a momentous challenge to achieve the aims of a bilingual Ireland, reinstating the spoken Irish language, and adapting it to urban structures of 'the worlds of commerce, politics, official religion, the professions and printed word', from which it had been banished 'as a result of complex socio-economic and political circumstances' (Daly and Dickson 1990: 12). The use of the public sphere of the media was important in creating a forum for public discourse in Irish while many campaigns within the movement brought issues to light which helped to reinstate the language to some degree. Despite the success of these endeavours, the aims of a bilingual Ireland were not fully realised. Scholarly research on the Gaeltacht areas and on new speakers has brought both encouraging issues and some concerns to light,[1] while much important work has also been undertaken to give an overall view of the successes and failures of the revival movement.[2] It is beyond the scope of this paper to fully assess all these issues conclusively and indeed to fully evaluate the results of the Irish language revival. However, an examination of the revivalist ideology and the forums and methods used to promote that ideology are helpful in an analysis of linguistic change in Ireland.

This chapter will examine how the challenge of a bilingual Ireland was mounted in the revival period and how this affected the overall results of Irish language revival in the first part of the twentieth century. The revival period coincided with a watershed in Irish language journalism, merging the concept of new journalism with periodical culture. This provided a forum for the creation of an Irish reading public and public debate, gradually establishing a 'permanent' public sphere through the medium of Irish, assisted by the 'communications revolution' of the early twentieth century (Briggs and Burke 2002: 104). Periodical culture and journalistic sources form the basis therefore for much of the discussion.

Firstly an assessment of the journalistic context from which this concept developed from the end of the eighteenth century onwards sets the framework for the initial ideology which prompted this challenge. As print and journalistic sources were often perceived as tools for normalising language within the public sphere of the media, they provide a blueprint for the vision for this period of sociolinguistic change. Secondly, due to the dearth of reliable statistical evidence, a brief overview of the methods used and the achievements of the language movement in the twentieth century help in reviewing the level of language usage and competency. This focus on the visibility of the language using literary texts, campaigns, educational policies, and political influences, was instrumental in the acceptance of Irish as a second language in the public sphere. The chapter will conclude with an analysis of how the approach taken to language revival continued to influence language policy after the foundation of the State.

8.1 The early context of Irish language revival in print journalism

In Eoin MacNeill's first article in *The Ecclesiastical Record* (1891) where he expressed the hope 'that the West will no longer allow the East to take the lead in this movement',[3] he not only recognised the rich native linguistic heritage of the western seaboard communities in the revival movement, but also the need for those communities to take ownership of that heritage with strong leadership. Romaine's assertion that the 'metamorphosis of Irish from the first language of an impoverished and geographically remote population into the modern language of a privileged urban elite', is relevant. This can also be deemed as both the foundation and stumbling block in Irish language revival (Romaine 2008: 19). The leadership from the east significantly predates the revival period, as the journalistic forum was used as a source long before the onset of the revivalist mentality. The usage of newspaper material in the Ó Neachtain manuscripts indicates that such material was a recognised source for public debate and general dissemination of information. This may well define them as the seeds of Irish language journalism, which was seen as a tool for expanding the scope of Irish language usage in public discourse as part of the temporary public sphere (Uí Chollatáin 2011: 289; Briggs and Burke 2002: 102). This is an example of continuity between manuscript and not only print culture but news culture, which is helpful in an analysis of language revival where the journalistic forum played a significant role. The emphasis rested very strongly on intergenerational transfer in the early stages of the revival but it would rely on the print forum for its standard, as indicated by the writings in the first Irish language newspaper *An Claidheamh Soluis agus Fáinne an Lae* [The Sword of Light and the Dawn of Day] (1899–1932) in articles such as 'An Rud is Riachtanaighe' [The Necessary Thing] (*An Claidheamh Soluis* 25 March 1899). Scant statistical evidence is available between 1851 and 1881 from the question on Irish language speakers on census forms. Prior to 1881 the questions were inserted as a footnote and it would appear that not many bothered to fill them in accurately, but questions on spoken Irish were included in the main census post-1881. There was considerable under-reporting in the censuses in the nineteenth century, so there were more speakers than admitted, but in 1891, before the founding of the Gaelic League, only 0.8 per cent (20,953) of the Irish population claimed to speak Irish as their main language and only 14.5 per cent claimed to be able to speak Irish. From 1851 to 1901 those who reported that they had Irish, including those who spoke only Irish, reduced from 23.3 per cent to 14.4 per cent (1,524,286 in 1851 compared to 641,142 in 1901). In the 'Notes' column in *An Claidheamh Soluis* in 1902 there was a short analysis of the census figures based on the differences between the provinces. It stated that the net decrease of bilingual speakers over the decade since the last census was 21,764 but that 'Irish society is becoming so complex that the mere native has to fight a hard battle in order to establish his individuality' ('Notes', *An Claidheamh Soluis*, 2 August 1902).

In a sociolinguistic context, the Irish language revival emerged from three basic requirements in that society: (i) the need to re-establish Irish as a contemporary literary language in the 'worlds of commerce, politics, official religion, the professions and printed word', as referred to earlier, (ii) the need to foster and revitalise the living tongue of the surviving Irish-speaking areas and (iii) the need to continue to preserve the antiquities of the language. Census statistics were reported on an all-island basis up to 1926, therefore it is interesting that the ideological framework of the scholarly approach to language revival was outlined in the Belfast-based periodical *Bolg an tSolair* [Miscellany] as early as 1795:

At present there are but few who can read, and fewer that can write the Irish characters; and it appears, that in a short time, there will be none found who will understand an Irish manuscript, so as to be able to transcribe or translate it.

It is chiefly with a view to prevent in some measure, the total neglect, and to diffuse the beauties of this ancient and once-admired language, that the following compilation is offered to the public; hoping to afford a pleasing retrospect to every Irishman, who respects the traditions, or considers the language and compositions of our early ancestors, as a matter of curiosity or importance. ('Réamhrá / Preface', *Bolg an tSolair*, pp. viii–ix)

Bolg an tSolair was rooted in the concept of overall cultural revival as opposed to linguistic dominance alone. It was printed in an urban, industrialised, middle-class, non-sectarian pre-revival environment in a period of progressive developments in industry and learning. Mary McNeill's description of Mary Ann McCracken's house in Rosemary Lane aptly describes this environment as 'the precursor by a century of the Irish Gaelic Revival' (1960: 84). *Bolg an tSolair* adopted a scholarly approach, and research on the glossaries within it present an interesting picture of the initial seeds of Irish language revival. These provide insights on the state of the language at the time, linking it directly to the work of many scholars of the era who were assembling these glossaries as specific learning and research tools (Ni Mhunghaile 2010: 47–62; Uí Chollatáin 2012a: 107–33). The content ranged from 'An abridgement of Irish Grammar' with mini chapters on orthography, speech, the noun, the adjective, the pronoun, verbs, adverbs and syntax, to vocabulary lists. These lists covered many areas of speech, with topics such as the elements of nature, parts of the body, mankind in general, government, food and living habits, military terms, and the sea, for example. There was also a series of dialogues, between the farmer, priest, and merchant, 'on travelling', and it concluded with Charlotte Brooke's scholarly work and other well-known songs.

Early nineteenth-century journals with Irish language material, such as *Ancient Ireland* (1835) and *Fior Eirionnach* (1862), for example, followed this scholarly approach of *Bolg an tSolair*. The journals consistently focused on the preservation of the language and the 'reply' to the authorities as opposed to being exclusively concerned with language revival. However, the link between nationhood and language continued to prevail and the political climate dictated much of the linguistic trend that would follow. It was only towards the end of the nineteenth century that writers and commentarists acknowledged the demand for cultural nationality and political nationalism as ideals which worked together as opposed to single entities (Titley 2000: 48). When this came to the fore in the public sphere it also influenced the impetus of the language movement, which was very evident in the more defined path the movement now took. This combined approach was explored in the initial debate on the founding of *Irisleabhar na Gaedhilge/The Gaelic Journal*, and it dominated until the founding of the first Irish language newspaper:

> The GAELIC JOURNAL will be at once the organ of the Irish language movement, the willing medium of interchange of knowledge among the students of Irish, the record of much of our literature and traditional lore, and the clear and indubitable witness that our language is still a living tongue, a great instrument of thought, with a living literature, and with its powers of creating a living national literature still unimpaired. The existence of the GAELIC JOURNAL will in this way be a protest and a testimony against the national crime, by whomsoever perpetrated, whether by design or neglect perpetrated, of ignoring our national language and literature, and abandoning them to disuse and oblivion. (*The Gaelic Journal*, May 1895)

The Irish language was viewed as the 'instrument of thought' while the use of the periodical itself would be a testimony against the abolition of the Irish language in the public sphere.

The links between language and nationhood echoed here were the foundation stones on which the Irish-Ireland movement based their school of thought. Much of this philosophy was preceded by the work of the eighteenth- and nineteenth-century intellectuals Rousseau, Herder, Fichte, for example, and this outlook dominated the early pre-revival scholarly approach to language preservation in Ireland (Ó Conchubhair 2009; Ó Torna 2005: 19–30). Indeed, to view Irish language revival as a concept confined in thought and implementation to the island of Ireland alone presents a narrow and incomplete understanding of it. Furthermore, media sources in the nineteenth century are very insightful in assessing the links with the Irish language community abroad. In the article on census figures in *An Claidheamh Soluis* in 1901, referred to earlier, the total number of immigrants is given as 430,993 and refers to 'the immigration of Anglo-Germans and Anglo-Scotchmen' as being responsible for the complexity of Irish society which is ultimately affecting language usage. Immigrant Irish language newspaper and journal content in America also supports the usage of the forum in a communicative context in the mid-to-latter half of the nineteenth century (Nilsen 1997; Uí Chollatáin 2014a, 2011). The newspapers and *An Gaodhal* [The Gael] in Brooklyn, New York are strong examples of this, often functioning as directories, communication networks and focal points for cultural transmission. It is important to note the varied value of media in an immigrant and in a native context here (Hourigan 2007: 252). The decline of the language in the north-east of Ireland in the late eighteenth and early nineteenth century was attributed to mass emigration and in certain areas of Canada and North America at least, census analysis demonstrates that Irish language speakers appear to have been relatively prevalent in the first quarter of the nineteenth century (McMonagle 2012: 140).

Initial findings also indicate evidence of Irish language in Australia somewhat later (Noone 2012). While further research is needed, this points to a revivalist mentality which was developing with at least as much speed within the immigrant communities in the mid-to-late nineteenth century as that which took root in the native community in the last quarter of the nineteenth century. This is further reinforced by Breandán Mac Aodha's account of Father Eoghan O'Growney's role in the revival, recognising the need for textual learning while combining this with the 'willingness to learn from abroad' and to 'innovate' (Mac Aodha 1972: 21). Print culture and media forums were central to this communications revolution. It is not surprising therefore that the messages from Douglas Hyde's initial speeches in New York gained a significant following crossing geographical borders. Almost 100 years on from the foundation of *Bolg an tSolair*, parts of Hyde's speech to the New York Cumann Gaeilge, 16 June 1891, were printed in the Irish American newspapers at the end of June (*Gaelic American* 27 June 1891). These reached the newspapers in Ireland where they influenced Eoin MacNeill and Eoghan O'Growney. Hyde primarily claimed that the language was in a bad way but that it was not dead, stating that a bilingual Ireland would be better than a monolingual English one. He concluded by stating that if the Irish people wanted to stand together as one nation, then the link for this was to be found in the ancient language of Ireland, Irish.

This prompted MacNeill to write 'Why and How the Irish Language is to be Preserved' in the *Irish Ecclesiastical Record* in December 1891, an article which is basically a treatise on his vision for the progression of the language movement with some practical recommendations. He compares the energetic advancement of the Irish language among the Irish in America, Australia and England to that of the Irish at home who 'seem to lie under a spell of impenetrable apathy'. O'Growney then asked MacNeill to write a more definite article on ways in which the Irish language could be preserved and revived, and an English and Irish version entitled 'Toghairm agus Gleus Oibre chum Gluasachta na Gaedhilge do chur ar aghaidh i nÉirinn'/'A Plea and a Plan for the Extension of the Movement to Preserve and Spread the Gaelic Language in Ireland' was published in *The Gaelic Journal* in March 1893. This 13-point article stated that:

> No language has ever been kept alive by mere book-teaching....The language cannot live at all that does not live in the homes of the people....Whatever is worth doing is worth doing speedily. ('A Plea and a Plan for the Extension of the Movement to Preserve and Spread the Gaelic Language in Ireland', *The Gaelic Journal*, March 1893)

MacNeill's articles and O'Growney's article 'The Irish Language' (*Irish Ecclesiastical Record*, November 1890), highlighted the need to combine the scholarly approach with the language of the home. A coherent message was emerging to formulate a policy of action.

Acting on the correspondence that the article generated from the literary elite of Ireland and the response to Hyde's speech, 'The Necessity for De-anglicising Ireland' which he made as president of the Irish National Literary Society in Dublin on 25 November 1892, J. H. Lloyd and MacNeill took it upon themselves to contact a number of prominent people whom, it was deemed, might be interested in founding such a movement. This group came together on 31 July 1893 and the foundation of the Gaelic League ensued, with Hyde as President and MacNeill as honorary secretary. Furthermore, following MacNeill's earlier criticism in the *Ecclesiastical Record* article of the failure of the Irish at home to 'decently support a quarterly journal devoted to the culture of Irish', he was now provided with a forum to address this issue. He also took responsibility on a voluntary basis for the first term as editor of the League's first Irish language newspaper, *An Claidheamh Soluis*, from March 1899 to September 1901. MacNeill credited this newspaper venture with testing the 'reality' of the movement. This highlights the importance of a newspaper for language revival at that time, securing a place for, and participation of Irish language material in the global communication revolution:

> We gladly give our readers this month the tidings that a great step forward is about to be taken in the interests of the National language. A weekly newspaper in the Irish language is announced. For the past year or two, since the movement in favour of our native tongue began to take firm root in the nation, the uprise of a newspaper in Irish has been eagerly hoped and looked forward to....A correspondent of the

GAELIC JOURNAL put the case in plain words a few months ago, when he said if this movement is a reality, it should by this time be able to stand the test of supporting a weekly paper. ('Fáinne an Lae' [The Dawn of Day], *The Gaelic Journal*, November 1897)

The language movement was gaining momentum, but if Irish were to be adapted to urban structures of the modern world, the economic value of the Irish language would also be a key element of the revival. In his editorials in *An Claidheamh Soluis*, MacNeill often wrote about his belief in the role that the Gaelic League had to play, not only in cultural and language revival, but in economic survival. Referring to Greece, Finland, Bohemia, Hungary and East Prussia, he sometimes used examples of material prosperity in other countries where language revival had taken place. The absence of sound research methods dictate that these claims seemed to be based more on speculation than on hard evidence. However, they highlight the European focus, viewing the Irish language in comparison with other world languages as opposed to seeing it as a marginalised language on the western seaboard of Europe. This perspective is in keeping with the initial revival ideology but places it on an international scale, while acknowledging the new communication networks.

The focus would be on the spoken language of the people, 'caint na ndaoine', and this would serve as the basis for related revival activities over the next forty years or so. This approach, which embraced the use of the living language in the journalistic forum as the new 'reality', was in stark contrast to that of the nineteenth-century Irish language periodicals, which fostered a scholarly and cultural approach emphasising preservation of the language as opposed to fostering language usage. The new media venture would be a 'bona fide newspaper' whose success depended on a number of issues, not least, passing the 'test' of creating an Irish reading public:

> The test is about to be made and we are confident of a successful result.... The new journal will be a *bona fide* newspaper, intended to supply in Irish a summary of news and miscellaneous interesting matter as weekly reading for the ordinary household. In fulfilling this purpose it will attain the great end of creating an Irish-reading public. (ibid.)

The founding of a news periodical indicates that the previous use of periodicals as a 'reply' or cry of protest to the authorities would now be supplemented by a forum which would develop the ideals of the nation, via the ideology of the revival movement in a communicative forum. The role of the publications had moved from 'protesting' to the authorities to 'testing' the Irish public, which suggested a two-way interactive process. This Irish language discourse was supplemented by the material in English language newspapers of the era, where the Gaelic column developed into a forum for the Irish-Ireland movement in the local and national press (Uí Fhaoláin 2014; Mac Congáil 2011). However, this 'test' had its share of failures, one of the greatest being the absence of the core native Irish language community in this forum. While MacNeill hoped that the west would take the lead over the east in reinstating the language, the need to put social structures in place for the standard use of the language took precedence for urban revivalists at this point. Irish had been excluded from areas of administration in society, which created a setting which protected the living language as a rural language and the print language as one for public discourse. The economic value of the language was minimal, which was not helped by the labelling of all the Irish-speaking districts (except the Decies) by the Congested Districts Board as not being capable of surviving without outside assistance (Ó hAilín 1969: 91–100; Ó Torna 2005: 45–60). This left little use for a news periodical within the Irish-speaking districts, and Irish language usage at this point was rooted in domestic use and in rural occupations such as farming and fishing:

> Human speech, as we know, is a social phenomenon, which can develop and flourish only in a community. A very powerful factor in the development of a language is the environment in which the community lives. This is very evident in the language of the Gaeltacht districts, which abounds in all the shades of local colour. There is a richness of vocabulary, of idiom, of expression derived from the pursuits of everyday life, from the activities of field and farm and household, of hill pasture and fishing boat. (Ó Danachair 1969: 115)

This was the 'reality', and it was this localised language register with dialectical variation, rather than the emerging new print language, which prevailed at the start of the revival period. While the news forum provided support for the communication of the ideals and activities of the revival movement in the context of the social, political, educational, and linguistic environment of Ireland at the time, it was probably a step too far to claim that 'supporting a weekly newspaper' would be one of the most telling benchmarks in monitoring the success of the revival movement. The Irish-speaking districts needed major revitalisation, and the new 'Gaeltacht' was viewed as an ideal or Utopia for the urban revivalists. For the Gaeltacht community, dealing with 'real' economic issues prevented them from engaging fully with this revivalist vision and ideology. The lack of economic value on the Irish language decimated the Irish-speaking districts, leaving much work to be done for the revivalists on both sides of the linguistic borders, east and west. Interestingly, this had been touched on in Eoin MacNeill's earlier article in the *Irish Ecclesiastical Record* in 1891, acknowledging that English was the language of material progress, which resulted in Irish being 'despised', due primarily to its perceived worthlessness in economic terms:

> It is remarkable that, in general, those who have known Irish from infancy are less enthusiastic in the cause than those who have to labour for its attainment. The reason probably is that in their infancy Irish was a thing despised. (*Irish Ecclesiastical Record* 1891: 1105–6)

8.2 Language revival implementation

The aims of the Gaelic League were drawn up as giving precedence to the spoken tongue in the Irish-speaking districts and to bilingualism. The way in which this would be implemented was described in detail in *Irisleabhar na Gaedhilge* in November 1893 under the editorship of Father Eoghan O'Growney, again acknowledging the need for the west to eventually take the lead:

The Gaelic League

Their principle and their *raison d'être* in contradistinction to the bodies existing side by side with them is, that under present conditions it is impossible to save the Irish language by means of a movement directed wholly or mainly on educational lines. Their object, correlative with this principle, is to conduct the movement mainly on popular lines, imitating *mutatis mutandis* the general scheme of the method invariably and successfully employed by every practical movement of the day – the method modified to suit the exigencies of the case, of local organization and local demonstration.

In short, they purpose at the earliest opportunity to change the venue of their work from Dublin to the Irish-speaking people; to teach, exhort, and encourage them not to abandon this noble heritage of national speech; to enlighten them as to the real disgrace of such a desertion; to stimulate them by the striking examples of other races around us; to make them respect their native speech, and themselves for the possession of it; to eradicate finally that unworthy feeling of shame attached to the speaking of Irish which has been the worst enemy of the language – in this way both by principle and practice to secure that the Irish language will be handed down to ever-increasing numbers of Irishmen.... In the noted Bismarckian phrase, it is abundantly clear that the founders of the Gaelic League have 'seized the psychological moment'. ('The Gaelic League', *Irisleabhar na Gaedhilge*, Nov. 1893: 227–8)

What followed was a very progressive period in the production of Irish language print material, and in the campaigns to ensure usage and visibility of the Irish language. The revivalist approach attempted basically to preserve and revitalise the impoverished spoken language of the west, and to reinstate the language in an urban context.

The establishment of a permanent 'public sphere' was important but some of the language debates in *An Claidheamh Soluis* did not appear to exist for much of the native-Irish-speaking public in the west. In the context of the communication revolution however, the fostering and the practice of using the Irish language in a national journalistic context was laying a foundation by creating a discourse on issues which quite possibly would never otherwise have reached the public domain. This would eventually pave the way for Irish language movements rooted in the Gaeltacht areas of the twentieth century, 'Cearta Sibhialta na Gaeltachta' ['Civil rights of the Irish-speaking areas'] in the 1960s, Raidió na Gaeltachta in the 1970s and Teilifís na Gaeilge in the 1990s, for example. The use of this forum was viewed as synonymous with new perspectives of unity, progression and power: 'The newspapers have great power. There is nothing as powerful as them to progress the language shift among people' (*An Claidheamh Soluis*, 29 September 1913). Caoilfhionn Nic Pháidín emphasises the necessity of using Irish in the public domain during this period, be it in a literary context or everyday usage within the community, as being central to the fostering of a modern Irish language community (Nic Pháidín 1998: 59).

There was a strong reliance on the structures which needed to be put in place and the first ten years of the Gaelic League were characterised by great activity. The most significant and successful venture which provided a nationally recognised platform for the Irish language and its culture was the Oireachtas or 'literary assembly', which began on 17 May 1897. Alongside the forum for modern literature, it provided a focal rallying point for the development of the ideology of the Irish nation in which, it was hoped, the Irish language would now play a central role:

The Oireachtas will...fix universal public attention on the Irish language movement; it will help in obliterating the dialectical differences and in fixing the literary standard; it will make for the creation of a modern Irish literature; it will encourage and be a bond of union to all workers in the revival of Irish; and finally, it will rally the Irish nation for the maintenance of the national tongue. (McMahon 2008: 156–7)

This assembly of the Oireachtas was described as being reminiscent of the ancient tradition of assemblies in the broader European context, where social unity was deemed as important as linguistic and literary unity:

Common festivals have ever been a tie between individuals of a race...After community of blood and community of language, community of festivals was the strongest bond that held the various independent Greek republics together as one Greece. What the Pythean, the Olympic, the Nemean, and Isthmian games were to the Greeks, the assemblies of Tara, Emania, Carman, and Tailtenn were to the men of Ireland....The ancient assemblies are revived in the Oireachtas. The festival is the rallying point of the movement. It affords a centre for the thought of all Irish-Ireland. It makes for social as well as for linguistic and literary unity. ('The Oireachtas', *An Claidheamh Soluis*, 25 March 1899)

The repeated reference to 'community' here is also important, as clearly these gatherings were viewed as central to the creation of an Irish language community because they 'inspired the League faithful and gave them a sense that they and their neighbours were *connected* to something larger than themselves' (McMahon 2008: 165). This is even more important considering that being part of a greater society was the catalyst for the Gaeltacht community's learning and promoting the English language in the first place, albeit that this was not driven by a love of the English language but out of economic necessity (Greene 1972: 11). While not having any economic value per se, the Oireachtas placed a 'real' value on the cultural traditions and practices of the community language, creating its own cultural currency. In fact one of the better examples of the coverage of the angle of the movement in the United

States in *Irisleabhar na Gaedhilge/The Gaelic Journal* relates to this aspect of the first Oireachtas:

> Mr Patrick O'Byrne, of the Gaelic Society, New York, was present at a meeting of the Central Branch, Gaelic League, Dublin, on the 24th September, and was accorded an Irish welcome. In returning thanks, Mr. O'Byrne dealt with the present position of the movement in America, and continuing, said: – Your Oireachtas was, I think, taken up better by the Press in America than anything that has happened on this side of the Atlantic for some time past. The novelty appealed to them. The very idea of the Irish people having a literary competition in their own language in Dublin was so extraordinary that they eagerly took notice of it. They in America...were happy that such a very large measure of success had attended the efforts of the Gaelic League in establishing an institution having for its objects the literary cultivation of the tongue of our fathers. He considered that there were two great reasons which should induce every Irishman to join the movement for the preservation of the Irish language – first, it offered a common platform to those of different shades of political and religious thought; and secondly that it formed a strong bond of union between the Celtic peoples of Ireland, Scotland and Wales. He concluded by again thanking the meeting for the hearty welcome accorded him, and said that he might take it upon himself to say on behalf of the Gaelic Society of New York that anything they could do to assist them they would do. (*Irisleabhar na Gaedhilge/The Gaelic Journal*, October 1897: 95).

This was in fact the 'reality' which Eoin MacNeill and his contemporaries needed to address if the revival was to be a success. Literacy and modern literature would play a major part in this and, as a spin-off from these activities, literary groups were formed. These types of societies were central to the success of revival movements in other countries as well (Uí Chollatáin 2004: 32, 164–5).

The creation of a modern literature led to many debates on font types, language register and standards, terminology and orthography, which have been documented in scholarly works (Ó Conchubhair 2003; Mag Eacháin 2014; Mac Mathúna 2007). The font issue and the spoken language 'caint na ndaoine', were probably the most divisive and controversial issues, both of which were central to linguistic change and to an increase in literacy rates. Furthermore, the use of Gaelic or Roman font had significant impact in the later part of the 1920s and was used in government policy for publishing school texts (Uí Chollatáin 2006, 2012b). One of the best sources for explaining the fundamental issues of the argument for 'caint na ndaoine' is Liam Mac Mathúna's preface to the new edition of *Séadna* by Father Peadar Ó Laoghaire, the main advocate of the spoken language at the time (Mac Mathúna 2011). *Séadna*, similar to other literary works of the revival, was first published in periodicals and newspapers, and combined the literary value of the story with the folklore component, rendering both equal in the promotion of the language but from different perspectives.

By 1919, the Gaeltacht situation had still not improved, which was a source of concern for some prominent language activists, as expressed by Liam Ó Rinn:

> I am afraid that that we won't have a proper natural literature in Irish until the Gaeltacht community wake up, not only with regard to the Irish language but with regard to the whole wide world. They have a sort of lethargy like someone who is trying to recover from illness. Or is it that they are kind of bewildered because the ancient Irish life they had is being cast aside without a new modern Irish life ready to put in its place? (*Irish Independent*, 13 December 1919: 6)

This probably best summarises the state of play which influenced the Gaeltacht mindset at this stage of the revival. Basically, the structures of the revival worked for the urban bilingual community of revivalists, but Gaeltacht speakers still needed English to take their place in the modern world. However, while they did not view their language as a 'reality' in this English-speaking world, they could no longer totally ignore its cultural value, a possibility which had only come to the fore at the end of the nineteenth and beginning of the twentieth centuries and which was further promoted through festivals of culture like the Oireachtas.

The revivalist debates and campaigns continued to ensure that the Irish language was rendered a visible part of the urban landscape. For example, it was a notable achievement when the first bilingual street nomenclature was put in place with Sráid Enrí/Henry Street, Dublin, in August 1901 (Uí Chollatáin 2004: 78). Other debates included the cases for Irish names on carts in Gaeltacht areas from 1899 to 1903 particularly; the campaign for the use of Irish addresses on letters with the Post Office, and the use of Irish in banks between 1900 and 1905 (Ibid.: 80, 113). These debates did not exert enough influence to make any real difference in language usage among the English-speaking public of the time, but their role in ensuring the visibility of the Irish language in an urban context was an important part of the ultimate successes of the Irish language revival for both urban and rural Irish speakers. Perhaps the most successful campaign was that of Irish as an essential requirement for the National University, which was debated successfully in *An Claidheamh Soluis* through the editorship of Pádraic Pearse, resulting in Irish becoming necessary for matriculation from 1913 onwards (Ibid.: 99–102; Ó Buachalla 1988). Clearly, the intellectual planning and execution of these decisions remain significant in the broader context of language community and culture down to the present day:

> Finally one must remember that in the act of Revival itself we are engaged in a new and absolutely audacious human and intellectual venture, the very planning of which and the very execution of which, will of itself help to give our culture a new dimension of experience and a unique quality of its own. In fact we are undertaking a cultural task the like of which was probably never before attempted by democratic means. It is more than likely indeed that the Gaelic League idea was one of the most exciting long-term ideas ever broached anywhere. But nobody in recent times has really presented it to the Irish people in these terms. (Ó Tuama 1972: 109)

The increasing pressure on the League to be politically involved meant that the foundation of the state was seen as a stepping stone to the final stage in the complete revival of Irish. The following extract from 1921 is upbeat with regard to the number of Irish writers but also highlights the cracks that were beginning to show due to lack of coherence in the approach that was being taken which, apparently, would be corrected by state policy or at least 'state assistance':

> Despite the war and politics a dozen Irish books were published from this time last year. That demonstrates that we have no lack of writers. As we will soon be masters in our own house, we should make better progress from now on. In order to render Irish language literature on a par with other world literatures in a few years, there are only two requirements: mutual support and state help. The support will be available in Cumann na Sgríbhneoirí [The Writers' Association], and if the members of the Association are fully serious about this, there is no doubt that the State will give them the help that they need. (*Irish Independent*, 19 December 1921: 4)

8.3 Language revival and twentieth-century Irish language policy

This state assistance mainly took the form of legislation, which placed Irish as the first language of the Irish state in the 1923 constitution, and of the implementation of an education system which favoured the Irish language as a subject as opposed to a living language. The education system is deemed as both a failing and a success of the Irish language revival movement. It provided the structures to teach the language successfully and ensured its necessity at the highest levels of the educational system, but:

> it unfortunately confined Irish and the Irish experience for many people to the classroom and left large areas of Irish life untouched. This meant that bilingualism was very often the result of an educational process rather than an organic phenomenon or intergenerational transfer. (Ó Murchú 2008: 32)

The isolation of the language as a marginalised learning activity ensured that the language standard was fostered and maintained, but the absence 'or limitations of domains in which that language [could] can be utilised' (Ó Curreáin 2008), have been a major stumbling block, a view also aired previously (Ó Cuív 1969: 130). John Horgan's assessment of the role of Irish language media in the Irish revival adds another dimension to this in the context of the communication revolution and the construction of a permanent public sphere, as mentioned at the start of this essay:

> The task of reviving the language as the main medium of communication for the majority of the population – an ideological objective which was all too frequently advanced by people with little knowledge of psychology, linguistics or education – was entrusted chiefly to the schools, and above all to the primary schools. In these circumstances, the role and the potential benefit, of Irish-language journalism was downplayed and even ignored. (Horgan 2001: 36–7)

Legislation has also continued to play a positive and necessary role in reinstating the Irish language. The status of Irish as the first nationally recognised language of the Irish state has compelled policymakers and language planners not only to recognise, but also to monitor its progress and developments, and/or its decline. This monitoring has secured benchmarks along which language revival can be assessed, indicating that this revival policy certainly halted the language shift from Irish to English to some extent at least.

This approach taken in 1923, allowing Irish the status of first national language, may well have been the saving of the Irish language if compared to other minority languages. Post-1926, the census only included the 26 counties and, even though the report does not differentiate between native speakers and learners, 19.3 per cent of the population claimed to be able to speak Irish (540,802 speakers out of a population of 2,802,452). In 1936 23.7 per cent (666,601 out of 2,806,905) claimed to be able to speak Irish. Although the success was noteworthy, the consistent neglect of the Gaeltacht community in the revival process continued. When the White Paper on the 1926 Gaeltacht commission was published in 1927, only 14 of the 82 recommendations were adopted. It was referred to as the 'Páipéar Bán' in the editorial in *An Claidheamh Soluis* in April 1929, using the dual meaning of 'bán' as the colour white and as land where nothing grows.

Helen Ó Murchú further develops the link between the economy, legislation and language, outlining that only two acts which involved the Irish language had an effect on economic life, An tAcht Árachais 1936 (Assurance Act) and An tAcht Iompair 1950 (Transport Act). Legislative and educational structures aid language revival and maintenance but these structures alone are not enough to change attitudes and secure language usage alongside language competence. It is essential that a community takes ownership of the language and to do that the members of the community need to use it, regardless of the level of competence. It could be said that this standard of usage was denied to the Gaeltacht community with the lack of commitment to the recommendations of the Gaeltacht Commission in 1926. However, without the goodwill of the national community in which the national language is being used, albeit in a minority or lesser-used capacity, language revival, maintenance and progression are challenging at best. In recent years, due to the continued research of Micheál Mac Gréil in reports in 1972–3, 1988–9 and 2007–8, clear points of reference have been established in asserting that a high level of positivity towards the Irish language among the general Irish population has been maintained over 20 years, from 1988–9 to 2008 (Mac Gréil 2009).

One would assume that the usage in Gaeltacht areas would surpass usage in the non-Gaeltacht speaking areas, but Dublin is the area showing the greatest increase in Irish speakers since 1891, further evidence of the east continuing to dominate the west despite Eoin MacNeill's hopes. The language may have 'metamorphised' in some areas, as a result primarily of Gaelscoileanna and such developments, and brought about a positive reclaiming of the language from a cultural majority, but there is much yet to be done. Also while economic climate is often blamed for the lack of success of the revival movement in the Gaeltacht areas, Ó Murchú claims that

> [...] in the real world few problems can be said to be wholly economic in nature – the economic aspects are inter-twined with their social and cultural dimensions. Culture is in the economy and the economy is in culture. And language lies at the root of both. (Ó Murchú 2008: 277)

To conclude, creating an awareness of the need to preserve the antiquities of the language was probably one of the greatest successes of the revival movement. Much needs to be done to ensure the future of editing manuscript material but this scholarly research is largely dependent also, as it always has been, on language usage to the highest professional and academic standards and on the fostering of the living tongue.

The need to foster and preserve the living tongue in the surviving Irish-speaking areas continues to be the greatest challenge. Generally, although a certain level of language competence was achieved, total language usage in an intergenerational context was not secured. The ideal of a bilingual Ireland was not fully realised, and the process of Irish language revitalisation remains challenging in the twenty-first century.

The revival and the subsequent developments in the twentieth century demonstrate that a living spoken language is in a constant condition of reinstatement and, to some extent, reinvention, but the challenge lies in the engagement of native speakers, regardless of geographical boundaries. The need to re-establish the language in all domains of modern Irish society has been addressed to some extent as a result of the revival movement and its aftermath. The tools and legislation have been put in place but much depends on language policy conforming to these structures. This will not guarantee that Irish will survive as a living language but it will help in securing a bilingual environment which would build on the ideals of the revivalists.

8.4 Conclusion

A language revival is no longer necessary in Ireland, but Irish needs to be incorporated into modern society to normalise the new 'reality' of language usage for the twenty-first century. The wealth of the traditional

Gaeltacht areas is the cornerstone on which the new Irish language will thrive, but this is no longer solely dependent on the traditional Irish Gaeltacht speaker. The established Gaeltacht areas are to the fore now in embracing new terminology associated with the worlds of 'commerce, politics, official religion, the professions and printed word' from which Irish had been banished 'as a result of complex socio-economic and political circumstances'. In this way the west and the east of Ireland are both finally taking ownership of the Irish language. The ideology on which the revival movement was founded is still very relevant in maintaining, building and supporting the language and in redefining the Irish language community, in which revival campaigns and media sources have played and continue to play a meaningful role. This role of the media is no longer ignored and the Gaeltacht and non-Gaeltacht Irish-speaking communities are probably more alert now to Ó Rinn's concept of the whole wide world, reasserting the status of the Irish language in a global context while acknowledging the continuity which was achieved by productive use of these forums in the revival period.

Notes

1. See Ó Curnáin (2007); Lenoach et al. (2012); Ó Giollagáin and Mac Donnacha (2008); Ó hIfearnáin and Ó Murchadha (2011); Ó hIfearnáin and Ní Neachtain (eds) (2012); Walsh and O'Rourke (2014).
2. See Billings (2014); Mac Aonghusa (1993); Mac Mathúna (2007, 2011); Mag Eacháin (2014); McMahon (2008); Nic Eoin (2005); Nic Pháidín and Ó Cearnaigh (eds) (2008); Ní Dhonnchadha (1981); Ó Conchubhair (2009); Ó Cuív (1969); O'Leary (1994); Ó Súilleabháin (1998); Uí Chollatáin (2004, 2006, 2011, 2012a, 2012b, 2014a, 2014b).
3. The allusion here is to the largely Irish-speaking west of Ireland versus the English-speaking east of Ireland.

References

Billings, Cathal (2014). 'Athbheochan na Gaeilge agus an Spórt in Éirinn 1884–1934' [The Revival of Irish and Sport in Ireland 1884–1934]. Unpublished PhD thesis, University College Dublin.

Briggs, Asa and Peter Burke (2002). *A Social History of the Media. From Gutenberg to the Internet.* Cambridge: Polity.

Daly, Mary and David Dickson (eds) (1990). *The Origins of Popular Literacy in Ireland: Language, Change and Educational Development 1700–1900.* Dublin: University College Dublin and Trinity College Dublin.

Greene, David (1972). 'The founding of the Gaelic League', in: Seán Ó Tuama (ed.) *The Gaelic League Idea.* Dublin: Mercier Press, pp. 9–19.

Horgan, John (2001). *Irish Media. A Critical History since 1922.* London and New York: Routledge.

Hourigan, Niamh (2007). 'Minority language media studies: key themes for future scholarship', in: Mike Cormack and Niamh Hourigan (eds) *Minority Language Media. Concepts, Critiques and Case Studies*. Clevedon, Buffalo, Toronto: Multilingual Matters, pp. 248–65.

Lenoach, Ciarán, Conchúr Ó Giollagáin and Brian Ó Curnáin (eds) (2012). *An Chonair Chaoch. An Mionteangachas sa Dátheangachas.* [The Blind Path. Monolingualism in Bilingualism.] Galway: Leabhar Breac.

Mac Aodha, Breandán S. (1972). 'Was this a social revolution?', in: Seán Ó Tuama (ed.) *The Gaelic League Idea.* Dublin: Mercier Press, pp. 20–30.

Mac Aonghusa, Proinsias (1993). *Ar Son na Gaeilge. Conradh na Gaeilge 1893–1993.* [For the Sake of Irish. The Gaelic League 1893–1993.] Baile Átha Cliath: Conradh na Gaeilge.

Mac Congáil, Nollaig (2011). 'Saothrú na Gaeilge ar nuachtáin náisiúnta Bhéarla na hAoise seo caite. Sop nó solamar?' [The Cultivation of Irish on English National News in the Previous Century], in: Réamoinn Ó Muireadhaigh (ed.) *Féilscríbhinn Anraí Mhic Giolla Chomhaill. Tráchtais don Athair Anraí Mac Giolla Chomhaill.* [Festschrift for Anraí Mhic Giolla Chomhaill. A Treatise for Anraí Mhic Giolla Chomhaill.] Baile Átha Cliath: Coiscéim, pp. 112–91.

Mac Gréil, Micheál (2009). *The Irish Language and the Irish People.* Maynooth: Survey and Research Unit, Department of Sociology.

Mac Mathúna, Liam (2007). *Béarla sa Ghaeilge: cabhair choigríche: an códmheascadh Gaeilge/Béarla i litríocht na Gaeilge 1600–1900.* [English in Irish. Help from the Foreign Country: Code-mixing of Irish and English in Irish Literature 1600–1900.] Baile Átha Cliath: An Clóchomhar Teoranta.

Mac Mathúna, Liam (ed.) (2011). *Séadna: an tAthair Peadar Ua Laoghaire.* [Séadna. Father Peadar Ua Laoghaire.] Baile Átha Cliath: Cois Life Teoranta.

McMahon, Timothy G. (2008). *Grand Opportunity. The Gaelic Revival and Irish Society, 1893–1910.* Syracuse: Syracuse University Press.

McMonagle, Sarah (2012). 'Finding the Irish language in Canada', *New Hibernia Review* 16.1 (Spring 2012): 134–49.

McNeill, Mary (1960). *The Life and Times of Mary Ann McCracken 1770–1866: a Belfast Panorama.* Dublin: Blackstaff Press.

Mag Eacháin, Conchúr (2014). *Téarmaíocht Ghaeilge na hAthbheochana.* [The Terminology of Revival Irish.] Baile Átha Cliath: Cois Life Teoranta.

Nic Eoin, Máirín (2005). *Trén bhFearann Breac. An Díláithriú Cultúir agus Nualitríocht na Gaeilge.* [Through the Speckled Land. The Displacement of Irish Culture and Modern Writing.] Baile Átha Cliath: Cois Life Teoranta.

Nic Pháidín, Caoilfhionn (1998). *Fáinne an Lae agus an Athbheochan (1898–1900).* [The Dawn of Day and the Language Revival (1898–1900).] Baile Átha Cliath: Cois Life Teoranta.

Nic Pháidín, Caoilfhionn and Séan Ó Cearnaigh (eds) (2008). *A New View of the Irish Language.* Baile Átha Cliath: Cois Life Teoranta.

Ní Dhonnchadha, Aisling (1981). *An Gearrscéal sa Ghaeilge 1898–1940.* [The Short Story in Irish 1898–1940.] Baile Átha Cliath: An Clóchomhar Teoranta.

Nilsen, Ken (1997). 'The Irish language in nineteenth century New York city', in: Ofelia Garcia and Joshua A. Fishman (eds) *The Multilingual Apple: Languages in New York City.* Berlin: Mouton de Gruyter, pp. 52–69.

Ní Mhunghaile, Lesa (2010). '"To open treasures so long locked up": Aidhmeanna agus cur chuige Charlotte Brooke ina saothar *Reliques of Irish Poetry* (1789)', *Léachtaí Cholm Cille XL*. Má Nuad: An Sagart, pp. 47–62.

Noone, Val (2012). *Hidden Ireland in Victoria*. Ballarat: Ballarat Heritage Services.

Ó hAilín, Tomás (1969). 'Irish Revival movements', in: Brian Ó Cuív (ed.) *A View of the Irish Language*. Dublin: Stationery Office, pp. 91–100.

Ó Buachalla, Séamas (1988). *Education Policy in Twentieth Century Ireland*. Dublin: Wolfhound Press.

Ó Conchubhair, Brian (2003). 'The Gaelic font controversy: the Gaelic League's (post-colonial) crux', *Irish University Review* 33.1: 46–63.

Ó Conchubhair, Brian (2009). *Fin de Siècle na Gaeilge. Darwin, an Athbheochan agus Smaointeoireacht na hEorpa*. [The Fin de Siècle of Irish. Darwin, the Language Revival and European Intellectualism.] Conamara: An Clóchomhar Teoranta.

Ó Cuív, Brian (1969). 'Irish in the modern world', in: Brian Ó Cuív (ed.) *A View of the Irish Language*. Dublin: Stationery Office, pp. 122–32.

Ó Curnáin, Brian (2007). *The Irish of Iorras Aithneach, County Galway*. Vols 1–4. Dublin: Dublin Institute for Advanced Studies.

Ó Curreáin, Seán (2008). 'Presentation from the Irish language commissioner', in: Fidelma Ní Ghallchóir and Blanca Nájera (eds) *Special EAFT Seminar. Minority Languages and Terminology Policies*. Vienna: Termnet Publisher, pp. 19–26.

Ó Danachair, Caoimhín (1969). 'The Gaeltacht', in: Brian Ó Cuív (ed.) *A View of the Irish Language*. Dublin: Stationery Office, pp. 112–21.

Ó Giollagáin, Conchúr and Seosamh Mac Donnacha (2008). 'The Gaeltacht today', in: Caoilfhionn Nic Pháidín and Seán Ó Cearnaigh (eds) *A New View of the Irish Language*. Dublin: Cois Life Teoranta, pp. 108–20.

Ó hIfearnáin, Tadhg and Máire Ní Neachtain (eds) (2012). *An tSochtheangeolaíocht: Feidhm agus Tuairisc*. [Sociolinguistics. Aim and Scope.] Baile Átha Cliath: Cois Life Teoranta.

Ó hIfearnáin, Tadhg and Noel Ó Murchadha (2011). 'The perception of standard Irish as a prestige target variety', in: Tore Kristiansen and Nikolas Coupland (eds) *Standard Languages and Language Standards in a Changing Europe*. Oslo: Novus, pp. 97–104.

O'Leary, Philip (1994). *The Prose Literature of the Gaelic Revival 1881–1921. Ideology and Innovation*. Pennsylvania: Pennsylvania State University.

Ó Murchú, Helen (2008). *More Facts about Irish*. Baile Átha Cliath: Coiste na hÉireann den Bhiúró Eorpach do Theangacha Neamhfhorleathana Teoranta.

Ó Súilleabháin, Donnchadh (1998). *Athbheochan na Gaeilge. Cnuasach Aistí*. [The Revival of Irish. A Collection of Essays.] Baile Átha Cliath: Conradh na Gaeilge.

Ó Torna, Caitríona (2005). *Cruthú na Gaeltachta 1893–1922*. [The Creation of the Gaeltacht 1893–1922.] Baile Átha Cliath: Cois Life Teoranta.

Ó Tuama, Seán (1972). 'The Gaelic League idea in the future', in: Seán Ó Tuama (ed.) *The Gaelic League Idea*. Dublin: Mercier Press, pp. 98–109.

Romaine, Suzanne (2008). 'Irish in the global context', in: Caoilfhionn Nic Pháidín and Seán Ó Cearnaigh (eds) *A New View of the Irish Language*. Dublin: Cois Life Teoranta, pp. 11-25.

Titley, Alan (2000). 'An náisiúntacht Ghaelach agus Náisiúnachas na hÉireann' [The Irish Nation and Irish Nationalism], in: Micheál Ó Cearúil (ed.) *An Aimsir Og. Cuid a Dó*, pp. 34–49.

Uí Chollatáin, Regina (2004). *An Claidheamh Soluis agus Fáinne an Lae 1899–1932*. [The Sword of Light and The Dawn of Day 1899–1932.] Baile Átha Cliath: Cois Life Teoranta.

Uí Chollatáin, Regina (2006). 'Iriseoireacht na Gaeilge, Conradh na Gaeilge, agus cúrsaí polaitíochta sna fichidí: Gluaiseacht amháin, trí mheán' [Irish journalism, the Gaelic League and the politics of the twenties: one movement and three media], in: Ruairí Ó hUiginn and Liam Mac Cóil (eds) *Bliainiris 6*. Rath Cairn: Carbad, pp. 173–202.

Uí Chollatáin, Regina (2011). 'Irish Language Revival and "cultural chaos": Sources and scholars in Irish language journalism', in: Erin Boon, A. Joseph McMullen and Natasha Sumner (eds) *Proceeding of the Harvard Celtic Colloquium. Volume XXX*. Cambridge, Boston: Harvard University, pp. 273–92.

Uí Chollatáin, Regina (2012a). 'Trasnú teorainneacha agus náisiún in iriseoireacht na Gaeilge sa naoú haois déag' [The crossing of borders and nations in Irish journalism of the nineteenth century], in: Fionntán de Brún and Séamus Mac Mathúna (eds) *Teanga agus Litríocht na Gaeilge i gCúige Uladh sa Naoú hAois Déag*. [Irish Language and Literacy in Ulster in the Nineteenth Century.] Béal Feirste: Institiúid Taighde na Gaeilge agus an Léinn Cheiltigh, Ollscoil Uladh [Belfast: Institute for Irish Research and Celtic Studies, University of Ulster], pp. 107–33.

Uí Chollatáin, Regina (2012b). 'Athruithe teanga agus caomhnú teanga i scéal an chló i ré na hAthbheochana' [Language shift and language preservation in print media in the revival period], in: Eoin Mac Cárthaigh and Jürgen Uhlich (eds) *Féilscríbhinn do Chathal Ó Háinle*. [Festschrift for Cathal Ó Háinle.] Conamara: An Clóchomhar, Cló Iar-Chonnacht, pp. 961–82.

Uí Chollatáin, Regina (2014a). 'Deisceabail agus soiscéalta. Ceannródaithe athbheochana agus fóram na hiriseoireachta' [Disciples and Gospels. Leaders of the Language Revival and the Journalistic Forum], in: Tracey Ní Mhaonaigh (ed.) *Léachtaí Cholm Cille XLIV*, pp. 22–45.

Uí Chollatáin, Regina (2014b). '*An Claidheamh Soluis agus Fáinne an Lae*. "The turning of the tide"', in Felix Larkin and Mark O'Brien (eds) *Periodicals and Journalism in Twentieth-Century Ireland*. Dublin: Four Courts Press, pp. 31–46.

Uí Fhaoláin, Aoife (2014). 'Language revival and conflicting identities in the *Irish Independent*', *Irish Studies Review* http://www.tandfonline.com/action/showCitFormats?doi=10.1080/09670882.2013.872388.

Walsh, John and Bernadette O'Rourke (2014). 'Becoming a new speaker of Irish: linguistic *mudes* throughout the life cycle', *Digithum* 16. Catalunya: Universitat Oberta de Catalunya.

9
Language, Politics and Identity in Ireland: a Historical Overview

Tony Crowley

9.1 Introduction

The Belfast Agreement (1998) brought about new constitutional arrangements between the Republic of Ireland and the United Kingdom, and a new structure of governance within Northern Ireland. Designed, amongst other aims, to end the violent conflict in Northern Ireland that had lasted almost 30 years, the agreement was arguably the most important political development within Ireland since the declaration of the Irish Republic in 1948. It is revealing therefore, that the text of the concord included the following general declaration:

> All participants recognise the importance of respect, understanding and tolerance in relation to linguistic diversity, including in Northern Ireland, the Irish language, Ulster-Scots and the languages of the various ethnic minorities, all of which are part of the cultural wealth of the island of Ireland. (Belfast Agreement 1998: 19)

In the context of a document that outlined the contours of a major historical settlement, this is a striking statement about the significance of language(s) in Ireland which indicates the continuing social and political status of 'the language question(s)' in Irish history. It will be the purpose of this chapter therefore, to present a short account of how and why language came to gain such importance in Ireland. Central topics in the analysis will be the role played by language in the imposition of colonial rule; in the incorporation of Ireland within the United Kingdom; in the movement to gain autonomy from British rule; and in the shaping of identity in both independent Ireland and Northern Ireland.

9.2 Language and colonial rule

In 1366, some two centuries after the Anglo-Norman invasion, the first legislative act of linguistic colonialism was passed by an Irish Parliament. The Statutes of Kilkenny were premised on a historical contrast:

> whereas at the conquest of the land of Ireland, and for a long time after, the English of the said land used the English language, mode of riding and apparel, and were governed and ruled, both they and their subjects called Betaghes, according to the English law… now many of the said land, forsaking the English language, manners, mode of riding, laws and usages, live and govern themselves according to the manners, fashion, and language of the Irish enemies. (Irish Archaeological Society 1843: 3, 5)

As a result of this cultural decline 'the said land, and the liege people thereof, the English language, the allegiance due our lord the king, and the English laws there, are put in subjection and decayed, and the Irish enemies exalted and raised up, contrary to reason'. To address the issue, the Statutes stipulated a series of measures, including one that,

> ordained and established, that every Englishman do use the English language, and be named by an English name, leaving off entirely the manner of naming used by the Irish; and that every Englishman use the English custom, fashion, mode of riding and apparel, according to his estate; and if any English, or Irish living amongst the English, use the Irish language amongst themselves, contrary to this ordinance, and thereof be attainted, his lands and tenements, if he have any, shall be seized into the hands of his immediate lord. (Irish Archaeological Society 1843: 11, 13)

On one reading the Statutes might be taken as evidence of a confident colonial state imposing its language and culture on the colonised. In fact, however, the edict implicitly reveals the complexity of the linguistic order in the medieval period, since rather than trying to control the Irish-speaking native population, the Statutes were directed at the colonisers in order to prevent the process of Gaelicisation. The focus was on the behaviour of those who lived in The Pale, the relatively narrow area of English rule: the 'English, or Irish living among the English'. In other words, the real problem for the colonial state in this period was not the fact that the vast majority of the subject people spoke Irish, it was that many of the colonialists were assimilating to the native culture.

The language struggle in medieval Ireland was not restricted to English and Irish, since the colonisers brought not only their own Norman language, they also imported the diverse languages of their soldiery (including Flemish, Welsh and Anglo-Norman). But as the contest of languages progressed, the significant relations developed between Irish, Latin, French and English. However, while French and Latin served as the languages of bureaucracy and administration, neither was used widely as a vernacular tongue and, over a significant period, French was gradually displaced by English as the main rival to Irish in Ireland. The spread of English was, however, a very limited process and one which depended on the uneven consolidation of colonial rule beyond the towns. The difficulty the colonisers encountered in this regard is revealed in various legislative acts. In 1465, for example, the Irish Parliament passed 'An act that the Irishmen dwelling in the counties of Dublin, Myeth, Vriel, and Kildare, shall go apparelled like Englishmen, and wear their Beards after the English Maner, swear Allegiance, and take English surname'. The aim of forcing the Irish living under English rule to conform to English culture included the crucial issue of naming, and the heads of families were ordered to adopt 'an English surname of one town, as Sutton, Chester, Trim, Skryne, Cork, Kinsale: or colour, as white blacke, browne: or arte or science, as smith or carpenter: or office, as cooke, butler' on pain of 'forfeyting of his good yearely' (Stat. Ire. 1786: 5 E 4. c. 3). But the most notable feature of these efforts to prescribe linguistic change is their failure, as exemplified by the exemptions that so often accompanied the apparently rigorous strictures. Thus the municipal archives of Waterford in 1492–3 recorded an order that no one 'shall plead or defend in the Irish tongue' in local courts, and that if necessary an English speaker had to be employed for the purpose. Importantly, however, an exception was made 'if one party be of the country' (which probably means outside the city), 'and then all such shall be at liberty to speak Irish' (Historical Manuscripts Commission 1885: 323). A more striking sign of the weakness of early colonial language policy is the fact that when one of Poyning's Laws in 1495 reaffirmed the Statutes of Kilkenny, it made an exception of 'those that speaketh of the Irish language' (Stat. Ire. 1786: 10 H7. c. 8).

The turning point came as part of a larger process of centralisation and consolidation undertaken by the later Tudors. The key text was Henry VIII's 'Act for English Order, Habit and Language' (1537) which elaborated on a point noted in the Statutes of Kilkenny almost two centuries earlier:

> there is again nothing which doth more contain and keep many of [the King's] subjects of this his said land, in a certain savage and wild kind and manner of living, than the diversity that is betwixt them in tongue, language, order and habit, which by the eye deceiveth the multitude, and persuadeth unto them, that they should be as it were of sundry sorts, or rather of sundry countries, where indeed they be wholly together one body, whereof his highness is the only head under God. (Stat. Ire. 1786: 28 H 8. c.xv.)

Given the importance of this insight, the act contained a warning:

> whosoever shall, for any respect, at any time, decline from the order and purpose of this law, touching the increase of the English tongue, habit, and order, or shall suffer any within his family or rule, to use the Irish habit, or not to use themselves to the English tongue, his Majesty will repute them in his noble heart ... whatsoever they shall at other times pretend in words and countenance, to be persons of another sort and inclination than becometh the true and faithful subjects. (Stat. Ire. 1786: 28 H 8. c.xv.)

In other words, whatever the Irish Lords in particular said about their political allegiance to the crown, adherence to the English language was to be considered a touchstone. Failure to use English was to be taken as a sign of political dissent.

With the extension of English power in Ireland, the ever-increasing bureaucratic and administrative demands of the colonial state necessitated the use of English, at least in those areas where crown rule was consolidated. And yet despite this development, the fact is that the imposition of English was a remarkably slow process that took place over centuries and remained patchy, at least until the end of the eighteenth century. That does not mean, however, that the 'Act for English Order, Habit and Language' was simply another failed legislative effort. Notwithstanding the ineffectiveness of Henry's edict as an instrument of rapid linguistic change, its significance lies precisely in its articulation of the link between cultural identity (the 'manner of living' that involves 'tongue, language, order and habit') and political allegiance. This ideological tenet became central to colonial language policy and was summarised in Edmund Spenser's dictum that 'the speech being

Irish, the heart must needes bee Irish' (which led Spenser to believe that state policy should follow previous practice since 'it hath ever beene the use of the Conquerour, to despise the language of the conquered, and to force him by all meanes to learne his') (Spenser 1633 [1596]: 48, 47). More importantly perhaps, the putative connection between linguistic identity and political allegiance was one that came to haunt colonialism; it became the basis of Irish cultural nationalism's entire political project.

9.3   After the Union: an English-speaking Ireland

There were a number of legal attempts that sought, directly or indirectly, to impose English in Ireland, yet it is clear that the impact of legislation on spoken Irish was very limited.[1] For example, the antiquarian, John Windele, estimated that in the early eighteenth century, two-thirds of the Irish population used Gaelic as their everyday language (1,340,000 from a total of just over 2 million) (J. W. [John Windele] 1857: 243). And it was claimed that by the end of the century, more than half the population were, perforce or by choice, Irish speakers: 'at least eight hundred thousand of our countrymen speak Irish only, and there are at least twice as many more who speak it in preference' (Stokes 1799: 45). Yet though the pace of anglicisation may have been slow, such surveys indicate that significant linguistic change was underway in the eighteenth century. If these figures are correct (and they are the best available), there was a clear acceleration of a process that developed even more quickly in the following century. For the 1851 census reported that less than a quarter of the population spoke Irish, of whom fewer than 5 per cent were monoglot, while the 1911 census recorded slightly more than 13 per cent as Irish speakers, with fewer than 3 per cent monoglot (Crowley 2005: 158). The shift is startling: from around 66 per cent to 15 per cent in less than 200 years. But given that the use of law as the instrument of linguistic change was relatively ineffective, how was this situation brought about? There are two principal factors: economics and cultural hegemony, both of which played important roles in the incorporation of Ireland within the United Kingdom after the Act of Union (1800).

Given the nature of colonialism, economic imperatives were bound to influence the use of language and there is evidence of an early understanding of this point. In the early eighteenth century, for example, Edward Nicolson argued that English was already the medium of economic exchange for the young: 'there is hardly a boy of 16 years old in Ireland but can understand and speak English. Their parents encourage

them to it for their own trading and dealing with their English land-
lords' (Nicolson 1715: 27). Later, the material benefits associated with
English were made clear in Arthur Young's *Tour in Ireland* (1780), in
which he recorded that 'Lord Shannon's bounties to labourers amount
to 50l a year. He gives it to them by way of encouragement; but only
to such as can speak English, and do something more than fill a cart'
(Young 1780: vol. 2, 50). Such practices led to an ordering of English
and Irish in terms of economics and affect. Anderson argued that for
the native speaker, Irish was the 'language of social intercourse', whereas
English was 'the language of barter, or worldly occupations; taken up
solely at the market' (Anderson 1818: 54). Coneys put the point in
starker terms: 'English is the language of his commerce – the Irish the
language of his heart' (Coneys 1842: 73).

Despite the linguistic effects brought about by economic pressure,
however, the co-option of Ireland into the United Kingdom following
the Act of Union (1800) was made problematic by the fact that significant (if decreasing) numbers of the Irish remained Irish-speaking.
It followed therefore that the political project of union had to be
matched by a cultural attempt to hasten anglicisation. There were two
main aspects to this process. First, as Joseph Lee has noted, the expansion of the anglophone state (including measures which were, ironically,
intended to meet nationalist demands), meant that English became the
medium for a wide variety of forms of work, social mobility and preference (Lee 1989: 666). Second, the impact of the state's economic policies
meant that English became a necessity for basic survival as the growth
of the cities drew workers away from rural Ireland (where the majority
of Irish speakers were born) to lives that were almost exclusively conducted in English. In addition, the devastating effects of the Famine and
the state's response to it not only caused a further massive population
shift away from the countryside, it also taught the rural poor an important lesson. As emigration became a way of life, Irish parents eagerly
sent their children to the state-funded national schools which taught
entirely in the language they needed in Britain and America. The clarity
of the parents' motivation was noted by an education commissioner: 'it
is natural to inquire how this strong passion for education could have
possessed a people who are themselves utterly illiterate . . . Their passion
may be traced to one predominant desire – the desire to speak English'
(Keenan 1857–8: xx).

Yet though the role of economics as a driver of linguistic change
was crucial, it does not quite explain the nature of the shift since as
Lee has noted, the economic argument 'would explain the acquisition

of English, but not the loss of Irish' (Lee 1989: 662). This is indeed a puzzling question: why did Irish people apparently make the judgement that English could only be learned if Irish were dropped? After all, bilingualism had formed part of the linguistic experience of Ireland for a considerable period of time. The answer lay in the cultural status which was increasingly attached to the English language in the nineteenth century. For although English had been the dominant language of economic life for a considerable period, the incorporation of Ireland into the United Kingdom brought with it the construction of English as the culturally hegemonic language and Irish as the stigmatised and secondary form.

There is evidence that the cultural as well as practical elevation of English began in the early eighteenth century, as Aodh Buidhe Mac Cruitín, poet, linguist and member of the bardic class, noted:

(1) na flatha ba fairsing in Éirinn uair...
   ur éirigh Galla agus ceannaithe caola an chnuais
   le tréimhse eatortha ag teagasc a mbéas don tsluagh;
   do réir mar mheallaid a mbailte dob aolta snuadh
   tá Béarla i bhfaisean go tairise is Gaeilge fuar.

   Consider the rulers who once were generous in Ireland...
   until foreigners and the cunning avaricious merchants came
      between them
   teaching their own customs to the people
   according as they seduce our fairest towns
   English becomes fashionable and Irish decays.

   (Ó Cuív 1986: 397)

Later in the eighteenth century the 'fashionability' of English amongst the Irish middle class in Ireland led to a remarkable confidence in their own form of the language. Nowhere was this more clearly articulated than in the *Essay on Irish Bulls* (1802) by Maria and Richard Lovell Edgeworth, in which they made the bold claim that 'the Irish, in general, speak better English than is commonly spoken by the natives of England':

The English which [the Irish] speak is chiefly such as has been traditional in their families since the time of the early settlers in the island. During the reign of Elizabeth and the reign of Shakespeare, numbers of English migrated to Ireland; and whoever attends to the phraseology of the lower Irish, may, at this day, hear many of the phrases and expressions used by Shakespeare. Their vocabulary has been preserved in its near pristine purity since that time, because they have not had intercourse with those counties in England which have made for themselves a jargon unlike to any language under heaven. (Edgeworth and Edgeworth 1802: 199–200)

Evidently, at least amongst the urban middle class, the elevation of English as the prestige form was well underway by the end of the eighteenth century. In relation to the rural poor, however, the construction of English as the culturally hegemonic form took longer and was brought about by two modes of institutional practice whose influence was both paradoxical and particularly effective: the Catholic Church and political nationalism.

After the legalisation of the Catholic colleges in 1782, English was used as the language of Irish Catholic higher education and one practical effect of this policy was the lack of support for the teaching of literacy in Irish, as Conor McSweeny noted: 'An Irish prayer-book is a thing which the poor Irish peasant has never seen. Not only has he not been taught the language which he speaks, but his clergy have never encouraged, and have sometimes forbidden him to learn it' (McSweeny 1843: vii, 55). The Church's decision that the future lay with English led to peculiar scenes:

I have seen an Irish bishop, with mitre on head and crozier in hand, delivering an elaborate English discourse to an Irish congregation, while a priest stood in the pulpit interpreting it sentence by sentence. This prelate was the son of an Irish peasant, born and reared in one of the most Irish districts in Ireland. Many of his audience might have been, and probably were his playmates in childhood and boyhood, and must have heard him speak the language of his father and mother; but he had never learned it, and was now too distinguished a dignitary of the church, to remember anything of the language of the vulgar herd he had left below him. (McSweeny 1843: vii, 55)

This practical elevation of English and derogation of Irish was denounced bitterly by a contributor to the revivalist journal *An Claidheamh Soluis* (The Sword of Light) at the end of the century: 'the priests are more to blame for the decay of Irish than any other class of the population ... The priests are to blame as a body for their attitudes towards English' (Ruadh 1899: 454).

The general message from the Catholic Church (though there were important dissenting figures), was reinforced by the other national influence on the cultural life of the majority of Irish speakers: the movement for political independence. From the revolutionary United Irishmen of 1798 to the Land Leaguers and the Irish Parliamentary Party of the late nineteenth century, purely political nationalism resolutely set its face against the use of the Irish language. From one perspective, this tactic made sense, since English was the language in which politics was conducted in the metropolitan centre, but at a deeper level, the use of English tied Ireland culturally ever more closely into the Union. Like Irish-speaking parents, Irish politicians appear to have thought that they had to drop Irish in order to use English. The enigma is particularly pointed in the case of Daniel O'Connell, in practical terms the most successful leader of Irish political nationalism. A native Gaelic speaker, O'Connell admitted that 'the Irish language is connected with many recollections that twine around the hearts of Irishmen', but, he added, 'the superior utility of the English tongue, as the medium of modern communication, is so great, that I can witness without a sigh the gradual disuse of the Irish' (Daunt 1848: 14–15). Following O'Connell's lead, in both the political and cultural spheres, Irish became the language of memory and affect while English was the language of utility and modernity. In practice, as a later commentator noted, 'the Irish-speaking Irishman' was given 'the choice of learning English, and using English, or of being shut out from every public function of life in his own country' (Ó hEigceartaigh 1918: 17).

After Union, a combination of forces, many of which had been emergent for a considerable period, created a new linguistic situation in which English became not only the dominant language of everyday life for the majority in Ireland – the medium of economics, education, family life, religion and even political aspiration – but also the culturally hegemonic language of prestige and status. As a corollary, Irish became an unmodern language of poverty and exclusion. Thomas Davis, the Young Irelander, noted that 'the middle classes [thought] it a sign of vulgarity to speak Irish' (Davis 1914: 105). Perhaps more significantly, a later observer noted that the 'illiterate Irish-speaking peasant' appeared to regard Irish as 'the synonym of poverty and misery' and to consider that 'many of the evils from which they suffer are traceable to its continued use' (Flaherty 1884: 13–14). With the spread of such sentiments, the cultural project of sealing Ireland's place in an English-speaking United Kingdom seemed to have been achieved.

9.4   The Irish language and independence

In 'The Necessity for De-Anglicising Ireland', a speech given to the National Literary Society in Dublin in 1892 (in the run-up to the Second Home Rule Bill), Douglas Hyde noted an incongruity:

> What the battleaxe of the Dane, the sword of the Norman, the wile of the Saxon were unable to perform, we have accomplished ourselves. We have at last broken the continuity of Irish life, and just at the moment when the Celtic race is presumably about to largely recover possession of its own country, it finds itself stript of its Celtic characteristics ... it has lost all that [it] had – language, traditions, music, genius, and ideas. Just when we should be starting to build up anew the Irish race and the Gaelic nation ... we find ourselves despoiled of the bricks of Irish nationality. (Hyde 1986: 157)

To remedy the problem, Hyde set out a cultural agenda at the heart of which was the Irish language:

> Every Irish-feeling Irishman, who hates the reproach of West-Britonism, should set himself to encourage the efforts which are being made to keep alive our once great national tongue. The losing of it is our greatest blow, and the sorest stroke that the rapid Anglicisation of Ireland has inflicted upon us. In order to de-Anglicise ourselves we must at once arrest the decay of the language. (Hyde 1986: 160)

Given the broad economic, political and cultural context set out in the previous section, the prospects for Hyde's project must have seemed slim, even though his talk was instrumental in the founding of Conradh na Gaeilge/The Gaelic League in 1893. And yet, 20 years later, on the eve of the events that marked the beginning of the end of British rule in Ireland, no less a figure than Padraig Pearse declared accurately that the 'coming revolution' would be brought about by 'the men and movements that have sprung from the Gaelic League' (Pearse 1952: 91).

The possibility of a gap between political autonomy and national independence was first fully articulated by Hyde (though it had been foreshadowed in the work of Davis and the Young Irelanders in the 1840s). Such sentiments were relatively common after the fall of Parnell, when, as W. B. Yeats noted, 'a disillusioned and embittered Ireland turned from parliamentary politics' (Yeats 1955: 559). In fact Yeats advocated just such a shift away from purely political nationalism 'to a partly intellectual and historical nationalism … with the language question as its lever' (Yeats 1955: 237). And the distinction was explored in the first pamphlet published by the Gaelic League, Fr. Michael O'Hickey's *The True National Ideal*:

> [Nationality] is the outcome, the resultant, the culmination of many things, of which political autonomy is but one – very important doubtless, but by no means the only or even the chief, thing to be considered. You may have a nation without political autonomy – not, I admit, a nation in all its fullness and integrity; but I emphatically insist that autonomous institutions, failing all other elements and landmarks of nationality, do not constitute a nation in the true sense. (O'Hickey 1900: 1–2)

Given the apparent disjuncture between the achievement of Home Rule and what Hyde called the rupturing of 'the continuity of Irish life', O'Hickey asked the crucial questions: 'what is a nation? Or, in other words, what is nationality?' Acknowledging features such as tradition, history, literature, and institutions, O'Hickey asserted that 'none is more fundamental, none more important, none strikes deeper roots, none is more far-reaching in its results than a national language. This truth the Dutch clearly grasped, and have enshrined in a proverb – "No language, no nation"' (O'Hickey 1900: 2). The principle was reflected in one of the Gaelic League's mottos: 'Tír gan teanga, tír gan anam' (A country without a language is a country without a soul) and it signalled a new primacy for culture. For underpinning the Gaelic League's campaign was the belief that only culture could prevent the promise of independence from becoming an empty gesture of political formalism. Specifically, only the revival of the Irish language could guarantee a nation worthy of the struggle to escape British rule.

At the end of the nineteenth century, then, the Irish language found a new role as the central factor in the constitution of the nation's cultural identity (there had been academic interest in Irish from the mid-eighteenth century, but its focus was antiquarian and did not include the contemporary spoken language). At times this culturalist tendency skirted the dangers of disregarding the need for political independence. D. P. Moran, for example, a key figure in the Irish-Ireland movement, claimed that when young Irish men and women could speak Irish as well as English, 'then there will be a genuine Irish nation – whoever may be making the laws – which economic tendencies, battering rams, or the Queen's soldiers will be powerless to kill' (Moran 1905: 27). For the most part, however, the Irish language was taken to be the repository of the nation's past and, therefore, for that very reason, its future:

> A people's language tells us what they were even better than their history. So true is this that even if the people had perished and their history had been lost, we might still learn from their language – and in language I include literature – to what intellectual stature they had attained, what was the extent and direction of their moral development, and what their general worthiness. (Kavanagh 1902: 1)

This form of cultural nationalism produced a mode of identity politics in which the Irish language was used to pit Irishness against Englishness. In many cases this took the form of an insistence on the importance of defending the cultural distinctiveness of Irish (and indeed other endangered languages) against the predations of empire. Thus Dermot Chenevix Trench asserted pointedly that 'national language movements are not as a protest against the abolition of barriers of race in the interests of human solidarity, but against the forcible extermination of a racial genius through the pressure of political and economic circumstance' (Trench 1912: 29). All too often, however, the debate followed the pattern of differentiation, ordering and evaluation that is typical of identity politics. This produced a variety of rhetorical tropes, some of which belonged to the discourse of biological racism. Trench, for example, referred to 'the Irish larynx' as 'the counterpart of Gaelic phonetics', and asked his reader if s/he wanted to live in 'an Ireland which reflects your racial type?' (Trench 1912: 27, 32), while in a similar vein, O'Hickey warned of the dangers of Anglicisation:

> We may, to all intents and purposes, cease to be Gaels; we may, in a sense, become West Britons; further we cannot go – Saxons we cannot become. Should the worst befall, it were better, in my opinion, to be something that could be clearly defined and classed; for anything at all would seem preferable to a mongrel, colourless, nondescript racial monstrosity evolved somewhere in the bosom of the twentieth century. (O'Hickey 1900: 4)

Indeed on occasion, cultural nationalists such as Moran were explicit about the benefits of racial discourse:

> Racial hatred is a bad passion at the best, and one which it appears to me, is absolutely unjustifiable on moral grounds, unless in so far as it is impersonal and complementary to a real desire to keep intact the distinctive character, traditions, and civilisation of one's own country. (Moran 1905: 67)

Such thinking led to some absolutist conclusions. Kavanagh described the English as 'a people with whom [the Irish] have nothing in common but a common humanity' since 'nature itself has drawn a broad line of separation, I must say a triple line, geographical, moral and intellectual' (Kavanagh 1902: 10). While a leader in *An Claidheamh Soluis* in 1917 asserted simply that 'An Irishman, however bad, is better than an Englishman, however good' (O'Leary 1994: 211).

Though dominant, such sentiments were not unchallenged and from a socialist perspective Frederick Ryan argued that 'the mere desire to speak another language does not of necessity correlate at all with the active desire for political freedom... if the people are content to let the substance of their liberty go, for the gew-gaw of a new grammar, so much the better – for the reactionaries' (Ryan 1904: 217–18). And even within the Gaelic League there was an ongoing debate between 'nativist' and 'progressive' elements over tactics and strategy. In fact in many ways the League itself was the epitome of a modern mass movement whose focus on education depended on innovative methods which inspired cultural confidence in a country greatly in need of it. Yet despite such tendencies, by far the League's greatest achievement was the consolidation of cultural nationalism's fundamental principle as the cornerstone of the national independence movement. Indeed, although the League's goal of reviving the language (or even halting its decline), was largely unattained by the time of independence in 1922, there can be no doubt that by that point, the idea behind the slogan 'tír agus teanga' (country and language) was firmly embedded in the national consciousness. In other words, over a remarkably short period of time, the cultural hegemony of the English language in Ireland had been challenged and, at least in principle if not in practice, weakened. As Michael Collins noted, the Irish language had played a central role in the struggle for independence and its place in the new Ireland seemed certain. The future was full of linguistic promise, even if it had yet to be realised:

We only succeeded after we had begun to get back our Irish ways, after we had made a serious effort to speak our own language, after we had striven again to govern ourselves. How can we express our most subtle thoughts and finest feelings in a foreign tongue? Irish will scarcely be our language in this generation, nor even perhaps in the next. But until we have it again on our tongues and in our minds, we are not free. (Collins 1922: 100)

9.5 Language, identity, politics

Yet if the association of language and identity was linguistic nationalism's most notable legacy, then its achievement was ambivalent. For as noted in Section 9.2 above, the linking of language, national identity and political allegiance was not a new development in Ireland. In fact it was first produced by the colonists as part of their policy of linguistic colonialism; from *The Statutes of Kilkenny* (1366) to Henry VIII's 'Act for English Order, Habit and Language' (1537), language use was taken to signify identity in the most simple and crude way. As the colonial adventurer Fynes Moryson put it somewhat disingenuously in his *Itinerary* (1617): 'communion or difference of language, hath always been observed, a spetial motive to unite or allienate the myndes of all nations... And in generall all nations have thought nothing more powerfull to unite myndes then the Community of language (Moryson 1903: 213). Yet though this belief arose precisely from the political and cultural order imposed by colonialism, it was not theorised and popularised within Europe at least until the end of the eighteenth century. At that point, largely under the influence of the German Romantic and idealist traditions, questions of language, identity and politics again rose to the forefront of crucial debates.

It is important to put this work in context, since many of the key thinkers involved in theorising these issues were situated in locations which gave them a sharp understanding of the politics of language. Johann Gottfried Herder, for example, one of the early and most significant thinkers in this line, worked in Riga, a city which belonged to the Russian Empire but in which German was the prestige language. Surveying this state of affairs, Herder commented:

Has a people anything dearer than the speech of its fathers? In its speech resides its whole thought-domain, its tradition, history, religion, and basis of life, all its heart and soul. To deprive a people of its speech is to deprive it of its one eternal good.... The best culture of a people cannot be expressed through a foreign language; it thrives on the soil of a nation most beautifully, and, I may say, it thrives only by means of the nation's inherited and inheritable dialect. With language is created the heart of a people. (Cited in Fishman 1989: 105)

Herder's forging of an absolute bond between a people's entire way of life and its language was to be enormously influential. Translated into political terms, the linkage was incendiary, as illustrated by Fichte's observation in the *Addresses to the German Nation* (1808) that 'it is beyond doubt that, wherever a separate language is found, there a separate nation exists, which has the right to take charge of its independent affairs and to govern itself' (Fichte 1968: 49). Such sentiments swept across Europe and gave a cultural bent to nationalist movements seeking independence from occupying powers. In Ireland in the 1840s this included Thomas Davis and the Young Irelanders, and Davis articulated the point in terms that echo Herder:

to impose another language on a people is to send their history adrift among the accidents of translation – 'tis to tear their identity from all places – 'tis to substitute arbitrary signs for picturesque and suggestive names – 'tis to cut off the entail of feelings and separate the people from their forefathers by a deep gulf. (Davis 1914: 97–8).

The political conclusion was similar to that outlined by Fichte: 'a people without a language of its own is only half a nation. A nation should guard its language more than its territories – 'tis a surer barrier, and more important frontier, than fortress or river' (Davis 1914: 98).

It is important to historicise such claims in order to grasp their significance. In the context of anti-colonialism, the putative link between language and identity, specifically language and national identity, can be viewed as part of a progressive tendency designed to undermine the justification for colonial rule. In the quotes from Herder, Fichte and Davis given above, for example, this is precisely how the language and identity link operates: we have a language of our own, an identity of our own, therefore we should have autonomy. And there can be little doubt that this principle, embedded within cultural nationalism, played an important role in reshaping the political map in Europe and beyond from the late eighteenth century onwards. Yet it needs to be remembered that the origin of this link lay with the colonial project itself and was part of the justification of linguistic colonialism: they have an alien language, an alien culture, therefore we need to impose our language and culture on them. In fact both linguistic and cultural colonialism and linguistic and cultural nationalism depended on an act of homogenisation that elided a wide variety of differences in order to produce abstract forms – 'language', 'culture', 'identity' – which were then deployed in very specific circumstances for particular political ends. In the context of colonialism, the goal was the imposition of a language as a way of cementing colonial order and rule. In anti-colonial struggles, the aim was to use the apparently unitary language in order to foster identity as a way of opposing colonial rule. But what happened once colonial rule had been overthrown? What were the effects of the 'language', 'culture', 'identity' link in Ireland and, just as importantly, Northern Ireland after independence?

In the Irish Free State, and later the Republic of Ireland, Irish was recognised as the national language and the first official language (English was the second). And from the very inception of the post-independence state, attempts were made to revive Irish as an everyday language of communication. 'Compulsory Irish' was introduced as a central component in education policy, support (albeit limited) was given to the Gaeltacht areas, the language was standardised, and Irish was made a requirement for public service posts. Whatever the intention, however, and notwithstanding the expenditure of considerable resources, the project failed (and was recognised to have failed by the 1960s) in terms of its practical goal. This led to a paradoxical situation, described in an influential report by the Committee on Irish Language Attitudes Research:

> The average individual, for instance, in the national population feels rather strongly that the Irish language is necessary to our ethnic and cultural integrity, and supports the efforts to ensure the transmission of the language. At the same time, under present policies and progress, he is not really convinced that we can ensure its transmission. He has rather negative views about the way Irish has been taught in school and has a rather low or 'lukewarm' personal commitment to its use, although in this latter case, the average person has not sufficient ability in the language to converse freely in it. On the other hand, he strongly supports nearly all government efforts to help the Gaeltacht, but at the same time feels that the language is not very suitable for modern life. (Committee on Irish Language Attitudes Research 1975: 24)

The report indicated a general belief (supported by the facts), that the goal of making Irish a language of everyday life had not been realised, despite a certain type of good will towards the language on the basis of its role in 'ethnic and cultural integrity'. But at a more significant level, what the report showed was that in the context of the failure of the language revival project, all that remained was the idea of the language as a marker of identity. This was recognised in a later report, *The Irish Language in a Changing Society: Shaping the Future* (1988), which noted 'a widening gap between the symbolic significance attached to Irish as an official emblem of national identity, and its use as a richly expressive vernacular in everyday life' (Bord na Gaeilge 1988: xvi). Ironically, it may well be that it was precisely its role as cipher for identity that undermined the use of the language itself, precisely because the identity for which the language was supposed to stand was a conservative, outmoded form which did not reflect the realities of a changing Ireland. In any case, the fate of Irish has been clear for a long time: 'if it is to survive at all it will be as a second language rather than as the main language of society' (Ó Riagáin 1997: 173).

If Irish in Ireland became a marker of national identity rather than the language of national life, then what of its role in Northern Ireland? The attitude of the Northern Irish state was dismissive from the start. Defending the abolition of state funding for Irish teaching in schools in 1933, for example, the then Northern Irish Prime Minister James Craig, Lord Craigavon, commented: 'what use is it to us here in this progressive, busy part of the Empire to teach our children the Irish language? What use would it be to them?' (Maguire 1991: 11). This effectively summed up the antipathetic attitude of the state through to the 1990s. At that point, however, and building on promises made during the peace process, Irish language activists consolidated the real achievements made from the 1960s onwards in the form of Irish-speaking communities that had been established across Northern Ireland (most notably in Belfast). This Northern revival has produced a remarkable growth in the number of Irish speakers in Northern Ireland, a large number of Irish-medium schools, and the establishment of the Belfast Gaeltacht at the heart of the Falls Road (no small achievements given the situation only twenty-odd years ago). In this situation, unlike that in the Republic, it is precisely the role of the language as a marker of identity that has allowed it to flourish. That said, however, in the context of a bitter conflict that lasted almost 30 years, and a society that remains divided on sectarian grounds, the use of Irish as a 'badge of identity' remains problematic. Even if they do not intend to do so, Irish speakers are perceived as making a statement about (non-British) identity every time they open their mouths, which means that the language continues to attract the attention of sectarians. This includes a prominent Loyalist member of the Stormont Assembly whose response to Sinn Féin members' use of Irish in parliamentary debates was to begin a speech with the words 'curry my yoghurt can coca coalyer' (a parody of 'go raibh maith agat, Ceann Comhairle').[2] All of which indicates how far the situation remains from the Belfast Agreement's recognition of 'the importance of respect, understanding and tolerance in relation to linguistic diversity' in Northern Ireland.

9.6 Conclusion

This chapter has sought to trace the bare outlines of the relations between language, politics and identity in Ireland over a long historical period. Given the fact that Ireland was subject to colonialism, incorporation within the United Kingdom, and then partition (resulting in the creation of a sectarian state), it is little surprise that language has been embroiled in the complex social relations that have been played out on the island. Under the specific pressures of Irish history, language (in the form of Irish, English, Ulster Scots ...), was reduced by various forces (some reactionary, some progressive) to little more than a marker of identity. Homogenised, made abstract, forced to fit prescriptive models of identity, the languages of Ireland have not been viewed historically as 'part of the cultural wealth of the island of Ireland', but as the means to foster division, to impose rule, and to create cultural and political hierarchy.

Notes

1. Legislation included: The Statutes of Kilkenny (1366); 'An Act that the Irishmen dwelling in the counties of Dublin, Myeth, Vriel, and Kildare, shall go apparelled like Englishmen, and wear their Beards after the English Maner, swear Allegiance, and take English surname' (1465); 'An Act for the English Order, Habit and Language' (1537); 'An Act for the Uniformity of Common Prayer and Service in the Church' (1560); 'An Act for the Erection of Free Schools (1570); 'An Act for the Explaining of some Doubts Arising upon an Act Entitled, An Act for the Better Execution of his Majesty's Gracious Settlements of his Majesty's Kingdom of Ireland' (1665); 'An Act to Restrain Foreign Education' (1695); 'His Majesty's Royal Charter for Erecting English Protestant Schools in the Kingdom of Ireland' (1733); and 'The Administration of Justice (Language) Act (Ireland)' (1737).

2. The insult led to the exclusion of Gregory Campbell, MLA, from Stormont for a day: http://www.belfasttelegraph.co.uk/news/politics/gregory-campbell-banned-in-absentia-over-curry-my-yoghurt-irish-language-stunt-30719543. html downloaded 14 November 2014.

References

Anderson, Christopher (1818) *A Brief Sketch of Various Attempts which Have Been Made to Diffuse a Knowledge of the Holy Scriptures through the Medium of the Irish Language*. Dublin.

Belfast Agreement: an Agreement Reached at the Multi-Party Talks on Northern Ireland (1998). London: The Stationery Office.

Bord na Gaeilge (1988). *The Irish Language in a Changing Society: Shaping the Future*. Dublin: Bord na Gaeilge.

Collins, Michael (1922). *The Path to Freedom*. Dublin: Talbot Press.

Committee on Irish Language Attitudes Research/An Coiste um Thaighde ar Dhearcadh an Phobail I dtaobh na Gaeilge (1975) Dublin: The Stationery Office.

Coneys, Rev. (1842) 'The Irish language', *The Nation*, 5.

Crowley, Tony (2005). *Wars of Words: the Politics of Language in Ireland 1537–2004*. Oxford: Oxford University Press.

Daunt, W. J. O'Neill (1848). *Personal Recollections of the Late Daniel O'Connell, M.P.* Dublin.

Davis, Thomas (1914). *Essays Literary and Historical*. Dundalk: Dundalga Press.

Edgeworth, Maria and Richard Edgeworth (1802). *Essay on Irish Bulls*. London.

Fichte, J. G. (1968). *Addresses to the German Nation*, ed. G. Armstrong Kelly, New York: Harper.

Fishman, J. (1989) *Language and Ethnicity in Minority Sociolinguistic Perspective*. Clevedon: Multilingual Matters.

Flaherty, Donal (1884). 'Practical hints towards preventing the decay of Irish in the Irish-speaking districts', in: *Proceedings of the [Society for the Preservation of the Irish Language] Congress Held in Dublin*. Dublin.

Historical Manuscripts Commission (1885). 'Archives of the municipal corporation of Waterford' in: *Historical Manuscripts Commission Report*, 10, Appendix v, Dublin.

Hyde, Douglas (1986). 'The necessity for De-Anglicising Ireland', in: B. Ó Conaire (ed.) *Language, Lore and Lyrics: Essays and Lectures of Douglas Hyde*. Dublin: Irish Academic Press.

Irish Archaeological Society (1843). 'The Statutes of Kilkenny' (1366), in: *Tracts Relating to Ireland*. Dublin: Irish Archaeological Society.

J. W. [John Windele] (1857). 'Present extent of the Irish language', *Ulster Journal of Archaeology*, First Series, 5: 243–5.

Kavanagh, Rev. P. F. (1902). *Ireland's Defence – Her Language*, Dublin: Gaelic League.

Keenan, P. J. (1857–8). 'Twenty-third Report of the Commissioners of National Education in Ireland', i, 143–4, *House of Commons Papers*. London.

Lee, Joseph (1989). *Ireland 1912–1985 Politics and Society*. Cambridge: Cambridge University Press.

McSweeny, Conor (1843). *Songs of the Irish*, vii. Dublin.

Maguire, Gabrielle (1991). *Our Own Language: an Irish Language Initiative*. Clevedon: Multilingual Matters.

Moran, D. P. (1905). *The Philosophy of Irish Ireland*. Dublin: Duffy.

Moryson, Fynes (1903). *Shakespeare's Europe. Unpublished Chapters of Fynes Moryson's Itinerary* (1617), ed. C. Hughes. London: Sherratt and Hughes.

Nicolson, E. (1715) 'Letter to the Secretary, Society for Promoting Christian Knowledge', in *Analecta Hibernia* (1931): 2.

Ó Cuív, Brian (1986). 'Irish language and literature, 1691–1845', in: Theodore W. Moody and W. E. Vaughan (eds) *A New History of Ireland*, vol. IV, 'Eighteenth Century Ireland, 1691–1800'. Oxford: Clarendon.

Ó hEigceartaigh, P. S. (1918). 'Politics and the language', *Samhain*, Dublin: Curtis, pp. 1–8.

O'Hickey, Rev. M. P. (1900). *The True National Idea*. Dublin: Gaelic League.

O'Leary, Philip (1994). *The Prose Literature of the Gaelic Revival, 1881–1921 Ideology and Innovation*. Pennsylvania: Pennsylvania University Press.

Ó Riagáin, P. (1997). *Language Policy and Social Reproduction in Ireland 1893–1993*. Oxford: Clarendon.

Pearse, Patrick H. (Padraig) (1899). 'The "Irish" Literary Theatre', *An Claidheamh Soluis*, 1.10.

Pearse, Patrick H. (Padraig) (1952). *Political Writings and Speeches*. Dublin: Talbot.

Ruadh, Donnchadh (1899). 'Irish in County Wexford', *An Claidheamh Soluis*, 1.29.

Ryan, Frederick (1904). 'Is the Gaelic League a progressive force?', *Dana: an Irish Magazine for Independent Thought* 7: 216–20.

Spenser, Edmund (1633). 'A View of the State of Ireland' (1596), in: Sir James Ware (1633) *The Historie of Ireland Collected by Three Learned Authors*, Dublin.

Stokes, Whitley (1799). *Projects for Re-Establishing the Internal Peace and Tranquility of Ireland*. Dublin.

The Statutes at Large Passed in the Parliaments Held in Ireland (1786–1801). 1310–1800. 20 vols. Dublin.

Trench, D. C. (1912). *What is the Use of Reviving Irish?* Dublin: Maunsel.

Yeats, W. B. (1955). *Autobiographies*. London: Macmillan.

Young, Arthur (1780). *A Tour in Ireland, with General Observations on the State of that Kingdom*. 2 vols. Dublin.

10
Emigrant Letters: Exploring the 'Grammar of the Conquered'

Kevin McCafferty

10.1 Doing linguistic archaeology

A few lines from Moya Cannon's poem *Our Words* distil some of the essence of the evolution of new varieties of English in Ireland:

> (1) as the language of conquest
> grows cold in statute books,
> elsewhere, its words are subsumed
> into the grammars of the conquered
> I be, you be, he bees.

(Cannon 2007: 16)

As new Englishes developed over the last five centuries – an important outcome of English, later British, conquest and colonisation – their speakers took the English language and made it their own, creating new grammars in the process. One new grammatical feature that emerged in Irish English (IrE) is the habitual aspect of the declension rattled off by the poet. The interaction in speakers' minds of English/Scots verb forms and an Irish grammatical category resulted in an IrE distinction between indicative and habitual *be*: *She bees early* means something different from *She's early*. This habitual reflects a category that was (and is) present in the Irish language but not in most of the English and Scots varieties that contributed to the feature pool from which IrE emerged. The exception in British English (BrE) is the south-western dialects of England, which did contribute to the mix in colonial Ireland, though the habitual in south-west England is invariant *be*, rather than the conjugated form found in parts of Ireland (see the overview in Hickey 2007: 226–8). *Be* as a habitual marker is present in only 17 of the 76 varieties

(22 per cent) covered by Kortmann and Lunkenheimer's (2013) global survey of morphosyntactic variation; the number of varieties with conjugated habitual *be* must be much lower.[1] In this case, speakers of IrE literally subsumed the words of the language of conquest into their own 'grammar of the conquered'. *She bees early* is a product of the sociocultural mix created by British subjugation and colonisation of Ireland, followed by language shift from Irish to IrE.

Historical sociolinguistics adds the social dimension to the reconstruction of the histories of language varieties in their sociocultural context. This has been called a '[s]ocially-oriented linguistic archaeology' (Conde-Silvestre and Hernández-Campoy 2012: 4): historical sociolinguists dig into layers of textual evidence deposited over the centuries to answer questions about the histories of linguistic features and language varieties. They use insights and methods from sociolinguistics, combining linguistic and social data to study how language change originates and spreads.

English speakers first settled in Ireland in the twelfth century, and while its position was insecure enough throughout the Middle Ages, there is evidence for the survival of features of Medieval IrE into the Early Modern period and after (cf., e.g., Hickey 2005: 193–202, 2007: 48–84; Kallen 2013: 212–19). As the final conquest of Ireland slowly approached completion, the English language was boosted by large-scale British settlement of parts of the Irish Midlands from the 1550s, Munster in the 1580s, and Ulster in the seventeenth century, the latter following the ultimate Irish defeat in 1603. Thus, IrE as we know it today began to evolve largely from the mid-sixteenth century, when English and Scots colonists arrived in large numbers.[2] From about 1750, language shift among the Irish-speaking natives started gathering pace, and English spread into western and south-western Ireland; the island was overwhelmingly English-speaking by 1900.

For a variety of this age, historical sociolinguistic accounts of IrE must be based on evidence from written documents, texts that are, at best, direct or indirect representations of the English of the Irish at some degree of remove from the actual spoken word. Diaries, journals, notebooks and letters written by English-speaking Irishmen and -women are held in archives in Ireland and around the world. One of the largest is the *Irish Emigration Database* (www.dippam.ac.uk or www.qub.ac.uk/cms/collection/IED.htm), which forms the core of CORIECOR, the *Corpus of Irish English Correspondence* (McCafferty and Amador-Moreno, in preparation). Personal letters are often regarded as one of the text types most likely to record colloquial, non-standard, or even broad vernacular usage in the past. Such texts may reveal linguistic developments through time and space, both social and geographical.

The present paper introduces CORIECOR and outlines the usefulness of this corpus for the study of earlier IrE. The concern here is with the kinds of questions that might be asked of CORIECOR data, beginning with linguistic issues and proceeding to geo- and sociolinguistic ones. First, I begin with a section about the usefulness of letters for historical (socio)linguistic study, followed by a brief introduction to CORIECOR.

10.2 Using letters

Historians of Irish emigration have been using personal correspondence of ordinary men and women as important and revealing sources since Schrier (1997 [1958]) analysed emigrant letters to explain why so many Irish crossed the Atlantic in the nineteenth century. There is by now a large body of history based at least in part on personal letters. Such studies examine letters as historical documents whose contents provide answers to questions about, for instance: the underlying motivations for migration; mechanisms of migration; family and community relationships; or how the Irish integrated into new communities abroad. Letters can be a rich source of information on such topics, widening the perspectives of historians to include a broad spectrum of people belonging to different social strata, especially as literacy spread and postage became more affordable in the nineteenth century.

Letters have also provided data for linguistic studies, beginning as far as Ireland is concerned with Montgomery's (1989) survey of the possible Ulster roots of Appalachian dialect features. Linguists are less interested in the content of letters and more in the linguistic forms used in them. Such studies tell language history from below, tapping into a type of data that until recently was not used for writing the history of the English language (or any other). Language history has traditionally been based on literary texts and the writings of elites, people who tend to have more education, and whose language was relatively standardised. In contrast, collections of personal letters often contain texts written by people with little or no formal education, whose writing skills were comparatively rudimentary, and whose letters often reveal colloquial speech patterns, and sometimes broad local or regional vernacular features, because their writing is based, to some extent at least, on the evidence of their ears rather than acquired competence in standard English.

For historians, the non-standardness or vernacularity of letters may be problematical. Many personal letters in archives are not written in accurately spelt, grammatically correct standard English. Literacy levels in Irish society were low in the early nineteenth century (FitzGerald 2013); while literacy improved over time, rates remained comparatively low in Ireland until the end of the century, some 60–70 years after the National School system was established. Correspondence between people of only basic literacy often contains dialect words, non-standard grammar, and phonetic spellings that reflect the everyday English used by members of the Irish peasant and labouring strata. For the historian or social scientist, this is often seen as a drawback. The introduction to a collection of articles on emigrant epistolary practices speaks of:

> [...] the problem of making sense of the writings of the many poorly educated and marginally literate writers for whom the necessity of writing inspired an exercise that taxed their abilities to the limit. Decoding texts with inadequate paragraphing and punctuation, ungrammatical constructions, highly irregular spelling, and language that combines native regional dialect, borrowings from the tongue of the country of resettlement, archaic colloquialisms, and singular, individualized modes of expression is the common experience of those who read immigrant letters. (Elliott et al. (eds) 2006: 3–4)

This list of difficulties faced by the historian highlights precisely the kinds of features that make a text interesting linguistically. As noted by Montgomery, the 'less educated members of society [were] more likely to have speech intrude into their writing because their limited literacy made them more dependent on their ear' (2001a: 13). And Schneider remarks that: '[...] when persons who have had but limited experience in writing and exposure to the norms of written expression are forced to write nevertheless, their writing reflects many features of their speech fairly accurately' (2002: 75–6).

Such comments emphasise how closely writing may reflect speech patterns and directly address the 'bad data' issue raised by Labov (1994: 10–11), who regarded historical data as 'impoverished' because the written documents available to us have survived by chance, because the language of these documents may be influenced by the norms of dialects other than the writers' own vernaculars, because we can only know what they wrote, not how their words were understood, and because we know little about either the social position of the writers and the social structures of their communities. Contra Labov, Nevalainen and Raumolin-Brunberg point out that we can often find out a lot about the historical contexts in which letters were produced (2003: 26–8), and that many of the problems highlighted by Labov can be overcome by 'systematicity in data collection, extensive background reading and good philological work' (Nevalainen and Raumolin-Brunberg 2003: 26). Further advantages of using historical data are that we can offer real-time analyses based on, e.g., letter data that represents genuine communication, thus also overcoming the observer's paradox (Nevalainen and Raumolin-Brunberg 2003: 26–7). As linguists we want access to evidence of the speech of earlier times. Texts like personal letters, which may show the more or less direct influence of speech on the written word, constitute one of the best sources for evidence of non-standard or vernacular usage before the invention of sound recording. In a real sense, then, we might say that the historian's difficulty is the linguist's opportunity.

10.2.1 The *Corpus of Irish English Correspondence* (CORIECOR)

The *Corpus of Irish English Correspondence* (CORIECOR) was based originally on letters contained in the *Irish Emigration Database*. It now also includes further letter collections. The corpus currently contains over 6500 letters and some 3.5 million words. CORIECOR is probably the largest corpus of its kind for IrE available anywhere, and it is still growing. While it contains few letters from the late seventeenth and early eighteenth centuries, there is substantial material from the 1730s onwards, and coverage of the entire period from 1750 to 1940 is fairly solid.

While linguists using letters have often been primarily interested in studying the most vernacular letters available (e.g., Montgomery 1995; Kautzsch 2002; see also Schneider 2002), and sometimes the only letters admitted for study are those that show high levels of vernacular usage, the editorial policy of the CORIECOR compilers is more omnivorous: this corpus includes letters written by people whose language ranges across a broad spectrum, from the correct standard English of some of the better-educated correspondents, including members of the clergy, gentry and aristocracy, via merchants and others from the 'middling orders', to the non-standard or vernacular English of the peasant and labouring classes. When coupled with as much background biographical information as possible on the letter-writers, CORIECOR holds out the prospect of historical sociolinguistic analysis of the evolution of IrE.

CORIECOR is intended for long-term diachronic research on IrE. Documents of the kind collected there, representing people from many parts of Ireland, may permit us to trace the emergence and development of features of IrE through time, as well as studying stylistic, regional and social variation. CORIECOR may also be used for comparative studies of IrE and other varieties. In the following, I summarise the findings of two variationist studies using CORIECOR: an analysis of the linguistic conditioning of BE-deletion in IrE, which shows that IrE is unlikely to be the source of much of the well-known BE-deletion in New World Englishes; and a study of the variable use of first person *shall/will* that shows the use of *shall* to have declined in IrE in the nineteenth century and to have been related to an urban–rural split and geographical variation, as well as the degree of intimacy between correspondents. Before outlining these studies, let's first take a look at some of the kinds of features that may be encountered in personal correspondence.

10.3   Documenting linguistic features in personal letters

The usefulness of personal letters for the study of regional English may be demonstrated by looking at some features gleaned from the short passages cited in Schrier's classic historical study, which analysed 222 emigrant letters (1997 [1958]: 196). Schrier's citations were chosen to serve his historical aims. He had no interest in the language of the letters as such, and comments only in vague terms on the 'charm of expression inherent in the modes and manners peculiar to Irish speech [and their] air of unlettered eloquence' (Schrier 1997 [1958]: 23). Yet there are many interesting linguistic features in his quotations, including both universal non-standard features and vernacular features typical of IrE.

Some of the general non-standard features in the Schrier letters are listed in (2)–(4). These are not diagnostic of particular localities or regions and therefore do not constitute dialect or vernacular traits. Rather, these are widespread non-standard forms that occur in almost all Englishes.

(2)   [...] they work **cheaper** and are more submissive than the English speaking working man (Schrier 1997 [1958]: 34)

(3)   [...] they are **not** aloud to sell **no** more liquor in the state of Iowa (Schrier 1997 [1958]: 27)

(4)   There **is** no lords or earls in this Country that you have too put your hand too your hat for (Schrier 1997 [1958]: 31)

Adverbs appear in a number of citations lacking the –*ly* ending preferred in present-day standard English, as in (2). This zero adverbial form is frequent in non-standard English, being reported in all British varieties and 91 per cent of all varieties globally (Kortmann and Lunkenheimer 2013). Negative concord (or multiple negatives), as in (3), is another ubiquitous non-standard feature. Normative grammarians have been condemning negative concord for centuries, but it remains one of the most widespread non-standard features, reported from 80 per cent of Englishes worldwide and all British varieties, with the (perhaps dubious) exception of Orkney and Shetland English (Kortmann and Lunkenheimer 2013). Finally, existential-*there* with a singular verb and notional plural subject (4) is another feature found in all British varieties and 71 per cent of all varieties worldwide (Kortmann and Lunkenheimer 2013). These are such common features of the English language that their use in IrE letters only indicates relatively non-standard usage.

Other features in the Schrier citations are more peculiar to IrE. There are, in fact, more dialectal than non-standard features in the citations. Features classified as dialectal for current purposes not only deviate from standard English usage, but are also associated with a particular region; in this case, they are reported in the literature on IrE. They need not be exclusively IrE, though some are. Many dialectal features of IrE are shared with the British Englishes of regions that supplied settlers to the British colony in Ireland, notably Scots/Scottish English, and the northern and (south-)western dialects of England. The features highlighted in (5)–(7) are some of the dialect or vernacular features found in Schrier's citations.

(5) [...] **dont be laboring** under an idea that men are very scarce here (Schrier 1997 [1958]: 35)

(6) Indeed I **do be thinking** of ye when ye least suspect it (Schrier 1997 [1958]: 36)

(7) [...] servant girls **gets** from eight to twelve shillings per week and keep (Schrier 1997 [1958]: 29)

The negative progressive imperative in (5) is a uniquely Irish phenomenon that is not even included in Kortmann and Lunkenheimer's (2013) global survey. It is a likely transfer from Irish, based on a parallel construction there, that appears to emerge in IrE only in the nineteenth century: the earliest attestation in CORIECOR is from the 1810s, though it is attested in earlier literary texts, such as Maria Edgeworth's *Castle Rackrent* (1801; see Hickey 2007: 222). The *do be* V-*ing* construction in (6) is another variant of the habitual in IrE,[3] referring to regular or repeated activity. This habitual use of *do be* is not found in the BrEs included in Kortmann and Lunkenheimer (2013), though a *do be* habitual is present in 42 per cent of varieties worldwide. Finally, there are in Schrier's citations a number of examples of the Northern Subject Rule (NSR), as in (6), which is well-documented in varieties of IrE (cf., e.g., Montgomery 1989, 1994, 1997; Filppula 1999: 150–9; McCafferty 2003, 2004; Pietsch 2005; Hickey 2007: 179–82). This concord type is shared with Scots and northern varieties of English English, as well as certain North American and other varieties (cf. summary and references in McCafferty 2003: 108–11). Example (7) illustrates the *subject type constraint*, which permits the use of *–s* forms (also *is*, *was* and *has*) with plural NP subjects, whereas third person plural pronominal subjects (*they*) are ungrammatical with verbal *–s* forms. Kortmann and Lunkenheimer (2013) report the NSR in only 9 per cent of varieties worldwide.

These three vernacular features, then, represent one that is unique to IrE, one shared with many overseas varieties but rare in BrE, and one that IrE shares with input regions of Britain, but that is very rare in global terms. They are thus diagnostic of IrE in different ways, reflecting respectively influence from Irish only, a combination of Irish and British influence, and British influence only. This brief summary shows that citations in Schrier (1997 [1958]) not only contain forms widely typical of non-standard English, but also dialectal or vernacular features that set IrE apart from other varieties. This evidence suggests personal letters might be a rich source of data for the study of IrE speech patterns in the past. The next two sections use CORIECOR data to examine in detail the linguistic conditioning of BE-deletion, and then the linguistic and social conditioning of *shall/will* with first person subjects.

10.4 Variationist linguistic analysis: BE-deletion in Irish English, 1731–1840

There is a huge body of research on the deletion of copula/auxiliary BE in African American English (AAE) and English-based creoles; Rickford (1998) provides an enduringly useful summary. A major strand of this research attempts to document the creole origins of AAE by showing BE-deletion to be subject to similar linguistic conditioning in creoles and AAE. In this literature, BrE and IrE are mentioned, if at all, only to discount the possibility of 'British' dialect origins (e.g., Wolfram 1974: 522). Nevertheless, examples from Old English onwards are cited in Visser's (1963: 190–1) historical survey of English syntax, and scattered reports from Britain and Ireland show traces of BE-deletion at various times in northern England and Scotland (Melchers 1972; Macaulay 1991; Giner and Montgomery 2001; Tagliamonte and Smith 2002; Tagliamonte 2013). Hickey (2001, 2007) also reports BE-deletion from south-eastern Ireland, and suggests that the issue of British or Irish dialect input should be reconsidered, since BE-deletion 'may well have been much more common in Ireland in previous centuries and so could have been transported to the New World by Irish immigrants' (2007: 176). This issue is addressed below by comparing the grammatical conditioning of BE-deletion in CORIECOR with that reported in New World Englishes (Rickford 1998: 173–85, 187–92).

As regards the following grammatical environment, there is a broad distinction between copula and auxiliary uses of BE, and finer distinctions between predicate types within these categories. A robust finding since Labov (1969) is that there is a regular constraint hierarchy: deletion is more likely when BE is an auxiliary (before *gonna* and V-*ing*, usually in that order) than when it is a copula (before an Adjective, Locative or Noun phrase, most often in that order). The hierarchy thus predicts declining likelihood of BE-deletion from left to right:

gonna > V-*ing* > Adj. > Loc. > NP

In preceding grammatical environments, a subject-type constraint has been noted. Present-day African American Vernacular English (AAVE) shows an 'absolutely regular' pattern: a personal pronoun favours deletion more than an NP subject. On the other hand, in some creoles, deletion is favoured more with NP subjects than pronouns; others show little difference between these subject types (Rickford 1998: 184). Earlier AAE (Ewers 1996; Kautzsch 2002) and Gullah (Weldon 2003) align with the widespread AAVE pattern, favouring BE-deletion more with pronominal subjects. This suggests long-term diachronic continuity – at least since the early nineteenth century – in AAE and Gullah alike.

A third set of robust findings on which there seems to be broad consensus among scholars of AAE is that BE is (virtually) categorically present in certain contexts, including: past-tense and non-finite BE; first person *am*; clause-final and emphatic BE; BE in existential-*there* contexts; and BE with *what, it, that* and *this* (WITT) in subject position (Blake 1997: 59–63, 65–70). These conditioning factors allow us to compare BE-deletion in IrE with findings for AAE, providing a detailed framework for testing whether BE-deletion in IrE might have influenced New World Englishes. If BE-deletion in earlier IrE followed the same constraint hierarchy as AAE and creoles as regards the effects of both preceding and following grammatical environments, this would make a strong case for IrE input into New World varieties in this area of the grammar.

10.4.1 BE-deletion in CORIECOR

For earlier IrE, there is no mention of BE-deletion in any published work to date, though the present author has noted examples in CORIECOR (McCafferty 2014). These occur in a wide range of contexts, including copula uses like those in (8)–(10).

(8) Mr. and Mrs. Oliver and their brother came to see us the first evening, John Ø the same good-natured pleasing man that I remember him in Ireland (Mary Cumming, Co. Antrim/Down, 25 November 1811)

(9) [...] and my name Ø William = and I understood that I was my uncle's intended Heir (William Neely, in letter from Benjamin Neely, Co. (London) Derry, 24 June 1811)

(10) [...] the Europeans who land there find Purchases very high and Ø glad to come where they hear Lands are good & cheap (Rowan Dobbs, Co. Antrim, 19 September 1751)

Here, deletion occurs with NP complements in the following environment in (8)–(9), and with a past participle functioning as an adjective (10). The subjects are third person singular in (8)–(9) and third plural in (10).

Deletion of auxiliary BE is exemplified in (11)–(13). In (11), we see deletion in a past-tense passive, which is reported as rare in New World Englishes. Example (12) is a present progressive. And (13) shows deletion in an example of the present *be*-perfect. In (12) we also have an instance of deletion with a first person subject, which is reportedly rare in AAE, while the other subjects here are an indefinite pronoun (11) and an NP (13).

(11) [...] some few was [tried?] in Carrickfergus and Down; and all Ø acquit Except four or five whose crimes was Felony and suffered (Henry Johnston, Co. Down, 20 April 1773)

(12) Robert:/ I take this oppertunity of letting you know we are all in good health at present, I Ø hoping this will find you all in the same. (John Gordon, Co. Down, 26 April 1799)

(13) Nixon the apothecary Ø gone to Thos. Kean (John Caldwell, Belfast, 18 October 1802)

Table 10.1 BE-deletion in IrE: effect of following grammatical environment, 1731–1840 (n = 253)

	eighteenth c. (n = 96)		1801–10 (n = 17)		1811–20 (n = 35)		1821–30 (n = 43)		1831–40 (n = 62)		Total (n = 253)	
	N	%	N	%	N	%	N	%	n	%	n	%
going to	0	0	0	0	0	0	0	0	0	0	0	0
V-*ing*	21	22	2	13	5	14	6	14	15	24	49	19
Adjective	24	25	4	24	6	17	11	26	20	32	65	26
Participle	36	38	5	31	12	34	16	37	13	21	82	33
Locative	8	8	2	13	5	14	3	7	8	13	26	10
NP	6	6	2	12	6	17	7	16	6	10	27	11
Infinitive	1	1	1	6	0	0	0	0	0	0	2	1
Clause-final	0	0	1	6	1	3	0	0	0	0	2	1
	96		17		35		43		62		253	

Already, then, these examples indicate deviation from the typical New World pattern of BE-deletion. Let's look now at the detailed patterns in IrE for following and preceding grammatical environments.

The results of the analysis of following environments in IrE are summarised in Table 10.1 and Figure 10.1 in terms of the categories that

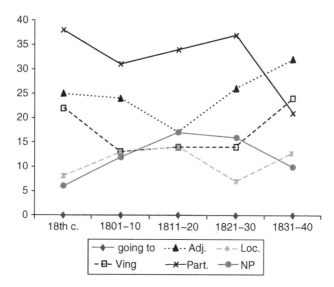

Figure 10.1 BE-deletion in IrE: effect of following grammatical environment, 1731–1840 (n = 253)

are widely used in AAE research, plus the inclusion of two further categories – infinitive and clause-final – which occur in total just three times in the CORIECOR data. The latter categories are normally excluded from studies of AAE, since BE is said to be categorical in these environments in AAE. They are indeed rare in IrE, too, but as Hickey (2001, 2007) has shown, clause-final deletion remains a feature of Waterford English today, so this environment should be considered in historical work on BE-deletion in IrE.

The most striking thing is the absence of tokens of BE-deletion in *going to* contexts, which numerous studies have shown is where deletion is most likely in AAVE. This may be because the *going to* future is a relatively recent innovation in the English language and it was not particularly frequent in earlier IrE.[4] In the CORIECOR data for the present study, there are just 80 tokens of *going to*, all with an overt BE-form.

The next divergence from the New World pattern is that the other auxiliary use of BE, V-*ing*, ranks only third out of six environments overall, accounting for just 12–24 per cent of the BE-deletion in the period under study. Across the board, it is the Adjective categories, whether dedicated adjectives or past participles in adjectival function, that rank first and second; combined percentages for these two categories account for an overall majority of BE-deletions throughout the period (51–65 per cent). The final two categories – Locatives and NPs – each account for an average of 10–11 per cent of all deletions. There is little difference between these two in terms of the likelihood of BE-deletion, though low token numbers might explain fluctuation between them. CORIECOR, then, produces this hierarchy for following grammatical environments:

Part./Adj. > V-*ing* > Loc./NP > *going to*

This is so radically different from the hierarchy widely attested for AAE and creoles that it seems safe to conclude that IrE is unlikely to have contributed much to BE-deletion patterns in the New World.

The CORIECOR results for preceding environments and contexts where it is claimed BE-deletion does not occur in AAE are summarised in Table 10.2 and Figure 10.2. Whereas AAVE favours BE-deletion most with pronominal subjects, IrE strongly favours deletion with NPs: nearly three-quarters of all BE-deletions occur with NP subjects in IrE. This is another striking divergence from the AAVE pattern. Personal pronoun subjects nonetheless account for 16 per cent of overall IrE BE-deletion. However, half of all these deletions (8 per cent) are with first person singular subjects, where AAVE does not usually delete BE. A further

Table 10.2   BE-deletion in IrE: effect of subject type, 1731–1840 (n = 253)

	eighteenth c. (n = 96)		1801–10 (n = 17)		1811–20 (n = 35)		1821–30 (n = 43)		1831–40 (n = 62)		Total (n = 253)	
	N	%	n	%	N	%	N	%	N	%	N	%
NP	77	80	7	41	21	60	27	63	47	76	179	71
Pers. pron.	14	15	1	6	7	20	7	16	12	19	41	16
I	8	8	1	6	3	9	2	5	7	11	21	8
Other pers. pro.	6	6	0	0	4	12	5	12	5	9	20	8
WITT	0	0	6	35	6	18	4	9	1	2	17	7
It	0	0	4	24	4	12	4	9	1	2	13	5
that	0	0	0	0	1	3	0	0	0	0	1	0.5
what	0	0	1	6	0	0	0	0	0	0	1	0.5
this	0	0	1	6	1	3	0	0	0	0	2	1
there	1	1	1	6	0	0	5	12	1	2	8	3
Others	4	4	2	12	1	3	0	0	1	2	8	3
	96		*17*		*35*		*43*		*62*		*253*	

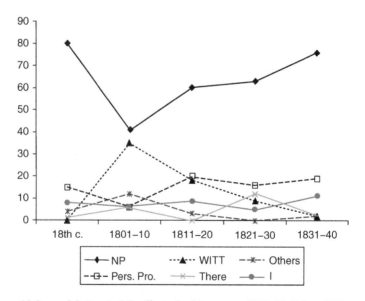

Figure 10.2   BE-deletion in IrE: effect of subject type, 1731–1840 (n = 253)

7 per cent of the BE-deletion in CORIECOR occurs in WITT (*what, it, that, this*) contexts, where deletion is also reportedly rare in AAVE. And 3 per cent of the IrE deletion occurs in existential-*there* environments, which again is a rare context for deletion in AAVE. In short, in terms of

both subject type and environments where AAVE does not usually permit BE-deletion, IrE deviates from the AAVE pattern on just about every point. However, we have also noted above that some creoles and diaspora varieties of AAE, as well as Earlier AAE, favour BE-deletion with NP subjects rather than pronouns, and allow (or allowed) deletion in WITT and existential contexts, just as IrE did until at least 1840. This suggests that there might be a possibility of IrE (and perhaps also BrE) influence on at least these BE-deletion patterns in Earlier AAE and creoles, though deletion in such contexts has apparently largely disappeared from AAVE since the nineteenth century.

This analysis of BE-deletion in IrE to 1840 suggests that deletion of copula and auxiliary BE in IrE and AAVE are largely unrelated phenomena. IrE is unlikely to have had any influence on the major BE-deletion patterns in the New World. On the other hand, some of the minor patterns may have been shared between IrE and AAE over a long period: where Earlier AAE, diaspora AAEs and some creoles diverge from present-day AAVE to some extent in deleting BE in these contexts, earlier IrE did so too. Irish migrants were in close contact with Africans in some of the major slave destinations – e.g., Barbados, Montserrat and Jamaica – during the eighteenth century (Rickford 1999: 177–84), and often worked as indentured servants alongside slaves on farms and plantations in the mainland North American colonies (Rickford 1999: 184–9). This may well be where IrE (and also varieties of BrE?) influenced BE-deletion patterns in the New World in the past. Further historical studies of more regional BrEs and New World varieties might confirm this hypothesis, if historical corpora were available.

10.5   Adding the socio: first person *shall/will* variation in Ireland, 1761–1890

For two reasons, we would not expect the distinction between first person *shall* and *will* with other grammatical persons to occur much in a corpus of IrE. First, for some 250 years, grammarians and commentators condemned the Irish inability to use *shall* and *will* 'correctly' (cf., e.g., Beal 2004: 96–7). Today, the decline of *shall* with first person subjects is also reported in both North American and BrE; as usual, American usage is assumed to be influencing British (e.g., Mair 2006: 100–3; Leech et al. 2009: 21, 71–83). But this change is often ultimately attributed to IrE and Scots influence on North American English (e.g., Jespersen 1909–49, vol. 4: 260; Mencken 1936: 179, 384; Kytö 1991: 336; Montgomery 2001b: 120, 133; Dollinger 2008: 239–41). Second, the grammarians' view may seem to be confirmed by the fact that first person *shall* is virtually non-existent in present-day IrE (Corrigan 2010: 64–5; Kallen and Kirk 2001: 71–3; Hickey 2007: 179; Amador-Moreno 2010: 44–5). However, a recent comparison shows that, while Dubliner Jonathan Swift (1667–1745) strongly preferred *will*, his close contemporary George Farquhar (1677–1707) had an equally strong preference for *shall* (McCafferty and Amador-Moreno 2014: 410), and Facchinetti (2000) found *shall* was used by speakers of IrE, at least by politicians and the upper classes, in the nineteenth century. However, since Facchinetti's data came from reports in *The Times*, it is possible, as she herself acknowledges, that English journalists and editors imposed *shall* on the Irish whose speech was being reported.

So what happened to *shall/will* in IrE? For comparative purposes, as in previous corpus-based studies (Kytö 1991; Dollinger 2008: 232), only full forms are counted, since *'ll* may be a contraction of either *shall* or *will*; however, the unambiguous contracted negative forms *shan't* and *won't* are included. In CORIECOR, there are in any case few contracted tokens. Examples of the forms counted are cited in (14)–(19).

(14) We **shall** only take care that his attendance shall be regular at Public Worship. (Carlile Pollock, 23 June 1789)

(15) However, if my Mother thinks proper I **will** take it at Glasgow (William Drennan, 25 January 1778)

(16) I **shant** neglect writing you often (Hamilton Young, 5 December 1787)

(17) and for that Reason I **will** Not Drink one half [kenn?] in his house this year (Thomas Shipboy, 9 November 1774)

(18) How **shall** I describe our sensation when we first saw this stupendous fancy of Nature (Robert Peel Dawson, 24 August 1838)

(19) if you write soon I **will** get it & **shall** reply at once (A. M. Faul, 8 September 1889)

Most of the data consists of first person *shall* and *will* in declarative clauses, both positive and negative, as in (14)–(17); contracted *shant* in (16) is one of the few negative contractions in the data (n = 16/1463, 1 per cent). Interrogatives like (18) are also infrequent (n = 12/1463, 1 per cent) and occur exclusively with *shall*. Finally, there are noteworthy tokens like (19), where both forms occur close together with the same first person subject.

Studies using CORIECOR indicate that usage in Ireland changed from predominant use of *shall* in the eighteenth century to *will* since the

Table 10.3   First person *shall/will* in IrE letters, 1761–1890 (n = 1463)

	Shall	%	Will	%	Total
1761–90	187	73	70	27	257
1831–40	204	45	254	55	458
1881–90	145	19	603	81	748
Total	*536*		*927*		*1463*

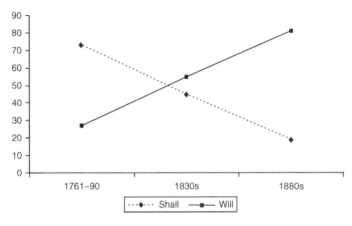

Figure 10.3   First person *shall/will* in IrE letters, 1761–1890 (n = 1463)

nineteenth (McCafferty 2011; McCafferty and Amador-Moreno 2012). The dramatic shift from the late eighteenth century to the late nineteenth is shown in Table 10.3 and Figure 10.3. Here we see, contra the tradition of normative commentary, just how frequent *shall* was in earlier IrE. In the earliest subperiod, 73 per cent of tokens were *shall*, and *shall/will* variation extended throughout the period studied. There is, however, a sharp decline in the proportion of *shall*, with *will* becoming the majority form by the 1830s. *Will* then consolidated its position, and was almost categorical in IrE by the 1880s, having reached 80 per cent use, and thus approaching categorical use in IrE. Thus, it was only in the latter half of the nineteenth century that IrE achieved its present-day exclusive use of *will* with first person subjects.

As for the influence of selected social constraints on *shall/will* variation in IrE from 1761 to 1890, I have tested the relative strength of three social factor groups that have been shown in previous studies to affect variation: intimacy, gender/sex, and geographical origin. Their

Table 10.4 GoldVarb analysis of *shall/will* in late eighteenth-century IrE (1761–90)

Corrected mean/input .728 — Log likelihood –124.064 — Total N 257

Factor groups/factors	wt.	%	N	Factor groups/factors	wt.	%	N
Intimacy				Gender			
Social superior	.99	70	10	Male	[.51]	76	231
Close nuclear family	.53	80	153	Female	[.35]	52	21
Other distant	.46	60	35	*Range*	*16*		
More distant family	.30	59	34				
Close personal friend	.27	70	23				
Range	*72*						
Place							
Tyrone	.68	80	46				
Belfast	.68	85	100				
Dublin	.65	79	29				
Down	.38	67	9				
(London)Derry	.25	52	29				
Other places	.37	61	31				
Antrim	.00	15	13				
Range	*68*						

Note that gender is not significant at 0.05 level; other factor groups are, however, significant.

influence is assessed using *GoldVarb X* (Sankoff et al. 2005) to analyse data extracted from CORIECOR using *WordSmith Tools 5.0* (Scott 2009). The data set consists of 1463 tokens of the full forms *shall* and *will* (and *shan't/won't*) across three subsamples: 1761–90, 1830s, and 1880s. The results are summarised in Tables 10.4, 10.5 and 10.6, with factor groups arranged in order of significance as indicated by the range of weightings within each factor group. GoldVarb weightings measure the likelihood of *shall*-use: scores over .50 favour *shall*, while weights below .50 disfavour that form, and scores around .50 are neutral. Table 10.4 presents the results for the late eighteenth century; here, two factor groups – intimacy and place – were statistically significant at the .05 level, while gender was not significant. In the analyses for the 1830s (Table 10.5) and 1880s (Table 10.6), all three factor groups were significant.

Although change tends to pattern along gender lines, Kytö (1991: 326) found the writer's gender had no effect on first person *shall/will* in seventeenth-century English. Nurmi, on the other hand, concluded that, in the Early Modern period, women led the shift to *will* (2003: 105–6), though the decline of *shall* began in men's usage in the sixteenth

Table 10.5 GoldVarb analysis of *shall/will* in IrE (1831–40)

Corrected mean/input .445   Log likelihood –264.491   Total N 458

Factor groups/factors	wt.	%	N	Factor groups/factors	wt.	%	N
Place				Intimacy			
Meath	.77	67	3	More distant family	.61	47	19
Other places	.72	58	31	Close nuclear family	.55	49	334
Tyrone	.58	52	89	Other distant	.51	38	16
Belfast	.58	48	101	Close personal friend	.26	26	74
Down	.56	45	40	*Range*	**35**		
(London)Derry	.53	52	107				
Armagh	.43	33	6	Gender			
Dublin	.43	33	3	Male	.55	44	341
Antrim	.19	17	78	Female	.37	44	115
Range	**58**			*Range*	**18**		

All factor groups significant at 0.05 level.

Table 10.6 GoldVarb analysis of *shall/will* in IrE (1881–90)

Corrected mean/input .127   Log likelihood –286.707   Total N 748

Factor groups/factors	wt.	%	N	Factor groups/factors	wt.	%	N
Place				Intimacy			
Wicklow	.91	67	15	Other distant	.75	35	29
Dublin	.90	64	14	Social superior	.63	50	10
Limerick	.84	29	7	Close nuclear family	.59	27	266
Armagh	.83	54	43	More distant family	.45	14	198
Antrim	.75	32	69	Close personal friend	.42	12	241
Fermanagh	.57	19	181	*Range*	**33**		
Down	.54	18	84				
Belfast	.47	15	39	Gender			
Other places	.46	15	68	Male	.57	17	461
(London)Derry	.43	10	93	Female	.46	25	276
Tyrone	.18	3	87	*Range*	**11**		
Donegal	.10	2	48				
Range	**81**						

All factor groups significant at 0.05 level.

century (Nurmi 2003: 95–7). In IrE, the gender effect is less than the effects of either intimacy or geographical origin, though there is a tendency for men to prefer *shall* more than women: women's weightings are consistently lower than men's. It is tempting to suggest that differential male/female literacy rates might have affected usage: men in

Ireland were more likely to be literate than women early in our period (Ó Ciosáin 1997: 44–5), and continued to lead in literacy rates until the 1881 census (Fitzpatrick 1990: 169, Table I). Men might, therefore, have been more disposed to use the 'literate' variant *shall*, associated with standard English and the upper classes (cf. also Facchinetti 2000).

Intimacy is defined for present purposes in terms of relationships between correspondents: family/non-family, closeness and social superiority. There is some indication that social distance favours the use of *shall*, but the picture is not straightforward. In the two subperiods for which we have data from correspondence addressed to social superiors, *shall* is a strong preference in these letters. Similarly, letters to 'close personal friends' consistently disfavour *shall*. However, letters to 'other distant' addressees (non-family, non-friends), which we might expect to favour *shall*, are fairly neutral in the first two subperiods and only show the expected effect of social distance in the 1880s. Letters addressed to 'distant family' also shift between strong selection against *shall* in the eighteenth century, favouring *shall* in the 1830s, and showing neutrality in the 1880s, which may well be due to letter-writers' personal preferences, and the precise nature of the relationship in each case. What appears to be happening here is that deference to older generations affects usage: *shall* is used more to older relatives, but not to people of similar age or younger.

Similar deference might account for the fact that letters between 'close nuclear family' vary between neutrality and favouring *shall*, which at first seems counterintuitive if we assume *shall* is the more formal variant. But what is happening here is that children defer to the authority of their parents, employing *shall* to signal respect, while writers are less inclined to do so in letters to siblings and children. That *shall* appears to be increasingly favoured in letters between nuclear family members as the nineteenth century progressed might reflect changing family structures: in the nineteenth century, Irish family relationships were hierarchical, and parents exerted a great deal of authority over their children, even into adulthood (Miller 2008). In these family categories, further subdivision by inter- versus intragenerational letters (e.g., from parent to child and uncle/aunt to nephew/niece or vice versa, and between coevals) might be revealing, though for the present data, small cell totals makes this unfeasible.

As regards geographical coverage, CORIECOR's regional bias towards the northern province of Ulster has been noted. While token numbers are small outside Ulster, there is no reason to suppose a North–South difference with regard to *shall/will*. The IrE results for the late eighteenth century suggest a rural–urban split: *shall* was strongest in urban centres like Belfast and Dublin, and weakest in rural Down, (London)Derry and Antrim.

Rural Tyrone appears to buck this trend, with a *shall* weighting equal to the urban areas. But much of the Tyrone data comes from correspondence between a merchant and his clients, so that this may be due to relative formality and deference, as much as regional difference.

In the 1830s (Table 10.5), regional patterns are more difficult to perceive, though the preference for *shall* persists in Belfast and Tyrone. The east–west pattern that we see later in the nineteenth century may be emerging in the *shall* preference of eastern locations: Meath and Down as well as Belfast. However, Armagh, Dublin and Antrim disfavour *shall* in this subperiod, and (London)Derry is neutral. By the 1880s (Table 10.6), a broad east–west split is discernible: with the exception of Limerick (with a small number of tokens from a single letter-writer), eastern areas (Dublin, Wicklow, Armagh, Antrim and Down) favour *shall*, as does Fermanagh, while Belfast is neutral. (London)Derry is weighted against *shall*, and Tyrone and Donegal weight heavily against *shall*-use. The general geographical distribution of *shall* suggests this form is used and maintained most in urban areas and in areas originally heavily settled by British colonists; these are also the regions that became English-speaking earliest.

The shift to first person *will* in North American English is unlikely to be due to Irish immigration, since *will* did not become the majority variant in IrE until the 1830s, and was still not quite categorical even in the 1880s. In IrE, the use of *shall* was constrained by social factors. While gender had little effect, women seemed to show a tendency to adopt *will* more readily than men. The women's behaviour is in line with Labov's principle that 'In linguistic change from below, women use higher frequencies of innovative forms than men do' (2001: 292).

Intimacy between writers and addressees appears to be an important constraint: increasing intimacy meant less likelihood of *shall*-use. However, this effect was apparently tempered by intergenerational deference or respect. Regional variation produced an urban–rural difference in the late-eighteenth-century data, with *shall* used more by writers from urban areas. By the 1880s, however, *shall* – by then much less frequent than in the previous century – was more likely to be retained in Dublin and the east coast region. This geographical distribution is interesting historically, given that the north-east and south-east regions centred on Belfast and Dublin became English-speaking before the rest of Ireland. Maintenance of the *shall/will* distinction in areas that have been English-speaking longest suggests it might be worth investigating this feature in relation to the spread of English from this eastern base into the west and south-west of Ireland, where Irish survived longer and the English language diffused more due to language shift than British settlement. It may be that areas settled by incoming British maintained older English usage longest, while speakers in areas shifting from Irish to English might never have acquired the subtle distinction between *shall* with first person and *will* with other grammatical persons. This possibility will be investigated in future research.

10.6 Conclusions

Letters and other personal documents can be useful sources of data for diachronic studies of IrE. Even the small number of examples found in Schrier's (Schrier 1997 [1958]) history of migration document the existence through time of non-standard, dialectal or vernacular features in the phonology and morphosyntax of IrE. At a very basic level, such documentation is useful for linguists wanting to know what forms actually occur in IrE at various times, and for giving us some idea of how long certain features have been present in this variety. Compared to Schrier's (1997 [1958]) brief citations, corpora containing texts of various types can provide enormous amounts of data on numerous well-known (and not so well-known) features of IrE.

The analyses offered above use the *Corpus of Irish English Correspondence* (CORIECOR) for variationist investigations of two language features, taking account of purely linguistic aspects of variation in one case, and relating variation to certain social factors in the other. BE-deletion is one of the lesser-known features of IrE. The factors affecting deletion of copula and auxiliary BE in IrE of the late eighteenth and early nineteenth centuries were very different from those at work in New World Englishes like AAE and English-based creoles today. Nevertheless, BE-deletion occurred at low rates in IrE in contexts that are often excluded from work on New World Englishes because they show (near-)categorical presence of BE. Given that the literature shows traces of BE-deletion in some of these contexts in Earlier AAE, diaspora AAEs and creoles, this might be an area of the grammar where IrE (and also BrE?) influence played some role in the past. At any rate, BE-deletion in such contexts in IrE is likely to have been part of the input into the feature pool that produced AAE and other New World Englishes, so that some IrE influence on BE-deletion cannot be entirely ruled out.

The account of *shall/will* variation in IrE shows the effects of certain social factors on the shift from *shall* in the late eighteenth century to *will* by the late nineteenth. The shift to *will* was probably led by women; the degree of intimacy between letter-writer and addressee played some role in determining the likelihood of using *shall/will*; and the writer's geographical origins also had some effect: it is suggested that rural–urban and east–west differences in *shall* maintenance or decline may have been related to patterns of British settlement and language shift from Irish to IrE.

Historical sociolinguistic study of IrE is a relatively new subfield, but it is one that holds great promise. CORIECOR is just one data set that lends itself to long-term diachronic research on IrE. From time to time, published editions appear of diaries, journals, notebooks and letters written by English-speaking Irishmen and Irishwomen held in archives in Ireland and around the world; data from these and histories based on them can supplement findings from a corpus like CORIECOR. Other sources may supply further data for comparison. For example, Irish newspapers in English are becoming available via online databases like *The British Newspaper Archive* (www.britishnewspaperarchive.co.uk), which currently gives access to a large number of Irish newspapers from 1750 onwards, and even more Irish newspapers from all over the country, dating from the eighteenth century onwards, are increasingly accessible via the *Irish Newspaper Archives* (http://www.irishnewsarchive.com/). The *1641 Depositions* (www.1641.tcd.ie) are a collection of eye-witness testimonies of the Irish rising of that year and its aftermath. And there are records of trials involving Irish people in databases like *The Proceedings of the Old Bailey* (www.oldbaileyonline.org). Finally, the *Corpus of Irish English* supplied on CD-ROM with Hickey (2003) offers a useful diachronic selection of texts, mainly dramas but also some prose and poetry, representing Irish English from the medieval period to the twentieth century. As these resources grow and more data sources become available, historical sociolinguistic approaches are bound to produce exciting new insights into the development of the 'grammar of the conquered' in IrE.

Notes

1. Most other habituals are equally rare in British English and show a distinct tendency to occur in the 'Celtic' areas – Wales, south-west England, Isle of Man – as well as British Creole and Maltese English (Kortmann and Lunkenheimer 2013).

2. Short introductions to the history of IrE are available in Filppula (1999: 4–11) and Amador-Moreno (2010: 16–30). Hickey (2007) provides the most comprehensive account to date in a single volume, while Corrigan (2010) deals in detail with English in Northern Ireland, and the companion volume by Kallen (2013) covers the Republic of Ireland.
3. The form *ye* might also be a vernacular second person plural pronoun.
4. Mair (2004) found the *going to* future was infrequent in English generally until the nineteenth century. A study of conservative dialects, including Cullybackey and Portavogie in Northern Ireland, showed it was less frequent in Northern Ireland than in any of the British locations (Tagliamonte et al. 2014: 83–4).

References

Amador-Moreno, Carolina P. (2010). *An Introduction to Irish English.* London: Equinox.

Beal, Joan C. (2004). *English in Modern Times 1700–1945.* London: Arnold.

Blake, Renée (1997). 'Defining the envelope of linguistic variation: the case of "don't count" forms in the copula analysis of African American Vernacular English', *Language variation and change* 9: 57–79.

Cannon, Moya (2007). *Carrying the Songs.* Manchester: Carcanet.

Conde-Silvestre, J. Camilo and Juan M. Hernández-Campoy (2012). 'Introduction', in: Juan M. Hernández-Campoy and J. Camilo Conde-Silvestre (eds) *The Handbook of Historical Sociolinguistics.* Oxford: Wiley-Blackwell, pp. 1–8.

Corrigan, Karen P. (2010). *Irish English, Volume 1 – Northern Ireland.* Edinburgh: Edinburgh University Press.

Dollinger, Stefan (2008). *New-dialect Formation in Canada: Evidence from the English Modal Auxiliaries.* Amsterdam: John Benjamins.

Elliott, Bruce S., David A. Gerber and Suzanne M. Sinke (2006). 'Introduction', in: Bruce S. Elliott, David A. Gerber and Suzanne M. Sinke (eds) *Letters across Borders. The Epistolary Practices of International Migrants.* New York: Palgrave Macmillan, pp. 1–25.

Ewers, Traute (1996). *The Origin of American Black English. Be Forms in the HOODOO Texts.* Berlin: Mouton de Gruyter.

Facchinetti, Roberta (2000). 'The modal verb *shall* between grammar and usage in the nineteenth century', in: Dieter Kastovsky and Arthur Mettinger (eds) *The History of English in a Social Context: a Contribution to Historical Sociolinguistics.* Berlin: Mouton de Gruyter, pp. 115–33.

Filppula, Markku (1999). *The Grammar of Irish English. Language in Hibernian Style.* London: Routledge.

FitzGerald, Garret (2013). *Irish Primary Education in the Early Nineteenth Century. An Analysis of the First and Second Reports of the Commissioners of Irish Education Inquiry, 1825–6.* Dublin: Royal Irish Academy.

Fitzpatrick, David (1990). '"A share of the honeycomb": Education, emigration and Irishwomen', in: Mary Daly and David Dickson (eds) *The Origins of Popular Literacy in Ireland. Language Change and Educational Development 1700–1920.* Dublin: Department of Modern History, Trinity College Dublin/Department of Modern Irish History, University College Dublin, pp. 167–87.

Giner, María F. García-Bermejo and Michael Montgomery (2001). 'Yorkshire English two hundred years ago', *Journal of English Linguistics* 29.4: 346–62.

Hickey, Raymond (2001). 'The south-east of Ireland. A neglected region in dialect study', in: John M. Kirk and Dónall P. Ó Baoill (eds) *Language Links. The Languages of Scotland and Ireland*. Belfast: Cló Ollscoil na Banríona/Queen's University Press, pp. 1–22.

Hickey, Raymond (2003). *Corpus Presenter. Software for Language Analysis with a Manual and 'A Corpus of Irish English' as Sample Data*. Amsterdam: John Benjamins.

Hickey, Raymond (2005). *Dublin English. Evolution and Change*. Amsterdam: John Benjamins.

Hickey, Raymond (2007). *Irish English. History and Present-day Forms*. Cambridge: Cambridge University Press.

Jespersen, Otto (1909–49). *A Modern English Grammar on Historical Principles*. Copenhagen: Ejnar Munksgaard.

Kallen, Jeffrey L. (2013). *Irish English, Volume 2 – the Republic of Ireland*. Berlin: De Gruyter Mouton.

Kallen, Jeffrey L. and John M. Kirk (2001). 'Convergence and divergence in the verb phrase in Irish Standard English: a corpus-based approach', in: John M. Kirk and Dónall P. Ó Baoill (eds) *Language Links: the Languages of Scotland and Ireland*. Belfast: Cló Ollscoil na Banríona/Queen's University Press, pp. 59–79.

Kautzsch, Alexander (2002). *The Historical Evolution of Earlier African American English. An Empirical Comparison of Early Sources*. Berlin: Mouton de Gruyter.

Kortmann, Bernd and Kerstin Lunkenheimer (eds) (2013). *The Electronic World Atlas of Varieties of English* [eWAVE]. Leipzig: Max Planck Institute for Evolutionary Anthropology. http://www.ewave-atlas.org/ (accessed 20 September 2013).

Kytö, Merja (1991). *Variation and Diachrony, with Early American English in Focus: Studies on CAN/MAY and SHALL/WILL*. Frankfurt am Main: Peter Lang.

Labov, William (1969). 'Contraction, deletion, and inherent variability of the English copula', *Language* 45: 715–62.

Labov, William (1994). *Principles of Linguistic Change, Volume 1: Internal Factors*. Oxford: Basil Blackwell.

Labov, William (2001). *Principles of Linguistic Change, Volume 2: Social Factors*. Oxford: Basil Blackwell.

Leech, Geoffrey, Marianne Hundt, Christian Mair and Nicholas Smith (2009). *Change in Contemporary English: a Grammatical Study*. Cambridge: Cambridge University Press.

Macaulay, Ronald K. S. (1991). *Locating Dialect in Discourse. The Language of Honest Men and Bonnie Lassies in Ayr*. Oxford: Oxford University Press.

McCafferty, Kevin (2003). 'The Northern Subject Rule in Ulster: how Scots, how English?', *Language Variation and Change* 15: 105–39.

McCafferty, Kevin (2004). '"[T]hunder storms is verry dangese in this countrey they come in less than a minnits notice [...]": the Northern Subject Rule in Southern Irish English', *English World-Wide* 25: 51–79.

McCafferty, Kevin (2011). 'English grammar, Celtic revenge? First-person future *shall/will* in Irish English', in: Raymond Hickey (ed.) *Studying the Languages of Ireland. A Festschrift for Hildegard L.C. Tristram*. Uppsala: Uppsala University Press, pp. 223–42.

McCafferty, Kevin (2014). '"*I dont care one cent what [Ø] goying on in great Britten*": *Be*-deletion in Irish English', *American Speech* 89.4: 441–69.

McCafferty, Kevin and Carolina P. Amador-Moreno (2012). ' "I will be expecting a letter from you before this reaches you": studying the evolution of a new-dialect using a *Corpus of Irish English Correspondence* (CORIECOR)', in: Marina Dossena and Gabriella Del Lungo Camiciotti (eds) *Letter Writing in Late Modern Europe*. Amsterdam: John Benjamins, pp. 179–204.

McCafferty, Kevin and Carolina P. Amador-Moreno (2014). '"[The Irish] find much difficulty in these auxiliaries [...], putting *will* for *shall* with the first person": the decline of first-person *shall* in Ireland, 1760–1890', *English Language and Linguistics* 18.3: 407–29.

McCafferty, Kevin and Carolina P. Amador-Moreno, in preparation. *CORIECOR. The Corpus of Irish English Correspondence*. Bergen and Cáceres: University of Bergen and University of Extremadura.

Mair, Christian (2004). 'Corpus linguistics and grammaticalization theory: statistics, frequencies and beyond', in: Hans Lindqvist and Christian Mair (eds) *Corpus Approaches to Grammaticalization in English*. Amsterdam: John Benjamins, pp. 121–50.

Mair, Christian (2006). *Twentieth-century English: History, Variation and Standardization*. Cambridge: Cambridge University Press.

Melchers, Gunnel (1972). *Studies in Yorkshire Dialects. Based on Recordings of 13 Dialect Speakers in the West Riding*. 2 vols. Stockholm Theses in English 9. Stockholm: Stockholms Universitet.

Mencken, Henry L. (1936). *The American Language*. Fourth edition. New York, NY: Alfred A. Knopf.

Miller, Kerby A. (2008). 'For "love and liberty": Irishwomen, migration, and domesticity in Ireland and America, 1815–1929', in: Kerby A. Miller, *Ireland and Irish America: Culture, Class, and Transatlantic Migration*. Dublin: Field Day.

Montgomery, Michael B. (1989). 'Exploring the roots of Appalachian English', *English World-Wide* 10: 227–78.

Montgomery, Michael B. (1994). 'The evolution of verb concord in Scots', in: Alexander Fenton and A. MacDonald (eds) *Studies in Scots and Gaelic*. Edinburgh: Canongate Academic, pp. 81–95.

Montgomery, Michael B. (1995). 'The linguistic value of Ulster emigrant letters', *Ulster Folklife* 41: 26–41.

Montgomery, Michael B. (1997). 'Making transatlantic connections between varieties of English: the case of plural verbal –*s*', *Journal of English Linguistics* 25: 122–41.

Montgomery, Michael B. (2001a). 'On the trail of early Ulster emigrant letters', in: Patrick Fitzgerald and Steve Ickringill (eds) *Atlantic Crossroads. Historical Connections between Scotland, Ulster and North America*. Newtownards: Colourpoint Books, pp. 13–26.

Montgomery, Michael B. (2001b). 'British and Irish antecedents', in: John Algeo (ed.) *The Cambridge History of the English Language, Volume VI: English in North America*. Cambridge: Cambridge University Press, pp. 86–153.

Nevalainen, Terttu and Helena Raumolin-Brunberg (2003). *Historical Sociolinguistics: Language Change in Tudor and Stuart England*. London: Longman.

Nurmi, Arja (2003). '*Youe shall see I will conclude in it*: sociolinguistic variation of WILL/WOULD and SHALL/SHOULD in the sixteenth century', in: David Hart (ed.) *English Modality in Context: Diachronic Perspectives*. Bern: Peter Lang, pp. 89–107.

Ó Ciosáin, Niall (1997). *Print and Popular Culture in Ireland 1750–1850*. London: Palgrave Macmillan.

Pietsch, Lukas (2005). *Variable Grammars. Verbal Agreement in Northern Dialects of English*. Tübingen: Niemeyer.

Rickford, John R. (1998). 'The creole origins of African-American Vernacular English: evidence from copula absence', in: Salikoko Mufwene, John R. Rickford, Guy Bailey and John Baugh (eds) *African-American English. Structure, History and Use*. London: Routledge, pp. 154–200.

Rickford, John R. (1999). 'Social contact and linguistic diffusion: Hiberno English and New World Black English', in: John R. Rickford, *African American Vernacular English: Features, Evolution, Educational Implications*. Oxford: Basil Blackwell, pp. 174–218.

Sankoff, David, Sali A. Tagliamonte and Eric Smith (2005). *Goldvarb X*. Toronto and Ottawa: University of Toronto and University of Ottawa. http://www.individual.utoronto.ca/tagliamonte/Goldvarb/GV_index.htm (downloaded 22 April 2010).

Schneider, Edgar W. (2002). 'Investigating variation and change in written documents', in: J. K. Chambers, Peter Trudgill and Natalie Schilling-Estes (eds) *The Handbook of Language Variation and Change*. Oxford: Basil Blackwell, pp. 67–96.

Schrier, Arnold (1997 [1958]. *Ireland and the American Emigration 1850–1900*. Second edition. Chester Springs PA: Dufour Editions.

Scott, Mike (2009). *WordSmith Tools 5.0*. Oxford: Oxford University Press.

Tagliamonte, Sali A. (2013). *The Roots of English. Exploring the History of Dialects*. Cambridge: Cambridge University Press.

Tagliamonte, Sali A. and Jennifer Smith (2002). ' "Either it isn't or it's not": NEG/AUX contraction in British dialects', *English World-Wide* 23: 251–81.

Tagliamonte, Sali A., Mercedes Durham and Jennifer Smith (2014). 'Grammaticalization at an early stage: future *be going to* in conservative British dialects', *English Language and Linguistics* 18: 75–108.

Visser, Fredericus Theodorus (1963). *An Historical Syntax of the English Language, Part One: Syntactic Units with One Verb*. Leiden: E. J. Brill.

Weldon, Tracy L. (2003). 'Copula variability in Gullah', *Language Variation and Change* 15: 37–72.

Wolfram, Walt (1974). 'The relationship of Southern White Speech to Vernacular Black English', *Language* 50: 498–527.

11
Society, Language and Irish Emigration

Raymond Hickey

11.1 The background to emigration

Emigration from Ireland is an enduring aspect of the country's history. Although it is recorded before the twelfth century, it is in the period after the Middle Ages that the beginnings of this emigration are to be found (see Table 11.1, Figure 11.1). Irish emigration must be seen in the context of England's involvement with Ireland. Initially, this consisted of the coming of relatively small numbers of English speakers, arriving with Anglo-Normans in the late twelfth century (Hickey 2007: Chapter 2). The English settled largely in the towns of the east coast, within the medieval area known as the Pale (Dudley Edwards 2005 [1973]). In the centuries after the coming of settlers from England the position of the Irish language actually strengthened. This was due in large part to the language shift from Anglo-Norman to Irish, above all by the land-governing settlers in the countryside. However, with the reversal of fortunes for the native Irish, due to military setbacks in the closing years of the sixteenth century, the situation for Ireland vis-à-vis England was to change permanently to the disadvantage of the Irish. A pivotal event in Irish history, or rather the perception of it, was undoubtedly the Flight of the Earls, a somewhat romantic label to refer to the departure of a number of Irish leaders from Lough Swilly near Derry in 1607. The decades after this event were characterised by increased immigration of people from Scotland and Northern England, who settled the land in Ulster (Robinson 1994 [1984]) and to a lesser extent in parts of Ireland to the south of this province (Canny 2001). This fact put pressure on the local Irish population who were in competition with the newcomers for agricultural resources. This situation was to form a recurrent theme in Irish history down to the twentieth century and would be responsible for most of the emigration from the country (Fitzgerald and Lambkin 2007). Often the competition was between native Irish and new, Scottish/English settlers; in some cases it involved only the Irish themselves and in yet other cases it was an internal issue for the Scottish settlers in Ulster. But the agricultural situation of Ireland was to dominate the country for three or even four hundred years after the beginning of the seventeenth century.

In addition to the economic circumstances within Ireland there were two other reasons for emigration. The first was forced emigration, i.e. deportation from Ireland, especially in the turbulent years of the mid-seventeenth century when the English authorities deported large numbers of Irish to the Caribbean to work on English-held islands like Barbados. There, landowners maintained sugar plantations from the middle of the seventeenth century, after the so-called Sugar Revolution (Higman 2000). There is a further subtype of emigration by deportation. This is where the Irish people affected were not resident in Ireland at the time. The deportations of Irish to Australia at the end of the eighteenth and in the early days of the nineteenth century, i.e. in the decades immediately following the initial settlement of 1788 in the Sydney area, took place from England, especially in the London area, where the overcrowded prisons housed many working-class English and Irish inmates.

The second major reason for emigration has to do with religious intolerance, whether perceived or actual. During the eighteenth century the tension between Presbyterians of Scottish origin in Ulster and the mainstream Anglican church, over the demands of the latter that the former take an oath and sacramental test, resulted in an increasing desire to emigrate (along with economic pressure), in this case to North America. But religion was probably not the sole reason for any emigration in the eighteenth century or any other time. The amount of land available in the New World was many times greater than what the Scottish settlers

Table 11.1 Timeline for emigration from Ireland during the colonial period

1600	1700	1800	1900
deportation of southern Irish to Caribbean	emigration by Presbyterians from Ulster to east of US	emigration of southern Catholics to urban eastern US	
	seasonal migration to Newfoundland from south-east Ireland	deportation, later emigration, to Australia + New Zealand	

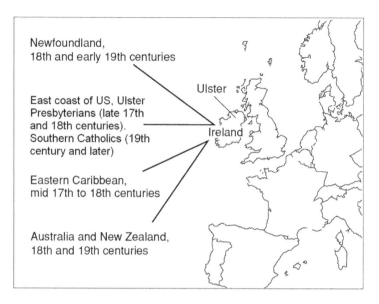

Figure 11.1   Major waves of emigration from Ireland to various destinations in the anglophone world

of the seventeenth century obtained in Ulster. As with so many other kinds of emigration from Ireland the main trigger for emigration was the economic situation, whether this was local or more general.

11.2   Assessing the linguistic evidence

Primary data on forms of English taken from Ireland to overseas locations are not readily available and scholars must resort to indirect sources in attempts at the reconstruction of features assumed to have characterised the transported forms of Irish English (Hickey (ed.) 2004). A certain amount is known about Irish English in previous centuries, given the literary portrayals of Irish characters, often of a satirical nature, in literary texts, usually plays; see the examples discussed in Hickey (ed.) (2010) for the sixteenth and seventeenth centuries and Hickey (2010) for the eighteenth century. Any consideration of earlier forms of Irish English must also bear in mind that some features which characterised such forms are no longer present, having been lost in the nineteenth century (Hickey 2008).

Sources for Irish English in the anglophone colonies would include vernacular reminiscences such as those contained in Corbyn (1970 [1854]) and utilised for linguistic analysis in Burridge (2010). But by far the most productive source of information on colloquial transported Irish English is familiar correspondence: there is a considerable body of letters written by emigrants back home to relatives and friends in Ireland. Such letters have already been used for linguistic analysis in Filppula (1999) and Hickey (2007). In addition, a large corpus of correspondence, documenting familiar Irish English, is currently under construction at the University of Bergen in Norway and has already been used for linguistic analysis (see McCafferty and Amador-Moreno 2012).

11.3   Across the Atlantic: emigration to the New World

In the title of this chapter the word 'language' has two references. One is to the Irish language, which is the heritage language from which the Irish shifted, at the latest after emigration but often before in preparation for this move. The second reference is to the features of vernacular Irish English which may have had an influence on forms of English at the locations of emigration during the colonial period, approximately 1600 to 1900. Both senses of language are actually related because with the shift from Irish, speakers engendered a variety of the English language which shows transfer features from this background language. Many of these features were later to form part of a distinct linguistic profile for the English language in Ireland.

11.3.1   The Caribbean

Although the Caribbean is an area which is not immediately associated with Irish influence, the initial anglophone settlement of the area, in the so-called 'Homestead Phase', did involve considerable Irish input. The island of Barbados was the earliest to be settled by the British (Holm 1994), as of 1627, and Cromwell in the early 1650s had a sizeable number of Irish deported as indentured labourers. This input to Barbados is important to Caribbean English for two reasons. The first is that it was very early and so there was Irish input during the formative years of English there (before the large-scale importation of slaves from West Africa). The second reason is that the island of Barbados quickly became overcrowded and speakers of Barbadian English moved from there to other locations in the Caribbean and indeed to coastal South Carolina and Georgia, i.e. to the region where Gullah was later spoken (Hancock 1980, Littlefield 1981).

The views of linguists on possible Irish influence on the genesis of English varieties in the Caribbean vary considerably. Wells (1980) is dismissive of Irish influence on the pronunciation of English on Montserrat. Rickford (1986) is a well-known article in which he postulates that southern Irish input to the Caribbean had an influence on the expression of habitual aspect in varieties of English there, especially because *do + be* is the preferred mode for the habitual in the south of Ireland (Hickey 2004b). This matter is actually quite complex and Rickford's view has been challenged by Montgomery and Kirk (1996).

11.3.2 The United States (i): Ulster Scots

Where religious circumstances led to a search for a better way of life abroad, one has emigration from Ireland. The earliest cases of this stem from the period immediately after the Reformation and its adoption by the English crown (early sixteenth century). After this many Catholics sought refuge on the Catholic continent, for instance in France, Spain and the area of later Belgium.

The situation in Ulster of the early seventeenth century was characterised by a combination of economic and religious factors. The religious motivation was rooted in such demands as the sacramental test which, according to an *Address of Protestant Dissenting Ministers to the King* (1729), was found by Ulster Presbyterians to be 'so very grievious that they have in great numbers transported themselves to the American Plantations for the sake of that liberty and ease which they are denied in their native country' (Bardon 1996: 94). But there is consensus among historians today (Miller 1985; Foster 1988: 215–16; Bardon 1996: 94) that economic reasons were probably more important, such as the increase in rents and tithes along with the prospect of paying little rent and no tithes or taxes in America. Added to this were food shortages due to failures of crops, resulting in famine in 1728/9 and most severely in 1741. Foster (1988: 216) stresses that the nature of Ulster trade facilitated emigration: the ships which carried flax seed from America were able to carry emigrants on the outward journey. Up to 1720 the prime destination was New England and this then shifted somewhat southwards, to Pennsylvania (from where the Irish frequently pushed further south, Algeo 2001: 13–14; Montgomery 2001: 126) and later to South Carolina. The rate of emigration depended on the situation in Ireland. In the late 1720s, in the 1760s and in the early 1770s there were peaks of emigration which coincided with economic difficulties triggered by crop failure or destruction in Ireland (Montgomery 2000: 244–5).

The option of emigration in the eighteenth century was open more to Protestants than to Catholics. The latter would equally have had substantial motivation for emigrating, after all the Penal Laws, which discriminated against Catholics in public life, were in force from at least the mid-seventeenth to the end of the eighteenth century. But emigration did not take place to the same extent with Catholics. It could be postulated that the Catholics lacked the financial means for a move to the New World. However, the Protestants who left were not necessarily in a financially better position, indeed many were indentured labourers who thus obtained a free passage. Foster (1988: 216) assumes that the Protestants were more ready to move and subdue new land (as their forefathers, who came from Scotland, had done in Ulster to begin with). The Protestant communities were separate from the Catholics and more closely knit. They were furthermore involved in linen production so that the cargo boats used for emigration would have been in Protestant hands.

The Ulster Scots emigration (Wood and Blethen 1997) is not only important because of its early date but because it established a pattern of exodus to America which, apart from Merseyside and to a lesser extent Tyneside, became the chief destination of Irish emigration in the northern hemisphere (Miller and Wagner 1994). Estimates suggest that throughout the eighteenth century emigration ran at about 4000 a year and totalled over a quarter of a million in this century alone (Duffy (ed.) 1997: 90–1).

11.3.3 The United States (ii): Southern Irish Catholics

Although the reasons for Irish people to leave the country became more economic after the seventeenth century, the role of the Church in the Irish diaspora should not be underestimated. The Catholic Church had a definite stance vis-à-vis emigration and used to send clergy to cater for Irish emigrants and attempted furthermore to regulate such essential social services as education.

Parallel to economically motivated emigration there was missionary activity overseas. This began in Africa – in Liberia at the behest of the then Pope Gregory XVI – in 1842 along with missionaries from the major European colonising nations in the scramble for Africa: France, Belgium, Holland and Germany. Despite the obvious Irish presence in this phase of African settlement there is no discernible influence of Irish speech on any form of English in Africa. In South Africa the numbers of immigrants from Ireland was under 1 per cent (mainly in the area of Grahamstown, north-east of Port Elizabeth) and hence insignificant for the development of English there, although the level of education, and hence the social position, of these immigrants was generally high.

The deportation of Irish convicts to Australia began in 1791 and within a decade there were over 2000 of them. By 1836 there were over 21,000 Catholics and only half of them were convicts by this stage. In 1835 a Catholic bishop was appointed. During the rest of the century the orientation of the Catholic Church in Australia towards a homeland, of which immigrants had no direct experience, diminished.

Of all countries which absorbed Irish immigrants it was the United States which bore the lion's share. The figure for the entire period of emigration to America is likely to be something in the region of 6–7 million (Montgomery 2001: 90) with two peaks, one in the eighteenth century with Ulster Scots settlers and the second in the mid-nineteenth century, the latter continuing at least to the end of that century. The greatest numbers of Irish emigrants went in the years of the Great Famine (at its height in 1848–9) and immediately afterwards, with a reduction towards the end of the century (Dudley Edwards 2005 [1973]: 149).

For the years 1847 to 1854 there were more than 100,000 immigrants per year. These Irish show a markedly different settlement pattern compared to their northern compatriots who left in the previous century. Whereas the Ulster Scots settled in Pennsylvania and South Carolina, the Catholic Irish, from the mid-nineteenth century onwards, stayed in the urban centres of the eastern United States, accounting for the sizeable Irish populations in cities like New York and Boston (Algeo 2001: 27; Montgomery 2000: 245). The reason for this switch from a rural way of life in the homeland to an urban one abroad is obvious: the memories of rural poverty and deprivation, the fear of a repetition of famine, were so strong as to deter the Irish from pushing further into the rural mid-west as opposed to, say, the Scandinavian or Ukrainian immigrants of the nineteenth century or the Germans in Pennsylvania in the eighteenth century.

The desire to break with a background of poverty explains why the Irish abandoned their native language. It was associated with backwardness and distress and even in Ireland, the leaders of the Catholics – such as Daniel O'Connell – were advocating by the beginning of the nineteenth century that the Irish switch to English as only with this language was there any hope of social betterment.

Diminished tolerance and their own desire to assimilate rapidly meant that virtually no trace of nineteenth-century Irish English was left in the English spoken in the eastern United States where the later Irish immigrants settled (but see Laferriere 1986 for possible traces in Boston English). In addition this emigration was quite late, and further removed from the formative years of American English, than the earlier Ulster Scots movement to the New World. Nonetheless, there may be some lexical elements from Irish in American English, such as *dig* 'grasp' < Irish *tuigim* 'understand', *phoney* 'bogus' < Irish *fáinne* 'ring' (putatively traced to the Irish practice of selling false jewellery) or *so long* 'goodbye' < Irish *slán* 'goodbye' where the transition from [s] to a velarised [ɫ] would suggest an extra syllable to English speakers.

11.3.4 Emigration to Canada

The Irish emigration to Canada must be divided clearly into two sections. The first concerns those Irish who settled in Newfoundland and the second those who moved to mainland Canada, chiefly to the province of Ontario, the southern part of which was contained in what was then called Upper Canada.

The oldest emigration is that to Newfoundland, which goes back to seasonal migration for fishing with later settlement in the eighteenth and early nineteenth centuries, and is a special case (Hickey 2002). The second layer is that of nineteenth-century immigrants who travelled up the St Lawrence River to reach inland Canada. There was further diffusion from there into the northern United States. The numbers of these immigrants are much lower for Canada, only a fifth (upwards of 300,000 for the entire nineteenth century) of the numbers which went to the United States. But seen relatively, this is nonetheless significant and some scholars maintain that elements of Irish speech are still discernible in the English of the Ottawa Valley (Pringle and Padolsky 1981, 1983).

11.3.4.1 *Newfoundland*

The Newfoundland settlement of Canada is unique in the history of overseas English. The initial impetus was the discovery of the abundant fishing grounds off the shores of Newfoundland, the continental shelf known as the Grand Banks. Irish and West Country English fishermen began plying across the Atlantic in the seventeenth century in a pattern of seasonal migration which took them to Newfoundland to fish in the summer months. The English ships traditionally put in at southern

Irish ports such Waterford, Dungarvan, Youghal and Cork to collect supplies for the long transatlantic journey. Knowledge of this movement by the Irish led to their participation in the seasonal migration. Later in the eighteenth century, and up to the third decade of the nineteenth century, several thousand Irish, chiefly from the city and county of Waterford (Mannion 1997), settled permanently in Newfoundland, thus founding the Irish community there (Clarke 1997) which together with the West Country community forms the two anglophone sections of Newfoundland to this day (these two groups are still distinguishable linguistically). Newfoundland became a largely self-governing colony in 1855 and as late as 1949 joined Canada as its tenth province.

Among the features found in the English of this area, which can be traced to Ireland, is the use of *ye* for 'you'-PL (which could be a case of convergence with dialectal English), the perfective construction with *after* and present participle, as in *He's after spilling the beer*, and the use of an habitual with an uninflected form of *do* plus *be*. Although Clarke (1997: 287) notes that the positive use of this is unusual in general Newfoundland English today – her example is *That place do be really busy* – it is found in areas settled by south-eastern Irish. This observation correlates with usage in conservative vernacular forms of south-eastern Irish English today (Hickey 2001: 13) and is clearly suggestive of an historical link.

There are also phonological items from Irish-based Newfoundland English which parallel features in south-eastern Irish English such as the use of stops for dental fricatives, syllable-final /r/, the weakening of word-final, post-vocalic *t*, the low degree of distinctiveness between /ai/ and /ɒi/ (cf. *bile* vs. *boil*), if present at all, and the use of an epenthetic vowel to break up a cluster of liquid and nasal as in *film* [fɪləm]. There are also reports of lexical items of putative Irish origin such as *sleeveen* 'rascal', *pishogue* 'superstition', *crubeen* 'cooked pig's foot', etc. (Kirwin 1993: 76–7; 2001). For a detailed discussion of these and similar features of Newfoundland English, see Clarke (2004) and Hickey (2002).

11.3.4.2 *Central Canada*

Central Canada was also settled by Irish. Here the Irish were among the earliest immigrants and so formed a 'charter group' and hence enjoyed a relatively privileged status in early Canadian society. By the 1860s the Irish were the largest section of the English-speaking population in Canada and constituted some 40 per cent of the British Isles immigrants in the newly founded Canadian Confederation. In mainland Canada the Irish came both from the north and south of the country, but there was a preponderance of Protestants (some two-thirds in the nineteenth and twentieth centuries) as opposed to the situation in Newfoundland where the Irish community was almost entirely Catholic.

The Protestants in Canada had a considerable impact on public life. They bolstered the loyalist tradition which formed the base of anglophone Canada. In the Canadian context, the term 'loyalist' refers to that section of the American population which left the Thirteen Colonies after the American Revolution of 1776, moving northwards to Canadian territory outside American influence where they were free to demonstrate their loyalty to the English crown. As these Irish Protestants were of Ulster origin they also maintained their tradition of organisation in the Orange Order, which was an important voluntary organisation in Canada.

In mainland Canada the Irish dispersed fairly evenly throughout the country, even if there is a preponderance in Ontario and in the Ottawa Valley. There is nothing like the heavy concentration of Scotch-Irish in Appalachia (Montgomery 1989) or that of later, post-Famine Irish in the urban centres of the north-eastern United States such as New York and Boston.

The influence of nineteenth-century immigration on Canadian English is not as evident as in Newfoundland. Nonetheless, one should mention one feature which Canadian English has partially in common with the English in the north of Ireland (Gregg 1973), what is known in linguistic literature as 'Canadian Raising' (Chambers 1973). The essence of this phenomenon is a raised point for the diphthongs /ai/ and /au/ before a voiceless consonant than before the corresponding voiced one: *house, lout* [hʌʊs, lʌʊt] but *houses, loud* [hauzɪz, laud]. Because of the so-called Scottish Vowel Length Rule this would have applied in Ulster Scots before voiced fricatives, as in *houses and mouthes*, leading to longer and more open diphthongs in such words.

11.4 The shortest route: the Irish in Britain

There is a long history of Irish emigrants in Britain, reaching back almost as far as that of the English in Ireland (from the late twelfth century onwards). But mass emigration only set in during the nineteenth century. And similar to the pattern of emigration to the United States in the late nineteenth and early twentieth centuries, the Irish congregated in areas where labour for industries like mining was wanting (O'Connor 1972, MacRaild 1999). It is estimated that by 1841 nearly 2 per cent of the population of England was born in Ireland (Dudley Edwards 2005 [1973]: 147). In Wales the percentage was much lower but there was a concentration in Swansea and Cardiff, cities which have always had connections with counterpart cities on the south coast of Ireland like Cork (O'Leary 2000). In Scotland the figures were much higher: 4.8 per cent of the population there was Irish-born and again these lived chiefly in the large cities – Glasgow and Edinburgh – which have a tradition of accepting migrant labour from Ulster.

As with the United States, the key period for the rise in the Irish sector of the population is the later 1840s. Between the censuses of 1841 and 1851 there was a jump from 49,000 to 734,000 Irish-born in Britain. This increase led to much friction between the English and Irish, especially as the Irish were frequently starving and diseased and in 1852, for instance, there were anti-Catholic, i.e. anti-Irish, riots in Stockport.

11.4.1   Liverpool

The areas of Britain which absorbed most Irish were Merseyside and its hinterland of Cheshire in the south and Lancashire in the north. The reason for this is obvious: the port of Liverpool is directly opposite Dublin and there was a constant ship service between the two cities.

The local dialect of Liverpool is Scouse and it is characteristic of its speakers to show a degree of fricativisation of /p, t, k/ in weakening environments such as in word-final position (Honeybone 2007; Watson and Clark 2016). Scholars such as Wells (1982) generally ascribe this to an independent development in Scouse. But one could also postulate that this is a relic of a former situation in Irish English. It is agreed that the Scouse fricativisation is typical of that section of the community which is directly derived from Irish immigrants. Furthermore, the Irish immigration into the Merseyside area took place chiefly in the first half of the nineteenth century. This was a period in which Irish in Ireland was relatively strong. Furthermore, the Irish who were forced to emigrate were the economically disadvantaged, which is tantamount to saying that they were Irish speakers or poor bilinguals. The latter group would of course have spoken a variety of English which was strongly affected by their native Irish and would thus have been likely to show lenition as a transfer phenomenon.

If this is the case then why is general lenition of all stops not a characteristic of modern Irish English? The explanation could be as follows. In the course of the nineteenth century the position of English strengthened as that of Irish was weakened. With this increased influence the least resistant idiosyncratic features of Irish English – lenition of labials and velars – would have been replaced by more standard pronunciations. In addition one can mention that the lenition of labials would have caused homophony as in word pairs like *cup* and *cuff*.

The generalised lenition in Scouse may well be a remnant of a wider and more regular distribution of lenition from Irish English which has been maintained, albeit recessively, in this transported variety of Irish English (see Hickey 1996 for a fuller discussion).

11.4.2   Newcastle upon Tyne

An area of England which falls outside the common pattern of poor rural immigration from Ireland is Tyneside. Here the Irish belonged to a higher social class and the influence of their speech has been general in Newcastle, as opposed to Merseyside, where in Liverpool it was largely restricted to the Catholic working-class population. House (1954: 47) in Beal (1993: 189) notes: 'In 1851, Newcastle, the most cosmopolitan of the north-eastern towns, had one person in every ten born in Ireland'. The possible convergent influence of Irish English in Tyneside (Mearns 2015) is noticeable in a number of grammatical parallels, for instance, it is the only variety of British English which shows *ye* as the second person pronoun (Upton and Widdowson 1996: 66–7), an obvious parallel with Irish English (though conceivably a survival from older forms of English as it is present in Scotland as well). Other parallels are the use of epistemic *must* in the negative (Beal 1993: 197). The use of singular inflection with third person plural verbs: *Her sisters is quite near* (Beal 1993: 194) is both a feature of northern English in general and of colloquial Irish English of the east coast, including Dublin. Failure of negative attraction is also attested for Tyneside English, e.g. *Everyone didn't want to hear them*, for *Nobody wanted to hear them* as is *never* as a negative with singular time reference (Beal 1993: 198).

Some of the features are reminiscent of northern Irish English, e.g. the use of double modals (not found in the south of Ireland and only very rarely in the north nowadays), especially in the negative in urban Tyneside, e.g. ... *they mustn't could have made any today* (Beal 1993: 195). This is also true of the use of a past participle after *need*, e.g. *My hair needs washed* for *My hair needs washing* (Beal 1993: 200). With these features one may be dealing with a geographical continuum, including Tyneside, and Scotland north of it. Indeed the use of a past participle after *need* would seem to have been taken to Northern Ireland by Scots settlers.

Not all the specific features of Tyneside speech point to possible Irish influence, e.g. the use of *for to* + infinitive is a common dialectal feature in the British Isles as is the use of *them* as a demonstrative pronoun (*I like them books*, Beal 1993: 207) and of course the use of singular nouns after numerals (*I lived there for ten year*, Beal 1993: 209). Items from phonology where convergence with Irish English input may have been operative are the following: (i) retention of word-initial /h-/ and (ii) retention of /hw/, [ʍ], e.g. *which* [ʍɪtʃ].

11.4.3 Middlesbrough

The city of Middlesbrough, since 1996 a unitary authority located in the former county of Cleveland, lies between County Durham to the north and North Yorkshire to the south (Llamas 2006: 96–7). The city is on the south bank of the Tees estuary. It was founded in 1830 when a railway was built in order to provide transportation for coal mined in the area, making Middlesbrough the first railway town. Iron works were founded in 1841 and iron ore was discovered in the region. Within a few decades Middlesbrough had become the largest producer of pig-iron in the world. This led to a phenomenal growth in the labour force and hence in the population so that within 40 years, by the 1870s, it had become a major town. By 1901 the population had increased to 91,000 from a mere 154 in 1831 (Llamas 2015; 2001).

The dramatic increase in population for Middlesbrough was fed from a number of sources, one of which was immigrant Irish. Due to the heterogeneous composition of the population it can be seen that by the census year 1851, there were no specifically Irish quarters in Middlesbrough. In addition no aversion to the Irish by the non-Irish was discernible at this time (Willis 2003: 20–4). The Irish section of the population had grown rapidly as seen in the increase from 6.3 per cent in 1851 to 15.6 per cent by 1861. By the 1870s one in five adult males was Irish, putting Middlesbrough second only to Liverpool in terms of the size of its Irish population.

Given the significant portion of Irish and the looser nature of its structure as a new town, as opposed to the much more established city of Sheffield, for instance, it is not surprising that an Irish influence is discernible in Middlesbrough speech, a legacy of nineteenth-century demographics. The similarity between Liverpool and Middlesbrough accents has been remarked upon repeatedly, including in the scholarly literature; see Kerswill and Williams (2000), with the Middlesbrough speakers being mistaken for Liverpool speakers. Jones and Llamas (2008) have also commented on this in the context of fricated /t/ in both areas.

Among the Middlesbrough features which can be seen as indicative of Irish are alveolar /l/, second person plural *youse* and vowel epenthesis in words like *film* ['fɪləm]. To these can be added fricated /t/ (Jones and Llamas 2008) and, importantly, a less common tendency to fricate word-final, pre-pausal /-k/ as in *back* [bax] (Llamas, personal communication). The lenition of labials, e.g, *cup* [cʌf], does not seem to occur. This fact matches the cline in Liverpool English where the preferential sites for lenition are (i) alveolar (*slit* [slɪt̞]), (ii) velar (*slack* [slax]) and (iii) labial (*slap* [slaf]).

It is no coincidence that both Merseyside and Teesside are dialect areas of Britain which show consonant lenition and that it is these areas which had the greatest input from (southern) Irish English. Add to this the folk perception experiments of Kerswill and Williams (2000), which linked the speech of the two areas, and the conclusion seems justified that the shared speech characteristics can be traced to nineteenth-century Irish migrants into these areas. The greater scope of stop lenition in both Liverpool and Merseyside would furthermore support the view that this is a kind of 'colonial lag', i.e. a remnant of wider lenition which was later narrowed in Ireland to alveolars due to the effects of supraregionalisation in the late nineteenth and early twentieth century.

11.5 Bridge to the North: the Irish in Scotland

The present chapter is concerned with identifying features of Irish English which might have been transported to locations outside Ireland. In the case of Scotland this endeavour must consider whether parallels between forms of Irish English and Scottish English are (i) historically continuations of earlier varieties of English or (ii) both due to transfer from Q-Celtic (Irish in Ireland and Scottish Gaelic in Scotland) during the language shift which affected both Ireland and Scotland. Furthermore, when considering possible parallels, it is sensible to examine forms of English in Ulster (Ulster Scots and Ulster English), rather than forms further south, given the geographical proximity of Ulster to Scotland and the historically attested emigration, which was often seasonal and driven by the search for work in Glasgow and west central Scotland and which has been typical of Ulster for the last two centuries. This latter situation, together with the seventeenth-century planting of Ulster by Scots, means that many features of English in Ulster may be imports from Scotland, i.e. that transportation was into, and not out of Ireland. For a discussion of features of Older Scots which have survived in Ulster, see Montgomery and Gregg (1997)

For the following discussion, vernacular Glasgow English has been examined (see Table 11.2). This has been investigated thoroughly by Caroline Macafee (see Macafee 1983 and 1994) and it is furthermore an urban vernacular which shows influence from Ulster English (from Co. Donegal across to Co. Down) due to emigration from the north of Ireland to the Glasgow region.

Table 11.2 Parallels between Glasgow English and Northern Irish English

---

In general vowel length tends to be determined by the Scottish Vowel Length Rule, where the phonetic environment following the vowel determines its length (Stuart-Smith 2008: 56–7; McClure 1994: 51). Basically, this also applies to Ulster Scots, as an imported feature, and has affected Ulster English to a certain extent. There is no trace of the rule further south in Ireland.

The fronted [ʉ] sound is shared with English in Ulster (and Ulster Irish). The sound can be fronted as far as [i] in Glasgow which gives pronunciations like *boot* [bɪt], *good* [gɪd], traditionally written as *buit, guid*, etc. These realisations are also typical of conservative Ulster Scots.

The non-retraction of /a/ after /w/, found in Glasgow, is also a conservative feature of Irish English in the north and south (mentioned by Sheridan 1781: 145).

The merger of the SQUARE and NURSE lexical sets in Glasgow is also found in northern Irish English, but not in southern forms. Macafee (1994: 225) considers this the result of Irish influence on Glasgow English.

The Glaswegian shift of /ð/ to /r/ (Stuart-Smith 2008: 62) is not a feature of Irish English, though the deletion of intervocalic /ð/ is a common northern feature, e.g. *northern* [nɔːɹn]. The use of [f] (TH-fronting) by younger speakers (Stuart-Smith 2004: 62) is probably an adopted feature from southern British urban vernaculars.

Vowel epenthesis in final clusters of /-lm/, e.g. *film* [fɪləm], and often extended to /-rl/ clusters, e.g. *girl* [gɛrəl], is an areal feature of both Ulster English and Irish as well as vernacular Scottish English and Scottish Gaelic.

L-vocalisation (McClure 1994: 48) is an established feature of Scots and continued in Ulster Scots.

Post-stop sonorant deletion, *col', ol'*, etc., is also shared with Irish English in the north and south.

The reduction of final, unstressed /o/ in *follow, yellow*, etc. is shared with both the north and south of Ireland.

The enclitic negative /-ne, nɪ/, common in vernacular forms of Scottish English, is shared with Ulster Scots, but not with southern Irish English, though they can be found sometimes in general forms of Ulster English.

/t/ epenthesis with *once* /wʌnst/ may be an Irish feature (McArthur 1992: 441).

Youse, yiz are probably imports from Ulster to Glasgow and western Scotland, but *you 'ns, yins* (< *you ones*) are Scottish in origin.

See as an opener highlighting a topic, e.g. *See football, I hate the stuff*, is not common in Ireland.

The form *ken*, equivalent to the pragmatic marker *you know*, is not found in Ireland.

There are a number of grammatical parallels between Scottish English and forms of Irish English. Some are very general, such as the past tense forms of verbs, e.g. *come* 'came', *done* 'did' (J. Miller 2008: 48) or the use of inflected verb forms with plural subjects, e.g. with the third person plural. However, verbal -*s* with the first person plural is not a common Irish feature (there is only one occurrence of *we was* in *A Corpus of Irish English* (Hickey 2003a) namely in Shaw's play *John Bull's Other Island*). Other features, like negative epistemic *must*, e.g. *This mustn't be the place* (J. Miller 2004: 53) are more exclusive parallels with Irish and northern British English.

Another grammatical parallel is the resultative O+PP word order as in *That's the letters written and posted* (J. Miller 2008: 56). Other features one could mention in this context is the overuse of the definite article, compared to more standard forms of English (J. Miller 2008: 59–60), the use of *than what* in comparatives, unbound *myself*. These last three features have clear parallels in Scottish Gaelic, as their equivalents in Ireland have in Irish, and can probably be regarded as transfer features originating in the historical language shift in Scotland. The widespread use of cleft sentences for topicalisation purposes (J. Miller 2008: 66–7) is similar to the situation in Ireland as is the preference for *that* as a relative pronoun with an animate antecedent.

11.6 The southern hemisphere: Australia and New Zealand

The anglophone southern hemisphere consists of three large countries, South Africa, Australia and New Zealand. The Irish emigration to South Africa was negligible, less than 1 per cent in total.

Anglophone settlement in Australia began in 1788 and in the 80 years up to 1868 various individuals were deported there from both Britain and Ireland. The Irish section of the population ranged somewhere between 20 per cent and 30 per cent. Given the sizeable number of Irish among the original settlers of Australia one would expect an influence on the formation of Australian English commensurate with their numbers. But the features traceable to Irish input are few and tenuous,[1] for instance the use of schwa for a short unstressed vowel in inflectional endings, e.g. *naked* British Eng: [ˈneikɪd], Australian Eng: [ˈnɛikəd] or the use of epistemic *must* in the negative, e.g. *He mustn't be in the office today*, 'He can't be in the office today' (possibly due to Scottish influence as well). Another candidate for Irish influence could be the retention of initial /h/, e.g. *hat*, *humour*, *home* all with [h-]. This sound has disappeared in urban vernaculars in Britain and its continuing existence in Australian English could be due to a degree of Irish influence. The occurrence of fricated [t̪] in word final, pre-pausal position might also be traced to Irish influence; see the discussion in Jones and McDougall (2006).

The low prestige of the Irish sector of the early Australian community is probably the chief reason for the lack of influence on later Australian English (the same holds for New Zealand as well). This lack of influence presupposes that the Irish community was easily identifiable and so easily avoidable in speech. It can be assumed that the language of rural immigrants from Ireland in the later eighteenth and during the nineteenth century was a clearly identifiable contact variety of Irish English and so its features would have been avoided by the remainder of the English-speaking Australian (or New Zealand) population. A feature of Australian English like negative epistemic *must* resulted from regularisation across the positive and negative, which the Irish had already carried out, and could have been adopted easily by the Australians they were in contact with.

Another fact which may be indicative of the status of early Irish settlers in Australia is that the inflected form of *you* for the plural, *youse*, is found in vernacular usage in Australia. This form is definitely of Irish origin (see Hickey 2003b for a detailed discussion) and was probably adopted by the English in Australia through contact with the Irish, but on a level, outside formal usage, which was characteristic of Irish English in the early years of this country.

11.7 Conclusion

Emigration from Ireland is a phenomenon whose motivation can be found in the social situations of the Irish throughout the centuries. The pressure to leave the country was generally self-perceived and self-motivated, with the exception of the relatively small number of deportations in the seventeenth century. The major anglophone locations of the northern and southern hemispheres were the prime destinations and in general the rural Irish chose to settle in the cities of the countries they emigrated to, probably due to traumatic experiences of rural life in eighteenth- and nineteenth-century Ireland. The emigrants became English native speakers at the new locations (if they were not native speakers before emigration), that is they abandoned the Irish language, often in preparation for emigration, especially in the second half of the nineteenth century. The Irish language was ultimately not to survive, although it was present in those cities which had a high Irish population, e.g. New York (Nilsen 2002). Irish emigration was not solely to anglophone regions. Many of those who emigrated to Canada settled in French-speaking, Catholic Québec (Grace 1993) while others availed of assisted emigration to other parts of the world, e.g. Argentina (Amador-Moreno 2012). In these cases the Irish also adopted the language of the host region or country, discontinuing the Irish language. In a similar fashion to other countries with a large diaspora, e.g. India, the role which the emigrants had to play in the life of the country they left was minimal, but their status in the new country was frequently considerable (see the discussions in Ó hAodha and Ó Catháin (eds) 2014) depending on the degree of integration and their participation in social life.

Note

1. Evidence for Irish features among the Irish-derived population in the nineteenth century is obvious in a number of accounts of life in early anglophone Australia (see the discussion in Burridge 2010). However, these features did not persist in Australian English of the twentieth century and later.

References

Algeo, John (2001). 'External history', in Algeo (ed.), pp. 1–58.
Algeo, John (ed.) (2001). *English in North America. Cambridge History of the English Language*, *Vol.* 6. Cambridge: Cambridge University Press.
Amador-Moreno, Carolina P. (2012). 'The Irish in Argentina: Irish English transported', in: Bettina Migge and Máire Ní Chiosáin (eds) *New Perspectives on Irish English*. Amsterdam: John Benjamins, pp. 289–310.
Bardon, Jonathan (1996). *A Shorter Illustrated History of Ulster.* Belfast: Blackstaff Press.
Beal, Joan C. (1993). 'The grammar of Tyneside and Northumbrian English', in: Milroy and Milroy (eds), pp. 187–213.
Burchfield, Robert (ed.) (1994). *English in Britain and Overseas. Origins and Development. The Cambridge History of the English Language. Vol. 5.* Cambridge: Cambridge University Press.
Burridge, Kate (2010). '"A peculiar language". Linguistic evidence for early Australian English', in: Hickey (ed.), pp. 295–348.
Canny, Nicholas (2001). *Making Ireland British 1580–1650.* Oxford: Oxford University Press.
Chambers, J. K. (1973). 'Canadian raising', *Canadian Journal of Linguistics* 18: 113–35.
Clarke, Sandra (1997). 'The role of Irish English in the formation of New World Englishes. The case from Newfoundland', in: Jeffrey L. Kallen (ed.) *Focus on Ireland*. Amsterdam: John Benjamins, pp. 207–25.

Clarke, Sandra (2004). 'The legacy of British and Irish English in Newfoundland', Hickey (ed.), pp. 242–61.

Corbyn, Charles Adam (1970) [1854]. *Sydney Revels (the Eighteen-Fifties) of Bacchus, Cupid and Momus; being choice and humorous selections from scenes at the Sydney Police Office and other public places, during the last three years.* [Presented by Cyril Pearl] Sydney: Ure Smith.

Dudley Edwards, Ruth with Bridget Hourican (2005) [1973]. *An Atlas of Irish History.* London: Routledge.

Filppula, Markku (1999). *The Grammar of Irish English. Language in Hibernian style.* London: Routledge.

Fitzgerald, Patrick and Brian Lambkin (2007). *Migration in Irish History, 1607–2007.* Basingstoke: Palgrave Macmillan.

Foster, Roy F. (1988). *Modern Ireland 1600–1972.* Harmondsworth: Penguin.

Grace, Robert J. (1993). *The Irish in Quebec. An Introduction to the Historiography.* Quebec: Institut Québécois de Recherche sur la Culture.

Gregg, Robert J. (1973). 'The diphthongs ɔi and ʌi in Scottish, Scotch-Irish and Canadian English', *Canadian Journal of Linguistics* 18: 136–45.

Hancock, Ian (1980). 'Gullah and Barbadian: origins and relationships', *American Speech* 55: 17–35.

Henry, Alison, Martin Ball and Margaret McAliskey (eds) (1996). *Papers from the International Conference on Language in Ireland. Belfast Working Papers in Language and Linguistics.* Belfast: University of Ulster

Hickey, Raymond (1996). 'Lenition in Irish English', in Henry, Ball and McAliskey (eds), pp. 173–93.

Hickey, Raymond (2001). 'The South-East of Ireland. A neglected region of dialect study', in: John Kirk and Dónall Ó Baoill (eds) *Language Links: the Languages of Scotland and Ireland.* Belfast: Queen's University Press, pp. 1–22.

Hickey, Raymond (2002). 'The Atlantic Edge. The relationship between Irish English and Newfoundland English', *English World-Wide* 23.2: 281–314.

Hickey, Raymond (2003a). *Corpus Presenter. Software for Language Analysis.* Including *A Corpus of Irish English.* Amsterdam: John Benjamins.

Hickey, Raymond (2003b). 'Rectifying a standard deficiency. Pronominal distinctions in varieties of English', in: Irma Taavitsainen and Andreas H. Jucker (eds) *Diachronic Perspectives on Address Term Systems.* Amsterdam: John Benjamins, pp. 345–74.

Hickey, Raymond (2004a). 'Development and diffusion of Irish English', in: Hickey (ed.), pp. 82–117.

Hickey, Raymond (2004b). 'English dialect input to the Caribbean', in: Hickey (ed.), pp. 326–59.

Hickey, Raymond (2007). *Irish English. History and Present-day Forms.* Cambridge: Cambridge University Press.

Hickey, Raymond (2008). 'Feature loss in nineteenth century Irish English', in: Terttu Nevalainen, Irma Taavitsainen, Päivi Pahta and Minna Korhonen (eds) *The Dynamics of Linguistic Variation: Corpus Evidence on English Past and Present.* Amsterdam: John Benjamins, pp. 229–43.

Hickey, Raymond (2010). 'English in eighteenth-century Ireland', in: Raymond Hickey (ed.) *Eighteenth Century English. Ideology and Change.* Cambridge: Cambridge University Press, pp. 235–68.

Hickey, Raymond (ed.) (2004). *Legacies of Colonial English*. Cambridge: Cambridge University Press.

Hickey, Raymond (ed.) (2010). *Varieties of English in Writing. The Written Word as Linguistic Evidence*. Amsterdam: John Benjamins.

Hickey, Raymond (ed.) (2015). *Researching Northern English*. Amsterdam: John Benjamins.

Hickey, Raymond (ed.) (2016). *Listening to the Past. Audio Records of Accents of English*. Cambridge: Cambridge University Press.

Higman, B. W. (2000). 'The sugar revolution', *Economic History Review* 53.2: 213–36.

Holm, John (1994). 'English in the Caribbean', in: Burchfield (ed.), pp. 328–81.

Honeybone, Patrick (2007). 'New-dialect formation in nineteenth century Liverpool: a brief history of Scouse', in: Anthony Grant and Clive Grey (eds) *The Mersey Sound: Liverpool's Language, People and Places*. Liverpool: Open House Press, pp. 106–40.

House, John W. (1954). *North Eastern England. Population Movements and the Landscape since the Early Nineteenth Century*. Newcastle: Department of Geography, King's College.

Jones, Mark J. and Carmen Llamas (2008). 'Fricated realisations of /t/ in Dublin and Middlesbrough English: an acoustic analysis of plosive frication and surface fricative contrasts', *English Language and Linguistics* 12.3: 419–43.

Jones, Mark J. and Kirsty McDougall (2006). 'A comparative acoustic study of Australian English fricated /t/, assessing the Irish (English) link', in: Paul Warren and Catherine I. Watson (eds) *Proceedings of the Eleventh Australasian Conference on Speech Science and Technology*. Canberra: Australasian Speech Science and Technology Association Inc., pp. 6–12.

Kallen, Jeffrey L. (ed.) (1997). *Focus on Ireland*. Amsterdam: John Benjamins.

Kerswill, Paul and Ann Williams (2000). 'Creating a new town koine: children and language change in Milton Keynes', *Language in Society* 29: 65–115.

Kirwin, William J. (1993). 'The planting of Anglo-Irish in Newfoundland', in: Sandra Clarke (ed.) *Focus on Canada*. Amsterdam: John Benjamins, pp. 65–84.

Kirwin, William J. (2001). 'Newfoundland English', in Algeo (ed.), pp. 441–55.

Kortmann, Bernd and Clive Upton (eds) (2008). *Varieties of English. Vol 1: The British Isles*. Berlin: Mouton de Gruyter.

Laferriere, Martha (1986). 'Ethnicity in phonological variation and change', in: Harold B. Allen and Michael D. Linn (eds) *Dialect and Language Variation*. Orlando: Academic Press, pp. 428–45.

Littlefield, Daniel C. (1981). *Rice and Slaves: Ethnicity and the Slave Trade in Colonial South Carolina*. Baton Rouge: Louisiana State University Press.

Llamas, Carmen (2001). 'Language variation and innovation in Teesside English'. Unpublished PhD thesis, University of Leeds.

Llamas, Carmen (2006). 'Shifting identities and orientations in a border town', in: Tope Omoniyi and Goodith White (eds) *The Sociolinguistics of Identity*. London: Continuum, pp. 92–112.

Llamas, Carmen (2015). 'Middlesbrough', in: Hickey (ed.).

Macafee, Caroline (1983). *Glasgow*. Amsterdam: John Benjamins.

Macafee, Caroline (1994). *Traditional Dialect in the Modern World. A Glasgow Case Study*. Bern: Peter Lang.

McArthur, Tom (1992). *The Oxford Companion to the English Language*. Oxford: Oxford University Press.

McCafferty, Kevin and Carolina P. Amador-Moreno (2012). 'A Corpus of Irish English Correspondence (CORIECOR): a tool for studying the history and evolution of Irish English', in: Bettina Migge and Máire Ní Chiosáin (eds) *New Perspectives on Irish English*. Amsterdam: John Benjamins, pp. 265–88.

McClure, J. Derrick (1994). 'English in Scotland', in: Burchfield (ed.), pp. 23–93.

MacRaild, Donald H. (1999). *Irish Migrants in Modern Britain 1750–1922*. Basingstoke, Hampshire: Macmillan Press.

Mannion, John J. (ed.) (1977). *The Peopling of Newfoundland. Essays in Historical Geography*. St John's: Memorial University of Newfoundland.

Mearns, Adam (2015). 'Tyneside', in: Hickey (ed.).

Miller, Kerby (1985). *Emigrants and Exiles: Ireland and the Irish Exodus to North America*. Oxford: Oxford University Press.

Miller, Kerby and Paul Wagner (1994). *Out of Ireland. The Story of Irish Emigration to America*. London: Aurum Press.

Miller, Jim (2008). 'Scottish English: morphology and syntax', in: Kortmann and Upton (eds), pp. 299–327.

Milroy, James and Lesley Milroy (eds) (1993). *Real English. The Grammar of the English Dialects in the British Isles*. London: Longman.

Montgomery, Michael (1989). 'Exploring the roots of Appalachian English', *English World-Wide* 10: 227–8.

Montgomery, Michael (2000). 'The Celtic element in American English', in: Hildegard Tristram (ed.) *Celtic Englishes II*. Heidelberg: Carl Winter, pp. 231–64.

Montgomery, Michael (2001). 'British and Irish antecedents', in: Algeo (ed.), pp. 86–153.

Montgomery, Michael and Robert Gregg (1997). 'The Scots language in Ulster', in Charles Jones (ed.) *The Edinburgh History of the Scots Language*. Edinburgh: University Press, pp. 569–622.

Montgomery, Michael and John M. Kirk (1996). 'The origin of the habitual verb *be* in American Black English: Irish, English or what', in: Henry, Ball and McAliskey (eds), pp. 308–34.

Nilsen, Kenneth E. (2002). 'Irish in nineteenth century New York', in: Ofelia Garcia and Joshua A. Fishman (eds) *The Multilingual Apple: Languages in New York City*. Second edition. Berlin: Mouton de Gruyter, pp. 53–71.

O'Connor, Kevin (1972). *The Irish in Britain*. London: Sidgwick and Jackson.

Ó hAodha, Mícheál and Máirtín Ó Catháin (eds) (2014). *New Perspectives on the Irish Abroad. The Silent People?* Lanham, MD: Lexington Books.

O'Leary, Paul (2000). *Immigration and Integration. The Irish in Wales, 1798–1922*. Cardiff: University of Wales Press.

Pringle, Ian and Enoch Padolsky (1981). 'The Irish heritage of the English of the Ottawa Valley', *English Studies in Canada* 7: 338–52.

Pringle, Ian and Enoch Padolsky (1983). 'The linguistic survey of the Ottawa Valley', *American Speech* 58: 325–44.

Rickford, John R. (1986). 'Social contact and linguistic diffusion: Hiberno-English and New World Black English', *Language* 62: 245–90.

Robinson, Philip (1994) [1984]. *The Plantation of Ulster. British Settlement in an Irish Landscape, 1600–1670*. Belfast: Ulster Historical Foundation.

Sheridan, Thomas (1781). *A Rhetorical Grammar of the English Language*. Dublin: Price.

Stuart-Smith, Jane (2008). 'Scottish English: phonology', in: Kortmann and Upton (eds), pp. 48–70.

Upton, Clive and John D. Widdowson (1996). *An Atlas of English Dialects*. Oxford: Oxford University Press.

Watson, Kevin and Lynn Clark (2016). 'Merseyside', in: Hickey (ed.).

Wells, John C. (1980). 'The brogue that isn't', *Journal of the International Phonetic Association* 10: 74–9.

Wells, John C. (1982). *Accents of English*. 3 Vols. Cambridge: University Press.

Willis, J. T. (2003). 'Integration or Segregation? The Irish in Middlesbrough in the 1850s and 1860s'. Unpublished MA thesis, Open University.

Wood, Curtis and Tyler Blethen (eds) (1997). *Ulster and North America: Transatlantic Perspectives on the Scotch-Irish*. Tuscaloosa, AL: University of Alabama Press.

Part III
Sociolinguistic Interfaces

12

Second-language Acquisition of Irish and the Role of Reading

Tina Hickey and Nancy Stenson

12.1 Introduction

A variety of sociolinguistic factors significantly affect success in promoting the acquisition of Irish as a first (henceforth L1) and second language (L2). These include societal attitudes toward Irish, parental support for Irish, teacher proficiency in Irish and pre-service preparation to teach it, the type of instructional methods adopted, the availability of appropriate materials and competing demands in schools. Given the small numbers acquiring the language as their first or dominant language, the majority of those engaged in learning Irish today are learning it as a second or foreign language. Here, we consider the sociolinguistic context of Irish language acquisition in today's Ireland, with particular emphasis on L2 acquisition and the role accorded to the development of Irish literacy in L2 contexts. We discuss the shift of focus in primary and secondary education to the development of oral language skills, which, in the context of continued losses in the native speaker population and limited exposure for L2 learners to Irish outside the classroom, has contributed to a serious decline in Irish reading, with concomitant negative effects on overall language skills. We argue that literacy in a second language offers a lifeline for minority languages, especially where learners are dispersed or have limited access to other proficient speakers, as is the case in most areas of Ireland outside Gaeltacht regions.

We begin with a brief outline in Section 12.2 of the contexts of Irish language acquisition. Section 12.3 presents a review of evidence regarding outcomes in Irish language achievement in primary education, with an overview of how the teaching of Irish has been framed historically, and a consideration of the relation between teaching Irish as a spoken language and Irish literacy in education. This leads to an exploration in Section 12.4 of the reasons underlying the disappointing results in achievement, based on analysis of data from two qualitative studies in which we conducted interviews with Irish language specialists and with teachers in mainstream (English-medium) schools. The interviews consider the impact of attitudes and motivation on children's learning, and particular attention is given to the value currently accorded to the teaching of Irish reading in the context of Irish L2 learning, and the approaches taken to it in mainstream schools. In Section 12.5 we situate these findings in terms of research on the role of literacy in second-language acquisition and the most recent curriculum developments and language planning strategies. We argue that, given the sociolinguistic realities of contemporary Ireland, more systematic attention to teaching Irish literacy would offer some benefits in addressing the challenges to L2 Irish acquisition in the mainstream school setting. The conclusion in Section 12.6 both summarises positive aspects of the contemporary language acquisition situation and identifies remaining concerns about the risks facing the language, as Irish L2 education enters a new phase, with curricular changes and a new strategy for the future of the language.

12.2   Irish language speakers and learners

Constitutionally designated the 'first official language' of the Republic of Ireland, Irish is nevertheless a minority language throughout the country, even to a growing degree in the officially designated Gaeltacht areas (see Ó Catháin, this volume, for further demographic details). Census 2011 found that 1.77 million (41 per cent of respondents) claimed ability to speak Irish, but of these, 59 per cent reported that they spoke Irish less often than weekly; only 34 per cent (596,366) spoke the language daily. Among the latter, the predominance of school-going L2 learners is clear from the fact that 87 per cent (519,181) of those reported as speaking the language daily did so only within the education system, and most of these were pupils aged 5 to 19 years. In contrast, just 4.3 per cent (77,185) reported speaking Irish daily outside of education. Over one-third of these resided in Gaeltacht regions, with the majority scattered throughout the Republic. Population figures thus include many second-language speakers of Irish of varying abilities who outnumber native speakers to a considerable degree.

In Northern Ireland, a growing minority of the population can also speak Irish to varying levels of proficiency; for example, Maguire (1990) discusses the effects of a revival movement centred on the Shaw's Road Irish-medium school in the latter decades of the last century. In the 2011

Census there, 11 per cent (184,898) of the population reported that they had an understanding of Irish (up 1 per cent from the 2001 census), but only about half this number reported that they can speak the language. Currently, 86 Irish-medium schools serve over 5000 preschool, primary and secondary pupils, constituting just over 2 per cent of the school population in Northern Ireland (Comhairle na Gaelscolaíochta 2014). Further afield, there are reports of growing numbers of adults (McCloskey 2008, Ó Conchubhair 2008) and children (Ó Broin 2012) learning Irish abroad. The Ireland-US (Fulbright) Commission's (IUSFC) comprehensive study of Irish instruction in the US identified 51 institutions of higher education and 36 non-academic organisations engaged in the teaching of Irish in 2011 (IUSFC 2011); since 2006, they have supported such classes by annually funding six Foreign Language Teaching Assistants on average to teach Irish in US colleges and universities. Ó Conchubhair (2008) also reviews Irish language teaching in England and Australia. Despite this evidence of increasing numbers of Irish learners outside Ireland, it remains the case that the largest numbers are still found in the educational institutions of the Irish Republic, and it is to this setting we now turn.

12.2.1 The Irish language in the educational system in the Republic

Irish language instruction has been a central part of the education system since the establishment of the Free State in the 1920s. Since that time, all pupils have studied Irish from school entry (about age four) as part of the regular curriculum and have been tested in it as part of their school-leaving examinations. Irish is a required subject for all primary pupils (except those exempted due to special educational needs). At second-level, Irish is compulsory up to the Junior Certificate examination at about age 15. Until 1973, a pass in Irish was required for an overall pass in the Leaving Certificate examination taken at about age 18 (Ó Riagáin 2008). Currently study of Irish is compulsory for the Leaving Certificate, but students are no longer required to pass Irish in order to pass the overall examination. Some pupils now opt not to take the subject seriously, although they are required to attend Irish lessons, which are offered at the levels of Higher, Ordinary and Foundation level. In 2014, only 85.6 per cent of students actually sat Irish in their Leaving Certificate examinations, a further drop on previous years. Concern has been growing at the increasing number of students seeking formal exemptions from studying Irish (cf. CoE/DES 2007) and while some of these can claim exemption on the grounds of having had a significant part of their education in other countries, others are exempted because of learning difficulties such as dyslexia. In parallel with the rise in those seeking exemptions, there has been a decline in the number taking the Higher Level course in recent years. Ní Laoire and Ó Laoire (2008) noted that only about a third of students took Irish at the Higher Level in 2008, compared to two-thirds taking Higher Level English.

It is noteworthy that concerns about the decline in take-up of Irish courses and the overall outcomes of the Senior Cycle brought about a significant change in the allocation of marks in the Leaving Certificate Irish exam from 2012, with an increase in the weighting of the marks for the oral component from 25 per cent to 40 per cent of the total, in an effort to improve Irish spoken skills and to encourage students to sit the exam.[1] One incentive for obtaining a Leaving Certificate qualification in Irish is its requirement for entry to the National University of Ireland, a group of universities in Dublin, Cork and Galway (University College Dublin, Maynooth University, University College Cork, University College Galway), although Ó Riagáin (2008) has questioned how long this will continue. Applicants for teacher training in the Republic of Ireland must achieve at least a grade C in the Higher Level course.[2]

12.2.2 The diversity of Irish language learning

Irish is now taught in a number of distinct contexts in contemporary Ireland. As the statistics above demonstrate, the overwhelming majority of daily speakers are engaged in learning Irish as a second language in school. Irish also continues to be acquired as the home language (or as one of the home languages along with English) in a minority of families. The decline in the number of such families means that even in Gaeltacht schools, Irish is the second language of a proportion of pupils but the first language of others, a situation which presents significant teaching challenges as the use of Irish in the home and community continues to drop (cf. Ó Giollagáin et al. 2007, Ó Giollagáin and Mac Donnacha, 2008). Outside of the Gaeltacht, the vast majority of Irish learners attend primary schools where English is the medium of instruction and Irish is a compulsory subject among 12 subjects in the curriculum. A minority of children in Ireland (6.4 per cent of primary pupils, in 180 primary-level Irish-medium schools across the 32 counties, according to Gaelscoileanna 2014) attend Irish immersion schools, called Gaelscoileanna, where Irish is the medium of instruction for all subjects except English. Overall, however, 95.5 per cent of primary schools teach through the medium of English, with Irish offered as a single subject at all grade levels from school entry at about age four.

A relatively recent development is the growing number of children whose home language is neither Irish nor English and who are learning English as an Additional Language, and Irish as their third or fourth language. Ó Laoire (2012) reports that approximately 10 per cent of the population were returned in the 2006 census as foreign-born speakers of other languages than English. Some of these developed an interest in Irish, and Ó Conchubhair (2008) commented on figures from Census 2006 indicating that between 4 per cent and 28 per cent of non-nationals in Ireland at that time (depending on place of birth) reported an ability to speak Irish. The analysis of the 2011 census does not provide comparable figures, but showed an increase of 124,624 in the number of non-nationals residing in Ireland since the 2006 census.

12.3 Learning of Irish as L2 and Irish achievement

It is clear that the original aspiration of spreading Irish to home use through acquisition in the schools (as discussed by, e.g. Ó Riagáin 2008, Ó Laoire 2012) has not succeeded, as the use of Irish in homes and society at large continues to decline (see Ó Giollagáin et al. 2007). The increase of anglophone children in Gaeltacht schools has had negative repercussions for the language development even of Gaeltacht children raised through Irish in the home (Hickey 2001; Ó Giollagáin and Mac Donnacha 2008). As English becomes the default language of peer group communication for the pupils, incomplete acquisition of Irish and English dominance is the result for many. As a result, performance in Gaeltacht schools on general measures of oral and written language skills is typically weaker than that of anglophone children in all-Irish schools outside the Gaeltacht. Outside the Gaeltacht, the Policy Profile prepared by the Council of Europe and the Department of Education and Science (CoE/DES 2007) declares an overall positive picture of Irish in the schools, based on the generally favourable attitudes toward Irish amongst the majority of the population and the steady growth of L2 learners in Ireland, even as the population of native speakers continues to decline (Ó Laoire 2005, Punch 2008). However, the gap between attitudes and achievement by L2 learners remains. Commenting on the outcome of both primary- and secondary-school Irish learning, Ó Riagáin (2008) argued that the low numbers taking higher-level courses for the Leaving Certificate indicate at best a moderate to negligible level of oral skills for the majority of school leavers. Murtagh (2003) points to the high levels of Irish attrition after graduating from school, even among those achieving good Leaving Certificate grades in Irish, but particularly among those from English-medium schools, as a result of the difficulty of forming Irish-speaking networks outside of school.

12.3.1 Primary school outcomes

Looking at achievement in Irish in primary school, reports from the Schools' Inspectorate likewise show consistently disappointing results in Irish achievement, despite extensive promotion of the language. Harris (2008) characterised the 1960s–1980s as a period of relative stability in Irish proficiency, although he cites three separate studies during the 1970s showing that a majority of teachers *believed* that the standard of pupils' Irish had declined since the 1960s. Harris et al. (2006) carried out a large-scale study of the Irish achievement of pupils in the final year of primary school (aged about 12 years), and compared their results to a previous national assessment in the late 1980s. They found a dramatic decline in the standard of spoken Irish achieved by pupils in this period, with 45 per cent of pupils failing to make even minimal progress in the Communication test and fewer than 10 per cent achieving mastery. Only about one-third of pupils in mainstream primary schools were found to have achieved mastery of the target objectives in Irish for their grade level (in contrast with 80 per cent mastery at grade 6 in Gaelscoileanna and 73 per cent mastery in Gaeltacht schools.) Moreover, the standards of attainment declined in the senior grades of primary school and still more in secondary school (Harris 2005). Eight years later, the most recent school inspection shows disappointingly little change (Hislop 2013). Inspectors found shortcomings with regard to the use of resources in 20 per cent of classrooms, leading to the conclusion that 'a sizable proportion of primary schools need to change their approach to the teaching of the Irish language' (Hislop 2013: 50).

12.3.2 Reading in Irish

Interestingly, Harris (2008) reports that, despite the negative perceptions from teachers about declining Irish achievement overall among pupils, one of his three studies from the 1970s revealed a perception among teachers that reading skills in Irish had in fact improved. However, actual performance in Irish reading appears to show a less rosy picture. Harris et al. (2006) found that more parents of 12-year-olds reported that their child had problems with reading in Irish (21 per cent) than reported problems with English reading (8 per cent) and they noted that schools differed more on Irish reading scores than they did on English reading or mathematics scores, indicating greater variability between schools in the teaching of Irish reading than in the teaching of English reading or mathematics. The Inspectorate Evaluation Studies (DES 2007: 60) report on Irish found that 'in approximately one third of classes, pupils had significant gaps in their skills of Irish word recognition and Irish reading comprehension'. The Chief Inspector's Report (Hislop 2013) shows further reason for concern about Irish reading achievement, since inspectors reported significantly less positive outcomes in Irish and Irish reading compared to English and mathematics, and noted that the teaching of Irish reading was problematic in as many as 24 per cent of lessons observed.

Psycholinguistic studies also show that children learning Irish as an L2 have specific difficulties with reading in Irish. Many of these findings converge on problems with Irish phonological awareness on the part of young readers, and a failure to decode Irish text in the way they have learned to decode English text. Parsons and Lyddy (2009) examined the Irish reading of eight-year-olds in Gaelscoil, Gaeltacht and mainstream schools. They found that the weakest readers' most frequent performance error took the form of refusal to attempt to read an Irish word, followed by (Irish) non-word substitutions and English real word substitutions. In contrast, the most proficient readers rarely refused to attempt an Irish word, and were more likely to make non-word errors. The high prevalence of refusal to attempt a word indicates a reliance on whole word recognition and a lack of decoding strategies, whereas the more successful readers' non-word errors point to greater use of a decoding strategy. The observation of English word-substitution errors among children reading Irish points to interference from English, and this was especially prominent among the weakest Irish readers, and was also noted by Hickey (2005, 2007), who observed words such as *ann* /a:n/ being misread as the English name 'Ann' or *siad* /siəd/ as 'said'. Hickey (2007) also showed that even high-frequency words with completely regular sound-spelling correspondences were misread by children in English-medium primary schools, and argued that this pointed to children engaging in guessing rather than decoding.

12.3.3   The changing role of literacy in the teaching of Irish

Ó Laoire (2005) provides an overview of the history of Irish language policy from the seventeenth century to recent times, which we draw on here in considering the changes in approaches to teaching the language in schools. The curriculum of 1922 identified four areas of focus for

Irish instruction, and placed reading at the centre of explicit instruction (Hyland and Milne 1992):

(1) a. Reading and spelling
b. Writing
c. Composition
d. Grammar

Although written skills clearly occupied a central curricular position at the outset, this was in the context of an aim to maximise the use of spoken Irish in the classroom as well, with a longer-term aim of Irish eventually becoming the medium of instruction wherever feasible. Infants' classes were to be taught entirely through Irish, along with as many other classes as possible. The policy succeeded to the degree that by the 1940s, 28 per cent of primary schools and 12 per cent of secondary schools were teaching all or some of their classes through Irish (Murtagh 2009). However, as the rule of teaching through Irish was relaxed from the 1950s onward (Ó Laoire 2005), the number of schools teaching through Irish declined, to a low of 20 schools in 1970. Despite the reversal of this decline in recent decades by the growth of Gaelscoileanna, the current total is still nowhere near the 40 per cent of schools teaching all or partly through Irish in the 1940s. Thus, far from being an option available to most children, Irish-medium education remains a minority model in the Irish education system.

From the 1960s, there was a change in teaching approach, and a shift of attention to oral language skills emerged. Audiolingual and audiovisual methods predominated in primary schools, with a prioritisation of developing oral skills replacing the reading and grammar focus of earlier years. The audiovisual materials developed for this course continued to be used until 1999, by which time they had long since become outdated and unsuitable (Harris et al. 2006). In 1999, a new primary curriculum was introduced (DES 1999), with a communicative approach to all four skills, and a focus on the living language. This is the curriculum currently in place, although a new curriculum is now being developed (the Integrated Curriculum). The 1999 curriculum calls for the introduction of L1 literacy in English from the first year of school, and formal reading in Irish is delayed until the fourth year (2nd class), to give time to build pupils' oral skills in Irish as well as initiating literacy in the native language before introducing it in the L2.[3] Irish remains a core subject, given approximately equal time with English and mathematics. The Department of Education and Skills recommends 3.5 hours per week be spent on the teaching of Irish.[4] According to McCoy et al. (2012), English-medium schools provide that, and a bit more to maths, but as much as 4.5 hours to English. What has changed most significantly is the reduction in time given to Irish outside the Irish lesson itself; although the recommendations remain regarding informal use of Irish throughout the day and the teaching of other subjects through Irish, the implementation of these recommendations appears to be weak. Fewer than a quarter of schools were found to teach through Irish outside of the Irish lesson itself (Harris and Murtagh 1999), and in as many as a third of classes observed by the Inspectorate (DES 2007), even the Irish lesson was taught through English, giving children little if any exposure to Irish as a natural medium of communication.

12.4 Factors contributing to lack of success

If language policy is, as Spolsky (2004) defined it, a network of conceptualised ideas on language beliefs, practices and management rooted in the traditions of national policy, Ó Laoire (2005) argued that Ireland lacks such a policy. This assessment echoes several articles in Ó Riagáin (ed.) (1988), a volume devoted to language planning in Ireland, and continues to be reiterated by these and other authors. On the one hand, as many have observed, the burden of revitalisation and spread of Irish was placed almost exclusively on the education system in the early days of Irish independence, with little attention to promoting language use and transmission through home and community. On the other hand, later efforts at language planning in Ireland placed greater emphasis on promoting economic development in the Gaeltacht, with an eye to slowing the high rates of emigration and thereby supporting language maintenance among native speakers. However, as was noted by Commins as early as 1988, the focus on economic development without due attention to the linguistic implications of policies implemented across multiple agencies led to unexpected negative linguistic consequences in the Gaeltacht, some of which were seen in the significant decline in Irish use documented in the comprehensive study of the Gaeltacht by Ó Giollagáin et al. (2007).

It is hardly news that the situation in Ireland is anomalous in that revitalisation efforts from the outset focused on the educational system instead of on promoting intergenerational transmission of Irish in the home. According to Fishman's widely cited taxonomy of language endangerment and revitalisation, assuring home use of an endangered language is a more urgent need than the establishment of its use in schools and government institutions. The emphasis on education-driven revitalisation in Ireland finds a measure of explanation in the particular Irish history of interactions among political, economic and demographic factors that led to both language shift in the eighteenth and nineteenth centuries and the revival movement of the twentieth, but the decision to focus on spreading the language through schooling seems to many in retrospect to have been premature, or at least incomplete. Extensive critical examinations of the Irish situation by Fishman (1991, 2000), Ó Riagáin (1988, 1997) Ó Laoire (1999) and others, make Ireland famous as a textbook case of language restoration efforts gone awry.

A major recent development with regard to language planning in Ireland was the publication of a new Strategy for the Irish Language 2010–2030, with cross-party support. It claims to take an evidence-based approach, and sets out ambitious objectives to treble the number of people who speak Irish on a daily basis outside the education system from 83,000 to 250,000; as well as increase by 25 per cent the number of people who speak Irish on a daily basis in the Gaeltacht. It targets a number of areas for action, from education, legislation and status to promoting family language transmission and Irish use in the Gaeltacht. One of its actions, the Family Language Support Programme, aims at supporting the use of Irish as the language of the home and community in the Gaeltacht, through a range of services for Gaeltacht families raising their children through Irish, extending from family language planning before a child's birth through preschooling, schooling and on to the teenage years. While it is too early as yet to assess implementation or outcomes of this strategy, it is significant that it includes positive measures to support home use of Irish, both within and outside the Gaeltacht, as well as retaining Irish as an obligatory subject to Leaving Certificate level.

It is against this policy backdrop that the various factors underlying the disappointing educational outcomes to be discussed in this section must be understood. Others such as Harris (2005) and Ó Riagáin (2008) have offered by-now-familiar lists of such factors, but here we will focus on the sociolinguistic factors relating to primary education and in particular the teaching of reading. To do so, we draw on data from two qualitative studies conducted in 2012–14, where we conducted semi-structured interviews with Irish language specialists and with primary school teachers, to gather views on standard practice and common challenges in teaching Irish reading. The first study included a sample of people who work with Irish professionally in various capacities: as secondary and university teachers of Irish, journalists, teacher educators and curriculum developers. Thirteen participants, 8 male and 5 female, were interviewed in Irish regarding their views on the teaching of Irish and Irish reading, the challenges of Irish spelling and related issues. Responses were transcribed verbatim and subjected to thematic analysis following Braun and Clarke (2006) to identify recurring themes and sub-themes in the responses. The second study consisted of interviews with primary teachers in English-medium schools. The same methodology was used, but interviews were conducted in English to avoid deterring potential participants who lacked confidence in their Irish. Teachers were asked about general priorities in the teaching of Irish, the role of reading in Irish classes, and the methods and challenges of teaching Irish and Irish literacy. Thirteen teachers (including one principal) were interviewed, 3 male and 10 female, with experience covering the range of primary classes. All quotations in the following sections are drawn from those interviews. The main themes to be considered here which emerged from the analyses of these data were the impact of societal attitudes towards Irish on L2 learners, the approach to Irish and Irish reading according to the experience of these participants, teachers' feelings about their preparation to teach Irish reading, and the challenges they perceived in finding appropriate materials.

12.4.1 Societal attitudes toward Irish

A strong theme to emerge from analysis of both sets of interviews was a perception of negative attitudes towards Irish among pupils at both primary and secondary levels, and lack of motivation to learn Irish in school. Respondents indicated that this negativity could be found at several levels. By the time pupils reach secondary school, the secondary teachers interviewed report extreme negativity toward Irish:

(2) Ar an gcéad dul síos, ní maith le formhór déagóirí na tíre seo Gaeilge.... Is fuath le níos mó déagóirí Gaeilge ná an méid a bhfuil an grá [acu] don teanga.[5] (M3)

[In the first place, most teenagers in this country don't like Irish ... more teens hate Irish than love it.]

Primary pupils, too, especially in upper grades, were noted to show declining enthusiasm for Irish.

(3) Attitude is the greatest challenge ... there's this negative 'I can't do it' – as if it's the most impossible language ever to learn. (T11-4th–6th class)

Motivation is a big big thing... pure motivation. In Infants, no – Infants just love it. Up to Second Class, it's all just games and fun. By the time [of] third and fourth, you start to hear [negativity] – and I'm not sure where it comes from, I think sometimes friends' opinion seeps through. (T6)

Looking at factors that contribute to this lack of motivation to learn Irish, pupils' perception of the low utility of Irish was cited as highly demotivating. Teachers reported the difficulty of convincing children of the use or value of learning Irish in an obviously bilingual context where they perceived no need for the language:

(4) I think that one of the biggest challenges facing Irish is that the children don't see a use to it, because everyone that speaks Irish also speaks English, and they find it difficult to understand why you would do it. (T6–4th class)

A second major theme emerging in these data related to the link between pupils' motivation to learn Irish and teacher commitment to teaching Irish. Some respondents commented on their perception of a widespread decline in interest in teaching Irish among both teachers and student teachers at both primary and secondary level, and noted how this affects pupils:

(5) Agus muna bhfuil spéis dá laghad agat dó, bhuel, bíonn meon diúltach agat, agus trasnaíonn sin go dtí na páistí, ach má thagann duine isteach go bhfuil an-suim agus spéis... spreag [ann sé] suim... sa Ghaeilge... (O1)

[If you haven't any interest in it, well you have a negative attitude, and that transfers to the children but if someone comes in with a lot of interest... that inspires interest... in Irish.]

Several of those interviewed referred to low levels of enthusiasm for teaching Irish among teacher colleagues, which they implied also led to Irish being relegated in status and receiving lower levels of preparation than other subjects:

(6) It is, kind of, the one that gets brushed off, you know, if there is something on... You know 'I've planned my history, so we'll do that, we'll leave Irish', that kind of attitude. (T8)

A related issue was the view of one specialist that the teaching of Irish is not given due consideration and preparation specifically in terms of second-language teaching, with the implication that this fed into pupils failing to make progress and consequent demotivation:

(7) Measaim nach dtugtar an tábhacht cheart do mhúineadh na Gaeilge mar múineadh dara teanga. (O1)
[I don't think that proper importance is given to the teaching of Irish as the teaching of a second language.]

Ní Ghallachair (2008) also supports this view.

Moving from the classroom level to the family level, another strong theme emerging from the data was the effect of negativity towards Irish in children's homes, and the difficulty for schools of counteracting this lack of family support. Interviewees noted that parents whose own experience of Irish was unsuccessful can often transmit negative attitudes to their children, perhaps unconsciously:

(8) You know, sometimes there can be a barrier, I suppose at home, the way it was taught years ago, and unfortunately that can be passed on to the children ... (T5)

Indeed, one teacher, when asked the single greatest challenge in relation to teaching Irish reading, identified the outlook from home. This may be directly tied to negative experiences of earlier teaching methods or it may be more indirect, through parents' demonstrating indifference or lack of confidence in their own Irish, illustrated by some of the teacher respondents reporting fewer questions about children's progress in Irish at parent teacher meetings.

Family lack of support for Irish includes pupils' siblings, who were also reported to be an important influence in the spread of negativity towards Irish. A fourth-class teacher described a student who had been a very successful and enthusiastic pupil in Irish initially but who suddenly had a change of heart:

(9) I think some of his older brothers and sisters started teasing him about Irish, and then all of a sudden he kind of shut off – you know, 'I'm not doing it' ... And now he's kind of like: 'Eh, Irish is not my thing.' (T6)

Overall, teachers commented repeatedly that this transmission of negative attitudes to Irish is difficult to combat in the school context. Nevertheless, as a principal whose school has a strong reputation for success and innovation in teaching Irish argued, this cycle must be broken in order to achieve better results:

(10) Unless we can change people's attitudes, you know, everything that we've been talking about here is pretty irrelevant. (TP1)

12.4.2 Classroom practices in teaching Irish and Irish reading

The most salient theme which emerged from the analysis of data from both the specialist and the teacher interviews referred to the focus on developing oral skills and the resulting minor role now given to Irish reading in mainstream schools at primary and secondary levels:

(11) My priority has always been getting them to speak it. I really don't care too much about any other aspect of it. (TP1)

S'í an aidhm is mó atá ar an múinteoir anois, ná an Ghaeilge labhartha (M1)

[The teacher's primary goal now is spoken Irish.]

Against the backdrop of this strong view emerging across the data regarding oral language as the main – or even sole – focus of the Irish classroom, it appeared that Irish reading is now viewed by some teachers as meriting relatively little attention in a communicative approach that emphasises *oral* communication:

(12) Níl an bhéim chéanna ar an léitheoireacht agus a bhíodh, mar sna bunscoileanna anois de réir chomh fada is féidir liom a dhéanamh amach, is cúrsaí cumarsáide go léir a bhíonn acu, agus bíonn cúrsaí comhrá agus mar sin ann. (S2)

[There isn't the same emphasis on reading that there used to be, because in primary schools now, as far as I can make out, it's all communicative and there are conversation courses and such.]

This was certainly not the intent of the 1999 curriculum (DES 1999), which is quite explicit that the communicative approach advocated was intended to cover all four skills of speaking, listening, reading and writing, but it seems that many teachers have construed this as an overwhelming focus on oral language skills relatively unsupported by literacy. This was highlighted by teachers' tendency, when asked how they teach Irish reading, to offer descriptions of how they teach oral Irish through games, drama, song and the like, with the result that many had to be prodded to talk about Irish reading at all. When asked to comment on how they approach the teaching of Irish reading, the majority reported using traditional methods, and general Irish language textbooks, rather than the more systematic approaches they take to English reading in their class and throughout their school:

> (13) I'd say Irish [reading] is just kind of left up to yourself. It's very haphazard, whereas the English programme of the school, it's a fixed programme. (T8)
>
> You just pick up bits and pieces [as materials for teaching reading] and it's not really a strategic approach ... (T3)

Overall, teachers indicated that it was not the norm in their experience of English-medium schools to use a reading series specifically developed to teach Irish reading systematically. This accords with Ó Faoláin's (2006) comments on how Irish reading has tended to be taught, and the problems arising from that, he argued, show a need for a more systematic approach to teaching Irish reading:

> The teaching of reading in Irish has had a tradition of using primarily the 'look and say' method with a large portion of contextual reading thrown in for good measure ... In Irish a new word had to be heard before it could be read ... This gave rise to a lack of clarity of structure which left the weaker pupil struggling with word identification and the more advanced pupil with difficulties in reading outside a very narrow curriculum. (Ó Faoláin 2006: 67)

Responses from teachers and teacher educators in our study support this observation regarding the teaching of Irish reading. They indicated that while it is now a widespread practice to use a phonics approach to introduce English reading, very few teachers in English-medium schools give systematic instruction in decoding in the early stages of teaching Irish reading. Instead, most indicated that they tend to teach Irish reading as they themselves were taught, typically a traditional approach relying on whole-word recognition rather than decoding strategies. Several teachers commented on teaching the spelling and reading of individual words and a few reported efforts to teach individual sound-spelling correspondences (the 'bh' = /v/ pattern was mentioned most) but not in a systematic way; then, when the time comes for formal instruction, as one teacher put it, 'kids are expected to just read'. Only one teacher interviewed reported using structured phonics materials for teaching Irish decoding skills, and indicated little enthusiasm from colleagues in taking up such instruction as a regular part of the school curriculum.

(14)   We're not using it officially across the school ... but we do use it in the classroom here, there's a program called *Fónaic na Gaeilge*. I would love to see it being used across the board, across the school in every Irish class. (T4)

Another teacher reported using an Irish spelling workbook series as a way of covering sound-symbol correspondences, but observed that use of structured materials in teaching Irish reading was infrequent among colleagues outside her school.

(15)   We work from a book called *Fuaimeanna agus Focail*, which is fantastic for, like, teaching phonics in Irish ... No, I don't [think other teachers use the materials] No I would say they don't.[6] (T7)

12.4.3   Teacher-preparation to teach Irish reading

Although the Curriculum Guidelines explicitly advise building linguistic awareness via comparison of Irish spelling with the patterns of English, most of the teachers interviewed indicated that they did not do so. Some were aware of the Guidelines' recommendation to teach linguistic awareness, but did not feel prepared to teach Irish systematically in that way. One teacher, who was very enthusiastic about teaching Irish in general, attributed this to lack of preparation to teach decoding in Irish in pre-service training:

(16)   Well, [decoding] that's definitely a part that I think I neglect a bit. And it's there in the curriculum. But I've had very little guidance in how to teach it. (T1)

This was supported by other teachers who commented that they felt ill-prepared to teach something that they did not understand:

(17)   To be honest ... about the spelling rules in Irish ... I don't think I was ever taught them. So I would find that very hard to teach. (T11)

I wish I'd had more training in how to teach it, because I kind of feel like I lack the proper knowledge behind it, so I teach it in whatever way I think fits. (T3)

In general, most of the teachers interviewed expressed a lack of confidence in their own understanding of the Irish spelling system and a lack of awareness of the patterns to be found therein. Reflecting on the pre-service training offered, teacher educators interviewed confirmed that little attention is given to Irish reading instruction or how Irish orthography works in colleges of education.

(18) Ní chaithim féin mórán ama ag ullmhú múinteoirí don léitheoireacht. (MO1)

[I myself don't spend much time preparing teachers for reading.]

Nuair a bhí mé ag múineadh Gaeilge do na múinteoirí sin, ní raibh aird dírithe ar litriú ar chor ar bith. (O4)

[When I was teaching Irish to those teachers, there was no attention paid to spelling at all.]

They reported that instruction is provided for the teaching of reading in English and indicated that it is assumed that teachers can carry this into the teaching of Irish. Indeed, 'literacy' as discussed in terms of policy is perceived to relate to English literacy, as one participant observed,

(19) Ní shílim go dtugtar mórán airde ar litearthacht na Gaeilge nuair atá oiliúint á cur ... nuair a labhraíonn siad faoi 'literacy', tá siad ag caint ar Bhéarla an t-am ar fad. (MS1)

[I don't think much attention is given to Irish literacy during training ... when they talk about 'literacy', they're talking about English the whole time.]

However, teachers interviewed indicated difficulties in adapting the skills acquired for teaching English literacy to teaching reading in Irish:

(20) I would have a background in literacy teaching, English, teaching reading and have done a lot of research myself in that area, but when it comes – I don't automatically transfer that knowledge to teaching Irish reading, that link has never ... up until this point there were two separate curriculums as such, and ... I didn't really think of teaching Irish in the same way [as English]. (T11)

One teacher educator commented that Irish reading should get more space as a topic in itself:

(21)   Is modúl ann féin an léitheoireacht, ba cheart go mbeadh modúl ann féin [di]. (O4)

[Reading [in Irish] is a module in itself; there should be a module for it itself.]

However, rather than gaining the attention it needs, it appears that the overcrowding of the primary curriculum, and, correspondingly, the teacher education curriculum, has led, in the perception of many, to a marginalisation of Irish instruction in teacher education overall:

(22)   Tá áit na Gaeilge, tá tábhacht na Gaeilge sa chóras oideachais laghdaithe go mór. Dá bhrí sin, ní dóigh liom go mbíonn go leor oiliúna ar aon rud i nGaeilge anois ag an gcuid is mó acu. (S2)

[The place of Irish, the importance of Irish in the education system has weakened a lot. So I don't think most of them get enough training in anything in Irish now.]

Both specialists and teachers interviewed pointed to the need for more professional development relating to Irish pedagogy at pre-service and in-service level, and for more language-specific literacy training. Asked what help would be most beneficial in supporting teachers in their teaching of Irish reading, one teacher replied:

(23)   I think maybe to be ***taught how*** to teach [Irish] reading, rather than making it up yourself. (T3)

12.4.4   Irish reading materials: Challenges

Although the language experts, particularly the curriculum developers and teacher educators, were on the whole quite positive about the improvement in materials available for reading, a recurrent theme was that, despite improvements in availability, there is still far too little to cover the different interest and ability levels of readers in Irish. A particularly salient theme in the teachers' data was their perceived lack of suitable teaching materials for the early stages of Irish reading. It must be noted that the situation regarding Irish reading materials has improved considerably in the last decade, partly due to the work of An Chomhairle um Oideachas Gaeltachta agus Gaelscolaíochta in the Republic and

ÁisÁonad in Northern Ireland. As a result, a range of Irish reading materials, including a course for teaching phonics in Irish are now in fact available, but the data here indicate that teachers in English-medium schools rarely avail of these materials. They reported that schools tend not to use such materials routinely for the introduction of Irish reading as is done for English reading, and library resources are usually weaker for reading in Irish than English, so teachers tend to feel left to their own devices, and struggle to find materials. Lack of time, or confidence or interest may contribute to teachers' dependence for Irish reading material on the general Irish textbook used in their class, as has been documented also in research and inspectorate reports (Harris et al. 2006, Hislop 2013).

(24)   What I see with my colleagues, Irish to them is just taking out the [text] book and doing *Bun go Barr* and that's Irish done, you know, they don't really enjoy it, they don't instil the love of it. (T7)

A minority of teachers interviewed did report efforts to access interesting and accessible texts in Irish through creative use of the internet, children's books and materials they prepare themselves:

(25)   I would take bits of a book that was an actual storybook that I might have read, and prepared them [the pupils] with that, rather than just do a textbook. I didn't use textbooks. (T2)

   No, I wouldn't stay with the textbook … there's lots of resources. On the internet, I suppose, and even then trying to get them to write out sentences themselves and read it, that sort of thing. (T3)

But the limitations of many teachers' awareness of what is available for Irish reading, the time constraints and curriculum pressure they experience and the decline in support for Irish and reading in general and in society at large, raise questions about the sustainability of such efforts even among the most dedicated, let alone those with lower levels of interest in the language:

(26)   Originally when I started teaching Irish, in primary school, I was using more a very active – 'cause this is the way we were trained in college, using puppets, and lots of different activities, and I did that for quite a while, but it was taking an awful lot of

my energy as a teacher. So gradually, as a teacher, I've had to space out my energies, so I have become more reliant on the [Irish text] books. (T1)

Of even greater concern perhaps is the apparent invisibility of many Irish reading materials. The majority of teachers interviewed were unaware of the existence of a phonics program for Irish, while those who were, indicated that they were alone among their colleagues in that awareness.

(27) I think the phonics program . . . that was made is very good, but I'm sure that only a handful of schools actually know that it exists. . . . I'd say I was the only person in my school that knew about that book, that particular course, and that went on it. I think there's a lot of things out there but I don't think people know about them or have access to them. (T8)

These issues and the most salient themes regarding the teaching of Irish emerging from these two groups of interviewees are discussed below in relation to national and international research.

12.5 Discussion

12.5.1 Attitudes and motivation to learn Irish

The interview data emphasise the impact of declining motivation to learn what many parents and pupils perceive as an increasingly marginalised subject. While surveys of the general population have consistently shown largely favourable attitudes toward Irish and toward continuing to teach the language in schools (Ó Laoire 2005), Ó Riagáin (1988) noted that the strength of positivity towards Irish lessened in the surveys done in the later 1980s compared to preceding surveys. A recent survey commissioned by the telecom company UPC found that one-third of 1000 adults surveyed said that they thought it would be more important to teach children computer skills than Irish (RTÉ News 2014). Looking at children's views of Irish, McCoy et al. (2012) drew on data from over 9000 9-year-old children in the *Growing Up in Ireland* database to compare their attitudes toward the three core subjects of English, mathematics and Irish. The children's views of Irish lessons were the least positive, with only 20 per cent of children reporting 'always' liking Irish (and between 25 and 33 per cent reporting 'never' liking Irish). In contrast, a small majority reported 'always' liking English, while attitudes toward mathematics were finely balanced between positive and negative views. Thus, while surveys of adults may still show general (if declining) support for the language, the evidence from teachers here and from children at the chalk face indicate demotivation to learn Irish, and significantly lower levels of enjoyment of learning Irish than they have when learning mathematics. In addition, as a result of low levels of satisfaction with Irish learning among several generations of pupils, many parents who did not enjoy learning it or are frustrated by their limited proficiency in Irish may transmit negative views of Irish to their children. In fact this theme emerged in the data from over two-thirds of the teachers interviewed.

12.5.2 L2 pedagogy and the role of Irish reading

It may be that at least some of the negativity towards Irish felt by pupils is due to frustration at their slow rate of progress in Irish as evidenced in the Irish achievement outcomes. The communicative approach advised in the 1999 curriculum represented a shift from the more behaviorist-inspired methodologies of preceding decades. The emphasis was very much on the development of oral Irish in the first few years of primary school, with reading introduced in second class. The 1999 curriculum advocated a four-skills approach to communicative language teaching, emphasising that written language skills are as important as oral skills and can (and should) be taught communicatively. The document stressed the importance of teaching linguistic awareness as part of both spoken and written language. The soundness of this recommendation is amply supported, not only by L2 research, but also by decades of reading research, from the seminal early work of Chall (1967) and Adams (1990), to a robust body of more recent work by Ehri (2003, 2007), and Adams (2011), among others, showing the importance of phonological awareness in the development of young L1 readers' ability to relate specific spelling patterns to the sounds of the language (phonological recoding, or decoding). Other research (e.g., Greaney 2003, Pikulski and Chard 2005, Rasinski et al. 2011) indicates that decoding skill is central to developing reading fluency, itself an essential component of successful text comprehension. Regarding the recommended pedagogical approach to literacy instruction, there is a body of evidence attesting to the value of systematic teaching of grapheme-phoneme (letter-sound) correspondences and developing whole-word recognition that is firmly based on automatised analysis of letters. This also applies to the promotion of repeated and extensive reading of a wide variety of books, recommendations which are supported by a number of reading meta-analyses: the National Reading Panel (NICHHD 2000), the National Early Literacy Panel (National Center for Family Literacy 2008) and the European EACEA (EACEA/Eurydice 2011). The consensus emerging from these studies is that children benefit from the provision of a solid foundation in decoding skills and a balanced approach that includes both bottom-up (code-based) and top-down (meaning-based) strategies, to provide the variety of skills needed to become a successful reader.

Yet the interview data here amplify the inspectorate evaluations, which showed that language-specific decoding skills for Irish do not appear to be taught systematically as the norm in English-medium schools. In fact, both the comments on the lack of systematicity in Irish reading instruction, and those on the lack of adequate preparation for the teaching of Irish reading in teacher education, hint at a marginalisation of reading instruction in Irish, a topic which has received little attention to date, and this marginalisation may be a contributing factor in the decline of general Irish language skills. The data here regarding the lack of a systematic approach to the early stages of teaching decoding skills specific to Irish orthography in mainstream schools shed further light on Parsons and Lyddy's (2009) findings (reported above in Section 12.3.2). The 2007 inspection report (DES 2007) indicated observation of analytic skills being taught in only 15 per cent of classrooms, with best practices (among which they included breaking down words in a structured way) seen in only 8 per cent. Some upper-level classes received no Irish reading instruction at all. The data also accord with Harris et al.'s (2006) observation of a reliance on the general Irish textbook in teaching Irish reading. This textbook is typically not a 'reader' but a general L2 textbook, with brief passages of dialogue and very short narratives whose function tends to be aimed at supporting oral language skills more than systematically fostering reading skills. As was found in the qualitative data, Harris et al. (2006) reported little reading in Irish for pleasure, and noted that real books in Irish were found in very few mainstream classrooms.[7]

A development that is relevant here is the official adoption of Strategy 2010–2030 for Irish, including retention of the language as an obligatory subject to Leaving Certificate level, and commitment to a curriculum which explicitly fosters 'both oral and written competence in Irish among students' (Government of Ireland 2010: 4). The statement that these aims are to be supported by increased investment in teacher pre-service and in-service education, and the provision of resources and textbooks to support innovative teaching, are to be welcomed. However, it appears that there is a need to engage in discussion and awareness-raising regarding the role and value of literacy in the second-language teaching of Irish in English-medium schools if these objectives are to be achieved. We have argued elsewhere (Hickey and Stenson 2011, Stenson and Hickey 2014) that not only is literacy development an essential component of second-language acquisition, even in classrooms where the emphasis is on oral language, but also that a systematic approach to early Irish reading instruction, with focus on developing language-specific decoding skills, is necessary to overcome the potential for negative transfer, or interference, from the already developing literacy in English.

There is, moreover, a considerable body of research indicating that L2 reading and other literacy-based activities in a second language offer valuable ways of developing L2 competence, not only as a tool for building vocabulary (Day et al. 1991, Day and Bamford 1998, Krashen 2004) but also as a vehicle for building, consolidating and enriching oral skills (Laufer 2003, Waring and Takaki 2003, Elley 1991). Nation (2001) examined the critical issue of building vocabulary in the second language, and what it means to really know a word, and Schmitt (2008) reviews some of the activities, many of them literacy-based, that effectively promote the different types of word knowledge in the context of the incremental nature of word learning. In the case of a threatened minority language such as Irish, where access to the spoken language outside of class is highly restricted for most pupils, Hickey (2009) discussed the importance of literacy in providing valuable linguistic input, crucial for the development of L2 skills. Hickey (2005) has also observed that reading in Irish can provide a bridge between the anglophone home and children's learning of Irish in school. Parents who do not feel comfortable trying to speak Irish with their children may be induced, with support, to read simple books in Irish to, and with, them. Repeated reading of texts and the resulting frequent exposure to the most common words have been shown to offer an effective way to build language skills as well as reading fluency (Stuart et al. 2000).

An integrated approach to language learning aims to equip learners with the range of different skills necessary to build and develop their language proficiency. Literacy is a vital weapon in the language learner's armoury, but for maximum benefit, decoding skills need to be fluent and automatic, rather than short-circuiting the extraction of meaning. Thus, approaches that can help to establish a bedrock of strong and reliable reading skills effectively increase the chances that L2 literacy will ultimately enable the learner to access beneficial input and positive experiences in the language, thus encouraging the virtuous circle of further reading offering L2 language-learning benefits. Tackling Irish reading systematically at the early stages is a vital step in allowing learners to access literacy later to help with extending vocabulary and to find more authentic and pleasurable outlets for using Irish as they continue through their primary school years and on into secondary school.

A new approach to teaching Irish as part of the new Integrated Curriculum (Ó Duibhir and Cummins 2012) is now being developed, drawing on international best practice as described in Harris and Ó Duibhir's (2011) review of research on effective language teaching. The evidence points strongly to the need for teachers to reach high levels of Irish proficiency and to receive high-quality pre-service and in-service education in second-language pedagogy. Teachers also need awareness of, and access to, high-quality materials for language teaching, which enable them to present Irish in positive and meaningful ways to pupils. This will also enable them to offer pupils opportunities to use Irish in the classroom outside the Irish lesson itself, as well as outside school. We have argued that a more effective use of Irish literacy-based activities and more reading, when taught effectively and according to best practices identified in the research and acknowledged in curriculum documents, can contribute significantly to these goals by increasing learners' access and exposure to the language. To accomplish this, teachers need the support of pre-service and continuing professional development for both their Irish skills and Irish-specific teaching, to prepare for teaching language-specific decoding skills effectively. They also need induction in the use of early reading materials such as *Fónaic na Gaeilge* (BELB 2011) and other resources that support automatised, fluent decoding as the foundation of Irish reading. The recent addition of a fourth year in the teacher preparation courses may also help if this additional time can be used, not only to build teachers' language skills (through Gaeltacht stays) but also for providing coursework in areas that have previously not been covered in the curriculum. These findings point to a need to use some of that time to provide more guidance to student teachers that specifically targets the teaching of Irish and Irish reading.

Finally, the materials that are already available need to be marketed more effectively to teachers in mainstream schools, rather than viewed as resources only for the Irish-medium sector, as currently seems to be the case, since many mainstream teachers appear to be entirely unaware of them. More widespread use of appropriate resources, so long called for by scholars, inspectors and teachers themselves, is essential to enable teachers to do their job where the teaching of Irish is concerned.

Provision of proper training and resources can have positive effects on teacher attitudes and enthusiasm for Irish, which in turn will be passed on to a greater number of pupils. Parents need to be educated too about the importance of showing support for their children's learning of Irish, and given assistance to find reasonable ways of providing that support.

12.6 Conclusions

The news is not all bad. The number of people claiming to be able to speak Irish continues to rise, and McCloskey (2008) describes the communities of Irish L2 speakers worldwide who embrace and use the language regularly. While they are a minority, their numbers do not seem to be shrinking, and they add a new dimension to a threatened language, rather like enlarging the gene pool. Literacy, including digital literacy, offers another dimension of access to this minority language. The increased accessibility of Irish-medium broadcasting has also enlarged the audience of Irish listeners, even if some remain passive users of the language. The Irish language is now a popular subject of study throughout the diaspora, where it was virtually unknown 30 years ago, and third-level educational opportunities in Irish are now available both in Ireland and abroad. For younger learners, the new curriculum being developed for the primary schools aims to integrate language instruction across skills, subjects and languages, and could be used to the benefit of Irish, provided the language 'gets its air time (T8)' and is not further marginalised under the pressures of the current [English] literacy/numeracy campaign or other new pressures such as a sudden perceived need to teach Chinese, or computer programming.

The 20-year Strategy for the Irish Language acknowledges the continuing language shift in the Gaeltacht, and this, coupled with the small number and size of viable Irish speech communities, means that the acquisition of Irish in schools remains a vital enterprise for the language's survival, even in Gaeltacht areas. Thus, it is of the utmost importance to maximise the effectiveness of that acquisition setting and offer learners every opportunity to build skills that will empower them as learners to build and develop proficiency in the language, so that they can gain satisfaction from their progress, rather than resenting their failure. Second-language reading, properly taught and properly developed as a language skill, can help by providing language input to learners beyond the classroom and introducing cultural and social worlds that might never be encountered through spoken language in the urban settings where most schoolchildren are learning Irish.

As noted above, the L2 learning of Irish is now situated in the context of the 20-year Strategy for the Irish Language, which encompasses many important goals such as increasing the visibility of Irish and opportunities to use it in daily life, increasing very significantly the number of people with a knowledge of the language and the number of daily users outside of education, enhancing teacher education and resources, protecting Gaeltacht speech communities and providing supports to encourage family language transmission. All of these are desirable goals, and show an admirable attempt to maintain and promote L1 acquisition as well as increase the achievement of L2 learners. However, it could be said that they have been the goals of every policy document since the start of the state, but little detail is provided, and no timeline, on exactly how they are to be implemented. Indeed, the document itself states that success will depend on the provision of resources to realise the goals, and in the past insufficient resources have been forthcoming. Time will tell whether the aspirations of this Strategy document, and other pending reforms, will bear fruit. For the Irish language, it may still be a case of 'Mair, a chapaill, agus gheobhaidh tú féar' [Live horse, and you will get grass].

Notes

1. This shift appears so far to have helped to stem the decline in the numbers taking the Higher Level course, which rose from 32 per cent in 2011 to 40 per cent in 2014.
2. It is worth noting also the growth in opportunities (and uptake) for third-level studies through the medium of Irish, apart from the traditional programmes in Irish language and literature found at all Irish universities. Ní Ghallachair (2008) lists four postgraduate-level degree or certificate courses in Irish in three third-level institutions, and the number has continued to rise. A survey of institutional websites shows that all universities and several institutes of technology now offer at least one such certificate, undergraduate or postgraduate degree programme in Irish.
3. In Gaeltacht schools and a number of Gaelscoileanna, in contrast, reading is introduced first in Irish or simultaneously in both languages.
4. This represents a considerable reduction from the five-hour minimum recommended in 1922 (Hyland and Milne 1992) and the average of 5.6 contact hours reported by Harris et al. (2006) in the 1970s.
5. The code 'T' indicates that a quotation is drawn from the sample of primary teachers interviewed in English, while 'M' indicates that a quote is from a secondary teacher interviewed in Irish, 'O' refers to a teacher educator and 'S' refers to other experts in the Irish interviews.
6. Despite the teacher's remarks, it should be noted, however, that this text does not provide comprehensive phonics instruction.

7. Teachers we interviewed also indicated that their classrooms and libraries often had a shortage of books in Irish; some classrooms do not have dictionaries for the children to use.

References

Adams, Marilyn J. (1990). *Beginning to Read*. Cambridge, MA: MIT Press.

Adams, Marilyn J. (2011). 'The relation between alphabetic basics, word recognition, and reading', in: S. Jay Samuels and Alan Farstrup (eds) *What Research has to Say about Reading Instruction*. Newark: International Reading Association, pp. 4–24.

BELB (2011). *Fónaic na Gaeilge: Fiosrú Focal. Lámhleabhar Teagaisc*. Belfast: Belfast Education and Library Board. Retrieved 17 December 2011 from: http://www. stmarys-belfast.ac.uk/aisaonad/comhaid/Fonaic_na_Gaeilge.pdf.

Braun, Virginia and Victoria Clarke (2006). 'Using thematic analysis in psychology', *Qualitative Research in Psychology* 3: 77–101.

Chall, Jeanne (1967). *Learning to Read: the Great Debate*. New York: McGraw Hill.

CoE/DES (Council of Europe/Department of Education and Science) (2007). *Language Education Policy Profile Ireland*. Strasbourg and Dublin: Language Policy Division, and DES.

Comhairle na Gaelscolaíochta (2014). Retrieved 23 September 2014 from www.comhairle.org.

Commins, Patrick (1988). 'Socioeconomic development and language maintenance in the Gaeltacht', *International Journal of the Sociology of Language* 70. Special issue on language planning in Ireland, Pádraig Ó Riagáin (ed.), pp. 11–28.

Day, Richard and Julian Bamford (1998). *Extensive Reading in the Second Language Classroom*. Cambridge: Cambridge University Press.

Day, Richard, Carol Omura and Motoo Hiramatsu (1991). 'Incidental EFL vocabulary learning and reading', *Reading in a Foreign Language* 7: 541–51.

Department of Education and Science (DES) (1999). *Primary School Curriculum/Curaclam na Bunscoile*. Dublin: Stationery Office.

Department of Education and Science (DES) (2007). *Irish in the Primary School: Promoting the Quality of Learning*. Dublin: DES Inspectorate Evaluation Studies.

EACEA/Eurydice (2011). *Teaching Reading in Europe: Contexts, Policies, and Practices*. Brussels: Education, Audiovisual and Culture Executive Agency.

Ehri, Linnea C. (2003). 'Systematic phonics instruction: Findings of the National Reading Panel.' London: DfES. Retrieved 1 June 2005 from http://www.standards.dfes.gov.uk/primary/publications/literacy/686807/ nls_phonics0303lehri.pdf.

Ehri, Linnea C. (2007). 'Development of sight word readings: Phases and findings', in: Margaret J. Snowling and Charles Hulme (eds) *The Science of Reading*. Oxford: Blackwell, pp. 135–54.

Elley, Warwick B. (1991) 'Acquiring literacy in a second language: the effect of book-based programs', *Language Learning* 41: 375–411.

Fishman, Joshua (1991). *Reversing Language Shift*. Clevedon: Multilingual Matters.

Fishman, Joshua (2000). *Can Threatened Languages be Saved?* Clevedon: Multilingual Matters.

Gaelscoileanna (2014). Retrieved 29 August 2014 from http://www. *gaelscoileanna* .ie/en/about/statistics/.

Government of Ireland (2010). *20-Year Strategy for the Irish Language 2010–2030*. Dublin: Stationery Office. Online document last retrieved 31 October 2014 from http://www.ahg.gov.ie/en/20-YearStrategyfortheIrishLanguage 2010-2030/.

Greaney, Keith (2003). 'Encouraging strategic decoding skills: Implications for reading teachers', in: Gerry Shiel and Ursula Ní Dhálaigh (eds) *Other Ways of Seeing: Diversity in Language and Literacy*, Vol 2. Dublin: RAI, pp. 113–19.

Harris, John (2005). 'The role of ordinary primary schools in the maintenance and revival of Irish', *Proceedings of the Fourth International Symposium on Bilingualism*, J Cohan, K.T. McAlister, K. Rolstad and J. MacSwan (eds). Somerville, MA: Cascadilla Press, pp. 964–77.

Harris, John (2008). 'The declining role of primary schools in the revitalisation of Irish', *AILA Review* 21: 49–68.

Harris, John and Lelia Murtagh (1999). *Teaching and Learning Irish in Primary School: a Review of Research and Development*. Dublin: Institiúid Teangeolaíochta Éireann.

Harris, John and Pádraig Ó Duibhir (2011). *Effective Language Teaching: a Synthesis of Research*. NCCA report #13. Dublin: NCCA.

Harris, John, Patrick Forde, Peter Archer, Siobhán Nic Fhearaile and Mary O'Gorman (2006). *Irish in Primary Schools: Long-Term National Trends in Achievement*. Dublin: Department of Education and Science.

Hickey, Tina (2001). 'Mixing beginners and native speakers in Irish immersion: Who is immersing whom?', *Canadian Modern Language Review* 57.3: 443–74.

Hickey, Tina (2005). 'Second language writing systems: Minority languages and reluctant readers', in: Vivian Cook and Benedetta Bassetti (eds) *Second Language Writing Systems*. Clevedon: Multilingual Matters, pp. 398–423.

Hickey, Tina (2007). 'Fluency in reading Irish as L1 or L2: Promoting high frequency word recognition', *International Journal of Bilingual Education and Bilingualism* 10.4: 471–93.

Hickey, Tina (2009). 'Developing biliteracy in Irish schools', in: Brendan Culligan (ed.) *The Changing Landscapes of Irish Literacy*. Dublin: RAI, pp. 197–209.

Hickey, Tina and Nancy Stenson (2011). 'Irish orthography: What do teachers and learners need to know about it, and why?', *Language, Culture and Curriculum* 24.1: 23–46.

Hislop, Harold (2013). *Chief Inspector's Report 2010–2012*. Dublin: Department of Education and Science.

Hyland, Áine and Milne, Kenneth (1992). *Irish Educational Documents, Vol. 2*. Dublin: Church of Ireland College of Education.

Ireland-US Fulbright Commission (IUSFC) (2011). *Interchanges: Irish Language Teaching and Learning in the US*. Dublin: Ireland-United States Fulbright Commission.

Krashen, Stephen (2004). *The Power of Reading: Insights from the Research*. Second edition. Portsmouth, NH: Heinemann.

Laufer, Batia (2003). 'Vocabulary acquisition in a second language: Do learners really acquire most vocabulary by reading? Some empirical evidence', *Canadian Modern Language Review/La revue canadienne des langues vivantes* 59.4 : 567–87.

McCloskey, James (2008). 'Irish as a world language', in: Brian Ó Conchubhair and Breandán Ó Buachalla (eds) *Why Irish?* Arlen House, Syracuse NY: Syracuse University Press, pp. 71–89. (Also available online at http://ohlone.ucsc.edu/~jim/PDF/notre-dame.pdf.)

McCoy, Selina, Emer Smyth and Joanne Banks (2012). *The Primary Classroom: Insights from the Growing up in Ireland Study.* Dublin: Economic and Social Research Institute.

Maguire, Gabrielle (1990). *Our Own Language.* Clevedon: Multilingual Matters.

Murtagh, Lelia (2003). 'Retention and Attrition of Irish as a Second Language'. Unpublished doctoral dissertation, University of Groningen.

Murtagh, Lelia (2009). 'The role of motivation in learning and using Irish among primary and second-level students', in: Sheila Drudy (ed.) *Education in Ireland. Challenge and Change.* Dublin: Gill and Macmillan, pp. 136–50.

Nation, I. S. P. (2001). *Learning Vocabulary in Another Language.* Cambridge: Cambridge University Press.

Nation, I. S. P. (2006). 'How large a vocabulary is needed for reading and listening?', *Canadian Modern Language Review* 63.1: 59–82.

National Center for Family Literacy (2008). *Developing Early Literacy: Report of the National Early Literacy Panel.* Jessup, MD: National Institute for Literacy.

National Institute of Child Health and Human Development (NICHHD) (2000). *Teaching Children to Read: An Evidence-Based Assessment of the Scientific Research Literature on Reading and its Implications for Reading Instruction.* NIH Publication No. 004769. Washington, DC: US Government Printing Office. Retrieved 30 October 2013 from http://www.nationalreadingpanel.org/Publications/publications.htm.

Ní Ghallachair, Anna (2008). 'Teaching and learning Irish today', in: Nic Pháidín and Ó Cearnaigh (eds), pp. 91–201.

Ní Laoire, Máire and Muiris Ó Laoire (2008). 'The challenges faced in the teaching of the Irish language at second level', *Public Affairs Ireland Journal* 50 (September 2008). Online article retrieved 10 October 2014 from http://www.publicaffairsireland.com/journal/archive/51-issue-50-september-2008/articles/838-the-challenges-faced-in-the-teaching-of-the-irish-language-at-second-level.

Nic Pháidín, Caoilfhionn and Seán Ó Cearnaigh (eds) (2008). *A New View of the Irish Language.* Dublin: Cois Life.

Ó Broin, Brian (2012). *Thógamar le Gaeilge Iad.* Dublin: Coiscéim.

Ó Conchubhair, Brian (2008). 'The global diaspora and the "new" Irish', in: Nic Pháidín and Ó Cearnaigh (eds), pp. 224–48.

Ó Duibhir, Pádraig and Jim Cummins (2012). *Towards an Integrated Language Curriculum in Early Childhood and Primary Education (3–12 years).* Research Report (#16). Dublin: National Council for Curriculum and Assessment.

Ó Faoláin, Dónal (2006). 'Developing a phonics programme in Irish for the teaching of reading in the Gaeltacht', in: Tina Hickey (ed.) *Literacy and Language Learning: Reading in a First or Second Language.* Dublin: RAI, pp. 65–73.

Ó Giollagáin, Conchúr and Seosamh Mac Donnacha (2008). 'The Gaeltacht Today', in: Nic Pháidín and Ó Cearnaigh (eds), pp. 108–20.

Ó Giollagáin, Conchúr, Seosamh MacDonnacha, Fiona Ní Chualáin, Aoife Ní Shéaghdha and Mary O'Brien (2007). *Staidéar Cuimsitheach Teangeolaíoch ar*

Úsáid na Gaeilge sa Ghaeltacht: Tuarascáil Chríochnaitheach. Baile Átha Cliath: Oifig an tSoláthair.

Ó Laoire, Muiris (1999). *Athbheochan na hEabhraise: Ceacht don Ghaeilge?* Dublin: An Clóchomhar.

Ó Laoire, Muiris (2005). 'The language planning situation in Ireland', *Current Issues in Language Planning* 6.3: 251–314.

Ó Laoire, Muiris (2012). 'Language policy and minority language education in Ireland: Re-exploring the issues', *Language, Culture and Curriculum* 25.1: 17–25.

Ó Riagáin, Pádraig (1988). 'Bilingualism 1973–1983: an overview', *International Journal of the Sociology of Language* 70. Special issue on language planning in Ireland: 29–51.

Ó Riagáin, Pádraig (1997). *Language Policy and Social Reproduction: Ireland 1893–1993.* Oxford: Clarendon Press, and New York: Oxford University Press.

Ó Riagáin, Pádraig (2008). 'Irish language policy 1922–2007: Balancing maintenance and revival', in: Nic Pháidín and Ó Cearnaigh (eds), pp. 55–65.

Ó Riagáin, Pádraig (ed.) (1988). *Language Planning in Ireland.* Special issue of *International Journal of the Sociology of Language* 70.

Parsons, Christine, and Fiona Lyddy (2009). 'Early reading strategies in Irish and English: evidence from error types', *Reading in a Foreign Language* 21.1: 22–36.

Pikulski, John J. and David J. Chard (2005). 'Fluency: Bridge between decoding and reading comprehension', *The Reading Teacher* 58: 510–19.

Punch, Aidan (2008). 'Census data on the Irish language', in: Nic Pháidín and Ó Cearnaigh (eds), pp. 43–54.

Rasinski, Timothy V., D. Ray Reutzel, David Chard and Sylvia Linan-Thompson (2011). 'Reading fluency', in: Michael L. Kamil, P. David Pearson, Peter Afferblach and Elizabeth B. Moje (eds) *Handbook of Reading Research, Volume IV.* New York: Routledge, pp. 286–319.

RTÉ News (2014). 'Survey suggests parents would like children to learn coding'. Retrieved 28 October 2014 from http://www.rte.ie/news/2014/1017/652936-coding.

Schmitt, Norbert (2008). 'Review article: Instructed second language vocabulary learning', *Language Teaching Research* 12.3: 329–63.

Spolsky, Bernard (2004). *Language Policy.* Cambridge: Cambridge University Press.

Stenson, Nancy, and Tina Hickey (2014). 'In defense of decoding', *Journal of Celtic Language Learning* 18: 11–40.

Stuart, Morag, Jackie Masterson, and Maureen Dixon (2000). 'Spongelike acquisition of sight vocabulary in beginning readers', *Journal of Research in Reading* 23.1: 12–27.

Waring, Rob, and Misako Takaki (2003). 'At what rate do learners learn and retain new vocabulary from reading a graded reader?', *Reading in a Foreign Language* 15.2: 130–63.

13

The Language of Irish Writing in English

Carolina P. Amador-Moreno

13.1 Introduction

The concept of 'perceptual dialectology' is defined by Preston (1999: xxv) as a sub-branch of *folk linguistics* that represents the interest in language use by dialectologists, sociolinguists and variationists. This area of investigation is particularly concerned with what non-specialists have to say about variation: 'Where do they believe it comes from? Where do they believe it exists? What do they believe is its function?' One of the principal techniques developed for perceptual dialectology in the 1980s included, for example, drawing boundaries on a blank map around areas where the respondents thought regional speech zones existed (Preston and Howe 1987), a method also employed by Hickey (2005: 99–105) in the context of Irish English, in order to test what conceptions of dialect areas non-specialist speakers had for Ireland. In Hickey's survey, the majority of the Dublin respondents distinguished between two forms of Dublin English: a northern, more vernacular form, and a southern form, which they referred to in the map returns as Dublin 4 (or D4). Such a division was also recognised by 39 per cent of the non-Dublin respondents. This distinction, together with prescriptive comments such as 'strong' or 'hard' to describe the north Dublin accent, or 'posh', 'snobbish', 'phoney' to refer to the Southside/Dublin 4 accent, is a good barometer with which to measure non-specialists' beliefs and attitudes towards the English spoken in Dublin.

The aim of this chapter is to discuss how non-specialised perceptions of Dublin English can be employed in order to signal current language use, as well as class, and gender differences. *Non-specialists* in this context refers to speakers who have had no formal linguistic training, and it includes those who may show a certain degree of linguistic awareness in their perception of language use. Fiction writers who use dialogue as a tool to imbue their stories with realism also fall into that category.

Many authors, as is well known, employ linguistic features that characterise natural conversation, including those who write memoirs, biographies and even standard non-fiction, because these features help them illustrate rather than just describe what they want to say. The type of information that can be gleaned from the use of dialogue, as I have argued elsewhere (Amador-Moreno 2010b, 2012: 22; Amador-Moreno and McCafferty 2015), helps authors construct characters without having to resort to descriptions. However, much of what is selected by fiction writers as representative of a particular type/group of speaker(s) is inevitably influenced by subjective factors: it reflects the author's own perception of how others speak. In such domains, representational practices can arise and become traditions (Hickey 2010: 14), both in the context of fiction and in the general public psyche, and stereotypes can become perpetuated. In the process of *enregisterment*, defined as that 'through which a linguistic repertoire becomes differentiable within a language as a socially recognized register of forms' (Agha 2003: 231), literary works are among the most influential elements that contribute to the systematic and structured use of what could be considered a linguistic shibboleth. In the Irish context, for example, the creation of the stereotypical figure of the *Stage Irishman* has often been based on linguistic characterisation through time (see Hickey 2007: 297–301, Walshe 2009: 5–14, Amador-Moreno 2010a: 89–109, and McCafferty 2010 for Northern Irish English specifically). In this sense, when examining the way authors represent dialects, it seems pertinent to consider what sort of socio-historical (or other non-linguistic) factors influence perception. Does fiction writing contribute to the creation of certain linguistic trends that may end up being associated with specific speech communities? Does the fact that certain authors show an interest in replicating real spoken discourse in their work influence readers' perception of how a particular speech community speaks? Or is the author's own perception of language use just a convenient tool that allows him/her to connect with readers? Reader/spectator/viewer identification clearly plays an important role in the success of a novel, a play, a film or a television programme. And, as Quaglio (2009: 13) puts it, 'it is through *language* that this identification is achieved and popular culture is expressed and reflected'.

This chapter discusses how the perception that fiction writers have of a particular dialect plays a key role in the process of enregisterment, a useful framework developed by Agha (2003) that combines various linguistic theories to describe how a set of linguistic features that start to be perceived as markers of socio-economic class, can end up being linked to place and *enregistered* as a dialect. One of the questions I ask is whether one set of linguistic forms could potentially be imported from another variety of English and become enregistered as a different variety through written fiction. In the present study I focus on one author, Paul Howard, and discuss how his depiction of the English spoken in Dublin is an important tool in the construction of the fictionalised identity of his characters. In his Ross O'Carroll-Kelly series, where the narrative style is built as an emulation of orality, the use of linguistic features, such as quotatives, conforms with the overall stylistic strategy employed by Howard in constructing the protagonist's narrative voice. In the sections that follow, I start by describing the value of the Ross O'Carroll-Kelly dataset for linguistic analysis; in Section 13.3 I explain why the analysis of quotatives is worth investigating; Section 13.4 discusses some issues in relation to how quotative forms are used in the novel *The Curious Incident of the Dog in the Nightdress* and their significance; and finally, Section 13.5 presents some concluding remarks.

13.2 A Dubliner's voice in fiction

Paul Howard, a Dubliner himself, and therefore, an *insider* in terms of awareness (Melchers 2010: 91–2; Wales 2010: 67–8), is a well-established writer in Ireland. His career as a fiction writer started with the creation of the character of Ross O'Carroll-Kelly [RO'CK], a satirical representation of a wealthy, chauvinistic young Dubliner in his twenties, from the south side of the city. The character of RO'CK came to life originally as part of a weekly column in the Irish *Sunday Tribune* in 1998 and his 'adventures' have been published to date in the same column format in *The Irish Times*. The column has so far given rise to a series of 14 novels, three plays and other Ross-related comedy writing. The novels display a type of humorous narrative that can be considered as the male variant of *Chick Lit*,[1] and has in common with its female-oriented counterpart[2] a confessional style derived from the fact that the story is presented as the oral narrative of the protagonist, Ross (O'Carroll-Kelly), 'as told to Paul Howard'. As Gorman (2013: 8) states, '[t]he format [of the series] is set out as a written text derived from an oral communication; therefore what is presented to the reader is an interlacing of speech/writing', a transcript of naturally occurring speech, which is what makes it interesting for the present study. This recording of speech in writing presents us with a type of narrative that is constructed as spontaneous discourse, crafting the impression that the protagonist is speaking directly to the reader (Ferris and Young 2006: 4). This technique, where the reader is treated as someone who is there to 'listen' to the story, purposely looks for an immediate connection with the reader, and such connection is further sought through an effective representation of dialect, which is the result of Howard's acute (though non-specialised) linguistic awareness. Much of the RO'CK comedy value derives from Howard's style and ability to capture the spontaneity of spoken Dublin English, which also explain, in part, how he has managed to take, as critic Dan Sheehan points out, 'what should have been a small-scale parody with a rapidly approaching sell-by date and turned it into one of the most enduring satirical figures in the Irish literary canon'.[3] Through the character of Ross, Howard provides the reader with the recorded speech patterns that characterise the wealthy south Dublin society that is the aim of his satire. In his attempt to capture the social class-based idiolect of this area of Dublin, Howard resorts, among other things, to eye dialect, as some literary critics have observed:

> Howard's dialogue sings, and he never misses the chance to subvert standard English in service of a larf. In Ross's parlance, cars are cors, guys are goys, body parts are body ports. Again and again the reader is compelled to wonder how the kind of airhead babble lampooned by Frank Zappa in *Valley Girl* 30 years ago came to be the official language of the Dundrum[4] generation. Ross's employment of the dreaded ascending line statement – whereby every other declaration is capped with a question mark, the legacy of too many hours watching *Friends* – and liberal pepperings of *like* would be intolerable in a so-called serious novel, but here, as send-up, it never gets old.[5]

Certain uses of the discourse marker *like* in the narrative presented by Ross do indeed sound like an importation from American English (Buchstaller and D'Arcy 2009) that has been appropriated by a very specific type of speaker in (the south side of) Dublin, to such an extent that authors like Howard employ it to characterise this type of speaker. Whether this is an illustration of the influence of spoken media on processes of language and dialect change or simply a case of a short-lived linguistic innovation that has been captured by Howard is something that would require further investigation: a balanced exploration of media engagement and media influence on the speech of young Dubliners would require the combination of speech data (fictional and non-fictional) with participant observation, as well as interviews and questionnaires,[6] but it is something worth considering.

The satirisation of prosperous Southside Dublin runs beside Howard's depiction of the more working-class and less prestigious Northside Dublin, both of which are represented through very specific linguistic features. Whereas Ross and his friends incarnate what Hickey (2005: 7–8) refers to as '*new* Dublin English', other characters from the Northside use 'local Dublin English'. The north–south divide that is represented in the novels is based on the linguistic differentiation between speakers generally coming from areas of high social prestige – those representing 'a section of the population which does not want to be identified with all too localised forms of Dublin English', and those who 'show strongest identification with traditional conservative Dublin life of which the popular accent is very much a part' (Hickey 2005: 6–7). The following excerpt from the novel *The Curious Incident of the Dog in the Nightdress* (2005) illustrates this linguistic differentiation (Tina and her son Ronan, who is also Ross's illegitimate son, are two characters from Dublin's Northside):

> I don't know what it is, roysh, but I can't stop thinking about Ronan. It's probably the whole father–son thing, blah blah blah, but I wake up in some bird's house in Booterstown this particular Sunday morning, roysh, and I bell Tina and ask her if it'd be okay to, like, call out to the gaff. She goes, 'Jaysus, you're not scared of out-staying your welcome, you, are ye?' and I'm there, 'Oh, but I just thought…' and she's like, 'I'm only messin' wi' ye, Ross. Ronan tinks de wurdled of ye. Come on out for yisser breakfast.'[7]

Apart from colloquial lexical items such as *bird, bell* or *gaff*, and the attempted phonetic rendering of words such as *roysh* (right), *tinks* (thinks), or *wurdled* (world), two other features call our attention as readers: on the one hand, the use of quotatives *she goes, I'm there*, and *she's like*, and, on the other, the insertion of *like* in mid-position (in 'it'd be okay to, *like*, call out to the gaff') which, as the review quoted above points out, sounds like a line taken from the sitcom *Friends*. Despite the fictional differences between the world recreated in *Friends* and in the RO'CK series, one of the things that the characters in the American sitcom and the Irish book saga may have in common is precisely the use of certain linguistic traits such as *like* as a discourse marker, and of *be* + *like*, *be* + *there*, and *go* as quotatives. Given that both settings try to recreate the effect of face-to-face interaction, the recurrence of linguistic features such as discourse markers and quotatives is to be expected, given that they characterise natural conversation and contribute towards rapport-building with the listener/reader.

The use of quotative forms such as *be + like, be + there,* and *go* form part of the linguistic repertoire of the Southsiders depicted in the RO'CK series. They are used for dramatisation, to frame direct quotations, as in the following excerpt:

> Emer turns around to me and goes, *'Oh my God,* I heard JP's totally flipped out', and I'm there, 'What do you mean, flipped out? He's just gone mad into God', and then Chloë goes, 'Oh, yeah, like he *needs* to be praying? He's loaded, Ross', and Emer's there, 'Yeah, I heard he's had a total breakdown. It's like, Oh! My! God!' and Chloë's like, 'I heard that, too. I heard it was like, *Aaahhh.* And I heard that from Wendy, who's, like, in the Institute with a girl who lives two doors down from his parents.'

In trying to create that effect of orality whereby Ross's storytelling positions the reader as listener, stories are dramatised by mimicking the characters in the narrative (in this case Emer, Chloë and himself). In previous work (Amador-Moreno 2012, 2015) I have argued that in naturally occurring spoken discourse, action-oriented narration generally calls for reported speech (Barbieri 2005: 231), and direct quotation is a common form of what Labov (1972) called *internal evaluation.* By putting words in the mouth of the characters, the teller communicates what happened from inside the story (Tannen 1982: 8), making it sound more dramatic.

In the context of narratives, quotatives are employed as a strategy to build on interpersonal involvement or to create a sense of identification. More specifically, in written narratives the use of quotatives allows the narrator to replay the speaker's reaction, as in face-to-face spontaneous conversation, and their use contributes to creating the effect of focus on interpersonal or emotional involvement, which is often foregrounded in real spoken narrative by oral features such as these. As was indicated above, Howard's narrative is presented to the reader as if a dialogue between Ross and the reader-as-listener had in fact been established from the outset, where the character-narrator manages to 'create the illusion of a sense of closeness with their readership because [he] appear[s] to be conveying [his] message directly' (Montoro 2012: 131). The incorporation of quotatives into the narrative, thus, creates that sense of intimacy that exists in conversations between friends, shortening the distance between speaker and listener (and between narrator and reader in this case).

The use of *be + like, be + there,* and *go* contributes to constructing the narration in a convincing fashion. In that sense, it could be argued that these features are an important part of the strategy deliberately employed by Howard to build rapport with the reader, who is able to recognise these speech features as characteristic of current spoken Dublin English (in some cases because they have actually witnessed similar scenarios occurring in real life).

The data to be analysed in what follows comes from the novel *The Curious Incident of the Dog in the Nightdress* (2005) (henceforth referred to as CIDN), which contains 91,839 words in total. This novel is representative of the style employed by its author,[8] and a corpus-analytic exploration of it provides interesting insights into how the narrative voice is constructed based on real spoken features of contemporary IrE. In Amador-Moreno (2015) I discuss how this construction may in fact affect the reader's evaluation of its effects, once certain recurrent forms such as discourse markers and quotatives are taken into account. In the present chapter I concentrate on the indexical meaning of the quotative forms that appear in the novel in order to assess how the choice of language or language varieties, linguistic features and language patterns may be revealing in terms of signalling in-group membership when relating narratives. I also argue that Howard's conscious decision to incorporate quotative forms into the novel and make them so salient is a clear indication of their existence in present-day Dublin English. His choice of linguistic features is not only a reflection of his reliability as an observer of contemporary Dublin speech, but also a sign of his strong interest in portraying his characters in a socially and linguistically realistic way through narration. Woven into the story of CIDN is Howard's concern with the display of sociolinguistic identities and attitudes towards contemporary Dublin English.

13.3 Why look at quotatives?

In the text surveyed here there is clear evidence of authorial sensitivity to high-frequency uses of quotative forms in real spoken Dublin English. A corpus-driven analysis of the novel reveals (Amador-Moreno 2012, 2015) that such frequency is replicated in Howard's writing in order to breathe realism into the story. And, although the recurrence of features like these may simply be a way of overgeneralising or exaggerating certain linguistic patterns for comic, thematic and even political purposes, as is often the case in writing (Ellis 1994: 139–40), in the context that this chapter focuses on, a corpus study of the novel shows how the repetition of certain patterns may carry a specific indexical meaning. Repetition of patterns in the form of clusters, or lexical bundles, as argued by Biber et al. (1999), are an important overall component of the representation of speech in a novel. Clusters, defined by Scott (2013) as

Table 13.1   Word list of 2-word clusters in CIDN

1	AND I	18	TO THE
2	AND I'M	19	THE OLD
3	I'M THERE	20	AND THE
4	IN THE	21	AND SHE'S
5	HE GOES	22	OUT OF
6	AND HE	23	HAVE TO
7	OF THE	24	HE'S LIKE
8	I GO	25	WE'RE TALKING
9	ON THE	26	AND THEN
10	I'M LIKE	27	OF A
11	AND SHE	28	AND IT'S
12	SHE GOES	29	OF COURSE
13	AND GOES	30	AT THE
14	I DON'T	31	ME AND
15	AND HE'S	32	SHE'S LIKE
16	TO BE	33	TO SAY
17	GOING TO	34	I JUST

'words which are found repeatedly together in each others' company, in sequence', have been known to be highly functional in real spoken interaction, as 'they reflect the interpersonal meanings (meanings which build and consolidate personal and social relations) created between speakers and listeners (writers and readers)' (Carter and McCarthy 2006: 835). In recent work (Amador-Moreno 2015), I point out that quotatives are among the most frequent 2-word clusters in CIDN. Table 13.1 shows the combinations *personal pronoun + go*; *personal pronoun + be + like*; and *I + be + there*, all of which introduce variation in the narrative as an alternative to more traditional quotative verbs such as *say*.

The use of quotatives and their rapid rise as a global innovation has been documented in most English-speaking countries, and this includes Ireland too. Its recent prominence in different spoken varieties of English is attested by the growing literature on this topic (e.g. Cukor-Avila 2002; Ferrara and Bell 1995 in the United States; Tagliamonte and D'Arcy 2004, 2007; Tagliamonte and Hudson 1999 in Canada, Buchstaller 2006, 2014; Durham et al. 2012, Macaulay 2001 in the UK, and Buchstaller and D'Arcy 2009 in New Zealand). Empirical analyses of quotatives in some of these studies have shown that the use of these forms is affected by external linguistic variables such as age, gender, ethnicity and language variety of the speaker, and by internal variables such as grammatical person of the subject, discourse-function of the quotation, and tense. In the section that follows I start by summarising my findings in relation to internal variables and then discuss the interplay between class, gender and linguistic variety in the novel, based on the use of quotatives.

13.4 The construction of male narration in Dublin English

Previous analyses of *like* as a discourse marker led on to a more detailed study of quotatives in the CIDN corpus. A comparison of the use of quotative forms in the CIDN dataset revealed (Amador-Moreno 2015) that of all the structures employed in the novel to report speech/thought, quotative *go* (preceded by subject), as in '...and we all go "Oh, yeah, roysh"', was the most recurrent, as shown in Figure 13.1.

Reports from several varieties of English have revealed that *go* is mainly a feature appearing at higher levels of frequency in the speech of young people (Tagliamonte and Hudson 1999; Macaulay 2001; Cukor-Avila 2002; Buchstaller 2006). A feature in flux (Britain 2010: 43), much of the literature dealing with this particular quotative has focused on its diffusion and sociolinguistic significance in comparison to *be like*. As Buchstaller (2006) points out, some researchers have suggested that *be like* will eventually push *go* out of the quotative system. However, if Howard's representation of Dublin English is to be taken as an indicator, what his rendering of quotatives in the present corpus shows is that,

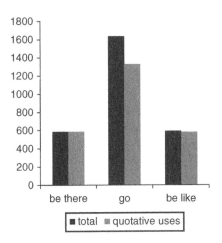

Figure 13.1   Quotative uses of *go, be there* and *be like*[9]

while the variants certainly exist side by side in present-day spoken Dublin English, no such push seems to be in progress.

Quotative uses of *like*, combining *subject + be + like* as in 'He answers the door and straight away I'm like, "Well?"', are also rather significant in the novel. They occur with pronominal forms (*I, he* and *she*) as shown in Table 13.1 above, as well as with first names, and we find them in the past tense, as well as in the present.

Quotative *like* is used to foreground reported speech and thought, as discussed by Ferrara and Bell (1995) and Romaine and Lange (1991), among others. The pattern *be + like* has been considered a case of grammaticalisation, where a single processing unit becomes automated (Tagliamonte and D'Arcy 2004), and it has received a large amount of attention in different varieties of English (e.g. Tagliamonte and Hudson 1999; Macaulay 2001; Tagliamonte and D'Arcy 2004; Buchstaller 2006). Its occurrence in Irish English has recently been studied by Höhn (2012), who compares the use of quotatives in two corpora: ICE-Jamaica (International Corpus of English – Jamaica component) and ICE-Ireland (International Corpus of English – Ireland component). Höhn's findings (2012: 273) indicate that although *go* and *be + like* are both present in the ICE-Ireland corpus, the most frequent quotative appears to be *say*. In the CIDN data, as shown in Figure 13.2 below, the use of quotative *say* (counting both present and past forms of the verb) is comparatively lower than the 'new' quotatives:[10]

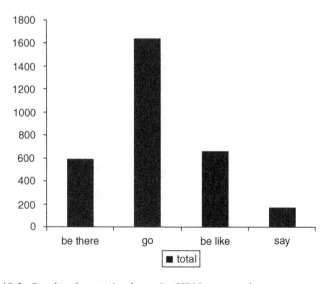

Figure 13.2 Results of quotative forms in CIDN compared

This is not surprising, given the fact that new quotatives, as argued above, have a more dramatic effect than verbs like *say* in narratives and have a stronger rapport-building effect than *say*. In the context of the novel, *say* is embedded in reported speech or else part of the cluster *as if to say*, which introduces reported thought. Notice, for example, the contrast (in terms of dramatic effect) between *be + going*, *be + like* and *be + there* and *say* in the following examples from the CIDN corpus:

(1) **I go**, 'Sorcha, can I remind you that we're still married', and **she's there**, 'Daddy **says** I can get an annulment', and **I'm like**, 'Don't change the subject', and there's this, like, silence on the line, roysh, then **she goes**, 'OH MY GOD! You don't know what an annulment is, do you?'

(2) After a few minutes **I go**, 'I think I've spotted a weakness in their back row', and Fionn **goes**, 'I know it was you, Ross', and I just stare at him, **as if to say**, basically, prove it, and **he's there**, 'She rang me. Your friend, Leilani. She felt bad about what she did', and I look at him **as if to say**, *Whatever!*

In Höhn's study, the new quotatives were almost exclusively restricted to private dialogues, the most informal type of register. Based on the premise that the less formal the interaction, the higher the use of direct quotation for narrative and involvement purposes, I have argued that Howard's rendering of new quotatives seems to tally well with Höhn's findings, and also with the conclusions in relation to its occurrence in ICE-Ireland reached by Kallen (2013: 191), who draws attention to the fact that 'the overall picture is one which suggests that speakers of Irish English adopted quotative *like* in ICE-related contexts sooner than their British counterparts'. As pointed out above, an important aspect of Howard's style is the imitation of the vividness often contained in private, informal interactions among friends. The use of *go*, *be + like* and *be + there + like* in the novel, therefore, contributes to a more realistic portrayal of the voices recreated in the story. The fact that the majority of the 'new' quotatives are used in the present tense in the corpus, as shown in Figure 13.3 below, is also in line with the stylistic effect sought by Howard.

When tracing the grammaticalisation pattern of *be + like*, Ferrara and Bell (1995), and later Barbieri (2005) too, observed that third person usage had increased over time and argued that this indicated a significant change from previous studies (e.g. Romaine and Lange 1991 on American English), where this structure was typically used for 'self-representation' (cf. a recent study by Durham et al. 2012, where they

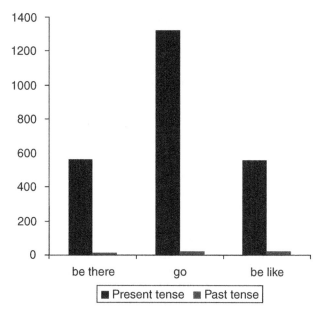

Figure 13.3   Past and present tense uses compared

notice first person respondents favouring *be + like*). Höhn (2012) shows that *be + like* was already used in IrE in the early 1990s, and became a lot more popular as time passed. Her findings point in a different direction to what Ferrara and Bell had predicted in relation to subject person usages: after analysing the development of *be + like* in the ICE-Ireland data, Höhn's study of IrE (comparing data from 1990–4 and 2002–5), leads her to the conclusion that there is no expansion of use from first-person to third person contexts as the frequency of *be + like* increases in IrE. In contrast, the present results based on the CIDN corpus seem to be more in line with the trajectory of development observed in the American English data, as shown in Figure 13.4 below.

However, as I have pointed out (Amador-Moreno 2015), given that Höhn's study does not focus on Dublin English only, the discrepancy between her data and the CIDN results in relation to *be + like* could be indicative of regional differences within IrE, or of other sociolectal differences that would need to be investigated in more detail. This discrepancy might also be simply due to the fact that the type of discourse genre that is represented in the CIDN corpus, lends itself better to reporting the speech of others.

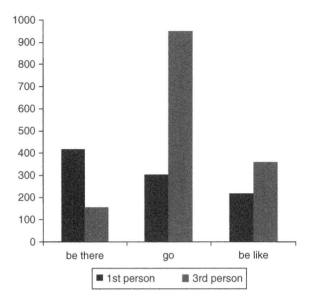

Figure 13.4 Distribution of quotatives across grammatical person

Figure 13.4 also shows that in the CIDN corpus, *go* is used more frequently to report the speech of others than to quote one's own speech. This seems to match Höhn's findings (2012), which reveal that in the case of quotative *go*, third person subjects become more frequent as time passes, following the trend observed by Barbieri (2005) in American English.

In contrast to its other two counterparts, the pattern *be + there*, as can be observed in Figure 13.4, seems to operate more consistently with first person subjects, which suggests a clear-cut distinction in terms of self-representation of the narrative voice vis-à-vis the voices of others. This forms part of the stylistic strategy that employs direct speech as a means of constructing a reliable narrator whose words are not actually reported, but witnessed within the fictional world in which they are produced (Short et al. 2002).

A curiosity in how the character of Ross reports the voices of others is to observe whether there is a correlation between the voicing of male/female speech and a particular quotative. Figure 13.5 shows gender preferences within third-person reporting in the CIDN corpus: as can be appreciated from the graph (shown in Figure 13.5), the type of 'male gossip' that Ross engages in involves first of all more talk about

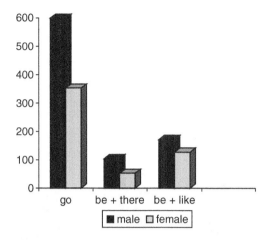

Figure 13.5 Reporting of male and female voices within third person subjects

what males say than about what females do. Of the three quotative forms, *go* tends to collocate more often with the reporting of male words/thoughts/actions, while in the case of *be* + *there* the number of times that this structure is used to report males is double the amount of female reporting. *Be* + *like* is the only quotative that is more or less balanced in terms of the reporting of both sexes.

In terms of how Ross's identity is signalled through his own voice, the 'speaker sex' factor as rendered in the novel is, of course, of great interest too. Sex differentiation in *be like* and *go* use has been suggested in studies dealing with quotatives, both from a perceptual perspective and when evaluating actual use. Early research on this feature focused on how people perceived it. For example, Blyth et al.'s (1990) attitudinal survey from the late 1980s (when the North American quotative system began to expand) showed that the majority of their respondents considered *be* + *like* as a female marker, associating it with California teenage girls. In Dailey-O'Cain's (2000) US study, 80 per cent of respondents identified *be* + *like* with women, whereas Buchstaller's analysis of UK data (2006) found that only 34 per cent of respondents associated *be* + *like* with women. Speaker's perceptions, however, do not necessarily correspond with actual language use. While Tagliamonte and D'Arcy (2006) suggest that sex differentiation in *be* + *like* use is evident in Toronto as new quotatives spread (see also Tagliamonte 2012: 249–58), the results obtained by Durham et al. (2012), in contrast, suggest 'a mild form of neutralization of the speaker sex effect' (Durham et al. 2012: 325), which seems to point in the direction of variability across communities. As they argue, 'social constraints on quotative variation often change from community to community, as patterns of linguistic variation map onto local social and stylistic differences in community specific ways' (Durham et al. 2012: 328). A comparison of the results obtained in two geographically close settings would lend further support to such argument: in his study of quotative use in Glasgow, Macaulay (2001) finds that young women tend to use quotative *like* more frequently. Working-class adult women used *go* most frequently, even though the overall picture showed that the adults in his survey used *say* as the most frequent quotative verb. Middle-class girls favoured the use of *be + like*, whereas middle-class boys preferred *go* as a quotative over *be + like*. In the Irish context, Höhn (2012) finds that *be + like* is equally frequent in male and female quotative use in ICE-Ireland, while quotative *go* represents a slightly larger proportion of female than male quotative use, and the traditional *say* occurs more frequently in male than female quotative use. When looking at the development of the forms, though, Höhn notices that the recent data shows a preference for *be + like* in male speakers, and that there is a clear trend shift in the use of *go* from female to male preference. *Say*, on the other hand, seems to evolve in the opposite direction: although in the first collection periods of her study it occurs most frequently in male speech, the opposite is true in more recent periods.

Given the prominent presence of *go*, and *be + like* in the speech of Ross, what Howard seems to be hinting at in his 'caricature' of southern Dubliners (which has an evident comic effect) is not only that both *go* and *be + like* are nowadays deeply embedded in the speech of Dublin middle-class male speakers in their twenties, but that *be + there* also has a role to play as part of the 'new' quotative repertoire in present-day Dublin English (see Figure 13.2 again for a comparison of *be + there* and *be + like*). The fact that *be + there* collocates most frequently with the first person pronoun would seem to indicate that (according to Howard's perception) Dublin middle-class males have a preference for this form when reporting themselves. The trend shift in the use of *go* from female to male preference observed by Höhn is clearly replicated in Ross's discourse (who comes across as a super self-centred individual), and it may also be indexical of the changes that Dublin English is undergoing at present. It also shows that, as pointed out by Durham et al. (2012: 327), as quotatives continue 'to diffuse globally, the social meaning associated with [their] use does not necessarily diffuse along with the surface form. Rather, individual communities adapt the innovation in the context of local social and economic conditions and local symbolism'. Indeed, this adaptation seems to have taken place in the context of Dublin, where the use of these quotative forms has come to symbolise the 'new'/'fashionable' speaker (see Hickey 2005: 7–8) as opposed to the 'local' speaker, highlighting linguistically the socio-economic divide between the north and the south sides of the city. Thus what in one variety of English may initially have been perceived as 'stigmatized, ungrammatical, and indicative of casual speech' (Blyth et al. 1990: 223), in another it might end up becoming a high-prestige form – or at least a clear social differentiator, if it continues to be identified as a dissociation marker (see Hickey 2005: 69–71). Whether or not the fictionalisation of this phenomenon will contribute to perpetuating the association between the use of quotatives and the 'new'/'fashionable' speaker, enregistering it as a dialectal feature characteristic of south Dublin speech, is something that we will be able to reevaluate in years to come. What is evident from the CIDN corpus is that the use of quotatives in present-day Dublin English is part of the current general perception of how Dublin middle-class male speakers narrate stories. The fact that Howard incorporates it so successfully in his writing, and the fact that readers respond to the fictionalisation of these forms, indicates that the use of these forms in Howard's writing are worth investigating. From a sociolinguistic perspective, then, the present study foregrounds the utility, value and richness of this type of data for investigation of sociolinguistic identities and (sociolinguistic) indices of community (cf. Vaughan and Clancy 2012).

13.5 Conclusions

This chapter started by referring to *perceptual dialectology* and by making the point that fictional writing also falls within the category of what can be considered 'nonspecialists' perceptions' of language use. Literary renderings of dialect, although certainly subjective, are among the most influential elements that contribute to the process of enregisterment, and to the social recognition of certain features as characteristic of a particular type of speaker. The old question of whether fiction creates or reflects reality is very much present in work dealing with literary dialect, and although it is not a new question, it is still a question that needs to be raised and to which this chapter contributes in a small way. By focusing on Paul Howard's writing, and on his use of quotatives, the chapter has explored how the author manages to convey issues related to gender and social class. The type of information that readers receive through the narrative voice helps them identify the main character more solidly, without the author having to resort to description. Some of the questions that were asked at the outset had to do with reader's as well as with author's awareness: whether fiction writing contributes to the creation of certain linguistic trends that may end up being associated with specific speech communities; or whether the fact that certain authors show an interest in replicating real spoken discourse in their work influences readers' perception of how a particular speech community behaves verbally. In the case of the RO'CK series, both trends probably feed off each other. Whether or not the use of quotatives in the novel will in future just reflect a linguistic fashion that ended up dying out is something that will be worth reconsidering. For the moment, what is interesting from a sociolinguistic viewpoint is what the modern reader is implicitly asked to reflect on: first of all, what type of speaker uses new quotatives in Dublin English? (what does it mean that a male speaker like Ross uses new quotatives?) and secondly, are new quotatives indexical of a particular social group in present-day Dublin English?

The discussion here has not revolved around how realistic Howard's writing is, nor whether his novels deserve the label 'literature'; rather, it has centred on the creative potential of his style, highlighting his ability to manipulate language in order to map social contexts and raise awareness among readers.

Corpus analysis of the patterning of quotative forms in the data points towards the prominence of *be + like, be + there* and *go* in narratives. What emerges from this study is a close correspondence with patterns associated with private speech, and the value of this type of data for sociolinguistic analysis. Further studies comparing Howard's perception of how quotatives function in contemporary Dublin English and real spoken data will help to determine the status of new quotatives in this particular urban variety and more broadly in Irish English in general.

Notes

1. As I have pointed out elsewhere (Amador-Moreno 2015), this genre is sometimes referred to as *Lad Lit*, *Dick Lit*, or *Cappuccino Fiction* (Montoro 2012).
2. An example of which in the Irish context would be Marian Keyes' writing.
3. Dan Sheehan, 'Roysh on the money', in *The Irish Times* (Saturday 9 October 2010), [Weekend Review], p. 10. Another critic, Patrick Freyne, also refers to Howard's place in Irish culture: 'A bit of an institution now in his own right, O'Carroll-Kelly is one of a pantheon of anthropomorphic Irelands (others include Cuchulain, Kathleen Ní Houlihan, Dev and Marty Whelan). It's hard

to imagine the place without him, and I believe that, in years to come, heavily footnoted editions of Paul Howard's long-running series will be the textbooks on early twenty-first-century Ireland' ('It's Good to Know We Can Rely on Ross', review of *The Shelbourne Ultimatum*, by Ross O'Carroll-Kelly, in *The Irish Times* (13 October 2012): Weekend ['Arts & Books']).

4. Dundrum is the name of a suburb on the south side of Dublin.
5. Peter Murphy, 'There's life in the old Rosser yet: Keeping up with the Kalashnikovs', *The Irish Times*, 27 September 2014.
6. For an interesting discussion of media influence on the spread of linguistic innovations like quotative *be + like* see Sayers (2014). A comparison of speech data from the UK and the US is also given by Tagliamonte and Roberts (2005), who analyse the representation of linguistic innovation (e.g. intensifiers *very*, and *so*) in *Friends*. See also Quaglio (2009) for a study comparing the language of *Friends* to natural conversation.
7. I am very grateful to Paul Howard and Patricia Deevy for giving me access to the electronic version of the novel. Extracts from *The Curious Incident of the Dog in the Nightdress* reproduced with kind permission of Penguin Books.
8. As I have pointed out in other work using this data, it is not the purpose of this chapter to validate the entire literary/fictional dialect of Paul Howard. Instead, its main purpose is to investigate quotatives in one novel, which is taken as representative of his writing. While a larger corpus of Howard's work might indeed provide a wider perspective on his style, the advantage of concentrating on just one of the novels is that the results produced are more manageable and easier to interpret pragmatically in their context (for a discussion of the advantages of using small, domain-specific corpora in pragmatic research see Vaughan and Clancy 2012).
9. The total count includes simple present and simple past tense forms of these quotatives (e.g. *go/goes/going/went*), which were retrieved using the concordancer suite in *WordSmith Tools*. The concordancer output for each quotative was then sorted manually to eliminate all instances that did not introduce direct quotation. Quotative uses of *go* also include the continuous form *going*, given its narrative function. For the purpose of this study, the structure *be + there + going* (e.g. 'and I'm there going, "Cool"') was counted as a separate quotative category, although it is included in the column of *go* in the figures shown here.
10. However one drawback of the ICE-Ireland corpus when using it comparatively is that it contains mostly speech produced by educated speakers, which makes it rather standard; also, her study does not differentiate between Northern Irish English and southern Irish English.

References

Agha, Asif (2003). 'The social life of cultural value', *Language and Communication* 23: 231–73.

Amador-Moreno, Carolina P. (2010a). *An Introduction to Irish English*. London: Equinox.

Amador-Moreno, Carolina P. (2010b). 'How can corpora be used to explore literary speech representation?', in: Anne O'Keeffe and Michael McCarthy (eds) *The Routledge Handbook of Corpus Linguistics*. London: Routledge, pp. 531–44.

Amador-Moreno, Carolina P. (2012). 'A corpus-based approach to contemporary Irish writing: Ross O'Carroll-Kelly's use of *like* as a discourse marker', *International Journal of English Studies. Special Issue: a New Approach to Literature: Corpus Linguistics* 12.2: 19–38.

Amador-Moreno, Carolina P. (2015). '"There's, like, total silence again, roysh, and no one says anything". Fictional representations of "new" pragmatic markers and quotatives in Irish English', in: Carolina P. Amador-Moreno, Kevin McCafferty and Elaine Vaughan (eds) *Pragmatic Markers in Irish English.* Amsterdam: John Benjamins, pp. 270–91.

Amador-Moreno, Carolina P. and Kevin McCafferty (2015). '"[B]ut *sure* its only a penny after all": Irish English discourse marker *sure*', in: Marina Dossena (ed.) *Transatlantic Perspectives in Late Modern English.* Amsterdam: John Benjamins, pp. 179–97.

Barbieri, Federica (2005). 'Quotative use in American English: a corpus-based, cross-register comparison', *Journal of English Linguistics* 33.3: 222–56.

Biber, Douglas, Stig Johansson, Geoffrey Leech, Susan Conrad, and Edward Finegan (1999). *Longman Grammar of Spoken and Written English.* Harlow: Pearson.

Blyth, Carl Jr., Sigrid Recktenwald, and Jenny Wang (1990). 'I'm like, "Say What?!"': a new quotative in American oral narrative', *American Speech*, 65.3 (Autumn 1990): 215–27.

Britain, David (2010). 'Grammatical variation in the contemporary spoken English of England', in: Andy Kirkpatrick (ed.) *The Routledge Handbook of World Englishes.* Abingdon: Routledge, pp. 37–58.

Buchstaller, Isabelle (2006). 'Diagnostics of age-graded linguistic behaviour: the case of the quotative system', *Sociolinguistics* 10.1: 3–30.

Buchstaller, Isabelle (2014). *Quotatives: New Trends and Sociolinguistic Implications.* Wiley-Blackwell.

Buchstaller, Isabelle and Alex D'Arcy (2009). 'Localized globalization: a multi-local, multivariate investigation of "be like"', *Journal of Sociolinguistics* 13: 291–331.

Carter, Ronald and Michael McCarthy (2006). *Cambridge Grammar of English.* Cambridge. Cambridge University Press.

Cukor-Avila, Patricia (2002). 'She say, she go, she be like: verbs of quotation over time in African American Vernacular English', *American Speech* 77: 3–31.

Dailey-O'Cain, Jennifer (2000). 'The sociolinguistic distribution and attitudes towards focuser *like* and quotative *like*', *Journal of Sociolinguistics* 4: 60–80.

Durham, Mercedes, Bill Haddican, Eytan Zweig, Daniel Ezra Johnson, Zipporah Baker, David Cockeram, Esther Danks and Louise Tyler (2012). 'Constant linguistic effects in the diffusion of *be like*', *Journal of English Linguistics* 40.4: 316–37.

Ellis, Michael (1994). 'Dialect as linguistic evidence: subject-verb concord in nineteenth century Southern literature', *American Speech* 69.2: 128–44.

Ferrara, Kathleen and Barbara Bell (1995). 'Sociolinguistic variation and discourse function of constructed dialogue introducers: the case of *be like*', *American Speech* 70: 265–89.

Ferris, Suzanne and Mallory Young (eds) (2006). *Chick Lit. The New Woman's Fiction.* New York and London: Routledge.

Gorman, Clare (2013). '"No border is guaranteed, inside or out": a reading of the speech/writing opposition within Paul Howard, a.k.a Ross O'Carroll-Kelly's

fictional series', *Otherness: Essays and Studies* 3.2. http://www.otherness.dk/
fileadmin/www.othernessandthearts.org/Publications/Journal_Otherness/
Otherness_Essays_and_Studies_3.2/No_border_is_guaranteed_Inside_or_Out_
Clare_Gorman.pdf, 10 June 2013.

Hickey, Raymond (2005). *Dublin English. Evolution and Change.* Amsterdam: John
Benjamins.

Hickey, Raymond (2007). *Irish English: History and Present-day forms.* Cambridge:
Cambridge University Press.

Hickey, Raymond (2010). 'Linguistic evaluation of earlier texts', in: Raymond
Hickey (ed.) *Varieties of English in Writing. The Written Word as Linguistic
Evidence.* Amsterdam: John Benjamins, pp. 1–14.

Höhn, Nicole (2012). 'And they were all like "What's going on?"': New quotatives
in Jamaican and Irish English', in: Marianne Hundt and Ulrike Gut (eds)
Mapping Unity and Diversity World-Wide: Corpus-Based Studies of New Englishes.
Amsterdam: John Benjamins, pp. 263–90.

Kallen, Jeffrey (2013). *Irish English. Volume 2 – The Republic of Ireland.* Berlin: de
Gruyter Mouton.

Labov, William (1972). *Language in the Inner City.* Philadelphia: University of
Pennsylvania Press.

Macaulay, Ronald (2001). 'You're like "why not?" The quotative expressions of
Glasgow adolescents', *Journal of Sociolinguistics* 5.1: 3–21.

McCafferty, K. (2010). '"[H]ushed and lulled full chimes for pushed and pulled":
Writing Ulster English', in: Raymond Hickey (ed.) *Varieties of English in Writing:
the Written Word as Linguistic Evidence.* Amsterdam: John Benjamins, pp. 139–
62.

Melchers, Gunnel (2010). 'Southern English in writing', in: Raymond Hickey
(ed.) *Varieties of English in Writing. The Written Word as Linguistic Evidence.*
Amsterdam: John Benjamins, pp. 81–98.

Montoro, Rocío (2012). *Chick Lit. The Stylistics of Cappuccino Fiction.* London and
New York: Continuum.

Preston, Dennis R. (1999). *Handbook of Perceptual Dialectology.* Volume 1. Dennis
R. Preston (ed.). Amsterdam: John Benjamins.

Preston, Dennis R. and George M. Howe (1987). 'Computerized studies of mental
dialect maps', in: Keith Denning et al. (eds) *Variation in Language: NWAV-XV at
Stanford, Stanford University.* Palo Alto, CA: Department of Linguistics, Stanford
University, pp. 361–78.

Quaglio, Paulo (2009). *Television Dialogue.* Amsterdam: John Benjamins.

Romaine, Suzanne and Deborah Lange (1991). 'The use of *like* as a marker
of reported speech and thought: a case of grammaticalization in progress',
American Speech 66: 227–79.

Sayers, Dave (2014). 'The mediated innovation model: a framework for researching media influence in language change', *Journal of Sociolinguistics* 18.2:
185–212.

Scott, Mike (2013). *WordSmith Tools.* Version 6.0. Oxford: Oxford University Press.

Short, Michael, Elena Semino and Martin Wynne (2002). 'Revisiting the notion
of faithfulness in discourse report/(re)presentation using a corpus approach',
Language and Literature 11.4: 325–55.

Tagliamonte, Sali A. (2012). *Variationist Sociolinguistics. Change, Observation,
Interpretation.* Malden and Oxford: Wiley-Blackwell.

Tagliamonte, Sali A. and Alex D'Arcy (2004). *'He's like, she's like:* the quotative system in Canadian youth', *Journal of Sociolinguistics* 8: 493–514.

Tagliamonte, Sali A. and Alex D'Arcy (2007). 'Frequency and variation in the community grammar: tracking a new change through the generations', *Language Variation and Change* 19.2: 199–217.

Tagliamonte, Sali A. and Rachel Hudson (1999). 'Be like et al. beyond America: the quotative system in British and Canadian youth', *Journal of Sociolinguistics* 3.2: 147–72.

Tagliamonte, Sali and Chris Roberts (2005). 'So weird; so cool; so innovative: the use of intensifiers in the television series Friends', *American Speech* 80: 280–300.

Tannen, Deborah (1982). 'Oral and literate strategies in spoken and written narratives', *Language* 58.1 (March 1982): 1–21.

Vaughan, Elaine and Brian Clancy (2012). 'Small corpora and pragmatics', in: Jesús Romero-Trillo (ed.) *Yearbook of Corpus Linguistics and Pragmatics 2013: New Domains and Methodologies.* Berlin: Springer, pp. 53–73.

Wales, Katie (2010). 'Northern English in writing', in: Raymond Hickey (ed.) *Varieties of English in Writing: the Written Word as Linguistic Evidence.* Amsterdam: John Benjamins, pp. 61–80.

Walshe, Shane (2009). *Irish English as Represented in Film.* Bern: Peter Lang.

14

Irish Society as Portrayed in Irish Films

Shane Walshe

14.1 Introduction

Discussions relating to Irish English and the media invariably focus on how the media are transforming or, indeed, threatening the way the English language is spoken in Ireland. Newspaper articles bearing headlines such as 'Leave upspeak to the, like, Americans?' (Behan 2005) or 'Janey Mac! Irish-English is banjaxed, so it is...' (Bielenberg 2008) tend to lay the blame for any change to Irish dialects squarely on the media. Although an examination into such claims would certainly be interesting, and similar research in the Scottish context has already been conducted by Stuart-Smith and Timmins (2014) in *Sociolinguistics in Scotland*, this is not the approach that will be taken here. Like Coupland in his influential 'The mediated performance of vernaculars', I, too, believe that it is unnecessary 'to limit the study of mediated dialect to a "vitality" agenda ("Will the mass media keep dialects alive or kill them off?") or to a "media effects" agenda ("Do the mass media influence the course of language change?")' (Coupland 2009: 297). Instead, it is possible to see the media as holding a mirror up to society and to examine language in film as evidence of art imitating life rather than vice versa. Thus, rather than exploring to what extent the media *shape* Irish English (hereafter IE), this chapter will instead examine to what degree the media *reflect* vernacular usage.

Although 'mass-mediated vernacular speech' – the representation of vernaculars in media products – has been treated with caution for being an artificial construction and thus of little use to linguistic research,[1] it is my contention that a corpus of fictional film speech can actually reveal much more about real language usage than was heretofore believed and can therefore be employed as a very useful tool in sociolinguistic research. As noted above, this is not necessarily a popular view, as for many people the notion that film speech accurately reflects real speech seems far-fetched. Their scepticism is supported by the fact that Kozloff has convincingly described just how far speech in movies differs from reality:

> In narrative films, dialogue may strive mightily to imitate natural conversation, but it is always an imitation. It has been scripted, written and rewritten, censored, polished, rehearsed, and performed. Even when lines are improvised on set, they have been spoken by impersonators, judged, approved, and allowed to remain. (Kozloff 2000: 18)

Moreover, as Hodson has noted, when it comes to the representation of regional dialects in film 'both production factors and audience comprehension places limits on the extent to which "real world" dialects are represented' (2014: 219). Nonetheless, despite such reservations, and in keeping with previous work (Walshe 2009), this study will treat the language in film as just another type of literary dialect,[2] since, like the dialogue in a play, it, too, is written down to be performed. The usefulness of literary dialect in linguistic research is widely recognised and, indeed, has already been attested several times in the IE context (e.g. Sullivan 1980; Hickey 2010). This chapter therefore builds on such work, examining to what degree fiction films succeed in accurately reflecting speech in Ireland – both North and South – and, by extension, whether a corpus of film speech can prove to be as valid as one of real speech when it comes to sociolinguistic research.

14.2   Methodology

14.2.1   Corpus composition: Ireland on film

It was originally my intention to conduct an all-encompassing sociolinguistic study, investigating how movies set in Ireland reflect differences in language usage between different classes, sexes, age groups, etc. However, as we shall see, Irish cinema proves to be surprisingly limited in the stories it tells, with many voices in Irish society effectively being silenced, something which, needless to say, is not ideal when one aims to do a comparative study of speech.

As has been noted elsewhere (Pettitt 2000), the Irish film industry is a very young one, which really only emerged in the late 1980s in the Republic of Ireland and a decade later in Northern Ireland. In terms of output then, the researcher is left with quite a small pool of films from which to compile a corpus. Indeed, it was difficult to even find 40 films set in the North which were available on DVD. However, once those had been found and transcribed, they became the touchstone against which a new corpus of films containing southern IE was compiled. This new corpus was necessary because there were major discrepancies between the periods of setting of the films in the northern corpus and those of the original southern one from Walshe (2009). This was due to the different themes which have preoccupied filmmakers in the two parts of the island of Ireland. In the North, the Troubles have invariably provided the subject matter for most films and, thus, they are mainly set during the late 1960s, '70s, '80s and '90s. In the South, in contrast, the 1970s and '80s have largely been ignored on film with a focus instead on the Irish heritage film 'typically set in the 1950s or earlier' (Pettitt 2000: 115) or on new genres set in the new millennium and dealing with urban crime or the effects of the Celtic Tiger. Thus, to achieve some degree of parity between the corpora, all films which are set prior to the 1960s (e.g. *The Wind that Shakes the Barley, Michael Collins, Angela's Ashes*) were removed from the 2009 southern corpus and replaced by ones that better reflect the composition of the northern one. The complete list of films in each corpus can be seen in the Appendix (Table 14.2).[3]

Once the initial problems of parity between the corpora had been overcome, further issues arose. Unlike sociolinguistic fieldwork, where one can carefully choose informants according to criteria such as age, class, sex, ethnicity, locality, etc., working with media products, as noted above, means working with the material that is available. As will be shown, such constraints complicated the analysis for a number of sociolinguistic categories.

14.2.1.1   Age

In contrast to a fieldwork scenario, where one can solicit accurate information regarding an informant's age, the age of a film character is generally unclear and the researcher has to resort to guesswork. One could rely on the actor's biographical data, but it is not uncommon for actors to play characters who are younger or older than they themselves are and, thus, accuracy is not guaranteed. In addition, there is the additional issue that certain age groups (the young and the elderly) are largely excluded because characters in their twenties to fifties tend to predominate in the movies in question.

14.2.1.2   Class

Again, where questionnaires would typically be able to gather information pertaining to an informant's social status, highest attained level of education, etc., film audiences are left to speculate regarding a character's class. Such guesswork can be informed by the character's occupation, residence, clothing, etc. but this is not the most reliable way of ascribing class. Making judgements on the basis of how the characters speak is also problematic, since speech is the independent variable under consideration and, thus, it is self-defeating to have it as a category in its own right. However, it is fair to say that there is a trend in Irish cinema to focus predominantly on the working class (cf. Ging 2013: 180). This is particularly the case for films related to the Troubles and urban crime.

14.2.1.3 Sex

Categorising characters according to their sex is much easier (despite the occasional transgender character, as in *Breakfast on Pluto*). However, in terms of facilitating a sociolinguistic study into variation in language use between the sexes, the corpus once again presents a major obstacle. The fact is that the majority of Irish films are very much male-centred with women frequently relegated to marginal roles as wives and mothers of gangsters, terrorists, prisoners, etc. This is particularly the case for Northern Irish films. Indeed, Holohan has commented on the fact that 'the silencing of female voices is a legacy of nationalist ideology which subordinated issues of female disempowerment to an overarching discourse of national emancipation' (2010: 29). O'Connell supports this notion, adding that Irish film production has been shaped by the emergence of largely male-centred genres with productions concerned with 'youth issues', 'the disaffected male youth', 'the social problem', 'Northern Ireland', 'New Laddism' and 'Ireland's underworld and criminal fraternity' (2010: 46). Thus, female speaking roles are much smaller and the amount of material available is not large enough for a sensible comparison on the basis of sex.

14.2.1.4 Ethnicity

Although Ireland has become more multicultural, such changes have been slow to be reflected in the films in the corpora, with only isolated examples of Irish characters of a different ethnic background and few occurrences of immigrants. If one regards religious communities in Ireland as ethnic groups (Catholics versus Protestants), even then the balance of representation is tipped very much in favour of the former. This is particularly remarkable in films set in Northern Ireland, where the Protestant community has traditionally been more numerous. However, this group very noticeably lacks a voice in northern films. This is because representations of the Troubles have been weighted very much in favour of the Catholic perspective (cf. McIlroy 1998 and McLoone 2008). Thus, another approach which could potentially have proven fruitful for sociolinguistic research turns out to be impossible given the material at hand.

14.2.1.5 Locality

Sociolinguistic comparisons of rural versus urban varieties also proved to be difficult given the focus of so many films on urban areas. Similarly, the spread of films according to regions is also uneven due to the predominance of Dublin and Belfast (as opposed to Cork, Limerick, Derry, etc.) as settings for the majority of movies. Again, this limits the comparisons that can be made between regions within each corpus. However, despite all the aforementioned limitations, the corpora nonetheless prove to be very useful for one particular type of sociolinguistic research, namely for analysing variation between the North and the South of Ireland and, thus, this will be the focus of the main analysis.

14.2.2 Corpus transcription and analysis

After the 80 films (40 northern and 40 southern) had been selected, all utterances containing IE features were transcribed, resulting in two corpora of around 32,000 words each. The various features were noted as either *occurring* or *not occurring*. The reason for this was that counting whether or not a feature occurred in a particular movie better reflected how likely it would be for viewers to encounter that feature if they were to watch any of the films. The actual number of occurrences of individual features per film was not measured, as high frequency in one movie may suggest one screenwriter's particular affinity for that feature but would skew the findings of the corpora in general (cf. Walshe 2009: 41). The results for each feature were then tabulated and compared between the northern and southern corpora, with the most striking ones being compared with the literature on IE. In addition, the data were measured against those from the SPICE-Ireland corpus and with the acceptability ratings for Hickey's *A Survey of Irish English Usage* (2004) to see whether they tallied with previous findings on the North-South distribution of features. SPICE-Ireland is the spoken component of ICE-Ireland and is divided quite evenly between Northern Ireland and the Republic (cf. Kallen and Kirk 2012). Hickey's survey, meanwhile, was conducted nationally and offers acceptability ratings for a variety of sentences, each containing a different feature of IE. Hickey acknowledges that the results are 'of relative value as they are not attestations but represent speakers' reactions to non-standard features. Nonetheless, they may well help to confirm or refute tendencies in the regional distribution of features' (2007: 164–5). In this sense, they were, indeed, invaluable. What follows, then, is a breakdown of the features from the film corpora which demonstrated the most significant differences on a North-South basis, and which, as we shall see, correspond well with the linguistic reality recorded by other scholars.

14.3 Morphology

14.3.1 Second person plural pronouns

IE has several possibilities for expressing the second person plural. In addition to the standard *you*, speakers can choose between *youse*, *yiz* and *ye*, as follows:

(1) a. '*Youse* two are getting married?' (*The Mighty Celt*)
 b. '*Yiz* are bored, aren't *yiz*?' (*Stand Off*)
 c. 'Oh, I missed *ye*, boys. I missed *ye*.' (*Into the West*)

As with all features under examination, the distribution of these pronouns varies between northern and southern varieties. According to Corrigan, the use of *youse* and *yiz* is 'extremely robust' (2010: 53) in northern IE, occurring among all ages and genders. This notion is supported by findings from Hickey's survey, which found acceptance rates for his sentence *What are youse up to?* to be between 79 per cent and 98 per cent in northern counties, whereas in the South the average acceptability was 60 per cent with the preferred second person plural form being *ye*. An exception was Dublin, and Leinster in general, where the acceptability of *youse* was much higher, averaging 74 per cent. Similar trends are apparent in the data from the film corpora, with *youse* occurring in 29 northern (73 per cent) and only 18 southern films (45 per cent) – 16 of which are set in Dublin. The *yiz* form, which Hickey found was marginally more acceptable in the North (55 per cent) than the South (51 per cent) also appeared in more northern than southern movies, namely 25 (63 per cent) versus 22 (55 per cent), while *ye* showed an opposite tendency, as one would expect, being favoured more in southern films, i.e. 15 (38 per cent) versus 8 (20 per cent). Again, the southern distinction regarding the use of *ye* in Dublin and the rest of the country is evident, with almost all of the 15 examples coming from films set outside the capital and the few instances that occur there being from characters who are not Dubliners themselves. Thus, with regard to second person plural pronoun usage, the film corpora provide us with our first indication that mediated language can serve well as a source of sociolinguistic insight, in that they echo the findings from other studies.

14.4 Syntax

14.4.1 Unbound reflexive pronouns

'Unbound reflexives' (UBRs), i.e. reflexive pronouns that are not bound to an antecedent, have long been a salient, if somewhat stereotypical, feature of IE (cf. Hickey 2007: 243). However, again, usage has been shown to differ between northern and southern varieties. For example, when Hickey tested the acceptability of the sentence *Himself is not in today*, he found that approval was low in the north of the country, ranging from between 5 and 8 per cent in Antrim and Down to over 25 per cent in Armagh (cf. Corrigan 2010: 55). The reasons for these discrepancies across the province are attributed by Hickey to the fact that these UBRs were influenced by transfer from the Irish substratum, meaning that one would expect lower results in counties like Antrim and Down where Ulster Scots is more prevalent and higher results where the Irish language persisted for longer, such as Armagh. This substratal theory is compelling, especially if one looks at Hickey's findings for the South, where the acceptability ratings are similar to those for Armagh, averaging around 23 per cent. Evidence of different usage patterns between North and South can also be found in the film corpora, where UBRs in the third person, i.e. *himself/herself* occur in only 2 Northern Irish films (5 per cent) compared with 9 southern ones (23 per cent). Examples include:

(2) a. 'Don't worry! I'll get *himself*.' (*A Belfast Story*)
    b. 'It might have been *herself* singing.' (*The Nephew*)

If one looks at other unbound reflexive pronouns (*myself, yourself,* etc.), a similar southern dominance is noticeable, with examples occurring in 12 movies from the North (30 per cent) compared to 21 from the South (53 per cent). Thus, mediated language use again appears to correspond to real language use, or at least acceptability.

14.4.2 The *after* perfect

Irish Englishes have a variety of ways of expressing the perfective, with the so-called *after* perfect being the most distinctive (Kallen 2013: 95). The structure describes an action which occurred immediately prior to the time of speaking or reference. It is generally found in the form, *be + after + V-ing*, as in all the examples from the film corpora. These include:

(3) a. '*Amn't I* just *after telling* ye I was in Hanley's?' (*The Guard*)
   b. 'Pat says his da *is after running* away from home.' (*The Snapper*)

The structure can also appear with a noun phrase (Kallen 2013: 96). Although it is one of the main features associated with the Irish, its distribution on the island is by no means uniform, with it occurring much less frequently in northern varieties. Corrigan notes that a reason for the rarity of this feature there compared to the other perfectives could be related to its origin. She states that since the *after* perfect is 'likely to have originated in Irish while the others are early English/Scottish forms, perhaps this has a synchronic effect on their distribution rather similar to the suggestions [...] that the most Gaelicised phonological features of varieties within NI are associated with certain regional and social groups (like SUE [South Ulster English] rather than US [Ulster Scots] and Catholics rather than Protestants)' (2010: 63). Hickey's survey found this indeed to be the case, with a mean acceptance of 88 per cent nationwide for his sentence *She's after spilling the milk*, but with the three lowest rates (as low as 58 per cent in Down) all 'to be found in east Ulster, the area of greatest Ulster Scots settlement historically' (2007: 206). The spoken component of ICE-Ireland also confirms this North-South divide, with only one instance of the *after* perfect in ICE-NI and 7 in ICE-ROI (Kirk and Kallen 2006: 96).

Given the overwhelming evidence from other studies that the *after* perfect is largely a southern feature, it is not surprising to find that the film corpora confirm this distribution, displaying a marked difference between the frequency of the structure in the northern corpus, namely 2 films (5 per cent), and the southern one, 16 movies (40 per cent). This lends further weight to the value of the film corpora for this kind of research.

14.4.3 Negator contraction

In Standard English, the contraction of *will* and *not* is *won't*. However, in many vernacular varieties, including those in Ireland, an alternative possibility is the contraction of the pronoun and *will* followed by *not*. Similarly, *have* and *not* are often realised with a contraction of the pronoun and *have* followed by *not* rather than as *haven't* (cf. Hickey 2007: 178). Examples of each include:

(4) a. '*I'll not* leave you, Liam.' (*Boxed*)
     b. 'Me, *I've not* done anything. I'm innocent.' (*The Most Fertile Man in Ireland*)

Hickey's survey found that there was quite a marked North-South divide regarding the acceptability of the lack of negator contractions. The mean for counties outside Ulster was 37 per cent, while in Ulster it was 77 per cent, with figures as high as 88 per cent in Belfast, Antrim and Down (2007: 273).[4] The high occurrence of the feature has also been attested for Northern Irish data by Tagliamonte and Smith (2002: 253) and Kirk and Kallen in the face-to-face conversations in ICE-Ireland, where they found that it occurred at a rate of 62.1 per cent in the North and 37.9 per cent in the South (2010: 188). A look at the film corpora reveals similarly clear differences, with the feature occurring in 21 northern (53 per cent) but only 6 southern films (15 per cent), once again echoing real linguistic behaviour.

14.4.4 *Will* for *shall*

The preference for using *will* rather than *shall* has long been a feature associated with the Irish. Indeed, in the nineteenth century, prescriptive handbooks warned Irish people against erroneously using the structure (Biggar 1897: 46–7). However, despite the strong associations of the phenomenon with speakers from Ireland, the film corpus reveals it to be very much a southern one, occurring in 18 southern (45 per cent) and only 7 northern movies (18 per cent).[5] Examples include:

(5) a. '*Will I* cook you your wee chops now or *will I* wait till your tea and make you a sandwich in the meantime?' (*Four Days in July*)
     b. '*Will we* head down the park first?' (*32A*)

While the findings above may come as a surprise, there is evidence to suggest that they are reflective of reality. In his survey, Hickey did not examine the acceptability of *will* for *shall*, but he did test the acceptability of the Standard English *shall* and discovered that his sentence *I shall have to leave soon* was regarded as 'no problem' by 59 per cent of the southern population, but as 'a bit strange' by 35 per cent and as 'unacceptable' by 6 per cent. Based on these results, one can make the assumption that the 41 per cent who found *shall* 'a bit strange' or 'unacceptable' are probably those who use *will* themselves. This is a comparable percentage to that from the southern film corpus (45 per cent). In contrast, 79 per cent of Hickey's northern respondents felt that *shall* was 'no problem', with the remaining 21 per cent probably being those who are likely to use *will* themselves, thereby closely reflecting the 18 per cent from the northern film corpus.

14.4.5 Imperatives

The negative imperative form *don't be* + V-*ing* is very common in varieties both north and south of the border. However, given the contexts of the material of SPICE-Ireland, it is perhaps not surprising that there were very few attestations of it there (only 3 examples). Nonetheless, the tendency was towards a northern distribution. This trend was reflected in Hickey's survey, where the imperative form received very high acceptance rates, once again demonstrating a slight preference in the North (96 per cent) compared with the South (90 per cent). The film corpora follow suit with *don't be* + V-*ing* appearing in 18 northern (45 per cent) and 16 southern (40 per cent) productions respectively, with examples including:

(6) 'Ah, *don't be gettin'* offended.' (*Calvary*)
(7) 'It's workin' for the Brits puttin' that food on the table, so *don't be complainin'*.' (*Bloody Sunday*)

If one looks more closely at this imperative, there is a noticeable difference with regard to the way it is used in each corpus. While in southern movies the form *don't be* + V-*ing* is most frequent, in the northern corpus, the imperative is often formed with an overt subject, as in *don't you be* + V-*ing*. The presence of the overt subject in imperatives, while also acceptable in Standard English, has already been noted as being particularly prevalent in the north (Corrigan 2010: 68; Henry 1995: 50–5). It appears both in *don't be* + V-*ing* structures and in regular imperatives where the verb and subject are inverted, as follows:

(8) a. '*Mind you* your language!' (*Good Vibrations*)
    b. '*Stay you* out of this, Aggie!' (*Middletown*)

Such structures in which subject and verb are inverted would be ungrammatical in southern IE and, accordingly, do not appear anywhere in the southern film corpus. Thus, whereas southern IE prefers the negative imperative without an overt subject, as in 13 of the 16 movies in which the structure appears, northern IE employs the subject frequently, i.e. in almost half the examples from the North (8 out of 18) in which *don't be* + V-*ing* occurs. Interestingly, the only example of *don't you be* + V-*ing* in SPICE-Ireland is also from Northern Ireland ('Oh no don't you be saying nothing Seanie'), further supporting the findings in the film corpora.

14.4.6 Relativisation

Relative clause marking can be achieved in a number of ways in IE. These range from standard relative pronouns *who, which* and *that* to non-standard ones, such as *at, as* and *what*. Alternatively, one can forego relative pronouns completely and have a zero subject relative pronoun (Hickey 2007: 260–1). Although the film corpora did not feature any of the aforementioned non-standard pronouns, the zero subject relative pronoun occurred quite frequently and is worth discussing, also in terms of its distribution. Examples include:

(9) a. 'He's the one man Ø can knit it all together and bring a lasting peace.' (*Divorcing Jack*)
  b. 'It's the British Ø have your son in jail, Mrs Quigley, not me.' (*Some Mother's Son*)

In their analysis of these structures in ICE-Ireland, Siemund and Beal found a slightly higher occurrence of what they term 'zero subject coordinators' in the North (16) than in the South (13) (2011: 263). This northern preference was also evident in Hickey's survey, where 30 per cent of northern respondents found the structure to be 'no problem' compared with 16 per cent down south. It is, thus, perhaps no surprise that the zero relative appeared much more frequently in the northern film corpus than in the southern one, occurring in 23 films in the former (58 per cent) and only 13 in the latter (33 per cent).

14.5 Lexis and discourse markers

14.5.1 *Grand*

Grand as a term of approval meaning 'fine' or 'splendid' is one typically associated with Irish speech (Hickey 2007: 363). Thus, it is no surprise that it appears in the film corpora. The surprising thing, perhaps, is the degree of difference in the rates of occurrence, with *grand* appearing in

15 northern films (38 per cent) and almost twice as many southern ones, namely 29 (73 per cent). Examples include:

(10) a. 'I'm *grand* and yourself?' (*Goldfish Memory*)
      b. 'Yeah, Jake's *grand*. He's with me.' (*What Richard Did*)

Unfortunately, Hickey's survey only tested the acceptability of morphosyntactic and occasional discourse features and, thus, we do not have information on the acceptability of lexical items. Moreover, there does not appear to be any mention of a North-South divide in any of the literature that mentions the feature. However, a perceptual dialectology study conducted by the author (Walshe 2010) and modelled on Hickey's survey revealed that when asked to comment on the acceptability of the sentence *No, thanks, I'm grand*, northern respondents had a lower approval rate, with one commenting, 'I think that is more of a southern expression. We don't say that as much in the North. "I'm doin' rightly" that's what people say or "I'm doin' alright." But *grand* is more of a thing that has come up to Northern Ireland a bit in recent years, but it definitely originates in the south.'[6] Whether or not this supposition about the origin is true, the findings in SPICE-Ireland for face-to-face conversations do, indeed, reveal a strong southern tendency for *grand*, with 40 of the 63 tokens occurring in ICE-ROI (Kallen 2013: 207), thereby once again confirming the findings of the film corpora and those in Hickey (in press).

14.5.2 Ma/Mam/Mammy

Different ways of addressing and referring to mothers are very common in the films and also reveal that the language in the movies compares quite well with previous corpora. Kallen, for example, has noted that *mammy* is used 15 times in ICE-ROI but only once in ICE-NI. He goes on to add that '[c]omparable use of *mam* occurs in ICE (NI) only twice from a Dublin speaker, but 19 times in ICE (ROI)' (2013: 161). The film corpora show that *mammy* does indeed appear in more southern films than northern ones, 19 (48 per cent) and 15 (38 per cent) respectively, and while that number is not as clear-cut as Kallen's findings, it is noteworthy that the majority of the uses in northern films are in those set in Derry, Armagh and the border counties and thus occurrences in these places may be more in line with southern usage, as was the case for the *after* perfect. Examples of *Mam*, meanwhile, are more in keeping with Kallen's findings, occurring in only 2 northern films (5 per cent) compared with 14 southern ones (35 per cent). Given that neither *mam* nor *mammy* are supposed to be synonymous with northern usage, it is not surprising that the remaining form of address/reference, *ma*, duly appears in more northern than southern movies, occurring in 30 (75 per cent) and 19 (48 per cent) productions respectively.

(11) a. 'It was me *mam's.*' (*Ondine*)
      b. 'Run on home to *mammy.*' (*War of the Buttons*)
      c. 'Alright, Victor, how's the *ma?*' (*Resurrection Man*)

14.5.3 Aye

Aye is a feature generally associated with Scottish English and, accordingly, is very salient in northern IE and comparatively rare south of the border. This notion is emphatically illustrated in SPICE-Ireland, where the northern data reveal 426 instances of *aye* compared to only 25 for the South. The film corpora display similarly clear-cut findings, with the feature occurring in 38 northern movies (95 per cent) compared to 3 southern ones (8 per cent). Examples include:

(12) a. 'I says, "*Aye*, go on, go ahead."' (*Jump*)
      b. 'I am, son, *aye.*' (*Mickybo and Me*)

14.5.4 Swear words

In the introduction to his dictionary on Irish slang, Share notes that the frequency of use of *fuck* and its derivatives among the people of Ireland have 'led to the Irish being regarded, by startled visitors, as the most foul-mouthed nation in Europe' (2005: x). When it comes to the film corpora, there is indeed plenty of evidence of the use of swear words, with a North–South division once more coming to the fore. This is particularly the case when one looks at the contrasting frequency of milder swearwords such as *bloody* and *bleedin'* and FECK and FRIG.

Since *bloody* and *bleedin'* are used in a similar fashion and also occur in other varieties of English, one might expect them to have a quite uniform distribution in Ireland. The film corpora, however, suggest that this is not the case, with *bloody* occurring in 22 northern films (55 per cent) compared with 10 southern ones (25 per cent).[7] This distribution is also reflected in the data from SPICE-Ireland, where *bloody* occurs 16 times in the North (40 per cent) versus 9 in the South (23 per cent). Film examples include:

(13) a. '*Bloody* waste of semtex it was.' (*Fifty Dead Men Walking*)
      b. 'The *bloody* peelers is here again!' (*Stand Off*)

The reverse is the case for *bleedin'*, which appears in only 1 northern movie (3 per cent) but 15 southern ones (38 per cent), albeit almost exclusively in Dublin films. Examples include:

(14) a. 'You're an awful *bleedin'* eejit, Mr Burgess.' (*The Snapper*)
b. 'What did you *bleedin'* call me?' (*Adam and Paul*)

Unfortunately, since there is only one instance of *bleedin'* in SPICE-Ireland, and that comes from the northern data, further research is necessary to examine whether a true North-South divide (or just a Dublin versus rest of Ireland one) really exists. A North-South contrast can, however, be seen in the use of FRIG versus FECK. *Frig* or some variant thereof occurs in 14 northern films (35 per cent) compared with 1 southern one (3 per cent). Examples include:

(15) a. 'Now ... *frig* off.' (*Mickybo and Me*)
b. 'Jeez, it's like a *friggin'* primary school in here sometimes.' (*Crossmaheart*)
c. 'What the *frig* are you at? he says.' (*Four Days in July*)

Tentative support for this notion of FRIG as a more northern feature is available in SPICE-Ireland, where it occurs 3 times in the northern material versus once down south. In contrast, SPICE-Ireland suggests FECK is more southern, occurring 5 times in southern material but never in the northern files. This southern tendency is more clearly expressed in the film corpora, where *feck* and its variants occur in only 4 northern films (10 per cent) compared with 15 southern ones (38 per cent). Examples of FECK include:

(16) a. 'I told him to *feck* off or I'd burst him.' (*A Man of No Importance*)
b. 'I wouldn't give that *fecker* the skin of a fart.' (*Mystics*)
c. 'What the *feck* are we waitin' for?' (*Irish Jam*)

14.5.5 *Ach/och*

In her monograph on English in Northern Ireland, Corrigan notes the saliency of the discourse markers *ach/och* in the region, saying that they are 'widespread amongst speakers irrespective of their age, ethnicity, gender, regional origins or socio-economic status' (2010: 99). She adds that they 'seem to be particularly noticeable to outsiders who often remark on them as unusual'. The term 'outsiders' could arguably be seen here to also extend to speakers of southern IE, as the features are very rare south of the border. This notion is substantiated by SPICE-Ireland, where *ach/och* occur a combined total of 92 times in the northern material compared with a mere 4 appearances in the southern data. This clear North-South divide was once again evident in the film corpora with *ach/och* occurring in 19 films from the North (48 per cent) and only 1 from the South (3 per cent), with examples including:

(17) a. '*Ach*, come on, Siobhan. It's a bit of fun, that's all.' (*The Closer You Get*)
      b. '*Ach*, Colum. How are ye doin'?' (*An Everlasting Piece*)

14.5.6   Clause-final *like*

Although *like* serves as a discourse marker in many varieties of English, there is one particular function which, although not exclusive to Irish Englishes, is more robust there, namely the use of clause-final *like* (Kallen and Kirk 2012: 56). This form employs *like* as a mitigator to mark the end of old information (cf. Corrigan 2010: 100) and was found in Hickey's survey to have a 59 per cent acceptability rate in the North compared to 43 per cent in the South. Data from SPICE Ireland, however, reveal a different picture, showing the feature as appearing 195 times in the NI material and 215 times in the ROI data (Kallen 2013: 192). It is in situations like this where conflicting information is available that the film corpora can hopefully provide further insights. In this case, the film data are more in keeping with the SPICE findings, reflecting a slight tendency in favour of clause-final *like* in 20 southern films (50 per cent) compared to 15 northern ones (38 per cent). Examples include:

(18) a. 'Fuck that, *like*.' (*What Richard Did*)
      b. 'Look, do you want to be my girlfriend for the next week? Exclusive, *like*?' (*Goldfish Memory*)

14.5.7   *What* as a tag

What, sometimes pronounced without the final 't', appears in IrE as a tag as a means of seeking assent or confirmation about what the speaker has just said (Harris 1993: 176). Examples include:

(19) a. 'Yeah, well. See you tomorrow, *wha'*?' (*Agnes Browne*)
      b. 'Keep it in the family, *what*?' (*The General*)

What as a sentence-final marker appears to be an overwhelmingly southern feature, appearing in 11 southern movies (28 per cent) and 1 northern one (3 per cent). Support for this southern trend is also offered by the ICE-Ireland corpus, where the feature is found 3 times, albeit solely in southern contexts.

14.5.8 *But* as a tag

As with the second person pronoun *youse*, the use of *but* as a tag, meaning 'though' or 'however', is typically associated with both Dublin English (McMahon and O'Donoghue 2004: 136) and northern varieties (Hickey 2004: 128). To that end, Kirk and Kallen were surprised that there were so few examples in their northern data: '[d]espite these possible associations of clause-final *but* with Scotland, we find that of the 11 occurrences of this feature in ICE-Ireland, only three are from ICE-NI' (2010: 202). Hickey's survey, in contrast, found that the acceptability of *but* as a tag was, indeed, higher in the North (35 per cent) than the South (20 per cent). Although the findings of the film corpora do not offer as clear a picture as Hickey's results, they too display a slight preference for *but* as a tag in northern films, namely 5 (13 per cent) compared with 4 (10 per cent) in southern movies, with all examples in the latter occurring, as one might expect, in films set in Dublin.

> (20) a. 'No, he's not here. Not going very far, *but*. The passport's here.' (*Jump*)
> b. 'He's right, *but*.' (*Boxed*)

14.5.9 Variable tags

Kallen and Kirk also look at variable tags as prominent features of IE. A variable tag is one that demonstrates 'a considerable degree of syntactic variability that is based on the main clause to which it is attached, but as a declarative tag it is a clearly different type from the canonical English tag question' (2012: 55). Such tags generally involve the use of *so* together with the verb which was used in the main clause (or an auxiliary), resulting in structures which affirm what has come before, as in the following:

> (21) a. 'You wouldn't know what to wear, *so you wouldn't*.' (*The Van*)
> b. 'Oh, I loved it, *so I did*.' (*Hunger*)

Kallen and Kirk found that the proportion of *so* tags was 'moderately greater from ROI (55%) than from NI (45%)' (2012: 112). Interestingly, this was one of the few times where the findings from the film corpora differed quite dramatically from those from the ICE corpus. Indeed, the films revealed not only that *so* tags were more common in northern Irish films, but that this was overwhelmingly the case, occurring in 19 northern (48 per cent) and 6 southern ones (15 per cent). Unfortunately, comparisons between the northern and southern distribution of this feature do not appear elsewhere in the literature and thus there is no way of confirming whether the ICE findings or those of the film corpora are more in keeping with the actual situation. This therefore would be an interesting avenue of investigation for the future. In this regard, it would also be interesting to examine whether a similar type of structure, namely repetition for emphasis, also differs in its distribution nationwide. Although there are no comparative data, the film corpora revealed that tags which work in a similar way to *so* tags, albeit without the use of the word *so*, occur quite frequently. Examples include:

(22) a. Ah, you're funny, *you are.'* (*Some Mother's Son*)
        b. 'I know a lot of things, *I do.'* (*The Mighty Celt*)

Such structures are not restricted to declarative sentences and indeed are more frequent in questions, as in the following:

(23) a. 'Did you not hear him, *did you not?'* (*Intermission*)
        b. 'Does it really hurt you, Sharon, *does it?'* (*The Snapper*)

All in all, these repetitions for emphasis occurred more in southern films than northern ones, appearing in 14 of the former (35 per cent) and 9 of the latter (23 per cent).

14.5.10 *See* as discourse marker

When comparing discourse markers between the northern and southern parts of SPICE-Ireland, Kallen and Kirk noted that 'uses of SEE as a discourse-marker are almost evenly divided between NI (51 per cent) and ROI (49 per cent)' (2012: 105). However, they were focusing on the use of SEE in collocations such as 'you see', 'I see' and 'do you see?' and ignored perhaps the most interesting use of SEE as a discourse marker, namely in introducing topic/comment structures (cf. Henry 1995: 131–5). This is a feature which, at least in terms of Irish varieties, appears to be unique to Northern Ireland:

(24) a. '*See me*, them ones have my head away.' (*Four Days in July*)
        b. '*See fuckin' me*, I have this town.' (*Resurrection Man*)
        c. '*See you*, Marley, you are a dickhead.' (*You, Me and Marley*)

This structure is not only found before direct objects as in the previous examples, but also with *if*/*when* clauses:

(25) a. '*See*, when this shop opens, there's to be no coming around lookin' for a donation for the Republican prisoners or the Loyal Orange Widows.' (*Good Vibrations*)
b. '*See*, when we get to Australia, I'm gonna get a pet kangaroo.' (*Mickybo and Me*)
c. '*See*, if it was me, I'd a never have come back.' (*Cherrybomb*)

In all, such uses of SEE occur in 11 Northern Irish films but no southern ones. Unfortunately, since there is no comparable data from elsewhere, this remains a feature that needs to be explored in more detail.

14.6 Summary

Following the approach taken by Kallen and Kirk (2012: 115), it is possible to present all the findings for the film corpora in one table summarising the percentage distribution between northern and southern Ireland for each of the features previously discussed and for a few others which showed clear trends, but couldn't be discussed due to the scope of the chapter, e.g. the predominantly northern *wee* and *wean* and the primarily southern *eejit* and *gobshite*. Thus, for example, if a feature like the *after* perfect appears in 18 films in total in the corpus, the percentage can be calculated on the basis of how many of those were in the South (16/18 = 89 per cent) and North (2/18 = 11 per cent) respectively. In keeping with Kallen and Kirk, Table 14.1 'denotes as "same or similar" the distribution range between 48 and 52 per cent; "near same" as between 53 and 56 per cent; "high" as between 57 and 69 per cent; and "very high" as above 70 per cent. The features which predominate in each zone can thus be compared in the table' (2012: 115).

14.7 Conclusion

As we saw at the beginning of this chapter, it turns out that Irish films do not lend themselves to an all-encompassing sociolinguistic analysis. This is because, at least in films set between 1960 and 2014, there has largely been a focus on telling the stories of young, working-class, white Catholic males, thereby silencing the voices of those who do not belong in that category.[8] Nonetheless, despite this drawback, the film corpora proved very useful for a variationist approach, enabling an

Table 14.1 Grammatical features in Northern and Southern Irish films

	Northern Irish Films				Southern Irish Films		
	Very high 70%+	**High 57–69%**	**Near same 53–6%**	**Same 48–52%**	**Near same 53–6%**	**High 57–69%**	**Very high 70%+**
Morphology		*youse* (62%)	*yiz* (53%)			*ye* (65%)	
Syntax	negator contraction (78%) *don't you* *be* + V-*ing* (73%)	zero relative (64%)	*don't be* + V-*ing* (53%)			unbound *myself/yourself*, etc. (64%) repetition for emphasis (61%)	unbound *himself/herself* (82%) *after* perfect (89%) *will* for *shall* (72%)
Discourse	*Ach/och* (95%) *See* (100%) *So* tags (76%)					final *like* (57%)	*what* tag (100%)
Lexis	*aye* (93%) *wee* (97%) *wean* (100%) *FRIG* (93%)	*ma* (61%) *bloody* (69%)			*mammy* (56%)	*grand* (69%) *eejit* (61%) *gobshite* (75%)	*mam* (88%) *FECK* (79%) *bleedin'* (94%)

338

interesting comparison between varieties of English in the north and south of the country. The findings revealed that the mediated language of film closely mirrors that of society and that trends and tendencies that were evident in the films were generally confirmed both by the extant literature and by data from SPICE-Ireland and/or Hickey's *A Survey of Irish English Usage*. What is more, the film corpora revealed trends regarding features that had received relatively little attention in terms of their distribution before, such as *what* as a tag, *don't you be* V-*ing*, *grand*, etc. On the few occasions when the findings in the films did not reflect those of the ICE corpus, this was largely due to the fact that certain features are more likely to occur in the more varied interactive contexts one encounters in films than in those which comprise the ICE corpus, such as legal cross-examinations, parliamentary debates and spontaneous commentaries, etc. Given the findings from the film corpora, I believe there is certainly sufficient evidence to support Coupland's claim that mediated language should be seen as 'a core sociolinguistic domain' (2009: 297) and that investigating the way that media products *reflect* language use in Ireland is just as valid as looking at the way they *shape* it.

A.1 Appendix

Table 14.2   Chronological list of Northern and Southern Irish films

	Southern films ordered according to the period they are set in	Northern films ordered according to the period they are set in
1960–1970	*Agnes Browne* (1999) *The Magdalene Sisters* (2002) *A Man of No Importance (1994)* *The Boys and Girl from County Clare (2003)* *War of the Buttons (1994)*	*The Butcher Boy* (1997) *Middletown* (2006)
1970–1980	*Last of the High Kings* (1996) *32A* (2007)	*Bloody Sunday* (2002) *Sunday* (2002) *Cal (1984)* *In the Name of the Father (1993)* *Mickybo and Me (2004)* *Nothing Personal (1995)* *Resurrection Man (1998)* *Breakfast on Pluto* (2005) *Good Vibrations* (2013)
1980–1990	*High Spirits* (1988) *The Commitments* (1991)	*An Everlasting Piece* (2000) *Fifty Dead Men Walking* (2008) *Hunger* (2008) *Some Mother's Son* (1996) *The Informant* (1997) *Angel* (1982) *Four Days in July* (1985) *H3* (2001)
1990–2000	*The Snapper* (1993) *Into the West* (1993) *The Van* (1996) *Trojan Eddie* (1996) *The Matchmaker* (1997) *The Nephew* (1997) *Waking Ned* (1998) *A Very Unlucky Leprechaun* (1998) *The General* (1998) *Ordinary Decent Criminal* (2000) *When the Sky Falls* (2000) *Veronica Guerin* (2003)	*You, Me and Marley* (1992) *The Boxer* (1997) *Crossmaheart* (1997) *Divorcing Jack* (1998) *The Most Fertile Man in Ireland* (1999) *Sunset Heights* (1999) *Omagh* (2004) *Shadow Dancer* (2012)
2000–Present	*About Adam* (2000) *When Brendan Met Trudy* (2000) *Rat* (2001)	*Mad about Mambo* (2000) *The Closer You Get* (2000) *Mapmaker* (2001)

On the Edge (2001)
Mystics (2002)
Intermission (2003)
Goldfish Memory (2003)
Dead Bodies (2003)
Cowboys and Angels (2003)
Adam and Paul (2004)
Dead Meat (2004)
Inside I'm Dancing (2004)
Irish Jam (2004)
Boy Eats Girl (2005)
Garage (2007)
Ondine (2009)
The Guard (2011)
What Richard Did (2012)
Calvary (2014)

Boxed (2002)
Man about Dog (2004)
The Mighty Celt (2005)
48 Angels (2006)
Cherrybomb (2008)
Five Minutes of Heaven (2009)
Wild about Harry (2009)
Stand Off (2011)
Jump (2012)
A Belfast Story (2013)

Notes

1. 'Linguists who use film dialogue as accurate case studies of everyday conversation are operating on mistaken assumptions' (Kozloff 2000: 19).
2. Literary dialect was defined by Ives as 'an author's attempt to represent in writing a speech that is restricted regionally, socially, or both' and that 'may attempt to approach scientific accuracy by representing all the grammatical, lexical and phonetic peculiarities that he has observed' (1950: 146).
3. This division of the film corpora is in keeping with the recognised linguistic boundary between northern and southern varieties of IE which stretches roughly from Dundalk and Drogheda in the east to Bundoran and Sligo in the west (cf. Tilling 1985: 20).
4. Even though Belfast is in County Antrim, Hickey treated them separately in his survey.
5. For this study, all examples are in the interrogative, as that is the form which most clearly shows that *will* and not *shall* is being used, because in affirmative sentences *I will* and *we will* are more likely to be contracted to *I'll* and *we'll*. Similarly, for the sake of clarity, interrogatives with the contracted forms are omitted.
6. The informant's intuition was correct. 'Rightly' only occurs in northern films, albeit only once, as was also the case in SPICE-Ireland. A more common expression used synonymously with *grand*, namely *dead on*, occurs 5 times, but only in northern Irish films. It, too, occurs only in SPICE-NI.
7. These do not refer to Bloody Sunday, an event one might expect to be mentioned frequently in a Northern context and which would skew the findings.
8. This is not to say that such an approach will not be possible in the future or, indeed, that such an analysis would not be feasible in terms of Irish television series. Shows such as *The Clinic* (2003–9), *Killinaskully* (2003–8), *Pure Mule* (2004–5), *Prosperity* (2007), *Love/Hate* (2010–14), *Moone Boy* (2012–) and *Mrs*

Brown's Boys (2010) include a variety of characters from varying walks of life in different genres and may be able to offer valuable sociolinguistic insights into IE usage since the turn of the century. Even then, though, an all-inclusive study of speech on the island would still be complicated by the dearth of series featuring northern varieties, with only *Give my Head Peace* (1998–2008), *The Fall* (2013–14) and *Number 2s* (2015) set in Northern Ireland.

References

Behan, Conor (2005). 'Leave upspeak to the, like, Americans?', *Irish Times*, 16 August.

Biggar, Francis J. (1897). *Our Ulster Accent and Ulster Provincialisms*. Belfast: Religious Tract and Book Depot.

Bielenberg, Kim (2008). 'Janey Mac! Irish-English is banjaxed, so it is…', *Irish Independent*, 9 February.

Corrigan, Karen P. (2010). *Irish English, Volume 1 – Northern Ireland*. Edinburgh: Edinburgh University Press.

Coupland, Nikolas (2009). 'The mediated performance of vernaculars', *Journal of English Linguistics* 37.3: 284–300.

Ging, Debbie (2013). *Men and Masculinities in Irish Cinema*. Basingstoke: Palgrave Macmillan.

Harris, John (1993). 'The grammar of Irish English', in: James Milroy and Lesley Milroy (eds) *Real English. The Grammar of English Dialects in the British Isles*. London: Longman, pp. 139–86.

Henry, Alison (1995). *Belfast English and Standard English: Dialect Variation and Parameter Setting*. Oxford: Oxford University Press.

Hickey, Raymond (2004). *A Sound Atlas of Irish English*. Berlin: Mouton de Gruyter.

Hickey, Raymond (2007). *Irish English. History and Present-day Forms*. Cambridge: Cambridge University Press.

Hickey, Raymond (2010), 'Irish English in early modern drama: the birth of a linguistic stereotype', in: Raymond Hickey (ed.) *Varieties of English in Writing. The Written Word as Linguistic Evidence*. Amsterdam: John Benjamins, pp. 121–38.

Hickey, Raymond (in press). 'The pragmatics of *grand* in Irish English', *Journal of Historical Pragmatics*.

Hodson, Jane (2014). *Dialect in Film and Literature*. Basingstoke: Palgrave Macmillan.

Holohan, Conn (2010). *Cinema on the Periphery. Contemporary Irish and Spanish Film*. Dublin: Irish Academic Press.

Ives, Sumner (1950). 'A theory of literary dialect', in: Juanita V. Williamson and Virginia M. Burke (eds) (1971). *A Various Language. Perspectives on American Dialects*. New York: Holt, Rinehart and Winston, Inc., pp. 145–77.

Kallen, Jeffrey L. (2013). *Irish English. Volume 2. The Republic of Ireland*. Berlin: de Gruyter Mouton.

Kallen, Jeffrey L. and John M. Kirk (2012). *SPICE-Ireland: a User's Guide*. Belfast: Queen's University Belfast.

Kirk, John M. and Jeffrey L. Kallen (2006). 'Irish Standard English: How standardized? How Celticized?, in: H. L. C. Tristram (ed.) *The Celtic Englishes IV*. Potsdam: Potsdamer Universitätsverlag, pp. 88–113.

Kirk, John M. and Jeffrey L. Kallen (2010). 'How Scottish is Irish Standard English?', in: Robert McColl Millar (ed.) *Northern Lights, Northern Words: Selected Papers from the FRLSU Conference, Kirkwall 2009*. Aberdeen: Forum for Research on the Languages of Scotland and Ireland, pp. 178–213.

Kozloff, Sarah (2000). *Overhearing Film Dialogue*. Berkeley and Los Angeles: University of California Press.

McIlroy, Brian (1998). *Shooting to Kill*. Wiltshire: Flicks Books.

McLoone, Martin (2008). *Film, Media and Popular Culture in Ireland. Cityscapes, Landscapes, Soundscapes*. Dublin: Irish Academic Press.

McMahon, Sean and Jo O'Donoghue (eds) (2004). *Brewer's Dictionary of Irish Phrase and Fable*. London: Weidenfeld and Nicholson.

O'Connell, Díóg (2010). *New Irish Storytellers. Narrative Strategies in Film*. Bristol: Intellect.

Pettitt, Lance (2000). *Screening Ireland. Film and Television Representation*. Manchester: Manchester University Press.

Share, Bernard (2003). *Slanguage. A Dictionary of Irish Slang*. Dublin: Gill and Macmillan.

Siemund, Peter and Kalynda Beal (2011). 'It-clefts in Irish English', in: Raymond Hickey (ed.) *Researching the Languages of Ireland*. Uppsala: Uppsala University Press, pp. 243–68.

Stuart-Smith, Jane and Claire Timmins (2014). 'Language and the influence of the media: a Scottish perspective', in: Robert Lawson (ed.) *Sociolinguistics in Scotland*. London: Palgrave Macmillan, pp. 177–96.

Sullivan, James P. (1980). 'The validity of literary dialect: Evidence from the theatrical portrayal of Hiberno-English forms', in: Lou Ann Matossian and Lisa Giles-Klein (eds) *Language in Society* 9. Cambridge: Cambridge University Press, pp. 195–219.

Tagliamonte, Sali and Jennifer Smith (2002). 'Either it isn't or it's not: Neg/aux contraction in British dialects', *English World Wide* 23.3: 251–81.

Tilling, Philip M. (1985). 'A tape-recorded survey of Irish English in its context', in: Dónall Ó Baoill (ed.) *Papers on Irish English. Irish Association for Applied Linguistics*, pp. 16–26.

Walshe, Shane (2009). *Irish English as Represented in Film*. Frankfurt: Peter Lang.

Walshe, Shane (2010). 'Folk perceptions of Irishness: Separating the Irish from the Oirish', paper presented at *New Perspectives on Irish English* conference, University College Dublin, 11–13 March 2010.

15

Translation and Society in Ireland, 1900–Present

Kathleen Shields

15.1 Introduction

Translation in Ireland from 1900 to the present day bears the strong imprint of social factors. While translations are often ignored and overlooked in favour of other larger and more pressing matters, they are nevertheless important indicators and vectors of social and cultural change. Translation movements and key translated texts can be mapped on to these moments of change, while conservative patterns can also be seen to endure. The two main languages under discussion are Irish and English (or Irish English), the direction of translation traffic between them being an indicator of their relative status. Irish is the language most frequently translated into English. However, translation to and from other languages, often involving the use of intermediary translations, also needs to be taken into consideration. Throughout the phases studied here the central and guiding question is: who are the translations for and why do the translators adopt the strategies that they do?

Translation in the first four decades of the twentieth century set a pattern that was to last until the advent of the digital age: literary translation predominates and plays a leading role in cultural and political debates while it is in the literary sphere that many political debates about cultural identity are played out. Conor Cruise O'Brien commented in the 1970s during the Northern Irish conflict that literature and politics formed an 'unhealthy intersection' in public debate (O'Brien 1975: 3). Unhealthy or not, the intersection is an important one and translations are at the very heart of it.

In the early years of the twentieth century, leading up to the 1916 Easter Rising and to the establishment of the Irish Free State in 1922, a wave of translating from Irish was part of the ongoing task of cultural self-definition. The work of the Irish Texts Society, which provided scholarly bilingual editions of major canonical texts in Irish, can be seen as continuing the consciousness-raising of the Gaelic League and of Douglas Hyde's mission to de-anglicise Ireland. As well as the works of the Irish Texts Society, other key translations from this period were Lady Augusta Gregory's *Cuchulain of Muirthemne* (1902), Kuno Meyer's *Selections from Ancient Irish Poetry* (1911), and James Stephens's *Reincarnations* (1918).

Paradoxically, these translations served as the basis for a new Irish literature in English and set a pattern for future new translations into English for many years to come. It was works like Douglas Hyde's translations in *The Love Songs of Connaught* (1893) that inspired Yeats and Lady Gregory to create a new literary Irish English. Seamus Heaney's *Sweeney Astray* (1983) is indebted to J. G. O'Keeffe's 1913 translation of *Buile Shuibhne* for the Irish Texts Society while Thomas Kinsella acknowledged the importance of the Society's translation of *Lebor Gabhala* or *Book of Invasions* for his translation, *The Táin* in 1969 (Kinsella 1970; Heaney 1983). During the twentieth century the literature in English was to take its place within an Anglo-American culture where translation tends to play a silent and ancillary role and where translations are praised when they achieve fluency and invisiblity (Venuti 1995: 1–39). For different motives therefore, both within the English-speaking and the Irish-speaking world there was often an indifference, even a wilful blindness to translation.

15.1.1 Irish language policy in the early twentieth century

Irish was designated as 'the first national language' in the constitution of the Irish State in 1922 (and again in the constitution of 1937), so that from its inception the state adopted a policy of Irish-English bilingualism. It was mainly the curricular reforms of the education system in independent Ireland that were meant to ensure that this policy of bilingualism was carried out. As John Coolahan writes of the school curriculum from 1922 to 1960,

> Inspired by the ideology of cultural nationalism it was held that the schools ought to be the prime agents in the revival of the Irish language and native tradition which it was held were the hallmarks of nationhood and independent statehood. Many people held that the schools in the nineteenth century had been a prime cause of the decline of the Irish language; under a native Irish government the process would have to be reversed. (Coolahan 1981: 38)

For the purposes of this discussion 'bilingualism' can be defined in two ways. For the individual, it is an ability to speak two languages and to switch between them. At the level of the group or society bilingualism can mean that two languages co-exist independently in parallel worlds, without translation or mediation between them necessarily taking place. In Ireland the policy of bilingualism led to some interesting attitudes towards translation which were to last for many decades: for cultural nationalists the first and native language is Irish. English, the second language, is a necessary evil into which translations have to sometimes be made for the purposes of clarification and exegesis. Since every Irish citizen should know the Irish language this means that translations are not really mentioned as they ought not to be taking place. Bilingualism can exist, but not translation or mediation between languages.

In reality, many writers to a lesser or greater extent used and understood Irish texts, if not translating from them, then mediating between the two languages. For this reason, right from the early years of the twentieth century, categories such as 'native' and 'foreign', 'source' and 'target', 'own' and 'other' were never straightforward. A further long-lasting consequence of the separation of the two languages was what Declan Kiberd called a state of 'quarantine' that existed between them and between the literatures in Irish and in English, a quarantine that started to come to an end in the 1980s with a wave of fresh bilingual texts (Kiberd 1979).

15.1.2 Translations in the early twentieth century

During the 1930s, practical steps were taken to reverse the direction of translation traffic between Irish and English. Since the nineteenth century most of the traffic had been in one direction, from Irish into English. Through the publications wing of the Department of Education, An Gúm, founded in 1926, the state sought to reverse this process by translating various genres (mainly popular prose fiction in English) into Irish (Cronin 1996: 156–61). Through the 1930s and 1940s many writers, editors, teachers and journalists produced translations from English, Spanish, French, German, Latin and Greek (Mag Shamhráin 1997). For instance Frederick William O'Connell produced *An Dr Jekyll agus Mr Hyde* (1929) while Risteard Ó Foghludha translated an anthology of world literature, and works such as *Fiche gearrscéal* (1930), a selection of stories by Daudet, Maupassant and Coppée. These translations were often quite creative. For example, Sean Ó Cuirrín in his translation *Dracula* (1933) turned Bram Stoker's work into a text for the 1930s, cutting out intertextual references to English literature, Greek mythology and to events of Stoker's time such as the emergent feminist movement and Anglo-American relations (de Brún 2007: 170–7, 183, 189). At the same time Ó Cuirrín recasts Stoker by writing in a concrete reporting narrative mode, drawing on the oral and rhetorical resources of the Irish language (de Brún 2007: 180, 185).

There was a logic to the translation experiment of An Gúm: Irish should not simply exist as the high form in a diglossic situation, used only for old literature, special occasions and state ceremonies while English was used for everyday life. (This is diglossia in Fishman's rather than in Ferguson's sense, pertaining to a relationship between two languages rather than between high and low forms in the same language. Whereas Ferguson defined diglossia as occurring in speech communities where 'two or more varieties of the same language are used by some speakers under different conditions' (1959: 325), Fishman (1967) expanded this definition to include a number of sociolinguistic situations, from stylistic differences within one language to the use of separate languages.) The purpose of these An Gúm editions was to provide a popular culture in Irish, with publications that were for light entertainment. However, the project, while it was idealistic, proved utopian in the face of the massive weight of London as a publishing centre.

During the 1920s and 1930s another kind of literary translation was taking place. This could be described as plurilingual translation by authors using and translating several languages. In the 1930s Samuel Beckett, Brian Coffey and Denis Devlin all translated French writers in different ways, particularly the poetry of French symbolists and of Paul Eluard. Denis Devlin and Thomas MacGreevy also translated their own work into several languages: Irish, Spanish, French and English. These writers have often been enlisted as figures of European Modernism and set against cultural nationalists in a binary fashion. However, translators like Coffey and Devlin perceived and used Irish as another modern European language and made translations of French writers into Irish. In the 1930s there was in European countries besides Ireland a wariness about language legislation, overt language planning and language policies that could all too easily be enlisted in the service of narrow nationalism and of fascism (Calvet 1987: 261–2). The European modernists' involvement with different languages is not necessarily a disengagement from society or politics, but rather a use of translation to counter the Herderian unity of language, literature and people.

These writers, by translating, construct a voice (or voices) in the interstices among languages. A succinct example is Thomas MacGreevy's poem 'Aodh Ruadh Ó Domhnaill'. In its English version it is the most anthologised of his poems and presents the speaker in Spain, searching for the grave of Aodh Rua Ó Domhnaill (MacGreevy 1991: 133–4). Yet as a text in English it refuses to be just an English poem and points to two other languages. This is how the poem begins in its English version:

> (1) *Juan de Juni*, the priest said,
>   Each J becoming H;
>
>   *Berruguete*, he said,
>   And the G was aspirate;
>
>   *Ximénez*, he said then
>   And aspirated first and last.

A negative of this same poem also exists in a French version as well as in Spanish, where it is the strangeness of the name in Irish that stands out (and there are no accents given on the Irish or the Spanish):

> (2) AODH RUADH O DOMHNAILL
>
>   Juan de Juni, el clerigo dijo,
>   Cambiando la J por H,
>
>   Berruguete, dijo
>   Y aspiro la G,
>
>   Ximenez, dijo entonces,
>   Aspirando el principio y el fin.

The Irish-English antagonism changes when seen from the wider perspective of European history. The plurilingual writers of the 1930s refract references to Ireland through translating in order to engage obliquely with their time. While this kind of writing was a relatively minor strand it anticipated some developments in translation that were to emerge at the end of the century.

15.1.3 Censorship and translation

The decades of the 1940s and 1950s were for various reasons a time of insularity and isolation: de Valera's 1937 constitution included new religious and corporatist elements while the church consolidated its authority and control in a great many areas of public life through schools, institutions and censorship (Keogh 1994: 96–104). The ambiguous policy of neutrality during the Second World War sealed Ireland off from the rest of Europe yet at the same time some 50,000 Irish men and women joined the British armed forces (Jackson 1999: 302–3). Economic protectionism and self-sufficiency meant also that the two decades saw high emigration (Garvin 2004). By virtue of their very nature, translations were bound to challenge cultural isolation, not only because they transmitted new ideas from outside the country, but also because translations from Irish radically questioned the status quo from within. Frank O'Connor as translator is a representative and towering figure, both in his prose and poetic work.

15.2   Translation of *Cúirt an Mheán-Oíche*

O'Connor was a theorist and practitioner of the Irish short story, and like his peers O'Flaherty and O'Faolain, shaped in part by his encounter with Russian literature in the 1940s, via intermediary English translations from Gogol and Dostoevsky. (Edward Garnett, the leading translator of Russian into English, who was Liam O'Flaherty's editor at Jonathan Cape in London, introduced O'Flaherty to Dostoevsky and Gogol.) George O'Brien has noted of O'Connor's short stories that he wrote them from psychological motives: the body politic had been taken care of in 1922, but the body personal, the body sexual and the body spiritual needed attention (O'Brien 2006: 453). This motive also underlies O'Connor's most controversial work, *The Midnight Court*, a translation of Brian Merriman's *Cúirt an Mheán-Oíche*, a light-hearted eighteenth-century satire.

Frank O'Connor's translation (1945) was banned for indecency and because the original debated topics that were burning issues at the time: natural children, frustrated female sexual desire, marriage, free love and clerical celibacy. It is important not to overstate the prevalence of censorship or to oversimplify it. Diarmaid Ferriter argues that cultural historians of the century perhaps tend to place too much emphasis on censorship, and he cites bestseller lists to show what people were actually reading as opposed to what was banned (Ferriter 2004: 10). Censorship under totalitarian regimes can also give rise to an uncomplicated narrative of the heroic translator, victim of an oppressive system (this is often how censorship in the dark years of the mid-twentieth century in Ireland is portrayed). However, as Maria Tymoczko says, 'in looking at the role of censorship in translation, we want to avoid buying into simplistic binary notions of victims and heroes in the translation process' (Tymoczko 2009: 30). In Ireland censorship came about through social consensus and constitutional means: not without opposition, for example Sir John Keane's tabling of a Senate motion in 1928 against the Censorship of Publications Act (1929). Its implementation often involved collaboration and adjustments, with government ministers and senior civil servants self-censoring and acceding to the demands of the Catholic Truth Society, which managed to gain the controlling vote on the Censorship Board (Ó Drisceoil 2005: 147). O'Connor deliberately chose *Cúirt an Mheán-Oíche* in an act of cultural redefinition, because it was a text with a reputation, openly positioning himself and Merriman together in an ironic relationship where he fires the first shot against the censors in an ideological battle.

Merriman's long narrative poem (composed around 1780) is itself an intriguing text, resisting straightforward interpretation. Its depiction of various forms of relations between the sexes was 'so energetic as to cause English language versions of the poem to be censored in Ireland in the mid-1900s, while the Gaelic original continued to circulate simultaneously in published scholarly editions as well as in the oral tradition' (Buttimer 2006: 344–5). *Cúirt an Mheán-Oíche* became a node of translation in the twentieth century, generating an extraordinary number of translations, for example an anonymous version by 'an intermediate teacher' (Frederick William O'Connell, 1909), by Aarland Ussher (1926), David Marcus (1953), David Greene (1968), Patrick C. Power (1977 [1971]), Cosslett Ó Cuinn (1987 [1982]) and Ciaran Carson (2005). A comparison of these reveals decade by decade changes in attitudes to sexuality, church dominance and feminism: Ó Cuinn's for example is notable for its sexual frankness and for the way that it constantly reminds the reader that the poem is a translation, while Patrick Power draws attention to the survival of the poem in the oral tradition of Munster. Others situate their language on a sliding scale between neutral English and more marked Irish English.

O'Connor's version is striking by virtue of the translation strategies that he deploys: he creates his own Brian Merriman, using irony and understatement while embedding personal autobiographical references in the text and writing in contemporary Irish English. In doing so he produces the Merriman poem not as a work of high literature but as a text of sociological importance, rather like the conversations of the Tailor and Ansty (also banned in 1942) which gave rise to heated Oireachtas debates and to the persecution of O'Connor's friends ('Oireachtas Historical Debates' 1942).

In his preface, O'Connor presents Merriman as an Enlightenment figure, someone who 'managed to read and assimilate a great deal of contemporary literature, English and French – Savage, Swift, Goldsmith and most of all Rousseau' (1945: 5–6). According to O'Connor, the part of the poem in praise of bastards derives from Rousseau and contemporary thinking on natural children: Merriman was in fact ahead of his time by two centuries. Admiring Merriman's audacity, he states: 'after all, he was writing in an Irish-speaking village in the eighteenth century things which even Yeats himself might have thought twice of writing in the English-speaking Dublin of the twentieth' (O'Connor 1945: 9). The target of the satire here is the Catholic Truth Society that controlled the Censorship Board to the extent that English language writers self-censored and thought twice before publishing. The retrograde decline from Merriman's day is linked to Catholicism: there is never likely to be a monument set up to Brian Merriman in Clare Street in Limerick where he died, 'for Limerick has a reputation for piety' whereas, according to the preface, 'the religious background of the Midnight Court is Protestant' (O'Connor 1945: 5). How does Frank O'Connor know this? Is it because of the arguments against celibacy of priests? The word 'Protestant' here is code for 'liberal' and 'not Catholic'. The main tenor of the translation is anti-church, rather than being written in the cause of sexual liberation. The preface has a knowing but disarming simplicity. With understatement it casts the drama in a land of fable, making it sound like Voltaire's *Candide*:

> The story of it is innocuous enough. The poet falls asleep, and in a dream is summoned to the fairy court, where the unmarried women of Munster are pleading their inability to get husbands. An old man replies by telling the story of his own marriage, and of how his young wife presented him with another man's child on his wedding night. The young girl rebuts the charge and tells the story of the marriage from the wife's point of view, and then the Fairy Queen sums up and gives judgement for the women, whose first victim is the poet himself. (O'Connor 1945: 6)

When Sir John Keane had tabled his motion in the Senate in 1928 against the Censorship of Publications Act he predicted that it would lead to the ban of significant literary works in Irish, such as *The Midnight Court* (Maume 2009). The reputation that the poem had acquired indicates that O'Connor knew that his translation was likely to be censored. By inserting autobiographical references into the poem, O'Connor positions himself alongside the Enlightenment Merriman that he creates in the preface.

As Liam P. Ó Murchú has noted, where Merriman simply refers to clerics, or clergy (*cléir*) O'Connor specifies hierarchical ranks: priest, curate, canon, etc. (Ó Murchú 2008: 138). There is an anti-clerical tone, specifically directed at the Catholic Church of the 1940s, that is added to the Merriman.

> (3)   Down with marriage! 'Tis out of date,
>   It exhausts the stock and cripples the state.
>   The priest has failed with whip and blinker
>   Now give a chance to Tom the Tinker
>
>   (O'Connor 1945: 34)

There is a vernacular energy to O'Connor's translation because it is written in the Irish English spoken in the 1940s. For instance, a girl speaks in the court, complaining of a shortage of men:

> (4)   Has the Catholic Church a glimmer of sense
>   That the priests won't marry like anyone else?
>   Is it any wonder the way I am,
>   Out of my mind for the want of a man?
>
>   (O'Connor 1945: 39–40)

In this way O'Connor pays tribute to the survival of Merriman in the oral tradition while also making the poem shockingly immediate. It is testimony to the power of the English translation that it was banned while the Irish original was not, as Frank O'Connor pointed out later in a letter to the *Irish Times*. 'The Censorship Board banned my translation; they did not ban the original... The implication of this was clear; that I had deliberately introduced material which was not to be found in any other edition, and that this material was sufficiently indecent to justify the banning of the whole work' (O'Connor 1946).

Not all translations from this period are radical however. In sociolinguistic terms drama translations from the time and throughout the century are rather conservative. One could cite by way of example Lord Longford's *School for Wives*, a translation of Molière made for the Gate Theatre tour of 1945, performed at the Gate in 1947, where the text is 'deliberately' given a 'slight... archaic flavour' and where the servants speak with one or two Hibernicisms (Longford 1948: 5). By comparison, Augusta Gregory's *Kiltartan Molière* (1910) is sociolinguistically radical to the extent that all of the characters of all social classes speak in 'Kiltartanese', a literary version of the Irish English spoken around Kiltartan. Yet the effect of this is to imply that Ireland is a classless society and to lose the speech distinctions that Molière had made between the servants and their masters.

15.3 Translation of the *Táin*

If Frank O'Connor's *Midnight Court* is an emblematic translation for Irish society in the 1940s, Thomas Kinsella's *Táin*, a translation of his composite and 'tidied up' version of the old Irish epic *Táin Bó Cuailgne* (Kinsella 1970: xi), is a key text for the modernising Republic of the 1970s and 1980s. Kinsella's version, as opposed to the much later one by Ciarán Carson (2007), was undertaken in the early 1960s and first published in 1969. It can be read as an anti-heroic, modernist and feminist rewriting of Augusta Gregory's *Cuchulain of Muirthemne* (Tymoczko 1999). Kinsella presents his translating of the *Táin Bó Cuailgne* as a reaching-back across centuries and a startling making-new for his readers in the present. If Kinsella's translation is fragmentary, then it has the designer fragmentariness of the modernist poem and in this respect the Le Brocquy black pen-and-ink illustrations play an important part in unifying the book. They exemplify a twentieth-century search for the 'impersonal' rather than a manuscript book illustration, as the artist explains in a note (Kinsella 1970: viii). The translation process involves blending, amplification and fragmentation of the source texts. The overarching strategy is to simultaneously alienate and appropriate the original texts, to stress the strangeness and primitive qualities of the old narrative (the alliterative patterns of *rosc*, for instance) while showing, through added glosses of place names and maps, that the topography is the same as that of present-day Ireland. Where Gregory's translation had bowdlerised, cutting out frank references to bodily functions, bizarre customs and heroic attributes and feats of violence, Kinsella's multiplies these (Leersson 1996: 203). Unlike Gregory, Kinsella is not detached from his readers, who are becoming increasingly urbanised and increasingly educated. Through reading, television, travel and migration, this public is in touch with aspects of the modern world which traditional education and censorship could no longer block out.

15.4 Bilingual text editions

While the aim of the *Táin* was to reconnect modern readers with an ancient past, quite a different translation enterprise can be seen in the many bilingual translations published during the 1980s and 1990s, when the Arts Council of Ireland adopted a policy of promoting Irish/

English bilingualism and of subsidising literary translations (for instance Ó Tuama and Kinsella 1981; Ó Direáin 1984; Bolger (ed.) 1986; Ní Dhomhnaill 1986). These can be described as bifocal or even multi-purpose translations undertaken for different constituencies of readers, whether for speakers of Irish as a first language who are also bilingual, whether for English speakers who can read and/or speak Irish with varying degrees of proficiency, or for monolingual English speakers. The bilingual collections are mainly intended for the second group of readers, to sensitise them to the interconnections between the two literatures and languages.

The bilingual editions were not uncontroversial, for two reasons. The first was their unidirectionality, the translation traffic always being from Irish to English. The second was that the English translations were feeding into world literature and overshadowing the Irish originals. Were texts being written in Irish with a view to being translated into English? The Irish language poet Biddy Jenkinson protested against those who believe that 'everything can be harvested and stored without loss in an English-speaking Ireland' and argued that for her, writing in Irish represented 'a stand here in the present among the outnumbered and beleaguered but determined survivors of Gaelic Ireland' (Jenkinson 1991: 33–4). Translation is not always a good thing, in her opinion.

15.5 Brian Friel's *Translations*

Biddy Jenkinson's point about the asymmetries of cultural exchange should not be confused with a more persistent attitude to translation deriving from the ideology of cultural nationalism, namely that translation from Irish is bad per se. This is the purely negative view of translation that is offered by Brian Friel's play *Translations*, a Field Day production presented for the first time in Derry in 1980 and restaged in Dublin, London and on Broadway. In the play, translation results in a wholesale loss of heritage and imaginative possessions. While Friel shows the Englishing of Irish place names to be the work of insensitive colonising British soldiers, in reality the translations for the nineteenth-century Ordnance Survey were done by great scholars of the Irish language such as John O'Donovan and Eugene O'Curry (Ó Catháin 2009). The encounter between the Latin- and Irish-speaking hedge-school master and the English officer is presented as happening with no cultural intermediaries present.

Translations, with the exception of the place names, unfolds entirely in English and translation is employed metaphorically to represent a fall from grace into English (and into loss of autonomy). It is interesting to contrast this play with the work of other Northern Irish writers of the period who translate in order to distance themselves from the troubled sectarian politics of the time. Derek Mahon, for instance, creates an alter ego through translation by including oblique references to 'expropriation' and home in his translations of Nerval and Rimbaud. Ciarán Carson similarly uses the distance that translation provides in order to refer, often with humour, to contemporary affairs in Northern Ireland and the world at large.

While the nationalist view of translation from Irish is a negative one, there is also in the culture at large a general indifference to translation and to the reality of languages other than English. This stems from Ireland's geographical position as a small, overwhelmingly English-speaking, country at the juncture between Britain and the United States, with a long history of emigration to these two countries.

15.6 Translation via intermediary texts

The great number of drama translations done from English into English is a good example of the dominance of English in Ireland, and a lack of engagement with the linguistic specifics and cultural resonances of original texts. One easy, if unethical and conservative, translation practice is the use of unacknowledged intermediary translations in English between the original and its Irish English translation. When Brian Friel writes for example about his *A Month in the Country*, after Turgenev, he works from 'a literal translation of Turgenev's text' and from this composes his own 'very free version' (Friel 1992: 7). Similarly, when Tom Kilroy does a new version of Chekhov's *Seagull*, set in the west of Ireland in the nineteenth century, it is not clear what text he is translating from. He is concerned to write against the 'many English versions' that tend 'to anglify Chekhov to a very English gentility, as if the plays were set somewhere in the Home Counties' (Kilroy 1993: 12). In this way the translators of the intervening English versions are hidden by the Irish playwright who does Chekhov or Ibsen or the Greeks. Frank McGuinness is an honorable exception to this practice in his naming and acknowledging of the intermediary translators. Hans-Christian Oeser, a translator who has won prestigious European translation awards for his work, takes issue with the practice, pointing out that it represents not only a blindness and indifference to the reality of translation, but also a kind of insularity, whereby intralingual translation (from unacknowledged English into English) is falsely presented as a new Irish engagement with another text in another language (Oeser 1996). The practice also fits in very well with a world publishing climate where English predominates as a 'pivot language', used increasingly in inter-mediary texts, and where the bulk of the literary translation traffic is from English into other languages and not the other way around (Bellos 2011: 210, 217, 233).

15.7 Translation and the education system

Throughout the twentieth century the most important institutional fac-tor that affected translations was the education system. The languages that were translated tended to be the languages taught in schools. From 1922 Irish was an obligatory and core subject up to school-leaving age in the Republic of Ireland, while it was not compulsory in Northern Ireland (Ó Buachalla 1988). Irish was and continues to be required for matriculation into the colleges of the National University of Ireland and was also required for entry into the Civil Service from 1937 until 1973. Until Minister of Education Donogh O'Malley introduced free secondary education in 1967, most children left school at 14, having studied Irish and English. Secondary education until then was class-based and charac-terised by a laissez-faire attitude on the part of the state (Coolahan 1981: 53). In secondary schools, before 1967, language and literary studies pre-dominated, with classics, particularly Latin, and English as the main languages, and French was also widely taught. Tom Garvin has argued that the teaching of Latin (for clerical and religious reasons) to the exclu-sion of modern languages put a brake on the economy for many years (Garvin 2004: 152–3).

Following both the introduction of free secondary education and Ireland's accession to the European Economic Community in 1973, Latin was dropped from school curricula and replaced by other lan-guages, French, Spanish and, for the first time, German. Thus the introduction of modern European languages and the extension of years at school coincided with the opening up of the economy to new trad-ing partners. This climate led to a more pragmatic approach to language learning and the setting up of formal translator training.

The main centre for institutionalised translator training is at Dublin City University, where the first degree programme in translation was set up in 1982, followed by a degree in translation studies at masters level (Kenny and Cronin 1995). Since 1989 University College Cork has also run a Masters in Translation Studies, preparing for the Institute of Lin-guists diploma. In both, translator training is mainly through English and Western European languages. Many translators in Ireland also learn on the job, often after taking degrees in modern languages. For the Irish Translators' and Interpreters' Association 'a translation degree is not essential but professional members must have some years of substantiated, consistent and contiguous experience in translation' (Keogh 1999: 8).

The Founding of the Irish Translators' Association (later the Irish Translators' and Interpreters' Association or ITIA) in 1986 was another step in the strengthening of translation as a profession. It is a network for its members, providing among other supports a code of practice, advice on payment and translation tools, and publishing a monthly newsletter. It differs from similar bodies in other European countries as it makes no separation between literary and non-literary translation, for the reason that similar difficulties of recognition are shared by all translators as well as interpreters.

15.8 Translation in present-day Ireland

In 1994 literary translation was given a more secure financial position with the founding of Ireland Literature Exchange (ILE), a not-for-profit organisation funded by the Arts Council and also directly by the government through Culture Ireland. To date it has given grants to both translators and publishers of translations of over 1500 works of Irish literature (in both Irish and English) into 55 different languages worldwide, as well as supporting translations from other languages (ILE 2014).

Nevertheless, despite the higher profile that translation now has and despite the growth in trade and contact with other European countries, English language monolingualism prevails. The US and Britain are of great economic importance to the Republic, and the officially monolingual cultures of these two countries can perhaps explain why the economic growth of the 1990s saw a corresponding decline in interest in foreign language learning as well as a decrease in the use and practice of Irish outside Irish-speaking households. Attitudinal support for languages does not necessarily mean concerted effort to learn them, to use them for work or to translate from them. Seán Ó Tuama's remarks about Irish can be extended to other languages also:

> favourable statistics regarding competence, and still more favourable statistics regarding attitudinal support, are not good indicators....of the position of Irish as an everyday spoken language in the country

as a whole. Indeed Irish is rarely heard as a normal spoken language.
(Ó Tuama 1989: 3)

Key factors have improved the climate for translation: translator training and accreditation, the establishment of a professional body, more
financial support for some kinds of translating, and finally the opening
up and strengthening of the economy. Since the turn of the millennium
the state has intervened in language policy and language planning.
New types of translating for different media have come to assume a
larger role, while literary translations no longer have the pre-eminence
that they once had as vectors for challenging or revising social norms.
Subtitling for television is a good example of routine everyday translation to which many have become accustomed, especially since the
advent of digital television. TG4, the Irish language television channel
founded in 1996, and since 2005 broadcasting in Northern Ireland as
well as in the Republic, adopted a policy of English and Irish subtitling
at its beginnings as Teilifís na Gaeilge. Viewing figures from Northern
Ireland are revealing: in an Ofcom survey on media consumption in
Northern Ireland in 2013 it is reported that TG4 is viewed at least once
a week by 13 per cent of the viewing public and viewed daily by 4 per
cent of Northern Ireland viewers. A further 9 per cent report that they
watch the channel weekly while 11 per cent of viewers watch it on a
monthly basis (TG4b). In the Republic of Ireland an average of 650,000
viewers a day watch the channel, and this figure exceeds 1 million people on major viewing days such as Christmas Day. In the early years of
TG4, the subtitles in Irish or English were optional and could be turned
on or off by the viewer. In recent years, while it is regrettable that the
subtitles are only in English and the viewer cannot turn them off, they
are nevertheless a good example of efficient, routine and everyday media
translation (O'Connell 2007).

In addition to media translation from Irish to English, the Official
Languages Act (2003) and the appointment of a Language Commissioner (Coimisinéir Teanga) for Irish meant a great increase in the
volume of translation of everyday texts from English into Irish. The aim
of the Act was 'to promote the use of Irish in public affairs and to ensure
the use of Irish by public bodies when communicating with the public
and/or providing services to the public', for example in letters, emails,
mail shots, information leaflets, reports, announcements and websites
(Coimisinéir Teanga 2014). Under the Act, public bodies have specific
duties to make sure information is available in the two languages of the
state.

After pressure from Irish language groups, the Council of Europe in 2005 amended the status of Irish from a 'working language' of the European Union to a full EU official language to apply on 1 January 2007. For practical reasons, in order to allow time for translator training, the Council decided that only regulations adopted by the European Parliament and the Council under the co-decision procedure have to be available in Irish. For other legislative acts there is a 'a temporary derogation for a renewable period of five years' (Council of Europe 2014). This arrangement is similar to the agreement reached on Maltese. In the wake of these two changes in the status of Irish there have been a number of specialist training courses leading to certification in translation, the Árd Diplóma sa Ghaeilge. While translator accreditation is ensured through this rigorous postgraduate examination, translators must also show evidence of regular work every two years.

In practice, government and EU recognition of the importance of Irish and a concomitant increase in translation activity does not necessarily lead to a corresponding increase in actual translation use. As Monica Heller argues, using Canadian French as an example, globalisation has brought about a 'commodification of language' with pressure towards standardisation for international communication alongside the 'valuing of local characteristics in order to legitimate control over local markets, and in order to attach a value of distinction to linguistic commodities in world markets of culture and tourism' (Heller 2003: 225). 'Linguistic minorities have been somewhat successful in playing the nation game' (Heller 2003: 227) and in the period of late modernity have 'turned vernacular competencies into valued locally distinctive goods'.

The ideology whereby each nation state was to have its language, in evidence in the early years of the Free State, has given place to a more pragmatic promotion of bilingualism for the individual citizen. Yet economic forces work in the opposite direction, making English monolingualism the norm. One study of multilingualism in Dublin, funded by the European Commission Lifelong Learning Programme, notes that the 2011 census recorded 182 different languages in use in the city, the main languages for each continent being Polish (Europe), Filipino (The Philippines, Asia), Yoruba (Nigeria, Africa) and Brazilian Portuguese (South America), while 26 per cent of these foreign language speakers were born in Ireland. Indeed, the authors note that the number of languages may even be greater than 182, because of the way the census questions were phrased (Carson et al. 2014: 6–8).

Yet this multilingualism in Ireland has not led to more translations of diverse languages or to agreement on what languages are to be translated. On the contrary, in health, education, policing and the courts a shortage of community interpreters is the norm, while translation is patchy and sporadic. (This contrasts with the situation in Northern Ireland.) It has been claimed that for court interpreting there is a reliance on translation agencies which do not check translators' experience or accreditation (O'Brien 2010). In the Republic of Ireland, a kind of US melting-pot model prevails, where everybody is expected to function through English and where the majority is made up of monolingual English speakers. It is important to distinguish between the 'multilingualism' of a society where languages coexist within a group and the 'plurilingualism' of the individual who can use more than one language (Observatoire européen du plurilinguisme 2014).

Ireland is both a monolingual and a multilingual society, with due respect being paid to the symbolic importance of bilingualism, and it is likely that it will become less multilingual with the passage of time. Since the Languages Act of 2003 most translation activity revolves around producing Irish texts for everyday use. At the same time the monolingual nature of the society means that English dominates, while very few translations from other languages are carried out. Monolingual cultures tend to be indifferent to translation, particularly when their language has become a global language, since, as Nicholas Ostler puts it in his study of lingua francas through the ages, a 'lingua franca culture' is a common language culture that does not translate (Ostler 2011: 150).

The tug between opposing cultural policies and economic realities evident in Ireland is writ large in the European Union. The economic policies of the Lisbon Treaty, which promoted economic mobility in the spheres of employment and education, and in its wake the use of English, sit uneasily alongside the Language and Multilingualism Policy of 2008 that aims to promote cultural diversity and cohesion (Wodak and Krzyżanowski 2011). Nevertheless, in cultural production in Ireland translation still plays a part, and for two reasons, as Michael Cronin points out. The languages of literature are more mixed up now because firstly 'the involvement of the Irish State with various aspects of bilingualism has meant that Irish Anglophones do not inhabit a wholly monoglot world' and secondly because of 'Ireland's incorporation into the turbomarket of the global English language' (Cronin 2011: 122–3). This means that Irish and Irish English are constantly being set against global English. Literary writing incorporates translation and plurilingualism into itself, somewhat in the manner of the 1930s experimental translation work of Beckett, MacGreevy, Coffey and Devlin.

15.9 Conclusion

In each of the four periods under study here, exemplary translations stand out by virtue of the manner in which they both reflect and shape the time during which they were produced: by defining the culture of the new nation; by challenging restrictive versions of this culture; by opening up to a wider Europe and the modern world; and by making translation an ordinary, everyday part of practical bilingualism. At the same time, we have seen a number of translations that are not particularly innovative or groundbreaking, particularly translations of drama. Conservative uses of translation and attitudes to other languages persist. To understand this we can point to Andrew Chesterman's concept of memes in translation theory, ideas about translation that spread, develop and replicate, like genes. 'Supermemes' can thus be very resilient, for example the idea that translators should remain invisible and that translation is an ancillary activity that need not be acknowledged (Chesterman 2000: 8–14). Yet standing out from this background of resilient ideas, each of the innovative examples studied here, such as the poetry and fiction translations of the 1930s, O'Connor's *Midnight Court*, Kinsella's *Táin* and TG4 subtitling, represents an experiment that tests a new relation between language and society.

References

Bellos, David (2011). *Is That a Fish in Your Ear. Translation and the Meaning of Everything*. London: Particular Books.

Bolger, Dermot (ed.) (1986). *An Tonn Gheal/The Bright Wave*. Dublin: Raven Arts.

Buttimer, Neil (2006). 'Literature in Irish, 1690–1800 from the Williamite wars to the Act of Union', in: Margaret Kelleher and Philip O'Leary (eds) *The Cambridge History of Irish Literature volume 1*. Cambridge: Cambridge University Press, pp. 320–71.

Calvet, Louis-Jean (1987). *La Guerre des langues et les politiques linguistiques*. Paris: Payot.

Carson, Ciarán (2005). *The Midnight Court. A New Translation of Cúirt an Mheán-Oíche by Brian Merriman*. Dublin: Gallery Press.

Carson, Ciarán (2007). *The Táin. Translated from the Old Irish Epic Táin Bó Cuailnge*. Harmondsworth: Penguin Books.

Carson, Lorna, Sarah McMonagle and Deirdre Murphy (2014). *Multilingualism in Dublin. LUCIDE City Report*. London: London School of Economics and Political Science.

Chesterman, Andrew (2000). *Memes of Translation. The Spread of Ideas in Translation Theory*. Amsterdam: John Benjamins.

Coimisinéir Teanga (2014). http://www.coimisineir.ie, accessed 18 October 2014.

Coolahan, John (1981). *Irish Education. Its History and Structure*. Dublin: Institute of Public Administration.

Council of Europe (2014). 'Irish' in 'Rules governing the languages in the institutions'. http://publications.europa.eu/code/en/en-370204.htm, accessed 23 October 2014.

Cronin, Michael (1996). *Translating Ireland. Translation, Languages, Cultures*. Cork: Cork University Press.

Cronin, Michael (2011). 'A dash of the foreign: the mixed emotions of difference', in: Kathleen Shields and Michael Clarke (eds) *Translating Emotion*. Oxford: Peter Lang, pp. 107–23.

De Brún, Sorcha (2007). '*Dracula* agus Seán Ó Cuirrín, cuid 1: ceisteanna cóirithe, téacsacha agus teanga' [*Dracula* and Seán Ó Cuirín, part 1: questions of arrangement, text and language], *Blianiris*: 166–203.

Ferguson, Charles A. (1959). 'Diglossia', *Word* 15: 325–40.

Ferriter, Diarmuid (2004). *The Transformation of Ireland 1900–2000*. London. Profile Books.

Fishman, Joshua A. (1967). 'Bilingualism with and without diglossia; diglossia with and without bilingualism', *Journal of Social Issues* 23.2: 29–38.

Friel, Brien (1992). *A Month in the Country. After Turgenev*. Oldcastle: Gallery Press.

Garvin, Tom (2004). *Preventing the Future. Why was Ireland so Poor for so Long?* Dublin: Gill and Macmillan.

Gregory, Augusta (1902). *Cuchulain of Muirthemne. The Story of the Men of the Red Branch of Ulster Arranged and put into English*. London: John Murray.

Gregory, Augusta (1910). *The Kiltartan Molière. The Miser. The Doctor in Spite of Himself. The Rogueries of Scapin* [translations of Molière]. Dublin: Maunsel.

Heaney, Seamus (1983). *Sweeney Astray. A Version from the Irish*. Derry: Field Day.

Heller, Monica (2003). 'Alternative ideologies of *la francophonie*', in: Roxy Harris and Ben Rampton (eds) *The Language, Ethnicity and Race Reader*. London: Routledge, pp. 225–42.

Ireland Literature Exchange (ILE) (2014). http://www.irelandliterature.com/, accessed 18 October 2014.

Jackson, Alvin (1999). *Ireland 1798–1998. Politics and War*. Oxford. Blackwell.

Jenkinson, Biddy (1991). 'A letter to an editor', *Irish University Review* 21: 27–34.

Kenny, Dorothy and Michael Cronin (1995). 'MA in translation studies at Dublin City University', *The Translator* 1: 241–60.

Keogh, Dermot (1994). *Twentieth-century Ireland. Nation and State*. Dublin. Gill and Macmillan.

Keogh, Michael (1999). 'The profile of a professional member', *Translation Ireland* 13.1: 8–9.

Kiberd, Declan (1979). 'Writers in quarantine? The case for Irish studies', *The Crane Bag* 3.1: 9–21.

Kilroy, Thomas (1993). *The Seagull*. Oldcastle: Gallery Press.

Kinsella, Thomas (1970). *The Táin*. Oxford: Oxford University Press [first published Dublin: Dolmen Press 1969].

Leerssen, Joep (1996). *Remembrance and Imagination. Patterns in the Historical and Literary Representation of Ireland in the Nineteenth Century*. Cork: Cork University Press.

Longford, Edward [Edward Pakenham 6th Earl of Longford] (1948). *The School for Wives* [translation of Molière]. Dublin: Hodges Figgis.

MacGreevy, Thomas (1991). *Collected Poems of Thomas MacGreevy*, Susan Schreibman (ed.). Dublin: Anna Livia.

Mag Shamhráin, Antain (1997). *Foilseacháin an Ghúim. Liosta de na Leabhair a d'Fhoilsigh an Gúm ó 1926 i Leith.* [The translations of the Gúm. A list of the books published by the Gúm since 1926.] Dublin: An Gúm.

Maume, Patrick (2009). 'Keane, Sir John' in: James McGuire and James Quinn (eds) *Dictionary of Irish Biography.* Cambridge: Royal Irish Academy and Cambridge University Press.

Meyer, Kuno (1911). *Selections from Ancient Irish Poetry.* London: Constable.

Ní Dhomhnaill, Nuala (1986). *Selected Poems/Rogha Dánta* [translated by Michael Hartnett]. Dublin: Raven Arts.

O'Brien, Carl (2010). 'Hundreds of court, Garda interpreters have no qualification', *Irish Times,* 7 June.

O'Brien, Conor Cruise (1975). 'An unhealthy intersection', *New Review* 2.16: 3–8.

O'Brien, George (2006). 'Contemporary prose in English: 1940–2000', in: Margaret Kelleher and Philip O'Leary (eds) *The Cambridge History of Irish Literature, Volume 2.* Cambridge: Cambridge University Press, pp. 421–77.

Observatoire européen du plurilinguisme (2014). http://www. observatoireplurilinguisme.eu/index.php?option=com_content&view= article&id=328&Itemid=89189047&lang=fr, accessed 18 October 2014.

Ó Buachalla, Séamas (1988). *Education Policy in Twentieth Century Ireland.* Dublin: Wolfhound Press.

Ó Catháin, Diarmaid (2009). 'O'Donovan (Ó Donnabháin), John (Seán)', in: James McGuire and James Quinn (eds) *Dictionary of Irish Biography.* Cambridge: Royal Irish Academy and Cambridge University Press.

O'Connell, Eithne (2007). 'TG4: 10 years on', *Estudios Irlandeses* available at http://www.estudiosirlandeses.org/reviews/tg4-10-years-on/, accessed 23 October 2014.

O'Connell, Frederick William [pseud. Conall Cearnach] (1929). *An Dr Jekyll agus Mr Hyde.* Dublin: Oifig an tSoláthair.

O'Connor, Frank (1945). *The Midnight Court. A Rhythmical Bacchanalia from the Irish of Bryan Merryman.* London: Maurice Fridberg.

O'Connor, Frank (1946). *Irish Times,* 'Letters to the Editor', 17 July.

Ó Cuinn, Cosslett (1987) [1982]. *The Midnight Court by Brian Merriman.* Dublin and Cork: Mercier Press [first published Cork: Mercier Press, 1982].

Ó Cuirrín, Seán (1933). *Dracula.* Dublin: An Gúm.

Ó Direáin, Máirtín (1984). *Tacar Dánta/Selected Poems* translated by Tomás Mac Síomóin and Douglas Sealy. Newbridge: Goldsmith Press.

Ó Drisceoil, Donal (2005). '"The best banned in the land": Censorship and Irish writing since 1950', *The Yearbook of English Studies* 35: 146–60.

Oeser, Hans-Christian (1996). 'Letter to the editor', *Translation Ireland* 10: 13.

Ó Foghludha, Risteard (1930). *Fiche gearrscéal.* [Twenty short stories.] Dublin: An Gúm.

Oireachtas Historical Debates (1942). http://historical-debates.oireachtas.ie/S/ 0027/S.0027.194212090003.html, accessed 25 September 2014.

O'Keeffe, J. G. (1913). *Buile Shuibhne.* London: Irish Texts Society.

Ó Murchú, Liam P. (2008). 'Aistriúchán/-áin Frank O'Connor de Chúirt An Mheonoíche le Brian Merriman' [The translation(s) of Brian Merriman's Midnight Court by Frank O'Connor], in: Charlie Dillon and Ríóna Ní Fhrighil (eds) *Aistriú Éireann.* [Translating Ireland.] Belfast: Cló Ollscoil na Banríona, pp. 131–45.

Ó Tuama, Seán (1989). 'Irish issue – Introduction', *Translation: the Journal of Literary Translation* 22: 3–7.

Ó Tuama, Seán, and Thomas Kinsella (1981). *An Duanaire 1600–1900: Poems of the Dispossessed*. Mountrath: Dolmen Press.

Ostler, Nicholas (2011). *The Last Lingua Franca. The Rise and Fall of World Languages*. Harmondsworth: Penguin.

Power, Patrick C. (1977) [1971]. *Cúirt an Mheán-Oíche/The Midnight Court* [translation of Merriman]. Dublin: Mercier Press.

Stephens, James (1918). *Reincarnations*. London: Macmillan.

TG4(a). TG4 viewing figures. 'Ofcom reports good viewing figures for TG4 in Northern Ireland', http://www.tg4.ie/en/corporate/news-releases/2013/010813.html, accessed 18 October 2014.

TG4(b). TG4 viewing figures in the Republic of Ireland. http://www.tg4.ie/, accessed 18 October 2014.

Tymoczko, Maria (1999). *Translation in a Postcolonial Context. Early Irish Literature in English Translation*. Manchester: St Jerome.

Tymoczko, Maria (2009). 'Censorship and self-censorship in translation: ethics and ideology, resistance and collusion', in: Eiléan Ní Chuilleanáin, Cormac Ó Cuilleanáin and David Parris (eds) *Translation and Censorship*. Dublin: Four Courts Press, pp. 24–45.

Venuti, Lawrence (1995). *The Translator's Invisibility. A History of Translation*. London: Routledge.

Wodak, Ruth and Michał Krzyżanowski (2011). 'Political strategies and language policies: the European Union Lisbon strategy and its implications for the EU's language and multilingualism policy', *Language Policy* 10.2: 115–36.

16
Sociolinguistic Information and Irish English Corpora

Elaine Vaughan and Brian Clancy

16.1 Introduction

The central part of this chapter presents the sort of sociolinguistic information that is retrievable from some corpora of Irish English (IrE) that currently exist. However, in order to fully explore and contextualise the research possibilities that corpora of IrE offer the sociolinguist, we probe the relationship – emergent, developing or with the potential to develop – between the core concerns of sociolinguistic research and contemporary corpus linguistics. Hence, the nature of language corpora and the fundamental aspects of the sort of analytical tools commonly used to mine them become relevant. An emergent consensus in most recent work on corpus linguistics and sociolinguistics (e.g. Friginal and Hardy 2014) is to take the view that as a methodological approach, corpus linguistics has much to offer sociolinguistics (and vice versa, though this is not as frequently discussed, see Kendall 2011). For the purpose of the present chapter, corpus linguistics is understood to be both an independent field of linguistic enquiry and a principled methodological approach to the analysis of linguistic data, one that is in the process of developing a strong, mutually beneficial research relationship with sociolinguistics, as evidenced in recent book-length treatments (e.g. Baker 2010, or Friginal and Hardy 2014). There are a number of reasons that this interdisciplinary relationship has developed, not least of which is the fact that corpus linguistics and sociolinguistics share what Baker (2010: 8–9) describes as 'fundamental tenets of best practice', *viz.*:

1. Both share a focus on naturally occurring language-in-use with context recognised as critical to the production and interpretation of language;

2. A quantitative orientation to data analysis is shared;
3. Both use sampling techniques to capture the range and complexity of language;
4. Both focus on variation across a wide range of linguistic features.

In other words, in essence, corpus linguistics and sociolinguistics overlap in their 'epistemology, focus and scope' (ibid: 9). One of the main concerns for sociolinguists in adopting a corpus-based methodology has been in relation to the type of sociolinguistic information currently available in corpora of different language varieties, a question which this chapter addresses in relation to IrE, but also the nature of what can be considered a corpus given that there is a long and strong tradition of gathering datasets of naturally occurring language-in-use – some large and some far smaller – for sociolinguistic research. This issue is considered below.

16.2   Corpora in corpus linguistics and sociolinguistics

Corpora (sing. *corpus*) are often described quite simply as databases of naturally occurring language, amenable to automated analysis; however, this is to understate what sorts of text collections are understood as corpora in the corpus linguistic sense. In early scholarly discussions of corpus linguistics as a distinct paradigm (in the Kuhnian sense) within linguistic analysis, a number of qualifying features of what a *corpus* might be began to emerge. These are described concisely by Flowerdew (2012: 3) and can be summarised as follows: a corpus

1. consists of authentic, machine-readable, naturally occurring language data;
2. is designed according to coherent, principled criteria;
3. is representative of a particular language or genre of language.

These criteria certainly limit the scope of which collections of texts might be described as corpora – and perhaps even exclude many datasets that sociolinguists may currently refer to as corpora. A consideration of what a corpus is or might be is therefore highly pertinent to any discussion of the relationship between corpus linguistics and sociolinguistics. If a corpus is defined loosely according to the criteria summarised by Flowerdew above, then it could be suggested that sociolinguists have been working with corpora, albeit 'unconventional' corpora for quite some time (cf. Beal et al. (eds) 2007 or D'Arcy 2011).[1] We have argued elsewhere (Vaughan and Clancy 2013) that size is not as important as research focus and design when it comes to corpus building, a position bolstered and inspired by McEnery et al.'s enlightened and practical approach to the question of size in corpus construction and the retrospective, or (re)consideration of 'collections of texts' as corpora:

> If specialised corpora which are built using a different sampling technique from those for balanced corpora were discounted as 'non-corpora', then corpus linguistics would have contributed considerably less to language studies. (McEnery et al. 2006: 2)

Add to this Baker's (2010) assertion of the common ground shared by both linguistic fields, and the overlap between corpus-based research and sociolinguistics has serious traction.

There are manifest advantages associated with the use of corpora in the study of sociolinguistics. Firstly, since the pioneering work of Labov (1972) who used a process of demographic sampling akin to that used in modern spoken corpora such as the British National Corpus to collect his data, sociolinguistics has needed access to spoken data. Corpora provide sociolinguists with access to spoken language that is naturally occurring, real-world and spontaneous. These elements of spontaneity and naturalness may seem to contrast with the sociolinguistic interview or other methods of data collection such as discourse completion tests; however, if we are flexible in relation to what we consider a 'corpus', and admit specialised, principled collections into the fold, this becomes less problematic. This sort of flexibility has challenged our conceptions of the nature of what is considered 'spoken' as well as what we might consider a corpus. In diachronic corpus studies, it has been argued that where there are no audio recordings available, we need to work with data that we can reasonably describe as representative of spoken language at a particular point in time. This orientation in blended research of many kinds has expanded the boundaries of both 'spoken-ness' and what can be considered corpora, or corpus-like. For example, Archer and Culpeper (2009: 288) refer to historical trial proceedings as 'speech-related data' and argue that these are as close to spoken language as we can get, for this time. Similarly, McCafferty and Amador-Moreno (2012) refer to personal letters as among the more 'oral' text types available for diachronic study, whereas Hickey (2003) centres the design of his corpus around drama – a written genre where the spoken word plays a central part. An important knock-on effect of the broadening of the sociolinguistic research paradigm, and, at least for some of it, a corollary broadening of what types of datasets and approaches might be available to analysts, has been a valuable discussion for both corpus linguists and sociolinguists regarding data and methods (e.g. Pichler 2010). The nature of corpus design criteria and the metadata preserved in corpus databases has much to offer sociolinguistic research questions, although with obvious caveats. As will be further explored below when we look at what corpora of IrE are available for sociolinguistic research, many corpora are annotated with sociolinguistic metadata. This includes information such as age, gender, level of education, ethnicity and so on, but some corpora also feature information such as the relationship between speakers, the level of formality and information about text, as well as context or genre type, and, as we will discuss, this allows researchers to compare language variation on a number of levels. However, this is not to say that the use of corpora (existing or specially designed) is unproblematic, or that corpora of naturally occurring spoken language particularly do not come with some caveats, as previously mentioned. One of the major issues in the use of corpora for any type of research, sociolinguistic or otherwise, is that the type of research that can be carried out is dependent on, and constrained by, the design and compilation of the corpus. Spoken corpora have tended to be transcribed orthographically – that is to say according to written language conventions primarily. This raises the issue of how, and in what ways, we represent the spoken language in written form, or what spoken language written down looks like, and how authentic it can be to the nature of spoken-ness (see, for example, Du Bois 1991). Hence, there are some problems associated with the marrying of corpus data and linguistic analysis more generally in relation to the nuanced representation of the spoken language (see Section 16.5). The corpus-based method, using an existing corpus or building something specialised, involves a certain degree of automated analysis, and a large degree of manual, post-hoc qualitative analysis. We will return to how automated analysis may inform close, qualitative analysis in Section 16.5, but before we move on, it is important to consider what information recorded as part of the compilation of a corpus might inform sociolinguistic research, and we do this by considering what kind of information might also qualify as a sociolinguistic variable.

16.3   The 'sociolinguistic variable'

A distinction between two orientations within sociolinguistic research, 'sociolinguistics' and 'the sociology of language' (e.g. Tagliamonte

2006), has often been suggested. The sociology of language deals with the relations between society and languages as wholes (Hudson 1996) and addresses sociopolitical aspects such as language maintenance and shift, language policy and planning and issues surrounding multilingualism. Sociolinguistics, on the other hand, is traditionally concerned with variation and change in language form and use – choice and selection of pronunciations, grammars or vocabularies according to categories such as male/female, socio-economic class or ethnicity, and so on. Although this distinction is somewhat contested (see Wardhaugh 2006: 13–17), corpus studies have, for the moment, allied themselves with the 'sociolinguistic' orientation. This orientation involves the study of the complex interaction between two primary variables – *linguistic* and *societal* (Friginal and Hardy 2014; Holmes 2001). Table 16.1 collates, adapts and expands a summary of possible linguistic and societal variables critical to sociolinguistic research identified by Friginal and Hardy (2014: 4–6).

As Table 16.1 illustrates, there are many societal variables that influence our choice of linguistic form and how we use it. Traditionally, sociolinguistic research has focused on sounds, words and grammatical

Table 16.1   Linguistic and societal variables investigated in sociolinguistics

Linguistic variables	Societal variables
Sounds, words and grammatical structures – Pronunciation, intonation, use of words and phrases	Social – Demographic information such as gender, age, sexuality, educational background, geographical information, class, income, etc.
Discoursal features – Overlap, latching, interruption, cohesive devices in writing, repair structures	Situational – Various communication contexts and registers – Speech community, social network theory, community of practice
Pragmatic features – Politeness, stance, taboo language, speech acts	Attitudinal and relational – Power, solidarity, roles and relationships, perceptions and attitudes
Communicative features – Pauses, response tokens, greeting and leave-taking	Temporal – Time periods, major historical events, migration patterns
Paralinguistic markers – Humour, silence, gesture, body language, emoticons	Other – Personality factors (introvert/extrovert)

structures (for example, whether or not we use the items *hood* or *bonnet* or how we pronounce /r/) and what this says about us as speakers or writers in terms of the factors already mentioned such as gender, social class or ethnicity. This traditional focus also encompasses the social significance of the relationship between the situational context and language choice. Factors such as the setting, topic and level of (in)formality are the primary focus here. It is within this traditional remit that we find the majority of corpus-based sociolinguistic studies. However, this traditional focus has broadened significantly and sociolinguists and, indeed, corpus sociolinguists are now concerned with a range of other factors.

16.4 Corpora of IrE available and suitable for sociolinguistic research

Table 16.2 describes a number of Irish English corpora that might be used for the purposes of sociolinguistic research, including information about their size, whether they are written or spoken, the time periods they represent, the metadata their databases contain, their availability to researchers and where to find further information about them. We have included the larger-scale corpora that have been compiled but have omitted many of the smaller-scale corpora that have been collected and used for IrE sociolinguistic research by individual researchers such as TravCorp[2] (Clancy 2011a, 2011b), other small corpora used in Filppula (1999) or those created by the Bonn project on variational pragmatics (e.g. Schneider 2005). We can see that the bigger corpora are indeed primarily written in nature. Written corpora are often larger than spoken corpora due to the financial and time demands involved in constructing a spoken corpus and also ethical and permission issues. The majority of corpora that are freely available to researchers are also written corpora. Although written texts arguably do not provide the same rich vein of social variables to be mined as spoken corpora do, as the majority contain only information about text type and date of publication, they do provide ample opportunity for the study of diachronic linguistic change in relation to Irish English. Indeed, McCafferty and Amador-Moreno (2012: 265) maintain that, despite a number of book-length treatments of IrE in recent years, 'there is a striking paucity of empirical research taking a long-term diachronic perspective'.

The spoken corpora such as the spoken component of ICE-Ireland, in contrast to the written corpora in Table 16.2, provide researchers with the largest amount of demographic variables. Indeed, modern spoken corpora are characterised by their attention to database information.

Table 16.2 Existing Irish English corpora

Corpus	Size*	Written or Spoken	Time period	Recorded metadata	Availability	Further information
New Corpus for Ireland (NCI)	c.30m Irish c.25m English	W	1880s–present day	Text-type; date of publication	On request	Foras na Gaeilge cconvery@ forasnagaeilge.ie
Corpus of Electronic Texts (CELT)	c.16.7m	W	1200s–present day	Text-type; date of publication	Yes	University College Cork http://www.ucc.ie/celt/
Parallel English-Irish corpus of legal texts	c.6.56m Irish c.6.45m English	W	1930s–present day	Text-type; date of publication	Yes	Fiontar (Dublin City University) http://www.gaois.ie/en/paradocs
Corpus of Irish English Correspondence (CORIECOR)	c.3m	W	c.1760s–early 1900s	Informant information; text-type; date of publication	Under construction	McCafferty and Amador-Moreno (2012)
A Corpus of Irish English	c.635,000	W	1330s–present day	Text-type; date of publication	Yes	Hickey (2003)

Table 16.2 (Continued)

Corpus	Size*	Written or Spoken	Time period	Recorded metadata	Availability	Further information
ICE Ireland and SPICE-Ireland	c.600,000 (S) c.400,000 (W)	S & W	1990–2005	Text-type; geographical information; gender; age; level of education; occupation; religion; first and other languages	Yes	Kallen and Kirk (2008) Kallen and Kirk (2012)
The Limerick Corpus of Irish English (LCIE)	c.1m	S	1998–2005	Context-type; goal-type; age; gender; geographical region; occupation; level of education	Restricted	Barker and O'Keeffe (1999)
The Northern Ireland Transcribed Corpus of Speech	c.300,000	S	1973–1980	Text-type; age; geographical region	On request	Kirk (1992)
A Corpus of Hiberno-English Speech	c.158,000	S	1970s–1980s	Text-type; age; gender; geographical region; level of education; occupation	No	Filppula (1999)
Dialects of English: Irish English	c.28,000**	S	2008	Age; gender; geographical region; religion; level of education	Yes	Corrigan (2010)

*All word counts, where necessary, have been generated using *WordSmith Tools 5.0* (Scott 2008).
**Approximate word count based on the 29 interview transcripts available on http://www.lel.ed.ac.uk/dialects/ni.html.

The two largest spoken corpora, LCIE and the Ireland component of the International Corpus of English (ICE-Ireland), contain 1 million words and 600,000 words of spoken IrE respectively. Both contain detailed demographic information such as age and gender and also information about where the speakers were born and where they lived at the time of recording (geographical information) and level of education. ICE-Ireland also details the religious background of the participants in the corpus, which is relevant as the corpus contains speech from both the Republic of Ireland and Northern Ireland. LCIE, on the other hand, was collected exclusively in the Republic. Also included as a spoken corpus in Table 16.2 is Corrigan's (2010) Northern Ireland contribution to the *Dialects of English* series (Edinburgh University Press). This series allows the systematic comparison of phonological features of different dialects. Although the word count appears small, this is solely based on available interview transcripts. The dedicated website also contains sound files of a reading passage task and a sentence task designed as a resource to allow the comparison of stylistic phonological variation – the interview representing the least formal speech style and the sentences the most formal (due to the greatest amount of attention being paid to the act of speaking). The recently released SPICE-Ireland (Kallen and Kirk 2012), in addition to being tagged pragmatically, is also prosodically tagged for intonation and word stress. As Table 16.2 shows, many of these corpora are freely available for potential sociolinguistic studies; there-fore, our attention now turns to how these might be usefully exploited for sociolinguistic gain through the use of a corpus-based method. We illustrate this through a consideration of the discourse/pragmatic item *shur* in IrE.

16.5   The corpus-based method: a sample and some observations

A consideration of the tools designed for use with corpora, and the type of quantification and analysis that they provide, is necessary in any dis-cussion of what a 'corpus-based' method might constitute. Corpora exist as electronic text files, and this means that they can be analysed via commercially and freely available concordancing software; we outline the automated analysis possible using concordancing software pack-ages such as *WordSmith Tools* (Scott 2008; commercially available) or *AntConc* (Anthony 2014; freely available) below, using a sample enquiry around a corpus-based analysis of the pragmatic marker *sure/shur(e)* in IrE. This is presented with two ends in mind. Firstly, it presents the tools themselves, and what automated processes can yield; secondly, it is possible to also highlight some caveats relating to how corpora might be harnessed for sociolinguistic enquiry as well as some limitations of corpora as they (to a large extent) currently exist. For this sample, we have selected *sure*, an example of what have been called *discourse* or *pragmatic markers* (or even *discourse-pragmatic markers*), rendered in the corpus we use as *shur(e)* to reflect a phonological reduction in the spoken mode related to function. This exemplar is fairly basic, but is really in the service of drawing out some points relating to how 'computerised corpora form a well-prepared basis for systematic, descriptive studies of instances of actual speech, for language variation and for how social context constrains communicative practices' (Andersen 2010: 548).

For the Limerick Corpus of Irish English (LCIE; described in Table 16.2 above), a decision was made at transcription stage to render the particular 'Irish English *sure*' as *shur(e)*. However, in practice, it was initially transcribed in three different ways, *sure, shure* and *shur*, due, in the main, to transcriber error. As a large-scale project in spoken language corpus terms, this is worth noting as it points to a couple of issues that researchers using corpora need to bear in mind – especially sociolinguists, for whom this sort of variation is the motivation and focus of research (Pichler 2010). Firstly, spoken language is hugely complex, and analysis can only proceed once the phenomenon (spoken language) has been captured in some way to allow for detailed observation. This presupposes a number of removes at which a spoken sample of language can be observed: we take a vibrant and mutable phenomenon, which exists only as sound waves (more often than not), and capture it according to written language conventions. It is thus 'represented', taken out of its original mode and context, though the transcriber attempts to be as faithful as possible to the original. Of course, the resultant 'static artefact' (Varenne 1992: 30) is not perfect; however, it is perhaps more pragmatic to operate sensibly within the boundaries of this imperfection than to ignore or overlook its potential.

16.5.1 Frequency

For the moment at least, and unless the researcher has access to the sources and resources to create the 'perfect corpus' (if such a thing exists), consulting existing corpora will mean that the analyst needs to be creative and thorough. For a discourse-level item like *sure/shur(e)*, this means anticipating the ways in which it might have been transcribed, and trawling a frequency list for those realisations. Frequency is one of the basic – and yet revealing and interesting – automatic processes available via corpus software. It represents 'entry-level' access to the corpus (cf. Baker 2006). For a corpus-driven approach, frequency of an item or items may justify further investigation. However, sociolinguistic insight could, and frequently does, identify a priori elements of language variation. A characteristic of word lists, the output view made possible by concordancing software, to point to a surfeit or dearth of an item in terms of frequency can be illuminating either way, we would argue. One characteristic of frequency lists is that they consist of mainly 'small', functional items, the interactional potential of which should not be underestimated (cf. Vaughan and Clancy 2013). The corpus-based approach has by and large been a comparative enterprise. Therefore, a frequency list is often all the more interesting when compared to, for example, a list from a different variety (taking the concept of variety as a broad one, at context level).

If we compare the raw frequencies for pragmatic marker *sure/shur(e)* in LCIE (1277 occurrences), with corresponding frequency of occurrence in SPICE-Ireland (194 occurrences) and then with the spoken component of the British National Corpus (BNC; 11 occurrences), it looks like there is a fairly solid quantitative basis to claim it as a pragmatic marker typical of Irish English, but, of course, all these corpora are different sizes: LCIE contains 1 million words; SPICE-Ireland, 600,000 words of spoken IrE, and the spoken component of the BNC, 10 million words.[3] In order to make frequency information for datasets comparable, *normalisation*, a basic but informative process, can be used. Normalised frequency (*nf*) can be achieved by using a simple calculation as demonstrated by Biber (1988). If we want to normalise per million words, for example, the calculation is as follows:

$$nf = \frac{\text{number of occurrences}}{\text{total number of words}} \times 1,000,000$$

When we normalise the frequencies for each corpus per million words, as in Table 16.3, we can see that *sure/shur(e)* is most frequent in LCIE.

Table 16.3 *Sure/shur(e)* in LCIE, SPICE-Ireland and the BNC normalised per million words

	LCIE	SPICE-Ireland	BNC
Raw frequency	1277	194	11
Normalised frequency	1277	310	1

Once a frequency list has been generated, another automatic procedure, the generation of keywords, can be harnessed. This creates the possibility for a different form of comparison, one that is based on *saliency*; in other words, what is most strikingly frequent or infrequent in relation to a comparative baseline, usually a frequency list from another corpus, or another component of the primary corpus being used. It is usual in corpus linguistic terms to ensure that this baseline corpus is a much larger corpus, comparatively, representative of the variety that is being investigated. The saliency measure is a cross-tabulation based on a statistical test (either chi-square or log-likelihood) to ascertain which items occur with unusually high or low frequency. Keywords are therefore not necessarily the most frequent words, but the most unusually frequent, or infrequent, words. This is a valuable measure in terms of sociolinguistic research, given that an item, or feature, of language may have been isolated for just that frequency or infrequency in a varietal context. The reference or comparison corpus used will obviously have an impact on what items or terms emerge as key.

Table 16.4 below shows the top ten keywords for LCIE when the spoken component of the BNC is used as a reference corpus (vocalisations such as *uh* and *hm* have been removed, as has extralinguistic information, such as laughter). In this view, *shure* is highlighted as a key.

16.5.2 Concordance

At this point, a third function, and one that involves a significant level of human intervention – especially if it is used as we suggest, in tandem with the metadata provided in the database for the corpus – is relevant.

Table 16.4 Top ten keywords in LCIE using BNC Spoken as reference corpus

	Keyword
1	like
2	**shure**
3	yeah
4	goin'
5	cause
6	tis
7	d'you
8	now
9	kind
10	grand

N	Concordance
1	<\$O8> the burgers over like . <$4> On his feet all day . <$1> **Shur** there's no way he'll be able for that like . <$E> speaker four
2	somewhere like . <$2> You've only thirty six cards MX . <$1> **Shur** I can't access it in U L where it is on the hard drive like .
3	<$1> Why? <$3> Look . Cos she looks at you sometimes . <$2> **Shur** half the dogs in Limerick are called Gizmo . <$4> That's the
4	first cousin . <$1> And he'll yeah he'll let you in with that accent . **Shur** didn't you get in no hassle the last time . <$3> Oh I did
5	there . So I mean that why I don't have it done . <$3> Yeah but **shur** you're not going to do anything like . <$1> I know but I still
6	I away <\$X> . Go <$X> way I away <\$X> from it . <$2> But **shur** or he could be working at the weekend you see . <$1> No
7	so young she wouldn't notice it . <$3> She wouldn't have a clue **shur.** <$4> We could've changed it . <$4> We could call her am
8	and what was the third one? <$3> Every second word is fuck **shur.** <$1> Yeah I watched a bit of it . <$3> There's fuck this
9	<$2> She's going to the Stable's drinking . <$1> Yeah I know **shur** I don't know why but she's after telling me ten times where
10	they made a lovely taglietelli vegetable thing . <$1> So FX told me **shur** FX is goin to make it some day . <$3> But I never took it
11	<$2> Definitely . <$1> Are you gutted about it? <$2> Big time . **Shur** wouldn't you be? <$1> Yeah . Why don't you go? <$2>
12	MX? <$2> No . <$3> No MX would be the wrong area all together **shur.** <$6> Did you meet the boss man? <$3> MX is just
13	. <$1> We're supposed to be makin the film this weekend **shur.** I wouldn't say that's goin to happen either now . <$3> Go
14	see if <$X> they're I they are <\$X> working . <$4> Yeah <$X> **shur** I sure <\$X> <$X> we'll I we will <\$X> plug them in there .
15	. <$3> She asked me did it mean they changed colour . <$X> **Shur** I sure <\$X> I didn't have a clue . <$4> You play with the

Figure 16.1   Sample of concordance lines for *shur* in LCIE (sorted one item to the left)

The concordance line view involves pre-selecting the item/s for analysis. The software searches the corpus and generates concordance lines that contain the item/s, the *node*, and the five or six words that occur immediately left and right of it. Figure 16.1 below shows 15 concordance lines for the *shur* rendering in LCIE.

By examining these concordance lines, we can formulate initial hypotheses using patterning of *shur* as our starting point. Looking at Figure 16.1, one feature of note is that a speaker tag such as <$1>, <$2>, etc. frequently occurs either as the first item to the left of *shur* (for example, line 1) or as the second item, for example before *but* is line 6, *yeah* in line 14 or *yeah but* in line 5. This may indicate that *shur* is often positioned as a turn initial item. Similarly, although to a lesser extent, a speaker tag occurs immediately to the right of *shur* in lines 7, 8, 12 and 13 indicating that it may also have a less frequent position as a turn final item. Previous research has shown that these positions are associated with particular discourse and pragmatic functions. Initial position is often commonly associated with discourse marking, whereas final position is associated with attention to face (Clancy and Vaughan 2012). Corpus software also makes it possible to interact with the complete original text file, as well as with the metadata. If we take the concordance line, *Shur wouldn't you be?* (line 11), it is possible to return to the original text and use the information from the original to see who is speaking. Extract 1 shows the original stretch of discourse in which *shur* is used.

Extract 1　<$1>　Is Nessa going to America she is?
　　　　　<$2>　Definitely.
　　　　　<$1>　Are you gutted about it?
　　　　　<$2>　Big time. Shur wouldn't you be?
　　　　　<$1>　Yeah. Why don't you go?
　　　　　<$2>　<$E> sniffs <\$E> Cos I can't get my J one. I'll be
　　　　　　　　over for holidays. That's my America fund there.
　　　　　<$1>　Mm hm.

A code is given to each file in LCIE, so that the database file contains all of the metadata. Therefore, it is possible to find out who is using the item, in this case, *shur*, the date the recording was made, the gender of the speaker, their occupation and level of education. Table 16.5 shows the sort of metadata preserved with the original recordings for LCIE.

Knowing that it is Speaker 2 (<$2>) who uses the item *shur* in Extract 1 means that it is possible to retrieve information about that situation and that speaker: the speaker was 20 years old in 2002 when the recording was made, male and a student (born and living in Cork). There is therefore the potential to create a highly contextualised, socially based picture of the use of *shur*. Comparing corpora designed according to the same criteria has meant that national varieties can be compared, and there is clearly great scope for this sort of comparative work, using available tools and metadata. We turn now to some relevant studies which have emerged from this tradition, and highlight some that harness corpora imaginatively and thoroughly, yielding great insight into situated linguistic phenomena.

16.6　Sociolinguistic case studies of Irish English using corpora

Thus far we have discussed the reciprocal benefits of the blend of corpus linguistics and sociolinguistics and illustrated, through a brief analysis of a pragmatic marker unique to Irish English *sure/shur(e)*, the potential of the automated processes the software makes available. We have also described in Table 16.2 the various corpora of Irish English that have been created and that can be used for the purposes of sociolinguistic research. Our attention now turns to these corpora and how they have been used to create an emerging sociolinguistic profile of IrE from both a synchronic and diachronic perspective. Interestingly, for the discussion of the blend of corpus linguistics and sociolinguistics, some of these corpora, for example, LCIE, were not created for an express

Table 16.5 Sample of metadata preserved in the LCIE database

Title	Rec_Year	Relationship	S1_age	S2_age	S1_BPlace	S2_BPlace	S1_Occupation	S2_Occupation
Family chatting in the kitchen	1998	intimate	48	23	Limerick	Limerick	Primary school teacher	Postgraduate student
Putting up the Christmas tree	1998	intimate	50	14	Limerick	Limerick	Steeplejack	Second level student
Decorating the house for Christmas	1998	intimate	23	14	Limerick	Limerick	Third level student	Second level student
Family chatting about the day	1999	intimate	19	24	Limerick	Limerick	Third level student	Third level student
Family and close friends chatting	2003	intimate						
Chatting in the car*	2001	intimate	20	20	Wexford	Wexford	Student	Tele-sales operator
Chatting in mobile home	2001	intimate	27	2.5	Manchester	Waterford	Secretary	Child
Arriving somewhere	2001	intimate	22	50	Cork	Cork	Student	Housewife
Morning after a night out	2001	intimate	22	50	Cork	Cork	Student	Housewife
Friends/Family chatting	2001	intimate	50	50	Cork	Cork	Housewife	Solicitor
Friends in the car chatting	2001	intimate	22	18	Cork	Student	Student	
Friends out walking	2001	intimate	22	18	Cork	Cork	Student	Student
Informal interview	1998	socio-cultural	23	17	Kildare	Killarney	Third level student	Second level student
Informal interview	1998	socio-cultural	23	17	Kildare	Limerick	Third level student	Second level student
Informal interview	1998	socio-cultural	23	17	Kildare	Bandon	Third level student	Second level student
Informal interview	1998	intimate	23	18	Kildare	Ennis	Third level student	Third level student
Informal interview	1998	socio-cultural	23	17	Kildare	Nenagh	Third level student	Second level student

sociolinguistic purpose, whereas others, for example, CORIECOR, were created specifically to examine sociolinguistic variation using corpus techniques. There are a number of studies that have highlighted the salience of the pragmatic marker *like* in Irish English in general, both in spoken and written language. Although *like* is by no means unique to IrE (see, for example, Andersen 2001; Tagliamonte 2005; D'Arcy 2007; Miller 2009), the marker (in addition to others such as *you know* and *now*) has emerged from corpus-based studies as a prominent item in the socio-pragmatic system of Irish English (see, for example, O'Keeffe et al. 2011; Vaughan and Clancy 2011). This is despite the fact that, as Amador-Moreno (2010) maintains, *like* can be considered a relatively new development in IrE. Kallen (2006) demonstrates how clause- or sentence-final *like* is more frequent in ICE-Ireland than in ICE-Great Britain. Schweinberger (2012) also uses the ICE suite of corpora and found a striking difference in frequency of *like* between IrE and South-Eastern British English in his data. He demonstrates how speakers of IrE prefer clause-final position *like*, primarily associated with mitigation, while British English speakers predominantly employ the marker in clause-medial position. These differences are attributed to the social meaning and covert prestige attached to the marker, pointing to the reluctance of middle-aged or older speakers of British English to adopt a feature stigmatised as being 'American'. In relation to the intimate context-type in LCIE, Clancy (2005, 2011a, 2011b) has shown that *like* is one of the most frequent hedging items in Irish family discourse. Clancy (2011a and b) has also built a corpus of family discourse from within the Irish Traveller community, a distinct ethnic group in Irish society, in order to demonstrate how factors such as ethnicity, age and level of education play a role in people's use of pragmatic markers. He found that pragmatic markers were more frequent in the discourse of settled, middle-class families than in Traveller families, where it is a relatively rare feature of their discourse. Factors such as ethnicity – the Traveller community prioritise family to such an extent that their social networks consist almost entirely of extended family – and level of education – two-thirds of all Travellers in Ireland are educated to, at most, primary level – play a large part in this discrepancy.

In addition to *sure/shur(e)* and *like*, *now* has also emerged from corpus-based studies as a key item in Irish English. Clancy and Vaughan (2012) have shown that *now* is more frequent in the spoken Irish English represented in LCIE than in other spoken corpora such as the British National Corpus (BNC),[4] the Corpus of Contemporary American English (COCA)[5] or the Scottish Corpus of Texts and Speech (SCOTS).[6] They, in part, attribute this frequency difference to the nature of the different corpus designs. For example, in terms of situational variables, the spoken component of the BNC contains spoken language from more formal settings such as debates, interviews or commentaries than is contained in LCIE. However, previous studies on *now* have maintained that it is more frequent in these formal speech contexts (see Aijmer 2002; Defour 2008) than in informal ones such as intimate discourse. Clancy and Vaughan's (2012) frequency results appear to contradict the previous literature concerning *now*, given that the data contained in LCIE is composed primarily of the intimate and socialising context-types, both of which can be classified as 'informal'. It has been shown that *now* is highly polysemous, functioning as a temporal adverb, a discourse marker or an intensifier, for example. Clancy and Vaughan (ibid.) maintain that it is the socio-pragmatic function of *now* that is pivotal in understanding the behaviour of the marker. This pragmatic function is markedly more frequent in informal Irish English than the sample of British English they compare it with (the spoken component of the BNC). In IrE, *now* functions in final position in the utterance to soften or mitigate face-threatening behaviour such as disagreement, challenge or evaluation, a function that is almost absent in the BNC data. This investigation of *now* in Irish English also highlighted an additional function of *now* as a deictic presentative. The most commonly recognised deictic presentatives such as the French *voici/voilà* or the Russian *vot/von* are examples of a linguistic item whose use is commonly accompanied by a gesture such as the presentation of food or drink (cf. Fillmore 1975: 41; Grenoble and Riley 1996). These addition functions performed by *now* in Irish English are essential to our understanding of sociolinguistic competence in the variety.

LCIE has also been used to explore variation in communicative features of language such as response tokens. O'Keeffe and Adolphs (2008) examined the occurrence of response tokens, verbal and non-verbal response to a speaker that indicate listenership without changing the speaker turn, for example, *yeah*, *right*, *no* or a simple head nod, in two corpora – the Cambridge and Nottingham Corpus of Discourse in English (CANCODE) and the LCIE. On an inter-varietal level, they found that in the British English data, response tokens were both more frequent and were comprised of a wider range of forms, but that the Irish English data demonstrated a greater degree of informality of use. These differences can be attributed to cultural idiosyncrasies across the two national varieties. The tokens *yes* and *quite,* which can be considered as formal options for responding to something that has been said, occur in

CANCODE but have no corresponding occurrence in the Irish English data. In contrast, Irish speakers favour a wider range of 'taboo' religious responses: in addition to *oh God* used in both datasets, Irish speakers also frequently use *Jesus* or *Jesus Christ*. O'Keeffe and Adolphs attribute the higher frequency of religious references to, paradoxically, the washing out of their previous force, but also see it as a mark of the continuing importance of religion in Irish society. An analysis of response token function was then carried out using two sub-corpora that were controlled for the social demographic variables of gender, age and socioeconomic class. They found that in the informal speech of co-habiting, middle-class, female speakers in their twenties, that there was no real variation at the level of response tokens' pragmatic function. This raises a number of interesting sociolinguistic questions regarding variation at the level of discoursal features between the two varieties – for example, do Irish people, because they use fewer response tokens, yield the turn less and interrupt more than British people?

In terms of diachronic variation in IrE, McCafferty and Amador-Moreno (2012) argue for an empirical diachronic approach to the study of IrE in the eighteenth and nineteenth centuries, a period when 'Irish English itself evolved and Anglophone settlement of North America and the southern hemisphere led to the development of American, Canadian, Australian, New Zealand, and other colonial Englishes' (p. 282). In Late Modern English, the progressive increased in frequency and acquired new uses, and diachronic corpora such as CORIECOR allow us to investigate the extent to which the spread of IrE contributed to this grammatical variation and change. In a pilot study using CORIECOR, McCafferty and Amador-Moreno (ibid.) found that in the late eighteenth century, the progressive became much more frequent in IrE and by 1840 it was four times more frequent than in 1770. At this time, it is also more frequent in the CORIECOR data than in matched British English data. They posit a number of sociophilological reasons as to why this might be the case. Firstly, the possessive may have grown in frequency in Late Modern English due to a corresponding growth in Irish emigration to other English-speaking countries such as the United States. Also, the rise in the use of the progressive at the time might be due to the rise in literacy levels of the lower classes. The rise of literacy levels in Ireland occurred at the same time as the decline in the use of the Irish language and the acquisition of English. This increase in literacy could have led to a colloquialisation of the language as 'more of the linguistic usage of lower social strata will be recorded in texts produced by members of those strata' (p. 280). This increase in literacy levels, they argue, could also be responsible for the shift from first person *shall* to *will* that occurred around the same time period (McCafferty and Amador-Moreno 2014). Interestingly, one of the quintessential features of the progressive in Irish English, the *after*-perfect, was found to be infrequent in the time period represented by CORIECOR.

The use of this quintessentially Irish English progressive in modern-day Irish English was the focus of O'Keeffe and Amador-Moreno's (2009) study of instances of the grammatical structure *be + after +* Verb-*ing* in LCIE. This progressive structure, an Irish language calque, is used to approximately convey the Standard English perfect aspect. Ninety-five occurrences of the structure were found in the 1-million-word LCIE and their functions classified. In relation to function, they maintain that this structure has a range of pragmatically specialised meanings in Irish English that cannot be replicated by any standard equivalent form. For example, in the context of narrative, they argue that this progressive acts as a 'metalinguistic trigger... heralding the main event of the storyline' (p. 529). In order to further investigate the structure's sociolinguistic profile, age and gender were taken into consideration. It was found that of the 95 occurrences, 73 per cent were used by females. In addition, this use of the progressive is particularly robust in the 18–25-year-old age category. O'Keeffe and Amador-Moreno argue that this marks the structure as core to the grammar of modern Irish English.

16.7 Concluding remarks

Where once the analysis of language varieties using language text corpora occupied a relatively obscure, niche position in comparison to other linguistic traditions more generally, it can be argued that it has come to prominence in the study of Irish English as a variety within the last decade at least. Much credit goes in particular to the contributions made by Kirk and Kallen and the ICE-Ireland project (see, for example, Kallen 2005 and 2006; Kallen and Kirk 2007), as well as the more-or-less contemporaneous Limerick corpus project (Barker and O'Keeffe 1999), as well as to the work of Hickey (2003). The increasing ease of recording and transcribing spoken language data (relatively speaking) has meant that in recent years, corpora and corpus methodologies are becoming more and more widely referenced. It could be argued that significant questions remain in respect of whether or not corpora are consulted in genuinely informed ways, and to what extent we can say that available corpora are equal to the tasks currently being asked of them. At the very least, it is possible to be open-minded and creative with existing resources, bearing in mind what they can and cannot tell us, or what they might provide partial or supporting evidence of. The possibilities of corpora and corpus linguistic methodologies for access to large quantities of authentic data, and swift, automatic analyses that would be not only laborious but potentially inaccurate if attempted manually, are the most often cited. However, it is arguably the emergent trend to blend corpus methodologies and other analytical and theoretical frameworks where the real value resides, though the potential is, as yet, not fully developed. As we have pointed out, it is only in recent years that book-length treatments of the beneficial relationship between corpus linguistics and sociolinguistics such as Baker (2010) and Friginal and Hardy (2014) have emerged. This situation is by no means unique – the blend of corpus linguistics and pragmatics has similarly come to the fore in recent years through the work of Romero Trillo (2008) and Aijmer and Rühlemann (eds) (2015).

There is still much work to be done in order that corpus linguistics be of further benefit to sociolinguistics (and, indeed, vice versa). The recent announcement of a new, publicly available 'Spoken British National Corpus 2014' is to be welcomed as it gives sociolinguists access to a contemporary demographically balanced corpus that will allow comparison with many of the formative spoken corpora that were primarily designed and constructed in the early to mid-1990s. This new BNC is being recorded on MP3 sound files which should address one of the main criticisms of spoken corpora levelled at them by sociolinguists – that access to good quality sound recordings is largely restricted or unavailable. In addition, advances in the design and construction of multi-modal corpora coupled with modern technology such as voice recognition software and digital recording, both audio and visual, should result in a corpus that allows sociolinguists to access sound, orthographic transcription and visual images simultaneously. The potential of these new corpora might also encourage a corresponding shift away from the dialectologically informed traditional focus on corpus-based sociolinguistic research, toward the outliers such as paralinguistic variation. In the Irish context, as we have shown, the larger spoken corpora of Irish English were finished in and around 2005; therefore, the time is ripe for an ICE-Ireland 2.0 or an LCIE 2.0 or indeed, a larger-scale corpus that is representative of both spoken IrE and Irish, and designed in a way that makes it both available to and suitable for not only researchers interested in sociolinguistics, but to those from a range of different linguistic and non-linguistic traditions.

Notes

1. Corpora are often written about just these sorts of binary terms: 'conventional' versus 'unconventional'; 'large' ('conventional') versus 'small' ('unconventional'), 'written' ('conventional') versus 'spoken' ('unconventional'). The reality is considerably more complex; perhaps a good translation of 'unconventional' here might simply be 'specialised'
2. This is a corpus of the speech of Irish Travellers which is currently being compiled by Brian Clancy at Mary Immaculate College, University of Limerick.
3. These counts refer to the use of *sure/shur(e)* as a pragmatic marker (***Shur** he never goes there*), and not as an adjective (*I'm **sure** I left it here*).
4. The spoken component of the BNC (10 million words) consists of demographically sampled texts complemented by texts collected by context-governed criteria (see www.natcorp.ox.ac.uk).
5. The spoken component of COCA contains over 90 million words of unscripted conversation from more than 150 television and radio programmes (see corpus.byu.edu/coca/).
6. The spoken component of the SCOTS corpus contains approximately 800,000 words of Scots and Scots English collected from a range of geographical locations featuring speakers of different genders, ages, occupations etc. (see www.scottishcorpus.ac.uk).

References

Aijmer, Karin (2002). *English Discourse Particles*. Amsterdam: John Benjamins.

Aijmer, Karin and Christoph Rühlemann (eds) (2015). *Corpus Pragmatics: a Handbook*. Cambridge: Cambridge University Press.

Amador-Moreno, Carolina P. (2010). *An Introduction to Irish English*. London: Equinox.

Andersen, Gisle (2001). *Pragmatic Markers and Sociolinguistic Variation: a Relevance-Theoretic Approach to the Language of Adolescents*. Amsterdam: John Benjamins.

Andersen, Gisle (2010). 'How to use corpus linguistics in sociolinguistics', in: Anne O'Keeffe and Michael McCarthy (eds) *The Routledge Handbook of Corpus Linguistics*. London: Routledge, pp. 547–62.

Anthony, Lawrence (2014). *AntConc Version 3.4.3*. Available online at: http://www.laurenceanthony.net/antconc_index.html (accessed 6 December 2014).

Archer, Dawn and Jonathan Culpeper (2009). 'Identifying key sociophilological usage in plays and trial proceedings (1640–1760): an empirical approach via corpus annotation', *Journal of Historical Pragmatics*, 10.2: 286–309.

Baker, Paul (2006). *Using Corpora in Discourse Analysis*. London: Continuum.

Baker, Paul (2010). *Sociolinguistics and Corpus Linguistics*. Edinburgh: Edinburgh University Press.

Barker, Gosia and Anne O'Keeffe (1999). 'A corpus of Irish English – past, present, future', *Teanga* (Yearbook of the Irish Association for Applied Linguistics), 18: 1–11.

Beal, Joan C., Karen P. Corrigan and Hermann L. Moisl (eds) (2007). *Creating and Digitizing Language Corpora, V.2: Diachronic Databases*. Basingstoke: Palgrave Macmillan.

Biber, Douglas (1988). *Variation across Speech and Writing*. Cambridge: Cambridge University Press.

Clancy, Brian (2005). '"You're fat. You'll eat them all."' Politeness strategies in family discourse', in: Anne Barron and Klaus Schneider (eds) *The Pragmatics of Irish English*. Berlin: de Gruyter Mouton, pp. 177–97.

Clancy, Brian (2011a). 'Complementary perspectives on hedging behaviour in family discourse: the analytical synergy of corpus linguistics and variational pragmatics', *International Journal of Corpus Linguistics* 163: 372–91.

Clancy, Brian (2011b). '*Do you want to do it yourself like?* Hedging in Irish Traveller and settled family discourse', in: Bethan Davies, Michael Haugh and Andrew Merrison (eds) *Situated Politeness*. London: Continuum, pp. 129–46.

Clancy, Brian and Elaine Vaughan (2012). '*It's lunacy now*: a corpus-based pragmatic analysis of the use of *now* in contemporary Irish English', in: Bettina Migge and Máire Ní Chiosáin (eds) *New Perspectives on Irish English*. Amsterdam: John Benjamins, pp. 225–46.

Corrigan, Karen P. (2010). *Irish English, volume 1 – Northern Ireland*. Edinburgh: Edinburgh University Press.

D'Arcy, Alexandra (2007). '*Like* and language ideology: disentangling the fact from fiction', *American Speech* 82: 386–419.

D'Arcy, Alexandra (2011). 'Corpora: Capturing language in use', in: Warren Maguire and April McMahon (eds) *Analysing Variation in English*. Cambridge: Cambridge University Press, pp. 49–71.

Defour, Tyne (2008). 'The speaker's voice: a diachronic study on the use of *well* and *now* as pragmatic markers', *English Text Construction* 1.1: 62–82.

DuBois, John W. (1991). 'Transcription design principles for spoken discourse research', *Pragmatics* 1.1: 71–106.

Filppula, Markku (1999). *The Grammar of Irish English: Language in Hibernian Style*. London: Routledge.

Fillmore, Charles (1975). *Santa Cruz Lectures on Deixis*. Bloomington, IN: Indiana University Linguistics Club.

Flowerdew, Lynne (2012). *Corpora and Language Education*. London: Palgrave Macmillan.

Friginal, Eric and Jack A. Hardy (2014). *Corpus-Based Sociolinguistics: a Guide for Students*. London: Routledge.

Grenoble, Lenore A. and Matthew Riley (1996). 'The role of deictics in discourse coherence: French *voici/voilà* and Russian *vot/von*', *Journal of Pragmatics* 25.6: 819–38.

Hickey, Raymond (2003). *Corpus Presenter. Software for Language Analysis*. Amsterdam: John Benjamins.

Holmes, Janet (2001). *An Introduction to Sociolinguistics*. London: Longman.

Hudson, Richard A. (1996). *Sociolinguistics*. Cambridge: Cambridge University Press.

Kallen, Jeffrey L. (2005). 'Politeness in Ireland: "In Ireland, it's done without being said"', in: Leo Hickey and Miranda Stewart (eds) *Politeness in Europe*. Clevedon: Multilingual Matters, pp. 130–44.

Kallen, Jeffrey L. (2006). '*Arrah, like, you know*: the dynamics of discourse marking in ICE-Ireland.' Plenary paper presented at Sociolinguistics Symposium, July, Limerick. Available online: http://www.tara.tcd.ie/bitstream/handle/

2262/50586/Arrah%20like%20y%27know.pdf?sequence=1 (accessed 2 December 2014).

Kallen, Jeffrey L. and John M. Kirk (2007). 'ICE-Ireland: Local variations on global standards', in: Joan C. Beal, Karen P. Corrigan and Hermann Moisl (eds) *Creating and Digitizing Language Corpora*, Vol. 1: Synchronic Databases. London: Palgrave, pp. 121–62.

Kallen Jeffrey L. and John M. Kirk (2008). *ICE-Ireland: a User's Guide*. Belfast: Cló Ollscoil na Banríona.

Kallen, Jeffrey L. and John M. Kirk (2012). *SPICE-Ireland: a User's Guide*. Belfast: Cló Ollscoil na Banríona.

Kendall, Tyler (2011). 'Corpora from a sociolinguistic perspective', *Revista Brasileira de Linguística* 11.2: 361–89.

Kirk, John M. (1992). 'The Northern Ireland Transcribed Corpus of Speech', in: Gerhard Leitner (ed.) *New Directions in English Language Corpora*. Berlin: Mouton de Gruyter, pp. 65–73.

Labov, William (1972). *Langauge in the Inner City: Studies in the Black English Vernacular*. Philadelphia: University of Pennsylvania Press.

McCafferty, Kevin and Carolina P. Amador-Moreno (2012). 'A corpus of Irish English correspondence: a tool for studying the history and evolution of Irish English', in: Bettina Migge and Máire Ní Chiosáin (eds) *New Perspectives on Irish English*. Amsterdam: John Benjamins, pp. 265–87.

McCafferty, Kevin and Carolina P. Amador-Moreno (2014). '"[The Irish] find much difficulty in these auxiliaries [...] putting *will* for *shall* with the first person": the decline of first-person *shall* in Ireland, 1760–1890', *English Language and Linguistics* 18: 407–29.

McEnery, Tony, Richard Xiao and Yukio Tono (2006). *Corpus-Based Language Studies: an Advanced Resource Book*. London: Routledge.

Miller, Jim (2009). 'Like and other discourse markers', in Pam Peters, Peter Collins and Adam Smith (eds) *Comparative Studies in Australian and New Zealand English: Grammar and Beyond*. Amsterdam: John Benjamins, pp. 317–38.

O'Keeffe, Anne and Svenja Adolphs (2008). 'Response tokens in British and Irish discourse: Corpus, context and variational pragmatics', in: Klaus Schneider and Anne Barron (eds) *Variational Pragmatics: a Focus on Regional Varieties in Pluricentric Languages*. Amsterdam: John Benjamins, pp. 69–98.

O'Keeffe, Anne and Carolina P. Amador-Moreno (2009). 'The pragmatics of the *be + after +* Verb-*ing* construction in Irish English', *Intercultural Pragmatics* 6.4: 517–34.

O'Keeffe, Anne, Brian Clancy and Svenja Adolphs (2011). *Introducing Pragmatics in Use*. London: Routledge.

Pichler, Heike (2010). 'Methods in discourse variation analysis: Reflections on the way forward', *Journal of Sociolinguistics* 14.5: 581–608.

Romero-Trillo, Jesús (ed.) (2008). *Corpus Linguistics and Pragmatics: a Mutualistic Entente*. Berlin: Walter de Gruyter.

Schneider, Klaus (2005). '*No problem, you're welcome, anytime*: Responding to thanks in Ireland, England and the USA', in: Anne Barron and Klaus Schneider (eds) *The Pragmatics of Irish English*. Berlin: de Gruyter Mouton, pp. 101–40.

Schweinberger, Martin (2012). 'The discourse marker LIKE in Irish English', in: Bettina Migge and Máire Ní Chiosáin (eds) *New Perspectives on Irish English*. Amsterdam: John Benjamins, pp. 179–202.

Scott, Michael (2008). *WordSmith Tools Version 5.0.* Liverpool: Lexical Analysis Software Ltd.

Tagliamonte, Sali A. (2005). '*So* who? *Like* how? *Just* what? Discourse markers in the conversation of young Canadians', *Journal of Pragmatics* 37.11: 1896–1915.

Tagliamonte, Sali A. (2006). *Analysing Sociolinguistic Variation.* Cambridge: Cambridge University Press.

Varenne, Hervé (1992). *Ambiguous Harmony: Family Talk in America.* Norwood, NJ: Ablex.

Vaughan, Elaine and Brian Clancy (2011). 'The pragmatics of Irish English', *English Today* 27.2: 49–54.

Vaughan, Elaine and Brian Clancy (2013). 'Small corpora and pragmatics', *The Yearbook of Corpus Linguistics and Pragmatics* 1: 53–73.

Wardhaugh, Ronald (2006). *An Introduction to Sociolinguistics.* Oxford: Blackwell.

Timelines

1 Language

Irish

5–6c	Primitive Irish: Remains of the language available in Ogam inscriptions (standing stones with personal names etched on the edge in a particular script). This is the period of Christianisation in Ireland (in 432 by St Patrick according to tradition). The early Celtic Christian church is particularly strong in Ireland and Scotland.
7c	Early Old Irish: Sources older than the main body of glosses.
8–9c	Classical Old Irish: Documented in glosses to religious works found in monasteries in continental countries like Germany, Switzerland and Italy.
10c–	Middle Irish: Available in legal texts, sagas as well as in works of literature contained in famous manuscript collections. Viking settlements are established in Ireland.
800–	Old Norse taken by Vikings to Ireland; loanwords appear later in Irish.
1169	Coming of the Normans (military conquest). Introduction of Norman French to Ireland; English speakers come in the retinue of the Norman lords.

Irish

13c–	Early Modern Irish: an increasingly fossilised form of language is found in praise poetry and emulations of older literary styles.
17c–	Modern Irish: Dialectal divisions become obvious (North, West, South). Appearance of regional differences in writing. Separation of Scottish Gaelic and Manx is complete.
1601	Irish and Spanish forces are defeated at Kinsale, Co. Cork. During the seventeenth century a vigorous policy of plantation is pursued, chiefly by Cromwell in the late 1640s and early 1650s. This leads to a concentration of Irish speakers in the poorer regions of the west of the country. Speakers from Ulster are also settled in north-west Connaught.
late 16c–17c	Irish clergy working on the continent, especially in Louvain, publish grammars and early dictionaries, e.g. the *Rudimenta Grammaticae Hibernicae* by Giolla Brighde Ó hEodhasa [O'Hussey] (c.1575–1614).
early 19c	Rapid decline of the Irish language sets in despite Catholic Emancipation in 1829.
1845–8	Potato famine occurs, affecting the poorer, mostly Irish-speaking areas.
late 19c	Decline is furthered by mass emigration. About 1 million speakers die and a further million emigrate in the ensuing exodus from the countryside.
1845	John Donovan *Grammar of Irish*, the first modern description of the language, appears.

English

12c	With the Anglo-Normans, varieties of English are established chiefly in the towns of the east coast, including Dublin.
early 14c	*Kildare Poems* A set of 16 poems, probably composed somewhere on the east coast of Ireland, between Dublin and Waterford.
1366	Statutes of Kilkenny A group of laws which, among many other things, proscribed the use of Irish by the Anglo-Normans and insisted that they use English. In order to be understood, the statutes were written in French.
1589	*Captain Thomas Stukeley*, the earliest dramatic piece satirising the use of English by the Irish, appears anonymously.
1781	Thomas Sheridan *A rhetorical grammar of the English language* is published. A prescriptive work, it includes an appendix suggesting corrections to Irish 'mispronunciations of English'.
1801	*Castle Rackrent* by Maria Edgeworth, considered the first regional novel in English, appears. Many Irish features are to be found in the speech of the characters.
1807	Jacob Poole publishes a glossary of the archaic English dialect in Forth and Bargy, Co. Wexford. This is more comprehensive than that by Charles Vallancey (1788).
1860	David Patterson *The Provincialisms of Belfast*, an important source of Belfast English at that time, appears.

1850–	Late Modern Irish: Irish-speaking areas are no longer geographically contiguous.
mid-late 19c	German works on Celtic, with the framework of Indo-European studies, are published, above all Johann Casper Zeuss's *Grammatica Celtica* in 1853 (revised by Hans Ebel in 1871) and Alfred Holder's *Alt-celtischer Sprachschatz* (3 vols 1896–1907).
1893	Conradh na Gaeilge (The Gaelic League) established.
20c	Late Modern Irish: Present-day Irish is spoken natively in areas which have been reduced greatly in size. There are now three main regions (Donegal, Connemara, Kerry, with remnants in West Cork and South-West County Waterford) with, at the very most, 50,000 native speakers left. However, there is a greater number of non-native speakers, with varying degrees of competence in the language, and a certain revival is taking place in large urban centres, notably Dublin and Belfast.
1910	Patrick W. Joyce *English As We Speak It in Ireland*. This is the first full length monograph on Irish English. The introductory sections on pronunciation and grammar still have a certain value.
1913	Holger Pedersen *Vergleichende Grammatik der keltischen Sprachen* is published. An abridged English translation appears in 1937.
1927	James Jeremiah Hogan *The English Language in Ireland* appears, a philological work on the development of Irish English since the Middle Ages.
1932	Thomas F. O'Rahilly *Irish Dialects Past and Present*, which contains references to English in the south-east of the country, is published.
1946	English translation of Rudolf Thurneysen *A grammar of Old Irish* is published in Dublin.
1957	Patrick Leo Henry *An Anglo-Irish Dialect of North Roscommon* appears. With this the modern era of research into Irish English begins. In the following decades several books and a large number of articles on the English language in Ireland, covering all aspects of its development and present-day forms, are published.

2 History

8000 BCE	First settlers appear in the north of Ireland, probably coming from Scotland.
3000 BCE	Arrival of Neolithic people in Ireland.
500–300 BCE	Probable arrival of Celts in Ireland; assimilation of previous non-Indo-European population.
c.130–80	Ptolemy gives a geographical sketch of Ireland.
c.400	Ireland has strong footholds in western Scotland (the kingdom of Dalriada) and south Wales; the Irish language is taken to Scotland.
432	St Patrick arrives and officially Christianises Ireland (date and person are contested).
795	Viking raids in Ireland begin from the north.
c.800	The Book of Kells, an illuminated manuscript of the four Gospels in Latin, is completed.
c.840	Dublin is founded by the Vikings as a base on the estuary of the Liffey.
c.900	Beginning of Middle Irish period.
1014	Battle of Clontarf signals the final decline of Viking power in Ireland.
1169	Anglo-Norman invasion in the south-east of the country (Wexford and Waterford) by Normans from Pembrokeshire, south-west Wales.
1172	Charter of Dublin issued; Anglo-Normans strengthen their presence in the city.
c.1200	Beginning of Early Modern Irish period (until c.1600).
1235	Anglo-Norman invasion of Connaught (Western province).
1315–18	Bruce invasion from Scotland with resistance to Anglo-Norman rule.
1366	The Statutes of Kilkenny, proscribing the Irish language and Irish customs, attempt to curb the rapid Gaelicisation of the Anglo-Norman settlers.
15c	Gaelic revival continues.
1509	Henry VIII King of England.
1541	Henry VIII accepted by Irish parliament as King of Ireland.
1549–57	Plantation of Laois and Offaly (centre of country).
1558	Elizabeth I, last of the Tudors, ascends the throne.
1586–93	Plantation of Munster.
1592	Foundation of Trinity College, Dublin.
1595–1603	Rebellion of Hugh O'Neill, Earl of Tyrone.
c.1600	Beginning of Modern Irish period.
1601	Irish and Spanish forces defeated by the English at Kinsale, Co. Cork.
1603	Death of Elizabeth I. Accession of James I (James VI of Scotland).
1607	On 14 September Ulster leaders leave for the continent ('Flight of the Earls'), depriving Ulster of native leadership.

1641	Rising by Ulster Catholics against Protestant settlers.
1642	Outbreak of civil war in England.
1649–50	Oliver Cromwell's campaigns in Ireland.
1652–3	Cromwellian confiscation of lands, regulated by the Act of Settlement.
1660	Restoration of the monarchy (with Charles II as king). The Cromwellian conquest is maintained.
1685	Death of Charles II and accession of James II (Catholic).
1690	Arrival of William III (of Orange) in Ireland. Battle of the Boyne (1 July).
1691–1703	Land confiscation follows.
1695	Beginning of a series of legislative measures against the Irish Catholics known as the 'Penal Laws' which were to last up to the beginning of the nineteenth century.
1713	Jonathan Swift becomes Dean of St Patrick's in Dublin.
1740–1	Famine breaks out in large parts of the country.
1796–8	Rebellion by the United Irishmen.
1801	Act of Union of Great Britain and Ireland comes into force (1 Jan.).
1823	Catholic Association founded, led by Daniel O'Connell.
1829	Catholic Emancipation Act.
1837	Reign of Queen Victoria begins.
1845	Potato blight appears in some counties and starts to spread. Beginning of the Great Famine (1845–9).
1849	Queen's Colleges (Belfast, Cork, Galway) established.
1850	Queen's University of Belfast founded.
1854	Catholic University of Ireland founded with John H. Newman first rector.
1867	Fenian rising takes place in five counties including Dublin.
1870	Home Rule movement launched by Isaac Butt. Gladstone's first Land Act recognises the rights of tenants.
1875	Parnell returned to parliament as member for Co. Meath.
1879–1882	'Land War' is waged.
1881	Parnell imprisoned; Gladstone's second Land Act.
1893	Second Home Rule Bill is introduced. Conradh na Gaeilge (The Gaelic League) is founded.
1899–	Literary revival gets well under way; Irish Literary Theatre founded.
1904	Abbey Theatre opened.
1908	Irish Universities Act establishes the National University of Ireland.
1916	Rising of rebels on Easter Monday in Dublin with an Irish Republic proclaimed on 24 April. In the Battle of the Somme the Ulster Division of the English army suffers severe losses.
1918	General election leads to success for the republicans.
1919–21	Anglo-Irish War (sporadic resistance to British presence) begins.
1920	Government of Ireland Act provides for separate parliaments for the north and south of the island of Ireland.

1922	The Irish Free State established, Northern Ireland excluded. The majority of the population is for the treaty in the ensuing election. Civil war begins.
1923	End of civil war. The Irish Free State admitted to the League of Nations.
1937	New constitution introduced by Eamon de Valera. The country is now officially called 'Éire' (this replaces 'Irish Free State', the former name). Irish is the main official language with English a further one.
1949	Ireland is declared a republic (18 April). Agreement that partition will be perpetuated. The official name of the country is now 'Republic of Ireland'.
1955	Ireland becomes a member of the United Nations.
1964	Talks on reconciliation between Seán Lemass (Republic of Ireland) and Terence O'Neill (Northern Ireland). Anglo-Irish free trade agreement is introduced.
1966	New University of Ulster at Coleraine, Co. Derry opened.
1968	Civil rights marches begin. Clashes in Derry.
1970	Provisional IRA begins a campaign of violence against British troops.
1972	Direct rule follows the suspension of the parliament of Northern Ireland.
1974	Power-sharing executive set up, but defeated by the Protestants in an all-out strike (May).
1985	Hillsborough Anglo-Irish Agreement is rejected by Protestants.
1990	Irish electorate vote for Mary Robinson as seventh President of Ireland, the first woman to hold this office.
1994	Both the IRA and the loyalist paramilitaries announce ceasefires.
1996	IRA ceasefire terminated.
1997	New Labour are victorious in British general elections.
1997	IRA declare a resumption of the 1994 ceasefire.
1998	Loyalist paramilitaries announce a ceasefire. 'Good Friday' agreement reached. It makes provision for two language bodies, The Ulster-Scots Agency/Tha Boord o Ulstèr-Scotch in Northern Ireland and Foras na Gaeilge (lit. 'The Irish foundation') in the Republic of Ireland.
1999–2015	Generally, the ceasefire still holds. No change in the political status of Northern Ireland.
2003	Official Languages Act introduced in Republic of Ireland. It provides for a language commissioner, Irish 'coimisinéir teanga', appointed by the President of Ireland.
2006	Census carried out in Ireland (April) registering, for the first time, the use of Irish outside the educational system as a daily language.
2007	Irish becomes an official language of the European Union on 1 Jan.

Glossary

Abbey Theatre A major theatre in Dublin which opened in 1904. It was closely associated with writers of the Irish Literary Revival, such as William Butler Yeats (1865–1939) and Lady Augusta Gregory (1852–1932), and saw the premieres of many of their plays and those of the writers John Millington Synge (1871–1909) and Sean O'Casey (1880–1964). The Abbey Theatre has been state-funded since its early days. The second major theatre in Dublin is the *Gate Theatre*, founded in 1928 as a theatre company by Hilton Edwards (1903–82) and Mícheál MacLiammóir (1899–1978). See Welch (1999); Morash and Richards (2013).

Act of Union of Great Britain and Ireland An act passed by the British parliament in 1800 and which came into force on 1 January 1801. Similar to the Acts of Union for Wales in 1534/1542 (Laws in Wales Acts) and for Scotland in 1707, this act led to the disbandment of the parliament in Dublin and to direct rule of Ireland from Westminster with all this implied in terms of loss of sovereignty. See Connolly (2002).

***after* perfective** A grammatical structure found in Irish English (and contact Scottish English) which indicates that an action has taken place recently and is of high informational value to the hearer, e.g. *Michael is after crashing the car*. See Hickey (2007: Chapter 4).

Anglo-Irish A reference, often found in literary and cultural studies, to individuals born in Ireland but with English ancestry and frequently of Protestant faith and with leanings towards England. At least formerly, the Anglo-Irish belonged to the landed gentry and were descended from the Ascendency. See Beckett (1976).

Anglo-Norman A reference to the type of French spoken in England after the Norman invasion of 1066 and which was taken to Ireland from West Wales in the late twelfth century (after the Norman invasion of Ireland in 1169). See Hickey (2007: Chapter 2).

Aran Islands (Irish: *Oileáin Árann*) A collective term for three islands in Galway Bay. The largest of these is 'Inishmore' (Irish *Árainn* or latterly *Inis Mór – Árainn*). It is largely Irish-speaking. The two smaller islands, *Inis Meáin* 'the middle island' and *Inis Oírr* 'the eastern island' (which is closest to the Co. Clare mainland) are both entirely Irish-speaking. The islands were the subject of a study, *The Aran Islands*, published in 1907, by John Millington Synge. See Welch (ed.) (1996).

Ascendancy Originally a reference to the Protestant ruling class in eighteenth-century Ireland. It later came to refer, as a rather vague term, to a putative Protestant elite in Ireland, usually on country estates. See McCormack (1985); Connolly (2002).

aspect One of three divisions of verbs (the other two being tense and mood). Aspect refers to the way in which an action is viewed by the speaker, i.e. as being finished (*perfective*), ongoing (*progressive*), recurring (*habitual*), etc. Put in a simple formula, tense specifies when an action took place and aspect how. See Hickey (2007: Chapter 4).

be **deletion** A feature of some varieties of vernacular Irish English, now apparently confined to the south-east of Ireland, whereby a finite form of *be* is missing in a so-called equative sentence, e.g. *Anthony [is] a great footballer.* See Hickey (2007: Chapter 4).

Behan, Brendan (1923–64) Dublin writer who in his relatively short life established a reputation as the living stage Irishman and wrote an autobiography *Borstal Boy* (1958). Time spent in prison provided the material for his play *The Quare Fellow* (1956). The later play *The Hostage* (1959) deals with national sentiments and the relationship with Britain. Similar to Sean O'Casey, Behan made liberal use of local Dublin English in his plays.

Belfast The capital of Ulster, at the estuary of the river Lagan in the north-east of the country. It was founded in the seventeenth century and expanded greatly with the development of such industries as shipbuilding in the nineteenth century. Linguistically, it is an amalgam of Ulster Scots and Mid-Ulster English inputs along with independent developments of its own. It is largely Protestant, though West Belfast has a Catholic majority. See Milroy (1981).

Belfast Agreement With this political accord (1998), also know as the Good Friday Agreement, two language institutions were recognised for the whole of Ireland (i) *Foras na Gaeilge*, lit. 'the Irish foundation', and (ii) *The Ulster Scots Agency* (Ulster Scots: *Tha Boord o Ulstèr-Scotch*), both intended to represent heritage languages in Ireland apart from English, preserving and promoting their cultures. The main offices of these institutions are in Dublin and Belfast respectively. See Lalor (ed.) (2003).

bilingualism The ability to speak two languages with native-like competence. With bilinguals one language will generally be dominant. Lay people often use the term if someone can simply speak a second language well. See Bhatia and Ritchie (eds) (2008).

blarney An impressionistic term for flattering, cloying speech which is supposed to be typical of the Irish. It has been known in this sense since the time of Elizabeth I, who is reputed to have used the term. The term derives from a stone on a rampart of Blarney Castle near Cork city which is supposed to give anyone who kisses it 'the gift of the gab'. Hickey (2007: Chapter 1).

Bliss, Alan Joseph (1921–85) An English philologist who, after moving to the chair of English language at University College Dublin, developed an interest in Irish English on which he published many articles and the monograph *Spoken English in Ireland 1600–1740* (1979). Although Bliss's ideas were not accepted uncritically he was in part responsible for the revitalisation of Irish English studies which began in the 1980s.

Boucicault, Dion (1820–90) A popular dramatist and actor from the Victorian era. Boucicault was successful with plays outside of Ireland (in England, America, Australia) written in an often melodramatic style. He was a keen observer of local dialect and his plays provide important attestations of linguistic features in Irish English of his time. Among his plays are *The Colleen Bawn* (1860), *Arragh na Pogue* (1864) and *The Shaughraun* (1875). See Welch (1996).

brogue A term stemming from the Irish word either for 'shoe' (*bróg*) or 'a knot in the tongue' (*barróg teangan*). The label has been used in the past four centuries for any strongly local accent of Irish English. Occasionally, the term is found outside Ireland as in 'Ocracoke Brogue' to refer to the local accent of offshore islands in North Carolina. Hickey (2007: Chapter 1).

Bunreacht na hÉireann 'Constitution of Ireland' An official document from 1937 which specifies in Article 8 that Irish is the first language of the then Irish Free State (since 1949, The Republic of Ireland) and that English is accepted as a second official language. See Lalor (ed.) (2003).

cant A term which has been used for the speech of Irish Travellers. It is taken by Irish scholars to stem from Irish *caint* 'talk' but the use in the New World can in fact be derived from French.

Carleton, William (1794–1869) Novelist and short-story writer from Co. Tyrone in the north of Ireland. Carleton knew rural Ulster, where he had grown up in poverty, very well. He portrayed many characters from this rural background using local forms of English there to portray their speech genuinely. See Welch (1996).

Catholic Emancipation Act An act passed by the English parliament in Westminster in 1829. It essentially repealed the various Penal Laws which discriminated against Catholics in public life in Ireland. The act paved the way for the introduction of general education for the entire populations of Ireland which came about with the foundation of so-called National Schools (primary level schools) in the 1830s. See Dowling (1971); Raftery and Fischer (2014).

Celtic A branch of the Indo-European family which spread from the European continent to the British Isles during the first millennium BCE. The split into two branches, a Q-branch, maintaining inherited /kw/, and a P-Celtic branch, in which this sound shifted to /p/, took place on the continent. Today there are six surviving languages (strictly speaking, four with native speakers): Q-Celtic with Irish, Scottish Gaelic and Manx (extinct) and P-Celtic with Welsh, Cornish (extinct, but with attempts at revival) and Breton. See Ball and Müller (2009).

cleft sentence A special type of sentence used for topicalisation purposes and which involves moving an element to the left and placing it in a dummy main clause with *it* as subject, e.g. *It's tomorrow we're leaving for Spain*. See Hickey (2007, Chapter 4).

Coastal Crescent A term used by Ulster Scots scholar Robert Gregg to describe a band running from Co. Down, south-east of Belfast, up to Antrim in the extreme north-east, through Co. Derry and across to north-east Donegal (but excluding the city of Derry). This area is that of strongest Scottish settlement and is where Ulster Scots is found in its most original form. See Corrigan (2010).

Connaught (Irish: *Connacht* 'Connaught', *Cúige Connachta* 'province of Connaught') The westernmost of the four provinces of Ireland, consisting of the counties Galway, Mayo, Roscommon, Sligo and Leitrim. The first two of these are very large and contain Irish-speaking areas along their coasts, e.g. in south-west Co. Galway (see following entry) and in north-west Co. Mayo. See *Leinster, Munster, Ulster*.

Connemara An area of flat land immediately west of the city of Galway extending out to the mountains on the west coast. It contains one of the few remaining Irish-speaking areas. 'Conamara' is the spelling in Irish. See Hickey (2011).

Conradh na Gaeilge/The Gaelic League An organisation founded in 1893 by Douglas Hyde and Eoin O'Neill, among others. Its aim was, and is, to further knowledge of the Irish language and hence promote its use in Ireland. In its early years it published an Irish journal, *An Claidheamh Soluis* ('The Sword of Light'), which lasted until 1932.

contact A situation in which speakers of two languages or varieties are continually in contact with each other, either due to geographical or social proximity or both. The mutual influence which results from such contact can and does lead to changes in the structure – or at least in the lexicon – of one or both languages. See Hickey (ed.) (2010).

contact Irish English A term describing varieties of English which are in contact with the Irish language via speakers in the few small remaining enclaves along the western seaboard where Irish is still spoken as a native language in a situation of unbroken historical continuity. See Hickey (2007, Chapter 4).

convergence A linguistic scenario in which two or more languages become increasingly similar in their structures, usually because of prolonged contact in a geographically delimited area. This convergence is realised by speakers adopting features of other languages they are in contact with and passing these features on to later generations. See Hickey (2007, Chapter 4).

Cork The second largest city in the south of Ireland. It has an easily recognisable accent with undulating intonational patterns which are found in the south-west in general (in counties Cork and Kerry) in both English and Irish. See Hickey (2011).

Corkery, Daniel (1878–1964) Irish writer, born in Cork and later professor of English literature at University College Cork. In language studies, he is known for his study of eighteenth-century Gaelic Munster – *The Hidden Ireland* (1925) – and for *The Fortunes of the Irish Language* (1954).

Corpus of Irish English A corpus of literary texts by Irish writers compiled by Raymond Hickey and covering the period from the late Middle Ages to the early twentieth century. The corpus is supplied with the book *Corpus Presenter*, see Hickey (2003).

Corpus of Irish English Correspondence A comprehensive corpus, largely consisting of emigrant letters written by Irish people, mostly from the north of Ireland, during the past few centuries. The corpus has been compiled and is supervised by Kevin McCafferty from the University of Bergen. See Amador-Moreno et al. (eds) (2015).

'Dart' accent A non-linguistic term which has been used in Dublin to describe a new pronunciation of English which arose there during the 1990s (previously referred to as a 'Dublin 4' or 'D4' accent). The reference is to the suburban railway line which travels through many upmarket residential areas where this accent is supposed to occur. Also called 'Dartspeak' or 'Dortspeak' (the latter spelling intending to reflect the raising of the START vowel, no longer a feature of this accent). See Hickey (2005).

de Bhaldraithe, Tomás (1916–96) Irish linguist and lexicographer. Born in Limerick and educated at University College Dublin where he was appointed Professor of Modern Irish in 1960. He is the author of important studies of Connemara Irish and of an *English-Irish Dictionary* (1959) which still remains the authoritative work for English to Irish translation.

Derry The second largest city in Ulster, on the banks of the river Foyle near where it enters the sea. It has always had a special status in west Ulster and, in the context of Northern Ireland, it is remarkable in having a Catholic majority. The label 'Londonderry' stems from the seventeenth century when London undertaker companies were commissioned to plant the city with English settlers. See Bardon (2001). On English in Derry city, see McCafferty (2001).

Dinneen, Patrick Stephen (1860–1934) Irish lexicographer. He was born in Co. Kerry and studied at University College Dublin. He was active in the Gaelic League and produced plays and translations. Dinneen is remembered for his *Irish English Dictionary* published in 1924 and revised in 1927. For many decades this remained the standard reference work in Irish lexicography. The Irish form of his name is Pádraig Ó Duinnín.

documentation The textual record for English in Ireland is not abundant for the first period (1200–1600), with the *Kildare Poems*, some minor pieces and city records forming the bulk of this. The second period (1600–) began with stretches of Irish English within English works, typically plays, often of a satirical nature. By the late eighteenth century the situation had changed and literature written by Irish writers and displaying features of Irish English at the time came to be published, e.g. the novel *Castle Rackrent* by Maria Edgeworth.

Donegal A large county in the extreme north-west of Ireland. It is geographically and linguistically a part of Ulster although not included in the state of Northern Ireland. The county also has a small community of Irish speakers along its north-west coast.

Doyle, Roddy (1959–) Irish novelist from Dublin whose novels reflect vernacular life in the city. These began with *The Commitments* (1987), *The Snapper* (1990) and *The Van* (1991), which form The Barrytown Trilogy. The novel *Paddy Clarke Ha Ha Ha* (1993) won the Booker Prize of that year. Doyle's narrative style is characterised by an abundant use of local Dublin dialect.

Dublin The capital of the Republic of Ireland, at the mouth of the River Liffey on the east coast. It is by far the largest city in the entire island, with nearly one-third of the Republic's population (over 1 million people) living in its metropolitan area. See Dickson (2014). For English in Dublin, see Hickey (2005).

Dublin Institute for Advanced Studies A state-funded research institution in Dublin with a School of Celtic Studies whose scholars publish work on Irish, mostly from an historical point of view. It also publishes books on Celtic studies in general.

Dublin Vowel Shift A reference to a series of vowel shifts which occurred in the 1990s in Dublin and which involved the raising of vowels in words like THOUGHT, NORTH and CHOICE as well as the fronting of the vowels in GOOSE and GOAT. This pronunciation became general for a generation growing up in Ireland from the 1990s onwards as this new Dublin usage became widespread throughout the Republic of Ireland. See Hickey (2005).

Dublin English A cover term for a group of varieties of English in the capital of the Republic of Ireland. English here has a long history going back to the late twelfth century. The vernacular varieties in the city have a distinct phonetic profile and non-local inhabitants of the city have in the past two decades or so avoided this by dissociating themselves from the local pronunciation (see previous entry).

east coast dialect area A reference to the east coast of Ireland, roughly from Dublin down to Waterford, where vernacular forms of speech show features which go back to the earliest days of English settlement, well before 1600.

Edgeworth, Maria (1767–1849) A prolific Anglo-Irish writer of novels, children's literature and, under the influence of her father Richard Lovell Edgeworth, of books on education. Her first novel *Castle Rackrent* (1800) about a dissolute Anglo-Irish family is generally regarded as the first regional novel in English and contains much dialect in its passages of direct speech.

emigration The transportation of Irish people to colonies in the New World and the southern hemisphere began in the seventeenth and late eighteenth centuries respectively, when many Irish were deported to Caribbean islands such as Barbados. Emigration, both voluntary and involuntary, continued throughout the eighteenth and nineteenth centuries with a large exodus of Ulster Scots from the north of Ireland to the Appalachian region of the later United States and a significant emigration of southern Irish to the USA and Canada in the nineteenth century, triggered above all by the Great Famine. See Fitzgerald and Lambkin (2007); on the transportation of Irish English, see Hickey (ed.) (2004).

emigrant letters Correspondence between emigrants in the overseas colonies and members of their families as well as friends back in Ireland. Such letters are linguistically interesting as they were usually written by relatively uneducated persons whose written style can be assumed to be close to their spoken language.

enregisterment A process whereby linguistic features of a variety become associated with its speakers and where a general awareness of these features arises. In the Irish English context such enregistered features would include the use of stops for fricatives, e.g. *dis, dem dose* for 'this, them, those' or the unraised MEAT vowel suggested in spellings such as *Jaysus* or *crayture*.

European Union In 2004 a considerable expansion of the European Union took place with a number of East European countries acceding to the union. This led to a greater freedom of movement for people from these countries. Among the latter was Poland, but also the Baltic states Lithuania, Latvia and Estonia, from where many people came to Ireland in search of employment.

first period (1200–1600) One of the two main divisions in the history of Irish English. It begins with the Anglo-Norman invasion in the south-east in 1169. By 1600, Gaelic resurgence, and with it that of the Irish language, had come to an end. The seventeenth century saw the importation of newer varieties of English on a wide scale in both the north and south of the country. See *second period*.

Forth and Bargy Two baronies in the extreme south-east of Ireland, in Co. Wexford, where a particularly archaic form of English, stemming from the late medieval period of settlement in Ireland, was spoken up to the beginning of the nineteenth century. *Yola*, the form of the word 'old' in the dialect, came to be used as a reference to the dialect itself.

fricative *t* A reference to the manner in which Irish people pronounce the sound /t/ between vowels or after a vowel and before a pause (in so-called weak positions) as in *city* or *pit*. This *t* sounds like /s/ but has less of a hissing quality and should not be confused with the *s* of English, i.e. the Irish pronunciations of *kit* and *kiss* are not identical. The fricative *t* is ubiquitous in the south of Ireland and common in the north as well. It is also found, as a transferred feature, in the speech of the Irish-derived community in Newfoundland; the Australian use of a similar sound may be connected to Irish input in the formative years of Australian English.

Gaelic A generic term for the Q-Celtic branch of the Insular Celtic languages consisting of Irish, Scottish Gaelic and Manx. In a Scottish context, the bare term 'Gaelic' or 'Gallick' (reflecting the Scottish pronunciation) is taken to refer to Scottish Gaelic.

Gaelscoileanna lit. 'Irish schools', Irish-medium schools which are in considerable demand in the Republic of Ireland and, to a lesser extent, in Northern Ireland. Instruction is in Irish and in general this leads to considerable fluency in second-language Irish by pupils. However, they do not normally continue using the language after they finish such schools, as the poor results for the use of Irish outside the educational system in the censuses of 2006 and 2011 have shown.

Gaeltacht A collective term in Irish (used in the singular) denoting the Irish-speaking districts in Ireland. The geographical limits of the Gaeltacht were set down by the government during the mid-twentieth century, but now (2015) only part of the Gaeltacht population are native speakers of Irish. Proposals have been put forward recently to redefine districts within the Gaeltacht to reflect more accurately the use of Irish there.

Gaoth Dobhair (English 'Gweedore') A townland and parish on the north-west coast of Co. Donegal which constitutes the largest Irish-speaking region in that county. It is adjoined to the immediate south by *Na Rosa* and to the north by *Cloich Cheannfhaola*, and somewhat further north again by *Ros Goill*, where Irish is still spoken by some very few speakers.

gender-differentiated language use Recent language change in Dublin, and by extension in the rest of the Republic of Ireland, has been driven by young lower-middle-class females, both the Dublin Vowel Shift of the 1990s and the recent Short Front Vowel Lowering. Because males lag behind in these changes, a gendered-differentiated use of language has arisen, e.g. in the onset centralisation of the GOAT vowel; that is, a word like *go* is much more likely to be pronounced as [gəʊ] by females than males.

Gerald of Wales (1146?–1223?) Latin: Giraldus Cambrensis, was a Norman Welsh monk and chronicler from Pembrokeshire. He is mainly known to posterity for two works, *Expugnatio Hibernica* ('The Conquest of Ireland') and *Topographia Hibernica* ('The Topography of Ireland') in which unflattering portraits of the Irish are given.

Great Famine, The (1845–8) A famine which broke out in Ireland due to the failure of the potato crop after a blight spread from the continent. In began in 1845 and reached its peak in 1847 – 'Black '47' – the worst year of the blight. In all, it is assumed that about a million people died of starvation and at least a further million emigrated to the New World. The reduction in population with both events, famine and emigration, was greatest amongst Irish speakers, accelerating the language shift to English in the second half of the nineteenth century.

Gregory, Lady Augusta (1852–1932) A writer, chiefly of plays, and a prominent figure of the Irish Literary Revival. For many years she was the patron of W. B. Yeats, who spent much time at her estate in Coole, Co. Galway.

hedge school A term referring to the informal and strictly speaking illegal education provided for Catholics before the Catholic Emancipation Act of 1829 and the establishment of National Schools (primary schools) in the 1830s. See Dowling (1968 [1935]).

Heuser, Wilhelm An early twentieth-century German scholar whose main achievement is the publication of *Die Kildare-Gedichte* 'The Kildare Poems' (Bonn, 1904), a critical edition of MS Harley 913 in the British Museum which has formed the outset for many later studies of these poems.

Hibernia The Latin word for Ireland, possibly deriving from the word for 'winter', but more likely from the name of an ancient tribe, the *Everni*, mentioned by Ptolemy as the *Iverni*, and associated with Ireland.

Hogan, James Jeremiah Irish philologist of English and professor at University College Dublin. His *The English Language in Ireland* (1927) gives a good philological overview of the development of Irish English from the late Middle Ages. His *An Outline of English Philology, Chiefly for Irish Students* (1934) contains many remarks on Irish English usage of his day.

Howard, Paul (1971–) London-born Irish journalist and novelist who is known for the successful series of novels featuring the South-Dublin figure of Ross O'Carroll Kelly as he manoeuvres his way through life in Dublin during the economic boom years of the Celtic Tiger and beyond. Written in racy dialect, the novels' style reflects the urban vernacular of a younger generation of South Dubliners.

Hyde, Douglas (1860–1949) Irish scholar and statesman, born in Castlerea, Co. Roscommon. He studied at Trinity College Dublin and began collecting and translating Irish folklore and poetry, publishing much of this as *Love Songs of Connacht* (1893) along with a *Literary History of Ireland* somewhat later (1899). He was a co-founder of the Gaelic League and active in the promotion of the Irish language. From 1909 to 1932 Hyde was professor of Irish at University College Dublin. He was elected first President of Ireland under the Irish constitution of 1937 and served a period from 1938 to 1945.

ICE-Ireland The Irish component of the *International Corpus of English*, compiled by Jeffrey Kallen of Trinity College Dublin and John Kirk of Queen's University Belfast and produced in 2008. It consists of a part for the Republic of Ireland and one for Northern Ireland. There is a dedicated website for the corpus at http://www.qub.ac.uk/sites/ICE-Ireland/.

Ireland, Republic of That section of the island of Ireland which achieved independence in 1922 and was known as the Irish Free State until the proclamation of a republic in 1949. It consists of 26 of the 32 counties of Ireland.

Ireland, Northern See **Northern Ireland.**

Irish The name for (i) the people of Ireland and (ii) the Celtic language (Irish *Gaeilge*) still spoken by a small minority, chiefly on the western seaboard. The latter is a Q-Celtic language, first attested in writing in interlinear glosses from the seventh century and still spoken today as a community language in three separate areas in the south, middle and north of the western seaboard of Ireland. Four broad periods are recognised in the history of the language, Old Irish (600–900), Middle Irish (900–1200), Early Modern Irish (1200–1600) and Modern Irish (1600 to the present).

Joyce, James (1882–1941) Dublin-born Irish novelist who is chiefly known for his novel *Ulysses* (1922), the story of one day in Dublin, 16 June 1904. In this work and his two other novels, *Dubliners* (1914) and *A Portrait of the Artist as a Young Man* (1916) Joyce made use of features of local Dublin dialect in stretches of direct speech. See Welch (ed.) (1996).

Joyce, Patrick Weston (1827–1914) Historian, geographer, place-name researcher and linguist. Joyce was born in Co. Limerick, educated locally, became a teacher in Clonmel and later studied at Trinity College Dublin. His main achievement in onomastics is *The Origin and History of Irish Names of Places* (3 vols, 1869–70) for which he used his good knowledge of Irish in explaining the composition of names. As a historian and geographer he made his name with *The Geography of the Country of Ireland* (1883) and *A Social History of Ancient Ireland* (2 vols, 1907). He is also the author of *A Grammar of the Irish Language* (1878) and *Old Celtic Romances* (1879). In Irish English studies he is remembered for *English As We Speak It in Ireland* (1910) (reprinted with new introductions in 1979 and 1988), which was remarkable for its time.

Keating, Geoffrey/Seathrún Céitinn (1570–1644) An Irish writer and priest working in the south of Ireland after having studied in Bordeaux. He fell out of grace with the authorities of his time and while in hiding gathered material for his monumental history of Ireland, *Forus Feasa ar Éirinn*, lit. 'the foundation of knowledge about Ireland', in which he defended Irish culture against the encroachment of English Protestant culture. He is also the author of some religious works, none of which were published during his lifetime but which were popular after his death.

Kildare Poems Sixteen pieces of verse of Irish origin in the Harley 913 manuscript in the British Library. It is the most comprehensive record of early fourteenth-century Irish English. The title comes from the eponymous poem in 'The Hymn of Michael of Kildare'. See Lucas (ed.) (1995), Hickey (2007: Chapter 2).

Kiltartanese An ironical reference to a style of literary English developed chiefly by Lady Augusta Gregory in the late nineteenth century. This style shows the heavy influence of Irish grammar and was reputedly typical of the speech of inhabitants of the barony of Kiltartan, south Co. Galway, where Gregory's estate,

Coole, was located. This style was further developed by John Millington Synge in his plays.

language death An emotive term sometimes applied to those situations in which a language ceases to exist. A well-studied instance of language death is Scottish Gaelic in East Sutherland in the north-east of Scotland (Dorian 1981), which was progressively abandoned from one generation to the next and during this process the grammar of the language showed clear signs of disintegration, for example in its morphological system. In some instances the very last speaker of a language may be identified, e.g. it is reported that Dolly Pentreath (1692–1777) was the last native speaker of Cornish and that Ned Maddrell (1877–1974) was the last speaker of Manx.

language shift A situation in which speakers of a language abandon this and move to another language with which they are in contact, usually over a prolonged period. This shift happened historically in Ireland with the move from Irish to English for the great majority of the population. Because the shift was characterised by unguided adult second-language acquisition in a non-prescriptive environment many structures of Irish were transferred to English, some of which became permanent features of later Irish English.

Leinster (Irish: *Laighin* 'Leinster', *Cúige Laighean* 'province of Leinster') One of the four provinces of Ireland in the east, south-east of the island consisting of the following counties: Carlow, Dublin, Kildare, Kilkenny, Laois, Longford, Louth, Meath, Offaly, Westmeath, Wexford and Wicklow, none of which contains a historically continuous Irish-speaking area. Dublin is located in this province. See *Connaught, Munster, Ulster.*

lexical sets A convention, introduced by John Wells in the early 1980s (see Wells 1982), which uses single words, written in capital letters, to represent sets of words with similar pronunciations. For instance, the FACE lexical set refers to all words which have the vowel deriving from Early Modern English /e:/ irrespective of how this is actually pronounced in a present-day variety (usually slightly diphthongised).

Limerick Corpus of Irish English A text corpus compiled at the University of Limerick in the early 2000s intending to represent a range of registers and varieties of Irish English with a view to later linguistic analysis.

malapropism The use of a word which is not the one which is intended. Such use occurs because of the phonetic similarity between the intended word and the one actually used, e.g. saying *ulster* for *ulcer* in Irish English. The term derives from one Mrs Malaprop in the play *The Rivals* by Richard Brinsley Sheridan, a character whose speech is replete with such phonetic near-hits.

MacAlister, Robert A. S. (1870–1950) Dublin archaeologist and professor at University College Dublin. He is renowned for many books on the archaeology of pre-Celtic Ireland. For Irish English studies his relevance is as author of the linguistically naive but nevertheless copious book *The Secret Languages of Ireland* (1937).

Mac Neill, Eoin (1867–1945) Irish politician and scholar best known today for his part in the struggle for Irish independence which preceded the founding of the Irish Free State in 1922. Before that he was active in Irish language affairs, having founded *Conradh na Gaeilge* (The Gaelic League) with Douglas Hyde. In 1908 he was appointed professor of early Irish history at University College Dublin.

McCurtin, Hugh (1670–1755) Irish poet and lexicographer. He was born in Co. Clare and educated privately by his cousin. He studied in France and returned to Ireland around 1714. In language studies he is known for two books: (1) *The Elements of the Irish Language, Grammatically Explained in English*, published in 1728 in Louvain and (2) an incomplete *English-Irish Dictionary* published in Paris in 1732.

Meyer, Kuno (1858–1919) German scholar who at the end of the nineteenth and beginning of the twentieth century published much on Celtic literature and philology. In 1903 he founded the *School of Irish Learning* for the promotion of scholarly work on the language and its literature.

Midlands The centre of Ireland, which is a flat expanse bordered by the hills and mountains which occupy the coastal regions of the country. This expanse stretches from an area west of Co. Dublin as far as the Shannon, linking up with east Clare, Galway and Mayo. On a north–south axis it is delimited by the border with Northern Ireland in the north, and to the south by a line running roughly from Limerick across to Dublin.

Mid-Ulster English A linguistic term referring to the speech of that section of the population of Ulster which is derived from English settlers of the seventeenth century. It is one of the two major linguistic groupings in Northern Ireland, the other being Ulster Scots.

modal One of a small set of verbs which are used with other verbs to indicate obligation, possibility, necessity, etc. *Can, might, may, could, would* are examples. These verbs are all irregular but in Irish English one of them has been made regular, i.e. the negative of *must* is not *can't* but *mustn't* as in *He mustn't be Scottish*.

Moryson, Fynes (1566–1630) An Elizabethan writer who travelled to Ireland and reported on his experiences there in a manner similar to Richard Stanyhurst.

Munster (Irish: *Mumhain* 'Munster', *Cúige Mumhan* 'province of Munster') One of the four provinces of Ireland, in the south, south-west of the country, consisting of the counties Clare, Tipperary, Limerick, Cork, Kerry and Waterford. Only the last three have Irish-speaking areas today. See *Connaught, Leinster, Ulster*.

New English A label sometimes used for English settlers who arrived in Ireland in the sixteenth and seventeenth centuries and who were Protestants. These settlers were different from the older Catholic English who had come to Ireland in the late Middle Ages. See *Old English*.

New Irish A recent label used for those people who live in Ireland but who were not born there, e.g. the many recent emigrants from Eastern Europe.

Northern Ireland A constituent part of the United Kingdom which consists of six counties of the historical province of Ulster. It was created in 1922 as an option for those inhabitants of the north-east of Ireland who wished to remain within the British union. The majority of its population are Protestants, largely descendants of original Scots or Northern English from the seventeenth century, but there is a sizeable Catholic minority in the region as well.

Northern Irish The Irish language as spoken today in pockets along the coast of Co. Donegal (particularly the region called Gaoth Dobhair/Gweedore) and on Toraigh/Tory Island off the north-west coast of the county.

Ó Cadhain, Máirtín (1906–70) Irish novelist, academic and political activist. He was appointed professor of Modern Irish in Trinity College in his later years. Among his best known works are the *Cré na Cille* 'The Clay of the Churchyard' and the short-story collection *Idir Shúgradh agus Dáiríre*, lit. 'jest and seriousness'.

O'Casey, Sean (1884–1964) Dublin writer of realistic plays at the beginning of the twentieth century. Among these are *The Shadow of the Gunman* (1923), *Juno and the Paycock* (1924) and *The Plough and the Stars* (1926). All of these are written in local Dublin English, to represent which O'Casey adapted the orthography of English. His later plays, such as *The Silver Tassie* (1928), are generally regarded as less successful.

Ó Cléirigh, Míchél (1575–1645) Irish chronicler and lexicographer. Born in Co. Donegal, he entered the priesthood and became a Franciscan in Louvain. He is best known for his *Annála Ríoghachta Éireann*, a chronicle of Irish history from its beginnings down to 1616. Because it was a collaborative work with others it is usually referred to in English as *Annals of the Four Masters*. Ó Cléirigh was also the author of *Foclóir* [Irish dictionary] (1643, Louvain), which is among the earliest lexicographical works for Irish.

O'Donovan, John (1806–61) Irish scholar born at Attateemore, Co. Kilkenny. He received an education at a local hedge school and later on in Waterford. During the 1830s he travelled widely in Ireland collecting language and folklore material as part of his work for the Ordnance Survey Office in Dublin. Later, in the 1840s, O'Donovan worked academically preparing an edition of *Annals of the Four Masters*. Nowadays he is chiefly known for his *A Grammar of the Irish Language* which appeared in 1845.

Ó hEódhasa, Giolla Brighde (1570–1614) Irish scholar born in Co. Fermanagh and educated in Ireland. He went abroad, first to France and then to Louvain where he entered the Irish Franciscan College of St Anthony. He lectured in theology and published his *An Teagasg Críosdaídhe* [The teaching of Christ] (Antwerp,

1611; Louvain, 1614). Ó hEódhasa is known to language studies for his treatise on the Irish language, *Rudimenta Grammaticae Hibernicae*, an original work which contains a classification of nouns by declension as in Latin.

Old English A reference to the English (and Anglo-Norman) settlers in pre-Reformation Ireland, i.e. the descendants of the late medieval settlers who came at the end of the twelfth century. This group assimilated largely to the native Irish.

O'Rahilly, Thomas Francis (1883–1953) Irish scholar born in Kerry and educated at University College Dublin. In 1919 he was appointed Professor of Irish at Trinity College Dublin and later moved to Cork, then back to Dublin and was finally professor at the School of Celtic Studies in the Dublin Institute for Advanced Studies, where he was made director in 1941. O'Rahilly wrote widely on literary and historical topics. His linguistic reputation rests on his monograph *Irish Dialects, Past and Present* (1932), a survey of the development and geographical distribution of different forms of Irish with notes on Scottish Gaelic and Manx.

Pale A term for the area of Dublin, its immediate hinterland and a stretch of the east coast down to the south-east corner which was first settled by the English and which was fairly successful in resisting increasing Gaelicisation up to the sixteenth century. The varieties of English in this area still show features which stem from late medieval Irish English whereas those further west in the country show greater influence from Irish.

P-Celtic One of the two major branches of Celtic, consisting of Welsh and Breton and perhaps revived Cornish. It is distinguished by the survival of Indo-European /k^w/ as /p/, e.g. Welsh *pen* 'head', cf. Irish *ceann*.

Penal Laws A collective term for a series of laws which were introduced successively from 1697 onwards and which led to the disenfranchisement of the native Catholic population. They were finally repealed with the Catholic Emancipation Act of 1829.

plantation The forced introduction of a non-native population by land seizure and planned settlement on this land. Such plantations were carried out at various points in Irish history, the most successful of which were the Scottish plantations in Ulster in the seventeenth century.

Poole, Jacob (1774–1827) A Protestant minister, born in Growtown, Co. Wexford, into a Quaker family. He is known in Irish English studies for his glossary of the Forth and Bargy dialect, which he compiled in the first years of the nineteenth century. This glossary is much more comprehensive than that of Charles Vallancey, published in 1788, and contains a few text pieces (songs) in an appendix. It was later edited by William Barnes in 1867.

Presbyterians Non-conformist Protestants who are particularly strong in Scotland and who came from there to Ulster in the seventeenth century.

Proceedings of the Old Bailey A large collection of court proceedings from the Old Bailey in London. The depositions and testimonies are frequently in vernacular English (depending on how verbatim the court clerks did the transcriptions) and have been used for the linguistic analysis of Irish English. See Hickey (2007, Chapter 4).

provinces and counties Ireland is divided today into four provinces and 32 counties. The provinces are roughly equal in size, but the counties vary as do the number of them in each province. The main Irish-speaking areas are in the provinces of Munster, Connaught and Ulster (Leinster does not have any historically continuous Irish-speaking areas). Ulster consists of nine counties, three of which are in the Republic of Ireland. The remaining six form Northern Ireland and are frequently referred to in Irish as *Na Sé Chontae* 'The Six Counties'.

prosody All elements which go beyond the individual sounds in speech. This includes word stress, rhythm and intonation, all of which can be quite specific to a particular variety.

Q-Celtic One of the two major branches of Celtic, consisting of Irish, Scottish Gaelic and Manx. It is distinguished by the survival of Indo-European /kʷ/ as /k/, e.g. Irish *ceathair* 'four', Welsh *pedwar*.

quotatives Parts of speech which are used to indicate a stretch of direct discourse. The particle *like* is commonly used by young speakers as a quotative in varieties of English today, including those in Ireland, e.g. *She was like 'no way am I going there'*.

Raidió na Gaeltachta An entirely Irish language radio service which was founded in 1972 and which broadcasts daily across Ireland with approximately equal representation of Northern, Western and Southern Irish varieties.

Received Pronunciation The standard pronunciation of British English. This stems originally from the speech of the middle and upper classes in London. In the course of the nineteenth century it developed into a sociolect, particularly when adopted by the public schools of the higher social classes, and attained a wide distribution in Wales and Scotland as well.

Republic of Ireland Since 1949 the official name for the south of Ireland (excluding Northern Ireland). With the declaration of a republic, Ireland left the Commonwealth and formally achieved a greater degree of independence from the United Kingdom.

retentionist view A standpoint in Irish English studies where considerable weight is accorded to regional English input to Ireland, i.e. dialect and archaic features of English were retained in Ireland. This stance implies that Irish did not play a central role in the genesis of Irish English.

revival of Irish (Irish: *athbheochan na Gaeilge*) A movement which began in the late nineteenth century and which became official policy in independent Ireland after 1922. The revival was not a success, judging by the continual decline in the numbers of native speakers, although partial knowledge of the language did increase in the twentieth century due to compulsory Irish in primary and secondary schools in the Republic of Ireland.

RTÉ (Raidió Teilifís Éireann 'Irish Radio and Television') The Irish radio and television network, a semi-state body which began radio broadcasting in 1926 and television in 1961. Until the 1990s it had a monopoly in broadcasting and was important in the dissemination of non-vernacular varieties of Irish English, especially those from Dublin, throughout the country.

Scottish Gaelic A form of Q-Celtic which was introduced to Scotland from Ireland from about 500 CE onwards. By the end of the Middle Irish period (900–1200) Scottish Gaelic, as attested in entries in the twelfth-century *Book of Deer* (associated with the abbey of Deer in Buchan), is taken to have diverged significantly from Irish, something confirmed later by the early-sixteenth-century *Book of the Dean of Lismore*.

Scouse The city dialect of Liverpool which, due to heavy Irish immigration to the Merseyside region in the nineteenth century, shows not insignificant traces of Irish English, e.g. in the realisation of dental fricatives as stops.

second period (1600 to the present) The second main division in the history of Irish English. In the early seventeenth century the widespread settlement of Ulster by people from Scotland took place. By the middle of this century, newer varieties of English were being imported in the south. These newer varieties fed directly into modern forms of Irish English.

Shaw, George Bernard (1856–1950) Shaw was born in Dublin but moved to England as a young man, where he was to remain for the rest of his life. Of the very many plays which he wrote in his long career as a dramatist, only one deals explicitly with national cultural differences, *John Bull's Other Island* (1904). There is a limited representation of Irish English speech in this play.

Shelta The assumed language of the Irish travelling people of which only a little is known (vocabulary and some grammatical features). The jargon is scarcely accessible today and not assumed to be the robust native speech of travelling people, even if this was in fact once the case.

Sheridan, Thomas (1719–88) Sheridan was born in Co. Cavan and died in London. His career was quite varied, covering activities as a writer, actor and lecturer on elocution. In the history of Irish English Sheridan is remembered as the author of *A Rhetorical Grammar of the English Language* (1781) which contains a section on the Irish pronunciation of English. He is also the author of a successful *General Dictionary of the English Language* (1780, 2 volumes) and an earlier *A Course of Lectures on Elocution* (1762). His son was the playwright Richard Brinsley Sheridan. See Sheldon (1967).

Short Front Vowel Lowering A recent process in many native varieties of English across the world whereby the vowel in the DRESS lexical set is lowered and that in the TRAP set is lowered and retracted, e.g. *dress* [dræs] and *trap* [trap]. This type of lowering is now found with young females in Dublin and may well spread to other groups in other areas. In Dublin the vowel in the KIT set is not appreciably lowered.

'slit' *t* See fricative *t*.

Spenser, Edmund (1552–99) Born in London, Spenser moved to Ireland in 1580 and settled on a large estate in Co. Cork. Spenser's *View of the Present State of Ireland* (written in 1596 but not published until 1633) is a typical document of its time, expressing the opinion that the Irish should be converted to the Protestant faith and anglicised or else suppressed by military means. Spenser is known generally as the author of *The Fairie Queene*, most of which was composed in Ireland.

South-West An area in the south-west of Ireland, which consists primarily of the two large counties Cork and Kerry, and which has a number of distinct features, such as nasal raising – the words *pen* and *pin* being pronounced identically – and distinctive intonational patterns.

Stage Irishman, the A stereotype which began to appear in English drama in the seventeenth century. The term is popularly used to denote anyone who displays supposedly Irish traits, such as flattering, flowery language and melodramatic behaviour.

Standard Irish (Irish: *An Caighdeán Oifigiúil*) A standard for modern written Irish orthography and morphology (but not pronunciation), established by the government in the 1940s and 1950s, and published in a book of this name in a definitive form in 1958 and reprinted many times since, see Government of Ireland (1958).

Stanyhurst, Richard (1547–1618) Stanyhurst received his school education at Kilkenny and later in England. On his return to Ireland with his tutor Edmund Campion he dedicated himself to Irish history. Stanyhurst revised a *History of Ireland* which Campion had put together hastily in 1571 and it appeared along with his own *Treatise containing a Plaine and Perfect Description of Ireland* in *Holinshed's Chronicles* (1577). Although Stanyhurst's attitude to the Irish was condescending, much in the Elizabethan tradition, his work forms the only historical source of remarks on language use in Ireland before 1600.

Statutes of Kilkenny (1366) A set of laws which, among many other things, proscribed the use of Irish by the Anglo-Normans in Ireland and insisted that they use English. In order to be understood, the statutes were written in French. In the event they were quite ineffectual.

subordinating 'and' A grammatical structure, once typical of forms of English influenced by Irish, in which a concessive clause is introduced by *and*, e.g. *They* *went out walking and it raining.* There is an exact structural equivalent to this in Irish: *Chuaigh siad amach agus é ag cur báistí,* lit 'went they out and it at putting rain.GEN'.

substratist view A standpoint in Irish English studies where considerable weight is accorded to structural transfer from Irish into English (see the example in the preceding entry). This stance implies that regional English input was correspondingly less important in the genesis of Irish English.

supraregionalisation A process which is assumed to have taken place in late nineteenth- and early twentieth-century Ireland and to have been triggered by the rise of general school education for the native Catholic Irish. It consisted of the replacement of salient dialect features by more mainstream ones. Because of this, vernacular forms of speech (for middle-class speakers) lost their local identity and became 'supraregional'.

Survey of Irish English Usage A survey, carried out by Raymond Hickey in the early 2000s with over 1000 respondents in different parts of Ireland, which aimed at ascertaining the acceptability of several non-standard features of Irish English among speakers of different ages and both genders. See Hickey (2007, Chapter 4 for a full discussion).

Swift, Jonathan (1667–1745) Apart from his pamphlets, political writings and satires, Swift wrote the short piece *A dialogue in Hybernian stile between A & B* (*c.*1735) in which he satirised the Irish-influenced speech of the English planters who had come to Ireland in large numbers in the seventeenth century. The item *Irish eloquence* contains material similar to that of *A dialogue in Hybernian stile between A & B* but was arranged in the form of a letter.

Southern Irish A reference to forms of Irish spoken in the southern part of the western seaboard of Ireland, i.e. on the tip of the Dingle peninsula in Co. Kerry. Irish was spoken in other parts of the South as a native language into the twentieth century, e.g. in parts of Co. Cork and on Ring peninsula in Co. Waterford but has all but disappeared there.

Synge, John Millington (1871–1909) Synge was born in Dublin of Protestant stock and educated at Trinity College and the Royal Irish Academy of Music. Encouraged by W. B. Yeats to go to the Aran Islands to experience the genuine life and customs of the Irish peasantry, Synge described his sojourns there in the book *The Aran Islands* (1907) in which he claimed that he had heard all the linguistic structures which he used in his plays when eavesdropping on local inhabitants. How genuine Synge's language is remains a matter of debate. He is the author of the following plays which embody his distinctive style: *The Shadow of the Glen* (1903), *Riders to the Sea* (1904), *The Well of the Saints* (1905), *The Playboy of the Western World* (1907), *The Tinkers' Wedding* (1907), *Deirdre of the Sorrows* (1909).

TG4 An Irish language television channel which began broadcasting in 1996. Unlike Raidió na Gaeltachta, it allows some English programmes and so appeals to a wider audience, above all to groups of interested viewers outside the Irish-speaking areas.

Tír Chonaill The preferred term in Irish for Co. Donegal, especially the Irish-speaking regions of this county. The name means 'country of Connell'.

traditional Irish A reference to the speech of older native speakers with greater competence in Irish than in English and whose command and use of Irish is not usually guided by a knowledge of the written language.

traditional Irish English A reference to rural English spoken during the twentieth century in areas in which Irish was still found or where the language had only recently disappeared. This type of English showed many lexical items from Irish which often displayed a similar phonological structure and the same stress pattern as in the Irish original.

transfer A process whereby speakers of a language adopt and incorporate features of a further language into their own. Transfer presupposes language contact and is at a premium in scenarios of language shift.

Ulaidh, Cúige Uladh (English: 'Ulster; Province of Ulster')

Ullans A term for (written) Ulster Scots which has been formed on analogy with Lallans, the Lowland Scots term for itself. It is also the name of a journal.

Ulster (Irish: *Ulaidh* 'Ulster', *Cúige Uladh* 'province of Ulster') One of the four provinces of Ireland, in the north of the country, consisting of the counties Derry, Antrim, Down, Armagh, Tyrone, Fermanagh (the six counties of Northern Ireland) as well as Monaghan, Cavan and Donegal (in the Republic of Ireland). Only Donegal has a historically continuous Gaeltacht area today, though there is a small urban Gaeltacht in Belfast (Co. Antrim). Up to the early twentieth century Irish was still spoken in the Glens of Antrim, on Rathlin Island, in the mountainous region of central Tyrone and in parts of south Armagh. Forms of English in the province are Ulster Scots in rural areas along the so-called Coastal Crescent and Mid-Ulster English, stemming from imported varieties of Northern English, in the centre of the province. See *Connaught, Leinster, Munster*.

Ulster Scots The language of the Scottish settlers and their descendants in the coastal regions in the north and north-east of Ulster. Much assimilation and mixing has taken place in the past few centuries especially in Belfast. Ulster Scots has undergone a considerable revival in recent years.

universalist view A kind of 'third way' in Irish English studies seen as complementing both the substratist and retentionist views (see relevant entries). In essence, it assumes that there are universals of unguided adult second-language acquisition which are similar in many ways, but not identical to creolisation. These are assumed to be responsible for many of the specific structures, such as aspectual distinctions, which arose during the language shift from Irish to English.

universities in Ireland The universities of the Republic of Ireland are the following: Trinity College Dublin (TCD, founded in 1592, the sole constituent college of the University of Dublin), Dublin City University (DCU, founded in 1975, with university status since 1989) and University College Dublin (UCD), the largest in the country, which is a continuation of the Catholic University of Ireland, founded in 1851 with John H. Newman as its first rector (1854). With the establishment of the National University of Ireland (NUI) system in 1908 University College Dublin came into being as its main constituent college. The others are NUI Galway and NUI Cork, both continuations of the Queen's College system, established in 1845. NUI Maynooth arose by separating from St Patrick's College (founded in 1795) as a secular university in 1997 (as of 2015 called Maynooth University). The University of Limerick (UL), like DCU, was a National Institute of Higher Education which also gained university status in 1989 (since 1991 Mary Immaculate College has been linked to UL). In addition there are a number of Institutes of Technology, four in Dublin and ten others in urban centres around the country (Athlone, Carlow, Cork, Dundalk, Galway, Letterkenny, Limerick, Sligo, Tralee, Waterford). In Northern Ireland Queen's University Belfast, like Cork and Galway, was chartered in 1845, becoming a university in 1850. Ulster University (2014–) was previously the University of Ulster (1982–) and the New University of Ulster (1968–). It incorporates four campuses – Belfast, Coleraine, Jordanstown and Derry – the latter stemming from the theological Magee College (1865).

vernacularisation A process in which non-local speakers style-shift downwards to achieve a vernacular effect. An example of this would be the use of *youse* or *yez* for the second person plural in Ireland. This is normally avoided by non-local speakers but can be employed when deliberately switching to a vernacular mode.

vocabulary There is a tradition of collecting and publishing local words as word-lists and smaller dictionaries (see relevant entries in Hickey 2002). Although such vocabulary is not always current in modern urban speech it provides a record of varieties of English with clear traces of the shift from Irish. For larger collections of specifically Irish English lexis, see Dolan (2012), Ó Muirithe (1996a, b; 1997) and Share (2003).

Wagner, Heinrich (1923–88) Swiss German scholar who carried out extensive research into Irish (in Donegal) and compiled a *Linguistic Atlas of Irish Dialects* (4 vols, 1958–64). In 1959 he published *Das Verbum in den Sprachen der Britischen Inseln* 'The verb in the languages of the British Isles' in which he assumed that there were many areal features — involving verbal aspect — shared by forms of English and the Celtic languages of the British Isles.

Welsh A P-Celtic language still spoken by considerable numbers of speakers in present-day Wales. The sounds of Welsh are different from Irish with a more symmetrical distribution. The grammar has a similar system of initial mutations to Irish (grammatical categories are indicated by changes to the initial sounds of words).

Western Irish A reference to forms of Irish spoken in the middle of the western seaboard of Ireland. Irish is still a daily language in the area west of Galway city, particularly in Cois Fharraige and the areas around An Cheathrú Rua, Ros Muc, Cill Chiaráin, Carna and on the Aran Islands (in Galway Bay). Although north-west Co. Mayo is geographically part of the west, Irish spoken there is of a northern character as the dialect stems from earlier in-migrants from further north.

Zeuss, Johann Kaspar (1806–56) Commonly regarded as the founder of Celtic studies as a modern academic discipline. He was born in Franconia, went to school in Bamberg and studied in Munich. After working as a secondary-school teacher for a while he accepted an offer of a professorship in Munich, but for reasons of ill health he relinquished this and returned to Bamberg. His main publication is his monumental *Grammatica Celtica*, published (in Latin) in 1853 shortly before his death. A second edition, revised by Hans Ebel, appeared in 1871.

General Bibliography

The following items are those referred to in the above glossary but also include general references about language, literature, history and culture in Ireland which readers can use as orientations when first coming into contact with these fields.

Amador-Moreno, Carolina P. (2010). *An Introduction to Irish English*. London: Equinox.

Amador-Moreno, Carolina P., Kevin McCafferty and Elaine Vaughan (eds) (2015). *Pragmatic Markers in Irish English*. Amsterdam: John Benjamins.

Ball, Martin and Nicole Müller (2009). *The Celtic Languages*. Second edition. London: Routledge.

Bardon, Jonathon (2001). *A History of Ulster*. Second edition. Belfast: Blackstaff Press.

Bardon, Jonathon (2013). *A History of Ireland in 250 Episodes: a Sweeping Single Narrative of Irish History from the End of the Ice Age to the Peace Settlement in Northern Ireland*. Dublin: Gill and Macmillan.

Beckett, J. C. (1976). *The Anglo-Irish Tradition*. London: Faber and Faber.

Bhatia, Tej and William C. Ritchie (eds) (2008). *The Handbook of Bilingualism*. Malden, MA: Wiley-Blackwell.

Brady, Anne M. and Brian Cleeve (1985). *A Biographical Dictionary of Irish Writers*. Mullingar: The Lilliput Press.

Brearton, Fran and Alan Gillis (eds) (2012). *The Oxford Handbook of Modern Irish Poetry*. Oxford: Oxford University Press.

Canny, Nicholas (2001). *Making Ireland British 1580–1650*. Oxford: Oxford University Press.

Cleary, Joe and Claire Connolly (eds) (2005). *The Cambridge Companion to Irish Culture*. Cambridge: University Press.

Connolly, Sean J. (2002). *The Oxford Companion to Irish History*. Second edition. Oxford: University Press.

Corrigan, Karen P. (2010). *Irish English, Volume 1 – Northern Ireland*. Edinburgh: Edinburgh University Press.

Craig, Patricia (1998). *The Oxford Book of Ireland*. Oxford: Oxford University Press.

Cronin, Mike (2001). *A History of Ireland*. Basingstoke: Palgrave.

Crowley, Tony (2000). *The Politics of Language in Ireland 1366–1922: a Source Book*. London and New York: Routledge.

Crowley, Tony (2005). *Wars of Words: the Politics of Language in Ireland 1537–2004*. Oxford: Oxford University Press.

Deane, Seamus (1986). *A Short History of Irish Literature*. London: Hutchinson.

Dickson, David (2014). *Dublin: the Making of a Capital City*. London: Profile Books.

Dolan, Terence (2012) [1998]. *A Dictionary of Hiberno-English. the Irish Use of English*. Third edition. Dublin: Gill and Macmillan.

Dorian, Nancy (1981). *Language Death: the Life Cycle of a Scottish Gaelic Dialect*. Philadelphia: University of Pennsylvania Press.

Dowling, Patrick J. (1971). *A History of Irish Education*. Cork: Mercier.

Dowling, Patrick J. (1968) [1935]. *The Hedge Schools of Ireland* (original edition, London: Longmans), reprinted Cork: Mercier Press.

Doyle, Aidan (2015). *A History of the Irish Language. From the Norman Invasion to Independence.* Oxford: Oxford University Press.

Dudley Edwards, Ruth with Bridget Hourican (2005) [1973]. *An Atlas of Irish History.* London: Routledge.

Duffy, Seán (2000). *The Concise History of Ireland.* Dublin: Gill and Macmillan.

Duffy, Seán (ed.) (2005). *Medieval Ireland: an Encyclopedia.* London: Routledge.

Duffy, Seán (ed.) (2012). *Atlas of Irish History.* Third edition. Dublin: Gill and Macmillan.

Filppula, Markku (1999). *The Grammar of Irish English. Language in Hibernian Style.* London: Routledge.

Fitzgerald, Patrick and Brian Lambkin (2007). *Migration in Irish History, 1607–2007.* Basingstoke: Palgrave Macmillan.

Foster, Roy F. (1988). *Modern Ireland 1600–1972.* Harmondsworth: Penguin.

Foster, Roy F. (2007). *Luck and the Irish: a Brief History of Change 1970–2000.* London: Allen Lane.

Foster, Roy F. (2014). *Vivid Faces: the Revolutionary Generation in Ireland, 1890–1923.* London: Allen Lane.

Foster, Roy F. (ed.) (1989). *The Oxford Illustrated History of Ireland.* Oxford: Oxford University Press.

Government of Ireland (1958). *Gramadach na Gaeilge agus Litriú na Gaeilge. An Caighdeán Oifigiúil.* [The grammar and spelling of Irish. The official standard.] Dublin: Stationery Office.

Hand, Derek (2014). *A History of the Irish Novel.* Cambridge: Cambridge University Press.

Harte, Liam (ed.) (2007). *Modern Irish Autobiography. Self, Nation and Society.* Basingstoke: Palgrave Macmillan.

Hennessey, Thomas (1997). *A History of Northern Ireland 1920–1996.* Dublin: Gill and Macmillan.

Hickey, D. J. and J. E. Doherty (2003). *A New Dictionary of Irish History from 1800.* Dublin: Gill and Macmillan.

Hickey, Raymond (2002). *Source Book for Irish English.* Amsterdam: John Benjamins.

Hickey, Raymond (2003). *Corpus Presenter. Software for Language Analysis. With a Manual and* A Corpus of Irish English *as Sample Data.* Amsterdam: John Benjamins.

Hickey, Raymond (2005). *Dublin English. Evolution and Change.* Amsterdam: John Benjamins.

Hickey, Raymond (2007). *Irish English. History and Present-day Forms.* Cambridge: Cambridge University Press.

Hickey, Raymond (2011). *The Dialects of Irish, Study of a Changing Landscape.* Berlin: de Gruyter Mouton.

Hickey, Raymond (ed.) (2004). *Legacies of Colonial English. Studies in Transported Dialects.* Cambridge: Cambridge University Press.

Hickey, Raymond (ed.) (2010). *The Handbook of Language Contact.* Malden, MA: Wiley- Blackwell.

Hickey, Raymond (ed.) (2011). *Researching the Languages of Ireland.* Uppsala: Uppsala University.

Kallen, Jeffrey L. (2013). *Irish English, Volume 2 – the Republic of Ireland*. Berlin: de Gruyter Mouton.

Keating-Miller, Jennifer (2009). *Language, Identity and Liberation in Contemporary Irish Literature*. Basingstoke: Palgrave Macmillan.

Kiberd, Declan (1995). *Inventing Ireland. The Literature of the Modern Nation*. London: Jonathan Cape.

Kiberd, Declan (2000). *Irish Classics*. London: Granta Books.

Kiberd, Declan (2005). *The Irish Writer and the World*. Cambridge: Cambridge University Press.

Kiberd, Declan and Gabriel Fitzmaurice (eds) (1991). *The Flowering Tree – An Crann faoi Bhláth. Contemporary Irish Poetry with Verse Translations*. Dublin: Wolfhound Press.

Kiely, Benedict (ed.) (1981). *The Penguin Book of Irish Short Stories*. Harmondsworth: Penguin.

Kinsella, Thomas (ed.) (1986). *The New Oxford Book of Irish Verse*. Oxford: University Press.

Knott, Eleanor and Gerard Murphy (ed.) (1966). *Early Irish Literature*. London: Routledge and Kegan Paul.

Lalor, Brian (ed.) (2003). *The Encyclopaedia of Ireland*. Dublin: Gill and Macmillan.

Lenox-Conyngham, Melosina (ed.) (1998). *Diaries of Ireland. An Anthology 1590-1987*. Dublin: The Lilliput Press.

Lucas, Angela (ed.) (1995). *Anglo-Irish Poems of the Middle Ages*. Dublin: Columba Press.

Lydon, James (1998). *The Making of Ireland. From Ancient Times to the Present*. London: Routledge.

Lyons, Francis S. L. (1971). *Ireland since the Famine*. London: Fontana.

Macafee, Caroline (ed.) (1996). *A Concise Ulster Dictionary*. Oxford: University Press.

Mac Anna, Ferdia (ed.) (1995). *The Penguin Book of Irish Comic Writing*. Harmondsworth: Penguin.

Mac Annaidh, Séamas (2001). *Illustrated Dictionary of Irish History*. Dublin: Gill and Macmillan.

McCafferty, Kevin (2001). *Ethnicity and Language Change. English in (London)Derry, Northern Ireland*. Amsterdam: John Benjamins.

McCone, Kim, Damian McManus, Cathal Ó Háinle, Nicholas Williams and Liam Breatnach (eds) (1994). *Stair na Gaeilge. In ómós de Phádraig Ó Fiannachta* [The History of Irish. In honour of Pádraig Ó Fiannachta]. Maynooth: Department of Irish.

McCormack, W. J. (1985). *Ascendancy and Tradition in Anglo-Irish Literary History from 1789–1939*. Oxford: Clarendon Press.

McCormack, W. J. (2001). *The Blackwell Companion to Modern Irish Culture*. Oxford: Blackwell.

McLoughlin, Michael (1996). *Great Irish Speeches of the Twentieth Century*. Dublin: Poolbeg.

Mac Mathúna, Liam (2007). *Béarla sa Ghaeilge: Cabhair Choigríche: An Códmheascadh Gaeilge/Béarla i Litríocht na Gaeilge 1600–1900*. [English in Irish. Help from the Foreign Country: Code-mixing of Irish and English in Irish Literature 1600–1900.] Baile Átha Cliath: An Clóchomhar Teoranta.

MacRaild, Donald H. (1999). *Irish Migrants in Modern Britain 1750–1922.* Basingstoke, Hampshire: Macmillan Press.

McRedmond, Louis (1996). *Modern Irish Lives. Dictionary of Twentieth-Century Biography.* Dublin: Gill and Macmillan.

Miller, Kerby and Paul Wagner (1994). *Out of Ireland. The Story of Irish Emigration to America.* London: Aurum Press.

Milroy, James (1981). *Regional Accents of English: Belfast.* Belfast: Blackstaff.

Mitchell, Frank and Michael Ryan (2001). *Reading the Irish Landscape.* Dublin: Townhouse.

Moody, T. W. and F. X. Martin (2001) [1967]. *The Course of Irish History.* Dublin: Mercier Press.

Morash, Chris and Shaun Richards (2013). *Mapping Irish Theatre. Theories of Space and Place.* Cambridge: Cambridge University Press.

Nic Pháidín, Caoilfhionn and Seán Ó Cearnaigh (eds) (2008). *A New View of the Irish Language.* Dublin: Cois Life.

Ó Gráda, Cormac (1999). *Black '47 and Beyond: the Great Irish Famine in History, Economy, and Memory.* Princeton, NJ: Princeton University Press.

Ó hIfearnáin, Tadhg and Máire Ní Neachtain (eds) (2012). *An tSochtheangeolaíocht: Feidhm agus Tuairisc.* [Sociolinguistics. Aim and scope.] Baile Átha Cliath: Cois Life Teoranta.

Ó Muirithe, Diarmaid (1996a). *Dictionary of Anglo-Irish. Words and Phrases from Irish.* Dublin: Four Courts Press.

Ó Muirithe, Diarmaid (1996b). *The Words we Use.* Dublin: Four Courts Press.

Ó Muirithe, Diarmaid (1997). *A Word in your Ear.* Dublin: Four Courts Press.

Ó Riagáin, Pádraig (1997). *Language Policy and Social Reproduction: Ireland 1893–1993.* Oxford: Oxford University Press.

Ó Snódaigh, Pádraig (1995). *Hidden Ulster. Protestants and the Irish Language.* Belfast: Lagan Press.

O'Sullivan, Patrick (ed.) (1992). *Irish World-Wide: History, Heritage, Identity.* 6 Vols. Leicester: University Press.

Ó Tuama, Seán and Thomas Kinsella (eds) (1981). *An Duanaire 1600–1900: Poems of the Dispossessed.* Dublin: Dolmen Press.

O'Toole, Fintan (1999). *The Irish Times Book of the Century.* Dublin: Gill and Macmillan.

Paor, Liam de (1986). *The Peoples of Ireland. From Prehistory to Modern Times.* London: Hutchinson.

Pierce, David (ed.) (2000). *Irish Writing in the Twentieth Century. A Reader.* Cork: University Press.

Poirtéir, Cathal (1995). *The Great Irish Famine.* Dublin: Mercier Press.

Raftery, Deirdre and Karin Fischer (2014). *Educating Ireland: Schooling and Social Change, 1700–2000.* Dublin: Irish Academic Press.

Regan, Stephen (eds) (2008). *Irish Writing. An Anthology of Irish Literature in English 1789–1939.* Oxford: Oxford University Press.

Reid, Gerard (ed.) (1999). *Great Irish Voices. Over 400 Years of Irish Oratory.* Dublin: Irish Academic Press.

Robinson, Philip S. (1984). *The Plantation of Ulster: British Settlement in an Irish Landscape, 1600–1670.* New York: St. Martin's.

Ruprecht Fadem, Maureen E. (2015). *The Literature of Northern Ireland. Spectral Borderlands.* Basingstoke: Palgrave Macmillan

Seymour, St John D. (1970). *Anglo-Irish Literature 1200–1582*. New York: Octagon Books.

Share, Bernard (2003). *Slanguage. A Dictionary of Slang and Colloquial English in Ireland*. Second edition. Dublin: Gill and Macmillan.

Sheldon, Esther K. (1967). *Thomas Sheridan of Smock Alley*. Princeton, NJ: University Press.

Smyth, W. J. and K. Whelan (eds) (1988). *Common Ground: Essays on the Historical Geography of Ireland*. Cork: University Press.

Swift, R. and S. Gilley (eds) (1989). *The Irish in Britain 1815–1939*. London: Pinter.

Tóibín, Colm (ed.) (2001). *The Penguin Book of Irish Fiction*. Harmondsworth: Penguin.

Tóibín, Colm and Diarmaid Ferriter (2001). *The Irish Famine. A Documentary*. London: Profile Books.

Tracy, Robert (1998). *The Unappeasable Host. Studies in Irish Identities*. Dublin: University College Dublin Press.

Trevor, William (1984). *A Writer's Ireland. Landscape in Literature*. London: Thames and Hudson.

Trevor, William (ed.) (2010) [1989]. *The Oxford Book of Irish Short Stories*. Oxford: University Press.

Walshe, Shane (2009). *Irish English as Represented in Film*. Frankfurt: Peter Lang.

Welch, Robert (ed.) (1996). *The Oxford Companion to Irish Literature*. Oxford: Oxford University Press.

Welch, Robert (1999). *The Oxford Companion to Irish Literature*. Oxford: Oxford University Press.

Welch, Robert (ed.) (2000). *The Abbey Theatre, 1899–1999. Form and Pressure*. Oxford: Oxford University Press.

Wells, John C. (1982). *Accents of English*. 3 Vols. Cambridge: Cambridge University Press.

Wilson Foster, John (2006). *The Cambridge Companion to the Irish Novel*. Cambridge: Cambridge University Press.

Woodham-Smith, Cecil (1962). *The Great Hunger*. London: Hamish Hamilton.

Index

Dublin English
  background, 20
  change in the 1990s, 25
    differentiation by speaker age, 26
    Dublin Vowel Shift, 25
  different varieties, 21, 22
    fashionable, 22
    mainstream, 22
    non-local realisation of STRUT
      vowel, 26
    non-local realisation of T, 26
  documentation, 20
  geography, 21
  hypercorrection, 21
  negative diagnostics, 26
  relationship with American English,
    27
  relationship with British English, 27
  Short Front Vowel Lowering, 28
    DRESS vowel, 29
    KIT vowel, 29
    LOT and THOUGHT vowels, 30
    present extent, 31
    TRAP vowel, 29

Ireland
  cities
    Belfast, 4, 6
    Derry, 5
    Dublin, 5
  expansion of European Union, 3
  language and politics
    Belfast Agreement, 198
    colonial rule, 199
    Essay on Irish Bulls (1802), 204
    evaluation, 215
    Irish after independence, 207
    numbers of Irish speakers, 203
    O'Hickey, Michael, 208
    post-union Ireland, 202
    role of Catholic Church, 206
    role of identity, 211
    status of Irish in independent
      Ireland, 213
  official languages, 4
  Polish section of population, 3, 4
  present-day languages, 3, 45
  Statutes of Kilkenny, 199
  travelling population, 7
Irish
  code-switching, 81
    domains and triggers, 87
    evaluation, 100
    informality marker, 85
    methodology, 94
    micro-interactional study, 93
    popular perceptions, 100
    research background, 83
    role and manifestation today, 101
    role in identity construction, 92
    socially diagnostic variables, 95
    sociolinguistic overview, 85
    stylistic/narrative device, 91
    the concept of nation, 60
  education
    Gaelscoileanna, 42, 272
  future of the language, 55
    evaluation, 56
    in the Gaeltacht, 55
    outside the Gaeltacht, 56
  Gaeltacht (Irish-speaking regions), 4
  government
    Údarás na Gaeltachta, 54
  history
    language change, 48
    sixteenth to twentieth century, 46
  language and media, 60
    cosmopolitan ideology, 76
    evaluation, 77
    liberal ideology, 67
    nationalist ideology, 63
    neoliberal ideology, 71

Irish – *continued*
  protectionist ideology, 64
  recent language attitudes, 71
  language shift and language death,
    43
  media
    Raidió na Gaeltachta, 42
    TG4, 42
  present-day situation, 41
  scholarship
    O'Donovan, John, 5
    Zeuss, Johann Kaspar, 5
  second-language acquisition, 269
    attitudes towards Irish, 279
    the educational system, 271
    evaluation, 293
    language learning, 272
    reading in Irish, 274
    role of literacy, 275
    speakers and learners, 270
  shift and revival, 176
    An Claidheamh Soluis, 180
    Bolg an tSolair, 178
    discussion in print journalism,
      177
    evaluation, 193
    The Gaelic Journal, 180
    Hyde, Douglas, 181
    implementation, 185
    Irish Ecclesiastical Record, 181
    MacNeill, Eoin, 177
    O'Growney, Eoghan, 181
    Oireachtas, 186
    twentieth century, 191
  speech community / network of
    speakers, 52
Irish English
  areal features, 15
    morphology, 16
    phonology, 16
    syntax, 16
  corpora, 365
    British National Corpus, 380
    concordances, 376
    Corpus of Contemporary
      American English, 380
    corpus-based methods, 373
    evaluation, 383

examination of sociolinguistic
  variables, 368
frequency considerations, 374
interrogation software, 373
keyword occurrence, 376
list of available corpora, 370
list of available corpora for Irish
  English, 371
metadata in corpora, 378
role in sociolinguistics, 366
Scottish Corpus of Texts and
  Speech, 380
sociolinguistic case studies,
  378
structure and content, 366
data sources, 35
enregisterment, 31
  grammatical forms, 33
  levels of indexicality, 32
  older features, 32
  orthographical representations,
    32
  orts for *arts*, 34
  vocabulary items, 33
feature sources
  suggestions, 18
Forth and Bargy, 5
grammar
  youse or *yez*, 15
history, 8
  Anglo-Normans, 9
  Boucicault, Dion, 11
  Carleton, William, 10
  Edgeworth, Maria, *Castle Rackrent*,
    10
  Experiences of an Irish R.M., 11
  First Period (1200–1600), 9
  hedge schools, 12
  input from England, 13
  Irish Literary Revival, 10
  Joyce, James, 11
  Kildare Poems, 9
  lack of Great Vowel Shift, 14
  language shift, 12
  Lowland Scots, 9
  renewed anglicisation, 9
  Second Period (1600–), 10
  Sheridan, Thomas, 5, 20
  supraregionalisation, 14

Swift, Jonathan, 11
vernacularisation, 15
language use, 107
  age and gender, 112
  evaluation, 122
  ICE-Ireland, 115
  regional focus, 109
  relationship to British and
    American English, 108
  social status and ethnic identity,
    112
  tag questions, 114
literature
  Howard, Paul, *The Curious Incident*
    of the Dog in the Nightdress,
    301
  Stage Irishman, 300
non-native varieties, 35
portrayal in films, 320
  character age, class, sex, 322
  character ethnicity, 323
  comparison with *A Survey of Irish*
    English Usage, 324
  comparison with SPICE-Ireland,
    324
  film corpus, 321
  locality, 324
  Northern and Southern films, 321
  regional dialects, 321
  themes of films, 322
  vernacular usage, 320
pragmatics, 34
pronunciation
  reflex of velarised L, 15
  unraised Middle English long
    e, 15
  word stress patterns, 12
relationship to English, 3
research
  International Corpus of English –
    Ireland, 7
scholarship, 4
  Bliss, Alan, 6
  contact explanations, 7
  Henry, Patrick Leo, 6
  Hogan, James Jeremiah, 6
  Joyce, Patrick W., 6
  language planning, 7
  retentionist viewpoint, 7

rural forms of language, 5
  urban sociolinguistics, 5
sociolinguistics, 19
  external influences, 19
  influence of Dublin, 20
  new pronunciation, 20
terminology, 8
  Anglo-Irish, 8
  brogue, 8
  Hiberno-English, 8
  Irish English, 8
  Mid-Ulster English, 8
  Ulster Scots, 8
translation, 344
  An Gúm, 346
  censorship, 348
  code-switching, 348
  cultural self-definition, 344
  diglossia, 347
  early twentieth century, 345,
    346
  English domination, 360
  European Union policy, 360
  evaluation, 361
  Friel, Brian, *Translations*, 354
  Irish language policy, 345
  Irish Texts Society, 345
  Merriman, Brian, *Cúirt an*
    Mheán-Oíche, 349
  multilingualism, 359
  present-day situation, 357
  role of the education system,
    356
  The *Táin*, 353
  use of intermediary texts, 355
vocabulary, 17
  archaisms and regionalisms, 17
  lexicography, 19
  transfer from Irish, 17
  transfer of idioms, 13
Irish history
  early Ireland, 133
    application of Schneider's
      Dynamic Model, 135, 148
    evaluation, 150
    linguistic and cultural contacts,
      134
    mechanisms of language contact,
      134

Irish history – *continued*
    post-1200 contacts, 143
    post-medieval period, 148
    pre-1200 contacts, 136
    early modern Ireland, 154
    attitudes to English, 156
    eighteenth-century Ireland,
        158
    evaluation, 172
emigrant letters, 218
    analytical value, 220
    *Corpus of Irish English
        Correspondence* (CORIECOR),
        222
    evaluation, 238

linguistic features in personal
    letters, 223
Proceedings of the Old Bailey, 239
emigration, 244
    destinations, 246
    England, 253
    evaluation, 260
    linguistic evidence, 246
    motivation, 245
    the New World, 247
    Scotland, 257
    timeline, 245

Ulster Scots, 4, 34
    revival, 4
    vocabulary, 5